NEMO·ME·IMPVNE·LACESSIT

The Arms of the Kings of Scots

COLLINS

SCOTTISH
CLAN
& FAMILY
ENCYCLOPEDIA

George Way of Plean and Romilly Squire

Foreword by

The Rt Hon. The Earl of Elgin KT
Convenor, The Standing Council
of Scottish Chiefs

HarperCollins*Publishers*

HarperCollins Publishers
PO Box, Glasgow G4 0NB

First Published 1994

ISBN 0 00 470547 5

Reprint 9 8 7 6 5 4 3

A catalogue record for this book is available from the British Library

Illustration acknowledgements

All heraldic illustrations by Romilly Squire except for
  Standards on pp. 65, 69, 77, 85, 91, 103, 105, 109, 121, 123, 133, 135, 137, 147, 151, 165, 181, 185, 189, 195, 199, 207, 209, 211, 217, 225, 231, 237, 249, 251, 257, 259, 267, 271, 273, 277, 281, 283, 285, 301, 303, 305, 307, 309, 311, 319, 321, 323, 337 and 339 by the late Don Pottinger LVO (reproduced by kind permission of Mrs Fay Pottinger)
  Standards on pp. 75, 83, 89, 129, 141, 143, 219, 221, 227, 247 and 325 by Jenny Philips
  Full achievements of arms on the endpapers, foreword and on pp. 79, 99, 131, 203, 297 and 313 reproduced from *The Scots Peerage* by Sir James Balfour-Paul
Photographs on pp. 23, 39, 50, 51 and 54 by Graham Lees
Line illustrations on pp. 32 and 33 by Roy Boyd
Illustration and maps on pp. 12, 31 and 62 by Iain Robinson
All other illustrations by HarperCollins Publishers

The Publishers wish to thank the following for their permission to reproduce illustrations:
William Drummond Moray of Abercairney and the Scottish National Portrait Gallery (p. 37); Lyon Office (pp. 44–45, 52[left], 53); Stuart C. MacBride (pp. 56–57); Patrick Barden (p. 60)

All tartans were kindly supplied by Peter MacArthur & Co. Ltd, Hamilton, except for those on pp. 69, 75, 87, 105, 131, 143, 155, 157, 163, 175, 191, 301 and 305 which were provided by the Scottish Tartan Society, Pitlochry

Reprographics by CMR Graphics Ltd., East Kilbride
Page make-up on Quark XPress® version 3.2 by Pintail Design and Marketing Ltd, Glasgow

Printed in Hong Kong

There has long been the need for an accurate and informed volume which would guide the host of the occasionally curious through the maze which is the family and clan story in Scotland. This need has now been fulfilled with this book which encourages the reader along the correct, if at times tortuous, path of understanding. It is this most important element which has been achieved – an honest understanding of a great part of the history of the nation of the Scots and how it was created around the character of chiefly leadership. This leadership was not wholly confined to military achievement and other characteristics and flashes of brilliance enliven the pages. Let there also be no doubt that, while much of the record inevitably covers the head or chief of the name or clan, there is yet remembrance of many others in kinship

This is indeed a collection in which the reader may revel in due but humble pride, encounter sheer survival, share in cunning artifice and, above all, realise with thankful joy that he or she bears a name of honour and repute. Then comes the overall pleasure of knowing that there is nothing else in the world quite as comparable or half as enduring.

The Rt Hon. The Earl of Elgin and Kincardine KT
Broomhall, Dunfermline

To Jean Parlett and Ann Gauld who made this possible
and to Michael, Younger of Plean, who makes it worthwhile

There are few subjects more likely to cause spirited debate amongst Scotsmen than that of family history. However, it cannot be denied that much that has been written on this subject has been over romanticised and in the words of the late Lord Lyon, Sir Thomas Innes of Learney, owed more to 'the souvenir shop than to the scientist'. When we were approached to edit, compile and contribute to this work, we were particularly pleased to note that our fellow contributors were not only experts in their subjects but were actively working and researching in their fields in Scotland. The credit for assembling the team and steering us from commission to publication goes to James Carney, our Senior Editor at HarperCollins Publishers, without whose patience and talent this work would not have been possible. The essays of Professor Macinnes and Alasdair Campbell of Airds will leave the reader in no doubt as to the origin and nature of the Scottish clans and that most vexed of subjects, tartan. It is hoped that this book will not only appeal to those generally interested in Scottish family history but will also be of practical use to those seeking accurate information on heraldry, genealogy and the law, customs and practices of the clan system.

When embarking upon a task of this scale, it was necessary to establish criteria to place the work within a manageable framework. After the introductory essays the book is divided into two alphabetical sections and numerous appendices. The first section provides information on the member clans of the Standing Council of Scottish Chiefs, as at the date of publication. The Council admits to membership chiefs who have been officially recognised by the Lord Lyon, King of Arms and whose heraldry includes hereditary supporters. The second section describes the clans and families who are not currently members of the Council but who have a coat of arms recorded in the *Public Register of All Arms and Bearings in Scotland*, indicating that the clan or family is, or was, organised.

The fact that a clan or family is excluded from membership of the Council of Chiefs is in no way a reflection on its standing as there are many technical legal reasons why the Lord Lyon may not recognise a chief. An obvious example of this is that of Innes, the family name of the present Lord Lyon himself, whose rightful chief – the Duke of Roxburghe – cannot be recognised as he bears the compound surname, Innes-Ker. The reader will find such niceties explained in the chapter on the law and the clan.

In the second section it has not always proved possible to determine precisely the coat of arms of some clans or families as they might be recognised in the future by the Lord Lyon if a claimant were to petition for recognition as chief. In such cases we have described those arms which we believe are most likely to be accepted as the undifferenced or plain arms of the name. In some cases, the shield of a clan chief or family head is divided into four or more parts, each of which illustrates a line of descent. Where these so-called 'quartered' coats appear, we have endeavoured to identify the shield which most prominently displays the chiefly arms of the name in question and have labelled each quarter by name. Where the Lord Lyon has appointed a commander to a chiefless clan, we have described the arms of the present commander, rather than speculate on what might be the arms assigned to a future chief unless this is beyond dispute, as in the case of Clan MacGillivray. We have standardised the heraldic terms used and, in particular, have deleted references to aspects of the heraldry personal to the individual rank and honours of the present chief, which may not automatically be transmittable to his or her successors, for example, the badge of a baronet. These matters are explained in both the chapter on heraldry and the glossary of heraldic terms. We have elected to adopt the system for spelling Gaelic surnames used by George Black in *The Surnames of Scotland* (1993 edition) set out on page XLIII of that work.

We are deeply indebted to the Lord Lyon King of Arms, Sir Malcolm Innes of Edingight KCVO, WS and to the Lyon Clerk and Keeper of the Records, Mrs C. G. W. Roads MVO, Carrick Pursuivant, for their assistance during our writing of the text. The unprecedented access permitted to the Registers, and the other records of the Lyon Court, together with the personal advice and encouragement offered has given this work a scope and depth which would otherwise have been impossible. Uniquely, permission was granted to reproduce paintings from the Lyon Register itself for the purpose of illustrating the high art of what is now recognised as the finest heraldic manuscript in the world. It was that art which first captured our imagination and fired an early interest in the mysteries of heraldry and the heroic deeds and legends which it recounts. For this, we both owe much to the late Don Pottinger LVO, Islay Herald. His artistic genius and the warmth and friendship he offered many years ago to two, no doubt over-opinionated, young men, can never be repaid and will not be forgotten. His widow, Fay Pottinger, kindly gave permission for Don's work on the standards of Scottish Chiefs to be reproduced and as a small tribute, a number of standards which were devised after Don's work was completed, have been commissioned from Jenny Philips, Herald Painter to the Court of the Lord Lyon, in the style which will always be associated with the Pottinger name. It should be noted that not all of the Pottinger standards conform to the blazon of the present chiefly arms.

It would have been impossible to produce this work without the co-operation of the members of the Standing Council of Scottish Chiefs, many of whom contributed, or made helpful comments upon, texts relating to their clans or families. Our particular thanks to the Convenor of the Council, The Right Hon. The Earl of Elgin and Kincardine KT for his encouragement and for agreeing to contribute the foreword.

Similarly, to all the clan secretaries, sennachies and historians whose help made this task possible, we extend our thanks and for their special assistance we would wish to acknowledge the advice assistance and contributions of Sir Crispin Agnew of Lochnaw Bt., Rothesay Herald; John Armstrong, Chairman, Clan Armstrong Trust; John L. B. Bell; Charles Burnett KStJ, Ross Herald; Charles Davidson, Clan Dhai Society; William Drummond-Moray of Abercairney; Peter Drummond Murray of Mastrick, Slains Pursuivant; Colin Forrester, Clan Forrester Society; Dr John Little, Clan Little Society; David Lumsden of Cushnie, Toiseach of Clan Lumsden; Archie Lumsden, Sennachie to Clan Lumsden; James Macarthur of Milton, Commander of Clan Macarthur; Martin Macintyre, Ceann-cath of Clan Macintyre; Archie Macpherson MA, LLB, Clan Macpherson Society; Dr William Marshall, Clan Keith; David Morgan, Clan Mcphee Society; and Henry Tilling KStJ.

Rosemary Way and Ewan Notman were conscientious and hard working researchers whose work is greatly appreciated while Valerie Macinnes carefully undertook the task of translating our manuscripts into the modern wonder of the computer floppy disk, never complaining about the obscurity of some of the language or the endless revisions that were necessary. The staff at the Lyon Court and all at Beveridge & Kellas must be thanked for their many kindnesses and for putting up with our frequent flights from euphoria to panic.

Although we are indebted for the advice and assistance we have received from all those mentioned above, all errors and omissions remain ours alone.

George Way of Plean and Romilly Squire
Edinburgh, 1994

Contents

List of Contributors

George Way of Plean LLB (hons), SSC, FRSA, FSA(Scot)
Baron of Plean; Secretary of the Standing Council of Scottish Chiefs; Partner, Beveridge & Kellas WS, Leith.

Romilly Squire OStJ, DA, FRSA, FSA(Scot)
Heraldic artist in the Court of the Lord Lyon; Deputy Secretary of the Standing Council of Scottish Chiefs; Officer, and Limner of the Priory of Scotland, of the Most Venerable Order of St John.

Allan Macinnes
Burnett-Fletcher Professor in History and Head of Department, History and Economic History Department, University of Aberdeen

Alastair Campbell of Airds
Unicorn Pursuivant of Arms and one of Her Majesty's Officers of Arms for Scotland; Member of the Court of the Lord Lyon and Chairman, Advisory Committee on Tartans to the Lord Lyon; Chief Executive, Clan Campbell; Archivist to the Duke of Argyll, Inveraray Castle

Patrick Barden PhD, FSA(Scot)
Chairman, Heraldry Society of Scotland; heraldic flagmaker

Kathleen B. Cory FSA(Scot)
Professional genealogist

List of Sources

Manuscripts

Balfour's Manuscript, Lyon Office

Thomas Crawfurd's Manuscript

Sir Robert Forman's Manuscript (otherwise known as *Workman's Manuscript*) Lyon Office, 1566

Lyon Register (see *Public Register of all Arms and Bearings in Scotland*)

Pont's Manuscript Lyon Office, 1624

Public Register of all Arms and Bearings in Scotland Lyon Office, 1677–

Published works

Adam, Frank *The Clans, Septs and Regiments of Scotland* Edinburgh, 1908

Agnew, Sir Andrew *The Hereditary Sheriffs of Galloway* Edinburgh, 1893

Anderson, Herbert *Notarial Protocol Book Dumfries* Edinburgh, 1914

Anderson, M. O. *Kings and Kingship in Early Scotland* Edinburgh, 1973

Anderson, William *The Scottish Nation* Edinburgh, 1873

Anderson, A. O. *Early Sources of Scottish History* Edinburgh, 1922

Angus, William *Pitfirrane Writs 1230–1794* Edinburgh,1932

Balfour-Paul, Sir James *Ordinary of Scottish Arms* Edinburgh, 1903

Balfour-Paul, Sir James *Scottish Family History* Edinburgh, 1930

Balfour-Paul, Sir James *The Scots Peerage* Edinburgh, 1904

Barrow, C. W. S. *Kingship and Unity. Scotland 1000–1306* London, 1981

Barrow, C. W. S. *The Anglo-Norman Era in Scotland* London, 1981

Barrow, C. W. S. *The Kingdom of the Scots* London, 1973

Bell, Robert *Ulster Surnames* Belfast, 1988

Black, George *The Surnames of Scotland* Edinburgh, 1993

Buchanan of Auchmar, William *A Brief Enquiry into the Highland Clans* Glasgow, 1723

Burke's General Armory London, 1989

Burke's Landed Gentry London, 1846

Burke's Peerage London, 1846

Campbell, R. *Scotland since 1707* Oxford, 1971

Crawfurd, George *Lives of the Officers of the Crown in Scotland* Edinburgh, 1726

Cunningham, A. *The Loyal Clans* Cambridge, 1932

Dalrymple, Sir James *Scottish History* Edinburgh, 1707

Donaldson, Gordon *Scotland: James V–VII* Edinburgh, 1990

Donaldson, Gordon *Scottish Historical Documents* Edinburgh, 1970

Duncan, Archibald *Scotland – the making of the kingdom* Edinburgh, 1975

Elvin, Charles *A Dictionary of Heraldry* 1977

Elvin, Charles *Elvin's Mottoes Revised* 1977

Ferguson, Joan *Scottish Family Histories* Edinburgh, 1986

Grimble, Ian *Scottish Clans and Tartans* London, 1973

Innes of Learney, Sir Thomas *Scots Heraldry* Edinburgh, 1978

Innes of Learney, Sir Thomas *Tartans of the Clans and Families of Scotland* Edinburgh 1964

Kay, John *Edinburgh Portraits* Edinburgh 1842

Laing *Calendar of Laing Charters* Edinburgh, 1899

Lawrie, Sir Archibald *Early Scottish Charters* Edinburgh, 1905

Lenman, B. P. *The Jacobite Risings 1689–1746* London, 1980

Levenax Cartularium London, 1837

Lynch, Michael *Scotland – A New History* London, 1991

Macdonald of Castleton, Donald *Clan Donald* Loanhead, 1978

MacFarlane, Walter *Genealogical Collections* Edinburgh, 1900

MacGibbon and Ross *Castellated and Domesticated Architecture in Scotland* Edinburgh, 1887

Mackenzie of Rosehaugh, Sir George *Science of Herauldrie* Edinburgh, 1680

Metcalfe, W. *A History of Paisley* Glasgow, 1908

Mitchison, Rosalind *A History of Scotland* London, 1982

Nisbet, Alexander *System of Heraldry* Edinburgh, 1816

O'Hart, John *Irish Pedigrees* Dublin, 1881

Pitcairn, Robert *Criminal Trials of Scotland* Edinburgh, 1833

Pitscottie, Robert Lindsay of *History and Chronicles of Scotland* Edinburgh 1911

Sellar, W. *The Origins and Ancestry of Somerled* Scottish Historical Review, 1966

Shaw, D. *History of the Province of Moray* Edinburgh, 1827

Smith, Annette *Jacobite Estates of the Forty-Five* Edinburgh, 1982

Smout, T. C. *A History of the Scottish People 1560–1830* London, 1969

Smyth, Alfred *Warlords and Holy Men* Edinburgh, 1974

St Andrews *Liber Cartarum Prioratus Sant. Andrew* Edinburgh, 1841

Stoddart, Robert *Scottish Arms 1370–1678* Edinburgh, 1881

Tranter, Nigel *The Fortified House in Scotland* Edinburgh, 1977

Watson, W. J. *Celtic Place Names of Scotland* Edinburgh, 1926

Youngson, A. J. *After the Forty-Five* Edinburgh, 1973

11

County Towns ●

Scale

0 10 20 30 40 50 miles

ORKNEY

Kirkwall

SHETLAND

Lerwick

(inset)

Outer Hebrides

Lewis

Harris

Stornoway

N.Uist

Benbecula

S.Uist

Eriskay

Canna

Rum

Muck

Eigg

Coll

Tiree

Iona

Scarba

Colonsay

Jura

Islay

Gigha

Barra

Skye

Portree

Mull

ARGYLL

Inveraray

DUNBARTON

Dumbarton

Rothesay

BUTE

Arran

SUTHERLAND

CAITHNESS

Wick

Dornoch

ROSS
AND
CROMARTY

Dingwall

Nairn

NAIRN

Inverness

MORAY

Elgin

BANFF

Banff

Huntly

ABERDEEN

INVERNESS

Fort Augustus

Glenfinnan

Fort William

Braemar

Aberdeen

KINCARDINE

Stonehaven

ANGUS

Montrose

Blair Atholl

Dunkeld

PERTH

Scone

Perth

Forfar

Dundee

Arbroath

CLACKMANNAN

KINROSS

Cupar

St. Andrews

FIFE

Kinross

Stirling

Alloa

STIRLING

Dunfermline

Linlithgow

W. LOTHIAN

Haddington

EAST
LOTHIAN

Renfrew

Paisley

RENFREW

Glasgow

Edinburgh

MIDLOTHIAN

Duns

BERWICK

Hamilton

LANARK

Lanark

Peebles

PEEBLES

Berwick
upon
Tweed

Ayr

AYR

Selkirk

SELKIRK

Jedburgh

ROXBURGH

DUMFRIES

KIRKCUDBRIGHT

Dumfries

WIGTOWN

Wigtown

Kirkcudbright

Whithorn

ENGLAND

The old counties of Scotland.

Clanship: A Historical Perspective

PROFESSOR ALLAN MACINNES

The most distinctive feature of Scotland's history, nationally and internationally, is probably that of clanship and the predominantly Highland clans. Too often, however, writings on the clans give precedence to literary romanticism over historical realism. In order to see the clans in their true historical perspective, the examination of five key themes is essential – the origins of the clans, the structure of clanship, clanship and disorder, the clans and the Royal House of Stewart and the aftermath of Culloden.

ORIGINS OF THE CLANS

Mythological founders have often been claimed by clans, reinforcing both their status and a romantic and glorified notion of their origins. Most powerful clans appropriated for themselves fabulous origins based on Celtic mythology. Thus the political rivalry between Clan Donald, who claimed to be descended from either Conn, a second-century king of Ulster, or Cuchulainn, the legendary hero of Ulster, and the Campbells, who claimed Diarmaid the Boar as their progenitor, was rooted in the Fenian or Fingalian cycle. On the other hand, others such as the McKinnons and the McGregors were content to claim common ancestry from the Alpin family who united the Scottish kingdom in 843. Only one confederation of clans, that of the MacSweens, Lamonts, MacLeys, MacLachlans and MacNeills, who emerged to prominence in Knapdale and Cowal in the twelfth century, can trace one line of their ancestry back to the fifth century – to Niall of the Nine Hostages, High King of Ireland. In reality, the progenitors of the clans can rarely be authenticated further back than the eleventh century and a continuity of lineage in most cannot be detected until the thirteenth and fourteenth centuries.

The emergence of the clans has less to do with ethnicity than with political turmoil and social opportunity. The Scottish Crown's reconquest of Argyll and the Western Isles from the Norse in the thirteenth century, following on from the pacification of Moray and the northern rebellions in the twelfth and early thirteenth centuries, created opportunities for lay and even ecclesiastical warlords with the assistance of their immediate kindred, to impose their dominance over diverse localities whose indigenous families accepted their protection, either willingly or by force. Although these warrior chiefs can be primarily categorised as Celtic, their origins range from Gaelic to Norse-Gaelic to British. Moreover, the political instability and dislocation which resulted from the Wars of Independence fought against the English Crown had, by the outset of the fourteenth century, created further scope for Celtic territorial expansion. It also allowed an influx of Anglo kindreds such as Camerons, Frasers, Chisholms, Menzies and Grants, whose ethnic origins ranged from Anglo-Norman to Anglian to Flemish, to move into the Highlands.

Another significant milestone in the emergence of clanship also arose during the Wars of Independence with the introduction of feudal tenures to regulate landholding, as Robert the Bruce sought to harness and control the martial prowess of the clans through the award of charters. Comprehensive grants of lands and the right to dispense justice in the name of the Crown were given to chiefs and leading gentry of the clans prepared to support the national cause against the English kings. Thus, the MacDonalds were elevated over the MacDougalls, with whom they shared common descent from Somerled, the great Norse-Gaelic warlord of the twelfth century. The subsequent political and cultural aggrandisement of the MacDonalds as Lords of the Isles, over the next two centuries, has tended to obscure the fact that they, like their acquisitive rivals, the Campbells, owed their position not only to their strong ties of kinship and local association, but also to the acceptance and promotion of their territorial influence by the Scottish Crown. Clanship was thereby essentially defined as a product of local association, kinship and feudalism. It is this feudal component, grounded and reinforced by Scots law, which separates clanship from tribalism, and which historically differentiates Scottish clans from aboriginal groups in Australasia, Africa and the Americas.

In the Highlands as in the Lowlands, shared local affinities and assumptions were reflected in the dominance of lordship based on family affiliations until the seventeenth century. In the Highlands, however, clanship had an added cultural association with the Gaelic language. Hence, the territory settled by the indigenous clans was designated Scottish Gaeldom.

THE STRUCTURE OF CLANSHIP
The authority of the clan
Clanship contained two complementary but distinct concepts of heritage. The collective heritage of the clan, their 'duthchas', was their prescriptive right to settle the territories over which the chiefs and leading gentry of the clan customarily provided protection. This concept meant that the personal authority of the chiefs and leading gentry as trustees for their clan was recognised by all clansmen; thus justification for and recognition of the chief's authority came from below and from within the clan itself. However, the wider acceptance of the granting of charters by the Crown, and by other powerful landowners to the clan chiefs, chieftains and lairds defined the estates settled by their clan as their 'oighreachd', and gave a different emphasis to the basis of the clan chief's authority. This concept was one of individual heritage, warranted from above, and it institutionalised the authority of chiefs and leading gentry as landed proprietors – owners of the land in their own right, rather than as trustees for the clan's collective good. The absence of this land concept differentiates the clanship of the Irish from Scottish Gaels. Of

course, the two concepts could co-exist, and from the outset of clanship in Scotland, the 'fine' – the clan warrior elite – strove to be landowners as well as territorial warlords.

Clans and the law
Whereas in the middle ages the concept of duthchas held precedence, the balance was tilting in favour of the concept of oighreachd in the early modern period. This shifting balance reflected the continuing importance of Scots Law in shaping the structure of clanship. In addition to the award of charters to the fine, continuity of heritable succession was secured by the acceptance of primogeniture. The 'tainistear', the heir to the chief, was usually the direct male heir and although attention has tended to focus on those clans where the direct heir was set aside in favour of a more politically accomplished or belligerent relative, disputes over succession were not characteristic of the Highlands beyond the sixteenth century; indeed, by the seventeenth century, not only was the setting aside of primogeniture a rarity, but male succession over several generations was increasingly governed and restricted by the law of Entail which prevented the division of landed estates among female heirs and thus the loss and alienation of clan territories.

The legal process primarily used to settle criminal and civil disputes within clans was that of arbitration. Within the clan, the offending and aggrieved parties put their respective case to an arbitration panel drawn from their leading gentry and over which their chief presided. In disputes between clans, the chiefs served as the procurators (legal agents) for the offending or aggrieved parties before an arbitration panel drawn from equal numbers of leading gentry from each clan and presided over by a neighbouring chief or landlord. The decision of the arbitration panel, from which there was no appeal, was recorded in the most convenient Royal or Burgh court. Arbitration was based on reparations, known as assythment, rather than retribution. The compensation awarded to the aggrieved party took account of such variables as the age, status and family responsibilities of the victim, as well as the nature of the crime. On payment of reparation the offending party was indemnified against any further action for redress. The process depended ultimately on the willingness of clans to make prompt reparation, a situation made more likely by the regular contracting of bands of friendship between clans which made standing provision for arbitration. Again, these bands had the force of law and were recorded in the most convenient Royal or Burgh court.

Clans and social ties

The most important forms of social bonding in the clans, in addition to legal bands, were fosterage and manrent. The marriage alliance, which reinforced links with neighbouring clans as well as kinship within territorially diverse families, was also a commercial contract involving the exchange of livestock, money and land through payments which in the case of the bride was known as the 'tocher' and for the groom, the 'dowry'. The gentry of the clan were expected to underwrite the contracts made by their chiefs or leading lairds, a legal obligation which grew in importance as increasing numbers of marriage contracts were made outwith Gaeldom in the course of the seventeenth century. Marriage ties, even when forms of trial marriage such as handfasting had been repressed in the wake of the Reformation, were the least durable aspect of social bonding. Conversely, fosterage, the bringing up of the chief's children by favoured members of the leading clan gentry and in turn, their children by other favoured members of the clan, cemented ties of such intensity that it was not regarded as exceptional for foster-brothers to sacrifice themselves in protecting their chiefs. The commercial facet of this relationship reinforced feelings of clan cohesion in making particular provision, usually in the form of livestock, for foster-children on their reaching adulthood or on the death of their foster-parents.

The third form of social tie was manrent.

This was a bond contracted by the heads of satellite families who did not live on the estates of the clan elite, but to whom they affiliated to ensure territorial protection. Bonds of manrent were reinforced by calps, the payment of death duties. On the death of these satellite heads, their families usually paid their best cow or horse to the chief in recognition of his protection and as a mark of personal allegiance. Although calps were banned as oppressive by Parliament in 1617, the need for protection could not be proscribed by legislation and manrent continued covertly. While manrenting was apparently less frequent, bands were made less to create new ties of dependency then to renew protection after a lapse of a generation, and notably after the political divisions occasioned by civil wars in 1644–47 and 1689–90.

The management of the clan

All members of the clan living on the estates of the chief and leading gentry paid rents and calp; those outwith the estates paid calp only. Such payments, which could be in money, in kind and in labour, were channelled through the tacksmen, the lesser gentry who served as the lynch-pins of clanship and the clan system and who gave tangible force to protection, hospitality and the productive use of clan resources. Until the advent of written leasing in the sixteenth century, the tacksman's holdings were held from the clan chief or his lairds according to oral tradition. Their role was essentially that of managers who aimed to attain a comfortable sufficiency for the farmers, crofters and cotters as well as the clan nobility. As the environment of Scottish Gaeldom was not particularly conducive to farming, the objective required the adaptation of customary rents and services owed by clansmen to the fine through the balanced management of landed resources, commercial demands and man-power.

The basic unit of management for every tacksman was the baile or township, which supported anything from four to over sixteen families, who were each assigned individual holdings but worked the land communally. Within this context, the tacksmen adapted customary estate management: they oversaw the reallocation of strips of land in open fields held as run-rig by the individual families within each township; arranging for crop manuring and herding; and organising the movement to summer pasture on upland and island shielings. They collected rents (from which they apportioned a share), and were responsible for controlling the amount of crops sown, work-services to be performed and numbers of livestock to be grazed. Incoming and newly inheriting tenants were given loans of seed-corn, livestock and tools – which were known as steel-bow – their needs having been assessed by the tacksman. The tacksman also played a key role in the rounding up and marketing of cattle by droving to the Lowlands.

Their managerial role, however, has tended to be subsumed by their military role as mobilisers of the clan host. Notwithstanding the martial exhortations of bards and other Gaelic poets, and the impressive numbers of clansmen that could be mobilised expeditiously on the passing round of the fiery cross, the calling out of the host was as much social and recreational as military. The host was mobilised particularly during the summer downturn in the agrarian cycle to provide gainful employment for clansmen who might otherwise drift into banditry. Thus, the month of August was traditionally assigned for the hunts, where the chiefs and their noble kinsmen and guests were attended by their followers to act as beaters and to engage in a variety of virile sports which have come down to posterity as Highland games. A large turnout of followers was also expected for weddings and funerals. A chief who failed to secure a large turn-out of his clansmen was deemed to have detracted from his own personal standing. The substantial mobilisation of the host to perambulate and control the estates of the clan elite served as a discouragement to the territorial ambitions of other chiefs or landlords. However, the calling out

of the host for social and recreational reasons was not without a large measure of military ambivalence as these occasions – which were especially noted for copious consumption of strong drink – could degenerate into disorder often caused by disputes relating to individual rank and precedence fanned by a highly developed sense of personal honour.

CLANSHIP AND DISORDER

The association of the clans with disorder was partly the product of their turbulent origins and was particularly marked by the disputes surrounding the break-up, forfeiture and abortive attempts at restoration of the Lordship of the Isles in the late fifteenth and early sixteenth centuries. Public perceptions of unruly elements within Gaeldom tended to make the blanket association of clanship with feuding and banditry commonplace, a perception that was not discouraged at the Scottish Court or by central government after the Union of the Crowns in 1603.

Territorial dispute

Feuding was essentially an issue of territorial hegemony – the outcome of the failure of the estates comprising the oighreachd of the clan elite to match up to the territories claimed as the collective duthchas of their clan. On the one hand, the clan gentry were frustrated that some of their clansmen were obliged to pay rents to other landlords; on the other, acquisitive clans, most notably the Campbells and the Mackenzies, were prepared to play off territorial disputes within and among clans to expand their own landed influence. Feuding on the western seaboard, which was conducted with such an intensity that the Macleods and Macdonalds on Skye were reputedly reduced to eating dogs and cats in the 1590s, was further compounded by the involvement of the indigenous clans in the wars of the Irish Gaels against the English Tudor monarchy in the sixteenth century. Indeed, within these clans there had evolved a military caste, the 'buannachan', who were regarded as members of the lesser gentry, even although they were purely warriors and not managers, and who migrated seasonally to Ireland to fight as mercenaries. When not contracted by the Irish Gaels, they lived parasitically off their own clan. The plantation of Ulster by James VI drove a wedge between the Gaels which eventually resulted in the redundancy of the buannachan within a generation. Their redundancy was an integral aspect of a Crown-inspired programme, which commenced with the Statutes of Iona of 1609, to assimilate the chiefs, their chieftains and gentry into Scottish landed society. Despite the opportunities created for perpetuating feuding in the civil wars between Covenanter and Royalist during the 1640s, chiefs and leading clan gentry, like their landed counterparts in the Lowlands, preferred increasingly to settle landed disputes by recourse to law. Following the restoration of the monarchy in 1660, the incidents of feuding between clans declined markedly. The last clan feud which led to a battle actually occurred at Mulroy on 4 August 1688, when the Macdonalds of Keppoch successfully resisted the government backed efforts of the Mackintosh chief of the Clan Chattan to take over their territory in the Braes of Lochaber.

Reiving

The decline of militarism among the clans was further evident in the phasing out of the 'creach', a ritualistic rite of passage whereby the young men of the clan demonstrated their virility by removing livestock from neighbouring clan territory. By the seventeenth century the most prevalent form of reiving or plundering was the 'spreidh', essentially a freelance operation involving rarely more than ten associates which usually preyed on the Lowland peripheries of Gaeldom. Livestock 'lifted' by these raiders could usually be recovered through the payment of 'tascal' – information money – and the guarantee of an indemnity from criminal prosecution. Conversely, certain clans, such as the MacFarlanes in the southern and the Farquharsons in the eastern Highlands offered their services as a professional watch for their Lowland neighbours, although their

rates for protection could not be dissociated from accusations of 'blackmail'. Continuance of such reiving can be linked geographically to the Macgregors in the southern and eastern Highlands and to the clans of the Lochaber region – clans in which the chiefs and nobles had little or no title to the territories settled by their clansmen. Yet even here, the acquisition of comprehensive landed titles by the Cameron chiefs in the course of the seventeenth century resulted in a marked decline in freelance reiving by the Lochaber clansmen.

From the later sixteenth century, central government, in the shape of the Scottish Privy Council, had demanded generally that clan leaders provide bands of surety promising the orderly conduct of themselves and their clansmen, who were defined not only as the tenants on their estates but all followers who owed territorial allegiance, including anyone resident within their bounds more than twelve hours. Although these bands carried considerable financial penalties including the forfeiture of land and title for persistent non-compliance, their issue was also recognition that Gaeldom could not be governed without the co-operation of the chiefs. Moreover, as the bands required the regular attendance of the clan leadership in Edinburgh, their sojourns to the Lowlands became increasingly prolonged. Absenteeism, in turn, led to the accumulation of debts which could only partially be recouped through raising rents. 'Wadsets', or mortgages, were increasingly used by the fine to raise money, particularly after the civil wars of the 1640s confirmed their commitment to Scottish as against Gaelic politics. With the expansion of droving in the later seventeenth century, tacksmen had sufficient funds to finance these mortgages which led to an acquisition of landed status themselves as the debts were secured against the revenues of the chief's estates. When the debts could not be discharged, the tacksmen acquired the land itself. The consequent expansion of land ownership amongst the tacksmen and lesser clan gentry meant that they, in turn, became liable for bands of surety. By the 1680s, this expansion of land ownership meant that for the first time the estates of the clan elite, held individually as their oighreachd, largely coincided with the territories settled collectively as the duthchas of their clan. The acceptance of responsibility by the expanded elite for the conduct of clansmen settled on their townships as tenants can directly be related to the decline of banditry as well as feuding.

Despite the growth of social responsibility amongst the landed proprietors, freelance reiving persisted. This can be attributed primarily to the proliferation of 'cateran' bands, groups of up to fifty bandits, who had thrown over the social constraint of clanship and were usually led by a renegade member of the clan gentry. These bands were also for hire, mainly on the peripheries of Gaeldom, where their principal employment was as thugs, settling or exacerbating landed disputes between Lowland lords and lairds. Within the Highlands, they remained a parasitic influence on clanship, their numbers being readily augmented in the social dislocation resulting from the civil wars of the 1640s and the Jacobite rebellions of 1689, 1715 and 1745. Successive Scottish governments, intent on taking punitive military action against the clans – including the forcible exaction of taxes – deliberately confused clanship with banditry. This defamatory and crude association was continued with less intelligence and growing virulence by successive British governments in the aftermath of the Treaty of Union of 1707 and the abolition of the Scottish Privy Council the following year. Official smearing with a charge of banditry was an integral, if blatant, aspect of anti-Jacobite propaganda because of the overwhelming identification of the clans, politically and militarily, with the Royal House of Stewart.

THE CLANS AND THE ROYAL HOUSE OF STEWART

Notwithstanding the forfeiture of the Lord of the Isles in 1493, the Scottish Crown under the house of Stewart from the mid-fourteenth to the outset of the seventeenth century had no coherent policy towards Gaeldom other

than occasional military expeditions to daunt refractory clans. After the Union of the Crowns in 1603, James VI did not abandon the military option. Indeed, he rigorously expropriated three clans – the Macdonalds of Kintyre and Islay, the Macleods of Lewis and the Macdonalds of Ardnamurchan – and proscribed another, the Macgregors. However, he was also resolved that chiefs and their leading gentry should be bound over as de facto agents for local government, a policy followed less systematically by his son, Charles I, whose political power in Scotland was eclipsed by the emergence of the Covenanting movement in 1638.

The civil wars

Clan support for the house of Stewart as hereditary rulers of Scotland was based primarily on the projection of traditional values of clanship onto the national political stage. As the chiefs were the protectors of the clan duthchas, so were the Stewarts trustees for Scotland. At the same time, clan support for Charles I during the civil wars of the 1640s was essentially reactionary. The clans who declared unequivocally for the Royalist cause were fighting less in favour of that absentee monarch than against the Covenanting movement which was making unprecedented demands on the Scots for ideological, financial and military commitment. More especially, the clans were reacting against powerful noble houses, pre-eminently those of Argyll and Sutherland, whose public espousal of the Covenanting cause masked their private pursuit of territorial ambitions. Conversely, aversion to the hitherto pervasive influence of the powerful pro-Royalist house of Huntly persuaded some clans in the central Highlands to side with the Covenanters and others to remain neutral. Civil wars divided the clans no less than the rest of Scotland, although religious affiliation was not such a divisive issue among them even although the Campbells and other Covenanting clans were in broad sympathy with Presbyterianism.

However, religion was a principal factor influencing clans to come out for the Jacobite rising in 1689. The sporadic efforts of Catholic missions in the Highlands had served to solidify the opposition of former Royalist clans to the deposition of James VII. However, the spread of Episcopalianism during the Restoration era was more significant in attracting support from hitherto neutral clans and in persuading former Covenanting clans to adopt a neutral standpoint. Episcopalianism not only provided a religious complement to the hierarchical nature of clanship, but inculcated a spirit of obedience and submission to royal authority throughout Gaeldom. Accordingly, the replacement of James VII by William of Orange was interpreted as a breach of patriarchal duty by Gaelic poets for whom the sundering of genealogical continuity imperiled the lawful exercise of government which, in turn, subverted the maintenance of a just political order. Far from being tyrannical or oppressive, James VII had won favour among the clans when, as Duke of York during his brother's reign, he instituted the commission for pacifying the Highlands in 1682 which, for the next three years, had sought the willing co-operation of chiefs and leading clan gentry in maintaining order. Moreover, James had proved notably responsible in redressing the acquisitiveness of the house of Argyll in particular and all Campbells in general.

The clans and Jacobitism

Following the death of James in 1701, clan support for his son James, 'the Old Pretender', and his grandson Charles Edward, 'the Young Pretender', was boosted by widespread public antipathy in Scotland to the passage of the Treaty of Union in 1707. However, as the Union had underwritten the establishment of Presbyterianism and had opened up English and imperial markets, it had won some support and the subsequent Risings of 1715, 1719 and, above all, 1745, again took on the character of civil wars in Scotland. Rebellions were marked by militant divergence of opinion among Highland clans as well as Lowland families. Such were the divisions in the clans caused by the Forty-Five, that clansmen in Skye and Wester Ross blatantly defied their more cautious chiefs to support 'the Young Pretender'. More audaciously, the Mackintosh chief of Clan Chattan raised a company for the British government, of whom all but nine deserted to join the six hundred clansmen raised by his wife for Prince Charles Edward. Militarily, the attraction of the Highlands for the launching of Risings was the ready mobilisation of the clan hosts. Moreover, social occasions such as the hunts, involving Lowland landlords as well as the clan elite, provided convenient cover to plot rebellion, as was demonstrated by the Earl of Mar, the Jacobite commander in 1715; he used the excuse of a hunt on his Braemar estates to assemble his forces in order to raise the Jacobite standard and launch the Fifteen. The British government in London found it difficult to take prompt military action against Highland insurgency because of communication difficulties, both with the predominantly Gaelic-speaking people and also across unfriendly terrain. Yet, as manifest by the fluctuating nature of clan support in all Jacobite risings, the further away the campaigns progressed from the Highlands, the more the appeal of the cause diminished as the clans' traditional territories remained unprotected. However, the greatest political and strategic contradiction lay in the attempt of the Jacobite claimants to reconcile their main goal – the English throne – with their military support, which was almost exclusively Scottish and predominantly clannish; a contradiction that ultimately proved to be the fatal flaw in the two campaigns which came tantalisingly close to success in 1715 and 1745.

Each Jacobite failure was marked by government reprisals of varying degrees of barbarity against the clans. Frustrated by the continuance of the Jacobite clans in arms for two years after the outbreak of rebellion in 1689, the government of William of Orange contrived the massacre of the MacDonalds of Glencoe in February 1692. Forfeiture of land among certain clans followed the risings of 1715 and 1719, but the government's attempted pacification of the Highlands by Disarming Acts in 1716 and 1725 mainly gained compliance from clans favourably disposed to the British establishment. The greatest severity followed the Jacobite defeat at Culloden in April 1746. Captured Jacobites, if they survived imprisonment and show trials in Carlisle, York and London, were usually shipped off to the plantations of the American South or the Caribbean. As a sop to English public opinion, the now anachronistic obligation to give military service to chiefs and nobles in return for landholding was abolished, along with the right to dispense justice enshrined in the feudal heritable jurisdictions; the government seemed unaware that these latter rights were in fact predominantly the preserve of the Lowland landed classes and were not in fact the bedrock of Highland society at all. Further repressive legislation rigorously enforced disarmament and banned such cultural trappings as the wearing of tartan. Speaking Gaelic was proscribed.

THE AFTERMATH OF CULLODEN

Clanship, as the working basis of Highland society, was destroyed after the Forty-five. The most critical external contribution was that of the Duke of Cumberland, son of George II and commander of the government forces. Having contemplated the wholescale transportation of the Jacobite clans, Cumberland settled instead for a draconian purge of Scottish Gaeldom by authorising the wanton butchery perpetrated by the government troops. The policy, which might now be called ethnic cleansing, was a disgrace, and one of the major troughs for British imperialism.

A more insidious contribution to the demise of clanship, however, was that made by the clan leaders themselves in their commercial determination to place greater emphasis on their individual rights as landowners (oighreachd) at the expense of their customary role as trustees for their clans (duthchas). The episodic establishment of

Independent Companies – an early form of the later Highland regiments – from the Restoration era had to undermine their traditional role as protectors of their clan territories. The abolition of the Scottish Privy Council in 1708 was also the end of central government's attempts to govern the Highlands in co-operation with the traditional hierarchy of the clans.

The threat of renewed forfeiture persuaded some chiefs, including the Mackenzies and the MacDonalds of Sleat to abstain from the Forty-Five. Other chiefs, including Clanranald and Glengarry, thought the campaign so ill-advised that although they permitted contingents of their clansmen to fight for the Jacobite cause, they personally stayed at home; the latter chief dissociated himself from his Jacobite clansmen. The distinctly pro-government chief of the Mackays of Strathnaver actually advised Cumberland that it was easier to conquer than to civilise the Highlanders.

For almost two decades prior to the Forty-Five, clansmen were leaving the Highlands for the Americas, either being led from Argyll, the central Highlands and Sutherland by clan gentry seeking to re-establish a traditional lifestyle in Jamaica, Georgia, New York and the Carolinas or as victims of land raids in the Hebrides designed to secure cheap labour for the colonial plantations. The clan elite's desire for higher rents from the profits of the thriving droving trade, at the expense of the tacksman, led to acquiescence in the emigration of the first group; to the second they turned a blind eye. Culloden and the ultimate failure of Jacobitism in Scotland provided the psychological escape clause for those chiefs and other members of the clan hierarchy intent on throwing over traditional obligations of clanship. They were generally marked by a preference for absenteeism allied to the agricultural improvement of their estates; oighreachd now replaced rather than complemented duthchas. The ground was prepared for the Highland Clearances and the emasculation of the working system of clanship.

The Law of the Clan

GEORGE WAY OF PLEAN SSC

The name 'clan' is derived from the Gaelic word 'clanna', meaning 'children'. The expansion of the power base of a single family group was inevitable as successful leaders extended their territories and thereby their ability to support larger groups of people, all acknowledging their paternal authority. The line of families extending from the chiefly line has been likened to a social pyramid with the chief at its apex, spreading down towards an ever broadening base; this arrangement of extended families was known in the Celtic polity as the 'fine' system. As Skene explained in *Celtic Scotland:*

> The fine system was one of the more important social features of the clan, not indeed as a means of succession but from the emphasis it gave to the concept of expanding branches, and the manner in which it developed biological communities within the Clan community keeping the pyramid always of manageable proportions. The gilfine consisted of a number of related households and was the minimum family commune. It was composed of five persons by which we understand not five individuals but five Heads. It represented the descendants of a grandfather as an actual working unit. Far from the title Chief being a rare one in Celtic civilisation, the popular unit was evidently the gilfine group under a gilfine Chief.

The chief was required to govern wisely, and he was assisted in this by numerous officers, managers and an entire household of 'civil servants'. If the chief was not well versed in law or was incapable of military leadership, these functions were delegated to a deemster or 'judex', or the war leader or 'ceann-cath', respectively. The tradition of an independent legal profession was well known throughout the Celtic lands, and judges (known as 'brehons') were highly respected individuals

whose office tended to be hereditary. The ceann-cath was usually a member of the chief's immediate family and often might have been the most suitable head of a major gilfine of the clan or perhaps the most likely heir if the chief were a youth or had no sons. There were no specific functions of the ceann-cath save in leading the war band and doing whatever might be necessary in times of military crisis. Following the chief himself in rank was the 'tainistear', who was the heir nominated by the chief during his own lifetime. The immediate family of the chief formed a kind of council known as the 'derbhfine', or true line. The heads of the individual gilfines, or houses into which the clan was divided, were known as 'ceann-tighes' which has generally been translated as 'chieftain'. (The precise definition of this term has proved extremely problematic when it has come before the Courts; see page 27 below.) The gentry of the clan, the 'duisne-uasail', constituted the only real rank gradation between the chief and his clansmen. They would have been originally denominated by their larger landholdings but in more modern times the term has become synonymous with an armiger, i.e. a person having their own grant of arms. As the Crown and its courts came to be called upon to settle disputes concerning chiefs and their clan rights, it became increasingly important to distinguish between chiefs and all their various descendants and, in particular, the principal cadets or gilfine houses. The development of a regulated and scientific system of heraldry was to become the key to this.

HERALDRY, THE LAW AND THE CLAN SYSTEM

According to the eighteenth-century heraldic authority, Nisbet, the purpose of heraldry is

> not merely show and pageantry as some are apt to imagine, but to distinguish per-

sons and families; to represent the heroic achievements of our ancestors and to perpetuate their memory; to trace the origin of noble and ancient families and the various steps by which they arrived at greatness; to distinguish the many different branches descended from the same families and to show the several relations which one family stands to another.

The Lyon Court

The Scottish Crown recognised the crucial role that heraldry played in fifteenth- and sixteenth-century society and invested its principal Officer of Arms, the Lord Lyon King of Arms, with considerable powers. A strong central court was established by a series of Acts of Parliament, culminating in that of 1672 which established the Public Register of all Arms and Bearings in Scotland, which has been maintained ever since. This Act made it unlawful for any person to bear arms which had not been properly registered, and decreed that all future grants of arms must be so recorded. As the clan system was at the heart of Scottish society and heraldry, it is not surprising that it soon became a dominant force in the development of Lyon Court practice and procedure.

The best definition of a clan provided by a heraldic authority is contained in Nisbet's *System of Heraldry*, published in 1722: 'A social group consisting of an aggregate of distinct erected families actually descended, or accepting themselves as descendants of a common ancestor, and which has been received by the Sovereign through its Supreme Officer of Honour, the Lord Lyon, as an honourable community whereof all of the members on establishing right to, or receiving fresh grants of, personal hereditary nobility will be awarded arms as determinate or indeterminate cadets both as may be of the chief family of the clan.' A clan is therefore a community which is both distinguished by heraldry and recognised by the sovereign.

The centre of this honourable community is the chief, who was invested with the twin symbols of Celtic and feudal power. First, he would possess the principal lands and, more importantly, the coat of arms showing his place in the honourable community. He would be the only person entitled to display the undifferenced shield of arms, i.e. without any marks of dependency upon any other noble house. Second, he would have, through his family connection and personal qualities, the loyalty of his people, giving the group coherence and a sense of permanence. Chiefship is therefore a title of honour and dignity within the nobility of Scotland. Any claimant to such a title must establish, to the satisfaction of the Lord Lyon representing the sovereign, that he or she is entitled to the undifferenced arms of the community over which they seek to preside. The Lyon Court operates within the Scottish judicial structure and the Lord Lyon sits in state in full judicial attire. The normal rules of evidence apply and the Lord Lyon is assisted in judicial proceedings by the Lyon Clerk. In important cases he is also entitled to seek the assistance of his Lords Assessors: these are the Lord High Constable of Scotland (the Earl of Erroll) and the Duke of Hamilton. It is the determining of chiefship which is among the Lyon Court's central work and according to Sir Thomas Innes of Learney, a former Lord Lyon,

> The determination of Chiefship either ministerially or judicially, is a matter of much more than academic importance and one which is really the basis of Scottish heraldry. Most Lyon Court litigations have been directly or indirectly connected with this. Not only from its social importance as a binding force in the community, but for the prevention of discord and uncertainty as well as the importance the subject gives to Scottish heraldry, it is manifestly expedient that such disputes should be capable of the conclusive settlement so effectively provided by a Court, and Office of Honour, deriving from the High

Sir Malcolm Innes of Edingight KCVO, the Lord Lyon King of Arms, in his judicial robes. This is the attire worn by the Lord Lyon when presiding over cases brought before the Lyon Court to determine such matters as chiefship and peerage.

Sennachie and embodying the relative nobiliary corpus juris of the Law of Arms.

Many important cases have come before the Lyon Court in the twentieth century and perhaps the most significant in recent years was an action in 1990 to determine rights in the chiefly House of Dunbar of Mochrum. The case is important for the procedures and the process which were followed. The Lord Lyon sat in a courtroom normally used by the Appeal Court in the Court of Session in

Edinburgh. The petitioner was represented by Sir Crispin Agnew of Lochnaw, Baronet, who wore, in addition to his advocate's wig and gown, the uniform of Unicorn Pursuivant and the Nova Scotia Baronet badge worn by all chiefs of Clan Agnew since 1629. The respondent was represented by a distinguished Queen's Counsel. The Crown had also entered the proceedings, being represented by the Lord Advocate, the most senior Scottish law officer and a member of the British Cabinet. The Lord Lyon's decision in the case was not accepted and an appeal was then heard in the Inner House of the Court of Session and ultimately the case was resolved in the House of Lords in London. This demonstrates not only that the Lyon Court is a fully integrated part of the Scottish judicial system, but also that clan rights have survived to this day, not just as a historical curiosity or romantic ideal, but as part of Scotland's heritage, worthy of the attention of the highest courts of the land.

Lawful possession of the undifferenced coat of arms of the first family is, therefore, clearly central to chiefship. However, it is recognition by the sovereign, which is of paramount importance. This was demonstrated by a case which took place in 1960, concerning the ancient and distinguished family of Spens. It has long been accepted that the grant of a peerage by the Crown where the title consists solely of the name of a Scottish armorial family was appropriate only to the chief or head of that family. Thus it was held that when a junior cadet of the chiefly house of Spens received a patent of nobility from the Crown as Baron Spens, he had been recognised by the sovereign as the head of the family, even although genealogically senior claimants existed. Lord Spens petitioned, and was granted the undifferenced arms of his family, to which he would not otherwise have been entitled. The judgment issued by the Lord Lyon contained a specific reservation that the arms would descend only to the heirs of Lord Spens bearing the peerage title, and if this title became extinct the arms would revert to the genealogically senior line of the family. In this case, then, the grant of arms followed recognition by the sovereign. There does exist one legal bar to a claimant taking up a clan chiefship even if he is entitled to the undifferenced arms. This occurs where the holder has two family names hyphenated together (known colloquially as a double-barrelled surname). It was established in the case of Campbell-Gray, Petitioner, in 1950 that no person may bear a compound or double-barrelled surname and be recognised as a chief. This is for the fairly obvious reason that the compound surname is held to be a new name and is not simply the aggregate of the two or more parts. The solution to this problem, which has been adopted by some chiefly families, is to drop the hyphenated aspect of the compound surname and simply add the additional names as forenames. The Duke of Buccleuch, Chief of Clan Scott, now incorporates his additional family names of Montagu and Douglas in the name Montagu Douglas Scott, without the offending hyphens and therefore has the recognition of the Lyon Court.

The process of a gilfine, or house within the clan, breaking off and forming a clan in its own right was not uncommon in past centuries. Yet this process of the community growing and perhaps separating into related but distinctive branches is not simply a relic of the past, but can still be a positive force in modern practice. This is to some degree illustrated by a recent dispute in the Court of the Lord Lyon between Sir David Nicolson of Lasswade Baronet, The Lord Carnock, and Nicolson of Scorrybreac. The House of Scorrybreac had emigrated to Australia in the nineteenth century. A petition was presented to the Lyon Court and the arms of Nicolson of Scorrybreac were duly recorded. There had been no matriculation of arms for a chief of Clan Nicolson for centuries. Nicolsons throughout the world recognised Scorrybreac as the only known leader of the clan. Lord Carnock presented a petition seeking the undifferenced arms of Nicolson and thereby recognition as chief of that name. His Lordship was successful in his petition.

Thereafter, Scorrybreac petitioned the Lord Lyon for recognition that his house and followers were truly an independent clan, Macneacail. The Lord Lyon accepted that although the arms of Scorrybreac demonstrated the family connection to Nicolson, nevertheless the West Highland Macneacails had in reality been independent for centuries. The Lord Lyon accordingly recognised their chief as Macneacail of Macneacail and Scorrybreac. The new chief, however, did not receive a grant of supporters.

The device of a heraldic supporter may appear, and is often believed, to be an integral part of the heraldry of a clan chief but this is emphatically not the case. Supporters (the splendid beasts, wild men and other devices which adorn the flanks of the shields of most clan chiefs) are 'additaments', or heraldic additions to the basic coat of arms, and are restricted to persons of rank, including peers of the realm, clan chiefs and other territorial magnates. They are marks of recognition by the Crown that the bearer is of high standing and may often represent in pictorial form some past heroic deed or other royal service rendered. They do not denominate any actual rank. This was most graphically pronounced by Lord Lyon Innes of Learney when he stated that 'supporters are incidents of Chiefship and other high persons. They are not *indiciae* of anything. They are exterior ornaments. A Chief was distinguished by his shield, surcoat and banner, not by supporters. No Chief went into battle with a stuffed dog and a golly nailed to the corners of his shield to show that he was a Chief. The idea is ludicrous.' However, the Lord Lyon has stated that the existence, or grant, of supporters can be conclusive evidence that arms are 'chiefly' in character where there is a dispute as to which shield of arms is that of the chief. The constitution of the Standing Council of Scottish Chiefs requires hereditary supporters for automatic membership. A chief without supporters may be proposed and, if elected, serve on the Council for his or her lifetime only. Each heir would require to be re-elected in the same manner.

Contrary to what is often believed, there is no specific armorial mark or symbol which denominates a clan chief, and in most respects the grant of arms when produced by the herald painters at the Lyon Court will look very similar to that of any other territorial noble. There has been a practice in the Lyon Court to allow only to clan chiefs a coronet around the top of the helmet from which the crest issues, but this practice is not yet universally established. The only truly unique heraldic device relating to a chief is the small triangular flag, known as a pinsel (which is more fully described on page 489).

SUCCESSION TO THE CHIEFSHIP

Once duly established in the Lyon Court, succession is governed by concepts of inheritance by heirs determined by blood. There are numerous references to the early Celtic practice of electing each successor to the chiefship; this was the role of the derbhfine, the true line. This body was, generally speaking, the nine most senior living descendants of a chiefly great grandfather, and in Ireland it was confined to persons connected only in the male line. In Scotland, derbhfines were not so restricted and electors and candidates could be connected by female lines and indeed, could be females. All the Scottish judicial and heraldic authorities confirm that chiefship can be held directly by a female heir, and several clans, including Fraser, Elliot, Maclachlan and Moffat, are most ably led by women. Even before the complete acceptance of succession by right of blood, the vagaries of an elective system were to some extent elided by the nomination of a successor by the chief before his death; this was the tainistear. It is doubtful if the chief could nominate anyone he wished; in general terms, most authorities indicate that the nomination required to be within the blood relations of the chief or it stood to be challenged. Lord Lyon Innes of Learney, following both Nisbet and Sir George Mackenzie of Rosehaugh, clearly distinguished between a nomination within the blood from that upon a complete stranger:

Tanistry [is] the right of each patriarch to settle succession, within the family, and only if he makes the settlement outwith that group, or seeks to alter an existing specific destination would the question of royal veto and therefore the need for Letters Patent arise, otherwise the heir or nominee makes up his title by matriculation. Unless the antecedent matriculation contains a specific destination all Arms in Scotland pass by succession or nomination in familia, the former admitting of possession on apparentcy, the latter necessarily involving immediate rematriculation to make up title.

The terms of any modern nomination seeking to determine the right of succession to a chiefship would accordingly require to be very carefully drafted indeed and would still be subject to the scrutiny of the Lyon Court.

The ad hoc derbhfine

However, the derbhfine has not entirely disappeared from the legal system, and it is to be found in the procedure followed where the whole chiefly line has been extinguished and no claimant to the undifferenced arms has come forward to the Lyon Court. In such a case, the Lord Lyon, exercising the delegated authority of the sovereign, may award the arms appropriate to the chief or head of any house by the petition of an 'ad hoc derbhfine'. It must be stressed that Lord Lyon does not, and cannot, rule on who should lead a clan in such a situation if there are rival nominees. The procedure requires one person to be selected by the ad hoc derbhfine who, if the Lord Lyon in his ministerial and executive capacity finds to be a fit and proper person according to the Law of Arms, may be granted the appropriate armorial ensigns, the symbol of his authority over his community. The procedure is initiated generally by an approach from a clan society or association to the Court of the Lord Lyon. An Officer of Arms, one of the Heralds or Pursuivants, is generally retained to oversee the necessary procedures and prepare the petition. The ad hoc derbhfine

is duly convened and advertisement of the procedure is generally ordered on a fairly wide basis to ensure that due notice is made and to give an opportunity for any heir to come forward and claim the chiefship by right of blood. As from 1 May 1992, the Lord Lyon King of Arms has issued guidelines in relation to ad hoc derbhfine as follows:

1. Any candidate selected and recommended to the Lord Lyon King of Arms requires to have been domiciled and habitually resident in Scotland for a period of three years before such recommendation and submission and must be so domiciled and resident at the time the recommendation and submission is made.
2. Membership of the ad hoc derbhfine shall consist of those who are in right of a Scottish coat of arms (matriculated within the last three generations to cover the holding of the armorial bearings on apparentcy or where the warrant authorise and the preparation of Letters Patent of Arms or an Interlocutor authorising matriculation of arms has been signed in favour of such a person at least a year and a day before they participate). The armorial bearings must be Scottish and those with a Scottish surname, but with arms granted by the English Kings of Arms or by the heraldic authority of any other State will not be acceptable. The owner of the armorial bearings will not require to be domiciled or resident in Scotland provided they otherwise qualify under this condition.
3. A person may also participate in the ad hoc derbhfine provided he owns lands in Scotland outwith a Burgh which is not a mere building plot. A properly recorded heritable title will require to be exhibited prior to participation in the ad hoc derbhfine.
4. Those with compound surnames may participate in an ad hoc derbhfine provided they otherwise qualify, but the last name of the compound surname will determine the family or clan to which the

owner of the compound surname belongs. Only those with a surname relevant to the ad hoc derbhfine may participate.

5. Only those in right of a substantive Scottish coat of arms may participate and eldest sons bearing arms with three or five point labels are excluded. Where the bearer of Arms which would qualify under these conditions is a minor, his tutor or guardian may not vote on his behalf. Any child who has reached the age of legal capacity, however, may vote in his or her own right.

The Lyon Court guidelines do not indicate the minimum number required to constitute an ad hoc derbhfine, although this has generally been stated in previous authorities as nine. The purpose of the procedure is to present to the Lord Lyon a suitable candidate and it is submitted that, provided the ad hoc derbhfine is composed of all those who are qualified to participate, and wish to, the exact number of the electors may not be entirely relevant. This, of course, begs the question that if there are not nine qualified electors, whether there is truly a 'community' which we have seen is essential to the basic definition of a clan. The support of the ad hoc derbhfine may also be fortified by an acclamation, possibly a petition, made by the wider body of clansmen. Such a petition may have no direct legal status but could be lodged as an additional production in the Lyon Court petition procedure. However, the issue before the Lord Lyon is the fitness of the nominee to bear the arms and not his apparent popularity within the clan.

The ceann-cath

As we have seen, succession by blood and by females often meant that the chief would not necessarily always be of full age or physically able to lead the clan in battle. This role was therefore fulfilled by the ceann-cath. This term, historically, could be applied to the war leader or commander, or to the head of the principal cadet line, or perhaps the most prominent gilfine house. The style has become

part of Lyon Court procedure where it is used for a person who has received a commission from the Lord Lyon to lead a chiefless clan whilst the search for a bloodline chief is made. This is an extension of Lyon's ministerial and executive jurisdiction which has been achieved by blending the authority of the Crown with the Celtic origins of the clan system. The process of proposing a candidate for the office of commander utilises the ad hoc derbhfine and the Lord Lyon's guidelines of May 1992 apply to this procedure in equal measure. Once the Lord Lyon has considered the petition to appoint a commander, he will, if so persuaded, grant a commission, usually for a period of five years. The commission can also be renewed. The text of a typical commission appears in Appendix 6.

In common with chiefs themselves, commanders do not receive any special heraldic insignia or device but they may petition for the grant of a pinsel. The commander's commission would be automatically terminated if a chief were recognised by the Lord Lyon. Commanders have been appointed to lead Clans Gunn, McPhie and McArthur, and several other petitions are believed to be pending.

Chieftain

In the traditional clan structure next in rank to the ceann-cath were the 'ceann-tighes', or chieftains. The definition of this title is a thorny subject which has caused much debate but from an examination of early writings including the Acts of the Scottish Parliament, it is clear that the title 'chieftain' has been used synonymously for that of 'chief', and that until recent times there was no practical difference. Indeed, the form 'chieftain' appears to have been more commonly used to mean 'chief' or 'head of a household' in many early documents. An Act of Parliament of 1597 refers to 'chiftains and chiefis of all clannis and the principallis of the brancheis of the saidis clannis duelland in the Heilands or bordouris'. To add to the confusion, 'chieftain' also derives from 'chiftane of the countrie', meaning a territorial noble who might be connected in blood to those living on his lands but equally might not. This comes from the French 'chevetainrie-propriété d'un chevetain-seigneur'. The majority of great feudal landowners in Scotland were, of course, within the clan system and hence the crisis of definition which has arisen. There is no doubt that the accepted modern style for the head of a clan is chief, and accordingly a chieftain in the modern sense must be something different. He must therefore be either a great feudal magnate, or the head of a gilfine branch house of a clan. Some authorities, including the late Sir Iain Moncreiffe of that Ilk, Albany Herald, Chief of Clan Moncreiffe, suggest that the title extends to the sons of a chief, perhaps on the analogy that they rank with the heads of gilfine and indeed may well found gilfine of their own. A popular misconception exists that a chieftain may be any person so named by the chief to a post of honour within the clan. This may partly have arisen from a judgment of the Appeal Court of the Court of Session in a case concerning Maclean of Ardgour, heard initially in 1938 and again in 1941. The Court categorically stated that the title of chieftain, when not synonymous with that of chief, was not determinable before the Courts. (Lord Lyon Innes of Learney stoutly rebutted the position adopted by the Appeal Court in that case, and those wishing a detailed analysis should refer to his annotations to chapter six of *The Clans, Septs and Regiments of the Scottish Highlands* by Frank Adam.) There is on record at Lyon Office a recent matriculation in 1982 of a chieftain of the Clan Maclennan, who was neither head of a branch or gilfine of the clan nor a territorial noble of Scotland. This was, however, a rather special case where the petitioner was accepted as being of the chiefly house and who had been passed over at an ad hoc derbhfine selection at his own request. The arms granted to him, along with the style of chieftain, were the undifferenced Arms of Maclennan surmounted with a permanent label charged with three eagles feathers. This is accordingly a case best considered unique to its own facts. There is no distinctive heraldic insignia appropriate to the title of chieftain and this status cannot be discerned in any way from the arms of the bearer. A chieftain, along with any other feudal noble, may petition for, and at Lyon's discretion receive, the additional grant of a guidon, or standard. The confusion over the title of chieftain and its position within the modern clan system may be partly alleviated by the avoidance of its use when referring to appointees of the chief to posts of honour within the clan. Such officers are now more usually styled 'commissioners' or 'lieutenants'. This practice has been approved by the Lord Lyon and by the Standing Council of Scottish Chiefs. The chief should provide his commissioner or lieutenant with a written commission or charter setting out his territorial jurisdiction, his powers, duties and a duration of his office. The commission may be for a fixed period of years but must always be at the chief's pleasure. The commissioner may be authorised to display an appropriate flag, and in some cases splendid chains of office have been presented. The title has no armorial significance but could be referred to in the text of a grant of arms as an office held by the petitioner.

Clansman

The criterion for determining a clansman is also a matter of dispute. The need for proved descent from a common ancestor related ultimately to the chiefly house is clearly far too restrictive. This is not to detract from the broad kinship and bloodbonds which a small nation, such as Scotland, can develop: it was suggested by the late Sir Iain Moncreiffe of that Ilk that around the time of the Union of the Crowns in 1603, one in every forty five persons claimed to be a member of a titled or chiefly house and consciously regarded themselves as noble.

Clans, as they developed their distinctive territorial base, would have comprised 'native' men who came to accept the authority of the dominant group in the vicinity. Chiefs would also accept allegiance from smaller communities and individual families by adoption, as well

The Earl of Elgin (left), the Convenor of the Standing Council of Scottish Chiefs, being presented with a commemorative diploma by the O'Conor Don, Prince of Connaught, at the Annual General Meeting of the Council in 1993. Lord Elgin is dressed in the uniform of the Royal Company of Archers. The O'Conor Don, descendent of the last High King of Ireland, attended the AGM on behalf of the Irish Council of Chiefs.

as from branches of the family not linked territorially to the main clan lands. Such alliances were sometimes the subject of elaborate ceremonial and developed into the system of written undertakings known as 'bonds of manrent'. The gradual process of absorption of other families into the main clan is to some degree responsible for the system of septs or sub-names. A clansman can be said to be one who professes allegiance to a chief and the other members of his noble community, whether by descent with a common name, territorial origin or adoption, and who respects the Law of Arms in Scotland. The clansman who becomes an armiger, i.e. receives a grant of arms from the Lord Lyon in his own right, will form part of the duisne-uasail. This will be acknowledged by his receiving a coat of arms suitably differenced from the chiefly arms themselves. The status of a clansman is accordingly not a lowly one and as part of a noble community recognised by the Crown, he may wear his tartan and the bonnet badge of his chief with pride.

Clansmen may also acquire territorial designations, an aspect of Scottish culture which is often misunderstood. They are not titles of honour and carry no precedence of any kind in or out of the clan system. Sir Crispin Agnew of Lochnaw, Rothesay Herald, wrote in the *Journal of the Heraldry Society of Scotland* in 1982:

> There is nothing upper class about territorial designations, they merely distinguish each person by name in relation to their ownership of land. They were of particular use in early landowning times when many of the same name owned land in the same area and each was distinguished by his territorial designation. Formerly every owner of a named piece of land, outwith a Burgh, used his designation, or if a tenant was described as 'in' the land. Hence 'Macwilliam of Glen William' owns the glen, while 'Macwilliam in Glen William' is the tenant of the glen. It is unfortunate that the general use of territorial designations has fallen into disuse, except among the gentry with the result they have acquired a snobbish appeal which is not warranted. Any person in Scotland who owns the dominium utile of a named piece of land, usually an estate, farm or house and policies, outwith a Burgh, may and should be encouraged to add the designation to his name.

However, it should be remembered that membership of a clan is not an automatic right. Any chief may refuse membership or outlaw an existing member from the clan, thus depriving him of the privileges of that status.

Insignia and symbols of rank

Apart from tartan, the commonest external symbols of clan affiliation are bonnet badges and the eagles' feathers often associated with them. Bonnet badges take the form of the chief's crest encircled with the representation of a strap and buckle bearing the motto. The badge is generally made of silver or a silver-coloured base metal. Bonnet badges can be seen throughout pages 64–343. A sprig of the plant associated with the clan could be worn behind the badge if so desired. Armigers may wear the simple strap and buckle badge if they so please, but are also entitled to wear their own crest within a plain circlet bearing their motto. They are entitled to display one eagle's feather, either real or represented in metal. A chieftain may again wear the simple strap and buckle badge or his own crest within a circlet with motto. He may display two eagle's feathers. Chiefs wear their crest within a plain circlet with motto, and display three eagle's feathers. Circlets may be surmounted by any coronet or cap of rank to which the bearer may be entitled, or omitted entirely as a matter of personal taste. There is a case to be made out for the wearing of eagle's feathers by clan commanders, commissioners and lieutenants. These feathers would be marks of delegated authority and not of individual rank. The feathers would be worn only when performing the duties delegated to the officer by his commission and strictly within the limits of those duties. Two eagle's feathers would seem appropriate to represent the delegated or substituted authority granted to such persons to carry out their necessary duties on behalf of the chief himself. The feathers would be worn with the strap and buckle badge only or perhaps even a special variant of this designating the office of the wearer, and not with any personal crest badge of the office bearer, in order to distinguish them from those entitled to two eagle feathers by rank. The wearing of eagle's feathers is not a matter regulated either by the ordinary law of the land or the Law of Arms. The principles set out are accordingly those governed by custom, practice and to a large degree, simple good taste. The display of any number of eagle's feathers to which the bearer is not entitled is unwise. The imposter exposes himself to ridicule and demonstrates a profound lack of respect for the system to which he pretends adherence.

THE FUTURE OF THE CLAN SYSTEM

The Standing Council of Scottish Chiefs was formed in 1952 at a meeting called under the auspices of the Lord High Constable of Scotland. The first convenor was the tenth Earl of Elgin, a post now held by his son. Membership is open to Chiefs of Name with hereditary supporters, indicative of the status they have obtained, but there is also an elective procedure. The day-to-day administration is undertaken by the secretariat based in Edinburgh. Apart from dealing with requests for information and assistance from members, the secretariat is also involved in dealing with enquiries from clansmen and from manufacturers and craftsmen who wish to incorporate the heraldry of chiefs into their products. The Council, if satisfied that a manufacturer meets its criteria of quality and accuracy, will licence the products requested.

The Council meets once a year in full session to discuss matters of general interest and concern, and there is also a committee which meets more regularly, if required.

A close liaison is maintained between the Council and the Lyon Court, through which appropriate response can be made to developments in the law which may impact upon the traditions of the clans. This was demonstrated in 1992, when legislation concerning the fertilisation of human embryos by scientific methods was amended to ensure that protection originally extended only to peerage titles, was granted to clan chiefs only after representations made by the Lord Lyon and action in Parliament by members of the Council. The law must develop and adapt to meet the changing needs of modern society but it can still recognise the importance of our ancient cultural traditions at the same time. As Frank Adam commented:

> The clan system, which continued unchanged through nearly six centuries, has something inherently grand about it. Primitive it may have been but it is a primitive organisation which has steadily fulfilled the aspirations of humanity and was most admirably adapted to the needs of the communities it controlled.

Perhaps the next six centuries will be the real test.

Tartan and the Highland Dress

ALASTAIR CAMPBELL OF AIRDS

There is no clearer symbol of Scottish identity than tartan, particularly when worn in the form of a kilt. Tartan's popularity guarantees its use in a variety of situations but, attractive as it is, it is its underlying significance as a means of clan or family allegiance that gives tartan and the Highland garb its real appeal. While perhaps not unique, this identification is given by few other forms of dress, and certainly not in such a versatile form – the Highland dress can be used for every occasion from the most formal appearance in front of the monarch to attendance at an international football match, and from the smartest of ballrooms to walking the hill. Its symbolism is powerful and Neil Armstrong, the first man to walk on the moon, took a piece of his clan

tartan with him on his historic journey.

The kilt is now worn by all Scots, Lowlanders and Highlanders alike, although not very long ago the former recoiled in disgust from what they regarded as a primitive form of dress worn only by those dismissed as 'redshanks' whose naked nether limbs were pinched and red from exposure to the cold weather.

Part of its appeal doubtless lies in its warlike associations, summed up in the quote that 'a man in a kilt is a man and a half'. Sir Colin Campbell sent out the Highland Brigade at Lucknow during the Indian mutiny of 1857 with the order 'Bring furrit (forward) the tartan'; German intelligence during the First World War rated the kilted 51st Highland

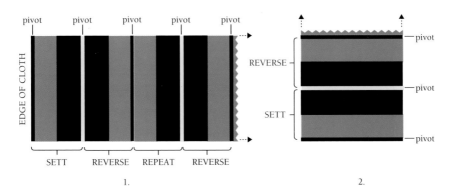

1.

2.

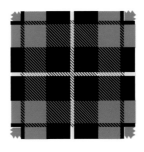

3.

The construction of a tartan. Although apparently complex, the design of tartan is often quite straightforward. A number of coloured stripes of varying width are woven from the edge of the cloth, running its full length. The basic sequence of stripes (the sett) is then reversed around a number of pivot points so that the stripes continually repeat and reverse across the width of the cloth, reminiscent of a medal ribbon. This woven sequence is known as the warp (1). The same sequence of stripes, the weft (2) is then interwoven at right angles to the warp to create the finished tartan (3).

Division – elsewhere the Highland troops had been described as 'The Ladies from Hell' – as the most formidable of all the Allied formations encountered by their army. The Cameron Highlanders were the last to wear the kilt in action, during the Second World War in France in 1940.

The whole subject has such a romantic appeal that the rather more prosaic facts concerning its origins and development tend to be overlaid by myth and fantasy. As a result it causes controversy which is all too often fuelled by emotion and wishful thinking rather than objective historical research and knowledge.

The exact derivation of the word 'tartan' is uncertain, but originally it referred to a type of material rather than to its pattern as is the case today. This pattern is created by the interweaving at right angles of the same sequence and proportions of coloured thread. In the majority of tartans this sequence is one

The typical wardress of the medieval Scottish warrior. Instead of expensive metal armour, a long heavily quilted coat, the 'leine croich', was worn, with a metal bascinet helmet and a chain mail coif protecting the more vulnerable areas of the head and neck. The figure illustrated here is based on a tomb carving found at Killian in Kintyre.

which can be repeated back or forward in either direction between two pivot points which can then be reproduced by multiplying each number to achieve the scale required. In practice, when the scale is a small one, some lines are given an inflated value to avoid their becoming invisible.

But this type of weaving is not exclusively Scottish, and similar forms can be found elsewhere. Its use is certainly very ancient and it was early to be found in the Highlands, its use spreading across Scotland in the eighteenth century, some time before the idea of using tartan as a means of identification of clan or family took root.

THE HISTORY OF THE KILT

The use of a simple length of material as a garment is, of course, one of the earliest forms of attire; perhaps one of the earliest instances of it on record in northern Europe is in its adoption at the end of the eleventh century by the Norse King Magnus Barefoot, who is said to have been given his nickname as a result.

The war dress of the medieval Scot was essentially the 'leine croich', a long, pleated coat which came down below the knees, its heavy pleats combining some form of protection with freedom of movement. It was worn with a pointed metal helmet, with the neck and shoulders protected by chain mail. Weapons were the spear and the double-handed claymore, a long double-handed sword with a cross hilt (nothing to do with the modern basket-hilted broadsword which is often erroneously given the name). Representations of medieval warriors so clad are to be found on many tombstones in Argyll and the Isles, from which it would appear that the dress was being worn right up to the early 1600s.

It was around this date that it appears the belted plaid, forerunner of today's kilt, became common wear. It has been suggested that this form of dress in fact was that of the Picts (the tribes who inhabited Scotland north of the borderlands) which was later adopted by the incoming Scots (who came from Ireland). Known as the 'feileadh breacan' or 'feileadh

Dressing in the feileadh mor. To dress, the wearer first set his belt on the ground and laid the pleated plaid lengthwise over it, with material below the belt approximating to the distance from his waist to the upper part of his knee. Lying down on top of the pleated material, he would then fold the unpleated ends across his front and, grasping the ends of the belt, buckle it around his middle (1). On standing up, something like today's kilt would result below the waist (2); after he had donned coat and waistcoat the surplus material hanging down would then be gathered up and secured under the belt and around the shoulders (3) in a number of possible variations which would vary according to the demands of weather, temperature, or the freedom of movement required (4).

mor' – the big kilt – it consisted of a width of tartan several yards in length. To dress, the wearer first set his belt on the ground and laid the plaid lengthwise over it with material below the belt approximating to the distance from his waist to the upper part of his knee. He would then kneel down and gather the cloth in pleats until only enough remained unpleated at either end to cover the front of his body.

Lying down on top of the pleated material, he would then fold the unpleated ends across his front and, grasping the ends of the belt, buckle it around his middle. On standing up, something like today's kilt would result below the waist; after he had donned coat and waistcoat the surplus material hanging down would then be gathered up and secured under

the belt and around the shoulders in a number of possible variations which would vary according to the demands of weather, temperature, or the freedom of movement required. At the close of the day, unbuckling the belt would once again convert the garment into a warm covering for the night.

There is much argument over the question of how and when the kilt as we know it today – the 'feileadh beg' or little kilt – developed. It is effectively the lower part of the big kilt separated from the upper half which now evolved into the later form of plaid. (It may be noted that the word 'plaid' in Gaelic means a blanket – nothing to do with the modern American usage of the word to denote tartan.)

Certainly the feileadh mor did restrict movement somewhat as evidenced during the clan conflict of Blar-na-Leine, 'The Field of Shirts', in 1544 between the Clan Donald and the Frasers, so called because both sides threw off their outer covering and fought to the death in their shirts. At some stage around the middle of the eighteenth century, the small kilt emerged and became increasingly popular; time could be saved by sewing in the pleats and a neater appearance resulted. Intense indignation is caused by the claim that the inventor of what is the kilt of today was in fact an Englishman named Rawlinson, who was in charge of a Lochaber iron-smelting works. The truth of the matter, however, will never be known.

TARTAN IN THE SEVENTEENTH AND EIGHTEENTH CENTURIES

A major subject of dispute is the antiquity of the practice of using tartan as a means of clan or family identification. Examples of ancient usage are very few in number but they do exist in two or three known instances. Apologists for the theory claim that the various thread-counts were recorded in the form of sticks around which were bound the correct number and sequence of coloured threads. However, no example of these pattern sticks has survived; hardly any setts, or patterns, among those in use today can be traced to early times, and there is no indication that they then had any sort of clan identity attached to them. Indeed, the evidence is very much the other way, as instanced by the patterns of such old plaids and scraps of tartan that have come down to us from before the closing years of the eighteenth century; these are very different from today's clan patterns, as are the tartans shown in those portraits of chiefs and lairds which have survived from the late seventeenth and eighteenth centuries. Indeed, few were painted in tartan, as their best clothes were seldom of this material, but of those that show the tartan it is evident that a number of different setts was often worn at the same time by the picture's subject and that none of them equate to the respective clan patterns of today.

This is borne out by the famous painting, 'Episode from the Scotch Rebellion', by Morier, of the Battle of Culloden in 1746, in which Barrell's Regiment is shown receiving the Jacobite charge. The Highlanders are shown clad in a whole variety of tartans, and each man is clothed in more than one sett, none of which can be identified as any of today's clan tartans. The models for the painting are said to have been Jacobite prisoners held at Carlisle Castle. Counter claims that the diversity of patterns shown might be due to their having borrowed garments from their neighbours to be painted in, or that the artist was inaccurate, do not stand up against the number of portraits painted at this period and later, which show conclusively that no organised system of clan or family identification through tartan existed at the time.

In fact, armies of this period (and subsequently) commonly used some form of badge in the head-dress as identification, such as the leaves of a plant or a scrap of paper or coloured ribbon. At Culloden, the Jacobites wore a bunch of white ribbon in their bonnets – the famous White Cockade – while the government forces were distinguished by a black cockade or a cross of red ribbon. (The contemporary story is told of a fugitive who was on the point of being cut down, abjuring his attacker, 'Hold hard, I'm a Campbell', to which the response was 'Where's your bonnet?' – this obviously being the vital clue to its wearer's identity, rather than his tartan.)

It has also been claimed that, rather than clan tartans, those setts classed as district tartans represent an ancient general system of identification. The theory rests heavily on the statement by Martin Martin in 1703 that it was possible to tell a man's residence by the pattern of his tartan. His claim is not corroborated by other contemporary writers and may mean no more than that certain patterns had gained popularity in certain areas – which is entirely possible. A recent work on the subject lists just under a hundred tartans with a geographical name. Leaving aside those with English and overseas titles which are of

The Government, 42nd or Black Watch tartan.

Highland Independent Companies, raised from shortly after the Restoration of 1660 onwards 'to Keep Watch upon the Braes', seem to have worn their own tartan, with no regulation. The first Highland regiments raised at the close of the seventeenth century wore the standard uniform of the line. But, from the raising of the final six Highland Independent Companies in 1725, an effort seems to have been made to standardise the tartans worn; this was certainly the case when these same companies were regimented in 1739 into what is now the Black Watch. The basic military tartan as worn by the original regiment is still worn by the Black Watch today – the familiar blue, green and black sett, whose sombre hues are said to have given the regiment its title. Frequently used by other regiments, it is also known as 'Government' or '42nd' as well as 'Black Watch'. It is worn as a clan tartan by Clan Campbell (usually today in lighter tones) and by such clans as the Grants, the Munros and the Sutherlands. The argument has been put forward for its having originated as the Clan Campbell tartan, as its use by the regiment, it is argued, was due to the large number of that clan serving in its ranks. In fact the reverse is almost certainly the case: the regimental tartan was adopted by the Campbells as theirs because so many of them were already used to wearing it when the whole idea of clan tartans became general. This would, of course, account for its use by the other clans mentioned, all of whom were involved in the Black Watch alongside the Campbells.

modern origin, there remain fifty-six whose names are Scottish. Of these, fourteen are post-1945 in origin and twenty-two are to be found on record prior to 1820. Of these twenty-two, the vast majority appear to be 'trade' names, found in Wilson's Pattern Book alongside such fanciful titles as 'Robin Hood', 'Rob Roy', 'Durham', 'Flora MacDonald' and 'Wellington'. Others include such doubtful examples as 'Lennox' from a portrait which is thought to be that of the Countess of Lennox; 'Strathspey' from a waistcoat worn by an officer thought to have served in the Grant or Strathspey Fencibles in the 1790s; while 'Dunblane', it appears, derives from a portrait of the English Duke of Leeds, whose secondary title was 'Viscount Osborne of Dunblane'. A mere handful show any sign of having possibly been used as true district tartans and the evidence for any general system as such remains unimpressive.

It was the army which was almost certainly responsible for the general acceptance of tartan as a means of identification. The early

Many later Highland regiments also used the same sett, either in its original form or with a slight differentiation, usually in the form of the addition of coloured over-stripes. For example, a yellow stripe was added by the 92nd Regiment, red and white stripes were added by the Mackenzie Lord Macleod's 73rd Regiment, and the same red and white, but in a different sequence, were added by the later Loyal Clan Donnachie Volunteers. The use of these modified sets by the regiments led to their adoption as clan tartans by, respectively, the Gordons, the Mackenzies and the Robertsons, the last as a hunting tartan. Other examples also exist.

As far back as 1700 there is evidence of the Royal Company of Archers – founded in 1672 and now The Queen's Body Guard for Scotland – wearing a uniform made of tartan akin to that given the name of Ogilvie today.

As the origins of the use of tartan as a means of identification lie with the army, so too in a large measure does the actual survival of tartan and of Highland dress after the Forty-Five rebellion. Part of the Government's punishment of the Highlands and its determination to quash any further threat of a Jacobite insurrection, was a proscription of the wearing of Highland dress and of tartan in any form by civilians. For the next thirty-seven years, it was only in the Highland regiments of the army that the Highland dress could legally be

A Highland soldier, c. 1744 showing an early representation of a Government tartan feileadh mor. Note how the plaid is being used to protect the lock of the musket from the elements.

worn. It was not until 1782 that the Marquess of Graham, acting as the spokesman of a campaign organised by the Highland Society of London, succeeded in a measure to overturn the ban. Paradoxically, it was at this time that there began the romanticisation of the Celt, a phenomenon which developed in the nineteenth century and which had an enormous influence on later images of Scottishness.

This romanticisation of, and subsequent lessening of suspicion towards the Highlanders, was manifest in a number of ways. The Romantic Movement in Europe in the late eighteenth century sought new forms of art and literature to counteract the Classical, and the publication by James MacPherson of the supposed works of the mythical Irish poet Ossian helped bring about a change in attitude to Gaels. MacPherson's work attained a popularity that spread right across Europe. Indeed, the bedside reading of the Emperor Napoleon in his campaigns was an Italian translation of Macpherson's book. The renown of the Highland regiments also had been steadily growing and they quickly attained an outstanding and glamourous reputation. By the end of the eighteenth century, the events of over fifty years previously began to appear less threatening, and 'Bonnie Prince Charlie' (who died in 1788) began to emerge as a figure of veneration. This change in attitude was also fostered by the writings of Sir Walter Scott, who, along with General Stewart of Garth, masterminded George IV's State Visit to Edinburgh in 1822 – the first to Scotland by the monarch for over two hundred years and the occasion of a quite extraordinary charade which, not unjustly, has been dubbed 'a Tartan Extravaganza'. Finally in the later nineteenth century, came Queen Victoria's love affair with the Highlands. Within a century the character, the image and the perception of Highlandness and Scottishness had been changed enormously. It was against this background that the modern system of clan tartans was to evolve.

James Moray of Abercairney displaying the very stylised Highland accoutrements worn at the State Visit of George IV in 1822.

THE DEVELOPMENT OF
THE MODERN TARTAN

One factor which has been decisive through-out the history of the development of the modern system has been the influence of the tartan manufacturers. At the close of the eighteenth century, the opportunities offered by tartan weaving on a large scale had become obvious to Border weavers and henceforth it was the large firms that they set up that became the main suppliers of tartan to the army and to private individuals alike.

The largest and most successful of these firms was that of Wilson's of Bannockburn, whose early order books give a most illuminating insight into the early naming of tartans. As with any marketing organisation it was important to maintain a steady flow of 'new products', and every year new patterns were introduced. Originally they were often identified only by a number but were subsequently made more attractive by being given a glamourous name – possibly that of some famous figure in history, real or fictional, or sometimes that of a well-known town or district.

The idea of individual tartans providing a clan or family identity was a most attractive one, which was adopted enthusiastically by both wearer and seller alike. A whole new market opened up, one that is still growing today. Chief and clansmen were all asking for 'their' tartan, a demand which the manufacturers were only too happy to meet. So it was, for instance, that Wilson's pattern known originally as 'no. 250', became known as 'Argyle' and, finally, 'Campbell of Cawdor'. And the manufacturers were eager to increase the number of customers by actively promoting the identification of more and more 'clan septs'.

With this sudden demand for clan tartans confusion was inevitable, as may be discerned today by the number of clans who claim the same tartan; ingenious solutions to the confusion were found: the Forbes and Lamont tartans which, derived from the basic military tartan with a white over-stripe, are claimed to differ from each other by the said overstripe being outlined, in the case of the Forbes tartan, by a thin black 'guard-line' – a distinction which it is quite impossible to pick up at a range of more than a few feet.

It was soon accepted that the authority for stating what was the correct tartan for a clan must be its chief. In 1815, the Highland Society of London began its collection of tartans with a limited number signed and sealed as correct by the chiefs of the clans concerned. Even at this stage, the idea that such setts must have been used in this fashion from the dawn of history was being encouraged. Some chiefs and chieftains, such as Robertson of Struan and the Marquess of Douglas, were considerably embarrassed, since – hardly surprisingly – they had no idea of what pattern was 'theirs'.

The first book on clan tartans appeared in 1831. *The Scottish Gael* was written by John Logan, one-time secretary of the Highland Society of London. It was followed in 1842 by *Vestiarum Scoticum* by two remarkable brothers who, after several changes of surname, eventually settled on that of Sobieski Stuart, claiming to be grandsons of Prince Charles Edward Stuart. Managing to convince many people, they claimed to possess an old manuscript, long held at the Scots College at Douai and dating from the sixteenth century, which gave details of some seventy five early clan tartans which, although only described in supposedly archaic language, enabled them to include illustrations of the setts concerned in their text. The original document somehow was never available for inspection. It was clearly a figment of the brothers' fertile imagination but a surprising number of today's clan tartans derive from it.

The Sobieski Stuarts' books, however, were merely among the earliest of a whole string of works on clan tartans which have appeared at regular intervals from then on right up to the present day. Often produced at the instigation of the cloth manufacturers, they usually include a potted history of each clan. Few of these works show any originality and most are merely rewrites of previous efforts on the subject and of dubious historical accuracy. There have been honourable exceptions, however, and for work on tartan itself, full credit should be given to, among others, the work of John Telfer Dunbar, Christina, Lady Hesketh, James Scarlett and, in particular, D. C. Stewart.

1.   2.

3.

Ancient (1), Modern (2) and Reproduction (3) versions of the Macdonald tartan illustrating the considerable colour variations that can be achieved by varying the dyes used for the fabric.

But identifiable tartans have grown from a trickle into a flood. Many clans have more than one tartan; there are a host of names who are distinguished by a tartan of their own although they have never constituted a clan; and against a list of around one hundred recognised clan chiefs today, records of some two thousand named tartans exist, of which a number represent public bodies or commemorate specific events.

VARIETIES OF TARTAN

In addition to the normal clan tartan, in some cases a clan may also have 'Hunting' or 'Dress' setts. The former is in less violent colours to act as better camouflage while out on the hill, the latter designed specifically for show, often in a pattern which contains a lot of white. This fancy, which is popular alike with tourists, manufacturers and professional Highland dancers, would appear to originate in the women's arisaid, or cloak, which was largely of undyed and therefore less expensive wool.

Confusion can be caused by the use of the descriptions of tartan as 'Ancient', 'Modern', 'Reproduction', 'Weathered' and 'Muted'. Strictly speaking, the first three have nothing to do with the antiquity of the pattern, but with the dyes employed. Early dyes were not particularly lightfast and rapidly faded or changed colour; to overcome this problem, in the mid nineteenth century 'Modern' aniline dyes were introduced. These produced much stronger, lasting colours, although they tend to be rather heavy and dark in tone. In the 1920s, the old vegetable dye colours were revived using modern methods, and these have become widely popular under the title of 'Ancient'.

'Weathered' and 'Muted' are used for tartans either dyed in colours which seek to reproduce the effect of ageing, sometimes by the interposing of a brown or drab thread between each coloured one.

There is no strict law which lays down the shade of colour to be employed, unless a sett specifically contains a lighter and darker form of the same colour. Campbell of Cawdor, for instance, contains both a light and a dark blue but one manufacturer's 'light blue' may in fact be darker than another's 'dark blue'. Red is red and green is green, whatever kind of red or green it is and many variations may be found; for this reason, the modern practice found in some cases of specifying such niceties as 'plum' or 'cerise' is to be deplored; there are too many possibilities of interpretation for such specifics to be clear and the Lord Lyon

will dissuade would-be users of such terms when they are put before him.

Another entirely modern conceit for which there is no historical foundation is the claim for symbolism in the colours employed – gold for the cornfields, green for the pinewoods, blue for the shining rivers, and so on. In some cases this has been carried as far as using threads of various colours in numbers which reflect a date or some other significant number, a fantasy which is unlikely to lead to good design.

As far as tartans are concerned, there is no overall system of control. As already stated, chiefs are considered the authority as to what tartans their clan should wear. Any tartan specified in a Grant of Arms by the Lord Lyon is registered by him, and clan chiefs recognised as such may have their tartans recorded in Lyon Court Books. Otherwise the rules are not strict. Any individual or organisation may have a tartan woven and claim it as theirs; whether it has any commercial success is, of course, another matter. Such tartans have become increasingly popular among commercial organisations or as a means to commemorate a particular event. The Scottish Tartans Society will, for a fee, research any such new sett and, if it does not clash with any previously recorded, include such a tartan in their records. The work they undertake is of great value but it has no official standing as such.

Similarly, there is no real restriction on the wearing of a specific tartan, apart from good taste. The typical statement 'my great-grandmother was a Macpherson therefore I have the right to wear the clan tartan' has no basis in fact. No such 'right' exists. Also, a man takes his father's identity only, and any claims made through the female line are not, strictly speaking, valid. In fact, there is nothing to stop anyone wearing whatever pattern of tartan takes their fancy but they should not, it is suggested, make invalid claims as to any reason they may have for doing so.

There are, however, shibboleths which exist over the wearing of different tartans at the same time: wearing two different tartans of your clan may be defensible, but wearing tartans of more than one clan is almost certainly not. Another concerns the 'correct' fashion in which a lady should wear her tartan sash over her evening dress. Lyon Office has issued a code of practice suggesting that the sash is worn over the right shoulder and tied in a bow over the left hip. It is doubtful whether such niceties have any historical base; in one area of the Highlands, certainly, it appears to have been the case that the sash was worn over the opposite shoulder from normal to indicate that the lady concerned was in 'an interesting condition' and therefore needed extra consideration on the dance-floor.

THE WEARING OF HIGHLAND DRESS

As already stated, the evolution of Highland dress as we know it today owes much to the military. Initially, the army very much followed the civilian dress of the day and adapted it to military purposes, but after the Proscription, the opposite became the case and civilian dress followed that of the military. Such characteristic features as the shoulder straps on today's jackets and the buttons on the sleeve are of military origin, the latter patterns once being found throughout the British Army as a means of discouraging the soldiery from wiping their noses on their cuffs.

The cuts of various forms of evening jacket can also be traced back to the late 1700s. The plaid became a separate garment and survives in military uniform today in two forms, the fly plaid, a vestigial piece of tartan draped from the left shoulder, usually worn by drummers, and the full shoulder plaid worn by pipers and bandsmen. The plaid is still carried as a length of tartan over the shoulder in civilian dress. Correctly used, it is a good form of protection against the weather.

The great kilt gave way to today's little kilt towards the end of the eighteenth century. Early kilts tended to consist of less material than today's for reasons of economy; they were worn much higher up the leg than is now fashionable and the sett of the tartan seems to

have been of a smaller scale. Recently, the hem of the kilt is being worn lower and lower – frequently to ridiculous lengths.

Sporrans started out as an entirely utilitarian leather pouch hung round the waist, drawn together by draw-strings and usually with a brass top or cantle; towards the second half of the eighteenth century the 'sporan molach', or hair sporran, made its appearance, and from then on the sporran became too decorative and heavy to be used in the field.

Waistcoats have become less common, although they may make a return. At present they have been replaced by the waistbelt – by day, this is normally a plain brass buckle on a broad leather belt, but increasingly, a silver-plate buckle with or without heraldic device is now often worn both by day and night.

Hose were originally made of cloth, usually a red and white dicing called 'cath dath' or 'war pattern'. They got hideously out of shape and even the ornate garters employed had difficulty in keeping them up. They were in due course replaced by knitted woollen hose which did not have the same problem. Today's white hose are of modern origin, originating in the 1960s as a poor substitute for diced or tartan hose for evening wear.

Dirks, originally worn as personal weapons, became part of the uniform of military officers and musicians only; in civilian attire their use was as an ornament for evening wear. They appear today only on the fullest of full-dress occasions. The 'sgian dubh', worn in the hosetop, became general wear only in the nineteenth century.

The round knitted bonnet, originally worn flat, towards the end of the eighteenth century was cocked up vertically and then decorated by an increasing number of ostrich plumes which eventually resulted in the military feather bonnet in which the original bonnet is virtually obscured. By creasing the unadorned bonnet front-to-rear, the Glengarry bonnet was created, worn as undress headdress by the whole British Army in late-Victorian times and once very popular as an article of civilian wear, although less so now. Bonnets as part of Highland dress are also worn less frequently. One observance of bonnet-wearing which is military in origin is that Lowlanders allow the ribbons behind their bonnets to fall, while Highlanders tie them in a knot.

Although the story by which the tartan kilt has become the national dress of Scotland is tortuous and myth-laden, and the way in which it is worn can vary from the sublime to the ridiculous, Highland dress is a powerful symbol of the wearer's pride in a Scottish ancestry and in Scotland itself. There are few, if any, other forms of national dress which can claim to make such a clear and unequivocal statement, and to be so instantly and widely recognisable.

Heraldry

GEORGE WAY OF PLEAN, ROMILLY SQUIRE AND DR PATRICK BARDEN

Heraldry, or armory, is a system of personal or corporate identification that first developed in Europe during the twelfth century and which is still in use today. It uses bright colours in recognisable and easily remembered arrangements together with objects, called 'charges', which are often caricatures of things found in real life. These colourful designs were first used on banners, shields and surcoats worn or carried by individual knights in battle and in tournaments; indeed, the term 'coat of arms' derives from the surcoat on which the heraldry was displayed. The medieval tournament or mock battle was a flamboyant sporting and social occasion which lent itself to the display of heraldry and probably to the development of the crest worn on top of the helmet. A miniature picture or sculpture of a formal arrangement of shield, helmet and crest was further used to identify a person on his seal and eventually on his tomb. This transition from heraldry worn or carried physically by its owner to its display on seals, charters and buildings led to the development of more elaborate design. Coronets or caps of rank were placed above the shield and supporters, usually fabulous animals, were placed on either side. The addition of a motto gives us the kind of arrangement which is familiar to us today in the arms of clan chiefs and others.

THE HEREDITARY NATURE OF ARMS

In order that heraldic symbolism would be able to identify the individual, rules evolved whereby each coat of arms could belong to only one person at a time. There is evidence that, at first, totally different designs were borne by different generations of the same family, or by brothers. Before long however, such variations ceased as coats of arms and other heraldic devices became inherited.

In some European countries, a system of 'patronymic arms' has grown up – persons bearing a particular name, although perhaps unrelated, are considered as having an equal right to the arms of that name. This is not the case in Scotland and it is essential in understanding Scots heraldry to realise that the rule concerning the individuality of heraldry was, and is, strictly applied under Acts of the Scottish Parliament of 1592 and 1672; even an eldest son may not bear his father's arms during his father's lifetime without a suitable difference being displayed. Consequently, the terms 'family arms' or 'clan crest' are meaningless in Scotland. Arms are strictly personal to the owner and their use or display by others, without permission, is illegal. On the death of the owner of a coat of arms, it descends to his heir, normally his eldest son, and in turn to the next heir and so on, for ever. Younger sons and their descendants called 'determinate cadets' inherit only the right to apply to the Lord Lyon for a version of their paternal arms. The arms granted carry a suitable mark of difference, governed by a system known as 'cadency'. It is entirely for the Lord Lyon to decide which differences to allow as he alone is cognisant of all the differences which have already been allotted and recorded in the *Public Register Of All Arms And Bearings In Scotland.*

Cadency and marks of difference

There are many methods by which the order of seniority of a family line can be shown in the differences allotted. Two of the most common systems of cadency are the border or 'bordure', most usual in Scottish heraldry, and cadency marks generally used in England and elsewhere. Both these systems are illustrated in the chart on page 44–45. These two methods, and others, can be and often are combined. The colours of bordures are determined in a set sequence by order of seniority amongst cadets. Where the bordure in the sequence happens to be of the same colour as the field

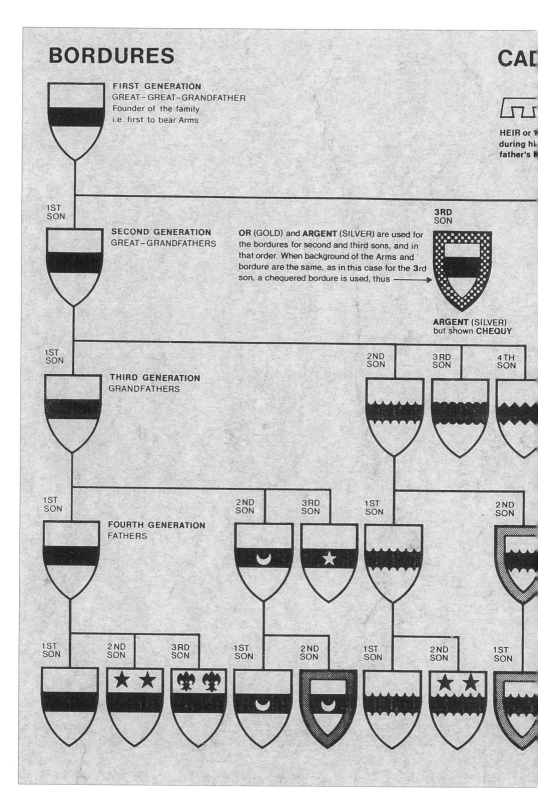

BORDURES

FIRST GENERATION
GREAT–GREAT–GRANDFATHER
Founder of the family
i.e. first to bear Arms

1ST SON

SECOND GENERATION
GREAT–GRANDFATHERS

OR (GOLD) and **ARGENT** (SILVER) are used for the bordures for second and third sons, and in that order. When background of the Arms and bordure are the same, as in this case for the 3rd son, a chequered bordure is used, thus ——▶

3RD SON

ARGENT (SILVER)
but shown **CHEQUY**

1ST SON

THIRD GENERATION
GRANDFATHERS

2ND SON

3RD SON

4TH SON

1ST SON

FOURTH GENERATION
FATHERS

2ND SON

3RD SON

1ST SON

2ND SON

1ST SON

2ND SON

3RD SON

1ST SON

2ND SON

1ST SON

2ND SON

1ST SON

2ND SON

1ST SON

CAD

HEIR or 1
during hi
father's **M**

Bordure and cadency marks.

CY MARKS

| 2ND SON | 3RD SON | 4TH SON | 5TH SON | 6TH SON | 7TH SON | 8TH SON | 9TH SON |

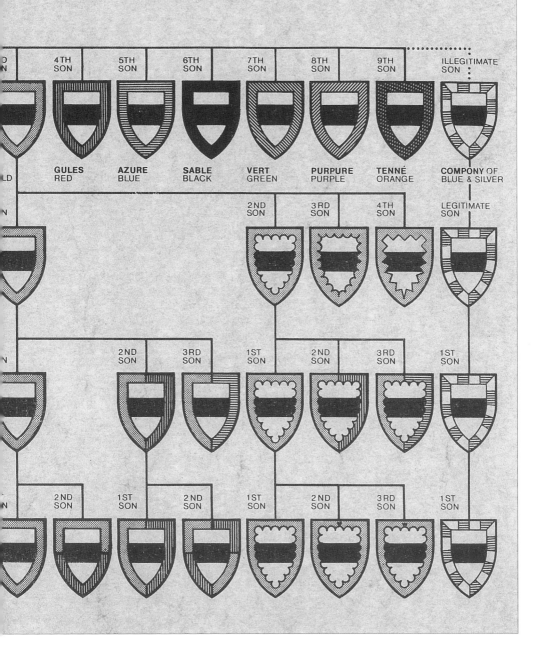

of the shield, it is made chequy of that colour and a contrasting one. The system continues in subsequent generations to show the seniority of descent, not from individual fathers, but from the founder of the House. Bordures can be further differenced by varying their inner edge in a set sequence of patterns. This combination of varying colours and patterns continues in a similar fashion for each subsequent generation. When these differences are not available to younger sons of the senior line, having already been used by junior cadets, an alternative system is used, such as adding small cadency marks or varying the edge of the main charge of the shield. An example of an alternative method of differencing can be seen in the arms of Campbell of Loudon where the chiefly or paternal arms in gold and black are merely re-tinctured as ermine and red without any other mark of cadency. A bastard is accorded a blue and white border called the 'bordure compony'. This is inherited by all his legitimate descendants thereafter. The usual English mark of illegitimacy, sometimes used in Scotland, is a 'baton sinister' which defaces the arms diagonally from the top right to bottom left of the shield. Royal bastards may have the baton in silver or gold as in the arms of the Dukes of Buccleuch.

The clansmen

Members of a clan or family who can show a probable relationship to the chief but who cannot provide acceptable evidence of their specific genealogical links are sometimes referred to as 'indeterminate cadets'. These and all who are unrelated in blood to the chief, or who cannot in any way prove their relationship, may apply to the Lord Lyon for a grant of arms in their own right. The design of the shield in such cases will almost certainly echo the chiefly arms and in this way, membership of a clan or family can usually be seen at a glance. There is no inherent right vested in clansmen to use or adapt in any way the arms of his chief or his family. Just as it is illegal to use another person's arms, it is equally so to invent or use bogus arms. The only heraldic device which may be used by a non-armigerous clansman is the so-called strap and buckle or clansman's crest badge. Examples of these are extensively illustrated throughout this work.

HERALDIC BLAZON

Clearly, to accurately identify someone by their coat of arms, it was necessary for rules to be established to describe the heraldry in words which could not be misunderstood. These rules, probably simple enough in earlier times, have developed over the centuries into a complex and thoroughly scientific system known as 'blazon'. Most standard works on heraldry describe in great detail the rules of blazon which is beyond the scope of this work. It may however be likened to an 'identikit' picture building up the elements one on top of the other in a set sequence. From the correct blazon, anyone versed in heraldry can instantly visualise the arms and with a little skill produce a drawing of them.

Although the written description of heraldry is a matter of law, the ability to depict the arms in any way in which the artist thinks fit has led to the vibrant and diverse art form which is heraldry today. It is an error to believe the arms as painted on the documents emanating from the Lyon office or any other heraldic authority, must be slavishly copied thereafter. These represent only the conventional interpretation adopted by one artist and another interpretation may look very different, but still be an accurate rendering of the blazon. The armiger may even request that his arms be painted in a particular style which may subsequently prove quite unsuitable for general use. A painting may also be commissioned for a particular purpose. For example, when arms were granted to a Scottish police force, they specifically requested that the painting be provided in such a way as to facilitate the manufacture of transfers which could subsequently be applied to patrol cars and other vehicles.

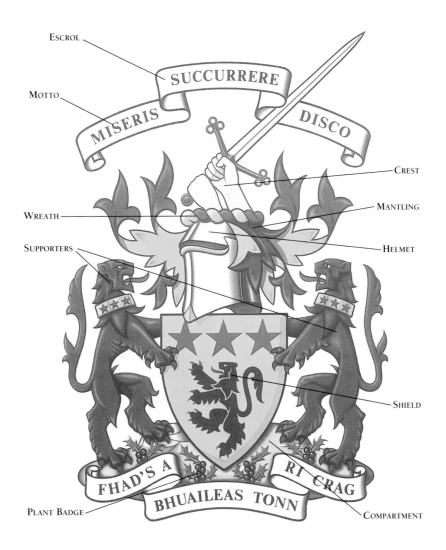

ESCROL

MOTTO

SUCCURRERE

MISERIS

DISCO

CREST

MANTLING

WREATH

HELMET

SUPPORTERS

SHIELD

FHAD'S A

RI CRAG

BHUAILEAS TONN

PLANT BADGE

COMPARTMENT

The full achievement of the Arms of MacMillan of MacMillan and Knap.

THE ACHIEVEMENT

In heraldry the various component parts of what is popularly called a coat of arms, are more properly collectively known as 'an achievement'. The foundation of everything is the shield to which may be added the helmet, mantling, wreath, crest, motto, coronet or cap of rank, robe of estate, compartment and supporters. In addition, there may also be special badges of rank or office as can be seen in the arms of the Dukes of Argyll or the Earls of Erroll.

The shield

The design depicted upon the shield is essential for positive identification of its owner and the display of the other elements without it is of restricted value. Although the other elements, such as the crest and motto may be, and are, used separately, the right to do so cannot exist without the authority to bear the arms as shown on the shield. The shield may be of any shape. This is normally dictated by the prevailing artistic tastes of the time and the need to accommodate the varied size or shape of the charges to be depicted. To avoid the more fanciful shapes commonly met with in past times, modern Scottish heraldic practice tends to favour strong and simple outlines. The shield is normally depicted, at the whim of the armiger or his artist, either upright or at an angle as if hanging by a strap. A few ancient families still have shields devoid of any charges and merely divided in two or more colours. However, practically all coats of arms consist of the shield with some device painted on it. The arms of a woman are depicted on a shield of oval shape or on a lozenge.

The helmet

Above the shield is usually placed a helmet, the design of which is determined by rank. The various types of helmet permitted in Scots heraldry are set out in the glossary. When helmets are shown in profile, they always face to the left, except where there are two or more helmets, in which case they may all face left or inwards towards the centre. Subject to these rules, the period and style of helmet vary, but should always conform to the period of the shield. In good heraldic design the scale of the helmet should reflect the realities of medieval armour where the great tilting helm was almost as tall as the shield.

The mantling

Originally no more than a simple piece of fabric worn from the helmet fulfilling the same function as a modern French Foreign Legionnaire's kepi, the mantling has been depicted by artists throughout the centuries in a more or less fanciful manner sometimes reaching ridiculous extremes. Although undoubtedly overdone in many cases, elaborate mantling has proved to be an extremely useful device enabling the artist to fill an awkward or unusual space within which the arms are to be depicted. This can often be seen in book plates or where arms are to be carved in stone or engraved on silver. There are rules governing the colours of mantling and its lining according to rank. The Sovereign uses

mantling of gold lined with ermine, whilst peers, and certain great Officers of State, use crimson lined with ermine. All others use the principal colour of the arms lined with the principal metal.

The wreath

The mantling is held in place by the wreath, sometimes called 'torse', a skein of silk with gold or silver cord twisted round it, placed as a fillet to cover the join between the crest and the helmet. It is conventionally illustrated by six pieces alternately of the principal metal and colour of the arms.

The crest

Upon the wreath is placed the crest. This may be a representation of almost any object, real or imaginary. In common with all other heraldic devices, crests face to the left unless specifically described as facing to the front or to the right. Clergymen do not normally use crests, displaying instead a special ecclesiastical hat, the form of which varies slightly according to individual rank within the church.

The arms of Keith O'Brien, Archbishop and Metropolitan of St Andrews and Edinburgh, depicting an ecclesiastical hat in place of crest and mantling.

The motto

Although popularly associated with battle cries, to which no doubt some mottoes do owe their origin, most authorities hold that mottoes first appeared upon standards and seals. The motto in an escrol forms part of the achievement and its position is always specified but, in most cases, is placed above the crest. Mottoes can be found below the shield, but usually only where there is more than one motto, or when a coat of arms is granted without a crest. The mottoes of clansmen usually reflect the same sentiments as that of their chief. Similar to the motto is the slughorn or *cri-de-guerre* which is only found in the heraldry of clan chiefs.

Coronets or caps of rank

Peers of the realm and feudal barons are entitled to place the coronet or cap (chapeau) appropriate to their individual rank, between the top of the shield and the underside of the helmet. In more simplified representations of the arms, a shield ensigned with the coronet or cap, is often considered to be a tasteful and striking design. In common with the peerage, whose various coronets are described in the glossary, the caps of the feudal baronage also vary. Barons of Scotland still in possession of their barony, are entitled to a red velvet cap lined with ermine. Those who represent baronial houses, but who no longer hold their fief, display a blue velvet cap lined with ermine. Barons of Argyll and the Isles follow the same rules but alter the lining to 'ermines'.

The robe or mantle of estate

In addition to coronets and caps, peers and barons may drape behind their shield a robe of estate appropriate to their rank. This practice, extensively employed in Continental heraldry, is often used artistically to replace or complement the need for over-elaborate mantling in certain situations.

The compartment

Below the shield may be a compartment, usually a depiction of a grassy mound, rocks or the sea. In the heraldry of clan chiefs the compartment will usually be embellished with the plant badge associated with the name. Some compartments are quite unusual, few more so than the monstrous man in chains below the shield of the chief of Clan Donnachaidh alluding to the assassin of James I apprehended by an ancestor. The compartment is only granted by the Lord Lyon as a special addition for persons of high rank and distinction.

The arms of Edward Leslie Peter of Lee showing the robe of estate and chapeau of a feudal baron.

Supporters

Usually standing upon the compartment, supporters are believed to have been devised to fill the blank spaces on either side of the shield and helmet when depicted upon a seal. In old Scots patents they were usually called 'bearers'. Regarded in Scotland as one of the highest honours, supporters are normally granted in pairs, although several examples of

The interior of the Lyon Office. The Lyon Registers can be seen in the cupboards beneath the main counter.

a single supporter can be found in the Lyon Register, such as the double-headed eagle of the City of Perth. Supporters are a mark of distinction and may be granted by the Lord Lyon either on a hereditary basis, or for the lifetime of a particular person. Hereditary supporters are only automatically granted to hereditary peers. Other distinguished persons, such as life peers, Knights of the Thistle and Knights Grand Cross of certain orders of chivalry also receive them as a matter of right but only for their own lifetimes. The Lord Lyon may make the grant hereditary as he did in the case of the Rt. Hon Lord Mackay of Clashfern, a life-peer, in recognition of his office as Lord Chancellor of Great Britain.

The badge

The crest itself, when used in certain ways, becomes a badge but some great men, including clan chiefs and others who may be considered to have 'a following' may be granted one or more additional heraldic badges. The commonest are based upon plants but they may also allude to some specific event in the history of the clan or family, such as the caltrap of the Drummonds, alluding to their

use at the Battle of Bannockburn in 1314. The badge can be used on its own and also appears on certain types of flag.

THE PUBLIC REGISTER OF ALL ARMS AND BEARINGS IN SCOTLAND

There is no better evidence of the diversity and splendour of heraldic art anywhere in the world than is to be found in the *Public Register of All Arms and Bearings in Scotland*, usually simply called the Lyon Register. Although private manuscript records of arms known as 'armorials', were maintained, few survived the destruction of Scottish records during Cromwell's occupation of Scotland in the mid seventeenth century. In 1672, an Act of the Scots Parliament sought to render previous legislation on the use of heraldry more effectual by creating a central public register similar to the Register of Sasines (Land Register), which had recently been successfully established. The new Act was highly successful but it took some five years to collate the vast amount of information which initially deluged the Lord Lyon.

Heralds travelled widely throughout Scotland rectifying honest errors, whilst

1.

2.

3.

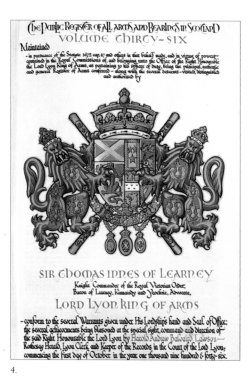

4.

The arms of various Lords Lyon showing the heraldic art of different periods. The arms are those of (1) Thomas Robert, Earl of Kinnoul, Lord Lyon 1804-66; (2) George Burnett, Lord Lyon 1866-90; (3) Sir James Balfour Paul KCVO, Lord Lyon 1890-1927; (4) Sir Thomas Innes of Learney GCVO, Lord Lyon 1945-69.

assiduously exposing the use of bogus arms. Undoubtedly, the fact that registration of existing arms was to be free only for a limited period contributed to the canny Scots' eagerness to comply with the Act. When the period of free registration came to an end in 1677, with the death of Lord Lyon Sir Charles Erskine of Cambo, the first volume of the Register was compiled and bound up under the supervision of the Lyon Depute, Robert Innes of Blairton. Since that time, all matriculations of existing arms and new grants have been chronologically recorded, on payment of ever increasing fees to Her Majesty's Treasury, in a series of massive volumes, each containing some 120 pages of vellum. Each entry contains a painting of the arms granted together with a manuscript text, setting out the personal details of the individual and the blazon.

Some of Scotland's greatest heraldic artists have worked on the Lyon Register over the centuries, making it the most magnificent manuscript of its kind in Europe. This is due, in no small measure, to the fact that successive Lords Lyon have rarely sought to influence the herald painters towards following a standardised or 'house' style and anyone consulting the Register will find themselves uniquely placed to trace the development of heraldic art from the 17th century to the present day. This is not to suggest that painters were free from the fashionable conceits which may have prevailed from time to time and the Register does contain its fair share of heraldic horrors.

In addition to recording in the Register, the Lyon Court issues to each petitioner a document on vellum with a painting of the arms recorded and the text as inserted in the relevant volume. Petitioners are nowadays given the option of commissioning the herald painter to further embellish their document with additional decorative art work. This can take any form that the Lord Lyon is prepared to sanction bearing in mind the essentially legal nature of the document. Regardless of

Two artistic interpretations of the arms of George Way of Plean. Both paintings were commissioned by the armiger, that on the left in the style of the seventeenth century and that on the right in a more contemporary style.

The installation of the Governor of Edinburgh Castle, 1979, showing the then Lord Lyon and several of the officers of arms: (heraldic officers left to right) the late Sir Iain Moncreiffe of that Ilk, Bt. (latterly Albany Herald); John Spens, Pursuivant (currently Albany Herald); the late Sir James Monteith Grant KCVO, Lord Lyon King of Arms; the late Don Pottinger LVO, Islay Herald; Malcolm Innes of Edingight (now Sir Malcolm Innes of Edingight KCVO, Lord Lyon King of Arms); the late Major David Maitland-Titterton, Ormond Pursuivant (latterly Marchmont Herald).

the skills with which the coat of arms is painted on the document, it must still be regarded as merely one artist's interpretation of the blazon, which other artists and crafts-men are free to reinterpret in their own way.

THE COURT OF THE LORD LYON KING OF ARMS

The importance of the office of the Lord Lyon is derived from the combination of functions vested in him which are not only heraldic but genealogical and ceremonial. He incorporates the pre-heraldic Celtic office of High Sennachie to the Royal line and as such, his certificate and presence was necessary for the coronation of Scottish kings. It is impossible to name these early Sennachies or to say who was the first Lyon King of Arms, as the office was designated in early charters and records only by surname and the title 'Lyon'. A Lord Lyon King of Arms, who received the rank of knight, was inaugurated in 1318 by Robert the Bruce at Arbroath Abbey. In 1399 Henry

Grieve is listed as 'King of Scottish Heralds'. He is the first King of Arms whose personal name is known. Matters became clearer by 1452 when it is believed that Duncan Dundas of Newliston was appointed. By the late six-teenth century the position of the Lord Lyon as a great officer of the Crown had become firmly established and, as has been often remarked, no herald in Europe exercises such powers of jurisdiction, is vested with such high dignity or possesses so high a rank. In his heraldic jurisdiction, Lyon stands in place of the Sovereign. Not only has the Lord Lyon jurisdiction to enforce the Laws of Arms, but he may prescribe new rules to meet changing circumstances which then have the force of law.

An example of this power relating to clans and families, can be found in the guidelines for the conduct of 'ad hoc derbhfine' used to recommend to the Lord Lyon candidates for clan commanders or vacant chiefships (see page 26). He is also a Judge of the Realm and most Lyon office business is conducted upon judicial lines. Scotland is probably the only country where a court of heraldry and genealogy operates on a daily basis and is fully integrated into the national judicial system. In addition to establishing rights to arms and pedigrees, Lyon has a penal jurisdiction con-

1.

2.

3.

4.

5.

6.

7.

8.

9.

The badges of Officers of the Court of the Lord Lyon: (1) Ross Herald; (2) Albany Herald; (3) Marchmont Herald; (4) Rothesay Herald; (5) Dingwall Pursuivant; (6) Kintyre Pursuivant; (7) Carrick Pursuivant; (8) Unicorn Pursuivant; (9) Lyon Clerk and Keeper of the Records.

cerned with protecting the rights of those who have properly recorded their arms. He is assisted in this by the Lyon Clerk and Keeper of the Records, and by a prosecutor, 'the Procurator Fiscal', who brings complaints relating to the misuse of arms, before the Court. It is only proper that the Crown, having taken fees in return for the exclusive right to armorial bearings, should extend its protection to these rights and Lyon can impose penalties such as fines, confiscation of items bearing falsely usurped arms and even imprisonment. The Lord Lyon's other official duties include jurisdiction in questions of 'name' and 'change of name' and on all questions relating to succession to chiefship, peerages and other titles of honour. He has the responsibility of preparing all state ceremonial in Scotland such as Royal proclamations, the investiture of Knights of the Thistle and the installation of the Governor of Edinburgh Castle.

The heralds and pursuivants

There are currently six officers of arms under the Lord Lyon, although at times this number has varied. The heralds are the senior officers of the Court and use such titles as Albany, Rothesay, Ross, Marchmont, Islay, or Snowden, whilst their junior colleagues, the pursuivants, are styled Kintyre, Unicorn, Carrick, Dingwall, Bute or Ormond. The Lord Lyon may also appoint temporary pursuivants usually known either as Falkland or Linlithgow pursuivant-extraordinary. Some great noble houses still maintain private officers of arms, recognised by the Lord Lyon, for example, Slains pursuivant to the Earl of Erroll, Garioch pursuivant to the Countess of Mar and Endure pursuivant to the Earl of Crawford.

The officers of the Court of the Lord Lyon, in addition to their ceremonial duties may be consulted by members of the public on heraldic and genealogical matters in a professional capacity similar to lawyers or other agents. They may appear to plead their client's case before the Lord Lyon or other courts of chivalry. Lyon may even authorise one of the private pursuivants to appear before him if this

is deemed appropriate in the circumstances.

The Lord Lyon and his officers all wear a special version of the uniform of the Royal Household, and, when appropriate, a tabard bearing the Royal Arms. The Lord Lyon's tabard is velvet and cloth of gold, those of the heralds are made of silk and those of the pursuivants, of taffeta. The uniform required to be redesigned in 1993 when, for the first time in history, a woman was appointed as an officer of arms. Mrs C. G. W. Roads MVO, who was appointed Lyon Clerk and Keeper of the Records in 1986, received her commission from the Lord Lyon as Carrick Pursuivant in 1992.

Court procedure
New grants

A person who wishes to apply to the Lord Lyon for a grant of arms either in his or her own name or for a specified ancestor, must present a written petition setting out their necessary personal details and any genealogical facts they seek to establish. They may prepare the petition themselves or seek the assistance of an officer of arms or a lawyer. The petition is lodged with the Lyon Clerk, who will require documentary proof of all statements made. There may follow some discussion with the Lyon Clerk to settle details and ensure the petition is in proper form to go forward for the Lord Lyon's consideration.

The Lord Lyon will then devise a suitable coat of arms and is normally willing to try to accommodate the wishes and ideas of the petitioner concerning design, in so far as possible, within the laws and rules of heraldry. It must however be remembered that this process is essentially legalistic. A petitioner who fails to request any element of the achievement to which they may otherwise be entitled, will find that this is omitted. Even clan chiefs who forget, or are not advised, to request additaments, such as the standard or pinsel, should they subsequently wish to acquire them must lodge another petition. Once the arms are agreed with the Lord Lyon, a court order, known as an 'interlocutor' is prepared. At this

TO · ALL · A[

whom These Presents Do or May Concern,
Knight Commander of the Royal Victor
Lord Lyon King of Arms, send Greeting

STUART

CRAWFORI

Burgess of Craft of the City of Aberdee
Aberdeen, Fellow of the Society of Ant
Fellow of the Institute of Directors, M
Chairman of the National Association o
St. John Bucksburn No. 795, Master Ma
Westhill, Skene, in the County of Aber
the Petitioner, born Johnstone in the
Dunbarton 9 September 1968 Sheena Hea
apparent, born Dumbarton in the Coun
sons, born Bellshill in the County of La
second son of the late William MacBrid
Mitchell, daughter of Archibald Knox; G
eldest son of James MacBride, and hi
there might be granted unto him such E
Laws of Arms, KNOW YE THERE
and Confirm unto the Petitioner and his

be severally matriculated for them, the following Ensigns Armorial, as depicted upon the
upon the 39th page of the 77th Volume of Our Public Register of All Arms and Bearing
Above the Shield is placed an Helm befitting his degree, with a Mantling Vert doubled Or a
charged with a cinquefoil Or, and in an Escrol over the same this Motto "BI GLIC", by de
same are, amongst all Nobles and in all Places of Honour, to be taken, numbered, accounted
IN TESTIMONY WHEREOF We have Subscribed These Presents and the Seal of
of the Reign of Our Sovereign Lady Elizabeth the Second, by the Grace of God, of the U
Territories, Queen, Head of the Commonwealth, Defender of the Faith, and in the Year of

A particularly fine example of Letters Patent granting arms to Captain Stuart C. MacBride.

O · SUNDRY

Malcolm Rognvald Innes of Edingight, ❖
er, Writer to Her Majesty's Signet, ❖ · ❖
❖~❖~❖~❖~❖~❖~❖~ WHEREAS, ❖

MACBRIDE

gess of Guild of the City of Aberdeen, Member of the Weaver Incorporation of ❖·❖
s of Scotland, Fellow of the Hotel Catering and Institutional Management Association,
of the Royal Institute of Public Health and Hygiene, Past Area ❖~❖
d Tables of Great Britain and Northern Ireland, Past-Master of Lodge
Sail, Chairman and Company Director, residing at 23 Westfield Gardens,
aving by Petition unto Us of date 6 March 1992 Shewn; THAT he, ❖
of Renfrew 18 May 1947 (who married Old Kilpatrick in the County of
aughter of John Caldwell, and has issue by her an eldest son and heir
Dunbarton 27 February 1969 Stuart Buchanan MacBride, and two younger
29 March 1971 Christopher David MacBride, and Scott Crawford MacBride) is   the
his wife (married Thornliebank in the County of Renfrew 6 February 1941) Helen ❖·❖
the Petitioner's said father (born 26 June 1915 and died 27 May 1984) was the ❖
Jeanie Rankin; AND the Petitioner having prayed that ❖~❖
Armorial as might be found suitable and according to the
that We have Devised, and Do by These Presents Assign, Ratify
dants with such due and congruent differences as may hereafter
n hereof, and matriculated of even date with These Presents ❖ ❖
tland, videlicet :- Vert, a garb within an orle of cinquefoils Or. ❖
a Wreath of the Liveries is set for Crest an oystercatcher Proper
ation of which Ensigns Armorial he and his successors in the · ❖
received as Nobles in the Noblesse of Scotland : ❖~❖~❖~❖~❖
ffice is affixed hereto at Edinburgh, this 26th day of March in
ingdom of Great Britain and Northern Ireland, and of Her ❖ · ❖
Lord One Thousand Nine Hundred and Ninety Three. ❖~❖~❖

the 42nd Year ❖
Other Realms and
❖~❖~❖~❖~❖

stage the statutory fees require to be paid and, immediately upon doing so, the petitioner may use the arms without having to wait for the arrival of the official painted document. The preparation of the grant of arms document and the painting in the Register cannot proceed until the entire text, and any extra decorative artwork required has been agreed with the Lyon Clerk. In due course the new grant will be signed by the Lord Lyon and sealed with the official Seal of the Court and sent to the petitioner. These splendid documents are then usually framed and given pride of place in the home or the premises of the petitioner.

Grants of arms are not only made to individuals, but to corporations, schools, colleges and other worthy bodies. When granting arms to someone for the first time, the Lord Lyon is acting in his ministerial capacity. His decision cannot be questioned or appealed to any other Court of law.

Matriculation of existing arms

Essentially this procedure is initiated in exactly the same way as an application for a new grant of arms. A petition is drawn up setting out precisely how and why the petitioner believes he or she is entitled to succeed to the arms or to be granted a suitably differenced version of their ancestral arms. Again, the Lyon Clerk receives the petition and confirms all necessary details and evidence to be produced. Lyon will then consider the petition and if it is contentious in any way, may order service of a copy on any person having an interest or right to challenge the claim made by the petitioner. He may also order Notices to be inserted in newspapers. He may then require the petitioner to prove his or her claim in open court, where the evidence will be heard and considered in very much the same kind of process as is followed in courts throughout the world. The parties may appear on their own or be represented by officers of arms or lawyers. If the dispute relates solely to heraldic matters, then the Lord Lyon's decision is final, but if wider issues of law arise, then his judgment can be appealed to the

Court of Session in Edinburgh and ultimately to the House of Lords. Thankfully most matriculations are uncontroversial and even where problems do arise, they can often be resolved without the necessity of a formal hearing. Once the petitioner's right has been established, the procedure for obtaining the use of the arms and the official painted document is the same as for a new grant.

THE MODERN USE OF HERALDRY

As has already been stated, heraldry developed as a means of identification and those who wish to use it should bear this fact in mind. The object should be to make identification as instant and as complete as possible. An armigerous person may use his arms in a great variety of ways which are still relevant to daily life. He may embellish his writing paper and engrave his silver, cutlery or glassware. Even today commissioning a full crested dinner service is not unknown. Manufacturers have become increasingly aware of the potential market for heraldic display and a whole range of products can be easily obtained. In Scotland, heraldry is much used in dress. The crest in silver is worn on the bonnet and the arms may appear on the buckle of the belt, the cantle of the sporran and on the handle and sheath of the dirk or sgian dhu. Jewellery for women, such as brooches and pins, lends itself to heraldic adornment. On their houses, armigers may carve or affix a full or partial representation of their arms, install stained glass windows and fly that most striking and historic means of heraldic display, the flag.

Flags and banners

National flags: since the Royal Navy introduced flags of a length twice their height it has become common to use British national flags of these proportions. Regimental colours however are in a length to height ratio of 5:4; where national flags are to be flown alongside square heraldic banners, they may also be square.

The Union flag: this is the correct flag flown by

citizens and corporate bodies wishing to show their loyalty to the United Kingdom. This should not be flown upside down; the broader white diagonals are upmost in the hoist.

The Saltire: blue with a white diagonal cross, this is the flag of St Andrew, patron of Scotland. It is the correct flag for Scots or Scottish corporate bodies to demonstrate their loyalty and nationality. It is in order to fly it alone or together with the Union flag.

The banner: this is the personal flag of an armiger which shows the arms, as depicted on the shield, and nothing else. Conventionally, the design is placed on the flag as if the flagstaff were to the left of a drawing of the shield. Thus, a rampant animal is said to 'respect' the staff, an eagle displayed looks towards the staff and so on. The design should go through the fabric so that on the reverse side all the devices will be turned round but will still respect the staff. It is quite wrong to use a banner of a plain colour with the owner's arms on a shield in the middle. This implies that the arms are of that colour with a small inescutcheon in the centre. It is equally wrong to show the helmet, crest, motto and supporters on the banner.

The purpose of a banner is to locate and identify its owner and it is the visual equivalent of his name. Flown over his house, it identifies his property; elsewhere, it indicates his presence. The size of a house banner will depend on the height of the building and the pole. It should be large enough to be identifiable from a reasonable distance. The best shape for a heraldic house flag is square, regardless of its size. A smaller banner may also be carried in processions, either by its owner or by his appointed bearer. Such a banner is usually made in fine fabric and may be fringed. Its proportions should be those of an upright rectangle about five wide by six deep.

The pipe banner: when an armiger has appointed a personal piper, he may provide

him with a banner to be attached to the base drone of the pipes. The same applies to an armigerous corporation, and where such a body has a pipe band, the pipe major attaches the banner to his pipes. The pipe banner may take various forms but is always shaped with an angle at the top corresponding approximately to the angle of the drone on the piper's shoulder. It then hangs down behind him and may end in a swallow tail, a double rounded end or any other way suited to the arms. The arms themselves are shown in the same manner as on a personal banner but are commonly turned so that they are right way up when the pipes are being played. A certain amount of distortion is allowed to enable the artist to fit the arms into the odd shape.

Pipe banners are also much used in the Highland regiments, where each company commanders' arms are borne on the pipes of the regimental band. Each regiment has its own tradition for the display of the arms and the regimental badge and these traditions are so well established as to have become acceptable even when they do not conform to the strict rules of heraldry. A pipe banner may have a different design on either side and in this case it needs to be rendered opaque by including a layer of black fabric between the two sides. A fringe may be added to any pipe banner, either plain or of the appropriate tartan.

The trumpet banner: rarely now called for, the trumpet banner consists of an approximately square banner of the arms, usually in very rich materials, fringed and tasselled according to taste and suspended from the trumpet by ribbons or straps. The arms are placed in such a way that the charges are right way up and facing away from the trumpeter when he is playing.

The street banner: where the only available flagstaff is attached to the facade of a building, the usual house flag is sometimes unsuitable. The design is often obscured due to its being at an angle or the flag is partly furled when there is no wind or blown over the staff when the wind eddies round the building. The street banner can be adapted to overcome these difficulties. In shape, the street banner is very like a large pipe banner. The charges upon it however should look outwards away from the buildings. The heaviest fabric which is practical should be employed and stiffeners may be sewn into the hems or fringes attached to the staff. A smaller form of the street banner may also be used for internal decoration, as for example in the great hall of a castle.

A gonfannon showing the impaled arms of Squire and Parlett.

The gonfannon: also known as a gonfalon, this is the form of banner often associated with the church where it is used in processions. Its essential feature is that it hangs from a horizontal bar which may in turn be suspended from a carrying staff. Not all church gonfannons are heraldic and many have highly decorated pictorial designs. Heraldic gonfannons are particularly suited to the internal decoration of historic buildings with arms

appropriate to the people and events associated with them. The gonfannon is capable of a variety of interpretations, the simpler the better. A rectangular upright banner of the arms with long tails of the livery colours is recommended.

The livery pennon: the livery pennon is a very simple flag consisting of the tinctures of the field and principal charge in the arms arranged on a long streamer parted horizontally and tapering to a point. Such a pennon has a practical value as a storm flag when, in high winds and rain, an expensive heraldic flag might quickly deteriorate. The livery pennon spaced along an avenue or around a games ground is an economical means of heraldically based decoration.

Special heraldic flags: all flags described so far may be used by any armiger. However, there are flags which are authorised specially by the Lord Lyon and are blazoned in the grant or matriculation of arms. These are the standard, guidon, pinsel and pennon, all of which are fully described in the glossary.

Manufacture: no material is wrong for a flag, although some are more suitable than others in certain situations. For external use, including naval flags flown at sea, the traditional woollen bunting has largely given way to modern synthetic fibres such as polyesters. Indoors, and for decorative purposes, silk, satin, damasks and brocade may be used, as well as finer spun polyesters. In general, the brightest possible colours give the best effect although luminescent dyes are not recommended. Gold and silver are represented by yellow and white respectively. However, special flags are sometimes decorated with gold thread or paint, as for example, to emphasise a coronet. Except in a few cases such as standards, fringes are regarded in Scotland as mere decoration, to be added or not according to the whim of the owner. If plain, they should be of the same metal as that which is predominant in the flag. They may also be made of alternate pieces of the principal colour and metal of the flag. Flags are a practical and prominent form of heraldic display and however they are made, it is essential that they are suitable for the purpose intended. In particular, flags to be flown on a flag pole must be light enough to lift in the wind or the effect will be lost.

For over 800 years, heraldry, and Scots heraldry in particular, has provided a unique and timeless opportunity to display bonds of kinship and cultural or historical association. Its use is not in any way a thing of the past as heraldry is still used to identify nations, seats of learning, companies and individuals. Indeed, many leading corporate bodies have now abandoned the logos and graphic designs created for them in the 1970s and 1980s in favour of classic heraldic designs. Nor is its use restricted to the old monarchies of Western Europe: South Africa has an efficient State Bureau of Heraldry whilst the Republic of Ireland maintains a Chief Herald who claims authority in heraldic matters relating to persons of Irish descent throughout the world. Even the disintegration of the Soviet bloc has contributed to the upsurge in interest in modern heraldry; the new Republic of Russia has countenanced the revival of a College of Arms which will design new coats of arms and register them along with the arms previously recorded by the former Imperial Russian officers of arms.

The sentiments which have driven this continued interest and respect for heraldry have been well expressed by the Canadian Heraldic Authority which was established in 1988:

> A wise nation encourages the development and use of symbols of sovereignty, community, family life and individual achievement. Over time, these devices become an important element in bringing the nation together, through recognition of a shared heritage, through the color and meaning added to public celebrations, through the decoration of public buildings, through the acknowledgement of contributions made by individuals and groups in the nation's story and through the enrichment of the nation's art and literature.

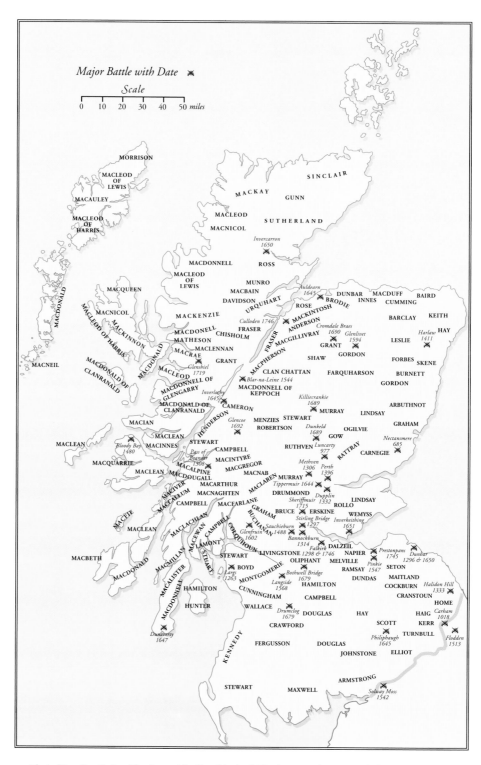

Member Clans
of the Standing Council
of Scottish Chiefs

AGNEW

This distinguished family have flourished in Wigtownshire and Galloway since the fourteenth century. The origin of the name is disputed, although it has generally been asserted to be Norman, from the Barony d'Agneaux. They first settled in England, but appear in Liddesdale in Scotland at the end of the twelfth century. A separate Celtic origin has also been suggested through the native Ulster sept of O'Gnimh, hereditary poets or bards to the great O'Neils of Clan Aodha Bhuidhe in Antrim who acquired the anglicised name of Agnew. The name was first written in English as O'Gnive, which later became O'Gnyw, and, latterly, O'Gnew. This would give the Agnews a common descent with other great names such as Macdonald and Macdougall through Somerled, the twelfth-century King of the Isles. The Agnew eagle crest may echo the similar device which appears on the shield of the descendants of Somerled

The fortunes of the family in Scotland were established when Andrew Agnew of Lochnaw was granted the lands and constableship of Lochnaw Castle in 1426. He was appointed hereditary Sheriff of Wigtown in 1451, an office still held by his direct descendents to this day. The sheriff's son, another Andrew, married a daughter of the chief of the Macdowalls, and it was from his second son, William, that the Lochryan branch of the family descended. Andrew Agnew of Lochnaw was killed at the Battle of Pinkie in 1547. Sir Patrick was MP for Wigtownshire from 1628 to 1633, and again from 1643 to 1647. He was created a Baronet of Nova Scotia on 28 July 1629. He died in 1661 and was succeeded by his eldest son, Andrew, who had been knighted in his father's lifetime and who was also returned as MP for Wigtownshire. He was created Sheriff of Kircudbright as well as Wigtown in the 1650s, when Scotland was part of the Protectorate with England. He married Anne Stewart, daughter of the first Earl of Galloway.

The family continued to prosper, and many alliances were made by inter-marriage with other prominent local families. The fourth Baronet married Lady Mary Montgomery, sister of the Earl of Eglinton. One of his grandchildren, Mary Agnew, married Robert McQueen who was to become notorious as the 'hanging judge', Lord Braxfield. Sir Andrew, the fifth Baronet, married his kinswoman, Eleanor Agnew of Lochryan, and produced no less than twenty-one children. He was a distinguished soldier who commanded the 21st Foot, later the Scots Fusiliers at the Battle of Dettingen in June 1743, the last occasion when a British monarch, George II, commanded troops in person. The king is said to have remarked that Sir Andrew's regiment had let French cavalry in among them to which Sir Andrew replied, 'Yes, please your Majesty, but they didna win back again'. Sir Andrew held Blair Castle, seat of the Duke of Atholl, against the forces of the 'Young Pretender', Prince Charles Edward Stuart, led by Lord George Murray in 1746. Murray, the Duke of Atholl's brother, had virtually starved out the garrison when he was ordered to lift the siege and return to

Standard

Inverness to meet the advance of the Duke of Cumberland. The office of hereditary sheriff became purely honorary on the abolition of hereditary jurisdictions in 1747, and Sir Andrew Agnew received the sum of £4,000 in compensation.

In 1792, Andrew Agnew, son of the sixth Baronet, renewed the family's links with Ireland when he married Martha de Courcy, daughter of the twenty-sixth Lord Kingsale.

Agnew

He died young and his son, the seventh Baronet, succeeded to the title and family estates when he was just sixteen years old. He married Madeline, daughter of Carnegie of South Esk, in 1816. He devoted himself to the improvement of his estates and almost completely rebuilt the Castle of Lochnaw. He became MP for the County of Wigtown and was a strong supporter of the movement to preserve the sanctity of the Sabbath.

Many of the the Irish Agnews were early emigrants to the new colonies in the Americas, and in particular to Pennsylvania. The castle and lands of Lochnaw have since passed from the family, but the world-wide family of Agnew has developed strong links with their Scottish homeland, largely through the efforts of the present chief, Sir Crispin Agnew of Lochnaw, eleventh Baronet. After a career in the regular army, he was called to the Scottish Bar and is now a distinguished advocate. He is also one of Scotland's leading heraldic experts and Rothesay Herald at the Court of the Lord Lyon. A thriving clan society exists and a tartan has been designed by the chief to further unite Agnews throughout the world.

ANSTRUTHER

In the early twelfth century, Alexander I granted the lands of Anstruther in Fife to William de Candela. Various origins have been attributed to him but nineteenth century research points to a descent from the Normans in Italy. It is known that William the Conqueror sought help from them and that a William, Count of Candela in Apulia, sent a son. The William de Candela who received the grant from Alexander was probably this son, or possibly his grandson as he did not die till the reign of Malcolm IV (1153–65). William de Candela's son, also William, was a benefactor of Balmerino Abbey, giving to the monks the site presently occupied by the Scottish Fisheries Museum in Anstruther. Henry, in the next generation, discontinued the name Candela and is described as 'Henricus de Aynstrother dominus ejusdem' in a charter confirming grants to Balmerino. His son, another Henry, accompanied the crusade of Louis IX of France to the Holy Land. He was obliged to swear fealty to Edward I in 1292 and again in 1296.

In the eighth generation, in 1483, Andrew Anstruther of Anstruther obtained confirmation of the barony and was among the Scottish nobles who fought at Flodden in 1513. He married Christina Sandilands who was descended from Sir James Sandilands of Calder and Princess Jean, or Joanna, daughter of Robert II. His younger son, David, fought at Pavia in 1520 in the king of France's Scots Regiment; his descendants died out in the male line with the death of the last Baron d'Anstrude in 1928.

Andrew's eldest son, John, married a Douglas of Loch Leven and their great-grandson, perhaps through this relationship with the Regent Morton, was chosen to be a companion of the young King James VI, who in 1585 appointed him Hereditary Grand Carver, an office confirmed by Parliament in the reign of Queen Anne and still held by the head of the family. In 1595 he became Master of the Household. His elder son, William, accompanied the king to England following the Union of the Crowns in 1603 and was made a Knight of The Bath at the coronation. He was a Gentleman of the Bedchamber to James VI, as was his younger brother, Sir Robert. The latter was a Privy Councillor and an ambassador to Denmark in 1620 and to the Holy Roman Empire, 1627–30; he acquired pictures abroad for the Royal Collection which was largely dispersed under the Commonwealth.

His son, Sir Philip, succeeded his uncle at Anstruther, fought on the Royalist side in the civil war and received Charles II at Dreel Castle after his coronation at Scone in 1651. Sir Philip was taken prisoner at Worcester later that year and his property was sequestered until the Restoration. His eldest son was a Privy Councillor and, as Lord Anstruther, a Lord of Session; his second son, Sir James Anstruther of Airdrie, became an advocate and Principal Clerk of the Bills in the Court of Session and the third son, Robert, was made a baronet in 1694 and acquired Balcaskie in 1698. Lord Anstruther's son, John, was made a baronet in 1700 and married Lady Margaret Carmichael, daughter of the second Earl of Hyndford. The fifth of these distinguished brothers was knighted and, as Sir Alexander Anstruther, married the Hon. Jean Leslie, granddaughter of the famous civil war general, David Leslie. General Leslie had been created Lord Newark in August 1661 with the title being restricted to heirs male of his body. Jean Anstruther's father, the second Lord Newark, died in 1694 and she assumed the title Baroness Newark in her own right. The two sons of Sir Alexander also claimed the Newark title, through their mother, and were accepted as such, even voting at the election of Scots representative peers to Parliament. It was not until 1790 that Sir Alexander's son, Alexander, the titular fourth Lord Newark, was challenged by the Duke of Buccleuch to prove his title. Lord Newark died only a year later and although his son briefly

used the title, he agreed to relinquish it in 1793.

His great-grandson inherited the Carmichael estates as heir general on the death of the last earl in 1817. The present chiefs of Clan Carmichael descend from him and no longer bear the name Anstruther. On the death of Sir Windham Carmichael-Anstruther in 1989, the seventh Baronet of Balcaskie, as heir male, became chief of the name of Anstruther, twelfth Baronet and Baron of Anstruther. The daughter of Sir William Anstruther-Gray, Coldstream Guards, first and last Baronet and Baron Kilmany, descends from the second Baronet of Balcaskie and is married to The Mcnab. Robert, elder son of the third Baronet of Balcaskie, was a Member of Parliament, served in the Scots Fusilier Guards and took part in the French Revolutionary wars, Abercromby's Egyptian Campaign and the Peninsular War. He commanded a brigade at Vimiero in 1808 and the rear guard during the retreat to Corunna, where he died in 1809. Sir John Moore, the commander-in-chief, was buried beside him at his own request in the Citadel in Corunna. The general's son and grandson, the fourth and fifth Baronets, were Members of Parliament and served in the Grenadier Guards. The sixth Baronet served in the Royal Engineers during the Bechuanaland campaign and in the First World War, he and his son Robert served in the Black Watch. The present Baronet, son of the latter, seventh of Balcaskie and twelfth of that Ilk, served in the Coldstream Guards during the Second World War and is Treasurer and Equerry to Her Majesty Queen Elizabeth the Queen Mother. Sir Fitzroy Anstruther-Gough-Calthorpe, descended from the general's younger son, was made a baronet in 1929. His great-grandson, Sir Euan, is the present third Baronet.

The chief's seat is still at Balcaskie in Fife. The house was built, probably about 1670, by Sir William Bruce, second son of Robert Bruce of Blairhall, a descendant of the Bruces of Clackmannan.

ARBUTHNOTT

ARMS
Azure, a crescent between three mullets Argent.

CREST
A peacock's head couped at the neck Proper.

MOTTO
Laus deo (Praise God)

SUPPORTERS
Two wyverns wings elevated, tails nowed Vert, vomiting flames Proper.

STANDARD
The Arms of Arbuthnottt of that Ilk in the hoist and of two tracts Azure and Argent, upon which is depicted the Badge three times along with the Motto 'Laus deo' in letters Argent upon two transverse bands Vert

BADGE
A peacock's head couped at the neck issuant from a chaplet of peacocks' feathers all Proper banded at the base with a riband Azure doubled Argent, and ensigned of a Viscount's coronet

This is a name of territorial origin, from the ancient lands of the same name in Kincardineshire. In early documents it is referred to as 'Aberbothenoth', and this has sometimes been translated as the 'mouth of the stream below the noble house'. This land has been in the hands of the same noble family for more than twenty-four generations, and has passed to the present Viscount of Arbuthnott. Hugh, who may have been of the noble family of Swinton, is believed to have acquired the lands of Arbuthnott by marriage to the daughter of Osbert Olifard, known as 'The Crusader', some time during the reign of William the Lion. Another Hugh, 'Le Blond', named presumably for his fair hair, was Laird of Arbuthnott around 1282. He appears in a charter of that year, bestowing lands upon the Monastery of Arbroath for 'the safety of his soul'.

Philip de Arbuthnott is the first of the name to be described in a charter as 'dominus ejusdem', or 'of that Ilk', in 1355. His son, Hugh Arbuthnott of that Ilk, was implicated in the murder of John Melville of Glenbervie, sheriff of the Mearns, around 1420. According to the traditional story, Sheriff Melville had made himself extremely unpopular with the local lairds by too strict an adherence to his jurisdiction. The Duke of Albany, who was at the time Regent of Scotland during the captivity of James I in England, is said to have become tired of endless complaints against Melville and exclaimed, 'sorrow gin that sheriff were sodden and supped in broo'. This was taken by the disgruntled lairds as a signal to kill the sheriff. The Lairds of Mathers, Arbuthnott, Pitarrow and Halkerton invited Melville to a hunting party in the Forest of Garvock. The unsuspecting sheriff was lured to a prearranged spot where he was killed by throwing him into a cauldron of boiling water. After he was truly 'sodden', each of the conspirators took a spoonful of the murderous brew. The Laird of Arbuthnott was ultimately pardoned for his participation in the affair and he died peacefully in 1446. His direct descendent, Sir Robert Arbuthnott of that Ilk, was elevated to the peerage as Viscount of Arbuthnott and Baron Inverbervie by Charles I to encourage him to support his cause.

Alexander Arbuthnott, who was descended from a younger branch of the chiefly house, was a distinguished cleric and staunch supporter of the Reformation in Scotland. He was Moderator of the General Assembly of the Church of Scotland which met at Edinburgh in April 1577. In 1583 he was directed by the Assembly to wait upon James VI to complain of various 'popish practices' still being permitted within the realm, and other grievances. He incurred considerable royal displeasure and he was placed under a form of house arrest within his college at St Andrews. His health seems to have declined, and he died before his forty-fifth birthday in October 1583.

Arbuthnott

Standard

Dr John Arbuthnott, the distinguished eighteenth-century physician and political humourist, also claimed near kinship to the chiefly family. He was educated at the University of Aberdeen but ultimately went to London to seek his fortune. In this he was assisted by a great stroke of luck. In 1705, he was in Epsom when Prince George, husband of Queen Anne, was suddenly taken ill, and he was summoned to the royal sickbed. The prince recovered, no doubt to the doctor's great relief, and Arbuthnott was appointed one of the royal physicians. He soon grew to be a

favourite and confidant of the queen, acquiring in the process a large circle of friends, including many of the leading politicians, wits and scholars of his time. He was admired by both Pope and Swift, particularly after the publication of his political satire, *The History of John Bull*. He even gained the respect of Dr Samuel Johnson, who described him as 'a man of great comprehension, skilful in his profession, versed in the sciences, acquainted with ancient literature and able to animate his mass of knowledge by a bright and active imagination'. Dr Arbuthnott died in September 1779.

The eighth Viscount of Arbuthnott was Lord Lieutenant of Kincardineshire and a representative peer for Scotland in Parliament from 1818 to 1847. The present chief and Viscount of Arbuthnott has contributed much of his life to public service, and has been awarded both the Distinguished Service Cross and the Order of the British Empire. He heads the Venerable Order of St John in Scotland, promoting their many charitable activities. The family seat is still at Arbuthnott House.

BANNERMAN

The name of Bannerman has its origin in the privilege held by ancestors of the family of carrying the royal standard in the tenth and eleventh centuries, and the arms of this family prominently proclaim this ancient and honourable office. It is not known when this right passed from the family, but according to one tradition it occurred in the late eleventh or early twelfth centuries, during the reign of either Malcolm III or Alexander I. The king is said to have arrived at the River Spey where a large enemy force had assembled on the opposite bank, believing themselves protected by the rising flood waters. The king was urged by his advisors not to attempt to cross the river until it fell, but he was enraged at the sight of the enemy and, unable to restrain himself, drove his horse into the water. Sir Alexander Carron, the king's chamberlain, perceiving his master's danger, seized up the royal standard and braved the raging waters, followed by the rest of the Scottish army. The rebels were put to flight and Carron was rewarded for his audacity by being named hereditary Standard Bearer to the King. His descendents still bear this privilege, and carry the Scottish royal banner at appropriate ceremonials.

In June 1367 David II granted land to Donald Bannerman 'dilecto medico nostro' of the lands of Clyntrees, Waterton and Weltown in the parish of Ellon in Aberdeenshire. The Bannermans were required to build a chapel where weekly mass was to be said for the repose of the soul of the king's father, Robert the Bruce. In 1370 the Abbot of Kinloss granted to the Bannermans land lying to the west of the city of Aberdeen.

The Bannermans became embroiled in the politics of north-east Scotland, which inevitably meant taking sides in the great feud between the powerful Gordons and their enemies the Forbeses, during the sixteenth century. The Bannermans generally were supporters of the Forbeses, but in 1608 Margaret Bannerman married George Gordon of Haddo, son of Sir John Gordon. He was to be a loyal supporter of the king and was later executed for opposing the National Covenant. Alexander Bannerman of Pitmedden also supported Charles I in his struggle against his Scottish presbyterian subjects, and his estates were only saved from forfeiture by passing them to his brother-in-law, Sir George Hamilton of Tulliallan. In 1644 Bannerman fought a duel with his cousin, Sir George Gordon of Haddo, and wounded him. The family lands were eventually restored to his eldest son, Sir Alexander Bannerman of Elsick, who was created a Baronet of Nova Scotia by Charles II on 28 December 1682. The royal patent proclaims that the title was for his constant loyalty during the rebellion (i.e., the civil war) and of the heavy calamities he had suffered on that account. His youngest son, Patrick, was to support the cause of the deposed Stuart monarchs, and rose in support of the 'Old Pretender' in 1715. He was Provost of Aberdeen, and presented a loyal address from the town to James VIII at Fetteresso, welcoming him to his ancient kingdom of Scotland. James, clearly delighted with the demonstrations of loyalty, promptly knighted Provost Bannerman. He was arrested after the failure of the rising and was conveyed as a prisoner to Carlisle to await execution, but he managed to escape, and went to France.

The Bannerman support for the Jacobite cause continued unabated, and Sir Alexander, son of the second Baronet, joined Prince Charles Edward Stuart with 160 men at Stirling in 1745 and was with his prince at the disaster of Culloden field in 1746. He escaped with his life, fleeing north to Dingwall and then to Sutherland. He ultimately escaped to France having narrowly escaped government troops at Elsick where he concealed himself in a secret closet. Sir Alexander Bannerman, fourth Baronet, was forced to sell the Elsick estates in face of a threat of forfeiture for suspected Jacobite intrigues.

Sir Alexander Bannerman was MP for the city of Aberdeen from 1832 to 1840, and thereafter Governor of the Bahamas and of Newfoundland. In 1851 he reacquired the house and estate of Elsick, but these passed through his only daughter to the Carnegie Earls of Southesk. The present chief of the Carnegies, the Duke of Fife, still resides at Elsick House.

Sir Henry Campbell Bannerman, Liberal Prime Minister of Britain from 1905 to 1908, was born in Glasgow in 1836. He assumed the name Bannerman through his mother after he entered politics in 1868. His first government post was financial secretary to the War Office but he rapidly rose through the ranks to become Secretary of State for War in 1886. He became a close friend of Edward VII who made him Prime Minister on the resignation of the Conservative administration of Arthur Balfour. He recognised talent and he appointed to his cabinet two future prime ministers: Herbert Asquith and David Lloyd George. Lloyd George was the first cabinet minister to come from a working-class background and Campbell Bannerman was criticised in some quarters for advancing him. With his health failing, Campbell Bannerman resigned in favour of fellow Liberal, Herbert Asquith, only seventeen days before his death in April 1908.

Sir Arthur Bannerman, twelfth Baronet, served in the Indian army and was political aide to the Secretary of State for India from 1921 to 1928. He was appointed a Gentleman Usher to George V and thereafter to Edward VIII and George VI. He was made a Knight Commander of the Royal Victorian Order in 1928.

John Bannerman, who died in 1969, was one of Scotland's greatest rugby players, winning no less than thirty-nine caps for his country. He was a passionate Scottish nationalist and a supporter of the Gaelic language. He was made a life peer as Lord Bannerman of Kildonan in 1967. The thirteenth Baronet, served in the Cameron Highlanders. An interest in languages led him to become a Russian interpreter, and after his military career he taught at Gordonstoun and Fettes College in Edinburgh. His son is the present chief.

BARCLAY

ARMS
Azure, a chevron Or between three crosses pattée Argent

CREST
*(on a chapeau Azure doubled Ermine) A hand holding a
dagger Proper*

MOTTO
Aut agere aut mori (Either to do or die)

SUPPORTERS
Two greyhounds Argent, collared Gules

T he Barclays were a family which came over from France with the Norman Conquest. The first spelling of their name was 'de Berchelai', believed to be the Anglo–Saxon version of 'beau', meaning 'beautiful', and 'lee' a 'meadow' or 'field'. The early settlers in Gloucestershire bore the Norman forenames of Roger and Ralph. Domesday Book lists them as owning twenty hamlets between the Rivers Wye and Usk. The Earls of Berkeley built Berkeley Castle as a fortress in 1153. Edward II was imprisoned and murdered there by his queen in 1327. The castle was so stout that its walls were only breached in the seventeenth century, during the civil war between Charles I and Parliament.

Some of the family went north to Scotland where they settled in the north-east at Towie, Mathers, Gartley and Pierston in Aberdeenshire. They also settled at Collairnie in Fife. Lord Roger de Berchelai, who is mentioned in Domesday, and, by tradition, his son, John, came to Scotland in the retinue of Margaret, sister of the Saxon Edgar the Aetheling, in 1067. She married Malcolm III, who bestowed various lands on her followers, including the lands of Towie to John de Berchelai.

The Barclays soon established themselves in strong positions in lands, offices and alliances, and took a notable part in national affairs, including the War of Independence. Sir Walter de Berkeley was Chamberlain of Scotland in 1165, and the duties of this high office would have kept him in close attendance upon his royal master, William the Lion. Sir David Barclay was one of the chief associates of Robert the Bruce and was present at most of his battles, particularly Methven where he was taken prisoner.

In the seventeenth century, a branch of the family was established at Urie near Stonehaven in Kincardineshire. The first Laird of Urie, Colonel David Barclay, was a professional soldier who served in the armies of Gustavus Adolphus, King of Sweden. He attained the rank of major and remained in service abroad until civil war broke out in his own country, when he returned home and became a colonel of a regiment of horse fighting for the king. He retired from active military service in 1647 and purchased the estate of Urie in Kincardineshire. After the Restoration he was committed prisoner to Edinburgh Castle upon a charge of hostility to the government, but he was soon liberated through the interest of powerful friends with whom he had served during the civil war. During his imprisonment he was converted to the Society of Friends (Quakers) by the Laird of Swinton who was confined in the same prison. His son, Robert Barclay, second of Urie, was also a Quaker, and published *An Apology for the true Christian Divinity as the same is held forth and preached by the people called in scorn Quakers* in 1675. The Apology, first published in Latin, was reprinted in English, German, Dutch, French and Spanish. Although the Quakers were generally persecuted, Barclay received great respect, even acquiring favour at the royal court. He moved with his family to London, and corresponded with Princess Elizabeth, niece of Charles I. In 1679 Charles II granted him a charter under the great seal, erecting his lands of Urie into a free barony. In 1682 the proprietors of East Jersey in America appointed him governor of that province, bestowing upon him five thousand acres of land. He never took up office but died at Urie in August 1690. David Barclay of Cheapside, the apologist's second son, founded Barclay's Bank.

There have always been close shipping and trading ties between the east coast of Scotland and Scandinavia and the lands around the Baltic, and the Barclays were involved in this trade. In 1621 Sir Patrick Barclay, Baron of Towie, the seventeenth Laird, signed a letter of safe conduct in favour

Barclay

of John and Peter Barclay who were merchants in the town of Banff and who wished to settle in Rostock in Livonia, on the shores of the Baltic. This letter is still extant, and is in the possession of Barclay descendents in Riga. The brothers became silk merchants and burghers. From Peter, in five generations, was descended Field Marshall Michael Andreas Barclay de Tolly, born 16 December 1761. He was made Minister of War in 1810 and two years later was given command of the Russian armies fighting against Napoleon. He avoided direct confrontation with the French and instead instigated a scorched earth campaign, leaving the country desolate through which the French troops were required to pass. The plan was a success, and retreat from Moscow in 1812 contributed greatly to Napoleon's final downfall. The appointment of a Scottish commander-in-chief was much resented by the Russian nobility, but nevertheless his capabilities were respected. Barclay de Tolly was created a prince by the Tsar, and his memory is still honoured in Russia, where his portrait hangs in the Hermitage in St Petersburg. He died on 25 May 1818.

ARMS
Argent, three cinquefoils Sable

CREST
A moor's head couped Proper wreathed Argent and Sable

MOTTO
Qui conducit (He who leads)

SUPPORTERS
*(on a compartment consisting of a stone wall Proper sur-
rounding a field Vert) Two angels Proper winged Or*

STANDARD
*Azure, a St Andrew's Cross Argent in the hoist and of two
tracts Argent and Sable, upon which is depicted the Crest
upon a chapeau Gules furred Ermine in the first compartment and the Badge in the second compartment, along
with the Motto 'Qui conducit' in letters Sable upon a
transverse band Or*

PINSEL
*Argent, on a Wreath of the Liveries a moor's head couped
Proper wreathed Argent and Sable within a strap Sable
buckled and embellished Or inscribed with this Motto
'Qui conducit' in letters of the Field and all within a
circlet Or fimbriated Gules bearing the title 'Borthwick,
Lord Borthwick' in letters Sable, the same ensigned of
a Baron's coronet, and in the fly on an Escrol Sable
surmounting a stem of two roses Gules leaved, barbed
and seeded Vert this Slogan 'A Borthwick' in letters of
the Field*

BADGE
*An angel Proper winged Or holding in the dexter hand a
cinquefoil Sable*

PLANT BADGE
A stem of two roses Gules leaved, barbed and seeded Vert

This name is of territorial origin, and it seems likely to have been assumed from lands on Borthwick Water in Roxburghshire. The family is one of the most ancient in Scotland and some recent research suggests that they may have come to Britain with Caesar's legions. It is traditionally asserted that the progenitor of this noble house was Andreas, who accompanied the Saxon Edgar the Aetheling and his sister, Margaret, later queen and saint, to Scotland in 1067. The family soon became prominent in Scottish affairs. Sir William Borthwick pos-sessed substantial lands in Midlothian and the Borders, and he obtained a charter confirming his lands of Borthwick around 1410; these were the lands after which the family were named. During the fifteenth century the Borthwicks acquired immense influence and became Lords of Parliament.

The first Lord Borthwick was one of the nobles who went to England as substitute hostages for the ransom of James I in 1425. He erected what remains one of the most impres-sive fortified dwellings in Scotland on a strong position near Middleton in Midlothian: the tower is over 110 feet high, with walls 14 feet thick, while the great hall is 50 feet long under a 37 feet-high vault. The castle has remained in the ownership of the Borthwick family to the present day. The first Lord Borthwick died some time before 1458 and is commemorated by a splendid tomb in the old church of Borthwick.

The Borthwicks fought alongside James IV at the ill-fated Battle of Flodden in September 1513, and met the same end as most of the flower of Scottish chivalry. William, Lord Borthwick, succeeded his father who fell at Flodden, and his prominence was emphasised by his being given command of the strategic Castle of Stirling and charged with the safety of the infant James V. John, Lord Borthwick, opposed the Reformation of the Scottish

Church and was an ardent supporter of Mary of Guise, the Queen Regent and mother of Mary, Queen of Scots. His adherence to the Church did not mean that he was in favour with clerical authority. In 1547, Lord Borthwick was excommunicated for contempt of the ecclesiastical court of the see of St Andrews. William Langlands, an officer of the court, was sent with the letters of excommunication for delivery to the curate of Borthwick. Langlands was seized by Lord Borthwick's servants who promptly threw him in the mill dam north of the castle and later made him eat the letters, mercifully having soaked them in wine. He was sent on his way having been warned that any other such communications would 'a' gang the same gait'. His son, William, was a staunch friend and confidant of Queen Mary, who was a frequent visitor to the castle. She took refuge there with her husband, Bothwell, but they were forced to flee when the castle was approached by a substantial force under Lords Murray and Morton. The queen is said to have escaped disguised as a pageboy.

Standard

The Borthwicks formed alliances with other noble and powerful families by marriage. William, Lord Borthwick, married the eldest daughter of Sir Walter Scott of Branxholm, ancestor of the Dukes of Buccleuch, and his son, James, married Margaret Hay, eldest daughter of Lord Hay of Yester, from whom descends the Marquess of Tweeddale. David Borthwick of Lochhill was a prominent lawyer who became the king's advocate, or principal legal adviser, in 1573. He may have been the first to bear the title, 'Lord Advocate', still in use today for the government's chief law officer in Scotland.

Not all the Borthwicks were nobles: one Robert Borthwick is named as Master Gunner

Borthwick

to James IV around 1509. He is said to have cast seven great cannons, called the Seven Sisters, which were lost when taken to the Battle of Flodden.

The Borthwicks adhered to the royalist cause during the civil war, and their castle was besieged after the Battle of Dunbar in 1650. The splendid fortress was spared from inevitable destruction when Oliver Cromwell offered Lord Borthwick honourable terms of surrender, which he accepted. He was allowed to leave with his family and goods unmolested. Thereafter the direct line failed and the title became dormant. Henry Borthwick of Neathorn was recognised as male heir to the first Lord by decision of the House of Lords in 1762 and he assumed the title, but died without issue ten years later. Various branches of the family disputed the right of succession in the eighteenth and nineteenth centuries, but in June 1986, Major John Borthwick of Crookston was recognised by the Lord Lyon, King of Arms, as the Right Honourable The Lord Borthwick of that Ilk and chief of the name and arms of Borthwick. He still lives on the ancient family lands and has two sons, so the succession to this most ancient title presently seems secure.

BOYD

This is said to be a descriptive name, deriving from the Gaelic, 'buidhe', meaning 'fair' or 'yellow'. The original fair-haired man is said to have been Robert, nephew of Walter, the first High Steward of Scotland. However, this derivation is challenged by Anderson, who points out that, as the High Stewards and most of their friends and dependents were of Norman origin, they would be unlikely to use a Celtic nickname for one of their close family. He believes the name to be of Norman or Saxon origin. Black asserts that the first Boyds were vassals of the Norman family of de Morvilles for their lands around Largs and Irvine.

Robertus de Boyd witnessed a contract between the Lord of Eglinton and the burgh of Irvine around 1205. Robert de Boyte is listed in the Ragman Roll of 1296, rendering homage to Edward I of England. Duncan Boyd was executed by the English in 1306 for supporting the cause of Scottish independence. Sir Robert Boyd was a staunch supporter of Bruce and was one of the commanders at the Battle of Bannockburn in 1314. His gallantry on the field of battle was rewarded by lands which were confiscated from the Balliols, including Kilmarnock, Bondington and other substantial holdings in Ayrshire.

The fortunes of the family continued to advance and they were raised to the peerage under the title, 'Lord Boyd of Kilmarnock' by James II. Lord Boyd was a trusted royal officer, and on the death of James II he was appointed one of the regents to the young James III, while his younger brother was appointed military tutor to the young king. The influence of the Boyd brothers on their young charge was considerable. Lord Boyd was appointed Great Chamberlain, and his son, Thomas, was married to Princess Mary, the king's sister, with the title of 'Earl of Arran'.

As the family had risen so high, it is not surprising that they made many powerful enemies. Those opposed to the Boyds began to conspire against them, and eventually persuaded the king that the ambition of this family was a threat to the throne itself. In 1469, Lord Boyd, his son, the Earl of Arran, and his brother, Alexander Boyd, were summoned to appear before the king and Parliament to answer charges brought against them. Lord Boyd, realising that appearance in Edinburgh would result in his death, made his escape to England. Sir Alexander, who was already a sick man, was brought before Parliament, and despite making a spirited defence he was executed for treason. The Earl of Arran had been abroad on state business, and on learning of the total reversal of his family's fortunes he accepted his exile, and was well received at royal courts throughout Europe. The king, who had now abandoned entirely his former mentors, summoned his sister back to Scotland, inducing her to come on the pretence that he might yet forgive her husband. The deluded princess returned, and was promptly detained by her brother who procured an annulment of her marriage.

Boyd

Standard

The family were restored to royal favour when Robert, a descendent of the younger son of the first Lord Boyd, received confirmation from Mary, Queen of Scots, of all the estates, honours and dignities of the family, with the title of 'Lord Boyd'. After the queen's escape from Loch Leven Castle, Lord Boyd was one of the first to join her at Hamilton, and fought at the Battle of Langside. He thereafter made many visits to her during her captivity in England. He died in 1590. The family adhered to the cause of the king during the civil war, and they received their reward after the Restoration when William, Lord Boyd, was created Earl of Kilmarnock in 1661. The third Earl opposed the Stuart claim during the rising

of 1715 and commanded a regiment of Ayrshire volunteers. His son, the fourth Earl, did not share his father's sympathies and fought for Prince Charles Edward Stuart, the 'Young Pretender', who appointed him a member of the Privy Council with the rank of general. He fought at the Battle of Culloden where he was captured. He was conveyed to the Tower of London and was beheaded on Tower Hill on 18 August 1746. All the Boyd titles were declared forfeit, but his eldest son succeeded through his mother to the earldom of Erroll in 1758, and assumed the name of Hay.

The eighteenth Earl of Erroll was created Baron Kilmarnock in the peerage of the United Kingdom in 1831. The twenty-second Earl of Erroll died in Kenya in 1941 leaving a daughter who, although entitled to succeed to the Scottish earldom of Erroll and the chiefship of Clan Hay, was excluded from the barony of Kilmarnock which, as a United Kingdom title, could only pass to males. Consequently, the brother of the twenty-second Earl resumed the name of Boyd and succeeded to the barony. The present chief is the seventh Lord Kilmarnock.

BOYLE

The Norman town of Beauville near Caen is the origin of this name. David de Boivil appears as a witness to a charter as early as 1164, and Richard de Boyville held the lands of Kelburn in Ayrshire around 1275. Henry de Boyville was keeper of the Castles of Dumfries, Wigtown and Kirkcudbright around 1291. Richard and Robert de Boyvil appear on the Ragman Roll of barons submitting to Edward I of England in 1296. Richard Boyle married Marjory, daughter of Sir Robert Comyn of Rowallan. Six generations later his descendent, John Boyle, was a supporter of James III, and was killed at the Battle of Sauchieburn in 1488. The family lands were forfeited, but his son, John, obtained their restoration when James IV once more established royal government. The family extended their holdings by successful marriages. The Boyles who settled in Ireland rose to become the powerful Earls of Cork, and are believed to descend from the same stock as the house of Kelburn.

The Boyles supported the cause of Mary, Queen of Scots, and later that of Charles I, suffering many hardships as a result. The family fortunes were restored when John Boyle of Kelburn was elected as a Commissioner of Parliament in 1681. His eldest son David, also became a Commissioner of Parliament and a Privy Councillor. He was raised to the Peerage as Lord Boyle of Kelburn in 1699, and was advanced to the title of Earl of Glasgow in 1703. He was one of the commissioners for the Treaty of Union with England, and in 1706 was appointed Lord High Commissioner to the General Assembly of the Church of Scotland. He staunchly supported the Hanoverian cause, and when the standard of the 'Old Pretender' was raised in 1715 he raised and armed troops at his own expense.

The third Earl followed a military career and was wounded at the Battle of Fontenoy in 1745 and again at Lauffeldt in 1747. He was also appointed Lord High Commissioner to the General Assembly, and held the office for nine successive years. Lady Jean, daughter of the first Earl, married Sir James Campbell, who also fought at Fontenoy, but died of the wounds he received. Their son succeeded to the Campbell earldom of Loudoun in 1782. Lady Augusta Boyle, daughter of the fourth Earl, married in 1891 Lord Frederick Fitz-clarence, son of William IV. David Boyle, a grandson of the second Earl, was a distinguished lawyer who was appointed Solicitor General for Scotland in 1807. He was elevated to the Bench and was ultimately appointed Lord President and Lord Justice General of Scotland in 1841. He retired from the Bench in 1852 after more than forty-one years of legal service.

The fourth Earl was also a soldier who commenced his career as a captain in the West Lowland Fencibles in 1793, rising to the rank of colonel in due course. He was appointed Lord Lieutenant of Renfrewshire in 1810.

His eldest son, John, Lord Boyle, was a naval officer who, in July 1807, was confronted by a superior French flotilla near Gibraltar. He bravely engaged the enemy but his vessel was overrun and Boyle was taken prisoner. He died unmarried, in 1818. His younger brother, James, became the fifth Earl in 1843, ending a promising career in the House of Commons. He too served in the Royal Navy and was made Lord Lieutenant of Renfewshire. He married Georgina Mackenzie in 1821 but the union was without issue.

When the fifth Earl died he was succeeded by his half-brother, the Hon. George Frederick Boyle. The succession of the sixth Earl was a catastrophe for the family fortunes. Educated at Oxford, George Boyle had been passionately interested in art and architecture. He was profoundly influenced by the Pre-Raphaelite movement and embraced not only its vision of form and beauty but extended it with his own taste for religious mysticism. He embarked on an ambitious building pro-gramme at Kelburn and funded the erection of

The full achievement of the Earl of Glasgow

churches all over Scotland. He bankrupted the entire estate and, in 1888, all his assets were put up for sale. Kelburn itself was only saved by the intervention of his cousin, later the seventh Earl.

The seventh Earl was a naval officer and Governor of New Zealand from 1892 to 1897. He had succeeded his cousin in 1890, and was additionally created Baron Fairlie of Fairlie in the peerage of the United Kingdom in 1897. This was to ensure him a seat in the House of Lords, as at that time only a limited number of Scottish peers could sit there. Elected by their fellow peers, they were known as representative peers. This system is no longer in operation.

The present head of the family and chief of the name succeeded his father, who was a distinguished naval officer, in 1984 as tenth Earl of Glasgow. He still resides at Kelburn Castle near Fairlie in Ayrshire, on the lands held by his family since the thirteenth century, and has done much to develop the family seat, which is now visited by Boyles from all over the world.

BRODIE

This most ancient family takes its name from the lands of Brodie near Forres in Morayshire. The family lost most of its early charters and other documents when the Gordons burnt the castle in 1645. Shaw suggests that the name itself is derived from the Gaelic word, 'brothaig', meaning 'ditch'. He suggests that they may have shared a common ancestry with the Morays and Inneses who were all settled along the Moray Firth in the twelfth century, pointing to the similarity of their coats of arms, each of which bears three stars.

Michael Brodie of Brodie received a charter of confirmation of his lands of Brodie from Robert the Bruce. The charter declares that Brodie held the thanage of Brodie by right of succession from his paternal ancestors. It has been suggested that the family may even have Pictish origins, being descended from the royal family who carried the name, 'Brude'. There is much evidence of Pictish settlement around Brodie, and although there is no certain proof of the claim, it must be considered as at least a reasonable explanation.

The Brodies were certainly prominent among the local nobility, and the name appears throughout the fifteenth and sixteenth centuries in charters of the diocese of Moray. John 'de Brothie' is recorded in a church charter attending on the Earl of Mar, Lieutenant of the North, in 1376. Thomas de Brothie, and his sons John and Alexander, are mentioned in connection with the Vicarage of Dyke, a living eventually bestowed on Alexander. Alexander Brodie of Brodie appears to have been a local judge as he was summoned before the Lords of Council in Edinburgh in January 1484 to give account of one of his verdicts. John of Brodie is mentioned many times as an arbiter of disputes particularly in 1492. He may be the same John of Brodie who assisted the Mackenzies in their battle against the Macdonalds at Blair-na-park in 1466. He witnessed a contract between the Calders and the Baron of Kilravock in 1482. His great-grandson, Alexander Brodie of Brodie, was denounced as a rebel, along with 126 others, in 1550 for attacking Alexander Cumming of Altyre and mutilating one of his servants. The rebel's eldest son David had his lands of Brodie erected into a free barony under charter of the Great Seal in July 1597. He had several sons; the second, Alexander, purchased the lands of Lethen and is ancestor to the Brodies of Lethen. The eldest son, another David, inherited the estates in 1626, but he died only six years later when they passed to his son Alexander, later the judge, Lord Brodie.

Alexander Brodie of Brodie, who was born in 1617, was a vigorous supporter of the reformed religion, and in 1640 he attacked Elgin Cathedral and destroyed its carvings and paintings, which he considered idolatrous. He represented Elgin in Parliament, and in 1649 was one of the commissioners sent to negotiate with the exiled Charles II his conditions for his return to Scotland. He was an able politician, as after the defeat of the royalist forces at the Battle of Worcester in 1651 he was summoned to London by Oliver Cromwell to consider a union between Scotland and England. He resisted attempts to appoint him to judicial office under the Protectorate, although he finally accepted after Cromwell's death in 1658. This brought him royal dis-favour after the Restoration, when he was fined for his actions. He died in 1679. In 1727 Alexander Brodie of Brodie was appointed Lord Lyon, King of Arms. A splendid portrait in his official robes still hangs in Brodie Castle. He was Lyon during the Jacobite rebellion of 1745 and attended on the Duke of Cumberland throughout his Scottish campaign. His son, Alexander, died in 1759, and the chiefship passed to a cousin, James Brodie of Spynie. He married Lady Margaret Duff,

Brodie

youngest daughter of William, first Earl of Fife, and was a talented botanist and agriculturist who made many improvements to the estate. His eldest son died in a drowning accident and the estate passed to his grandson, William Brodie, in 1824. William Brodie of Brodie was Lord Lieutenant of Nairn from 1824 to 1873.

There are other distinguished branches of this family, including the Brodies of Lethen and a distinguished family of English baronets who claim descent from the chiefly line. Sir Benjamin Collins Brodie, whose family are believed to have left Banffshire to settle in England around 1740, was one of the most distinguished surgeons of his time, and was president of the Royal Society. He was surgeon to both William IV and Victoria. He was created a baronet in August 1834. Brodie of Brodie still lives at Brodie Castle, but in 1979 the present chief placed it in the care of the National Trust for Scotland.

BRUCE

This name, now inextricably linked with the history of the Scottish nation through its association with the victor of Bannockburn, was ancient long before that momentous battle. It is believed that Adam de Brus built the castle at Brix between Cherbourg and Valognes in Normandy in the eleventh century, the ruins of which still remain. Robert de Brus followed William the Conqueror, Duke of Normandy, to England in 1066, and although he is thought to have died soon after, his sons acquired great possessions in Surrey and Dorset. Another Robert de Brus became a companion-in-arms to Prince David, afterwards David I of Scotland, and followed him when he went north to regain his kingdom in 1124. His loyalties were torn in 1138 when, during the civil war in England between Stephen and Matilda, who claimed to be the rightful heiress, David led a force into England. de Brus could not support his king, and resigned his holdings in Annandale to his second son, Robert, to join the English forces gathering to resist the Scottish invasion. At the Battle of the Standard in 1138, Scottish forces were defeated and de Brus took prisoner his own son, now Lord of the lands of Annandale. He was ultimately returned to Scotland, and to demonstrate his determination to establish his branch of the family in Scotland, he abandoned his father's arms of a red lion on a silver field and assumed the now familiar red saltire. The arms borne by the present chief allude to both elements.

William the Lion confirmed to the son the grant of the lands of Annandale made to his father by David I. Robert, fourth Lord of Annandale, laid the foundation of the royal house of Bruce when he married Isobel, niece of William the Lion. She also brought extensive estates, both in Scotland and England. Princess Isobel's son, another Robert, known as 'the competitor', was at the time named heir to the Scottish crown. However, his claim was challenged by the birth of a son to the daughter of his wife's elder sister, who was married to John Balliol. On the death of Alexander III in 1286 there commenced the contest for the succession to the Crown between Bruce and Balliol. The death of the child heir to the throne, Margaret, the Maid of Norway, in 1290, opened the competition for the succession once more, and to avoid a civil war, the rival claimants asked Edward I of England to act as arbiter. In 1292 Edward found in favour of John Balliol. But Edward was not content to advise on the selection of a new monarch, and asserted a right of overlordship in Scottish affairs. Balliol attempted armed resistance but was decisively defeated at the Battle of Dunbar in 1296. His defeat left the leadership of Scotland in the hands either of the powerful Comyn family or of the Bruces. Robert the Bruce met with John Comyn on February 1306 in the Church of the Minorite Friars at Dumfries. Bruce stabbed his rival in the heart, and his companions dispatched the rest of the Comyn party. Within weeks Robert was crowned king and began a long, hard campaign to make his title a reality, culminating in the Battle of Bannockburn in 1314. He set about rebuilding the shattered nation and it is a considerable tribute to his leadership and abilities that he substantially achieved his objectives. In 1370 the first Stewart monarch succeeded to the throne by right of descent from Marjory, Bruce's daughter.

Standard

Thomas Bruce, who claimed close kinship with the royal house, organised with Robert the Steward (later Robert II) a rising in Kyle against the English in 1334. He received in recompense part of the Crown lands of Clackmannan.

Sir Edward Bruce was made commendator

Bruce

of Kinloss Abbey and appointed a judge in 1597. In 1601 he was appointed a Lord of Parliament with the title of 'Lord Kinloss'. He accompanied James VI to claim his English throne in 1603 and was subsequently appointed to English judicial office as Master of the Rolls. In May 1608 he was granted a barony as Lord Bruce of Kinloss. His son, Thomas, was created first Earl of Elgin in 1633. The fourth Earl died without a male heir and the title passed to a descendent of Sir George Bruce of Carnock. This branch of the family had already been created Earls of Kincardine in 1647, and thus two titles were united.

The seventh Earl of Elgin was the famous diplomat who spent much of his fortune rescuing the marbles of the Parthenon (the Elgin marbles) which were at that time falling into utter ruin. His son was an eminent diplomat and Governor General of Canada. He led two important missions to the Emperor of China. He was Viceroy of India, a post also held by the ninth Earl of Elgin from 1894 to 1899. The present chief – the eleventh Earl of Elgin and fifteenth of Kincardine – is prominent in Scottish public affairs and is convenor of the Standing Council of Scottish Chiefs.

BUCHAN

ARMS
Argent, three lion's heads erased Sable langued Gules

CREST
(upon a chapeau Gules furred Ermine)
A sun shining upon a sunflower full blown Proper

MOTTO
Non inferiora secutus (Not having followed mean pursuits)

SUPPORTERS
(on a compartment embellished with sunflowers Proper).
Dexter, a heron with an eel in its bill all Proper; sinister, an antelope Argent attired Or, collared Sable, the collar charged with three sunflowers Proper

STANDARD
The Arms of Buchan of Auchmacoy in the hoist and of two tracts Argent and Sable, upon which is depicted the Badge three times along with the Motto 'Non inferiora secutus' in letters Argent upon two transverse bands Gules

PINSEL
Argent, a sun shining upon a sunflower full blown Or upon a Wreath Argent and Sable surrounded by a strap Sable, buckled and embellished Or, inscribed with the Motto 'Non inferiora secutus' in letters Or, all within a circlet also Or, fimbriated Vert, bearing the name and style 'Buchan of Auchmacoy' in letters Sable, the same ensigned of a chapeau Gules furred Ermine, and in the fly on an Escrol Sable surmounting a sunflower Proper, this Slogan 'Auchmacoy' in letters Argent

BADGE
An eagle displayed Azure, on its head a chapeau Gules doubled Ermine, armed, beaked and membered Or, holding in its claws an escutcheon of the Arms of Buchan of Auchmacoy, and in each claw a sunflower slipped and leaved Proper

PLANT BADGE
Sunflower

A name derived from the district of Buchan which comprises the north-eastern part of Aberdeenshire and part of Banffshire. The ancient mormaership, or earldom, of Buchan came into the hands of the Comyns, who were later deprived of it after their defeat at the hands of Robert the Bruce. Buchan was thereafter conferred on Alexander Stewart, the feared Wolf of Badenoch, natural son of Robert II. The geographic name would, however, have been used by notable inhabitants of the district, even although they may have had no provable connection with the great earls.

Black lists Ricardus de Buchan as clerk to the bishopric of Aberdeen around 1207. William de Buchan held land in Aberdeen before 1281. Sir Thomas de Boghan appears on the Ragman Roll rendering homage to Edward I of England in 1296. His lands were around Edinburgh, and his seal bears an eight-rayed figure which may be the derivation of the shining sun which forms part of the chief's crest.

It cannot be accurately ascertained when the Buchans gained the lands of Auchmacoy, but Andrew Buchan of Achmakwy was one of the assize appointed to settle the boundaries of the lands of St Peter's Hospital in 1446. Auchmacoy seemed to have been in the family's hands from the beginning of the fourteenth century, but it was in 1503 that Andrew, generally reckoned to be the second chief, received a charter to the lands from James IV.

The Barons of Auchmacoy were staunch royalists and firm supporters of the Stuarts throughout the seventeenth century. Thomas, the third son of James Buchan of Auchmacoy, was a professional soldier who learned his trade in the wars in France and Holland. He served in Douglas's Scots Regiment, raised for the king of France, until 1686, when he was commissioned colonel in the Earl of Mar's regiment by James VII. Loyal to his commission, he joined Viscount Dundee to fight for his deposed monarch. After Dundee's death at Killiecrankie in 1689, Buchan was appointed commander-in-chief of all Jacobite forces in Scotland, receiving his commission from the king in Ireland. He returned to Scotland in April 1690 where he met at Keppoch with chiefs sympathetic to the Jacobite cause. It was resolved to delay the general muster of the clans until the summer, but General Buchan was to harry the enemy with his force of

Standard

twelve hundred foot. On 1 May 1690 at Cromdale, Buchan was taken by surprise by a strong government force under General Mackay. Buchan escaped, regrouped his men, and joined forces with the Farquharsons. The Highland reinforcements encouraged Buchan to take the offensive again. He marched from Abergeldie through the Mearns towards Aberdeen but he was soon opposed by the Master of Forbes and a strong force of cavalry. Buchan cleverly disposed his troops to give an appearance of numerical superiority and his ruse was successful. Forbes retreated towards Aberdeen, causing panic in the city. Buchan, however, had no intention of attacking the city and turned towards Inverness. General Mackay's forces however, marched to intercept him, and Buchan's Highlanders drifted away into their home glens. Buchan was allowed to go into exile in France, but he fought again at

the Battle of Sheriffmuir in 1715 and was still in communication with the exiled royal family when he died in 1721.

James Buchan, fourteenth of Auchmacoy, was recognised by the Lord Lyon as chief of the name in April 1830. The title then passed through his only daughter, Louisa, to her cousin, Sir Norman Sinclair, eighteenth Earl of Caithness. He petitioned the Lyon Court in April 1913, taking the surname and arms of Buchan of Auchmacoy. His daughter, Lady Lucy Buchan, married Sir Thomas Innes of Learney, the great Lord Lyon, in 1928. She was the mother of Sir Thomas's younger son, the present Lord Lyon, Sir Malcolm Innes of Edengight. The earl's eldest daughter, Lady Olivia, became the seventeenth of Auchmacoy. Her son changed his name in 1949 to be recognised by the Lord Lyon as chief of the Buchans. The chief's seat remains at Auchmacoy House near Ellon.

Alexander Buchan was an eminent British meteorologist who first observed what were to become known as Buchan Spells: departures from the normally expected temperature occurring during certain seasons. Buchan established the weather map as the basis for weather forecasting. John Buchan, born in August 1875, was a clergyman's son, educated at the Universities of Glasgow and Oxford before being called to the Bar in 1901. He served in the colonial service in South Africa and this inspired his literary career. His most famous work was *The Thirty-nine Steps*, popularised by the motion picture directed by Alfred Hitchcock. In 1935 he was appointed Governor General of Canada and was created first Baron Tweedsmuir.

BURNETT

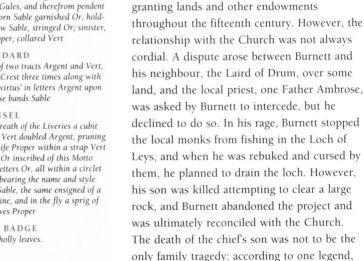

This ancient family claims Norman descent, but it is possible that the name is also connected with the great Saxon family of Burnard who held estates in England before the Norman Conquest. The Saxon 'beornheard' means 'brave warrior'. It seems likely that the family, now calling themselves de Bernard, first came to Scotland on the return of David I from England, and they appear to have settled in Roxburghshire. Alexander Burnett was a faithful adherent of Robert the Bruce, and on the defeat of the English he was rewarded by a grant of land in the royal Forest of Drum, together with the title of forester. In the main hall of the ancient seat of the Burnetts' Crathes Castle, pride of place is still given to an ancient and splendid ivory horn said to have been presented by Bruce as a symbol of the barony and title bestowed upon Burnett.

Nisbet states that the Burnetts were great benefactors of the Church, and they appear granting lands and other endowments throughout the fifteenth century. However, the relationship with the Church was not always cordial. A dispute arose between Burnett and his neighbour, the Laird of Drum, over some land, and the local priest, one Father Ambrose, was asked by Burnett to intercede, but he declined to do so. In his rage, Burnett stopped the local monks from fishing in the Loch of Leys, and when he was rebuked and cursed by them, he planned to drain the loch. However, his son was killed attempting to clear a large rock, and Burnett abandoned the project and was ultimately reconciled with the Church. The death of the chief's son was not to be the only family tragedy: according to one legend, the ghost of a cousin of the family once haunted Crathes Castle, seeking her lost love.

Bertha de Bernard came to stay at Crathes where she soon fell in love with one of her cousins. Sadly for the young lovers, the boy was already betrothed to a daughter of the powerful Hamiltons. The Hamilton match was dear to the ambitions of Lady Agnes Burnett who arranged for her son to be sent on an embassy to England by James V. Bertha pined for her sweetheart but then mysteriously died. Lady Agnes was suspected of poisoning the girl to ensure she could not obstruct the family advancement but nothing could be proved. Bertha's father returned from the wars in France and laid a curse on his kinsmen. Thereafter a 'Green Lady' haunted Crathes and her appearances always heralded death and destruction for the family until she disappeared in the seventeenth century.

Sir Thomas Burnett, who had been created a Baronet of Nova Scotia in April 1626, was a staunch supporter of the Covenant, but he was also related to the great Marquess of Montrose, and entertained him at Crathes Castle and accompanied him on his march towards Aberdeen. His son, the third Baronet, was Commissioner for Kincardineshire in the last Scottish Parliament and was strenuously opposed to the union of Scotland and England which was ultimately to be effected in 1707. On the death of Sir Robert Burnett of Leyes without issue, the title passed to his cousin, Thomas Burnett of Criggie.

The seventh Baronet was an officer in the Royal Scots Fusiliers and served throughout the American Wars, being taken prisoner after the surrender of General Burgoyne at Saratoga in 1777. The family's great military traditions were carried on in more recent times by Major General Sir James Burnett of Leys, thirteenth Baronet, who commanded a brigade in the First World War and was colonel of the Gordon Highlanders. He was mentioned in dispatches eleven times and was awarded the Distinguished Service Order twice. He was appointed a companion of the Order of the Bath, and decorated by France with the Legion of Honour. His grandson is the present chief, and he still lives on the family lands although Crathes Castle, one of Scotland's greatest historic monuments, is now in the care of the National Trust for Scotland.

Other distinguished Burnetts include

Burnett

Robert Burnett, raised to the Scottish judiciary as Lord Crimond in 1661 and whose son, Gilbert, became an eminent historian and clergyman. In 1698 he was appointed preceptor to the Duke of Gloucester, son of Queen Anne.

James Burnet of Monboddo, the eminent eighteenth-century lawyer, philosopher and judge, was born in 1714, the son of George Burnet and Elizabeth Forbes, sister of the laird of Craigievar. A descendant of the eleventh laird of Leys, he studied law in the Netherlands and at the University of Edinburgh before being admitted to the Faculty of Advocates in 1737. He came to prominence as one of the counsel in the famous peerage case, 'the Douglas Cause'. He became a sheriff in 1764 and a supreme court judge, with the title 'Lord Monboddo', three years later. He was an intellectual with varied interests including the origins of man; he was ridiculed for his belief that man was related to apes and originally had tails. He also, however, believed in mermaids and satyrs. The poet Robert Burns was a frequent guest of Monboddo at his house in Edinburgh. He died in 1799 at the age of 85.

Charles Burnett, a prominent museum curator, is Ross Herald at the Court of the Lord Lyon.

CAMERON

There are several theories concerning the origin of this name: one states that they are descended from a younger son of Camchron, a king of Denmark, but the more likely explanation is that the first authentic chief of the clan, Donald Dubh, was descended either from the Macgillonies or from the mediaeval family of Cameron of Ballegarno in Fife. Donald Dubh married an heiress of the Macmartins of Letterfinlay, and by his prowess and leadership, united the confederation tribes which became known as the Clan Cameron. He is believed to have been born around 1400, and he and his successors were known as captains of Clan Cameron until the time of Ewan Macallan, in the early sixteenth century, when the lands of Lochiel were united by charter into the Barony of Lochiel. Ewan's father, Alan Macdonald Dubh, the twelfth chief, was reckoned to be one of the bravest captains of his time. It was during his lifetime that the feud began with the Mackintosh clan, which was to continue sporadically for about three hundred years.

Ewan Macallan was one of the great Cameron chiefs, well favoured at court and very successful in all he undertook. The untimely death of his eldest son, Donald, was a great blow to him and, resolved to give up the world, he went on pilgrimage to Rome. The pope ordained that he should build six chapels to expiate his sins – the church at Cilachoireil, Roy Bridge, is on the site of one of these chapels. He later supported the heir to the Lordship of the Isles in an unsuccessful revolt, was apprehended by Huntly, and executed at Elgin. A renowned clansman known as Taillear Dubh na Tuaighe (Black Tailor of the Axe), who was a fearless warrior, was a natural leader of the clan during the sixteenth chief's minority. He later left Lochaber and settled near Dunoon. There are many descendents of his, bearing the name of Taylor, who are loyal adherents to the Clan Cameron. The next great chief was Sir Ewen, who was born in 1629 and died in 1719. As a young man, his education was overseen by the Marquess of Argyll, but his allegiances were altered after a trip to Edinburgh, where he witnessed the execution of Montrose and heard of his exploits. He became an implacable enemy of the Parliamentarian forces and fought many battles to preserve the independence of his clan. In 1682 he was knighted by the Duke of York in Edinburgh, and he took part with Dundee in the Battle of Killiecrankie in 1689 in support of James VII. As a soldier, he was fearless and as a chief, he was loved, trusted and admired by his clansmen. His grandson, known as the 'gentle Lochiel', was an enlight- ened chief who tried to improve the lot of his clansmen. When Bonnie Prince Charlie landed in Scotland in August 1745, the chief, as a staunch Jacobite, felt duty bound to meet him, and was eventually won over by the prince to support his cause with all his clan. The history of the Forty-five is well known, but if Lochiel had not come out with his clan, the rising might never have taken place, and the chief always felt guilty that he had allowed his better judgment to be thwarted by the prince's natural charm. He died in France in 1748, mourned by friend and foe alike.

Cameron

Standard

The savage repercussions which followed the disaster of Culloden altered the Highlands beyond recognition. The Cameron clan lands were forfeited, their houses burned, and their cattle removed or shot. The chief's wooden house, situated near the present House of Achnacarry, was destroyed. Today, only its stone gable remains, together with a summer house by the River Arkaig. In 1784 the estate was returned to Donald, grandson of the gen- tle Lochiel, subject to a large fine. He decided

to build a new house at Achnacarry which he started in about 1802, with the help of James Gillespie, the prominent Scottish architect. The project was later abandoned but his son, Donald, the twenty-third chief, completed the building which today stands by the banks of the River Arkaig, unaltered except for a wing added by his grandson.

The Cameron Highlanders, who have always had a very close association with the clan, were raised by an outstanding soldier leader, Alan Cameron of Erracht, in 1793. Donald, twenty-fourth chief who died in 1905, was a Member of Parliament for Inverness- shire for seventeen years and a member of the Royal Commission enquiring into the griev- ances of the crofters in 1883. His son, Donald Walter, twenty-fifth chief, was a soldier, and at the outbreak of the First World War he raised four new battalions of Cameron Highlanders. In 1934 Lochiel was created a Knight of the Thistle and subsequently appointed Lord Lieutenant of Inverness-shire. The present chief, who succeeded his father in 1951, was also created Lord Lieutenant in 1971, and a Knight of the Thistle in 1973.

CAMPBELL

Traditional genealogies place the origin of this clan among the ancient Britons of Strathclyde, but the first Campbell in written records is Gillespie, in 1263. Early grants of land to him and his relations were almost all in east-central Scotland, although the family's first connection with Argyll appears to have come about some generations before, with the marriage of a Campbell to the dynastic heiress of the O'Duines, who brought with her the Lordship of Loch Awe. Through this connection the clan took its early name of Clan O'Duine, a name which was later supplanted by the style Clan Diarmid, from a fancied connection with a great hero from early Celtic mythology, Diarmid the Boar. The original seat of the clan was either Innischonnel Castle on Loch Awe, which was in Campbell hands by the early fourteenth century, or Caisteal na Nigheann Ruaidhe on Loch Avich. The Campbell landholdings spread, with Craignich, Avaslotnisk, Melfort and Strachur, together with other lands of Cowal, being early additions, and the family's power soon spread throughout Argyll.

At first the Campbells were under the domination of the Macdougal Lords of Lorne who killed the Campbell chief, Sir Cailen Mor Campbell, in 1296. (All subsequent Campbell chiefs have taken as their Gaelic patronymic, 'MacCailein Mor'). However, this situation was reversed in the time of his son, Sir Neil, a staunch ally and companion of Robert the Bruce, by whom he was rewarded with extensive grants of land forfeited by the Lords of Lorne and other enemies in Argyll. It was this that gave initial impetus to the rise to power of the Campbells in the west Highlands. The king also gave his sister in marriage to Sir Neil, who appears to have disposed of his existing wife for this better offer, a common practice at a time when noble marriages were primarily a means of forging alliances. This royal marriage resulted in a son, John, who was created Earl of Atholl.

John was killed at the Battle of Halidon Hill in
1333, and with no heir to succeed, the title and
lands passed out of Campbell hands. However,
this close royal connection may have helped to
ensure the emergence of the Loch Awe branch
as the chiefly line of the Campbells. The
Macarthur Campbells of Strachur may well have
been senior by primo geniture, but their chance
of pre-eminence failed when a projected marriage with the MacRuari heiress to Garmoran
was prevented by her family. The lands later fell
into the hands of the expanding Clan Donald,
but not before a charter had been made out to
her intended husband, Arthur Campbell, a
younger son of Strachur. This gave rise to the
celebrated incident in 1427 when James I executed both John Macarthur, a descendent of the
disappointed bridegroom, and the then
MacRuari chief in order to settle the quarrel
over the right to Garmoran.

Campbell

Standard

Throughout the fifteenth century the
Campbells gave steady support to the Crown
in an area where royal influence was under
severe pressure, first from the rival Crown of
Norway and then from the descendents of
Somerled, former Lord of the Isles, with the
eventual emergence of the Crown's most powerful rival in the Macdonald Lordship of the
Isles. The Lordship of the Isles was broken by
the Crown by the end of the fifteenth century,
leaving the Campbells the main power in the
area. Thereafter they continued to act as the
chief instrument of central authority in the
region. This long struggle for supremacy, and
with it, the headship of the Gael, may be said
to be the real cause for the ancient enmity
between the Campbells and the Macdonalds.

In 1445, Sir Duncan Campbell of Loch
Awe became Lord Campbell. In 1457 his
grandson and heir, Colin, was created Earl of

Argyll. He married one of the three daughters
of the Stewart Lord of Lorne, and through a
financial deal with his wife's uncle, he brought
the Lordship of Lorne to the Campbells, with
not only much land and the stronghold of
Dunstaffnage, but the important dynastic significance of a title which represented the senior
line of the descendents of Somerled; from then
on the Campbell chiefs quartered the galley of
the Isles in their Arms. His uncle, another
Colin, also married another of the Stewart
daughters and founded a line which was to
rival that of Loch Awe in terms of power and
importance – the Campbells of Glenorchy,
later Earls of Breadalbane. The Earls of
Breadalbane were to build themselves the pala-
tial Taymouth Castle, at the east end of Loch
Tay, which still stands to this day. It was said
at one time that Breadalbane could ride for a
hundred miles across his family's possessions
which stretched from Perthshire to the
Atlantic.

The Campbell family held other earldoms,
in the north and south of the country. As Earls
of Loudoun they held land in Ayrshire and
spawned a host of lairdships there; and they
gained the thanedom of Cawdor from the
Calders as a result of the marriage of an infant

Calder heiress to one of Argyll's sons, founding the great house of the Earls of Cawdor.

However, internal rivalry for the chiefship led to a feud which threatened to split the clan. Campbell of Cawdor, a guardian of the young seventh Earl of Argyll, was murdered in 1592 during a conspiracy by some of the other guardians, which threatened the child's life and that of his brother. None of the principal conspirators was brought to justice, but the young earl survived a suspected poisoning attempt to become an able soldier and unite the clan.

Campbell support for central government brought rewards. In 1607 Archibald, seventh Earl of Argyll, was granted former Macdonald lands in Kintyre, while in 1615 Campbell of Cawdor was allowed to purchase Islay and most of Jura which had previously belonged to the Macleans of Duart.

The civil war and the invasion of the Irish Macdonalds into Argyll in support of the great Montrose brought wholesale death and destruction, and at Inverlochy in 1645 the clan suffered the biggest single defeat in its history. Archibald, the eighth Earl, attempted to maintain a precarious balance between his espousal of the Covenant and his support for Charles II's attempts to win his father's throne. But it was a balance too fine to be maintained, and the earl was executed for treason after the Restoration. His son, the ninth Earl, was staunch in his loyalty to the Protestant religion and he, like his father, was executed, this time as a result of his support for the rebellion of Monmouth against the king.

The Revolution of 1688 once more restored the family fortunes, and in 1703 William of Orange created the tenth Earl, Duke of Argyll and Marquess of Lorne and Kintyre, with a string of lesser titles. The second Duke was one of the first officers of the British army to be promoted to the rank of field marshall; his military skills were said to be equal to, if not greater than, those of his renowned contemporary, Marlborough, and he became commander-in-chief of the British army. He was succeeded by his brother, the

most influential man in Scotland and a proponent of the Treaty of Union of 1707.

The success of the Campbells owed much to a remarkable succession of chiefs, although they could not have achieved what they did without the support of their people. Throughout their history the chiefs managed to combine their role of Highland clan chiefs with a strong presence at court, which insured them a leading part in the affairs of Scotland, Great Britain and the Empire. In the days when allegiances were expressed by bonds of manrent, the chiefs of a dozen clans swore allegiance to Argyll, whose superiority as lord extended to the Outer Hebrides, and his clansmen possessed great swathes of Scotland both within and without the bounds of the Highlands. They were difficult neighbours and their success, and the ways in which they achieved it, brought them many enemies, but no-one could gainsay those achievements. Shortly before 1745 the strength of Clan Campbell was put at a total of some five thousand men.

The rise of Empire opened up many other opportunities to serve the Crown, and no less than sixteen regiments of the British army were at one time or another raised by members of the clan. The Argyll and Sutherland Highlanders, descended from Lochnell's 98th (later 91st) Highlanders still wear the Duke's boar's head as their cap badge and charge to the Campbell battle-cry, 'Cruachan'. The intense pride of the Campbells in their ancestry was illustrated when Queen Victoria's daughter, Princess Louise, became engaged to the Marquess of Lorne, the ninth Duke's heir, in a marriage which was sensational in its day. The news was apparently told to an old lady in Inveraray, who is said to have replied, 'Ach weel, Her Majesty'll be a prood wumman the day, wat wi' her dochter gettin' mairrit on the son of MacCailein Mor'.

Campbells have spread out across the globe and have prospered. Geographic features throughout the world are called after the family, and although there are now fewer Campbells still owning lands in the Highlands,

Campbell of Breadalbane

Campbell of Cawdor

the family still prospers there. No less than four new Campbell peerages have been created since the end of the Second World War to add to the fifteen Campbell families who have already been distinguished in this way. Much of the ancestral lands are still in family hands, including the Castles of Inveraray, Dunstaffnage and Cawdor. MacCailein Mor is often to

be seen at great state ceremonials in his capacity as hereditary Great Master of the Royal Household. The Clan Campbell is now organised as a world-wide association with a permanent base at Inveraray Castle which is still the family home of the twelfth Duke of Argyll and twenty-sixth chief.

CARMICHAEL

ARMS
Argent, a fess wreathy Azure and Gules

CREST
A dexter hand and arm in pale armed and holding a broken spear Proper

MOTTO
Tout jour prest (Always ready)

SUPPORTERS
Dexter, a knight armed at all points and plumed with three ostrich feathers holding in his dexter hand a Marischall's baton all Proper; sinister, a horse of war Argent furnished Gules.

STANDARD
Azure, a St Andrew's Cross Argent in the hoist and of two tracts Argent and Azure, upon which is depicted the Crest in the first and third compartments and the Badge in the centre compartment along with the Motto 'Tout jour prest' in letters Argent upon two transverse bands Gules

BADGE
A horse of war Argent furnished Gules within a circular wreath Azure and Gules

The Carmichaels have been settled on the lands in the upper ward of Lanarkshire from which they derive their name, for almost eight hundred years. The lands of Carmichael were originally part of the broad Douglasdale territory granted to the Douglases by Robert the Bruce in 1321. Robert de Carmitely resigned claims to the patronage of the church of Cleghorn around 1220. Robert de Carmichael is mentioned in a charter of Dryburgh Abbey in the year 1226. Later, other Carmichaels are mentioned in charters of the Douglas family until, between 1374-84 Sir John de Carmichael received a charter of the lands of Carmichael from William, Earl of Douglas. This Sir John was one of the knights who supported the Douglas faction in their struggle for power in Scotland and in their forays across the English border. The granting of this large piece of Douglas territory was undoubtedly a reward for the martial prowess of Sir John and the Carmichael men. The barony of Carmichael was confirmed to the head of the family in 1414 and it extended at its greatest extent to over fourteen thousand acres in the parishes of Carmichael, Pettinain and Carluke.

The traditional hero of the Carmichael family is Sir John de Carmichael of Meadowflat, later of Carmichael, who fought in France with the Scottish army sent to the aid of the French in their resistance against an English invasion. On March 22 1421, at the Battle of Beauge, Sir John rode in combat against the English commander and unhorsed him, breaking his own spear in the action. His victim was the Duke of Clarence, a Knight of the Garter and brother of Henry V of England. Carmichael's victory so demoralised the English that they fled from the field. To commemorate this deed, Carmichaels bear the broken spear as their crest.

Catherine, daughter of Sir John Carmichael of Meadowflat, captain of Crawford

Castle, became the mistress of James V, bearing him a son who was half-brother to Mary, Queen of Scots. The king built the Castle of Crawfordjohn in Clydesdale for her and as a place for them to meet undisturbed. In 1546 Peter Carmichael of Balmedie took part in the slaying of Cardinal Beaton in his Castle of St Andrews. He is said to have struck the cardinal repeatedly, presumably with a dagger. He was one of a group of four conspirators and for his crime he was sentenced to the galleys, serving at the oars with the reformer, John Knox. He was later imprisoned but escaped, disguised as a friar mendicant.

Sir John Carmichael, known as 'the most expert Borderer' was chief from 1585 until he was murdered in 1599. John was a favourite of James VI and was knighted at the coronation of James's queen, Anne, and was subsequently sent on a diplomatic mission to England. He was captain of the King's Guard, Master of the Stables, warden of the west marches and a Privy Councillor. He was later ambushed and shot after arresting some Armstrongs during a disturbance in the lands between Annan and Langholm. Sir John's brother, Archibald Carmichael of Edrom, later prosecuted the murderer and obtained justice.

Sir James Carmichael, first Lord Carmichael was created a Baronet of Nova Scotia in 1627 and raised to the peerage in 1647. His son, William, married Grizel, daughter of the Marquess of Douglas, and their son, John, succeeded his grandfather as second Lord Carmichael. In 1701 he was created Earl of Hyndford, Viscount Inglisberry and Nemphlar, and Lord Carmichael of Carmichael. The five succeeding Earls of Hyndford all held high offices of state and often served in the army. However, their loyalties shifted with the times. The first Lord Carmichael was a staunch supporter of Charles I but his son, although knighted by the king in 1633, took the side of Parliament, along with his brother, Sir Daniel. He commanded the Clydesdale Regiment at Marston Moor in 1644 and at Philiphaugh the following year, where the royalist forces under the

Carmichael

Marquess of Montrose were defeated. The remaining brothers, Sir James Carmichael of Bonnytoun and Captain John Carmichael, were royalists. The former fought at the Battle of Dunbar in 1650, and the latter was killed at Marston Moor, where he must have taken the field against his own elder brothers.

The third Earl, known in the family as 'the great Earl', was a staunch supporter of the Hanoverians, and was an ambassador in the service of George II. He was also noted as an agricultural improver, laying out large sums to plant trees and gardens and improve the soil. The sixth Earl died unmarried in 1817, when the family titles and honours became dormant and the great estates of Carmichael passed to Sir John Anstruther of Anstruther, Baronet, who descended through a daughter of the second Earl of Hyndford. For one hundred and sixty-three years the Carmichael-Anstruthers were the proprietors of Carmichael, and made it their seat until the death in 1980 of Sir Windham Carmichael-Anstruther, eleventh Baronet. The present chief, Richard Carmichael of Carmichael, has worked tirelessly to support the Clan Carmichael Society which now has branches throughout the world.

CARNEGIE

I n 1358 Walter de Maule made a grant of the lands and barony of Carnegie, lying in the parish of Carmylie, to John de Balinhard. There is no certain record of the origin of the de Balinhards, save that their lands were near Arbroath. Nisbet suggests that the de Balinhards were related to the Ramsays. but there is no direct evidence of this. Duthac de Carnegie acquired part of the lands of Kinnaird in Forfarshire around 1401, and subsequently obtained from Robert, Duke of Albany, Governor of Scotland, a charter dated 21 February 1409, confirming him in these lands. Duthac was killed at the Battle of Harlaw in 1411, leaving an infant son, Walter. Walter Carnegie of Kinnaird fought at the Battle of Brechin in May 1452 under the standard of James II borne by the Earl of Huntly. The rebels, commanded by the Earl of Crawford, were defeated. Crawford later burned Kinnaird in revenge. Walter later rebuilt the house using a corner of the old foundations, and it remained largely unaltered until the time of Sir Robert Carnegie who enlarged it, probably around 1555.

John Carnegie of Kinnaird fought and died at the Battle of Flodden in September 1513. His son, Sir Robert, who extended Kinnaird, was appointed one of the judges of the College of Justice in 1547 and sent to England the following year to negotiate the ransom of the Earl of Huntly, Chancellor of Scotland, who had been captured at the Battle of Pinkie. It is said that he was the first Carnegie to claim that his ancestors were cup bearers to the kings of Scots, the family arms bear an antique cup as a reference to this royal office.

Sir Robert's son, John, extended the family lands and was a faithful and loyal adherent to Mary, Queen of Scots. He, unlike many, never abandoned his loyalty to the queen. He died without issue in 1595, and the estates passed through his younger brother. Sir David Carnegie, born in 1575, was created Lord Carnegie of Kinnaird in April 1616. He was advanced to the rank of Earl of Southesk in June 1633. Sir John Carnegie, the second son of David Carnegie of Panbride and brother of David, first Earl of Southesk, was also elevated to the peerage in 1639 as Lord Lour, and in 1647 he was created Earl of Ethie. In 1662 he procured an exchange of his titles of Earl of Ethie and Lord Lour, for those of Earl of Northesk and Lord Rosehill.

James, second Earl of Southesk, attended on the king in exile, Charles II, in Holland in 1650 and was one of the Commissioners chosen for Scotland to sit in the Parliament of England during the Protectorate. He succeeded his father in 1658, although he was nearly killed in a duel with the Master of Gray in London in 1660. The younger son of the third Earl was not so fortunate in his duelling career and was killed in Paris in 1681 by William, son of the Duchess of Lauderdale. The Carnegies were Jacobites, and although the fourth Earl took no part in opposing the Revolution of 1688, he thereafter shunned the royal court. He had married Mary, daughter of the Earl of Lauderdale, by whom he had an only son, James, the fifth Earl. He followed the 'Old Pretender' in the rising of 1715, and for this he was attainted by Act of Parliament and his estates forfeited to the Crown. In 1717 a special Act of Parliament was passed to enable the Crown to make some provision for his wife and children. Sadly, the royal provision for the fifth Earl's children could not protect them from the high rate of infant mortality at that time, and both died young. The earl himself died in France in 1730, and the representation of the family then devolved on Sir James Carnegie of Pittarrow, who was descended from a younger son of the first Earl of Southesk. This line had been created Baronets of Nova Scotia in 1663. The sixth Baronet, Sir James Carnegie, was a distinguished soldier who was able to secure in 1855 an Act of Parliament reversing the attainder and restoring the titles of Earl of Southesk

Carnegie

and Lord Carnegie of Kinnaird and Leuchars with their original precedence. The ninth Earl harkened back to his family's early ancestry when he chose the title of 'Baron Balinhaird' on his elevation to the peerage of the United Kingdom in December 1869.

The Carnegies, in common with most Scottish noble families, sought to secure their fortunes by judicious and powerful alliances by marriage. No such alliance was more splendid than that of the eleventh Earl who, as Lord Carnegie, married Her Highness Princess Maude, younger daughter of the Princess Royal and granddaughter of Edward VII. The princess assumed the title of her husband on her marriage in accordance with the English custom, although she retained her royal status. On her death, her son, as well as being heir to his father's earldom of Southesk and the chiefship of the Carnegies, inherited the dukedom of Fife, the title of his maternal grandfather. The eleventh Earl died in 1992 and his son, the Duke of Fife, succeeded to the chiefship. He thereafter decreed that the subsidiary title of the dukedom, borne by the heir apparent, would be Earl of Southesk in honour of his Carnegie ancestors.

CATHCART

The lands of Cathcart take their name from the River Cart in Renfrewshire. 'Caeth-cart' itself means the 'strait of Cart'. The progenitor of this noble family appears to have been Rainaldus de Kethcart who, as early as 1178, was witness to a charter of the king's steward to Paisley Abbey. William de Kethcart, his son, was witness to a charter around 1200, exchanging with the Abbey of Paisley the lands of Knoc for lands lying near Walkinshaw. Alan de Cathcart sealed a charter of resignation to the Abbot of Paisley of lands at Culbeth in 1234. His daughter, Cecilia, married John de Perthick, who later made over all her lands in the village of Rutherglen to the Abbey of Paisley, around 1262. William de Cathcart, Alan's son, was one of the Scottish barons who submitted to Edward I of England in 1296 and is listed on the Ragman Roll. He was succeeded by Sir Alan de Cathcart who was a staunch supporter of Robert the Bruce in the struggle to regain the independence of Scotland. He then followed the king's brother, Edward, and was one of a party of only fifty knights who, under cover of dense fog, surprised a much superior English force under Lord St John in Galloway, and routed them. He survived the War of Independence and in a deed making a gift to the Dominican Friars of Glasgow in 1336 he is designed as 'Dominus Ejusdem', generally translated as 'of that Ilk'. He was related to the Bruces through his wife, the sister of Sir Duncan Wallace of Sundrum, who had married Eleanor Bruce, Countess of Carrick. His grandson, Sir Alan de Cathcart, successfully extended his patrimony, obtaining several estates in Carrick. In 1447 he was raised to the peerage with the title, 'Lord Cathcart'. He obtained lands in Ayrshire, including the estate of Auchencruive which was to become the principal seat of the family until 1718. He became Constable of the royal castle at Dundonald and in 1485 he was appointed

Master of the Artillery. Alan, son of the second Lord Cathcart, along with his two half-brothers, Robert and John, was killed at the Battle of Flodden in 1513. The third Lord Cathcart was killed at the Battle of Pinkie in September 1547.

Alan, fourth Lord Cathcart, was a fervent Protestant and a promoter of the Reformation, particularly in the west of Scotland where his influence was greatest. At the Battle of Langside in 1568 he fought with his men on the side of the Regent Moray against the army of Mary, Queen of Scots. The ancient Castle of Cathcart was near the field of battle and there is a viewpoint from which the queen is said to have awaited the outcome of the engagement.

Charles Cathcart, the eighth Lord, was born around 1686 and was to have a distinguished military career. In 1709 he became a major in the Scots Grays and was later appointed colonel of the regiment. At the outbreak of the Jacobite rising of 1715 he joined the Duke of Argyll at Stirling with a detachment of dragoons. At the indecisive Battle of Sheriffmuir, Cathcart's troops outflanked the Jacobite forces. He was later sent to Ireland with the rank of major general. The ninth Lord Cathcart also opposed the restoration of the Stuart monarchy, having been appointed an aide-de-camp to the Duke of Cumberland. He fought at the Battle of Culloden, where he was wounded. In February 1768 he was appointed ambassador at St Petersburg and was well received by the Empress Catherine. He wore a patch on his cheek, apparently to cover a scar received at Fontenoy, and when he insisted on wearing this, even for his portrait by the great Sir Joshua Reynolds, he earned himself the soubriquet 'Patch Cathcart'. His eldest son, William, later tenth Lord Cathcart, accompanied his father to Russia. On his return to Scotland he took up legal studies and was called to the Bar in 1776. When he succeeded to his father's title he gave up his legal career and returned to the army. He rose to the rank of lieutenant general, and

The full achievement of the Earl of Cathcart

was commander-in-chief of the forces in Ireland in 1803. He was created a Knight of the Thistle. In 1807, as Napoleon's troops were about to take control of Denmark, Lord Cathcart with Admiral Gambier successfully besieged Copenhagen, capturing the Danish fleet of over sixty vessels together with naval stores and munitions. He was rewarded with the additional titles of 'Viscount Cathcart of Cathcart' and 'Baron Greenock'. In June 1814 he was advanced to the title of 'Earl Cathcart'. The second Earl also had a distinguished military career and served throughout the Peninsular War and at the Battle of Waterloo in 1815. He was commander of the army in Scotland and governor of Edinburgh Castle from 1837 to 1842. His brother, Frederick, maintained the family's connection with Russia when he was appointed Minister Plenipotentiary at the Court of St Petersburg in 1820, and was made a Knight of the Russian Order of St Anne. The chiefly line has maintained its military traditions and the father of the present chief held the rank of major general.

CHARTERIS

ARMS
*Quarterly, 1st & 4th, Argent, a fess Azure within a
double tressure flory counterflory Gules (Charteris);
2nd & 3rd, Or, a lion rampant Gules, armed and langued
Azure*

CREST
A dexter hand holding up a dagger paleways Proper

MOTTO
This is our Charter

SUPPORTERS
*Two swans, wings elevated Proper, gorged with an Earl's
coronet Proper*

Chartres, the French city famed for its cathedral, is claimed as the origin of this name. William, a son of the Lord of Chartres, is said to have come to England with the Norman Conquest, and his son or grandson came north to Scotland with the retinue of David I. One of the earliest references to the name is found in a charter to the Abbey of Kelso around 1174, where the name appears in its Latin version, de Carnoto. In 1266 a charter of confirmation provides evidence of four generations: Robert de Carnoto, knight, is said to be the son of Thomas, who was himself son of Thomas, son of Walther. Sir Thomas de Charteris was appointed Lord High Chancellor of Scotland by Alexander III in 1280, the first person to hold this office who was not also a clergyman. Andrew de Charteris rendered homage to Edward I of England in the Ragman Roll of 1296, but soon took up arms to fight for Scotland's independence, for which his estates were forfeited to Balliol, the English-sponsored King of Scots. His son, William, was an adherent of Robert the Bruce and was with him when Comyn was slain at Dumfries in 1306. Sir Thomas Charteris, now styled 'of Amisfield', faithfully supported the Scottish Crown and was appointed ambassador to England. In 1342 he was appointed Lord High Chancellor by David II. He was killed in 1346 at the Battle of Durham. A feud appears to have developed between the Charterises and the Kilpatricks of Kirkmichael. In Pitcairn's *Criminal Trials of Scotland* it is recorded that in March 1526 John Charteris of Amisfield, his brother and his two sons were charged with the murder of Roger Kilpatrick, son of Sir Alexander Kilpatrick of Kirkmichael. A more noble dispute occurred in 1530, when Sir Robert Charteris, the eighth Laird, fought a duel with Sir James Douglas of Drumlanrig in what was said to have been one of the last great chivalric contests. It was fought with all the observance of a medieval tournament with heralds and the king himself watching from the castle walls. The joust was apparently fought with such fury that Charteris' sword was broken and the king had to send his men-at-arms to part the combatants.

In 1641 Sir John Charteris of Amisfield was appointed one of the Commissioners of Parliament to confirm the Treaty of Ripon. He was a supporter of the National Covenant but was not prepared to rise against the king. He was imprisoned in Edinburgh in 1643 and released in March 1645, having provided security for his good behaviour. He joined the forces of the Marquess of Montrose after the Battle of Kilsyth, and was with the royal forces when they were surprised by Lesley's cavalry at Philiphaugh in September 1645. His brother, Captain Alexander Charteris, was one of Montrose's staff and followed him on his ill-fated campaign in Caithness in 1650. He was captured and along with the great Marquess was conveyed to Edinburgh for trial. He was executed on 21 June 1650, beheaded by the Scottish version of the guillotine, 'the maiden'. It was perhaps poetic justice that this machine was also used to execute Montrose's arch rival, the Marquess of Argyll, after the Restoration. The Borders estates passed through an heiress to Thomas Hogg, who later assumed the name of Charteris. Colonel Francis Charteris, the male representer of the family purchased lands near Haddington, which he renamed Amisfield to recall his family's ancient seat in Nithsdale. He left an only daughter, Janet, who married the Earl of Wemyss, and her second son, the Honourable Francis Wemyss, later fifth Earl, inherited the substantial estates of his maternal grandfather, and in consequence assumed the name and arms of Charteris. The Charteris estates near Haddington are now sold but the

magnificent Palace of Gosford House, partly by Robert Adam, is still the seat of the Earl of Wemyss and March, chief of the name of Charteris.

Another branch of the family which long disputed the chiefship with their Dumfriesshire cousins were the Charterises of Kinfauns in Perthshire. They are said to have received the lands of Kinfauns as a reward for supporting the cause of Robert the Bruce against the English. The Ruthvens, who held considerable sway over Perth from their nearby Castle of Huntingtower, often disputed the authority of the Charterises, which led to a bitter and bloody feud. In 1544 Patrick, Lord Ruthven, was elected Provost of Perth, but at the instigation of Cardinal Beaton, who suspected Ruthven of Protestant sympathies, he was deprived of the office, and John Charteris of Kinfauns was appointed in his stead. The city declined to acknowledge Charteris, and barred the gates against him. Charteris, along with Lord Gray and the Lesleys, gathered armed forces and attacked the town. They were repulsed by the Ruthvens assisted by their neighbours the Moncrieffs, and Charteris was forced to flee. The Ruthvens remained Provosts of Perth until William Ruthven, Earl of Gowrie, was executed in 1584. In 1552 John Charteris had been killed by the earl's heir in the High Street in Edinburgh.

The family was not always involved in violent conflict, however: Henry Charteris was an eminent printer and bookseller in Edinburgh, and is credited with publishing the famous *Ane Satyre of the Thrie Estaitis* of Sir David Lyndsay, which is still performed today. The printer's son was to become Professor of Divinity and a Regent of the University of Edinburgh.

CHATTAN

There are many theories on the origin of this unique group of families which did not follow the ordinary pattern of other Scottish clans, but rather became a community or confederation, consisting of various descendents of the original ancestors. They were distinguished by the wildcat which figures prominently in their heraldry. One theory states that they came from the Catti, a tribe of Gauls driven out by the Romans; another says they took their name from Catav in Sutherland. The most widely accepted, however, says they descended from Gillichattan Mor, the great servant of St Cattan. Gillichattan was probably the co-arb, or baillie, of the abbey lands of Ardchattan. Around the time of Malcolm II they became possessed of lands at Glenloy and Loch Arkaig, where Torcastle became the chief's seat. Little is certain until the clan became established around Lochaber at the close of the thirteenth century. In 1291, Eva, daughter of Gilpatric, or Dougal Dall, of Clan Chattan in Lochaber, married Angus Mackintosh, sixth of Mackintosh. After his marriage to Eva, Angus lived for some time at Torcastle in Glenloy, but due to the enmity of Angus Og of Islay he withdrew to Rothiemurchus. The Camerons, claiming that the lands around Arkaig had been abandoned, occupied them by right of conquest. Thereafter a long and bitter feud was fought between the Camerons and Clan Chattan which lasted until 1666. In 1370 four hundred Camerons made a raid into Badenoch but while returning home with their spoils they were met at Invernahavon by a strong force of Mackintoshes supported by the MacPhersons and Davidsons. The Camerons were defeated, but the battle was the origin of feuding between the MacPhersons and the Davidsons. In 1503 the Camerons rebelled against the king and ravaged Badenoch. Despite several bloody encounters, it took some three years to quell the insurrection.

Prior to the fourteenth century, Clan Chattan appears to have been a conventional clan though little is known of it. Subsequently, however, it evolved into a confederation or alliance of clans made up of (a) the descendants of the original clan (Macphersons, Cattanachs, Macbeans, Macphails), (b) Mackintoshes and their cadet branches (Shaws, Farquharsons, Ritchies, McCombies, MacThomases), and (c) families not originally related by blood (MacGillivrays, Davidsons, Macleans of Dochgarroch, MacQueens of Pollochaig, Macintyres of Badenoch, Macandrews). By the eighteenth century the clans in and around Strathairn (Shaw, Macbean, Macphail, MacGillivray) looked to Mackintosh as their chief, having none of their own, but whether this was as Clan Chattan or Clan Mackintosh is unclear, the histories of both clans being inextricably entwined.

Chattan

The Reformation and the general turmoil in Scotland after the downfall of Mary, Queen of Scots, was a difficult time for the confederation, the MacPhersons in particular having become disaffected. In an attempt to consolidate their power a gathering was summoned in 1609 by William Mackintosh of Benchar, the uncle of the seventeenth Mackintosh chief who was still in his minority, to meet at Termit, where the leaders of the families swore a bond of union and loyalty to Mackintosh.

Standard

In the risings of 1715 and 1745 Clan Chattan declared for the Stuarts, and suffered as a consequence. Among the dead and captured after the Battle of Preston in 1715 were numbered many bearing Clan Chattan surnames, especially MacGillivrays. The Mackintosh chief was imprisoned until August 1716 and he died at Moy in 1731. When Bonnie Prince Charlie returned in 1745 to promote his father's claim to the throne, the chief of the Mackintoshes was an officer of George II in command of a company of the Black Watch. He did not rally to the prince's call to arms, but his wife, Anne, daughter of Farquharson of Invercauld, raised the confederation in his absence, selecting MacGillivray of Dunmaglas as commander. Under him the Clan Chattan Regiment fought at the Jacobite victory of Falkirk in 1746. It is of note that there were separate Macpherson and Farquharson regiments.

The suppression of the Highlands after the Forty-five undermined the nature of the confederation, and its members largely sought independent destinies. The major families continued to dispute the vestiges of power, but no more violently than in heated debate before the Court of the Lord Lyon. As early as September 1672, the MacPherson claim had been swept aside by the Lord Lyon, and Mackintosh was declared to be chief of the name of Mackintosh and of the Clan Chattan. The chiefs of Clan Mackintosh continued as captains of Clan Chattan until 1947, when Duncan Alexander Mackintosh of Torcastle was recognised by the Lord Lyon as thirty-first chief of Clan Chattan. The present chief lives in Zimbabwe.

CHISHOLM

The family was known in the Borders as early as the reign of Alexander III. The name derives from the Norman or French, 'chese', 'to choose' and the Saxon, 'holm', meaning 'meadow'. Their lands were at Chisholm in the parish of Roberton in Roxburghshire. One of the earliest recorded members of this family is John de Chesehelme, who was mentioned in a bull of Pope Alexander IV in 1254. Richard de Chesehelme of Roxburghshire rendered homage to Edward I of England and is listed in the Ragman Roll of 1296. The seal he used shows a boar's head which remains this family's principal device to this day. There is a tradition that two Chisholm brothers saved the life of the king when he was attacked by a ferocious wild boar. It is somewhat fancifully suggested that the armorial supporters granted to the Chisholm chiefs are said to represent the two brothers. By way of reward for the deed the family were granted lands in Inverness-shire, and they achieved prominence in the north when, in 1359, they gained control of an important stronghold. Robert de Chisholme was appointed constable of Urquhart Castle on the shores of Loch Ness in succession to his maternal grandfather. He had been knighted by David II and was taken prisoner at the Battle of Neville's Cross in 1346. He was later ransomed and lived to become sheriff of Inverness and justiciar of the North. His son, Alexander, married Margaret, heiress to the lands of Erchless, and Erchless Castle was to become the seat of the clan.

The family remained staunchly Catholic during the early years of the Reformation, and the Chisholms of Cromlix in Perthshire provided three successive Bishops of Dunblane. The third and last of these Chisholm bishops was later to become Bishop of Vaison near Avignon. They were implicated in Catholic intrigues which threatened the stability of the new reformed faith in Scotland. In 1588 it was alleged that William Chisholm, Bishop of Vaison, came in secret to Scotland bearing personal letters from the Pope promising that if the Scottish Crown acknowledged papal authority, the Holy See would ensure that the impending Spanish Armada did no harm to the realm. The news that the Armada had sailed later that year put the Church of Scotland into a state of general alarm and they took steps to neutralise Catholic sympathisers by summoning them before the General Assembly in Edinburgh for questioning. The son of Sir James Chisholm of Cromlix was amongst those brought before the Assembly although no charges were brought at that time. Sir James was, however, denounced in 1592 for 'traffiking in sundry treasonable matters against the true Religion' and was excommunicated at St Andrews in September 1593. During the seventeenth century the clan chiefs became Protestant, but they remained tolerant of the Catholic faith. Roderic Maciain Chisholm was active in the 1715 rising under the Earl of Mar. Chisholm of Crocfin, an aged veteran, led two hundred men of the clan at the Battle of Sheriffmuir. The family estates were forfeited to the Crown and sold, but a pardon was granted in 1727 and most of the lands were purchased back from MacKenzie of Allangrange. The Chisholms still adhered to the Jacobite cause, and when Bonnie Prince Charlie raised his father's standard in 1745, Roderick, a younger son of the chief, was appointed colonel of a battalion. Of the Chisholms who fought at Culloden, less than fifty survived, and Roderick was among the fallen.

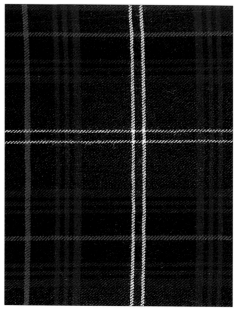

Chisholm

Standard

After Culloden, the 'Young Pretender' was obliged to trust his life to seven of his devoted followers, and three of these – Alexander, Donald and Hugh – were Chisholms. They slept in a cave in Glenaffric and scavenged for food. Having conveyed the prince to the coast of Arisaig, Hugh Chisholm shook hands with him and vowed never to shake hands with another man. He lived to a ripe old age and is said to have kept his vow. The Chisholms were, however, more wary than they had been in the 1715 rising, and both the chief and two of his other sons did not openly support the Stuart cause. The Chisholm lands were accordingly preserved.

In the mid eighteenth century Ruairidh, the twenty-second chief, tried to raise money by increasing his tenants' rents, precipitating the mass emigration from the Chisholm lands to the New Worlds overseas. Alexander, the twenty-third chief, attempted to reverse this decline, but he died in 1793 leaving an only daughter, Mary, and the chiefship devolved upon his half-brother William. He made over most of the family land to sheep grazing and the emigrations continued.

In 1887 the chiefship passed through an heiress to James Gooden-Chisholm of Surrey. However, his descendents have since abandoned their English name, and once more The Chisholm takes his place in the Council of Chiefs.

COCHRANE

Tradition has it that the Cochrane ancestry goes back to a Viking invader who settled in Renfrewshire between the eighth and tenth centuries. In keeping with the character of their traditional ancestor, the Cochranes took as their heraldic beast a boar; the three boars' heads adorning the chief's shield were said to mark the exploit of a warrior who is reputed to have slain three wild boars then terrorising the countryside. The name of Cochrane may be the combination of two Gaelic words, meaning 'the roar of battle' or 'battle-cry'. There is another, more fanciful explanation which states that, in ancient days, there was a great battle in which an early member of the family fought with such outstanding bravery as to bring about victory for his side. In recognition of his exceptional valour, his leader singled him out from the other warriors and clapping him on the shoulder, called him 'coch ran', meaning 'brave fellow'.

In his *History of Paisley*, Metcalfe refers to the purchase by William, Lord Cochrane, of the lordship and barony of Paisley from the Earl of Angus in 1653, stating that 'the Cochranes who had been connected with the county of Renfrew for upwards of five hundred years now took up their residence in the Palace of Paisley', which puts their original settlement back to the early 1100s. The first certain record of the name appears to be Waldev de Coveran, who appears as witness to a charter in 1262. William de Coveran is mentioned as a person of consequence in the Ragman Roll of 1296, rendering homage to Edward I of England. John de Coveran appears in 1346 as a witness in the election of an abbot of Paisley. Again in 1366, Goseline de Cochran is witness to several grants made by Robert the Steward to Paisley Abbey, which he assumed into his particular patronage. de Cochran appears to have been in particular favour with Robert II, as he appears frequently as a witness in royal charters of that time. William de Cochran of that Ilk obtained from Robert II a charter of the lands of Cochran, which had hitherto been held as vassals of the High Steward of Scotland. About 1350 Robert II built a castle at Dundonald in Ayrshire. It became a favourite residence of both himself and his son, Robert III; both monarchs were to die there, the latter in 1406.

The Dundonald estate, with its castle, came into Cochrane hands around 1638, and it was from these lands that the first Earl of Dundonald, William Cochrane, took his title in 1669. The chiefship had almost been lost at the beginning of the seventeenth century, when William Cochrane of that Ilk was unable to produce a male heir. However, he made prudent provision in the marriage negotiations of his daughter, Elizabeth, requiring that her husband assume both the name and the coat of arms of Cochrane. Sir John Cochrane, the eldest son of Elizabeth and her husband, Alexander, was a colonel in the army of Charles I, and in 1650 became ambassador to Poland for the exiled Charles II.

There then followed a most remarkable succession of chiefs who served their country with distinction, both on land and at sea; they have been called the fighting Cochranes. In October 1745, the seventh Earl, a supporter of the Hanoverian succession, had his horse shot from under him at the West Port of Edinburgh while Jacobites were in possession of the capital. The most renowned of the fighting Cochranes was undoubtedly Thomas, the tenth Earl, who, in 1801, was in command of a brig and its crew of only fifty-four men. He boarded and captured a Spanish frigate of thirty-two guns and a complement of over three hundred men. This was considered a feat almost unparalleled in British naval history. In 1807, before he inherited the earldom, he became a Member of Parliament although still

Cochrane

a serving officer. A dedicated sailor and compassionate officer, he attacked the corruption and abuses which riddled the Admiralty of his day, and as a consequence he made many enemies. He was ultimately prosecuted on a trumped-up charge of financial irregularity, was convicted and was struck off the Navy List. In 1817 he accepted an invitation from Chile to organise and command its navy. He helped to secure independence, not only for Chile but also Peru, Brazil and Greece. In 1832, a more liberal government restored him to all of his previous privileges, and he was promoted to rear admiral. He is buried in Westminster Abbey. The fourteenth Earl of Dundonald, father of the present chief, was born in 1918. He served with the Black Watch from 1938, and during the Second World War he was on the staff in North Africa, Sicily, Italy and Greece. After the war he served in Germany and with the War Office until retiring in 1953.

COLQUHOUN

The lands of the Colquhouns lie on the shores of Loch Lomond. Umphredus de Kilpatrick received from Malduin, Earl of Lennox, the estates of Auchentorily, Dumbuck and Colquhoun during the reign of Alexander II. The chief's early stronghold was Dunglas Castle, which perched on a rocky promontory above the River Clyde near the royal castle of Dumbarton. Later chiefs of Colquhoun were to be appointed governors and keepers of Dumbarton Castle. The barony of Luss, from which the chiefs now derive their territorial designation, came to the Colquhouns by marriage, when Sir Robert of Colquhoun married the heiress of the Lord of Luss around 1368. Sir John Colquhoun of Luss was appointed governor of Dumbarton Castle during the minority of James II, and was murdered in 1439 during a raid at Inchmurrin. He was succeeded by his son, also Sir John, who rose to be Comptroller of the Royal Household, and extended considerably the family estates. In 1457 he received a charter incorporating all his lands into the free barony of Luss. The forests of Rossdhu and Glenmachome together with the lands of Kilmardinny, followed a year later. In 1474 he was part of the embassy to Edward IV of England, seeking to negotiate a marriage between the infant James IV and Edward's daughter, Cecilia. He fought at the siege of Dunbar Castle, held by rebels against the king, where he was killed by a canonball. The Colquhouns also controlled the Castle of Camstradden, which had been obtained by a younger son of Luss in 1395. The sixth Colquhoun Laird of Camstradden was a renowned knight who fought at the Battle of Pinkie in 1547.

The strategic nature of the Colquhoun lands made them particularly vulnerable to clan raids, sometimes of great ferocity. In 1603, Alasdair Macgregor of Glenstrae marched into Colquhoun territory with a force of over four hundred men. His band followed a track along the eastern hills above Loch Long. The chief of the Colquhouns, who was granted a royal commission to suppress the Macgregors, assembled his followers and neighbours, and with a force of five hundred foot and nearly three hundred horse, advanced up Glen Fruin to repel the Highland raiders. Macgregor split his force in two and while the Colquhouns and the main Macgregor force locked in deadly combat, the second band of Macgregors outflanked their foes and attacked from the rear. The Colquhouns were caught in a vice and were driven into the Moss of Auchingaich where their cavalry were useless. It is believed that over two hundred Colquhouns were killed. The ancient enmity between the Colquhouns and the Macgregors gradually subsided until, at the end of the eighteenth century, the chief of Colquhoun and the chief of Clan Gregor visited Glen Fruin and shook hands on the very site of former slaughter.

Colquhoun

Standard

Sir John Colquhoun, the eleventh Laird of Luss, was created a Baronet of Nova Scotia on 30 August 1625. He was accused in 1632 of absconding with his wife's sister, Lady Catherine Graham, daughter of the Earl of Montrose. It was alleged that he had used witchcraft and sorcery to accomplish his intrigue. He, perhaps wisely, did not return to answer the charges, and as a fugitive he was excommunicated and his estates forfeited. The estates were recovered, after much negotiation, by Sir John's eldest son in 1646. Sir Humphrey Colquhoun, fifth Baronet, represented Dunbartonshire in the last Scottish Parliament in 1703, and strongly opposed the Treaty of Union. On 30 March 1704, having no male heir, he resigned his baronetcy to the Crown and obtained a new patent, allowing the title

to pass on his death to the male issue of his daughter's husband, James Grant of Pluscardine. When Pluscardine's elder brother died, he succeeded to the substantial estates of his father and once more assumed the name of Grant. He was ancestor of the Earls of Seafield and the Barons Strathspey, on whom the baronetcy devolved. Sir James Grant Colquhoun, fourth son of James Grant and Ann Colquhoun, succeeded to the Colquhoun estates, and built the grand mansion of Rossdhu which is still the seat of the chiefs today. He was made a baronet on 27 June 1786.

Sir Ian Colquhoun, the seventh Baronet of the new creation, and father of the present chief, was a distinguished and popular figure in Scottish society. He was mentioned in dispatches no less than five times in the First World War and twice wounded. He was created a Knight of the Thistle and was Lord High Commissioner to the General Assembly of the Church of Scotland. A member of the Royal Commission on ancient and historical monuments in Scotland and some time Rector of Glasgow University, he was at the forefront of the movement to preserve Scotland's ancient monuments and countryside.

COLVILLE

This ancient Norman name probably derives from the town of Colvile between Caen and Bayeux in Normandy. The name first appears in Scotland when Philip de Colville is found as a witness to a charter by Malcolm IV to the Monastery of Dunfermline some time prior to 1159. He was later one of the hostages for the release of William the Lion under the Treaty of Falaise in 1174. He was granted the baronies of Oxnam and Heton in Roxburghshire, together with other lands, particularly in Ayrshire. Thomas de Colville, his son, was witness to several charters of William the Lion between 1189 and 1199. He was unjustly suspected of treason against the Crown, and was for a time imprisoned in Edinburgh Castle, but he regained royal favour and died on his own estates in 1219. His son, William de Colville, acquired the barony of Kinnaird in Stirlingshire, which remains the seat of the family to this day. He granted a lease of part of his barony to the Abbot of Holyrood House in a charter which was confirmed by Alexander II in September 1228.

E'stace, the heiress of Sir William Colville of Oxnam, was married to Sir Reginald Cheyne of Inverugie, an elderly knight who died around 1291, leaving his widow considerable wealth. She swore fealty to Edward I of England and appears on the Ragman Roll of 1296 holding lands in Aberdeen, Ayr, Banff, Forfar, Inverness and Kincardine. Nisbet in his *System of Heraldry* attributes the foundation of the fortunes of the Colvilles to her considerable abilities. A grant by E'stace de Colville to the Abbey of Melrose of the church at Ochiltree was later confirmed by Robert Colville in 1324, in a charter which describes him as 'Baro baronial de Ochiltree' – Baron of the barony of Ochiltree. The baron made donations to the monks of Kelso and in 1350 his charter to the barony of Ochiltree was confirmed by David II. Thomas Colville of

Oxnam, probably a grandson of the baron, was one of the gentlemen selected to accompany Princess Margaret, daughter of James I, to France for her marriage to the Dauphin, later Louis XI, in 1436. Four years earlier, Robert Colville had stood as one of the substitute hostages for the ransom of James I necessary to secure the king's release from English captivity.

In 1449, Sir Richard (or Robert) Colville slew John Auchinleck, a favourite of the Earl of Douglas. To avenge Auchinleck's fate, Douglas laid waste all the lands belonging to Colville and besieged and took his castle at Kinnaird, with great loss of life. Robert Colville of Hilton fell with his king at the Battle of Flodden in September 1513. His son, Sir James Colville of Ochiltree, was appointed to the office of Comptroller of the Royal Household in 1527. He exchanged his lands of Ochiltree with Hamilton of Finnart for the barony of East Wemyss and Lochorshyre in Fife in 1530. As Sir James Colville of Easter Wemyss, he was appointed a judge of the Supreme Court. He was later accused of treason, and his estates were annexed by the Crown, but his forfeiture was recalled in 1543. Sir James Colville, third of Easter Wemyss, was a distinguished soldier who fought in France for Henry, Prince of Navarre, later King Henry IV. He returned to Scotland in 1582 along with Francis Stewart, Earl of Bothwell, loaded down with commendations from his French patrons. In 1604 he was raised to the peerage with the title of 'Lord Colville of Culross', which title the chiefs still bear. The second Lord Colville, who had succeeded to his grandfather's title in 1620, died without issue in 1640. His cousin was heir to the title but did not assume it, and it remained dormant until 1723. John Colville, 'de jure' seventh Lord Colville, was a soldier who served at Churchill's great victory of Malplaquet in 1709. In 1722 he made up title as heir to the second Lord Colville, but a petition to the king claiming the Peerage was referred to the House of Lords for enquiry. On 27 May 1723 the House was found in favour of Colville, who was placed on the Roll of Peers. He continued his military career and later rose to command a battalion at the siege of Cartagena in 1741, where he died. He left a large family who all followed successful military careers. The Honourable Charles Colville commanded the 21st Regiment of Foot at the Battle of Culloden in 1746, and died in 1775, having achieved the rank of lieutenant general. The Honourable Alexander Colville joined the Navy in 1731 and soon obtained his own command. In 1744 he became captain of the *Leopard,* a fifty-gun frigate. He was promoted to commodore, and obtained command of the *Northumberland,* which sailed to America in 1755. During the winter of 1759 the French laid siege to Quebec. Alexander, now Lord Colville, received orders to take his squadron to the relief of the city as soon as the St Lawrence River was free of ice. He set off as the spring thaw commenced, against the advice of local mariners, and succeeded in bringing his squadron safely off Quebec. His arrival forced the French to raise the siege and retreat. He was promoted to the rank of Vice Admiral in 1769.

Sir Charles Colville served with distinction in the Peninsular War (1808–14) and at the Battle of Waterloo. He was created a Knight Grand Cross of the Order of the Bath. His two elder brothers both died leaving no issue, and his son, Charles, succeeded to the peerage. He was Chief Equerry to Queen Victoria and Lord Chamberlain to Queen Alexandra. On 12 July 1902 he was created Viscount Colville of Culross in the peerage of the United Kingdom. Sir Stanley Colville, brother of the second Viscount, was a rear admiral and commander-in-chief at Portsmouth between 1916 and 1919. He received some of the highest honours his country could bestow, including the Grand Cross of the Order of the Bath. The present Viscount, the thirteenth Lord Colville of Culross, succeeded to the title in 1945.

CRANSTOUN

The origin of this name is territorial, from the lands and barony of Cranstoun in Midlothian. The lands may have been named from the Anglo–Saxon for 'place of the crane', a bird which appears both on the shield and as the crest of this noble family. Another suggestion is the 'tun' or 'dwelling place' of Cran or Cren, which both appear as forenames in Saxon chronicles. Elfrick de Cranstoun was witness to a charter by William the Lion to the Abbey of Holyrood. He also appears in a deed between Roger de Quincy and the Abbot of Newbattle around 1170. Thomas de Craystoun is recorded, in the reign of Alexander II, as making a donation of lands near Paiston in East Lothian to the Church, for the welfare of his soul and those of his ancestors and successors. Hugh de Cranstoun appears on the Ragman Roll of Scottish barons swearing fealty to Edward I of England in 1296. Randolphus de Cranston, son and heir of '*dominus de eodem*', made a donation to the Abbey of Newbattle in 1338. Thomas de Cranston received a charter to his lands of Cranston from David II.

The Cranstons of that Ilk prospered until the late sixteenth century, when they became embroiled in the volatile contemporary political situation. Thomas and John Cranston, descendants of the house of Cranston of that Ilk, were among those accused of treason in 1592 for assisting the Earl of Bothwell in his attack on the Palace of Holyrood House. In June 1600 Sir John Cranston of that Ilk was indicted for harbouring his kinsmen, forfeited traitors, and only obtained a stay of the proceedings against him on the intervention of the king. On 23 August 1600, another Thomas Cranston, the brother of Sir John Cranston, was executed at Perth for complicity in the Gowrie Conspiracy to kidnap James VI. Sir John Cranstoun of Morristoun, captain of the Guard to James VI, was raised to the peerage with the title of 'Lord Cranstoun' on 17

November 1609. Around the same time the Reverend William Cranstoun was minister of Kettle in Fife. He was a staunch Presbyterian who resisted the attempts of the king to introduce bishops into the Scottish Church. He fell into great disfavour with the authorities, and they attempted to prevent him preaching. He was in the middle of a sermon when the king's commissioners charged him to cease, advising him that another had been appointed to preach in the church. Cranstoun, nothing daunted, replied, 'But the Lord and his Kirk have appointed me, therefore, beware how you trouble this work'. He continued his sermon without interruption but he was formally 'put to the horn', i.e. declared in contempt and an outlaw. On 10 May 1620, John Spottiswood, Archbishop of St Andrews, convened a full ecclesiastical court and Cranstoun was deprived of his charge despite his advanced age and obvious sincerity.

Cranstoun

The third Lord Cranston supported the royalist cause in the civil war and fought at the Battle of Worcester in 1651 where he was taken prisoner. He languished in the Tower of London and his estates were sequestrated, save for a small portion which the Commonwealth allowed to his wife and children for their support. William, fifth Lord Cranstoun, sat in the last independent Scots Parliament where he was a supporter of the Treaty of Union. George Cranstoun, a descendant of the fifth Lord, was an eminent lawyer and judge. He had originally been intended for a career in the army, but after studying law he became an advocate and, ultimately, Dean of the Faculty of Advocates in 1823. In 1826 he was elevated to the Bench, taking the title, of 'Lord Corehouse'. He was an excellent scholar who was particularly well versed in the classics, and a friend of Sir Walter Scott, with whom he had studied at Edinburgh University. He entertained the great author at his seat of Corehouse in Lanarkshire. James, eighth Lord Cranstoun, was a distinguished officer in the Royal Navy who commanded HMS *Bellerophon* in a squadron of only seven ships which was attacked on 17 June 1795 by a French fleet three times larger. After a running battle which lasted more than twelve hours, the French were completely defeated, and eight ships of the line were destroyed. Lord Cranstoun was later appointed Governor of Grenada, but before he could set foot upon the island, he died, it is believed of lead poisoning, in 1796. The peerage became extinct in 1813.

Lieutenant Colonel Alastair Cranstoun of that Ilk and Corehouse was recognised as chief in 1950. He was a distinguished soldier and holder of the Military Cross, and was military attaché in Lisbon. He died in 1990, when he was succeeded by the present chief who still lives at Corehouse.

CRICHTON

ARMS
Argent, a lion rampant Azure, armed and langued Gules

CREST
A dragon spouting out fire Proper.

MOTTO
God send grace

SUPPORTERS
Two lions Azure, armed and crowned Or

The lands of Kreitton formed one of the earliest baronies around Edinburgh, and are mentioned in charters of the early twelfth century. Thurstan de Crechtune was a witness to the foundation of the Abbey of Holyrood House by David I in 1128. Thomas de Crichton, who is believed to have been Thurstan's son, was one of the Scottish nobility who swore fealty to Edward I of England and is listed in the Ragman Roll of 1296. Thomas had three sons, each of whom extended the family's holdings. William, his second son, married Isabel de Ross, heiress to the barony of Sanquhar in Dumfriesshire.

A descendent of this line, Sir Robert Crichton of Sanquhar, was sheriff of the county of Dumfries in 1464 and Coroner of Nithsdale from 1468 to 1469. His eldest son, Robert, was created a peer with the title of 'Lord Crichton of Sanquhar' by James III in 1487. The title does not appear to have brought the family great happiness. William, third Lord of Sanquhar, was killed in the house of the Regent Arran around 1552 by Lord Semple. The sixth Lord Sanquhar died in disgrace, being accused of complicity in the murder of a fencing master who, years before, had accidentally blinded Crichton in one eye. The title passed through a younger line, and thereafter to the family of Crichton-Stuart, the present Marquesses of Bute.

Sir William Crichton, another descendent of Thomas de Crichton, was Chancellor of Scotland during the minority of James II, being appointed to this high office in 1439. Following the death of his rival, the Earl of Douglas, Sir William organised the infamous 'black dinner' at Edinburgh Castle, of which he was at the time the governor. The young King James was in residence at the castle, and the new Earl of Douglas and his brother were invited to be guests of honour at a royal banquet. After dinner, the two Douglases were dragged from the boy king's presence and executed on the Castle Hill. The Douglas clan, never slow to take revenge, laid siege to Edinburgh Castle and Crichton, perceiving the dangers, surrendered the castle to the king and an uneasy truce was declared. The Douglases made at least one further unsuccessful attempt to assassinate the chancellor. He was sent in 1448 to arrange the marriage of the king with Mary, daughter of the Duke of Gueldres, having been raised to the peerage with the title of 'Lord Crichton'. The second Lord Crichton obtained through marriage the barony of Frendraught in Banffshire. The third Lord joined the Duke of Albany in his rebellion against his royal brother, James III, and garrisoned the Castle of Crichton against the king. The rebellion failed, and as a consequence the Crichton estates were forfeited for treason. The Castle of Crichton, the ruins of which still form a prominent landmark south of Edinburgh, passed through various hands, including the celebrated Earl of Bothwell, ill-fated third husband of Mary, Queen of Scots.

Perhaps the most celebrated Crichton was James, the son of the Lord Advocate of Scotland during the reigns of both Queen Mary and her son, James VI. He has passed into history as 'the Admirable Crichton' on account of his superb mental and physical prowess. He is reputed, by the age of twenty, to have mastered all the knowledge of his time, and could speak and write at least ten languages. He was also a superb equestrian, a feared swordsman and accomplished in all social graces. On leaving university at St Andrews, he travelled to Paris, where he challenged professors of the city to dispute with him on any branch of science or literature, offering to answer them in any one of his ten languages. It is claimed that fifty doctors appeared to put to him questions of mind-bending complexity which he disposed of with ease. The next day he attended a public joust and was declared champion of the field. He is said to have displayed his skills to the pope on a visit to Rome and so impressed the Duke of Mantua that he asked him to be tutor to his son, Vincenzo. It seems that the young man did not take to his new mentor. At a carnival in July 1582 Crichton was set upon by a gang of masked bandits, who discovered that his reputation was not mere vanity. He promptly killed five of his attackers and turned to dispatch the sixth and obvious leader of the pack. On discovering that his opponent was none other than his young pupil, he dropped his guard, whereupon Vincenzo stabbed Crichton in the heart. The people of Mantua were shocked, and nine months of court mourning was to follow.

Another James Crichton was raised to the peerage of Scotland as Viscount Frendraught in 1642. He accompanied the great Marquess of Montrose on his disastrous expedition in March 1650. At Invercarron, when Covenant forces under Colonel Strachan defeated the royalist army, Lord Frendraught is said to have given his horse to Montrose to enable him to escape from the field. Frendraught was severely wounded and taken prisoner, but he died before he could suffer public justice. The present chiefly line descends from the Crichtons of Frendraught, and the family now make their home at the splendid Castle of Monzie near Crieff. The father of the present chief did much to unite his scattered kinsmen and was a prominent member of the Council of Chiefs.

This name is sometimes said to derive from the Gaelic 'Macdara', meaning 'son of oak'. The Darrochs who settled around Stirling appear to derive their name from the lands of Darroch near Falkirk, where there may once have been an oak grove. The chief's coat of arms bears three oak trees in deference to this legend. John Darroch was baillie of Stirling in 1406. John Darach de Cruce is mentioned in 1445, and may be the same as John Darraugh who was Commissioner to Parliament for the burgh of Stirling in 1450. Mariote Darrauch was nurse of Lady Margaret, second daughter of James II, in 1462. Marion Darroch of Stirling protested in 1471 that she had not given consent to the alienation of an annual rent due to her. Jacobus Darroch was a notary public who appears as a witness to a charter relating to the lands of the Stirlings of Keir around 1477.

The Darrochs were, however, most numerous on the islands of Islay and Jura, where they were part of the mighty Clan Donald. The Clann Domhnuill Riabhaich took their name from a corruption of the Gaelic 'dath riabhach', meaning 'brindled colour'. This is said to have been adopted to distinguish them from the many fair-haired inhabitants of Jura, who were known as 'dath buidhe', from which the modern name 'Bowie' derives. In 1623 the Mic ille Riabhaich appear on a bond acknowledging as their overlord and protector Sir Donald Macdonald, first Baronet of Sleat, while he promises due protection to them in return. The patronymic of the chief became settled as 'McIllriech'. From McIlliriech of Jura descended the family who became Barons of Gourock, the port on the Clyde. Duncan Darroch, who was born on Jura sometime before the middle of the eighteenth century, left to make his fortune abroad, ultimately settling in Jamaica. He prospered, amassed a considerable estate and determined to return to his native soil. In

1784 he acquired the lands and barony of Gourock from the Stewarts of Castlemilk. He matriculated arms and in the Lyon register was designated as 'Chief of that ancient name the patronymik of which is McIliriech'. The supporters assigned to him by the Lord Lyon are presumably an allusion to his sojourn in exotic lands. In 1791 he married Janet, daughter of Angus Maclartie, a prosperous Greenock merchant, by whom he had several children. He was succeeded by his son Duncan, who commanded the Glengarry Fencibles, rising to the rank of lieutenant general. In 1799 he received public acknowledgment of his work by Marquess Cornwallis, who congratulated him on bringing the regiment into a fine state of discipline and efficiency. The general married Elizabeth, granddaughter of Sir James Cotter of Rockforest, Baronet. His eldest son, another Duncan, succeeded as third Baron of Gourock and followed a military career. As Major Darroch of Gourock he married Susan Parker, the daughter of the Laird of Fairlie in Ayrshire, who amassed a fortune from the West Indies trade. From this point it became traditional for the heir to the chiefship to be named Duncan, and this has continued to the present day.

The fourth Baron acquired the estate of Torridon in Ross-shire in 1873. Educated in England, he became a lawyer and was called to the Bar. He was, however, still Deputy Lord Lieutenant of Renfrewshire until his death in 1910. Miss Margaret Darroch of Gourock married in July 1927 the chief of Clan Mackintosh, Rear-Admiral Lachlan Mackintosh of Mackintosh, the father of the present chief. She actively assisted the Mackintosh in clan matters and eventually published a definitive history of her new family which is still highly regarded by modern historians. Duncan Darroch, sixth Baron of Gourock, the father of the present chief, was a distinguished soldier who served in the Argyll and Sutherland Highlanders in both world wars, retiring with the rank of lieutenant colonel. He was a member of the Royal Company of Archers (the monarch's bodyguard in Scotland) and Commandant of the Cadet Corps for Stirlingshire.

Not all the Darrochs went to the mainland, however: in 1658, Dugald Darroch presented fifty psalms translated into Gaelic to the Church authorities, who declared them unacceptable in their construction. He then collaborated with other Gaelic scholars in Campbeltown, and ultimately a corrected version, known as the Caogaed ('Fifty'), was published in Glasgow in 1659. Dugald continued to minister to his congregation in Campbeltown, conducting services both in Gaelic and English. William Darroch, the minister of Kilchrenan and Dalavich, was a son of the manse, born around 1675. He was ultimately deposed from the ministry, allegedly for neglect of proper family worship.

DEWAR

ARMS
Or, a chief Azure

CREST
*Issuant from a Crest-cornet Or of four (three visible)
strawberry leaves, a dexter arm vambraced, brandishing
a sword Proper, hilted and pommelled Or*

MOTTO
*Quid non pro patria (What will a man not do for his
country)*

On Compartment
Virtute et solertia (By virtue and by skill)

SUPPORTERS
*Dexter, a knight in armour, resting his exterior hand
upon a sword, point downwards Proper; sinister, a figure
of St Fillan Proper holding in his exterior hand a crozier
Argent*

STANDARD
*The Arms of Dewar of that Ilk in the hoist and of two
tracts Or and Azure, upon which is depicted the Crest in
the first and third compartments and the Badge in the
second compartment along with the Motto 'Quid non pro
patria' in letters Or upon two transverse bands Sable*

BADGE
*Within a mascle Azure an anchor in pale with a serpent
twisted about the shank, his head reared above the top of
the same, Proper*

The lands of Dewar near Heriot in the south-east of Edinburgh, were clearly possessions of this family, but whether they gave their name to the lands or took it from them is not known. In common with so many Scottish families, a legend exists to demonstrate physical prowess. A savage wolf is said to have been plundering the district around Heriot, and land was offered as a reward for the man who would dispatch the beast. Dewar is said to have achieved the task and received his promised bounty.

The earliest historical reference to an organised family named Dewar appears in the Ragman Roll, where Thomas and Piers de Deware of Edinburghshire swore fealty to Edward I of England in 1296. In 1474 Lord Borthwick granted a charter confirming to William Dewar his lands of Dewar. The family were to grow in prominence and were styled 'of that Ilk' in various charters in the sixteenth and seventeenth centuries. William Dewar of that Ilk sold the lands of Dewar and moved to nearby Carrington, and it is from this family that the present chiefs descend.

The representation of the chiefly line passed to the nephew of William Dewar of that Ilk, James, who is believed to have been a mariner. The family became successful merchants and purchased the barony and estate of Vogrie near Gorebridge in 1719. David Dewar of Vogrie was Postmaster General of Leith and Edinburgh, and his son matriculated arms in 1747.

The estate became a hive of industry when coal was discovered at the end of the eighteenth century, and by 1842 the Vogrie Colliery was producing superior-quality coal which was much in demand. Scotland's first gunpowder mill was also established on the Vogrie estate, and was powered by water wheels. The fifth Laird of Vogrie, who died in 1869, lived much of his life in India, where he was a High Court judge. His brother,

Alexander, sixth of Vogrie, served with the Bengal cavalry, and although he was responsible for building the mansionhouse which still stands at Vogrie today, he enjoyed it for only five years of his life. At its greatest extent the estate extended to almost two thousand acres, and today this has dwindled to around two hundred and fifty. The present chief, who was recognised by the Lord Lyon in 1990, is the only son of Vice Admiral Kenneth Dewar, born in 1879, who was an aide to George V. He at one time commanded HMS *Royal Oak*. He was a fierce critic of the Navy of his time, and wrote a highly regarded book on its training, administration and command system in 1939. The present chief and his heir both served as professional soldiers, each attaining command of their respective regiments.

Only the great Bell Tower still remains of the once proud Augustinian monastery of Cambuskenneth, founded in 1140 by David I. Robert the Bruce held several of his parliaments there and it was the sepulchre of the tragic James III, murdered after the Battle of Sauchieburn in 1488. Dewars are recorded in the nearby Royal Burgh of Stirling as early as 1483, but it is not until the seventeenth century that a distinct branch of the family styled 'Dewar of Cambuskenneth' can be said to exist. In 1710, John, elder son of Patrick Dewar of Cambuskenneth, was fined £50 for causing 'blood and riot'. From this line descends Peter de Vere Beuclerk Dewar, author of a definitive history of the Dewars in 1991, who in addition to being a member of the Royal Company of Archers, has served as Falkland Pursuivant Extra-Ordinary on many occasions.

The Dewar family whisky business was transformed into a major Scottish company through the drive and acumen of John Dewar, born in 1856. In 1917 he was created Baron Forteviot of Dupplin. The family seat at Dupplin Castle, built between 1828 and 1832, was one of the grandest houses in Scotland, but it has since been demolished to make way for a more conveniently sized dwelling. The title remains in the family, which is still closely connected to the whisky industry.

Donald Campbell Dewar, son of a Glasgow doctor, has been Member of Parliament for Garscadden in Glasgow since 1978. A lawyer by profession, he is one of Scotland's most prominent politicians and a candidate for high office in any future Labour government.

Another derivation of the name comes from the Gaelic 'Deoradh', meaning 'pilgrim', which was often a soubriquet given to a person who had custody of one of the relics of a saint. The most distinguished of the five Highland families who bore the name of Dewar were the Dewar Coigerachs, custodians of the staff of St Fillan, a Celtic saint and abbot believed to be of royal blood, who died in 777. St Fillan founded a priory, later known as Strathfillan, where he was buried. Robert the Bruce, who was impressed by the many stories of miracles worked by the presence of the saint's relics, had the staff brought with the Scots Army to Bannockburn in 1314. After his victory, he endowed a church in St Fillan's honour. Originally a simple wooden staff, it was elaborately decorated in later centuries, and is now an outstanding example of fourteenth-century Scottish craftsmanship. The valuable relic was held by the family until the late seventeenth century when it was sold to Macdonell of Glengarry but they later regained possession of it. In the nineteenth century they emigrated to Canada, taking the saint's relic with them. It was later returned to the Society of Antiquaries of Scotland. This priceless artefact of the early Celtic church is now preserved in the National Museum of Antiquities in Edinburgh. In 1905 the Lord Lyon granted arms to Donald Dewar of Canada, granting him behind his shield 'two croziers of St Fillan in Saltire, being the insignia of the Office of the Hereditary Keeper of the Crozier of St Fillan'. Differenced arms were also recorded for the keepers of other relics of St Fillan, including his left arm bone, his meser or missal, and his bell.

DRUMMOND

One of the families residing on the edge of the Highlands, the Drummonds have always played a prominent part in Scottish affairs. The parish of Drymen lies to the west of Stirling and appears to have derived its name from the Gaelic, 'dromainn', meaning a 'ridge' or 'high ground'. The traditional legend narrates that the first nobleman to settle at Drymen was Hungarian, having accompanied Edgar the Aetheling and his two sisters to Scotland in 1067 on their flight from William the Conqueror. The royal fugitives were warmly received by Malcolm III, who married one of the royal sisters, Margaret, later to be made a saint. The first chief appearing in written records was Malcolm Beg, Chamberlain of Lennox, who married Ada, the daughter of the Earl of Lennox and who died some time prior to 1260. Gilbert de Dromund of Dumbarton appears on the Ragman Roll of Scottish noblemen submitting to Edward I of England in 1296. Malcolm de Drummond also swore fealty to Edward at this time. Despite this, the Drummonds firmly supported the cause of Bruce and Scottish Independence, and after the Battle of Bannockburn the king bestowed upon them lands in Perthshire. It is supposed that the four-spiked pieces of iron called 'caltrops', which form part of the heraldic emblems of the Drummonds, allude to Sir Malcolm's promotion of the use of these weapons, which were highly destructive of the English cavalry.

In 1357, Annabella Drummond married, John, High Steward of Scotland, later Robert III, and she exercised considerable influence over her husband. Sir John Drummond rose to great power during the reigns of James III and IV. He was created a peer with the title of 'Lord Drummond' in 1488, a title borne today by the present chief. In one famous incident he was confined in Blackness Castle for having struck the Lord Lyon, King of Arms, for allegedly slighting his grandson, the Red Earl of Angus, and was only released a year later. His son, David Drummond, also fell foul of royal justice after a feud with another family resulted in his violation of the right of sanctuary. He did not escape with imprisonment, and instead paid with his life.

Around this time the Drummonds built a new castle at Concraig, and named it Drummond Castle. It is now the Scottish seat of the Earls of Ancaster, whose family name is Drummond-Willoughby. James, the fourth Lord Drummond, was created Earl of Perth in 1605.

Standard

Drummond

The family were staunch supporters of the Stuart kings, both during their quarrels with Parliament and after the exile of James VII. The third Earl joined the Marquess of Montrose in August 1645 and was taken prisoner at Philiphaugh the following month. James, the fourth Earl, was appointed Lord High Chancellor of Scotland in June 1684. On the accession of James VII he openly declared himself a Catholic, and enjoyed high royal favour. He was one of the founder knights at the revival of the Order of the Thistle in 1687. When James abdicated, the Edinburgh mob plundered the earl's town house and he himself became a prisoner for nearly four years in Stirling Castle. He was freed in 1693 and went to Rome. He was summoned to France by his king, who bestowed upon him the Order of the Garter and raised him to the rank of Duke of Perth. His brother, the Earl of Melfort, also one of the founder knights of the Order of the Thistle, was with the king during his campaign in Ireland in 1690. The brothers so impressed their French hosts that their duchesses were accorded the jealously guarded right to sit in the royal presence. James

Drummond, later the second Duke, was one of the first to join in the rising of 1715. He formed a daring plan to seize Edinburgh Castle and commanded Jacobite horse at the Battle of Sheriffmuir. He escaped to France and his estates were forfeited. The third Duke joined Bonnie Prince Charlie on his arrival at Perth in September 1745. He followed his prince into England and captured Carlisle. His brother, John, later arrived with troops sent to assist in the rising by the king of France. At the Battle of Culloden, the duke commanded the left flank, and after the defeat of the Jacobite forces he was forced to flee. His escape was a harrowing ordeal and he died on the passage to France in 1746. The estates and titles of the Drummonds were once again declared forfeit.

In 1853 George Drummond, Duc de Melfort, Comte de Lussan and Baron de Valrose in the peerage of France, was restored by Act of Parliament to the title of 'Earl of Perth', together with various subsidiary titles. The sixteenth Earl of Perth was the first secretary general of the League of Nations and his son was a Minister of State and a member of the Privy Council.

DUNBAR

The town and port of Dunbar has figured prominently at various points in Scottish history and the family whose name it bears is of ancient Celtic origin. Gospatrick, Earl of Northumberland, received the lands of Dunbar and other parts of Lothian from Malcolm III. His son witnessed the foundation of the great Abbey of Holyrood House in 1128, and was accorded the rank of earl. He made donations to the Abbey of Kelso and is recorded in various charters. Patrick of Dunbar married Ada, natural daughter of William the Lion, around 1184 and was created justiciar of Lothian. Earl Patrick's daughter received as part of her dowry the lands of Home, establishing the line that was later to be created Earls of Home in the seventeenth century. Her brother, Patrick, went to the Crusades, and died in 1248 at the siege of Damietta in Egypt. Patrick 'Black Beard', Earl of Dunbar, was one of the competitors for the Crown of Scotland at Berwick in 1291 through his royal great-grandmother, Ada. His wife was a Comyn and held Dunbar Castle for Balliol, but was forced to surrender it in April 1296. The tenth Earl, another Patrick, sheltered Edward II of England at Dunbar after his flight from the field of Bannockburn in 1314. Historians have suggested that if the king had been seized by Dunbar he might have been forced to make peace with Robert the Bruce, thereby preventing further years of bloodshed. Despite his apparent treachery, the earl made his peace with his cousin the king, and was present at the Parliament at Ayr in 1315 which settled the succession of the Scottish throne. He was appointed governor of Berwick, where he was besieged by Edward III. He surrendered to the English and the town was refortified and garrisoned by English troops. Dunbar renounced any allegiance to the English king, as a result of which his castle was besieged by the Earl of Salisbury. Command of the castle fell to Dunbar's wife, commonly called 'Black Agnes', who performed her task with vigour. The English attacked the castle with all the technology of fourteenth-century siegecraft, and when they brought up a machine which, from its shape was called 'the sow', she personally directed its destruction by rocks hurled from the castle walls. As the English fled for their lives she is said to have scoffed, 'behold the litter of English pigs'. The siege lasted nineteen weeks and Salisbury eventually retired, leaving Black Agnes in possession of her husband's fortress.

The tenth Earl was one of the most powerful nobles in Scotland, with vast estates. In 1388 he accompanied the Earl of Douglas into England and fought at the Battle of Otterburn. He had arranged a marriage for his daughter with the Duke of Rothesay, son of Robert III, but through the influence of the Douglases the marriage did not take place. The earl was incensed by this slight to his family pride, and retired to his estates in England. He was eventually reconciled with the Douglases and returned to Scotland in 1409. George, the eleventh Earl, succeeded to his father's title and vast estates in 1420, and was prominent in public affairs. His wealth, however, was to be his undoing: James I coveted the Dunbar estates and imprisoned the earl on trumped-up charges of treason, so the earldom and the estates were forfeited to the Crown. The last earl died in England in 1455.

Dunbar

Standard

The family had established a number of branches, including the Dunbars of Mochrum (to which house the present chief belongs), of Northfield, Hempriggs, Durn, and Both. It is a tribute to the distinction of this name that each of these five branches achieved the rank of baronet. Gavin Dunbar, Archbishop of

Glasgow and Lord High Chancellor of Scotland in the reign of James V, was a younger son of Sir John Dunbar of Mochrum. He distinguished himself at the University of Glasgow and in 1514 became Dean of Moray. In 1524 he was appointed Archbishop of Glasgow. He weathered the first storms of the Reformation and although reckoned a good and learned man, was criticised for his participation in the persecution of Protestants instigated by Cardinal Beaton. Sir James Dunbar of Mochrum was created a Baronet of Nova Scotia in March 1694 with a special royal honour of a grant of supporters 'Imperially Crowned'. The second Baronet served in the Duke of Marlborough's cavalry with great distinction. He was recognised as chief on the death of Ludovic Dunbar in 1744. Sir William Dunbar, ninth Baronet, was Registrar General from 1902 to 1909. The title of the present chief was established only after a celebrated court case in 1990 first heard before the Lord Lyon, King of Arms, then appealed to the Supreme Court in Edinburgh, and finally concluded in the House of Lords in London.

DUNDAS

The ancestry of this ancient family is said to be traced from Helias, son of Hutred, a younger son of Gospatrick, Prince of Northumberland. The first reliable record of the family is found in the reign of William the Lion when Serle de Dundas appears in deeds of that period. Serle de Dundas and Robertus de Dundas both appear on the Ragman Roll of Scottish nobles submitting to Edward I of England in 1296. Sir Archibald Dundas was a favourite of James III and was employed by him several times on important missions to England. The king intended to bestow high rank upon his ambassador, but died before he could do so. James IV did, however, bestow lands upon Dundas, including the island of Inchgarvie with the right to build a castle there.

George Dundas, the eighteenth Laird, was a staunch presbyterian who fought in the Wars of the Covenant. He was a member of the committee for the trial of the great Marquess of Montrose. He was subsequently given command of Linlithgowshire and charged with its defence against the forces of Oliver Cromwell. George Dundas, twenty-third Laird, was a captain in the East India Company and died in a shipwreck off the coast of Madagascar in 1792.

The principal branches of the family were Dundas of Blair Castle, Arniston, Duddingston, and Fingask. William Dundas of Kincavel, ancestor of the Dundases of Blair, was a Jacobite who was imprisoned for his part in the rising of 1715. The founders of the house of Arniston, which was to acquire distinction through high legal and political office, were senior cadets of the chiefly house of Dundas. Sir James Dundas, first of Arniston, was governor of Berwick in the reign of James VI. His eldest son, Sir James Dundas, was knighted by Charles I in November 1641 and sat as member of the Scottish parliament representing Mid-Lothian. He was a loyal subject but violently disapproved of his king's interference with the Church of Scotland and in particular with plans for the re-introduction of bishops. Consequently, he was one of the first signatories to the National Covenant. When the monarchy was restored in 1660, he was offered a seat on the supreme court bench, in spite of not being a professional lawyer, and he eventually accepted the post, taking his place with the title 'Lord Arniston' in May 1662. He did not serve the court long as he refused to sign the declaration, required by law in 1663, accepting that both National and Solemn League Covenants had been unlawful. Arniston promptly resigned rather than accept the oath, but his vacancy was not filled for nearly eighteenth months whilst his friends tried to persuade him to return. He offered to do so only if the declaration was amended to refer solely to the 'Solemn League and Covenant' and even then only in so far as it led to 'deeds of actual rebellion'. He did not resume his seat and died at Arniston in 1679. His eldest son, Robert Dundas of Arniston, was made a judge ten years after his father's death and to honour his memory, he took the title 'Lord Arniston'. The family were thereafter to provide no less than two Lords President of the Court of Session. Henry Dundas, first Viscount Melville, was a distinguished politician. In 1775 he was appointed Lord Advocate and thereafter Treasurer of the Navy. In 1791 he became Secretary of State for the Home Department at a time when the country was in crisis after the outbreak of the French Revolution. On 21 December 1802 he was raised to the peerage as Viscount Melville and Baron Dunira. His splendid town mansion in St Andrew Square in Edinburgh is now the headquarters of the Royal Bank of Scotland. In the original plan for Edinburgh's Georgian New Town, the site of Melville's house was to be a church to balance that built in Charlotte Square which lay at the other end of George Street, which linked the two. The viscount

Dundas

preferred the site for his own home, and so great was his influence that the plan was simply ignored. He died in 1811, and his statue stands on a lofty column in the centre of St Andrew Square.

Sir David Dundas was born in Edinburgh in 1735. He was a distinguished soldier, rising ultimately to be commander-in-chief of the British army in 1809. Other branches of the family were also ennobled, including Sir Thomas Dundas of Kerse, who was created Lord Dundas of Skea in 1794, and whose descendants became first Earls, and then Marquesses of Zetland. The second Marquess was Secretary of State for India from 1935 to 1937. Admiral Sir Charles Dundas of Dundas, twenty-eighth chief, was an aide-de-camp to George V and principal naval transport officer during the First World War. The present chief lives abroad, but many of the great Dundas houses, including Dundas Castle and the splendid eighteenth-century mansion of Arniston, are still homes of members of the family.

DURIE

The origin of this name is uncertain, but it is thought to derive from the French 'Du Roi', indicating that the family probably came to Britain with the Normans. Some research suggests that they may have come to Scotland as part of the entourage of Queen Margaret in 1069. They settled in Fife and although there are accounts of Duries in that ancient kingdom as early as 1119, it is generally accepted that they rose to prominence as administrators to Princess Joan, sister of Henry III of England, who married Alexander II (1214–49). They were granted the estate of Craigluscar, near Leven, where a house, built in 1520, has a stone shield bearing the Durie arms and the initials of a George Durie and his wife, Margaret Bruce. Craigluscar remained in the family until the 1900s.

The family's prominence in Fife can be seen throughout the thirteenth and fourteenth centuries where the name appears in various important charters. Duncan de Dury was a witnss for Malise, Earl of Strathern, around 1258. Other documentary references include Francis de Douery (*c.* 1250), Malisius (Malise) de Douery (*c.* 1350), Michael de Douery (*c.* 1373), John de Douery (*c.* 1406) and Richard de Douer (1405); it is from the latter individual that the main line is descended.

Burntisland Castle (now known as Rossend) was built in 1382 and has an armorial tablet above the entrance bearing the Durie arms and the date '1554'. Occupied for a time by Mary, Queen of Scots in 1563, it and most of the extensive Durie properties were confiscated by the Crown at the Reformation and the estates were sold around 1614 to Sir Alexander Gibson who, when he became a judge in 1621, took the judicial title, 'Lord Durie'.

Abbot George Durie (1496–1572) attained high position in both Church and State. he was Commendator, and the last Abbot, of

Dunfermline (1530–61) before the Reformation. He appeared in Parliament on several occasions between 1540 and 1554 and was appointed an Extraordinary Lord in July 1541. He became a Lord of the Articles and a member of the Governor's 'Secret Counsale' in 1543 and a Lord of Council and Session, and Keeper of the Privy Seal, a year later. A staunch supporter of Queen Mary, his position at court was well established under her and her mother, the Queen-Dowager. A bitter opponent of the new faith, he brought his own cousin, John Durie, a monk, to trial for proclaiming the new teaching. The Queen and the Queen-Dowager wrote several letters to their resolute friend while in their distress, and employed him on diplomatic missions to the court of France. He later fled there, taking with him the relics of Queen Margaret of Scotland for 'safe keeping' from the new order.There is a persistent story that Abbot George was canonised, founded on Dempster's *Historià Ecclesiastica* of 1627 which refers to Nicolaus Sanders' book, *De Visible Monachia Ecclesiae*. The mystery is compounded by the fact that Sanders' book was published in 1571 while it is thought that the abbot died in 1572.

The turmoil of the Reformation disrupted several Duries' lives. Abbot George's brother, Andrew Durie, Abbot of Melrose and Bishop of Galloway (1541), was despised by the reformer, John Knox. John Durie, minister of Edinburgh, was imprisoned in Edinburgh Castle in 1580. Robert Durie, minister of Anstruther, was sentenced to be exiled for attending a proscribed General Assembly of the Church. The family's strong adherence to Rome was continued by George's sons, George and John, who were educated at the Scots' Colleges in Paris and at Louvain. John joined the Jesuits and there is little doubt that he was 'Jesuit Durie', implicated in the conspiracy to release Mary, Queen of Scots and to depose Elizabeth I of England.

George's other son, Henry, through whom the family line runs, held the lands of Craigluscar. His wife, Margaret McBeth (Macbeith) was renowned for her skill with herbs. A favourite of Anne of Denmark, she attended the births of the royal children born at the Palace of Dunfermline. She was particularly successful in treating children's illnesses and supposedly saved the life of the future Charles I when other physicians had failed. John Durie, minister of Dalmeny, was also in favour with the Stuart monarchy. In 1621, he went to Oxford to study its library system with Archbishop Laud's approval. He travelled extensively in Europe and much of his work was published, including *The Reformed Librarie-Keeper,* in 1650.

In the later seventeenth century, a subsequent George Durie was a captain in Louis XIV's Scots guards and also a provost of Dunfermline. Several of his brothers fought in Flanders and a Belgian family line, 'du Ry', has been traced to them. In 1812, during repair work to Dunfermline Palace, an important Durie relic was discovered. The Dunfermline Annunciation Stone, which depicts the Archangel Gabriel announcing the impending birth of Christ to Mary, was probably carved as a door architrave and displays the arms of Abbot George Durie, giving it a probable date of around 1540. The stone is now in the care of Historic Scotland.

The Duries were chiefless for some time until the recognition in 1988 of Lt Col. Raymond Varley Dewar Durie of Durie. He established his descent through his grandmother, Elizabeth Durie of Craigluscar, from Abbot George. He served in the Argyll and Sutherland Highlanders for 35 years and was in Shangai when it fell to the Japanese; he escaped by making a journey of 2,000 miles to Chungking for which he was mentioned in despatches. As assistant military attaché, he was responsible for the evacuation of wounded from HMS *Amethyst* in 1949 during the Chinese civil war. He is the co-compiler of a Chinese-English military dictionary.

ELIOTT

Outside the small circle of the nobility and gr·at landed families, few individuals or their kin are well recorded in Scottish medieval history, but the obscurity surrounding the origin of the Eliotts, who suddenly make their appearance as a distinct clan with a chief in the late fifteenth century, is unusual even by the sparse standards of such records. This lack of information can probably be traced to the destruction of the old castle at Stobs in a fire in 1712, when all the family documents, with a single exception, were burnt.

According to family tradition, the Ellots (as the name was then spelt) came from Angus at the foot of Glenshie, and moved to Teviotdale at the time of Robert the Bruce. It is true that to move from the north to the Borders, as suggested by the Eliott tradition, would be considered as exceptional. However, in 1320 there occurred in Liddesdale an event of some note which might lend credence to the tale. In that year, William de Soulis, one of the most powerful nobles in Scotland, whose family had for nearly two hundred years held the Lordship of Liddesdale, was convicted of treason against Robert the Bruce and imprisoned for life. All his lands were forfeited. Two years later Liddesdale, together with the great Borders fortress of Hermitage Castle, was made over to Bruce's illegitimate son, Robert. On the occasion of so sudden and dramatic a change in the lordship, it would scarcely be remarkable for Bruce to ensure his hold on the strategically important frontier region by encouraging the settlement of a loyal and tested clan – such as the Ellots – in the district.

It is known from a Berwickshire pedigree that Ellot of Redheugh was living in the early 1400s. John Elwalde from Teviotdale is recorded in 1426. Robert Ellot of Redheugh appears as the tenth chief in 1476, and from that time the formal history of the clan can be said to have begun. In 1470 he built a strong tower on a cliff overlooking the ford on Hermitage Water. This was one of about one hundred strong towers belonging to the Ellots which were dotted around Liddesdale, which they shared with the Armstrongs, another of the great Borders riding clans.

They fought at Flodden where Robert, thirteenth chief, was killed along with James IV and the flower of Scottish nobility. In 1565 a deadly feud developed between the Ellots and their neighbours, the Scotts. Scott of Buccleuch, ancestor of the present duke, executed four Ellots for the minor crime of cattle rustling. Three hundred Ellots rode to avenge their kinsmen. The losses on both sides were heavy, but the Scotts thought better of matters, and came to terms with the Ellots. Their next opponent was James Hepburn, the great Earl of Bothwell and future husband of Mary, Queen of Scots. In a skirmish around Hermitage Castle Bothwell was wounded, and in reprisal a royal force of nearly four thousand men devastated the lands of the Ellots and their neighbours in 1569.

Eliott

Standard

The Union of the Crowns in 1603 marked the beginning of the end for the border reivers. There were many summary executions, and around this period many Borderers accepted the offer of a new life in Ulster during the plantation, when much of the province was colonised. Robert Eliott of Redheugh went into exile in Fife, leaving his broad lands in Liddesdale. It was around the 1650s that the 'i' was introduced into the name of Ellot.

Sir Gilbert Eliott of Stobs became chief in 1673. He was created a Baronet of Nova Scotia by Charles II in December 1666. The third Baronet remodelled the old Tower of Stobs into a mansion house around 1764, although it was subsequently rebuilt after a fire. His second son, Augustus, was a distinguished soldier

who was rewarded for his spirited defence of Gibraltar in 1782 with a peerage. He was created Lord Heathfield, but this title became extinct within one generation. Another branch of the chiefly family acquired the lands of Minto in 1703. This line has produced some persons of distinction, and were created baronets in 1700. Sir Gilbert Eliott of Minto was a diplomat who served first in Corsica, then in Vienna, finally becoming Governor General of Bengal. He returned from India in 1813 to be created Earl of Minto and Viscount Melgund. The present Earl of Minto is prominent in local government in the Borders, although the magnificent mansion house of Minto has had to be demolished. The estate of Stobs also passed from family hands at the turn of this century. For a time the chiefs resided in America, but in 1932 the tenth Baronet reclaimed the ancient holding of Redheugh where he died in 1958. The present chief is the daughter of Sir Arthur Eliott, eleventh Baronet and twenty-eighth chief. There being no bar to female succession to a Scottish chiefship, she assumed her father's seat on the Council of Chiefs, but the baronetcy passed to a male heir.

ELPHINSTONE

The lands of Airth lie close to the barony of Plean in Stirlingshire. The family which took their name from this land, and probably erected the first castle at Plean, were known as 'de Erth'. The de Erths ended in an heiress, and the lands which were acquired by her husband near Tranent in East Lothian were probably named in memory of her family. The name first appears in East Lothian in a deed of about 1235 by Alanus de Swinton, where mention is made of the 'de Elfinstun.' de Swinton's son, John, is probably the same John who acquired the lands, to become John de Elfinstun. However, according to one tradition, the family claimed descent from Flemish knights called Helphenstein. Yet another version of the family history suggests that the name derives from 'Alpin's tun' – the farmstead of Alpin.

Sir John de Elfinstun married Margaret of Seton, the niece of Robert the Bruce. A descendent, William Elfinstun, became rector of Kirkmichael at the age of twenty-five. He studied Civil and Canon Law in Paris, eventually becoming Professor of Law in that university. In 1484 he was appointed Bishop of Aberdeen and later Lord High Chancellor of Scotland, a post he held until the death of James III in June 1489. In 1494 he obtained from Pope Alexander VI a bull for the founding of a university in Aberdeen. King's College was built in 1500. Besides building and designing a university, he left a large sum to erect and maintain a bridge across the River Dee at Aberdeen. After the death of James IV at Flodden, the bishop quit his see and left for Edinburgh to assist in restoring peace to his ruined country. He died soon after his arrival in the capital in October 1514. He left his compilations on Canon Law and other writings which can be found in the College in Aberdeen. A cousin of the bishop, Sir Alexander Elphinstone, was created Lord Elphinstone by James IV and fell with his king on Flodden Field. It is said that he bore a striking resemblance to the king, and was at first mistaken for him during the battle. His son, Alexander, the second Lord, was killed at the Battle of Pinkie in 1547. The fourth Lord Elphinstone was appointed in 1599 a judge of the Supreme Court of Scotland and later Lord High Treasurer.

A cadet branch of the family were made peers with the title Lord Balmerino. They were staunch Jacobites and the 6th Earl was taken prisoner after Culloden. He was beheaded in August 1746 displaying such courage that many onlookers were moved to tears.

The eleventh Lord Elphinstone was lieutenant governor of Edinburgh Castle. One of his younger brothers, George Keith Elphinstone, was a distinguished naval commander. He served with great distinction on the American station, the squadron of ships which served to protect British shipping interests off the eastern coast of America. In 1795 he was made vice admiral and commanded the fleet which captured the Cape of Good Hope and compelled the Dutch fleet to surrender without firing a gun. His reward was an Irish barony. He was later promoted to the rank of admiral, and created Baron Keith of Banheath, only to be advanced once more, to the rank of Viscount in 1814. William George Keith Elphinstone, the viscount's nephew, was a colonel at the Battle of Waterloo in 1815. In 1837 he was promoted to major general and was commander-in-chief of the Bengal army, where he led the disastrous Afghan campaign of 1841. He was to face a court martial, but the effects of long service and the Indian climate spared him this indignity, and he died before proceedings could be commenced. John, the thirteenth Lord, was Governor of Madras and a lord-in-waiting to Queen Victoria.

Elphinstone

The full achievement of Lord Elphinstone

ERSKINE

This name was originally derived from the lands of Erskine on the south of the Clyde in Renfrew, and the name itself may be from the ancient British for 'green rising ground'. Henry de Erskine was proprietor of the barony as early as the reign of Alexander II. He was witness to a charter by the Earl of Lennox of the patronage and tithes of Roseneath to the Abbey of Paisley around 1226. John de Irskyn appears on the Ragman Roll of Scottish nobles submitting to Edward I of England in 1296. His son, Sir John de Irskyn, had a son and three daughters, the eldest of whom married Thomas Bruce, brother of King Robert. A second daughter, Alice, married Walter, the High Steward of Scotland.

The Erskines were staunch in their support of the Bruce family and Sir Robert de Erskine became an illustrious and renowned figure in his time. He was appointed by David II constable and keeper of the strategic royal Castle of Stirling. (The present chief still holds this royal office, greeting the monarch at the gates of the castle on state occasions.) In 1350 he was appointed Lord Great Chamberlain of Scotland and justiciar north of the Forth. In 1371 he was one of the nobles who established the succession to the throne of Robert II, grandson of the great Bruce and first of the Stewart dynasty. In the mid fifteenth century the family claimed one of the great Celtic titles when Alexander, Earl of Mar, died in 1435. Alexander was a Stewart who claimed the title through his wife, Countess of Mar in her own right. Sir Robert Erskine, who had been created Lord Erskine, now claimed the ancient earldom by right of his descent from Isabella, Countess of Mar. The king, however, refused, insisting that the earldom now belonged to the Crown because the last male holder had been a Stewart. Despite this dispute with the king, the Erskines became guardians to young James IV and were there-

after to be guardians to five successive generations of royalty.

Alexander, third Lord Erskine, constructed a massive tower in 1497 at Alloa,
which was to be the seat of the chiefs for the
next three hundred years. His son was killed
at Flodden in 1513 and it was John, fifth Lord
Erskine, who became guardian and tutor to
James V. The ill-fated Mary, Queen of Scots
came to the Erskines when she was still a
baby, and spent the first five years of her life
around Alloa and Stirling Castle. She bestowed
upon Lord Erskine a new title of 'Earl of Mar',
although without the former precedence. (This
was later to cause considerable legal difficulties, and although the Erskine Chiefs are Earls
of Mar and Earls of Kellie, there is also a
Countess of Mar in her own right who is also
a member of Council of Chiefs.) In 1582, Lord
Erskine took part in the raid of Ruthven,
which placed the young James VI in the hands
of an extreme faction of the Protestant nobility
for nearly a year. Erskine was exiled as a
result, but was ultimately restored to royal
favour and became Lord High Treasurer of
Scotland in 1616.

Erskine

Standard

The ability to change political allegiance
according to the pragmatic needs of survival
or the desire for gain was a skill not unknown
to the Scottish nobility, and the sixth Earl of
Mar, born in 1675, had the aptitude to such
an extent that he has passed into history as
'bobbing John'. He was a supporter of the
union and seemed reconciled to the
Hanoverian succession, but when he attended
court in London in 1714 he was not offered
the post of Secretary of State for Scotland, and
considered this to be a direct insult. He
promptly returned to his ancestral lands and,

raising the standard of the 'Old Pretender',
James VIII, he called out his own clansmen
and all loyal supporters of the house of Stuart.
He had soon gathered an army of over ten
thousand clansmen. The earl led his Jacobites
to Dunblane where he met an indifferent royal
force under the Duke of Argyll. The Battle of
Sheriffmuir, which was fought on 13
November 1715, was inconclusive and,
although Mar's forces were probably victorious, they left the field without inflicting any
severe damage upon Argyll, who then claimed
a victory for himself. The rising was a failure
and Mar fled to France, whereupon his title
and lands were forfeited. The estates were purchased by another branch of the family in
1724. The earl received the Jacobite title of
Mar, but this was abandoned in 1824 when
the Erksines were restored to the earldom of
Mar and the attainder on the family was lifted.
The earldom of Kellie, which had been
bestowed in 1619 on a younger son of the
chiefly line, became united with the earldom
of Mar in 1835.

FARQUHARSON

arquharsons trace their origin back to Farquhar, fourth son of Alexander Cier (Shaw) of Rothiemurcus, who possessed the Braes of Mar near the source of the river Dee in Aberdeenshire. His descendants were called Farquharsons, and his son, Donald, married Isobel Stewart, heiress of Invercauld. Donald's son, Finla Mor, was the real progenitor of the clan. The Gaelic patronymic is MacFionlaigh Mor. He was royal standard bearer at the Battle of Pinkie, where he was killed in 1547. From his lifetime onwards the clan grew in stature, important branches being founded through the nine sons of his two marriages, in particular those of Craigniety, Monaltrie, Whitehouse, Finzean, Allanquoich, Inverey, Tullochcoy, Broughdearg, and Achriachan. In addition to those who bear the name Farquharson and the other variations which clearly denominate the descendants of Farquhar, there are other families which are acknowledged to be septs or dependents, having close affiliation by tradition, and they include the names Hardie, MacCardney, MacCuaigh, Grassick, Riach, Brebner and Coutts.

The Farquharsons were not as numerous as some of their predatory neighbours, and in 1595 they joined the confederation known as Clan Chattan by a bond of manrent to the chief of the Mackintosh, acknowledging him as their 'natyff cheiff'.

When the Erskines set out to reassert their claim over the ancient Earldom of Mar at the end of the sixteenth century they were opposed around Braemar by the increasing power and prominence of the Farquharsons. John Erskine, 'de jure' eighteenth Earl of Mar, built a castle at Braemar to defend his lands, but this ultimately passed into the hands of the Farquharsons themselves. The clan's fierce reputation led to their being known as the fighting Farquharsons, and they were staunch supporters of the Stuarts. Donald Farquharson of Monaltrie fought with Montrose in 1644, and the family later supported Charles II. John Farquharson of Inverey, known as the Black Colonel, declared for James VII and followed Graham of Claverhouse, the famous 'Bonnie Dundee', in 1689. He burned Braemar Castle and was a thorn in the flesh of the government until his death in 1698. In the rising of 1715, John Farquharson of Invercauld joined the Clan Chattan regiment of which he was colonel, but was taken prisoner at Preston, later being transferred to London and held in Marshalsea Prison for ten months.

Undaunted, the Farquharsons supported Bonnie Prince Charlie and at Culloden were led by Francis Farquharson of Monaltrie, the Baron Ban who was nephew and commissioner to John. He was taken prisoner and condemned to be executed at the Tower of London, only being reprieved along with two other Highland officers on the very morning set for their execution. However, he remained a prisoner and was later paroled, not being permitted to return to Scotland for over twenty years.

Farquharson

Standard

His cousin, Anne, daughter of Invercauld, became famous in the Jacobite cause. She was married to Angus, chief of Mackintosh, who was a serving officer in the Black Watch. In her husband's absence she called out Clan Mackintosh who joined their allies of Clan Chattan. The Mackintosh had the misfortune to be captured by the forces of Prince Charles Edward at the Battle of Prestonpans, and was sent home to his estate at Moy, having given his parole not to take up arms against the Jacobite cause for one year. It is claimed that on his arrival he was greeted by his wife: 'Your servant, captain', to which he retorted, 'Your servant, colonel', after which she was forever known as Colonel Anne. She afterwards saved

the prince from an attempt to capture him when resident at Moy. Colonel Anne found herself imprisoned at Inverness after Culloden, but was released after six weeks. Anne's father, John, had succeeded his brother, William, who died unmarried in 1694. John died in 1750 and was succeeded by his son, James, who died in 1805. From his marriage to Amelia, daughter of Lord George Murray, the renowned Jacobite general, eleven children were born but sadly all but his youngest daughter, Catherine, predeceased him. In 1815 she was recognised by Lyon Court as chief of the name of Farquharson. She was succeeded by her son, James. On the death in 1936 of James's descendent, Alexander Haldane Farquharson of Invercauld, the arms were confirmed to his daughter, Myrtle Farquharson of Invercauld, but she was killed in an air raid in 1941. The succession then passed to her nephew, the present chief, Captain Alwyne Compton Farquharson of Invercauld. Much of the ancestral estates still remain in the family hands, and Braemar Castle is fully restored and now open to the public. The Braemar Highland Gathering is now world famous, having enjoyed royal patronage since the reign of Queen Victoria.

The sons of Fergus have spread across Scotland, from Ross-shire in the north to Dumfriesshire in the south-west. The Gaelic patronymic, 'MacFhaerghuis', is translated alternatively as 'son of the angry' or 'son of the bold and proud'. Although tradition seeks to attribute a common ancestry to the various distinct families bearing this name, there is no real evidence to support this. Indeed, the heraldry of the chiefly family is quite different from other examples relating to families of the same name. The Argyllshire Fergussons claim descent from Fergus Mor mac Erc, a very early king of the Scots of Dalriada. The boars' heads which appear on most shields of this family indicate a connection with the early Scots of Dalriada, who came from Ireland across Argyll. There is evidence linking the Fergussons living in Ayrshire and Dumfries with Fergus, Prince of Galloway an important figure in the reigns of David I and Malcolm IV. He restored the church at Whithorn, founded the Abbey of Dundrennan and died at the Abbey of Holyrood in 1161. The Earls of Carrick descended from this Fergus.

The Fergussons held the lands of Kilkerran, probably from the twelfth century, but the first certain record is John Fergusson of Kilkerran in 1464. He may have been descended from John, son of Fergus, one of the witnesses to a charter of Edward Bruce signed at Turnberry shortly after the Battle of Bannockburn in 1314. By 1600 there were Fergussons all over the southern part of Carrick, all of whom acknowledged Kilkerran as their chief. They sided with the Kennedys in their feud with the Lairds of Bargany and were part of the Earl of Cassillis's band in the skirmish around Maybole in 1601 when Bargany met his death.

The Ayrshire Fergussons adopted the Protestant faith during the Reformation. Sir John Fergusson of Kilkerran fought for the royalist cause in the civil war. The Kilkerran estates fell heavily into debt and it fell to one of Sir John's grandsons to restore the family fortunes. Sir John Fergusson, born around 1653, became a distinguished lawyer and a member of the Faculty of Advocates in 1681. He was created a Baronet of Nova Scotia in November 1703. His son, James, became a judge of the Supreme Court in 1735 with the title, 'Lord Kilkerran'. General Sir Charles Fergusson of Kilkerran, seventh Baronet, served in the army for almost forty years. His early career took him in 1895 to Egypt and later to the Sudan. In 1914 he was the youngest major general on the army list. He served throughout the First World War and was later military governor of occupied German territory. From 1924 to 1930 he was Governor General of New Zealand. The present chief still lives at the splendid Kilkerran House in Ayrshire.

Standard

The Fergussons of Dunfallandy may well have a quite separate descent, but their heraldry proclaims them as cadets of the principal house of which Kilkerran is the recognised head. They have supporters which mark them out as a principal branch of importance. The lands of Dunfallandy and the house which still bears this name lie near Pitlochry in Atholl. Atholl Fergussons appear in the Act of Suppression drawn up by the Privy Council in 1587, and Dunfallandy was ordered to give security for the good behaviour of his followers. They were ardent Jacobites who came out in both the Fifteen and the Forty-five. Dunfallandy himself was captured and was fortunate to escape execution at Carlisle in 1746. General Archibald Fergusson of Dunfallandy served in India under the East India Company for many years. He was

Fergusson

wounded at the Battle of Seringapatam in 1799. In 1812 he rebuilt Dunfallandy House, where his descendents lived until very recently.

Other distinguished branches of the family include the Fergussons of Pitfour, one of whom became a High Court judge in 1765 with the title of 'Lord Pitfour'. His son, Lieutenant Colonel Patrick Fergusson, invented the first breach-loading rifle used by the British army and patented in 1776. Ronald Fergusson of Raith, Viscount Novar, was MP for Leith from 1886 to 1914, when he was appointed Governor General of Australia. His ancestor, General Sir Ronald Fergusson, was a distinguished soldier who was praised by the Duke of Wellington for his gallantry during the Peninsular War of 1808–14, and is perhaps now best known for the famous double portrait of him and his brother, Robert, in the uniform of the Royal Company of Archers (the monarch's bodyguard in Scotland). The Fergussons were not, however, without culture, and Robert Fergusson, who died in 1774, was the poet most admired by Robert Burns, who venerated his work and took it as his model.

FORBES

In that part of north-east Scotland which spreads itself from the mountain ranges of Aberdeenshire to the coast of Banff and Buchan, lie the lands of the Clan Forbes; here the great houses and estates of the clan – once there were no fewer than one hundred and fifty of them – were situated along the winding rivers that flow eastwards and northwards especially along the valley of the Don. Overlooking the Don today stands Castle Forbes, built in 1815 by James Ochoncar, seventeenth Lord Forbes, and still occupied by the direct descendents of Duncan Forbes upon whom the original lands were conferred in a charter dated 1271 by Alexander III.

The Forbes family grew in power in Aberdeenshire throughout the fourteenth century. Sir John Forbes of the Black Lip had four sons: William became the progenitor of the Pitsligo line; John was ancestor of the Forbes of Polquhoun; Alistair of Brux founded the lines of Skellater and Inverernan; while Alexander, his eldest son, fought in the victory at Harlaw in 1411 alongside the Earl of Mar against the invading hordes led by Donald of the Isles, and was elevated to the peerage some time between 1443 and July 1445, when he took his seat in Parliament. Since then the title has been handed down through successive generations, and on the union roll of 1701, Forbes was the premier Lordship of Scotland, a precedence held to this day.

James, son of the first Lord Forbes, himself had three sons: William, the third Lord Forbes; Duncan, who founded the family of Forbes of Corsindae and Monymusk; and Patrick of Corse, squire to James III, whose line later became Baronets of Craigievar.

Throughout the fifteenth and sixteenth centuries, a long and bitter struggle was waged against the great house of Gordon, although the Forbeses' traditional enemies were the Leslies. In the 1520s these feuds reached a climax, with murders by both sides occurring constantly. One of the most prominent of those killed by the Forbes faction, Seton of Meldrum, was a close connection of the chief of the Gordons, the Earl of Huntly. Huntly soon became involved in a plot aimed at the Master of Forbes, son of the sixth Lord, who was heavily implicated in the Seton murder. In 1536 Huntly accused the master of conspiring to assassinate James V by shooting at him with a canon. The Master was tried and executed, but within days his conviction was reversed and the Forbes family restored to favour. However, the damage to relations between the Forbes and Gordons was irreparable, and for the remainder of the century the feud reduced Aberdeenshire to an unparalleled state of lawlessness. The Reformation added religion to the differences already existing between the clans, as the Gordons remained defiantly Catholic but the Forbeses favoured Protestantism. The Forbeses' traditional enemies, such as the Leslies, Irvines and Setons, attached themselves to the Gordon faction and thereby remained Catholic, while the Keiths, Frasers, Crichtons and others formed a Protestant opposition of which the Forbeses were the heart. The feud culminated in 1571 in two battles, at Tillieangus and Craibstone. Druminnor, then Lord Forbes's seat, was itself plundered, and in the same month the Gordons followed this with the massacre of twenty-seven Forbeses of Towie at Corgarff. Two Acts of Parliament were required to force the clans to put down their arms.

In 1582, James VI confirmed his 'trusty and well beloved cousin', Lord Forbes, in the 'lands which have been in continuous possession of his family in times past the memory of man'. However, the struggle of the previous decades had drawn the Forbeses deep into debt, making it necessary in later years for them to sell much of their land.

Through all these 'local' troubles, and indeed into this present century, members of the family have achieved military distinction for their country. James Ochoncar, the seventeenth Lord Forbes, was an officer in the

Forbes

Coldstream Regiment of Footguards for twenty-six years, rising to the rank of general, having served as second-in-command of the British forces in Sicily in 1808 before commanding the Cork and Eastern districts in Ireland. It was during his time in Ireland that a castle was built near Alford on the site of the old family home of Putachie, and the seventeenth Lord is generally regarded as responsible for the building and for the layout of the estate. Today Castle Forbes is the home of his great-great-great-grandson. The present chief of the clan, Nigel, twenty-second Lord Forbes, lives at Balforbes on the south side of the River Don, which bisects the 'modern' Forbes estate. He followed his father, Atholl, twenty-first Lord, into the Grenadier Guards and fought throughout the major campaigns of the Second World War, before becoming military assistant to the High Commissioner for Palestine, General Sir Alan Cunningham. Like his father and many earlier holders of the title, he was elected to serve as a representative peer for Scotland in the House of Lords, and was Minister of State for Scotland in the Conservative government of Harold Macmillan in 1958–59.

FORSYTH

A s with so many families whose history stretches back before the twelfth century, the derivation of this family's surname is uncertain. If the name is Celtic in its origin, it may derive from the Gaelic personal name 'Fearsithe', meaning 'man of peace'. It may, however, allude to a place of peace, and refer to a particular place, or lands. One tradition provides a Norman descent from Forsach, one of the Norsemen who settled on lands on the River Dordogne in Aquitaine. The Viscomte de Fronsoc accompanied Eleanor de Provence to London to marry Henry III and lived at the English court from 1236 to 1246. It is believed that his family obtained lands in Northumberland, and thence to the Borders of Scotland.

William de Fersith appears on the Ragman Roll of Scottish noblemen submitting to Edward I of England in 1296. Osbert, son of Robert de Forsyth, received a grant of lands at Sauchie in Stirlingshire from Robert the Bruce sometime after March 1306. He distinguished himself at the Battle of Bannockburn and received confirmation under the great seal of the realm of his lands in 1320. Osbert's son was appointed the king's macer and constable of Stirling Castle in 1368. Fersith the clerk is recorded receiving a royal pension of one hundred pounds per annum from Robert II. The family became established around Stirling and many prominent burgesses and civic dignitaries bore the name.

David Forsyth of Dykes in Lanarkshire acquired his lands some time prior to 1488. His seal bore heraldry similar to the arms of de Fronsoc, and he specifically claimed them as his ancestors. There was a Forsyth castle at Dykes until it was demolished in 1828. A branch of the family left Dykes and moved to Inchnoch Castle in Monkland and their descendents spread the family throughout Ayrshire and around Glasgow.

William Forsyth, baillie of Edinburgh

around 1365 had, with other issue, a son, William, who, in 1423, moved to St Andrews and subsequently acquired the barony of Nydie. This was a fief of the Archbishops of St Andrews. Alexander, fourth Baron of Nydie, was sheriff depute of Fife, and the arms assigned to him are recorded in Balfour's manuscript. Alexander died at Flodden in 1513. His grandson, James, married a substantial heiress, Elizabeth Leslie, granddaughter of the Earl of Rothes and great-granddaughter of James III. The Forsyths of Nydie had little choice thereafter but to tie their fortunes to their extremely powerful relatives. They acquired lands around the royal Palace of Falkland, and in 1538 John Forsyth was appointed king's macer and thereafter Falkland Pursuivant. It is from the Falkland Forsyth lairds that the present chief descends.

Forsyth

Standard

Another branch of the family settled near Monymusk, and William Forsyth represented Forres in the Parliament of 1621. The Reverend Alexander John Forsyth was a pioneer in the development of modern firearms and his work led to the invention of the percussion lock, which replaced the flint lock in the eighteenth century. He received a modest Crown pension for an invention which in today's terms would have brought him enormous wealth. William Forsyth, born at Old Meldrum in 1737, was a distinguished horticulturalist. He went to London where he studied at the botanical gardens in Chelsea. In 1784, he was appointed Chief Superintendent of the Royal Gardens at Kensington and St James' Palace. He researched actively and was particularly interested in plant diseases. He discovered a composition which inhibited

certain diseases common to fruit trees and received a grant from Parliament to assist in publishing his findings in order to make his work widely available. In 1802 he published a *Treatise on the Culture and Management of Fruit Trees* which proved so popular that the first three editions were sold out. He was made a Fellow of the Society of Antiquaries and of the Linnean Society. He died in his beloved gardens at Kensington in July 1804. In honour of his name, there is now a genus of plants termed 'forsythia'.

The Reverend Peter Taylor Forsyth was born in Aberdeen in 1848. He studied at Aberdeen University before going to Germany for post-graduate research where he gained a high reputation for his strong Protestant theology. He was Principal of Hackney Theological College in London and published his most influential work, *The Person and Place of Jesus Christ*, in 1909.

The present chief was recognised by the Lord Lyon in 1970. He has restored Ethie Castle near Arbroath, now the clan seat, making the family motto highly appropriate.

FRASER

The Frasers probably come from Anjou in France, and the name may derive either from Fredarius, from Fresel or from Freseau. It has also been suggested that they descend from a tribe called Friselii in Roman Gaul, whose badge was a strawberry plant.

They first appeared in Scotland around 1160, when Simon Fraser held lands at Keith in East Lothian. About five generations later Sir Simon Fraser was captured fighting for Robert the Bruce, and executed with great cruelty by Edward I in 1306. His cousin, Sir Alexander Fraser of Cowie, Bruce's chamberlain, was the elder brother of another Sir Simon Fraser, from whom the Frasers of Lovat descend. He married Robert the Bruce's sister, Mary, who for a time was imprisoned by the English in a cage hung from Roxburgh Castle wall. Simon's grandson, Sir Alexander Fraser of Cowie and Durris, acquired the castle now called Cairnbulg and the lands of Philorth by marriage with Joanna, younger daughter and co-heiress of the Earl of Ross in 1375. Eight generations later, in 1592, Sir Alexander Fraser of Philorth received from James VI charters creating the fishing village of Faithlie, which he had transformed into a fine town, also improving the harbour, which became a burgh of regality and a free port, called Fraserburgh. He was also authorised to found a university in the town, but the scheme was short-lived, falling victim to the religious troubles of the times. When plague hit Aberdeen in 1647, staff and students from King's College were evacuated to the town for two years, but now a street name and some lettering carved on a wall are all that remain of the early seat of learning.

The eighth Laird of Philorth also built Fraserburgh Castle, later the Kinnaird Head Lighthouse, and in doing so bankrupted himself, being forced to sell the Castle of Philorth, which passed out of the family for over three hundred years until the nineteenth Lord Saltoun bought it back in 1934.

The ninth Laird married the heiress of the Abernethy Lords Saltoun, and their son became the tenth Lord Saltoun. The present chief, as well as bearing the undifferenced arms of Fraser, has also a 'grand coat' which quarters the arms of Abernethy, Wishart and Ross. The tenth Lord Saltoun was severely wounded at the Battle of Worcester in 1651, but survived thanks to his servant, James Cardno, who rescued him from the battlefield, hiding and nursing him until he finally got his master home to Fraserburgh. In 1666 he built a house a mile from Fraserburgh which he called Philorth House, where the family lived until it was burned down in 1915. Sir Alexander Fraser of Durris was personal physician to Charles II. He was educated at Aberdeen and soon acquired a reputation for general scholarship but particularly in medicine. He accompanied the king throughout his campaign in 1650, but seems to have been unpopular with some of the more extreme Covenanters because of his progressive scientific opinions. After the Restoration in 1660, he sat in the Scottish Parliament although he was still prominent enough in court circles to feature in the diaries of Samuel Pepys. He died in 1681. The family took no part in the Jacobite rebellion.

Standard

The sixteenth Lord Saltoun commanded the Light Companies of the First Guards in the Orchard at Hougoumont on the morning of the Battle of Waterloo in 1815. It was he who, later in the day, first noticed the Imperial Guard emerge from the hollow where they had been hiding all day, and drew the Duke of

Fraser

Wellington's attention to them. The nineteenth Lord Saltoun was a prisoner of war in Germany for most of the First World War. He became a member of the House of Lords from 1936 and devoted himself to numerous public works, and latterly to promoting the Royal National Lifeboat Institution (RNLI). He died in 1979 at the age of 93.

Other branches of the family also prospered. Andrew Fraser of Muchalls was raised to the peerage in June 1633 with the title, 'Lord Fraser'. He completed the early work on Castle Fraser which stands south of the River Don near Inverurie. This magnificent castle, entirely reminiscent of a French chateau, is now fully renovated and in the care of the National Trust for Scotland. The peerage conferred on Andrew Fraser fell dormant in the eighteenth century. The nineteenth Lord was succeeded by his daughter, Flora Fraser, twentieth Lady Saltoun. She is married to Captain Alexander Ramsay of Mar, a great-grandson of Queen Victoria, and he and Lady Saltoun are officially members of the royal family.

Arms
*Quarterly, 1st & 4th, Azure, three fraises two and one Argent (Fraser);
2nd & 3rd, Argent, three antique crowns two and one Gules (Bisset)*

CREST
A buck's head erased Proper

MOTTO
Je suis prest (I am ready)

SUPPORTERS
Two bucks rampant Proper

The Frasers of Lovat descend from Sir Simon Fraser, brother of Sir Alexander, chamberlain of Robert the Bruce. It is thought that Sir Simon Fraser married the heiress to the Bisset lands around Beauly, and this is how the family of Lovat came to be settled there. The first certain record linking the lands of Lovat to the Frasers is in 1367 when Hugh Fraser is styled 'dominus de Loveth et portionarius de Ard' (lord of Lovat and portioner of Ard). The Gaelic patronymic of the Lovat Frasers is 'MacShimi', meaning 'son of Simon', and it was in use at least at the beginning of the fifteenth century.

Around 1422, the Frasers acquired lands at Stratherrick by Loch Ness, together with part of Glenelg. Although the exact date of creation is uncertain, some time between 1456 and 1464, Hugh Fraser was raised to the peerage as Lord Lovat or Lord Fraser of Lovat. Around 1511, the chiefs established their seat at Beaufort Castle, which is still inhabited by them. The present castle is relatively modern, but occupies roughly the same site as previous strongholds which were destroyed in the thirteenth and eighteenth centuries.

The Lovat Frasers had their fair share of clan feuds and battles but amongst the most memorable, and bloody, was with the Macdonalds of Clanranald in 1544. The chiefship of Clanranald was in dispute and Lord Lovat was the uncle of one of the warring claimants, Ranald 'Galda' (the stranger), whose cause he took up. Lovat, with over four hundred of his best men, joined forces with the Earl of Huntly, the Lieutenant of the North, to crush the Macdonalds and make Ranald chief. The combined force marched to Inverlochy in Lochaber from where they successfully established Ranald's control of Moidart by taking Castle Tirrim. Huntly then decided to split his force from the Frasers and returned to his own territory. The expedition was cut short and

Lovat led his men up the Great Glen towards Glenmoriston. The decision to divide their forces for the return journey may indicate that Lovat and Huntly thought the Macdonalds were no longer a threat, but this was to prove a fatal miscalculation for the Frasers. The Macdonalds had been stalking the invaders but held back so long as they were numerically inferior – a position which reversed once Huntly's men were gone. They moved swiftly to outflank Lovat and fell upon the unsuspecting Frasers on a stretch of wild marshland to the north of Loch Lochy. The battle became known as Blar-na-leine – 'the field of shirts', when the heat of day compelled the Highlanders to throw off their heavy plaids or 'feileadh mor' to fight in their shirts. (Some modern scholars dispute this translation, asserting that it really refers to the marshy ground.) Lovat was outnumbered and could have fought a rearguard action to try and cover his escape, but instead he bravely led his men forward into a pitched battle. Lovat, his son and heir, along with hundreds of his men, were killed in the fierce fighting with victory falling to the Macdonalds. Lovat and his son were buried in the priory at Beauly. The defeat was a setback but the real power of the clan was largely undiminished.

The family multiplied rapidly and established many cadet branches, including the Frasers of Reelig with their castle at Moniack, Inverallochy, Fingask, and many others. The ninth Lord Lovat had four daughters but no son, and his widow arranged a marriage for Amelia, the eldest daughter and heiress, with the Master of Saltoun, later twelfth Lord Saltoun. When his father was travelling to Castle Dounie to discuss the marriage details with Lady Lovat, Amelia's uncle, Thomas Fraser of Beaufort, and his son, Simon, later eleventh Lord Lovat, kidnapped him. He was held prisoner and threatened with death if he did not agree to abandon the proposed mar-

riage, which he promptly did. Simon, the kidnapper, when eleventh Lord Lovat, was famous as the 'old fox' of the Forty-five, plotting with both government and Jacobite forces, depending upon his assessment of where he thought his present advantage lay. He mustered the Frasers to support Prince Charles Edward Stuart in the autumn of 1745. At least one battalion (and some authorities say two) of Frasers fought at Culloden Moor in April 1746. They suffered heavy losses, and the whole Fraser country was ravaged by the troops of the Duke of Cumberland. Charles Fraser, younger of Inverallochy, although grievously wounded was summarily executed. MacShimi was captured at Loch Morar and taken to London, where he was beheaded on Tower Hill on 9 April 1747. His title and estates were declared forfeit. His son, Simon, was pardoned, and when George II began raising Highland regiments, Lovat formed first in 1757, the 78th Fraser Highlanders, who later fought with Wolfe at Quebec and later the 71st Fraser Highlanders who served faithfully in the American War of Independence. His brother, Archibald, later raised the 'Fraser Fencibles' during the Napoleonic War. He left no legitimate heirs, and in 1837 the peerage, which had been attainted, was restored to a cousin, Thomas Fraser of Strichen, a descendent of the fourth Lord Lovat. In 1899 Lord Lovat raised the Lovat Scouts to fight in the Boer War. The Scouts saw service in the First World War and in the Second, where MacShimi became a distinguished commando leader, being awarded both the Distinguished Service Order and the Military Cross. He died in 1995 shortly after tragically losing two of his sons in accidents within a matter of months of each other. He has been succeeded by his 18-year-old grandson, Simon Fraser, but the great Lovat estates, including Beaufort Castle, have had to be sold.

GORDON

The Gordons are one of the great families of the north-east of Scotland, and their surname has many suggested meanings, although the family originally were almost certainly of Anglo–Norman descent. There is also a tale which makes the first of the family the saviour of a Scottish king, in this case from a wild boar. This is said to explain the boars' heads which appear on the Gordon arms.

The first certain record of the name places the family in the Borders during the reigns of Malcolm IV and William the Lion. Richard de Gordon appears in numerous charters, and probably died around 1200. Sir Adam de Gordon was one of the wardens of the marches in 1300, and in 1305 was appointed one of the commissioners to negotiate with Edward I seeking settlement to the competition for the crown of Scotland. He became a staunch supporter of Robert the Bruce, and was one of the ambassadors sent to Rome to petition the pope to remove the excommunication which had been placed on Bruce after his murder of John Comyn. For his services the king granted to Gordon the lands of Strathbogie, which had been confiscated from the Earl of Atholl for treason.

The Castle of Strathbogie was to be renamed Huntly after a portion of the Gordon lands in Berwickshire. In 1436 Sir Alexander Gordon was created Lord Gordon, and his son was raised to the title of Earl of Huntly. The family became embroiled in the deadly battle for power between the king and the Douglases. Huntly was for the king, but when he moved his forces south, the Earl of Moray, kinsman and ally of the Douglases, devastated the Gordon lands and burned Huntly Castle. The Gordons were recalled and soon defeated their enemies. After the fall of the Douglases, the power of the Gordons grew unchallenged. Their control over their lands was almost regal, and the chiefs are to this day fondly referred to as 'Cock o' the North'. A grand new castle at Huntly rose from the ruins of the old, and it soon rivalled any of the great houses of the realm. In 1496 Huntly Castle hosted the marriage of the pretender, Perkin Warbeck, believed at the time to be one of the missing sons of Edward IV (the 'princes in the tower'), to Lady Catherine Gordon. James IV honoured the couple with his presence, although he was a frequent visitor to Strathbogie in any event.

George, fourth Earl of Huntly, became Chancellor of Scotland in 1547 and was a close confidant of the regent, Mary of Guise, the mother of Mary, Queen of Scots. The Gordons paid scant attention to the Reformation, remaining firmly Catholic. However, they disagreed with the young queen; Huntly died at Corrichie, leading his men against the royal army, and his son, Sir John Gordon, was later beheaded before Queen Mary at Aberdeen. The Gordons eventually made peace with the Crown, and in 1599 the chief was created Marquess of Huntly. The second Marquess was a fierce supporter of the royalist cause in the civil war, and his followers have passed into history as

Gordon

Standard

the Gordon Horse, which figured so prominently in the campaigns of the great Marquess of Montrose. Huntly's pride was such that he found it impossible to co-operate with Montrose, and some historians have suggested that had he done so wholeheartedly, the whole course of the war in Scotland might have been very different. Huntly was captured in Strathdon in December 1647 and was taken to Edinburgh, where he languished until March 1649, when he was beheaded. Lord Louis Gordon was restored to the family estates and titles in 1651, and was raised to the highest

rank of the peerage as Duke of Gordon in 1684.

The Gordons fought on both sides during the Jacobite risings of 1715 and 1745. The second Duke of Gordon followed the standard of the 'Old Pretender' at the Battle of Sheriffmuir in 1715. He later surrendered, but although he was imprisoned for a short period, no further proceedings were taken against him. The third Duke remained loyal to the Hanoverians when Prince Charles Edward Stuart reasserted his father's claim in 1745, but his brother, Lord Louis Gordon, promptly raised a regiment of two battalions. After Culloden he escaped to France, where he died in 1754. George, fifth Duke of Gordon, was a general in the army and for a time governor of Edinburgh Castle. He died without issue, and the dukedom became extinct. The marquessate passed to a kinsman, from whom the present chief descends.

Another branch of the clan were created Earls of Aberdeen in 1682. The fourth Earl was a Prime Minister in the mid nineteenth century. This branch, too, were advanced to the dignity of Marquess, and established their seat at Haddo House near Aberdeen.

GRAHAM

Despite a colourful tradition which asserts that Greme was a mighty Caledonian chief who broke the Antonine Wall driving the Roman legions out of Scotland, the likely origin of this family is Anglo–Norman; the Manor of Gregham, or Greyhome, is recorded in William the Conqueror's Domesday Book. When David I came to Scotland to claim his throne, Graham was one of the knights who accompanied him. Sir William de Graham was present at the erection of the great Abbey of Holyrood and witnessed its foundation charter.

The first lands the family acquired in Scotland appear to have been around Dalkeith in Midlothian. Sir Nicholas de Graham attended the Parliament in 1290 where the Treaty of Brigham, for the marriage of the infant heir to the Scottish throne, Margaret, the Maid of Norway, to Prince Edward of England, was agreed. Their acceptance in Celtic Scotland was assured when they married into the princely family of Strathearn, and from Malise of Strathearn they acquired the lands around Auchterarder which were to become their principal seat. Sir John de Graham was a companion-in-arms of Sir William Wallace, the great patriot. His bravery was legendary even in his own lifetime, and he was called 'Graham with the bright sword'. He fell at the Battle of Falkirk in 1298, and his gravestone and effigy can still be found in Falkirk Old Parish Church.

The family's landholdings and power grew throughout the centuries. They acquired the lands of Mugdock north of Glasgow, where they built a stout castle around 1370. Patrick Graham of Kincardine was created a peer in 1451 with the title, 'Lord Graham'. Two generations later they were created Earls of Montrose and in 1504 their hereditary lands of 'Auld Montross' were erected into a free barony and earldom of Montrose. The first Earl fell at the fateful field of Flodden in 1513.

By means of purchase and inheritance the Graham lands had become, by the late seventeenth century, among the richest in Scotland.

The name would have been remembered for the many great deeds of the family, but it passed into legend in the person of the fifth Earl and first Marquess of Montrose, James Graham, probably the most glamorous figure in Scottish history. A renowned scholar and poet, he was one of the leaders of the movement opposed to Charles I's attempt to introduce new practices of worship into the Scottish Church. Montrose signed the Covenant, but later decided not to take up arms against the king. He offered his services to the king, who gratefully accepted and created him captain general of the king's army in Scotland. This was a grand-sounding title, but the king's general was left to find his own army. The Grahams rallied to their chief, and they were joined by a large force of Highlanders led by Alasdair Macdonald, 'Colkitto'. The campaign of 1644–45 is one of the most remarkable in Scottish military history. At one point, Montrose seemed poised not only to hold Scotland for the king, but to drive south to ward off the certain defeat faced in England. However, on 13 September 1645, Montrose was taken by surprise at Philiphaugh in the Borders by a substantial force of Covenant cavalry under General David Lesley. The captain general escaped to the north, but his forces were massacred after they surrendered, and the royalist cause in Scotland seemed mortally wounded. In May 1646, Montrose received orders from Charles to disband his army and leave the kingdom. Charles had by this time placed himself in the keeping of the Scottish Covenanting forces in England, setting in motion the series of events which led him to the scaffold at Whitehall.

Montrose arrived safely in Norway and thereafter travelled extensively on the Continent. His military prowess, coupled with his own personal wit and charm, guaranteed the warmth of his reception. In Germany he was raised to the rank of mareschal, and offered field command. The French similarly

Graham

honoured him. He had done everything and more that could be expected of a loyal subject, but the glitter of royal courts and the power which was offered to him could not sway his belief that his duty and loyalty lay with his king. He was given commission by the newly proclaimed Charles II to recover Scotland. With the assistance of arms and supplies from Sweden and Denmark, Montrose landed in Orkney in March 1650. He reached the mainland but the anticipated rising of royalists did not materialise. At Invercharron in Ross-shire, the tiny royal army was totally defeated and Montrose forced to flee. He was betrayed, captured and transported to Edinburgh, where he was sentenced to death without the formality of a trial, and executed on 21 May 1650. After the Restoration, the Stuarts repaid their debt to the Grahams in some small measure by according the captain general's remains one of the grandest state funerals ever held in Scotland. The chiefs were raised to the highest rank of the peerage in 1707, when the fourth Marquess was created Duke of Montrose.

The third Duke of Montrose sat in Parliament, and was responsible for the Act which in 1782 repealed the prohibition on the wearing of Highland dress.

GRANT

ARMS
Gules, three antique crowns Or

CREST
A burning hill Proper

MOTTO
Craig Elachie (The rock of alarm)

On Compartment
Stand Fast

SUPPORTERS
*(on a compartment embellished with seedling Scots pines
fructed Proper)*
*Two savages, wreathed about the head and middle with
laurel, each bearing on his exterior shoulder a club
Proper*

STANDARD
*The Arms of Grant of that Ilk in the hoist and of two
tracts Gules and Or, upon which is depicted the Crest in
the first compartment, and the Badge in the second and
third compartments, along with the Slughorn 'Craig
Elachie' in letters Or upon two transverse bands Vert*

BADGE
*A sprig of Scots pine fructed Proper environed of the
circlet of a Baron's coronet*

PLANT BADGE
Seedling Scots pines fructed Proper

I t seems fairly certain that the ancestors of this clan would have come with the Normans to England, where the name is found in public documents soon after the Conquest. In 1229, Richard, Archbishop of Canterbury, is styled in Latin charters as 'Magnus', meaning 'great' or 'large' and in Norman or French translated as 'le grand'. The Grants first appear in Scotland in the middle of the thirteenth century when they acquired lands in Stratherrick through the marriage of one of the family with Mary, daughter of Sir John Bisset. From this union there came at least two sons, one of whom, Sir Laurence le Grand, became sheriff of Inverness. The Grants supported the interest of Bruce in the competition for the Scottish crown, and John and Randolph de Grant were taken prisoner at the Battle of Dunbar in 1296. They were later released, and around this time the family acquired the lands at Glenmoriston and Glen Urquhart which they still hold.

The victory of Robert the Bruce confirmed the Grants in their holdings in Strathspey, and whatever their southern origins they were now firmly established as Highland chiefs. The rich lands of the Spey valley provided the Grants with men and cattle, the key to power in the Highlands. Grant power was further consolidated when Sir John Grant married Maud, heiress of Glencairnie, a branch of the ancient princely dynasty of Strathearn. In 1493 the lands were erected into the free barony of Freuchie, and in 1536 Sir James Grant built a castle, called at one time Castle Freuchie, but renamed at the end of the seventeenth century as Castle Grant.

James Grant of Freuchie, called James the Bold, defended royal authority in the north during the insurrections there in the reign of James V. By way of reward, James granted Freuchie a charter exempting him from the jurisdiction of all royal courts except the Supreme Court in Edinburgh. When the

Reformation came to Scotland, the Grants soon became staunch adherents of the new doctrine, and they declared for the National Covenant in 1638. After the Battle of Inverlochy in 1645 they joined the Marquess of Montrose, and thereafter remained faithful to the royal cause. After the Restoration, the Laird of Grant was to have been rewarded with an earldom, but he died before the patent had been sealed. The Grants endeavoured to secure their territories by alliances with other clans, and they were particularly associated with the Macgregors. Indeed, some clan historians assert that the Grants, as well as the Macgregors, are part of the Siol Alpin, that is, those Highland clans whose chiefs descend from King Alpin, father of Kenneth Macalpin, first king of the Picts and Scots. After Clan Gregor was declared outlaw, a large number of Macgregors settled on Grant lands.

Grant

Standard

Ludovick Grant, the eighth Laird of Freuchie, was so rich and powerful that he was popularly called 'the Highland king'. He abandoned his family's past loyalties, and supported the government of Mary and William. They not only appointed Grant a colonel and sheriff of Inverness, but in 1694 the barony of Freuchie was granted the status of a regality, meaning that Grant was indeed almost king of his own lands, having power not only to punish most wrongdoers but also regulate commercial matters such as weights and measures. The regality was abolished along with all other heritable jurisdictions after the failure of the Jacobite rising of 1745. Although some individual members of the family were Jacobites, Clan Grant generally supported the house of Hanover during the risings of 1715 and 1745, so saving them from the relentless persecution inflicted on other Highland clans.

The Grants embarked upon an ambitious scheme to modernise their lands, even building a completely new town, Grantown-on-Spey, establishing mills and factories there. When, in 1811, Sir Lewis Grant of Grant inherited the Ogilvie earldoms of Seafield and Findlater, the chiefs gained a seat in the House of Lords. But the fifth Earl of Seafield and twenty-seventh chief of Clan Grant fell into a serious dispute with his brothers, which resulted in the Grant estates being disentailed. The consequence of this was that when the Seafield earldom, which can descend in the female line, parted company with chiefs of Clan Grant, the lands were lost. The chiefs, however, retained the independent peerage which had been created in 1817 under the title, 'Baron Strathspey of Strathspey.'

The Grants of Rothiemurchus, one of the principal branch families, still hold their lands around Aviemore, and other branches of the family also hold land in Strathspey. Castle Grant has sadly fallen into a state of neglect, but it is hoped that new owners will shortly restore it to its former glory.

GRIERSON

ARMS
Gules, on a fess Or between three fetterlocks Argent a mullet Azure

CREST
A fetterlock Argent

MOTTO
Hoc securior (More secure by this)

SUPPORTERS
(on a compartment embellished with bluebell flowers)
Two cats rampant guardant Sable each charged on the shoulder of a fetterlock Argent

STANDARD
Azure, a St Andrew's Cross Argent in the hoist and of two tracts Or and Gules, upon which is depicted three times the Crest upon a chapeau Azure furred Ermine, along with the Motto 'Hoc securior' in letters Argent upon two transverse bands Azure

PINSEL
Gules, displaying the Crest within a strap and buckle Proper with the Motto 'Hoc securior' in letters Or and within a circlet Or ensigned of a chapeau Azure furred Ermine the title 'Grierson of Lag' in letters Gules, and in the fly an Escrol Or with the Slogan 'Lag' in letters Azure along with a stem of bluebells Proper

PLANT BADGE
A stem of bluebells Proper

The personal name of Gregor is from the Greek word for 'vigilant' through its Latin translation, 'gregorius'. This was a popular name in the Middle Ages, particularly among the clergy. 'Grierson' is believed to be derived from this forename, and it has been conjectured that the family come from the same stock as the Macgregors. However, modern historians have refuted this, and no evidence exists to support the theory.

Gilbrid Macgregor received a charter from the Earl of March of lands at Dalgarnock in Dumfriesshire. Around 1408, the Griersons obtained the lands of Lag, which was to become the principal seat of the family. In a charter of 1420, Gilbert Grierson is described as 'armour bearer' to the Earl of Douglas. He married Janet, daughter of Sir Simon Glendinning, whose mother was Mary Douglas, daughter of the fourth Earl of Douglas and his wife, the Princess Margaret. This royal connection secured the early fortunes of the family and in 1460, Vedast Grierson of Lag built a strong tower on his lands. His son, Roger, obtained a royal charter in 1473 confirming his lands. He was killed at the Battle of Sauchieburn in 1488. The Lairds of Lag also followed James IV to the fateful field of Flodden in September 1513, where they met the same fate as much of the flower of Scottish chivalry. The Griersons declared for the infant James VI during the confrontation between his mother, Queen Mary, and the Protestant lords who held the child. Sir William Grierson of Lag was closely allied to the powerful Maxwell family, and he joined forces with them against the Johnstones of Annandale at the Battle of Dryfe Sands in 1593. He was knighted by James VI around 1608. His only son, Sir Robert, was succeeded by his cousin, also Robert, who was to become the first Baronet of Lag. Throughout the south and west of Scotland it was this Laird of Lag that for a time made the name of Grierson synonymous with terror and death, in his fierce persecution of the Covenanters during the reign of James VII. He was created a baronet of Nova Scotia in March 1685 and in the same year he surprised an illegal Covenanter service at Kirkconnell. In the struggle that ensued, most of the worshippers were killed and Lag was said to have refused to give them a decent burial. Whether the story was true or not, it was quickly spread, earning Grierson his feared reputation. One of the Covenanter martyrs was John Bell of Whiteside whose stepfather was Viscount Kenmure. Lord Kenmure was with Graham of Claverhouse in Kirkcudbright when they encountered Sir Robert and a quarrel broke out. Kenmure drew his sword and was only dissuaded from fighting a duel by the intervention of Claverhouse. He made a splendid alliance when he married Lady Henrietta Douglas, sister of the Duke of Queensberry. Surprisingly, the Griersons did not support the overthrow of James VII, and considered William and Mary to be usurpers. Sir Robert Grierson was arrested in 1689 and held a prisoner for some months until a substantial cash surety was paid. He was imprisoned on two subsequent occasions, being at one point accused of a conspiracy to counterfeit money. He was cleared of all allegations, but his ordeal had broken his health and he died in 1736. He has secured a measure of immortality, as the writer Sir Walter Scott drew on his life in the novel, *Red Gauntlet*. His eldest son, William, second Baronet, died only four years later without an heir, and his brother, Sir Gilbert, succeeded to the title. From him descended Colonel William Grierson of Bardennoch, one of the intimate circle of friends of Sir Walter Scott. His eldest son, Thomas Grierson, was a soldier who distinguished himself at the siege of Delhi in 1857,

but died later that year from wounds he had received. The eighth Baronet, Sir Alexander Grierson of Lag, was also a regular soldier, being commissioned into the 78th Ross-shire Highlanders. Sir Robert Grierson of Lag, tenth Baronet, served in the King's Own Scottish Borderers during the First World War. By that time a great portion of the Grierson lands had been lost, although the ruins of the Tower of Lag still stand to this day.

Sir George Abraham Grierson was a distinguished linguist who devoted much of his life to the study of the dialects of the Indian sub-continent. He studied mathematics at Trinity College, Dublin, where he discovered his ability to assimilate foreign languages and won prizes in Sanskrit and Hindi. He used this talent to obtain a government post in Bengal in 1873. He published two important works, *Seven Grammars of the Bihari Language* (1883) and *Bihar Peasant Life* (1885). In 1898, he began his life work, the *Linguistic Survey of India*, which ran to over eight thousand pages and contained information on over 364 languages and dialects. He was knighted in 1912.

Communication skills were also the first love of Dr John Grierson, born in Kilmadock near Stirling in 1898, and widely regarded as the father of the British documentary film movement. He was educated at the Universities of Glasgow and Chicago, making his first film in 1929, *Drifters*, a study of the lives of North Sea fishermen. He assisted in setting up the National Film Board of Canada in 1939 and on the outbreak of war made public information films for the government. He was a director of UNESCO and then film controller for the British Central Office of Information until 1950 when he embarked upon a career in television. He died in 1972. Other important branch families include the Griersons of Chapell, and of Dalgoner.

GUTHRIE

The lands known as Guthrie lie in Angus, and the family who took this as their name is one of the oldest in that county. The origin of the name is not known. There is a fable that the lands were named by an early Scots king after a fisherman 'gut three' fish to serve to his hungry Monarch. King William the Lion granted the lands of Gutherin to the Abbey of Arbroath around 1178. The family, who were royal falconers, subsequently purchased these lands. In 1299 the Laird of Guthrie was sent to France to invite Sir William Wallace to return to Scotland. The embassy was successful, and Guthrie landed with Wallace at Montrose.

The early family charters have been lost, but it seems certain that the family obtained the Barony of Guthrie by charter from David II. Alexander Guthrie of Guthrie witnessed a charter by Alexander Seaton, the lord of Gordon, to Lord Keith, in August 1442. In 1446 he acquired the lands of Kincaldrum near Forfar and became baillie of Forfar. Sir David Guthrie of Guthrie was armour bearer to the king and captain of the guard, later being appointed Lord Treasurer of Scotland in 1461. In 1468 he obtained a charter under the great seal to build a castle at Guthrie, and this remained the residence of the chiefs until very recently. In 1473 he was appointed Lord Chief Justice of Scotland. He greatly increased the family estates, and founded a collegiate church at Guthrie, the dedication of which was confirmed in a Papal Bull of 1479. His eldest son, Sir Alexander Guthrie, fell at Flodden in September 1513. The Guthries were quick to support the reformed religion in Scotland, and in 1567 signed a bond upholding the authority of the infant King James VI against that of his mother, Queen Mary. At this time the Lairds of Guthrie were feuding with their neighbours, the Gardynes, and Alexander Guthrie was assassinated at Inverpeffer. The Guthries retaliated in like manner, ultimately being saved from the consequences of their action by a royal pardon granted in 1618. Alexander Guthrie was one of the twenty-five gentlemen pensioners and an early ceremonial bodyguard commanded 'to attend the King's Majesty at all times in his riding and passing to the fields'.

The estate then passed through cousins until, in 1636, John Guthrie, Bishop of Moray, became the eleventh chief. He had been ordained at Perth, and had become minister of St Giles in Edinburgh in 1621. In 1623 he was consecrated Bishop of Moray and took up residence at Spynie Castle, the palace of the bishopric. The king's attempts to alter the style of worship in the Scottish Church eventually led to the outbreak of open hostilities, and in 1640 the bishop was forced to surrender his castle to forces under Colonel Monroe. He retired to his own estates of Guthrie, where he died in June 1643. His third son, Andrew Guthrie, fought with the great Montrose and was taken prisoner at the Battle of Philiphaugh. He was sentenced to death and beheaded by the Scottish guillotine, 'the maiden', at St Andrews in January 1646. His daughter, Bethia, married her kinsman, Francis Guthrie of Gagie, and thus the title and estates remained in the Guthrie family. James Guthrie, a scion of the chiefly house, was a Covenanter minister who became one of the movement's early martyrs. Ordained the minister of Lauder in 1638, he moved to Stirling in 1649, where he preached openly against the king's religious policies. He was in due course summoned before the Church of Scotland's General Assembly, whose authority he challenged, and for this was stripped of his office. He continued, however, to preach with great zeal, until he was arrested in February

Guthrie

1661. The trial was a farce and its outcome predetermined: James Guthrie was sentenced to death and was executed in June 1661.

The Guthries of Halkerton were another branch of this family who held their barony by right of the office of royal falconers in Angus. The title and office were only relinquished in 1747 under the terms of the Heritable Jurisdictions Act of that year. John Douglas Guthrie of Guthrie served in the cavalry during the Egyptian campaign of 1882 and married Mary, daughter of Duncan Davidson of Tulloch. Lieutenant Colonel Ivan Guthrie of Guthrie, the last chief to live at Guthrie Castle, was born in 1886. A distinguished soldier, he commanded the 4th Battalion the Black Watch and was awarded the Military Cross. The present chief resides in England and Guthrie Castle has been sold.

HAIG

ARMS
*Azure, a saltire between two mullets in chief and in base,
a decrescent and an increscent in fess Argent*

CREST
A rock Proper

MOTTO
Tyde what may

SUPPORTERS
*Dexter, a bay horse caparisoned, thereon mounted a
private of the Seventh (Queen's Own) Hussars, habited,
armed and accoutred Proper;
sinister, a bay horse caparisoned, thereon mounted a
lancer of the Seventeenth (The Duke of Cambridge's
Own) Lancers, habited armed and accoutred Proper*

'Tyde what may, what'er betyde, Haig shall be Haig of Bemersyde'. That was the prophecy made in the thirteenth century by the poet, Thomas the Rhymer. For eight hundred years Bemersyde has been continuously in the possession of the Haigs, from Petrus de Haga, founder of the family to the present chief, the thirtieth Laird and second Earl Haig. Nisbet asserted that the family was of Pictish or early British extraction, but the name de Haga is evidently Norman. Petrus de Haga, proprietor of the lands and barony of Bemersyde, appears as a witness to a charter of Richard de Morville, Constable of Scotland from 1162 to 1188, to the Monastery of Dryburgh. The fact that Petrus is mentioned in several charters as 'Dominus de Bemersyde' (Master of Bemersyde) is evidence that this family were considerable magnates even at that time.

de Haga was one of the noblemen charged by Alexander II with the apprehension of John de Bisset for the murder of the Earl of Athol at Haddington in 1242. The Barons of Bemersyde appear swearing fealty to Edward I of England in the Ragman Roll of 1296, but they wholeheartedly joined the struggle for Scottish independence and fought with Sir William Wallace at the Battle of Stirling in 1297. The sixth Laird followed the banner of Robert the Bruce to the Battle of Bannockburn, although he was only seventeen years of age at the time. He was killed at the Battle of Halidon Hill in 1333. Gilbert Haig was one of the commanders of the Scots host who defeated the Earl of Northumberland at Sark in 1449. He also opposed the rising power of the Douglas family. His son, James, was an adherent of James III and when that monarch's reign came abruptly to an end with his murder in 1488, Haig was forced into hiding until he could make peace with the young James IV.

William Haig of Bemersyde fell at Flodden in 1513. Robert, fourteenth Laird, avenged his father's death when, at Ancrum Moor in 1544, he captured Lord Evers, the English commander, and carried him in a wounded condition to Bemersyde where he died a few days later. Haig buried him in Melrose Abbey.

The Haigs became embroiled in the religious and political turmoil of the seventeenth century, enduring persecution for their own religious beliefs. William Haig, the nineteenth Laird, held the office of King's Solicitor for Scotland during the reigns of James VI and Charles I. Anthony Haig, the twenty-first Laird, was a member of the Society of Friends, or Quakers, and suffered a long period of imprisonment during the persecution of that sect. Four sons of the chief were killed fighting in the service of the king of Bohemia between 1629 and 1630.

In the nineteenth century, it seemed as if the prophecy of Thomas the Rhymer would come to nothing, as the future of the direct line of the Haigs then lay in the hands of three unmarried daughters, Barbara, Mary and Sophia. Before their deaths, they executed a deed transferring the succession to their cousin, Colonel Arthur Balfour Haig, of the Clackmannan branch of the family and who was descended from the second son of the seventeenth Laird of Bemersyde. He accordingly became twenty-eighth Laird and chief.

The father of the present chief was the first Earl Haig, commander-in-chief of the British Expeditionary Forces in France from 1915 to 1919. On leaving Oxford University, George Haig underwent his officer training and entered the 7th Hussars in 1885. He served in the Nile expedition of 1898 and fought at the Battle of Khartoum. He saw service throughout the Boer Wars where he served with distinction and was decorated for bravery. During the First World War, Haig was responsible for the policy of attrition followed by the British forces on the Western Front, a policy which made little real strategic impact until 1917 and has been the subject of great controversy since. He successfully halted

Haig

the German offensive by July 1918 and launched the Allied counter attack which ended the war four months later. He was created Earl Haig, Viscount Dawick and Baron Haig of Bemersyde on 29 September 1919. He was a Knight of the Thistle, a Member of the Order of Merit and received many other British knighthoods and foreign orders. Bemersyde was purchased from Arthur Balfour Haig in 1921 with money contributed by the people of the British Empire and presented to Lord Haig in recognition of the services he had rendered in the cause of freedom.

The Tower of Bemersyde was originally built in 1535, when its principal purpose was defence. It was improved in 1690, when large windows and fireplaces were introduced. The house was extended in the eighteenth and nineteenth centuries. In 1960 further alterations were carried out by the present chief to improve the overall design and proportions of the house. The second Earl Haig, who was page of honour to George VI at his coronation in 1937, is a distinguished artist and an Associate of the Royal Scottish Academy.

HALDANE

ARMS
*Quarterly, 1st & 4th, Argent, a saltire engrailed Sable;
2nd, Argent, a saltire between four roses Gules;
3rd, Or, a bend chequy Sable and Argent*

CREST
An eagle's head erased Or

MOTTO
Suffer

SUPPORTERS
Two eagles Proper

William the Lion bestowed the manor of Hauden on Bernard, son of Brien, between 1165 and 1171. A cadet of this house is believed to have settled in Strathearn, where he acquired lands which were later incorporated into the barony of Gleneagles, where the chiefs still reside today. The name has nothing to do with the noble birds whose feathers adorn the bonnets of chiefs; rather, it is derived from the Gaelic *eaglais*, meaning a church. The family charters include one from William the Lion to Roger de Hauden of the lands of Frandie near Gleneagles. Aylmer de Haldane appears in the Ragman Roll among the Scots barons swearing fealty to Edward I of England in 1296. He soon, however, allied his fortunes with those of Robert the Bruce in the struggle for Scottish independence. Sir Simon de Haldane received a charter of part of the lands of Bardrill in Strathearn from Sir John de Logy in 1312. He married Matilda de Arnot, and by this marriage he obtained extensive lands within the ancient earldom of Lennox. Sir John Haldane, third of Gleneagles, was Master of the Household under James III, sheriff principal of Edinburgh, and Lord Justice General of Scotland beyond the Forth. He resigned his lands in Perthshire, Stirlingshire and Fife to the Crown in 1482, and received a charter erecting them into the free barony of Gleneagles in 1482. Through his marriage to Agnes, daughter of Murdoch Menteith of Rusky, he claimed the earldom of Lennox. He began a lengthy lawsuit with John Stewart, Lord Darnley, which was finally concluded by a settlement whereby Lord Darnley retained the title to the earldom, and Gleneagles received as compensation one quarter of the lands. Sir James Haldane, fourth of Gleneagles, was appointed Governor of Dunbar Castle in 1505. In 1508 his son, the fifth of Gleneagles, obtained a charter erecting all his lands in Lennox and in Perthshire not already forming part of the land of Gleneagles into the barony of Haldane, with its chief seat at Rusky House. He was killed, along with many other Scottish nobles, at Flodden in 1513.

The Haldanes soon embraced the Reformation, and played a prominent part in the political upheavals which followed the overthrow of Mary, Queen of Scots. In 1585 they were part of the force which laid siege to Stirling Castle in an attempt to persuade the king to rescind the sentence of banishment on the Earl of Angus and other unruly Protestant nobles. James Haldane, brother of the Laird of Gleneagles, led an attack on the west port of the castle and engaged Sir William Stewart, colonel of the Royal Guard, driving him back. On the point of victory, however, Haldane was shot by Colonel Stewart's servant.

Sir John Haldane, the eleventh Laird, was a professional soldier who, with his brother, James, fought for Henry, Prince of Orange, in the Netherlands. He returned to Scotland and was knighted by Charles I in 1633. He represented Perth in Parliament, and was fervent in his support of the National Covenant. He heavily burdened his estates with debt by raising men and supplies. He is credited with the building of the present House of Gleneagles. He fought with the royalist army, leading his regiment against the forces of Parliament at the Battle of Dunbar in 1650. The Scots army, although numerically superior, was heavily defeated and Haldane was killed.

The sixteenth Laird, Patrick Haldane, had a remarkable career. He was Professor of Greek at the University of St Andrews and entered the University of Leyden in 1711. He turned to the law, and rose to be Solicitor General for Scotland in 1746. He was nominated to the Supreme Court Bench, but his appointment was opposed on the grounds that the Crown did not have the right to appoint a judge without the consent of the Court itself. The matter was taken to the House of Lords, which ruled in favour of the Crown. However, Patrick Haldane did not take up his seat on the Bench, having received another government appointment in the meantime. It was said that the objection, although raised on technical grounds, was in truth motivated by Haldane's political enemies. Patrick's son, General George Haldane, a professional soldier who fought at Dettingen in 1743 and Fontenoy in 1745, served under the Duke of Cumberland against the Jacobites in the campaign of the 'Young Pretender' between 1745 and 1746.

In 1820 the estates passed to the cousin of the eighteenth Haldane of Gleneagles, Admiral Adam Duncan, Viscount Duncan of Camperdown. One of Britain's most celebrated naval heroes, he took his title from his most renowned victory, at the Battle of Camperdown in 1797. The admiral's son, who, in 1831, was raised to the title of Earl of Camperdown, assumed the additional surname of Haldane. In 1918 the fourth Earl of Camperdown resigned his rights in the estate of Gleneagles in favour of his kinsman, James Chinnery-Haldane, eldest son of the Bishop of Argyll. His sons, Alexander, who succeeded as chief, and Brodrick became well-known in Scottish society. Brodrick is a renowned portrait photographer who still lives in Edinburgh. Alexander died in 1994 and the chiefship and estates passed to his nephew, Martin. The Haldanes also held, at one time, Airthrey Castle, which now forms the centre of the campus of Stirling University.

HAMILTON

It is believed that this family descends from a Norman, Walter Fitz Gilbert of Hambledon, who appears in a charter to the Monastery of Paisley around 1294. His lands appear to have been in Renfrewshire, but for his belated support of Robert the Bruce, the king rewarded him with lands in Lanarkshire and the Lothians. These included the lands of Cadzow, later to become the town of Hamilton.

Walter's son, David, fought for David II in 1346 at the Battle of Neville's Cross, where he was captured and held prisoner until a substantial ransom was paid. James, first Lord Hamilton, married Princess Mary, daughter of James III, in 1474. The issue of this marriage were clearly in line of succession to the throne, and Princess Mary's son was created Earl of Arran. The family extended the simple Castle of Brodick on the island of Arran, and in the nineteenth century the chiefs developed it into a splendid stately home. The second Earl of Arran was the heir to the throne of both James IV and Mary, Queen of Scots. He was appointed Regent of Scotland while the queen was still a child, and to secure his claim to the throne he proposed to marry his son to her. In the end the match did not take place, and Mary married the heir to the French throne. However, Arran had figured prominently in the marriage negotiations with France and, as a reward, he was created Duke of Chatelherault in the French peerage in 1548. When Mary's marriage to the Dauphin of France ended with his death, the Hamilton hopes of a royal match were again rekindled. He was sent into exile for five years in 1561 when he openly opposed Mary's marriage to Lord Darnley, but on his return he endeavoured to save the ill-fated queen, who stayed at Cadzow after her escape from Lochleven.

The fourth Earl of Arran and third Duke of Chatelherault became Chancellor of Scotland and keeper of both the strategic

Castles of Edinburgh and Stirling. In 1599 he was advanced to the rank of Marquess. His brother, Claud, was created Lord Paisley in 1587, and later Lord Abercorn. This branch of the family also prospered, Abercorn being translated into an earldom and ultimately a dukedom in 1868. The Dukes of Abercorn now have their seat in Ulster in the splendid house of Baronscourt.

The third Marquess was a staunch supporter of Charles I, who rewarded him in 1643 with a Scottish dukedom, making Hamilton the premier peer of Scotland. Hamilton led an army into England after the Scots had handed Charles over to Parliament, but strategic errors and the superiority of the English army resulted in his defeat at Preston in 1648. He was beheaded at Whitehall in 1649 shortly before the king. His brother, the second Duke, was a brave but less than competent soldier who was killed at the Battle of Worcester in 1651.

The title passed to Anne, the daughter of the first Duke. A woman of great intellect and determination, she inherited the title and estates heavily burdened by debts, a situation made worse by a legal dispute with her kinsman, the Earl of Abercorn, who challenged her right to succeed. She had married William Douglas, Earl of Selkirk, and set out to re-establish the family seat, laying the foundations for the building of a great palace. Her son, the fourth Duke, must have inherited some of the fire and energy of his mother, as he met his death in a duel in London in 1712. The affair was something of a scandal, as the parties' seconds also joined in, and after Hamilton killed his opponent, Lord Mohun, one McCartney promptly killed the duke. The

Hamilton

fifth and sixth Dukes extended the palace and built the splendid hunting lodge named Chatelherault, now part of a public park.

Alexander, the tenth Duke, completed the enlargement of Hamilton Palace and adorned it with spectacular works of art collected from all over the world. He was nicknamed 'Il Magnifico' and lived in truly regal style. He crowned his royal ambitions by marrying his son, William, to Princess Marie of Baden, a cousin of Napoleon III. The fourteenth Duke inherited his family's sense of adventure and in 1933 piloted the first aeroplane to fly over Everest. The fifteenth Duke is an engineer, a former RAF test pilot and an author. Hamilton Palace was demolished because of mining subsidence and the seat is now Lennoxlove, near Haddington.

HANNAY

The Hannays hail from the ancient princedom of Galloway. The original spelling of the name appears to have been 'Ahannay', and although its origin is uncertain, it may derive from the Gaelic 'O'Hannaidh', or 'Ap Shenaeigh'.

Gilbert de Hannethe appears on the Ragman Roll among the Scottish Barons submitting to Edward I of England in 1296. This may be the same Gilbert who acquired the lands of Sorbie. The Hannays were suspicious of the ambitions of the Bruces, and supported the claim of John Balliol who, through his mother, Lady Devorgilla, was descended from the Celtic Princes of Galloway. In the fifteenth and sixteenth centuries they extended their influence over much of the surrounding countryside, building a tower on their lands at Sorbie around 1550. The tower was the seat of the chief family of this name until the seventeenth century, when it fell into disrepair after the family were outlawed. In 1965 the tower was presented to a clan trust, and a maintenance scheme was put in hand.

There were many distinguished scions of the chiefly house, including Patrick Hannay, the distinguished soldier and poet whose literature, once highly regarded, is now almost forgotten. The grandson of Donald Hannay of Sorbie, he entered the service of Queen Elizabeth of Bohemia, the daughter of James VI and sister of Charles I, who became his patron. In 1619, Hannay published two eulogies on the death of Queen Anne, wife of James VI, and on his own death many eulogies were published. The best of these expresses the high regard with which Patrick and his kin were held:

> Hannay thy worth betrays well whence thou'rt sprung and that that honour'd name thou dost not wrong;
> As if from Sorbie's stock no branch could sprout but should with ripening bear golden fruit.

Thy Ancestors were ever worthy found
else Galdus' grave had grac'd no Hannay
ground.
Thy father's father Donald well was
knowne to the English by his sword, but
thou art showne by pen (times changing)
Hannays are active in acts of worth be't
peace or war.
Go on in virtue, aftertimes will tell,
none but a Hannay could have done so
well.

(Galdus was a resistance leader against the
Romans.)

Also from the house of Sorbie came James
Hannay, the Dean of St Giles' in Edinburgh,
who has passed into legend as the minister
who attempted to read the new liturgy in St
Giles' in July 1637. It was at Dean Hannay's
head that Jenny Geddes flung her stool crying,
'Thou false thief, dost thou say Mass at my
lug?' A full scale riot ensued, which ultimately
had to be suppressed by the town guard. In
1630, Sir Robert Hannay of Mochrum was created a Baronet of Nova Scotia. Other branches
descended from Sorbie include the Hannays of
Grennan, Knock, Garrie and Kingsmuir. At the
beginning of the seventeenth century the
Hannays of Sorbie became locked in a deadly
feud with the Murrays of Broughton, which
ended in the Hannays' being outlawed and
ruined. The lands and tower of Sorbie were
lost around 1640. One consequence of the
family's being outlawed was the emigration of
large numbers of Hannays to Ulster, where the
name is still found widely in Counties Antrim,
Down and Armagh. The Hannays of Newry are
reckoned to be the senior branch of the emi-
grant families.

In 1582, Alexander Hannay, a younger
son of Sorbie, purchased the lands of Kirkdale
in the Stewartry of Kirkcudbright. His son,

Hannay

John Hannay of Kirkdale, inherited the estate
and established the line which is now recognised by the Lord Lyon as chief of the name.
Alexander Hannay, a younger son of Kirkdale,
was a professional soldier who served in India,
where he rose to the rank of colonel. His
eldest brother, Sir Samuel Hannay of Kirkdale,
succeeded to the title and estates of his kinsman, Sir Robert Hannay of Mochrum, Baronet.
The next baronet, Sir Samuel Hannay, entered
the service of the Hapsburg Emperors, and
prospered sufficiently to build for himself a
grand mansion on his family lands. The house
is said to have provided the inspiration for Sir
Walter Scott's novel, *Guy Mannering*. Sir
Samuel died in 1841 and the baronetcy
became dormant. The estate of Kirkdale and
the representation of the family passed to Sir
Samuel's sister, Mary, and on her death in
1850 to her nephew, William Rainsford
Hannay. The present chief, who was recognised as Hannay of Kirkdale and of that Ilk in
1983, is his descendent.

HAY

This family descend from a member of
the de La Haye, powerful Norman
princes who followed William the
Conqueror to England in 1066. (William de
La Haye, cup bearer to Malcolm IV, was
claimed as ancestor by Sir William Hay of
Errol when he was raised to the peerage as
Earl of Errol in 1453.) The lands of Errol in
Perthshire were confirmed to William de Haya
by charter around 1172. The fortunes of the
family were secured when Sir Gilbert Hay
became one of the faithful comrades-in-arms
of Robert the Bruce, not only at the glory of
Bannockburn, but sharing the hardships of the
earlier campaigns. Gilbert was rewarded with
the lands of Slains in Aberdeenshire, but more
importantly with the office of Lord High
Constable of Scotland. Hay was first created
constable in 1309 and then, by charter dated
12 November 1314, the title was made hereditary. This dignity, which is still enjoyed by the
present chief, gives the holder precedence in
Scotland before every other hereditary honour,
saving only the royal family itself. The Lord
High Constable was responsible for the personal safety of the monarch, and was sword
bearer at coronations. He maintained a ceremonial royal guard, called the Durward of
Partisans, and has a theoretical jurisdiction
over persons indicted for riot or crimes of
bloodshed near the royal person.

Sir Thomas Hay, seventh Baron of Erroll,
brought royal blood into the family when he
married Elizabeth, daughter of Robert II. The
family were also descended from Celtic Kings,
through the marriages of David de La Hay to
Ethna, daughter of the Earl of Strathearn, and
of Gilbert, third Baron of Erroll, to Idoine,
daughter of the Earl of Buchan. Another Sir
Gilbert Hay fought for the cause of Joan of Arc
and attended the coronation of Charles VII of
France at Rheims. From this knight errant
descend the Hays of Delgatie, whose castle
near Turriff is now restored as the Clan

Centre. Sir William Hay of Delgatie served with Montrose as chief of staff during his campaign on behalf of Charles I. On the defeat of the royalist party, he was captured and imprisoned, finally being executed in 1650. Delgatie, having shared the fate of his commander, was accorded a state funeral after the Restoration, and is buried in St Giles' in Edinburgh.

The Hays did not embrace the Reformation, but in consort with other Catholic nobles, including the Gordons and the Red Douglases, negotiated with Philip II of Spain in the hope of bringing about an alliance. A campaign against the Protestant nobles, led by Argyll in 1594, ultimately led to James VI's declaring both Erroll and Huntly rebels, and they went into exile. Slains Castle was taken and blown up under the personal supervision of the king, and it has remained a ruin ever since.

Hay

Standard

A brief period of exile convinced Erroll of the wisdom of converting to the reformed religion, and he returned to Scotland and to royal favour. The Hays remained loyal to the Stuarts, and came out in both the Jacobite risings of 1715 and 1745. The thirteenth Earl received the Order of the Thistle from James VIII, the 'Old Pretender'. He was succeeded by his sister, Mary, who revelled in Jacobite intrigue, using the ruins of Slains Castle as a meeting point for Jacobite agents. She personally called out the Hays to fight for Bonnie Prince Charlie. On her death in 1758 the title passed to her great nephew, James Boyd, whose father, the Jacobite Earl of Kilmarnock, had been beheaded for treason in 1746. The Kilmarnock title had been forfeit for treason and James, in addition to the earldom of Erroll, assumed the surname of Hay and the chiefship of the clan.

The eighteenth Earl was Lord High Constable during George IV's visit to Scotland in 1822, and he lavished a fortune on the affair, which nearly ruined him. The nineteenth Earl, William Hay, fought in the Crimea where he was wounded at the Battle of Alma in 1854. He was passionately concerned for the welfare of his people, and founded the fishing village of Port Erroll. He provided the hard-pressed fishermen with good housing at a low rent, and dealt generously with the many widows that this hazardous calling produced. His son, Major General Charles Hay, twentieth Earl, saw action in the Boer War and commanded the Household Cavalry and was lord-in-waiting to Edward VII.

Other branches of the family rose to prominence, including the Hays of Yester, who were to become the Marquesses of Tweeddale. They built the great Adam mansion of Yester near Gifford in East Lothian. In 1950 Diana, Countess of Erroll, founded the Clan Hay Society, which now has branches throughout the world. She was married to the Scottish herald, Sir Iain Moncreiffe of that Ilk Bt, and their son is the present chief.

HENDERSON

here are three origins of this name from opposite ends of the kingdom. The Hendersons in the Borders seem simply to be the 'sons of Henry', and the name is often found in the variant of Henryson. They were not a significant power in the Borders, although they were still classed as a riding clan. William Henderson was chamberlain of Lochmaben Castle around 1374. He received from the king of England a pension when he was driven from his lands in the lordship of Lochmaben, and is believed to have died around 1395. From Dumfriesshire the family spread across into Liddesdale, but they do not appear in the list of border clans named by Parliament in 1594 in its attempts to suppress the border reivers.

From the Dumfriesshire family descended James Henderson, who became Lord Advocate around 1494 and was later appointed to the Bench. He acquired the lands of Fordell in Fife and there erected a fine fortified mansion. Fordell was to become the designation of the Lowland chiefs, and it is from this family that the present chief descends. The castle is no longer in Henderson hands, but it was restored this century by the former Solicitor General for Scotland, Sir Nicholas Fairbairn, QC. After the Hendersons left Fordell Castle at the end of the nineteenth century, many fine family portraits found their way into the collection of the National Portrait Gallery of Scotland.

Perhaps the most prominent of the Hendersons of Fordell was Alexander Henderson, who was born around 1583. He was educated at the University of St Andrews where he became a Master of Arts and, sometime before 1611, a Professor of Philosophy. He later became minister of the parish of Leuchars. He was violently opposed to Charles I's attempts to reform the Church of Scotland, and especially to the introduction of the new prayer book in 1637. He travelled to

Edinburgh to present a petition to the Privy Council, denouncing the new prayer book and stating that it had not received the sanction of either the General Assembly of the Church or of Parliament. Henderson, along with Johnston of Warriston, drafted the National Covenant which was first sworn and subscribed in Greyfriars Churchyard in Edinburgh in February 1638. Thousands of persons of all classes clamoured to subscribe. When the General Assembly met in Glasgow in 1638 they unanimously elected Henderson as moderator. He was in the forefront of church affairs and therefore of politics throughout the troubled reign of Charles I, and was also responsible for drafting the Solemn League and Covenant in 1643. When the king surrendered himself to the protection of the Scottish army in 1646, it was for Henderson that he sent to discuss a reconciliation with his disaffected subjects. Henderson met the king in an attempt to persuade him to accede to the Church's demands. He failed, and the attempt damaged his own health to such an extent that he died in August 1646. He is buried in Greyfriars Churchyard, the scene of his greatest triumph and site of a monument to his memory.

Thomas Henderson of Dundee, who began his career as a lawyer, became one of Scotland's greatest astronomers in the nineteenth century, and was appointed the first Astronomer Royal for Scotland.

The Hendersons in the north of the country lived in Glencoe, and took the English version of their name from the Gaelic Maceanruig, claiming descent from a semi-legendary Pictish prince, Eanruig Mor Mac Righ Neachtain, or 'big Henry son of King Neachtain'. Neachtain is said to have reigned from 700 to 724 and to have built the Pictish stronghold of Abernethy. It is not known when the sons of Henry first came to Glencoe, but it appears that their individual identity was lost when the last of their chiefs, Dugall Maceanruig, produced an heiress who, accord-

Henderson

ing to tradition, had a son, Ian Fraoch, by her lover, Angus Og of Islay. His son, called Iain Abrach, took as his patronymic MacIain, which was thereafter to designate the Macdonald chiefs of Glencoe. The Hendersons were not forgotten, however, and they traditionally formed the chief's bodyguard. When the house of MacIain of Glencoe was attacked by government troops in 1692 in what was later to be termed the Massacre of Glencoe, the chief's piper and personal attendant, big Henderson of the chanters, a man almost 6 feet, 7 inches in height and of prodigious strength, was among those killed.

In the far north the name Henderson arises again, but from a quite different source. Hendry, one of the younger sons of a fifteenth-century chief of Clan Gunn, hereditary crowners, or coroners, of Caithness, formed his own gilfine, or sept, which took his name. There is no obvious connection between the Caithness Hendersons or Mackendricks with either the Glencoe or Borders families.

The present chief, who established his rights before the Lyon Court, is a physician and lives in Australia.

HOME

A Borders family of immense power, the Homes are said to have been the descendents of the Saxon Princes of Northumberland through Cospatrick, Earl of Dunbar. Prior to 1266, William de Home appears in land grants to the Monastery at Coldstream. Geoffrey de Home submitted to Edward I of England in 1296. His son, Sir Thomas, married the heiress to the Pepdie estate of Dunglass.

Sir Alexander Home of Dunglass was captured at the Battle of Homildon in 1402. He later followed the Earl of Douglas to France, where he was killed in battle in 1424. He left three sons, from whom most of the principal branches of the family were to descend. His eldest grandson was created a Lord of Parliament, taking the title 'Lord Home' in 1473. He joined in the rebellion against James III, which ended in the death of the king. His son, the second Lord Home, became joint administrator of the Lothians and Berwickshire during the minority of James IV, and Great Chamberlain of Scotland in 1488. Lord Home and his followers formed part of the army levied by James IV for his invasion of England in 1513. At Flodden, Lord Home led the vanguard of Scots knights, and although he personally escaped the slaughter, many of his family and supporters were not so fortunate. Home was appointed one of the counsellors to the Queen Regent. When the regency was transferred to the Duke of Albany, the fortunes of the Homes suffered. Lord Home was accused of conspiring with the English and was arrested for treason, and he and his brother were executed in October 1516, after which their heads were displayed on the Tolbooth of Edinburgh. The title and estates were, however, restored to another brother, George Home, who on several occasions led his Border spearmen against the English. On the eve of the Battle of Pinkie in 1547 he was thrown from his horse and died of the injuries that he sustained. The Home lands were occupied by the English invaders and it fell to Lord Home's son, Alexander, the fifth Lord, to retake them in 1549. He supported the Reformation and sat in the Parliament which passed the Protestant Confession of Faith in 1560.

The politics of the reign of Mary, Queen of Scots were complex, and the Homes, along with many others, shifted their allegiance more than once. Lord Home, supported the marriage of Mary to Bothwell, but later led his men against the queen at the Battle of Langside. Fortunes shifted again, and in 1573 he was arrested and later convicted of treason against the young James VI. He was only released from Edinburgh Castle when his health had failed and he died a few days later. Despite his father's chequered political history, Alexander, the sixth Lord Home, was unswerving in his devotion to James VI, and was a royal favourite throughout his life. In 1603, when James travelled to England to take possession of his new kingdom, he stopped at Dunglass, and Lord Home then accompanied him to London. In March 1605 he was raised to the title of Earl of Home.

The third Earl was a staunch supporter of Charles I, and in 1648 was colonel of the Berwickshire Regiment of Foot. When Cromwell invaded Scotland in 1650 he made particular point of seizing Home's castle, which was garrisoned by Parliament's troops.

The Home allegiances were again inconstant during the Jacobite risings. The seventh Earl was imprisoned in Edinburgh Castle during the rising of 1715, and his brother, James Home of Ayton, had his estates confiscated for his part in the rebellion. When the 'Young Pretender' asserted his father's claim in 1745, the eighth Earl joined the government forces under Sir John Cope at Dunbar and later fought at the Battle of Preston. He rose to the rank of Lieutenant General and was appointed

Home

Governor of Gibraltar where he died in 1761.

Henry Home was a distinguished eighteenth-century lawyer who, on being elevated to the Supreme Court Bench in 1752, took the title of 'Lord Kames' after his family estate in Berwickshire. He was a noted author, and published several important works on Scots Law which are still highly regarded to this day. David Hume, born in 1711, has become perhaps the most highly regarded British philosopher of the eighteenth century.

The family came to public prominence in the twentieth century, when the fourteenth Earl disclaimed his hereditary peerage to become Prime Minister of the United Kingdom as Sir Alec Douglas Home. The title is only disclaimed for his lifetime, and may be revived by his heirs. His brother, William Douglas Home, is a distinguished author and playwright. The family seat is the splendid border estate of the Hirsel, from which the former Prime Minister named the life peerage bestowed upon him for service to the nation, as Lord Home of the Hirsel.

HOPE

ARMS
Azure, a chevron Or between three bezants

CREST
*A broken terrestrial globe surmounted by a rainbow
issuing out of a cloud at each end all Proper*

MOTTO
At spes infracta (But hope is unbroken)

SUPPORTERS
*Two female figures representing Hope in vestments Vert,
on their heads garlands of flowers, each resting her
exterior hand on an anchor all Proper*

T his name may be of native Scots origin, deriving from the Borders family of Hop or Hoip. John de Hop of Peeblesshire and Adam le Hoip both appear on the Ragman Roll of Scottish nobles submitting to Edward I of England in 1296. Nisbet suggests that another derivation of the name may be from the family de H'oublons of Picardy. The French 'oublon' means 'hop', and when translated into English it became Hope. The immediate ancestor of the principal line, John de Hope, is said to have come to Scotland from France as part of the retinue of Magdalen, first wife of James V, in 1537. He married and settled in Edinburgh, where he prospered and had a son, Edward, who was one of the commissioners for Edinburgh to the first General Assembly of the Church of Scotland in 1560. His grandson, Sir Thomas Hope, was appointed Lord Advocate by Charles I. He acquired the estate of Craighall in the parish of Ceres in Fife, which thereafter was the principal family designation.

Sir Thomas Hope of Craighall was one of the greatest lawyers of his time, and his work, Hopes Practicks, is occasionally referred to by Scots lawyers even today. In 1628 he was created a Baronet of Nova Scotia, and was one of the drafters of the National Covenant in 1638. He died in 1646, having seen two of his sons raised to the Supreme Court Bench. His eldest son, who succeeded to the Baronetcy, took the judicial title of 'Lord Craighall'. He is credited with having advised the exiled Charles II to 'tret with Cromwell for the one half of his cloak before he lost the whole'. The sixth Baronet sold the estate of Craighall in 1729 to his kinsman, the Earl of Hopetoun. Sir Thomas Hope, eighth Baronet of Craighall, was a distinguished agricultural improver, and the parkland known as The Meadows, bordered by the street known as Hope Park, on the south side of Edinburgh, were laid out by him. The sixteenth Baronet was a Member of

Parliament for Midlothian from 1912 to 1918, and served with distinction in both the Boer War and the First World War.

The Hopetoun branch of the family came from Sir James Hope, younger son of the great Lord Advocate, who acquired lands in West Lothian and took as his territorial style, Hopetoun. His son, John Hope of Hopetoun, drowned in the wreck of the frigate *Gloucester,* and it is believed that he died saving the Duke of York, later James VII. This act may have contributed to the meteoric rise of his son, Charles who, as soon as he became of age in 1702, was elected to Parliament for Linlithgow. He was quickly appointed to the Privy Council, and on 5 April 1703 was raised to the peerage as Earl of Hopetoun, Viscount Aithrie and Lord Hope. The great mansion of Hopetoun House was first planned during the first Earl's infancy, and it is today considered one of William Adam's masterpieces.

During the eighteenth century the Earls of Hopetoun amassed vast estates, until they came to own most of West Lothian as well as large parts of East Lothian and Lanarkshire. General Sir John Hope, later the fourth Earl, was a distinguished soldier who was with Sir John Moore at Corunna in 1809. He fought throughout the Peninsular War and returned safely to his ancestral estates. He was prominent in the revitalisation of the Royal Company of Archers (the bodyguard of the monarch in Scotland), of which he was to become captain general. He staged a magnificent reception for George IV at Hopetoun

Hope

House in 1822 during the king's famous visit to Scotland. John Adrian Hope, the seventh Earl, was Lord Chamberlain to Queen Victoria from 1898 to 1900. He was the first Governor General of the newly created Australian Commonwealth in 1900. He was created Marquess of Linlithgow in October 1902. The second Marquess was Viceroy of India from 1936 to 1943.

The family still reside at Hopetoun, which has now been placed in trust to preserve this great monument for the nation. The senior line of Hope, the Baronets of Craighall, also survive today, and are the claimants to the chiefship of this noble name.

HUNTER

A t Hunterston in Ayrshire is carefully preserved on a frail parchment a charter signed by Robert II on 2 May 1374, confirming the grant of land to William Hunter 'for his faithful service rendered and to be rendered to us in return for a silver penny payable to the Sovereign at Hunterston on the Feast of Pentecost'. To this day the Laird of Hunterston keeps silver pennies, minted in the reigns of Robert II and George V, in case of a royal visit to the district on the day appointed for the payment of his rent. William Hunter, who received this charter, is reckoned the tenth Hunter of Hunterston. In even earlier records, William and Norman Hunter appear using the Latin form of the name, 'Venator'. Aylmer le Hunter of the county of Ayr signed the Ragman Roll in 1296 as one of the nobles of Scotland submitting to Edward I of England.

By the fifteenth century the Hunters were hereditary keepers of the royal forests of Arran and the Little Cumbrae. It appears that they held this office from an early date, and the family claims a long descent from the holders of similar offices in England and Normandy before coming to Scotland. By tradition, an ancestor of the Hunters was with Rollo, the Viking, at the sack of Paris in 896, and was later appointed one of the huntsmen to Rollo's descendents, the Dukes of Normandy. The Hunters followed William the Conqueror's queen, Matilda, to England, and because of this their names are not included in the list of the companions of the Conqueror. The Hunter's wife was lady-in-waiting to Queen Matilda, and presumably had a hand in making the famous Bayeux Tapestry. It seems likely that the family came to Scotland early in the twelfth century at the invitation of David I, who was brought up with his sister at the Norman court in England, and were given the lands which eventually became known as Hunter's Toune.

In the sixteenth century the service to be rendered by the Hunters became chiefly military. John, the fourteenth Laird, died with his king at Flodden. His son, Robert, was 'trublit with sikness and infirmity', and in 1542 was excused from army service by James V provided he send in his place his eldest son and his tenant. His son, Mungo, succeeded his father in 1546, but was killed the following year at the Battle of Pinkie. In succeeding generations the Hunters became peaceful Lairds, tending their estates and looking after their tenants. Cadet branches of the family, as was the custom, made their own way in the world as soldiers or in the professions. Robert, son of the twentieth Laird, graduated at Glasgow University in 1643. He was minister of West Kilbride, where he bought land and so founded the Hunters of Kirkland. Robert, a grandson of the twentieth Laird, served under Marlborough and became Governor of Virginia and then of New York.

The early eighteenth century brought financial problems for the family. These were resolved by Robert Hunter, a younger son of the twenty-second Laird, who succeeded to the estate and managed it with such vigour and accomplishment that it has been said that he may be viewed as a second founder of his ancient family. He was considerate of his tenants, often remarking that they had held their occupancies from as early a period as he did himself. He died at the age of 86 and was succeeded by his daughter, Eleanora. She married her cousin, Robert Caldwell, a wealthy merchant and banker. He assumed the name Hunter, and together they began extensive improvements to the estate. They built the present Hunterston House, a fine example of late-eighteenth-century architecture. Their son altered and extended the house in 1835. He had two daughters: Jane, who married Gould Weston, and Eleanor, who married Robert William Cochran-Patrick. Jane Hunter Weston died in 1911 to be succeeded by her son, Lieutenant General Sir Aylmer Hunter-Weston, a distinguished soldier. He served on Kitchener's staff in the Egyptian War of 1896,

Hunter

then in the Boer War and later as.divisional officer to Sir John French, commander of the British Expeditionary Force in France from 1914 to 1915. In the First World War he was in the Gallipoli landings, and later commanded the 8th Army on the Western Front. He was awarded many decorations and honours, including the Distinguished Service Order and a Knighthood of the Bath. He served as MP for North Ayrshire and Bute for twenty-seven years, and commissioned the great architect, Sir Robert Lorimer, to restore the old Castle of Hunterston. He died in 1940 without issue, and on the death of his widow in 1954 the estate passed to the descendents of his mother's younger sister. Eleanora, granddaughter of Eleanora Hunter and Robert William Cochran-Patrick, and daughter of Sir Neil Kennedy Cochran-Patrick, succeeded, adopting the style, 'Miss Hunter of Hunterston'. In 1969 she passed the estate to her nephew, Neil, who was officially recognised by the Lord Lyon as twenty-ninth Laird and chief. Prior to his death in 1994, he had nominated by tanistry his eldest child, Pauline, to succeed him as chief; she has now been recognised in this position by the Lord Lyon.

IRVINE

E rewine and Erwinne are old English personal names, and Gilchrist, son of Erwini, witnessed a charter of the Lord of Galloway sometime between 1124 and 1165. The lands which first bore the name of Irvine appear to have been in Dumfriesshire. Family tradition asserts that the origin of the chiefly family is linked with the early Celtic monarchs of Scotland. Duncan Eryvine, whose eldest son settled at Bonshaw, was the brother of Crinan, who, through the lay Abbots of Dunkeld, claimed descent from the High Kings of Ireland. Crinan married the daughter and heiress of Malcolm II, and their eldest son became King Duncan, the monarch whose murder forms the basis for Shakespeare's *Macbeth*. William de Irwin was a neighbour of the Bruces, whose seat was at Lochmaben near Bonshaw. It is not surprising that the family supported their powerful neighbours and de Irwin became armour bearer and, later, secretary to King Robert. As a reward for twenty years of faithful service, William de Irwin was granted the royal forest of Drum in Aberdeenshire, which was thereafter to become the chief seat of the family. There was already a tower at Drum, probably built before the end of the thirteenth century as a royal hunting lodge. From this was to grow the stately Drum Castle, which remained in the virtually continuous occupation of the family until it was presented to the National Trust for Scotland for the benefit of the nation. It remains one of the most beautiful castles in Scotland.

The third Laird of Drum, the first of twelve Irvines who successively bore the name Alexander, was a knight of almost legendary prowess who followed the Earl of Mar to the French wars. He later fought at the Battle of Harlaw in 1411. This battle marked the last challenge by the Lords of the Isles to royal authority, and was fought only twenty miles from Drum itself. Sir Alexander de Irwyne engaged in single combat Maclean of Duart, the famous 'Hector of the Battles', and after a legendary struggle both died of the wounds each inflicted upon the other. The next Laird figured prominently in the negotiations to ransom James I from the English. When the king's release was secured he knighted de Irwyne. After the king's murder in Perth, Sir Alexander took control of the city of Aberdeen to try and restore order. The sixth Laird was also a peace maker, and was rewarded by James V in 1527 for his efforts to suppress 'rebels, thieves, reivers, sorcerers and murderers'. His eldest son was killed resisting the English invaders at the Battle of Pinkie in 1547. Alexander, the tenth Laird, was a staunch royalist and supporter of Charles I. He was sheriff of Aberdeen, and was offered the earldom of Aberdeen, but the king was executed before he could confirm the grant. Its being a royalist in a predominantly Covenanting district meant that Drum Castle was an obvious target, and it was ultimately attacked when the Laird was absent. A strong force with artillery surrounded the castle, and after Lady Irvine's surrender, it was occupied and looted. The laird's sons also fought in the civil war, and both were captured: Robert, the younger son, died in the dungeons of Edinburgh Castle, but his brother, Alexander, was set free after Montrose's victory at Kilsyth in 1645. Drum Castle was yet again assaulted, and this time not only was the castle completely ransacked but the ladies of the house were ejected and the estate ruined. Alexander survived the war to succeed his father as eleventh Laird, and yet again the royal offer of a peerage was made. This time the laird refused it when he discovered that the king was unwilling to offer reparation for the destruction of the Drum estates which had been endured while the family supported his cause. He later caused a local scandal when after the death of his first wife, he married a

Irvine

sixteen-year-old shepherdess from his estates, who was forty-seven years his junior.

The fourteenth Laird was a Jacobite and fought at the Battle of Sheriffmuir in 1715. He received a severe head wound in the battle and never recovered, dying after years of illness and leaving no direct heir. The estate passed to his uncle, John, and then to a kinsman, John Irvine of Crimond. The Irvines continued in their adherence to the Jacobite cause, and fought for Bonnie Prince Charlie at Culloden. The laird only escaped capture after the prince's defeat by hiding in a secret room at Drum. He then spent several years in France in exile, before being allowed to return to his estates. The twenty-second Laird fought with the Grenadier Guards in the First World War.

Other lines have been equally distinguished. Colonel John Irving of Bonshaw fought in the Abyssinian Campaign of 1867. His son, Sir Robert Irving of Bonshaw, was commodore of the Cunard Line and captain of the *Queen Mary*.

ARMS
Argent, a saltire Gules, on a chief of the Last three mullets of the First pierced of the Second

CREST
A spur rowel of six points Proper

MOTTO
Cave adsum (Beware I am present)

SUPPORTERS
Dexter, a horse at liberty Proper; sinister, a man in armour having a scimitar at his side Proper

STANDARD
The Arms in the hoist and of two tracts Argent and Gules, upon which is depicted a sprig of apple-blossom in the first and third compartments, and the Crest in the centre compartment, along with the Motto 'Cave adsum' in letters Or upon two transverse bands Sable

PLANT BADGE
Sprig of apple-blossom

A name derived from the French, 'jardin' meaning 'garden' or 'orchard'. Black suggests that this does not mean that the family were gardeners, but rather that their residence was near one. The family of du Jardon came over to England with William the Conqueror in 1066. The name is first encountered in Scotland prior to 1153, in charters to the Abbeys of Kelso and Arbroath, where Wmfredus de Jardin appears as a witness. Humphrey de Jardin witnessed a charter by Robert Bruce to the Abbey of Arbroath around 1178. The name is also met in the form 'de Gardinus'. Patrick de Gardinus was chaplain to the Bishop of Glasgow at the beginning of the thirteenth century. In 1245, Sir Humphrey de Gardino witnessed a resignation of lands in Annandale. Yet another variant is found in the Ragman Roll of nobles pledging fealty to Edward I of England in 1296: Jorden del Orchard appears on the roll rendering homage for his lands in Linlithgow.

The chiefly line appears to have established itself at Applegirth on the River Annan in Dumfriesshire by the fourteenth century. Their earliest stronghold was Spedlings Tower, which was abandoned in the late seventeenth century when the family moved across the River Annan to Jardine Hall, apparently to escape the ghost of an unfortunate miller who had been left to starve to death in the tower's dungeon. Sir Alexander Jardine of Applegirth was active in defending the Borders against the incursions of the English. It is narrated that in 1524, in company with Lord Maxwell, Sir Alexander engaged an English host near Carlisle, routed them and took nearly three hundred prisoners. In 1547, his son, John, faced English retribution when Lord Wharton, with a force of over five thousand men, overran Annandale. He ravaged the Jardine lands and forced Applegirth to submit. Later that year, with the help of French troops, the Jardines harried the English and exacted a terrible retribution for their humiliation.

The Jardines, following the Johnstons, supported Mary, Queen of Scots until her marriage to Bothwell, when they declared allegience to the infant King James VI. For his clan's support, Jardine was to receive a pension from the revenues of the Archbishopric of Glasgow, but this was never paid. His namesake, fourth in descent from Sir Alexander, married Lady Margaret Douglas, sister of the first Duke of Queensberry. His elder son, Sir Alexander, born in 1645, was created a Baronet of Nova Scotia on 25 May 1672.

The fourth Baronet, born in 1712, embraced the Catholic faith and lived on the Continent. He became a Knight of the Sovereign Order of Malta, taking a vow of celibacy. He died in Brussels in December 1790 when he was succeeded by his brother, Sir William. The seventh Baronet, yet another Sir William, distinguished himself as an author and editor of works on natural history. A nephew of Sir William, Frank Jardine, lived his life in unusual circumstances in Australia. Frank's father was an officer in the colonial service in Australia. On 16 October 1873, Frank married Princess Sana, the niece of Moliatoa, King of Samoa. His royal connections helped him to develop north-east Australia and the new state of Queensland. Frank called his Australian estate Lockerbie.

Dr William Jardine went to the Far East as a surgeon for the East India Company. In 1827 he went into partnership with James Matheson. The house of Jardine Matheson prospered, particularly after the Opium Wars established a strong British merchant base in Hong Kong. The company grew to dominate trade in the Far East and is still a name to be reckoned with today.

Another cadet of Applegirth was the Reverend John Jardine, born in 1716. He was an eminent clergyman, but was also one of the

Jardine

intellectual and literary elite of Edinburgh in the mid eighteenth century. In 1759 he was a member of the 'Select Society', some of whose other members included Adam Smith, David Hume and Allan Ramsay. He helped to launch the critical journal, *The Edinburgh Review*. He was appointed Dean of the Order of the Thistle and a royal chaplain. His son, Sir Henry Jardine, WS, became a lawyer, but he continued his father's academic and intellectual interests. He was Deputy King's Remembrancer in Exchequer for Scotland and was one of those present when the 'Honours of Scotland' were re-discovered in 1818. He was knighted in 1825 and later made a Fellow of the Royal Society of Edinburgh.

The father of the present chief, Sir William Jardine, twelfth Baronet and twenty-third chief, was active in promoting clan activities and served on the Committee of the Council of Chiefs. His work has been continued by his heir, Sir Alec, the twenty-fourth chief.

JOHNSTONE

This name is a simple patronymic. The Johnstones were at one time among the most powerful of the Borders clans. They settled originally in Annandale, and have for over six hundred years held extensive possessions on the western marches where they kept watch against the English freebooters.

The first recorded of the family was John Johnstone, whose son, Gilbert, is named in records dated after 1194; John must therefore have been a prominent settler before that date. Sir John Johnston, knight of the county of Dumfries, appears on the Ragman Roll swearing fealty to Edward I of England in 1296. His great-grandson was appointed one of the wardens of the western marches in 1381. His son, Adam Johnstone, was Laird of Johnstone before 1413, and took part with the Scottish army in the Battle of Sark in 1448. Adam's son took part on the royal side in the desperate struggle between James II and the Douglases, and was instrumental in the suppression of the rebellion of that great house by the Crown. He was rewarded by the king with a grant of the lands of Buittle and Sannoch near Threave Castle, formerly part of the Douglas lands of Galloway. Adam's eldest son, John, was the progenitor of the Annandale or main branch of the family, while another reputed son, Matthew, who was said to have married a daughter of the Earl of Angus, chief of the Red Douglases, was the ancestor of the Westerhall branch.

The Johnstones, unlike many of their neighbours, who raided one another's lands, 'sought the beves that made their broth' only in England but they had a hereditary feud with the Maxwells. Lord Maxwell, the head of this great family, was the most powerful man in the south-west of Scotland in the sixteenth century. He was slain, with many of his men, at the Battle of Dryfe Sands near Lockerbie on 7 December 1593. In turn, at a meeting held in 1608 to reconcile their differences, Johnstone was treacherously killed by the ninth Lord Maxwell. He paid with his life on the scaffold in 1614.

James Johnstone, the chief of the clan, was created Lord Johnstone of Lochwood by Charles I in 1633. Ten years later he was made Earl of Hartfell, which title was designated to him and his heirs male only. He joined Montrose after the Battle of Kilsyth in August 1645. He was captured at Philiphaugh, but was spared through the intercession of Argyll. The eldest son of Lord Hartfell, James, was imprisoned for a time with his father in the Castles of Dumbarton, Glasgow, St Andrews and Edinburgh. To recompense Lord Hartfell for the hardships he had suffered in the royal cause, Charles II created him Earl of Annandale and Hartfell, Viscount of Annan, Lord Johnstone of Lochwood, Lochmaben, Moffatdale and Evandal. As James, the Earl of Annandale and Hartfell, had at that time daughters as his heirs, the king granted a charter in 1662 erecting the land into a territorial earldom entailed to the heirs male of his body, and failing that to heirs female. Although James later had a son, William, this grant was to be of consequence two centuries later.

In 1701, William, third Earl of Hartfell and second Earl of Annandale and Hartfell, was raised to the rank of Marquess of Annandale. He held many important state offices including Secretary of State and President of the Privy Council. James, second Marquess of Annandale, died at Naples in 1730, having enjoyed the family dignities and estates for only nine years. His half-brother, George, third and last Marquess, who succeeded him, was found on 5 March 1747 to be incapable of managing his affairs, and a curator was appointed. On the Marquess's death in 1792 the family titles became dormant and the estates devolved upon his grand-nephew, James, third Earl of Hopetoun.

Unsuccessful attempts were made in the nineteenth century to revive the Annandale titles, but it was not until 1971 that real progress was made. It was decided to proceed

Johnstone

upon the basis of the charter of 1662, which re-granted the earldom of Annandale and Hartfell as a territorial earldom capable of descending through the female line. The first step was to confirm the Annandale families as chiefs of the Johnstones, and to update their family pedigree. On 16 February 1982, the Lord Lyon recognised Major Percy Johnstone of Annandale and of that Ilk as baron of the lands of the earldom of Annandale and Hartfell and of the lordship of Johnstone, Hereditary Steward of the Stewartry of Annandale and Hereditary Keeper of the Castle of Lochmaben. From there the case was presented to the House of Lords in June 1985, and the Court found in favour of Major Percy's son, Patrick, who is the present Earl of Annandale and Hartfell and chief of the name and arms of Johnstone.

Other senior branches of the clan also flourished, particularly the house of Caskieben. Sir George Johnston of Caskieben was created a Baronet of Nova Scotia on 31 March 1626. The third Baronet fought in the army of William of Orange at the Battle of the Boyne in 1690. The eleventh Baronet resides in America. The seat of the chief is the mansion of Raehills south of Moffat.

KEITH

A warrior of the Chatti slew the Danish General Camus at the Battle of Barrie in 1010, for which valour Malcolm II dipped three fingers into the blood of the slain and drew them down the shield of the warrior, thereafter named Marbhachair Chamuis, or 'Camus Slayer'. Ever since then, the chief of the Keiths has borne on his arms the same three red lines. This is depicted as early as 1316 on the seal of Sir Robert de Keth, marischal. Malcolm's victory at the Battle of Chathem in 1018 brought him into possession of Lothian, and Camus Slayer subsequently held the Lothian lands of Keth from which his progeny took their names. A Norman adventurer, Hervey, married the native heiress of Marbhachair and received a charter for the lands of Keth from David I around 1150. Hervey's son was styled 'Marischal of the King of Scots' in a charter of 1176, which office the family held until the attainder of George, tenth Earl Marischal. The Marischal was custodian of the royal regalia and charged with the safety of the king's person within Parliament.

Robert the Bruce granted Halforest, the Aberdeenshire royal forest, to his friend, Sir Robert de Keth, in 1308, and it was there that the Marischal built his castle. His nephew, Sir William of Galston, returned Robert's heart to Melrose Abbey after the demise of the Black Douglas at the hands of the Moors in Spain. By a charter of Robert in 1324, the office of marischal became hereditary in the family of Sir Robert de Keth, the cavalry commander at Bannockburn, conditional upon their bearing the ancient arms inherited from Marbhachair Chamuis. The young David II was escorted by Sir Robert the Marischal when he fled to the safety of France during Edward Balliol's usurpation.

Sir William the Marischal (1350–1407) added great estates in Buchan, Kincardine and Lothian to his existing patrimony when he married the heiress of Sir Alexander Fraser, the High Chamberlain. His brother, John, married the Cheyne heiress, bringing to the Keiths the massive Inverugie estate with its castle which later became the chief's seat of the earls marischal. Three of Sir William's offspring married children of Robert II, while another daughter married Sir Adam Gordon, progenitor of the Earls of Huntly, and to whom she took substantial estates, forming the foundations of that great family.

The third Lord Keith was elevated to the peerage as Earl Marischal in 1458, the only peer to be styled by his great office of state. The third Earl Marischal, with the Earl of Glencairn, invited the reformer John Knox to return to Scotland in 1559, while the fourth Earl founded Marischal College in Aberdeen, endowing it with the Greyfriars lands and introducing radical teaching protocols which were later to be adopted universally. George, the fifth Earl Marischal and the wealthiest nobleman in the land, undertook the embassy to Denmark which culminated in the marriage of James VI to Princess Anne of Denmark.

Keith

Standard

After the coronation of Charles II in 1651 at Scone, William, the seventh Earl, was captured and imprisoned in the Tower of London, where he remained until the Restoration, when the king appointed him a Privy Councillor and later Lord Privy Seal, in recompense for the great sufferings he and his family had endured in the royal cause. There were rewards for those who had hidden the Scottish crown jewels on the Keith lands after Charles's coronation: Ogilvie of Barras was created a knight baronet, and Marischal's brother, John, became Knight Marischal and later Earl of Kintore, with an augmentation to his arms consisting of the royal crown, sword and sceptre. Kintore's nephew, the eighth Earl

Marischal, was appointed a Knight of the Thistle by James VIII, the 'Old Pretender'.

The Keith family supported the Jacobite cause in the Forty-five, for which the tenth Earl and his brother, James, forfeited their lands, castles and titles. The Keith brothers thereafter played a part in Continental affairs during the eighteenth century. The earl was one of the very few Jacobite Knights of the Garter and also received Prussia's highest order, the Black Eagle. James was invested by the Tsarina with the Russian Imperial Order of St Andrew.

Keith of Ravelston and Dunnottar was recognised as a represener of the Marischals by the Lord Lyon in 1801. His nephew was dubbed Knight Marishal for George IV's visit to Edinburgh in 1822. The flamboyant ninth Earl of Kintore, who was Governor General of South Australia from 1889 to 1895, decimated the Kintore estates. The twelfth Earl of Kintore promoted the clan internationally and was instrumental in appointing a hereditary sennachie to preserve the family's history and traditions. The thirteenth and present Earl continues to reside on the Keith Hall estate in Aberdeenshire.

KENNEDY

ARMS
Argent, a chevron Gules between three cross crosslets fitchée Sable, all within a double tressure flory counter-flory Gules

CREST
A dolphin naiant Proper

MOTTO
Avise la fin (Consider the end)

SUPPORTERS
Two swans Proper, beaked and membered Gules

Cunedda, a chieftain of the Votadini tribe of Lothian, was sent by the Saxon leader, Vortigern, to south west Scotland to establish settlements intended to resist Picto-Scottish sea raids. These settlements spread down the west coast as far as north Wales. In the Celtic language, Cunedda was rendered as *Cinneidigh* (meaning ugly or grim-headed), and the name gradually became especially associated with the district of Carrick in Ayrshire. Gilbert Mac Kenedi witnessed a charter granting lands in Carrick to the abbey at Melrose in the early part of the reign of William the Lion, while Gillespie Kennedy is named as senechal of Carrick in charters during the reign of Alexander II. The Kennedys claimed blood kinship with the Earls of Carrick and supported Bruce in the War of Independence. They were rewarded when Robert II confirmed John Kennedy of Dunure as chief of his name and baillie of Carrick in 1372. His direct descendent, Gilbert was created Lord Kennedy around 1457 and was one of the regents of the infant James III.

A brother of the first Lord Kennedy, James Kennedy, was one of Scotland's best-loved bishops. He served briefly as High Chancellor of Scotland and was Bishop of Dunkeld, and later Archbishop of St Andrews. At St Andrews he founded St Salvator's College in 1455.

Hugh Kennedy of Ardstinchar served as commander of the Scots mercenary troops who fought for Joan of Arc at the siege of Orleans; hence Joan figures on the arms of Kennedy of Bargany. Sir David, third Lord Kennedy, was created Earl of Cassillis in 1509 and died at Flodden in 1513. The second Earl was murdered in 1527. Gilbert, third Earl, was one of four Scottish commissioners who were poisoned at Dieppe on their return from the marriage of Mary, Queen of Scots to the Dauphin in 1558. He had inherited his title at the age of twelve when one of his first acts was to sign, under duress, the death warrant of Patrick Hamilton, the first Scottish Protestant martyr. The fourth Earl earned an infamous reputation by 'roasting' Alan Stewart, Abbot of Crossraguel, in the black vault of Dunmore in order to obtain tracts of abbey land.

The sixth Earl of Cassillis, John, was Lord Justice General of Scotland from 1649 to 1651. He was a zealous Protestant, as was his son, the seventh Earl, and both were firm supporters of Parliament during the civil war. The Justice General sat in Cromwell's House of Lords. They suffered for their beliefs, but their estates remained largely intact. When the eighth Earl died without heirs there was a three-year court dispute to determine the succession. The House of Lords finally found in favour of Sir Thomas Kennedy of Culzean in preference to William, Earl of March and Ruglan. Sir Thomas's brother, David, an advocate, succeeded him in 1775 as tenth Earl, and was an active improver. He commissioned the architect Robert Adam to build the castle at Culzean, considered to be Adam's masterpiece.

On the death of the tenth Earl the title passed to a kinsman who had settled in America. Captain Archibald Kennedy was an officer in the Royal Navy who held estates in Hoboken in New Jersey and became the greatest property owner in New York. He tried to be neutral during the American War of Independence, and was accordingly mistrusted by both sides. Half of his New York properties were confiscated, including number 1, Broadway, which was appropriated by George Washington. His son, the twelfth Earl, was a close friend of the Duke of Clarence, who, on his coronation as William IV, created him Marquess of Ailsa. The second Marquess, Archibald Kennedy, was killed in a hunting accident in 1870. His son succeeded to the title at the age of twenty-two, and after his death in 1938 the family title was borne by each of his three sons in turn.

The Kennedys of Kermuck were hereditary constables of Aberdeen from at least 1413.

Kennedy

The family was outlawed in 1652, when the father and son of the family mortally wounded John Forbes of Watertown in a fracas. Captain William Kennedy, who was part Cree Indian, led an expedition to search for Sir John Franklin, the explorer seeking the Northwest Passage between the Atlantic and Pacific Oceans.

The Moray Kennedys came north with the possession of the earldom of Moray by Janet Kennedy and her son by James IV. She was sister to the third Lord Kennedy. The Clan Ulric in Lochaber are said by tradition to be descended from Ulric Kennedy, who had fled from Ayrshire because of his lawlessness. These Kennedys became a sept of the Camerons. Lieutenant General Sir Clark Kennedy of Knockgray served throughout the Peninsular War. At Waterloo in 1815, he was in command of the centre squadron of the Royal Dragoons and personally captured the eagle and colours of the 105th Regiment of French Infantry. His arms were augmented to incorporate these honours with the word, 'Waterloo'. The fifth Marquess presented Culzean Castle to the National Trust, but the chiefs still live on family land in Ayrshire.

KERR

The Kerrs were one of the great riding clans of the Scottish Borders, and their name is rendered in various forms, including Kerr, Ker, Carr and Carre. It stems from the old Norse, 'kjrr', meaning 'marsh dweller', and came to Scotland from Normandy, the French settlement of the Norse. A variant is found on the west coast of Scotland and particularly on the island of Arran, which has a separate derivation, taken from the Gaelic 'ciar', meaning 'dusky'. Nevertheless, family tradition asserts a Norman origin, from two brothers, Ralph and Robert (also called John), who came to Roxburgh from Lancashire. Which of the brothers was the elder has never been ascertained, but the senior branch of the family, the Kerrs of Ferniehurst, claim descent from Ralph, while their rivals, the Kerrs of Cessford, descend from John.

The influence of the Kerrs grew steadily throughout the fourteenth and fifteenth centuries, and by the time of the fall of the Douglases in the mid fifteenth century, the Kerrs had become Crown vassals with considerable influence. In 1451 Andrew Kerr of Cessford received a charter to the barony of Old Roxburgh, and in 1457 he was appointed warden of the marches. The family were confirmed in the barony and Castle of Cessford by a charter of 1493. Sir Andrew Kerr of Ferniehurst received a royal charter to the barony of Oxnam, and was appointed warden of the middle marches in 1502. This important and influential royal office was to pass in 1515 to another Sir Andrew Kerr, this time of the house of Cessford, who had fought at Flodden two years earlier. He was killed near Melrose while escorting the infant James V to Edinburgh in July 1526. His grandson, Mark Kerr, had his lands of Newbattle and Prestongrange erected into the barony of Newbattle by a charter of 1591, and in 1606 he was created Earl of Lothian. This title failed when his son died in 1624 without male issue. Sir Andrew Kerr of the Ferniehurst line was created Lord Jedburgh in 1621.

The third peerage to come to the family was the earldom of Ancram, which was bestowed upon Sir Robert Kerr who was descended from a younger son of Sir Andrew Kerr of Ferniehurst. Sir Robert of Cessford, who now spelt his surname with a single 'r', was created Earl of Roxburghe in 1616. To add to the plethora of honours showered on the family, Sir William Kerr, son of the Earl of Ancram, was granted a new earldom of Lothian in 1631. His son, Robert, who was advanced to the rank of Marquess, also succeeded to the earldom of Ancram on the death of his uncle. The Roxburghe title was later to be advanced to a dukedom, largely in return for supporting the political union of Scotland and England in 1707. The dukedom of Roxburghe was to pass through female lines until, in 1805, the chief of Clan Innes inherited the title and compounded his surname as Innes-Ker.

Kerr

Standard

The history of the rivalry between the two branches of the family is so complex that few who are not deeply interested can unravel it. If Ferniehurst supported young James V, then Cessford was for the Douglases. In the next reign Ferniehurst was a staunch supporter of Mary, Queen of Scots, and did not abandon her cause, even after her flight into English captivity; but Sir Walter Kerr of Cessford led his men against the queen at the Battle of Langside in 1568. The feud only came to an end when in 1631 William Kerr of Ferniehurst married Ann Ker of Cessford, and it is their descendents who are the present Marquesses of Lothian.

The first Marquess was Lord Justice General of Scotland. He had five sons and five daughters. One of these, Lord Mark Kerr, was a distinguished professional soldier and is reputed to have had a high sense of personal honour and a quick temper. He fought several duels throughout his military career but rose ultimately to the rank of general, and was appointed governor of Edinburgh Castle in 1745. His eldest brother, the second Marquess was created a Knight of the Thistle in 1705. Robert Kerr, one of the sons of the third Marquess, has the dubious distinction of being the only person of high rank killed on the Hanoverian side at the Battle of Culloden in 1746. His elder brother, later the fourth Marquess, commanded three squadrons of cavalry at Culloden and survived to serve under the Duke of Cumberland in France in 1758. Admiral of the Fleet, Sir Walter Talbot Kerr, a younger son of the seventh Marquess, was a naval lord at the Admiralty from 1899 to 1904.

The twelfth and present Marquess of Lothian lives at Ferniehurst Castle, although the principal seat of the family is the great mansion house of Monteviot. His son, Michael Ancram, is a Member of Parliament.

KINCAID

The Kincaids are said to descend from the ancient Earls of Lennox, the Galbraiths of Buthernock, the Grahames and the Comyn Lords of Badenoch. Their name appears to be territorial in origin, but its derivation is uncertain. One explanation is that it comes from the Gaelic, 'ceann cadha', the 'steep place' or 'pass'. A second translation may be 'of the head of the rock', and a third possibility is, 'the head of the battle,' which could refer to a later achievement in the family history.

An early reference to the name is found in 1238, when Alexander III granted the lands of the Kincade to Maldouen, third Earl of Lennox, who in the same year granted the lands to Sir William Galbraith, the fourth chief of that name. The Galbraiths' principal castle was originally Craigmaddie, but when the line ended in three sisters the estate was partitioned. In 1280, one of the sisters married a Logan, and they obtained confirmation of the lands of Kyncade by a charter from the fourth Earl of Lennox, and the family took their surname from the property. The Kyncade lands (now with a new spelling) extended from the River Glazert to the River Kelvin and were thought originally to consist of thirty thousand acres.

Although Kincaids have not made a great mark in Scottish history, one member of the family distinguished himself by gallant conduct against the English forces of Edward I, and in his valiant services in the successful recapture of Edinburgh Castle in 1296. The then Laird of Kincaid was made constable of Edinburgh Castle, an office he held until around 1314. It was during the reign of Robert the Bruce that the castle on the Kincaid shield was granted as an honourable augmentation to his armorial bearings as a reference to his feat.

When the Kincaids obtained their lands at the end of the thirteenth century they would have erected a tower or peel. There is no trace of this building today, but a house was built around 1690, enlarged in the mid eighteenth century and rebuilt in 1812.

From the late sixteenth century onwards, the family increased their landholdings in the east of the country. Firstly, as a result of an advantageous marriage, the Kincaids gained the estate of Craiglockhart near Edinburgh. In due course they added to this the estate of Bantaskin near Falkirk, the grim Blackness Castle near Linlithgow and the fields of Warriston, now a suburb of Edinburgh.

Malcolm Kincaid, who lost his left arm in a clan skirmish in 1563, was actively engaged in a feud in the 1570s with the Lennoxes of Woodhead. The luckless Malcolm was killed by a Stirling of Glovat in 1581. Some historians have commented that the feud with the Lennoxes is made remarkable by the fact that it was later by marriage to that very family that the Kincaid name was carried on to be re-established as an independent clan in the twentieth century. John Kincaid of Warriston was murdered in 1600 by one of his grooms who was in league with his wife. The conspiracy was detected and the groom forced to confess. The couple both suffered the ultimate penalty for their crime but, although the Lady of Warriston was beheaded in deference to her rank, the hapless groom was 'broken on the wheel'.

The Kincaids fought on the royalist side in the civil wars of the seventeeth century, campaigning largely in Ireland. The family suffered considerable hardship as a result of its adherence to the royal cause, and many of the name emigrated to North America. The family were later supporters of the Stuart cause in

Kincaid

exile, and following the rising in 1715 David Kincaid was obliged to leave Scotland, ultimately settling in Virginia. In 1746 four sons of Alexander Kincaid, Lord Provost of Edinburgh, and the King's Printer, fought a rearguard action after Culloden, but were ultimately taken prisoner and their doom seemed certain. However, they escaped and took ship for America, and they, too, settled in Virginia. At the end of the eighteenth century the principal line of the Kincaids married into the Lennox family and for most of the next two centuries the families were virtually synonymous. The Kincaids have now re-established themselves as an independent family and their present chief, Madam Kincaid of Kincaid, now represents her name on the Council of Chiefs.

LAMONT

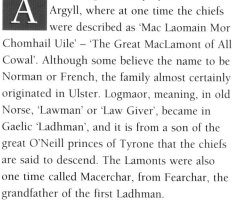

A name of great antiquity in south Argyll, where at one time the chiefs were described as 'Mac Laomain Mor Chomhail Uile' – 'The Great MacLamont of All Cowal'. Although some believe the name to be Norman or French, the family almost certainly originated in Ulster. Logmaor, meaning, in old Norse, 'Lawman' or 'Law Giver', became in Gaelic 'Ladhman', and it is from a son of the great O'Neill princes of Tyrone that the chiefs are said to descend. The Lamonts were also one time called Macerchar, from Fearchar, the grandfather of the first Ladhman.

The first certain record of the chiefs is found in charters of the early thirteenth century. Laumanus, son of Malcolm, granted to the monks of Paisley lands at Kilmun, together with the church of Kilfinan. These grants were confirmed in 1270 and again in 1295 by Malcolm, the son of Laumanus. In 1456 John Lamond is recorded as the baillie of Cowal. In 1466, probably the same John, now described as Lamond of that Ilk, disputed with the monks of Paisley certain rights relating to the lands which had been ceded to them by his ancestor two hundred years before. Later that century the direct line of the chiefs is believed to have failed, and the representation of the family passed to the Lamonts of Inveryne, later styled 'Lamont of Lamont'. They established their chief seats at the strong Castles of Toward and Ascog, which they held until their destruction by the Campbells in the seventeenth century. Sir Iain Moncreiffe of that Ilk, the celebrated twentieth-century herald and historian, asserts that Sir John Lyon, who became Thane of Glamis in 1372, was a son of the chiefly house of Lamont. He points out that the Lamont arms bear a silver lion on a blue shield, while the Lyons' bear a blue lion on a silver shield. Such a simple reversal of the colour scheme of a coat of arms was a recognised manner of differencing used by cadets.

An incident involving the chief of the Lamonts at the beginning of the seventeenth century is widely quoted by clan historians as a classic example of the Highland laws of hospitality. Lamont is said to have been hunting with some Macgregors when a dispute broke out. Macgregor, the Younger of Glenstrae, was stabbed by Lamont, who then fled, hotly pursued by the chief's son's men. Lamont is said to have reached Glenstrae, the home of the Macgregor chief whose son he had just killed. Lamont, claiming he was pursued by enemies, asked for shelter and protection, which Macgregor willingly gave. When his angry clansmen appeared and related the events of the night, the chief refused to allow his guest to be harmed in any way. He had given his word of protection and not even his great personal grief could overcome his sense of honour and obligation.

Lamont

Standard

Sir James Lamont of Lamont, chief of the clan in 1643, was a well respected and popular leader who was deeply interested in the welfare of his people. He declared for the royalist cause, which brought his clan into direct confrontation with his powerful Campbell neighbours. The Campbells had steadily encroached upon the Lamonts' ancient Lordship of Cowal, yet Lamont was initially hesitant to move against the Campbells. After Montrose's great victory at Inverlochy in 1645, however, the Lamonts laid waste the Campbell lands at Kilmun. In 1646 a powerful Campbell army invaded the Lamont territory and besieged the Castles of Toward and Ascog. Sir James Lamont surrendered the castles, having reached apparently honourable terms with the Campbells. The fortresses were to be handed over but the lives of the Lamonts were to be spared. However, not every chief adhered to his word with the sense of honour of

Macgregor of Glenstrae: on the surrender of the castles Sir James was thrown in a dungeon at Dunstaffnage, where he was held in terrible conditions for five years. Over two hundred clansmen, women and children were massacred, and the castles were reduced to ruins. The Lamont massacre was one of the charges brought against the Marquess of Argyll at his trial in 1661 following the Restoration of the Stuart monarchy. The Lamont chief presented a petition to Parliament in person, in which it was narrated that the Campbells acted with inhuman barbarism; one charge that they did 'cause hang upon ane tree near the number of thirty six persons most of them being special gentlemen of the name of Lamont and vassals to Sir James'. Argyll was already doomed for his treason, but the Lamont charges were in many ways more damaging to his reputation as a Highland chief. The Lamonts did not receive compensation, and their star remained eclipsed by their Campbell oppressors, whose power continued to grow unabated. The chiefs took up residence at Ard Lamont, where the last chief to live in Cowal was born in 1854. In 1893 the last of the clan lands were sold and the present chief lives in Australia.

LEASK

As with many Scottish families, there are several possibilities as to the origin of the name. It may be a diminutive of the Anglo–Saxon 'lisse', meaning 'happy'. In Norse it means 'a stirring fellow'. The late Professor Keith Leask of Aberdeen believed that Liscus, chief of the Haedui, a tribe of Gauls described by Julius Caesar in his Gallic Wars, was the ancestor of the Leasks. The Castle of Boulogne, once the possession of Charlemagne and one of the greatest fortresses in France, at one time belonged to a family called de Lesque. An early reference to the name is found in mention of Erik Leask, who was reputed to be chamberlain to his kinsman, the king of Denmark.

William de Laskereske appears on the Ragman Roll of 1296, submitting to Edward I of England. Around 1345 William Leask was granted a charter of confirmation by David II, son of Robert the Bruce, to his lands of Leskgoroune or Leskgaranne. He may be the same William Leysk who was recorded in the parish records of the church at Ellon in Aberdeenshire, in the following manner: 'William de Laysk, the elder, Lord of that Ilk, bequeathed a pound of wax yearly to the altar of the Holyrood in the church of St Mary of Ellon'. He also bequeathed from his lands at Logy a stone of wax for lights to be burned on the Sabbath and other feast days on his tomb and those of his wives, Alice de Rath and Mariota de St Michael. His seal was appended to the charter confirming the donations, along with that of the Bishop of Aberdeen, in 1380. The local kirk session records at the beginning of the seventeenth century show that William Lask of that Ilk and his tenants were regular attenders in the newly reformed church at Ellon. The second known chief, who was also baillie of the barony of Findon, inherited half of the lands of Henry de Brogan, Lord of Achlowne, in 1390. In 1391 he appears as a witness to a charter by the Earl of Orkney.

About the middle of the next century a younger son of Lask went to Orkney at the request of the then earl, who had formed an almost princely court around his splendid palace at Kirkwall. A branch developed there which can still show the longest unbroken male lines of the family.

In 1456, the third chief, Wilfred, signed a bond of manrent in favour of William Hay, Earl of Erroll, and resigned his lands in favour of his son and heir, Thomas. The connection with the Hays appears to have remained strong from this point onwards and when the Cheynes of Esslemont allied themselves with the Hay Earls of Erroll, their bond, dated 1499, was signed at the Chapel of Laske. William Lesk of that Ilk, the seventh chief, signed the oath of allegiance to the child James VI in 1574 following the deposition of his mother, Mary, Queen of Scots.

In 1615 the register of the Privy Council records a complaint from Alexander Leask that Adam Gordon, brother of the Laird of Gight, put violent hands upon him at the Yet of Leask and wounded him grievously. Later in the same year the Gordons again attacked the Leasks, setting upon the son of the chief, for which act George Gordon was outlawed. Yet again in 1616, William Leask of that Ilk was accosted by John Gordon of Ardlogy and a party of men with 'pistolets and hagbuts'. Alexander Leask of that Ilk was one of the noblemen who recorded his coat of arms in the newly established public register in 1672.

Disaster overtook the family at the end of the seventeenth century when they borrowed heavily upon their estates to invest in the ill-fated Darien scheme. This was a trading venture with Central America which was intended to rival the great East India Company

Leask

established in London. The lands chosen for the first settlement were disease-ridden, and most of the colonists and traders perished. Broken by debt, Alexander Leask of that Ilk, the thirteenth and last known chief in the unbroken line, gave up his estates, and the house of Leask became the residence of Robert Cumming. Little is then known of the family until the twentieth century when, in 1963, a descendent managed to buy back a portion of the family lands and established the Leask Society with the support of other prominent Leasks such as Lieutenant General Sir Henry Leask, sometime governor of Edinburgh Castle and General Officer commanding the Army in Scotland. In 1968 the Lord Lyon recognised the present chief for her lifetime and re-established a line of descent which has secured the bloodline for at least the next two generations.

ARMS
Argent, a saltire between four roses Gules

CREST
Two broadswords in saltire behind a swan's head and neck all Proper

MOTTO
I'll defend

SUPPORTERS
Two naked savages wreathed about the heads with roses Gules and about the loins with oak-leaves, holding in their exterior hands clubs erected Gules

STANDARD
Azure, a St Andrew's Cross Argent in the hoist and of two tracts Argent and Gules, upon which is depicted the Crest, upon a chapeau Azure furred Ermine, in the first compartment, and a rose Gules in the second compartment, along with the Motto 'I'll defend' in letters Argent upon a transverse band Azure

PINSEL
Argent, upon a Wreath of the Liveries the Crest within a strap Gules buckled and embellished Or, inscribed with the Motto 'I'll defend' in letters Or, all within a circlet also Or fimbriated Vert bearing the name 'Lennox of that Ilk' in letters Sable, the same ensigned of a chapeau Azure furred Ermine, and in the fly an Escrol Azure surmounting a rose slipped Gules, bearing this Slogan 'The Lennox' in letters Argent

PLANT BADGE
A rose slipped Gules

The ancient earldom which bore this name consisted of the whole of Dunbartonshire, as well as large parts of Renfrewshire, Stirlingshire and Perthshire. 'Leven-ach' signified in Gaelic a 'smooth stream'. From the ancient Celtic Mormears of Levenax sprang the Earls of Lennox who were to become joined to the royal house of Stewart. The origins of the earldom, which was well established by the twelfth century, are disputed, but one theory asserts that a Saxon baron by the name of Arkyll received lands in Dunbartonshire and Stirlingshire from Malcolm III, and by his marriage to a Scottish heiress had a son, Alwyn, first Earl of Lennox. However, it is claimed by other historians that the earldom was conferred by William the Lion upon his brother, David, Earl of Huntingdon, and that the family of Lennox was not established until after William's reign.

By the end of the thirteenth century the Earls of Lennox were among the most powerful nobles in the realm, and Malcolm, the fifth Earl, was one of the nominees supporting the Bruce claim to the crown of Scotland. In 1296 he led his Lennox men into England and besieged Carlisle. He swore fealty to Edward I of England and is listed in the Ragman Roll of that year, but he was also at the forefront of the struggle for Scottish independence and was one of the mainstays of Robert the Bruce. His son was present at the coronation of Robert II at Scone in 1371, although he died only two years later with no direct male issue. The earldom passed through his only daughter to Walter de Fasselane, who assumed the title of Earl of Lennox. Margaret Lennox and her husband resigned the title to the Crown, who regranted it to their son, Duncan, whose elder daughter, Isabella, married Murdoch, Duke of Albany and Regent of Scotland between 1419 and 1425. The connection with Regent Albany was to prove an unhappy one. On the return of James I from his imprisonment in England, Lennox fell victim to the king's hatred of all those connected with Albany, whose father had murdered the king's brother and who had presided over the decline of Scotland into disorder. The earl was beheaded in May 1425, although then in his eightieth year. His son-in-law, Albany, was executed, and his daughter, the widowed duchess, was imprisoned at Tantallon Castle in East Lothian with her son, Walter de Levenax, who was later transferred to the Bass Rock, and then to Stirling, where he was executed. The grieving widow and mother was eventually allowed to return to her island residence at Inchmurrin on Loch Lomond. The succession to the title was thereafter disputed, and the lands themselves were divided. The Duchess of Albany's sisters, Margaret and Elizabeth, both left descendents who claimed the vast estates. From Margaret Lennox descended the Menteiths of Rusky, and from Elizabeth, the Stewarts, later Lords Darnley.

John, Lord Darnley assumed the title of Earl of Lennox in 1488 and sat in the first Parliament of James IV. In 1503, Matthew, the second Stewart Earl of Lennox, obtained from James IV the hereditary sheriffdom of Dunbartonshire, which was made an adjunct of the earldom. In 1513, Matthew, along with the Earl of Argyll, commanded the right wing of the Scots army at Flodden, where he was slain. The younger son of the fourth Stewart Earl was Henry, Lord Darnley, the unfortunate husband of Mary, Queen of Scots. Darnley, who became King Henry upon his marriage, was later murdered, an act which was one of the factors leading to his widow's being deposed, and set in motion the events which led to her execution at Fotheringay Castle. The Earldom of Lennox consequently passed to the young James VI along with the other Darnley estates, which he later granted to his uncle, Charles, his father's younger brother. When he died without male issue the title was bestowed by the king on Esmé Stuart, the son of John, Lord de Aubigny, a younger son of the third Stewart Earl of Lennox and Governor

Lennox

of Avignon. He was recalled to Scotland by James VI in 1579, and in 1581 he was created Duke of Lennox and High Chamberlain of Scotland. His son, the second Duke, was additionally created Duke of Richmond in 1623. The dukedoms and the estates once more died out in a direct line and devolved on Charles II as the nearest male heir. He conferred the dukedom of Lennox and of Richmond upon Charles Lennox, his illegitimate son by his liaison with Louise de Kerouaille. The present Duke of Richmond, Gordon and Lennox, proprietor of the famous Goodwood Race Course, is Charles Lennox's direct descendent. In the nineteenth century the Lennoxes of Woodhead, later of Lennox Castle near Glasgow, claimed the right to succeed to the title and honours of the ancient Earls of Lennox, and although their claim to the peerage was never established, they were recognised as chief family of the name. The family sold Lennox Castle to the city of Glasgow in 1927, and their chief seat became Downton Castle near Ludlow. The present chief is in the almost unique position of having his grandmother, Madam Kincaid of Kincaid, as a fellow member of the Council of Chiefs.

LESLIE

T he progenitor of this great Scottish family is claimed as Bartolf, a Hungarian nobleman who came to Scotland in 1067 in the retinue of Edgar the Aetheling, brother of Margaret, later queen of Malcolm III. Bartolf was apparently a man of intellect and bravery, for which qualities Malcolm appointed him governor of Edinburgh Castle and bestowed on him estates in Fife, Angus, the Mearns and Aberdeenshire. It is said that he was carrying the queen across a swollen river upon his own horse. The queen almost fell from the horse, whereupon Bartolf cried out 'Grip fast', and as the queen took hold of his belt buckle she replied, 'Will the buckle bide'. The river crossing was accomplished, and to commemorate the event the family has the motto, 'Grip fast', and they still carry belt buckles on their shield. Bartolf established his principal holding in the Garioch district of Aberdeen, at a place known then as Lesselyn, where he built a castle. From Lesselyn the name has evolved to Lesley, of which spellings still vary widely. Bartolf's son, Malcolm, was created constable of the royal castle at Inverury which he held for David II, and his great-grandson, Sir Norman Lesley, acquired the lands of Fythkill in Fife, afterwards called Lesley, around 1282.

The chiefly line passed to a junior branch of the family from whom the present chiefs, the Earls of Rothes descend in a curious manner. In 1391 Sir Norman Lesley, believing his only son, David, to have been killed in the Crusades, settled his estates on his cousin, George Lesley. In 1398, shortly after Sir George had taken possession of the castle and lands, David returned from the Wars and claimed possession of his estate. Time has now shrouded in mystery the exact terms of the settlement that was reached, but the family resolved matters peacefully. Sir George's grandson, another George, was created a Lord of Parliament in 1445 as Lord Lesley of Leven, and had all his lands united into the barony of Ballinbreich. He was advanced to the title of Earl of Rothes sometime prior to 1458. The third Earl died at Flodden in 1513. George, the fourth Earl, was one of the Scottish commissioners at the marriage of Mary, Queen of Scots to the heir to the throne of France in 1558. George died in mysterious circumstances at Dieppe, along with the Earl of Cascillus and two others. It was popularly believed that they had been poisoned for refusing to allow the crown of Scotland to be settled on the Dauphin.

Leslie

Standard

Thereafter, the Lesleys abandoned politics for a time, for the less hazardous career of professional soldiery. Europe throughout the seventeenth century was an almost permanent battleground, providing ample employment for the younger sons of many Scottish noble houses. Lesleys fought in Germany, France, Sweden and the Baltic. Perhaps the most famous of the Lesley mercenaries was Alexander Leslie, who was recalled from the Continent to take command of the Army of the Covenant, and was later raised to the peerage as the Earl of Leven. His seat was the great Tower of Balgonie which he improved and extended. (Although the castle fell into ruin, the main tower has now been fully restored as a family home, and the present Laird is a prominent heraldic craftsman.) David Lesley, of the Rothes family, was also a Covenanter commander. He defeated Montrose at Philiphaugh in 1645 and was routed by Cromwell's troops at Dunbar in 1650. He was captured the following year and imprisoned in the Tower of London until the Restoration in 1660, being created Lord Newark in the following year. Sir Alexander Leslie of

Auchintoul became a general in the Russian army and Governor of Smolensk. The seventh Earl was created Duke of Rothes in 1680 by Charles II. He was a great favourite of the king and one of the most distinguished statesmen of his time. The dukedom died with him as he left no male heir, but under the terms of an earlier charter the earldom could pass through the female line, and thus the title was preserved.

The ninth Earl was Vice Admiral of Scotland and governor of Stirling Castle. He was a supporter of the Hanoverians, and in 1715 he commanded a regiment of cavalry at the Battle of Sheriffmuir. He sold much of the Rothes estates, although the magnificent Leslie House near Fife remained the seat of the earls until 1926. Leslie Castle in Aberdeenshire has also been fully restored in recent years by David Lesley, a prominent local architect. There have been many other distinguished persons of this name, including Harald Leslie, Lord Birsay, a judge of the Scottish Land Court and twice Lord High Commissioner to the General Assembly of the Church of Scotland.

LINDSAY

The Lindsays came to prominence both in England and Scotland in the late eleventh century. Sir Walter de Lindissie, 'noble and knight' accompanied David, Earl of Huntingdon, brother of Alexander I, to Scotland to claim his throne. His great-grandson, Sir William de Lindesay, sat in the Parliament of 1164 and was afterwards a justiciar. He held the lands of Crawford, the earldom of which was to ultimately be the premier title of the chiefs, but he sat in Parliament as Baron of Luffness in East Lothian. He acquired considerable wealth through his wife, Ethelreda, a granddaughter of the great Cospatrick ruler of most of Northumbria. His son, Sir David, married Marjory, a member of the royal family, and on his death in 1214 he was succeeded as third Lord of Crawford and High Justiciar of Lothian by his son, David, who also inherited the English estates of Limesay and Wolveray. One of his descendents, another Sir David, was High Chamberlain of Scotland in 1256 and later died on the Crusade led by Louis of France in 1268. His grandson, yet another Sir David, succeeded to the estates as Lord of Crawford and was one of the barons whose seal was appended to the letter of 1320 to the pope, asserting the independence of Scotland, and more commonly known as the Declaration of Arbroath. In 1346, his second son and heir, Sir James de Lindsay, married Ejidia, daughter of Walter the High Steward of Scotland and half-sister to Robert II.

Sir David de Lindsay took part in the famous tournament at London Bridge in 1390 in the presence of Richard II of England, at which Lindsay won the day and the admiration of the English king. On 21 April 1398 he was created Earl of Crawford. He was Lord High Admiral of Scotland in 1403 and sent as ambassador to England in 1406. Alexander, the fourth Earl, joined in the rebellion against James II and fought at the Battle of Brechin in

1452. The royal forces were victorious and the earl was attainted for treason, but he was later pardoned. His daughter, Elizabeth, married John, the first Lord Drummond, who was ancestor of Henry, Lord Darnley, the King Consort of Mary, Queen of Scots and the father of James VI. The fifth Earl rose high in royal favour and was successively Lord High Admiral of Scotland, Master of the Royal Household, Lord Chamberlain and High Justiciary. The sixth Earl fell at Flodden, in close attendance on his king, James IV.

Ludovic Lindsay, who had learned his trade as a soldier on the Continent, fought for Charles I during the civil war. He commanded a regiment of cavalry at Marston Moor and was later with Montrose at Philiphaugh in 1645, where he was captured. He died without issue, having first resigned his earldom to the Crown for regrant to his kinsman John, Earl of Lindsay. The title remained in this branch of the family until the nineteenth century, when it passed to the Earls of Balcarres. The Lindsays of Balcarres descended from a younger son of the ninth Earl of Crawford, who were created earls in their own right in 1650 for eminent services during the civil war. The first Earl of Balcarres was made hereditary governor of Edinburgh Castle, Secretary of State for Scotland and High Commissioner to the General Assembly. His younger son, Colin, later the third Earl, was a staunch Jacobite who fought during the rising of 1715 and only escaped being attainted for treason through the intervention of his life-long friend, the Duke of Marlborough. Alexander, the sixth Earl of Balcarres, became the twenty-third Earl of Crawford, and his descendent, the twenty-ninth Earl, is the present chief.

Another prominent branch of the family were the Lindsays of Edzell, who descended

Lindsay

from a son of the ninth Earl of Crawford. Although Edzell Castle to the north of Brechin is now largely ruinous, it is famed for its magnificent renaissance garden which has been completely restored, and is unique in Scotland. The garden was laid out by Lord Edzell, a judge of the Supreme Court who, as a youth, had travelled widely on the Continent. The Lindsays have also contributed another unique aspect of Scottish heritage through the work of Sir David Lindsay of the Mount. His play, *Ane Satyre of the Three Estaitis*, satirising the corruption in Church and State, was first performed in 1540 and still has relevance today. It has been successfully revived twice this century to high critical acclaim.

The present chiefs still reside at Balcarres in Fife, where they are prominent in local affairs. The earldom of Lindsay has also been revived, although this line now bear the compound surname of Lindsay-Bethune.

LOCKHART

In early times this name was spelt
'Locard' or 'Lokart'. Like so many
Scottish families, the Locards came
from England where they were among those
dispossessed of their lands by William the
Conqueror. There were Lockards near Penrith
in the twelfth century and later in Annandale,
where the town of Lockerbie is said to be
named after them. The family finally settled in
Ayrshire and Lanarkshire, where they have
held land for over seven hundred years.

The earliest paper in the family archives is
a charter of 1323. By this, Sir Symon Locard
bound himself and his heirs to pay out of the
lands of Lee and Cartland an annual rent of
£10. Stephen Locard, grandfather of Sir
Symon, founded the village of Stevenston in
Ayrshire, which would have been a hamlet or
ferm-toun, housing farmers and workers on
his estate. His son, Symon, acquired lands in
Lanarkshire and, like his father, called a village which he founded, Symons Toun (today
Symington) after himself. Symon, the second
of Lee, won fame for himself and his family
fighting alongside Robert the Bruce in the
struggle to free Scotland from English domination, and was knighted for his loyal service.
Sir Symon was among the knights, led by Sir
James Douglas, who took Bruce's heart on
Crusade in 1329 to atone for his murder of
John Comyn in the Church of Greyfriars in
1306, and his consequent excommunication.
Douglas carried the king's heart in a casket, of
which Sir Symon carried the key. The crusade
was ended prematurely when Douglas was
killed fighting the Moors in Spain, but to commemorate the adventure and the honour done
to the family, their name was changed from
Locard to Lockheart, which afterwards became
Lockhart. The heart within a fetterlock was
from then on included in the arms of the family, and the deed is also commemorated in the
motto.

As well as a new name, the family gained

a precious heirloom on the Crusade: the mysterious charm known as the Lee Penny. Sir Walter Scott used the story of its acquisition by the family as a basis for his novel, *The Talisman*. Sir Symon captured a Moorish amir in battle in Spain, and received from the man's mother as part of his ransom, an amulet or stone with healing powers. The amir's mother told Sir Symon that the stone was a remedy against bleeding, fever, the bites of mad dogs

Standard

and the sicknesses of horses and cattle. The amulet was later set in a silver coin which has been identified as a fourpenny piece of the reign of Edward IV. The coin is kept in a gold snuffbox which was a gift from Maria Theresa, Empress of Austria, to her general, Count James Lockhart. Such was the belief in the amulet's powers that a descendent of Sir Symon, Sir James Lockhart of Lee, was charged with sorcery, an offence which could carry the death penalty. After examining the accused the Synod of the Church of Scotland dismissed the case, because 'the custom is only to cast a stone in some water and give deseasit cattle thereof to drink and the same is done without using any words such as charmers use in their unlawful practices and considering that in nature there are many things seem to work strange effects whereof no human wit

can give reason it having pleast God to give the stones and herbs a special virtue for healing of many infirmities in man and beast'.

Alan Lockhart of Lee was killed at the Battle of Pinkie in 1547. Sir James Lockhart of Lee, born in 1596, was appointed a gentleman of the Privy Chamber by Charles I and was knighted. In 1646 he was appointed to the Supreme Court Bench, taking the title of 'Lord Lee'. A zealous royalist, he was captured at Alyth in 1651 and conveyed to the Tower of London. His son, Sir William, was a distinguished soldier who fought on the royalist side at the Battle of Worcester in 1651. He later became reconciled to Cromwell's Commonwealth and married the Lord Protector's niece. Consequently, he was not in favour with the restored Stuart monarchs after 1660 and made his home in France. He then campaigned on the Continent, where he achieved such prominence that Cardinal Mazarin, successor to Cardinal Richelieu, offered to make him a mareschal of France. He died in the Netherlands in 1675. James Lockhart, who inherited the estates in 1777, also saw service on the Continent where he rose to be a count of the Holy Roman Empire, a Knight of the Order of Maria Theresa and a general of that empress's imperial forces. The title of count became extinct when James's only son, Charles, died without issue.

Lee Castle and estates have been out of family hands for some time but the present chief, Angus Lockhart of the Lee, still manages substantial lands around Carnwath.

LUMSDEN

The manor of Lumsdene is first mentioned in 1098 when Edgar, King of Scots, and son of Malcolm III and Margaret, refounded Coldingham Priory in the county of Berwick, endowing it with the villages of Coldingham, Lumsdene, Renton and Swinewood. The first recorded possessors of the land, divided into Easter and Wester Lumsden, were Gillem and Cren de Lummisden who, between 1166 and 1182, attested a charter granted to the Priory of Coldingham by Waldeve, Earl of Dunbar. Gilbert de Lumisden appears as witness to charters between 1249 and 1262. The common ancestor of the Lumsdens, Adam de Lumisden of that Ilk, and his son, Roger de Lummesdene, did homage to Edward I of England in 1296, and their names appear, with the variations of spelling, on the Ragman Roll.

From Adam, the first recognised chief of the name of Lumsden, descended Gilbert, who married the heiress of Blanerne, as evidenced by a charter of 15 June 1329, and he later adopted her crest of a white-tailed eagle, or 'earne', devouring a salmon. This crest is still used by the Fife armigerous branch of the family. From Gilbert's eldest son, another Gilbert, descended the families of Lumsden, or Lumsdaine of Blanerne in Berwickshire, and Airdrie, Innergellie, Stravithie, Lathallan and Rennyhill in Fife. Gilbert's younger son, Thomas, held the lands of Drum and Conland in Fife and East and West Medlar, or Cushnie, in Aberdeenshire as confirmed by a charter in 1353. From him descend the northern Lumsdens of Cushnie-Lumsden, Tillycairn, Clova and Auchindoir. The family of Burgess-Lumsden of Pitcaple descend through a female line. The more recent Lumsden estates of Balmedie, Belhelvie, Sluie and Banchory belonged or belong to cadet branches of these families. The senior line of Lumsden did not register their arms in 1672, but two cadet houses, of Alexander Lumsden of Cushnie and

Sir James Lumsden of Innergellie, did so, both registering undifferenced arms. At present there are thirteen members of the Lumsden family who bear arms, either as matriculated cadet descendents of Alexander and Sir James or on grants in their own right.

Lumsdens appear in Scottish history as soldiers, scholars and statesmen, and also included merchants, barristers, surgeons, churchmen and soldiers. Sir James Lumsden served under King Gustavus Adolphus of Sweden during the Thirty Years' War, and he and his brother, William, returned to fight for the royalists in the civil war, after the Battle of Marston Moor in 1644. The Lumsdens of Cushnie sat as barons of the north in Parliament.

Andrew Lumsden, who was grandson of Sir Andrew, primate of Scotland in the Episcopal Church in 1713, and was descended from Andrew, third son of Robert Lumsden, Baron of Cushnie, was secretary to Prince Charles Edward Stuart during the 1745 rising. Attainted after Culloden, he fled to Rome where he became secretary and later Secretary of State to James VIII, the 'Old Pretender', until the latter's death in 1766, when he rejoined Prince Charles until 1768. He returned to Scotland in 1773 and was fully pardoned in 1778 by the Hanoverian government. His tartan waistcoat is preserved at Pitcaple Castle.

Another cadet of Cushnie, Sir Harry Burnett Lumsden of Belhelvie, a knight both of the Order of the Star of India and of the Bath, founded the elite Lumsden's Guides, who served on the North-West Frontier of India. He was the first to use 'khaki', an Urdu word meaning 'dust-coloured', and was the

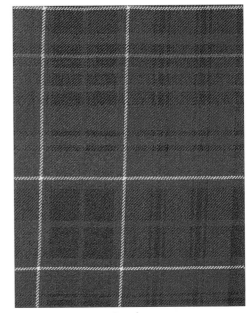

Lumsden

first to use uniforms of that colour; these were later to be universally adopted by the British army. John Lumsden of Cushnie was a director of the East India Company. Harry Leith Lumsden of Auchindoir founded the village of Lumsden in Aberdeenshire in 1825. Hugh Lumsden of Clova and Auchindoir was papal chamberlain to Pope Benedict XV.

The Lumsden Castle of Tillycairn has been splendidly restored in this century by the present Baron of Cushnie, and a gathering of the house of Lumsden was held there in 1988. The House of Lumsden Association was formed in 1972, and their work to gather together those of the name throughout the world reached a pinnacle in 1985, when the claim of the present hereditary chief was established in the Court of the Lord Lyon.

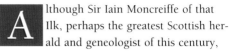

A lthough Sir Iain Moncreiffe of that Ilk, perhaps the greatest Scottish herald and geneologist of this century, believed that this family were of Celtic origin and descended from a younger son of the Lamonts, the generally accepted view is that they descend from a French family called de Leon, who came north with Edgar, son of Malcolm II, at the end of the eleventh century to fight against his uncle, Donald Bane, the usurper of the throne. Edgar was triumphant, and de Leon received lands in Perthshire which were later called Glen Lyon.

Roger de Leonne witnessed a charter of Edgar to the Abbey at Dunfermline in 1105. In 1372 Robert II granted to Sir John Lyon, called the White Lyon because of his fair complexion, the thanage of Glamis. Five years later he became Chamberlain of Scotland, and his prominence was such that he was considered fit to marry the king's daughter, Princess Jean, who brought with her not only illustrious lineage, but also the lands of Tannadice on the River Esk. He was later also granted the barony of Kinghorne. He was killed during a quarrel with Sir James Lindsay of Crawford near Menmuir in Angus. The family have descended in a direct line from the White Lion and Princess Jean to the present day, and their crest alludes to this. His only son, another John, was his successor, and he strengthened the royal ties by marrying a granddaughter of Robert II. Sir John's son, Patrick, was created Lord Glamis in 1445 and thereafter became a Privy Councillor and Master of the Royal Household. He had earlier discovered that being a courtier was not always an easy life, when he was one of those sent to England as a hostage in 1424 for the ransom of James I. John, the sixth Lord Glamis, was, according to tradition, a quarrelsome man with a quick temper. He married Janet Douglas, granddaughter of the famous Archibald 'Bell the Cat', and in the years following his death she suffered terribly for the hatred which James V bore to all of her name. Lady Glamis was accused on trumped-up charges of witchcraft and, despite speaking boldly in her own defence, her doom was preordained. She was burned at the stake on the castle hill at Edinburgh on 3 December 1540. Her death was much lamented, as she was 'in the prime of her years, of a singular beauty, and suffering all, though a woman, with a man-like courage, all men conceiving that it was not this but the hatred which the King carried to her brothers'. Her young son was also found guilty of conspiracy and sentenced to death, the sentence to be carried out when he had come of age. He was fortunate that he did not do so until after the king's death, when he was released. The king took possession of Glamis and plundered it.

The eighth Lord Glamis renounced his allegiance to Mary, Queen of Scots and served under the Regents Moray and Lennox. He was made Chancellor of Scotland and Keeper of the Great Seal for life, and his son, the ninth Lord, was captain of the Royal Guard and one of James VI's Privy Councillors. In 1606 he was created Earl of Kinghorne, Viscount Lyon and Baron Glamis. His son, the second Earl, was a close personal friend of the Marquess of Montrose and was with him when he subscribed to the National Covenant in 1638. He accompanied Montrose on his early campaigns in defence of the Covenant, but despite his great affection for the Marquess, he could not support him when he broke with the Scots Parliament to fight for Charles I. Lyon almost ruined his estates in supporting the Army of the Covenant against his friend.

In 1677 the third Earl of Kinghorne obtained a new patent of nobility, being styled thereafter Earl of Strathmore and Kinghorne Viscount Lyon, Baron Glamis, Tannadyce, Sidlaw and Strathdichtie. He paid off the debts he inherited from his father by skilful manage-

The full achievement of the Earl of Strathmore and Kinghorne

ment of the estates and was later able to alter and enlarge the Castle of Glamis. John, his son, although a member of the Privy Council, opposed the Treaty of Union of 1707. His son was a Jacobite who fought in the rising of 1715 at the Battle of Sheriffmuir in Tullibardine's regiment. He died defending his regiment's colours. In 1716 James, the 'Old Pretender', son of James VII, was entertained at Glamis. Thirty years later another king's son, but a much less welcome one, the Duke of Cumberland, stopped at the castle on his march north to Culloden. It is said that after he left the bed which he had used was dismantled.

Among the Jacobite relics now preserved at Glamis are a sword and watch belonging to James VIII, the 'Old Pretender', and an intriguing tartan coat worn by him. The youngest daughter of the fourteenth Earl of Strathmore and Kinghorne is HM Queen Elizabeth, the Queen Mother.

MACALISTER

This important family was one of the earliest branches to assert its independence from the great Clan Donald. Some doubt exists as to the exact progenitor of this clan, but it is now accepted they are the descendents of Alastair Mor, son of Donald of the Isles. Alastair first appears as a witness to a charter granted by his brother Angus, Lord of the Isles, to the Abbey of Paisley around 1253. The lands of Lowp, later to be the chiefly designation of Loup, are mentioned in a charter by James III confirming lands in Kintyre to the Lord of the Isles. In 1481, Charles Macalister was made constable of the Castle of Tarbert, and received a grant of lands in Kintyre. Charles was succeeded as chief by his son, John, who is the first to be styled 'of the Lowp'. The Castle of Tarbert was used by James IV as a naval supply base during his campaign to suppress the Lordship of the Isles. Clan Alastair occupied an influential position, although they were by no means a numerous clan, and therefore sought to secure their position by alliances with other houses. In 1591, Godfrey Macalister of Loup received a charter from the Earl of Argyll in relation to lands at Tarbert which they held until after 1745.

The Macalisters were not immune from family quarrels, and in 1598 Godfrey Macalister killed his tutor and guardian, Charles Macalister, and thereafter besieged his sons at their house at Askomull. In 1600 the island of Arran was invaded by the Macalisters, who seized the house and estates of John Montgomery of Skelmorlie, plundering possessions valued at £12,000 Scots. Two years later, Archibald Macalister, the heir of Tarbert, led his men, along with other clans of north Kintyre, to raid the prosperous island of Bute. It is said that a force of over twelve hundred men ravaged the Stewart possessions on the island, for which act Archibald Macalister was denounced as a rebel. In 1605 Archibald and his kinsman, John Macalister, tutor of Loup, were ordered to appear before the Privy Council and fined surety on pain of being denounced as rebels. Alexander Macalister, along with Angus Og, leader of the Macdonalds of Islay were found guilty of treason and after incarceration in the prison of the Tolbooth in Edinburgh, they were hanged. However, by 1623 Macalister of Loup was one of the justices of the peace for Argyllshire.

The Macalisters came to Stirlingshire some time in the fourteenth century, and during generations that followed their Celtic name was anglicised into its more familiar lowland version, Alexander. By the sixteenth century they settled on the estates of Menstrie only a few miles north-east of the mighty royal Castle of Stirling. William Alexander of Menstrie became a courtier under the patronage of the Earl of Argyll. He was instrumental in promoting the colonisation of the Scottish territories in Canada, known as Nova Scotia, and devised the scheme whereby those investing in the colony would receive the honour known as a Baronetcy of Nova Scotia. The scheme was a roaring success, although it did more to bolster the flagging royal finances than secure the development of the far-distant colony. There is a splendid room displaying the arms of the Baronets of Nova Scotia still preserved at Menstrie. He was rewarded by his grateful royal master first with a viscountcy, and then the earldom of Stirling. In 1631 Archibald Macalister of Tarbert visited his kinsman, William Alexander, now Earl of Stirling, at his Castle of Menstrie, and the earl procured for his guest election as a burgess of the royal burgh of Stirling in August of that

Macalister

year. It was during his kinsman of Tarbert's visit that the earl obtained an acknowledgment that he was chief of the Macalisters. This was, of course, entirely a product of the earl's vanity, and had no genealogical basis whatsoever.

By 1706 Tarbert had passed from the Macalisters into the possession of the Macleans. The chiefs continued to flourish on their lands of Loup and a younger son, Duncan, settled in Holland in 1717, where he rose to high rank in the army; his descendents can still be traced to this day. The chiefly family eventually sold off their estates in Kintyre, and the present chief lives in England. Glenbarr Abbey is the modern clan centre, displaying many interesting artifacts and mementoes of the name.

MACBAIN

There are several possible Gaelic origins for this name, but the most likely appears to be 'bheathain', meaning 'lively one'. This could also have been rendered as 'Mac'ic'Bheatha', or Macbeth, a name evocative of Scotland's early history. When Malcolm III deposed the line of Macbeth from the throne, his power was constantly challenged by the powerful noble families of Moray. Unrest continued in the region for several generations until, in the reign of Malcolm IV, the power of the mormaers of Moray was finally broken, and various members of the family sought refuge in other parts of the kingdom. According to tradition, the ancestor of the Macbains sought out his kin among the descendents of Gillichattan Mor, more commonly called the Clan Chattan. They bore on their shield the galley which is also borne by Macbain, alluding to their common ancestry. It is believed that Macbain formed part of the wedding party that accompanied Eva, daughter of Dougal Dall, sixth in line from Gillichattan Mor, on her marriage to Angus, chief of the Mackintoshes, in 1291. Macbain was welcomed by his Mackintosh hosts and settled around Inverness. In order to avoid further royal persecution, the Macbains joined the Chattan confederation of clans, and the chief's crest and motto clearly demonstrate this.

The earliest certain record of the name in its more modern form appears in an old Kinrara manuscript of the mid fourteenth century, which names both Bean MacMilmhor and his son, Milmor Macbean. The Macbains supported Robert the Bruce in the struggle for Scottish independence, and they are credited with the killing of the steward of the Red Comyn, whose master had been stabbed to death by Bruce himself in the Greyfriars Church at Dumfries in 1306. They fought at the Battle of Harlaw in 1411 along with the rest of the Chattan Confederation on the side of the Macdonald Lord of the Isles in the last serious attempt to wrest the ancient Lordship of the Isles from the grip of the king of Scots. They suffered heavy losses in what was otherwise an evenly matched battle, and in the history of Clan Mackintosh it is recorded that 'the Mackintosh mourned the loss of so many of his friends and people, especially of Clan Vean'. Paul Macbean, the twelfth chief, was weighed down by heavy debts and was forced to relinquish his lands around 1685. The present chiefly line descends from his younger son, the elder line having ended in a daughter, Elizabeth Margaret Macbean, who married Dougald Stuart around 1790, but died without issue. The loss of the lands of the clan at Kinchyle must have been sorely felt, but happily the present chief has continued the work of his father, who retrieved some of the clan lands and established the Macbain Memorial Park on the slopes above Loch Ness.

Macbain

Standard

The martial prowess of this clan has never been in doubt, and it is perhaps fitting that much of their history honours the memory and the feats of the greatest Macbean warrior, Gillies, one of the great heroes of the Battle of Culloden. The Macbains had supported the earlier Jacobite rising of 1715, and many were transported to the plantations in Virginia, Maryland and South Carolina after the Stuart defeat. This did not deter Gillies Mor Macbean, grandson of the twelfth chief, from taking up commission as a major to fight for Bonnie Prince Charlie, the 'Young Pretender'. On that fateful day in 1746, Gillies, a giant of a man said to be at least 6 feet 4 inches, saw government dragoons breaking through to assault the Highlanders in the flank. The major threw himself into the gap and, with his back to the wall, cut down thirteen or four-

teen of his assailants until he himself was mortally wounded. A Hanoverian officer called back his men in an attempt to save a brave fellow soldier, but Macbean was already dead. Other Macbains also distinguished themselves on that bloody field, and it was a Macbain who assisted Cameron of Lochiel, who was wounded and unable to walk, to escape to safety. Aeneas Macbean made good his escape after the battle by leaping repeatedly from one side of a stream to the other until his exhausted pursuers were forced to give up.

After Culloden the chief struggled to keep the remaining clan lands together, but they were finally sold in 1760. The military prowess of the clan continued unabated. Lieutenant General Forbes Macbean was appointed commander of artillery in Canada in 1778. William Macbean had an extraordinary military career, rising from the rank of private to that of major general, earning the Victoria Cross for gallantry during the Indian Mutiny of 1858. It was a Macbain who commanded the Gordon Highlanders against the Boers of South Africa in 1881. In this century the chiefly line has flourished, first in Canada and now in the United States.

MACDONALD OF MACDONALD

The Clan Donald, often described as
the most powerful of the clans, hold
as their eponymous ancestor Donald
of Islay, who succeeded his father Reginald or
Ranald, son of Somerled, Lord of the Isles in
1207. Somerled's campaigns spanned over
forty years, during which time he gained a
kingdom and the hand of Ragnhild, daughter
of King Olav the Red, Norse King of Man and
the Isles. The story of this match is part of the
origin legends of Clan Macintyre. The new
empire stretched from Bute to Ardnamurchan,
including Lorne, Argyll and Kintyre on the
mainland. On Somerled's death his realm was
partitioned between his heirs, each of whom
was to establish the fortunes of a great clan.
Dugall received Lorne, Mull and Jura, and
from him sprang the Macdougalls. Angus had
Bute, Arran and Garmoran (Moydart, Morar
and Knoydart), which passed through his
heiress, Jane, to the Stewarts. Reginald fell heir
to Islay and Kintyre, which passed in due
course to his son, Donald. Unlike his father,
who seems to have tempered personal valour
with a love of peace and culture, Donald was
an iron warrior. He perpetrated so many black
deeds in defence of his possessions that he
feared for his salvation, and went on a pilgrimage to Rome to seek absolution for his
sins from the pope. He died, probably in 1269,
when he was succeeded by Angus Mor.

When Alexander III determined to oppose
the nominal suzerainty of Norway over the
Hebrides, he provoked the launching of King
Haakon's Norwegian fleet, which anchored off
Largs in 1263. Angus Mor and his uncle,
Ruari, were technically vassals of Haakon, and
after his defeat at the Battle of Largs, con-
firmed in the Treaty of Perth in 1266, the king
of Scots became their overlord. An uneasy
truce existed for a time, and Angus's son,
Angus Og, came to the aid of Robert the
Bruce, leading his fierce clansmen against
Edward II of England at Bannockburn in 1314.

When Angus Og died in 1330, he left two sons. John, later Lord of the Isles, and Iain, from whom descended the Macdonalds (Maciains) of Glencoe. John's son, Donald, inherited the lordship in 1386. He unsuccessfully laid claim to the great earldom of Ross through his wife, Margaret, which led to the bloody Battle of Harlaw in 1411. After his defeat at Harlaw, Donald returned to his island fastness, and it was left to his son, Alexander, to reassert, this time successfully, their right to the earldom.

The power of the lordship reached its peak under Alexander's son, John, Earl of Ross and Lord of the Isles. Not since the time of Somerled had the isles enjoyed such independence, but his ambitions were to be John's undoing. He entered into the Treaty of Ardtornish with Henry VII of England in 1462, agreeing to accept the English king as overlord once James IV had been defeated. James, with customary decisiveness, acted swiftly, invading the isles and ultimately stripping John of all his titles in May 1493. Attempts were made over the next two generations to revive the lordship, but by 1545 it had become a forlorn hope. The various branches of the descendents of Donald gradually accepted Crown charters and recognition of their separate holdings. This was part of the successful royal policy to keep Clan Donald divided, and thereby less of a threat to central authority.

Macdonald of Macdonald

Standard

Various claims were made to the chiefship of the whole Clan Donald, but by the late seventeenth century, Hugh Macdonald of Sleat on Skye was recognised by the Privy Council as Laird of Macdonald. The lairds were first created baronets and then, in 1776, Lords Macdonald in the Irish peerage. The third Lord Macdonald sought to split the paramount chiefship with the peerage, from the house and baronetcy of Sleat, and an Act of Parliament was procured in 1847 to effect this. (The process is explained in the chapter on the Macdonalds of Sleat.) The dispute was resolved in 1947, when the present chief's father was recognised by the Lord Lyon as Lord Macdonald, high chief of Clan Donald, under whom are recognised the chiefs of Sleat, Clanranald and Glengarry. A recent petition to the Lord Lyon in favour of a claimant to be recognised as chief of the Macdonalds of Keppoch was unsuccessful, but may be resubmitted. A highly active Clan Donald Society now exists, with its centre at Armadale Castle on Skye. Lord Macdonald still lives on the island and is vice-convenor of the Council of Chiefs.

MACDONALD OF CLANRANALD

On a broken cross shaft found on the island of Texa off Islay is carved what is probably the oldest surviving likeness of a Macdonald. It depicts a typical fourteenth-century Celtic prince, wearing a quilted coat with chain-mail and a conical helmet, and armed with a great sword and a battle-axe. This is the Cross of Ranald, son of John of Islay, Lord of the Isles, by his marriage to Amy Macruari, the heiress to the great Lordship of Garmoran, a vast inheritance of lands between the Great Glen and the Outer Hebrides. There seems now little doubt that Ranald was the second and the eldest surviving son of John and Amy, and heir to the chiefship of Clan Donald. The succession did not, however, pass to him, but to Donald, his younger half-brother, whose mother was a daughter of Robert II and a Stewart princess. Ranald had received a charter from his father, confirmed by Robert II in 1373, of the greater part of the Macruari inheritance, including Moydart, Arisaig and Lochaber. Clan historians believe this was part of an arrangement whereby Ranald accepted being passed over as high chief. Ranald actively participated in Donald's installation at Eigg.

Ranald had five sons, including Alan, the eldest, who was to succeed as chief of Clanranald, and Donald, who founded the line of Glengarry. Alan Macranald died at his Castle of Tirrim in 1419, succeeded by his son, Roderick, who was a staunch supporter of the Lord of the Isles. Roderick, believed to have died in 1481, was succeeded by his eldest son, Alan. A capable and war-like chief, he led a raid into Lochaber and Badenoch in 1491, which culminated in the capture of Inverness Castle. Clanranald appears to have adjusted to the realities of royal power, and on the first visit of James IV to the Highlands, Alan Macruari was one of the few chiefs to render him homage.

Alexander, the seventh chief, led a comparatively peaceful life, marrying three times and raising a large family. He had an illegitimate son, John Moidartach, who was to succeed him in the chiefship. Why all of his other sons were passed over is a mystery, but it may have been that John was the fittest person to lead the clan to war, an ability which at that time was still an essential element of chiefship. He was expressly legitimated by an Act of the Privy Council on 15 January 1531. His rule commenced in the midst of turmoil: James V had annulled all charters given to the chiefs while he was still a minor, and the chiefs had rebelled. James led an expedition to the isles and Clanranald was arrested. In his absence, Ranald Gallda, another descendant of Alan Macruari, occupied Castle Tirrim. When the king died in 1542 the Earl of Arran became regent to the infant Mary, Queen of Scots. He promptly released the imprisoned island chiefs to use them as a counterbalance to the powerful Argyll. Ranald Gallda fled to his kinsman, Lord Lovat, while John gathered his forces to oppose Ranald. They met to the north of Loch Lochy in 1544 in a battle called Blar-na-leine, where Ranald was killed. John was acknowledged as chief of Clanranald in 1584 by James V's widow, Mary of Guise, the Queen Regent.

Macdonald of Clanranald

Standard

The chiefs of Clanranald were staunch supporters of Charles I, and played a distinguished part in Montrose's great victory at Inverlochy in 1645. The chief's son, Donald, followed Montrose in his other great victory at Kilsyth, where he led the charge which shattered General Baillie's Lowland infantry. John of Moidartach and Donald lived to see the Restoration in 1660. Alan, the fourteenth chief, succeeded Donald when he was only thirteen. Three years later, in 1689, he led his clan to join Viscount Dundee to fight for James VII. He was forced to flee to France, and for a time served in the French army. When the Stuart royal standard was unfurled on the Braes of Mar on 6 September 1715, Alan hurried to be first to rally to the Jacobite cause. His grateful monarch created him Lord Clanranald. He was killed at the head of his clan at the Battle of Sheriffmuir in November 1715. His brother, Ranald, assumed the chiefship, but spent the rest of his life in exile in France. Succession passed to Donald of Benbecula, who had also fought at Killiecrankie. It was his son, Ranald, who became famous during the rising of 1745 as Old Clanranald, to distinguish him from his dashing son, Ranald, Younger of Clanranald, who led the clan out for Bonnie Prince Charlie, the 'Young Pretender'. After Culloden, young Clanranald escaped to France but was allowed to return to Scotland in 1754.

The descendents of 'Young Clanranald of the Forty-five' died out in 1944, and the chiefship, or captaincy, passed to the heirs of Alexander Macdonald of Boisdale, a younger brother of the seventeenth chief. Ranald Alexander Macdonald, captain of Clanranald, the present chief, was recognised by the Lord Lyon in 1956.

MACDONALD OF SLEAT

The Macdonalds of Sleat descend from Uisdein or Hugh, younger son of Alexander, Lord of the Isles, who had died at Dingwall in 1449. Hugh was a man of power and ability, and sat on his brother's Council of the Isles. In 1495, after the Lords of the Isles had been forfeited, Hugh obtained a Crown charter to the lands he held. These he passed to his son, John, whose own sons plunged the clan into a period of death and destruction. John eventually married a daughter of Macleod of Harris by whom he had one son, Donald Hearach, but he also had at least four more sons, each by different mothers. Gilleasbuig Dubh, or Black Archibald, his son by a daughter of Torquil Macleod of Lewis, has been said by clan historians to have had a soul as dark as his complexion. He conspired with two more of his half-brothers, Angus Dubh and Angus Collach, to murder both Donald Hearach and the eldest of John's illegitimate sons, Donald Gallach. Black Archibald had Gallach strangled, and stabbed Donald Hearach in the back after inviting him to dinner to view a new galley he had built. Reprisals followed, and Archibald's half-brothers both died violent deaths. Archibald became, in this manner, the sole surviving son of John. He paid the penalty for a life of blood when he was murdered by his nephews, Ranald and Donald Gruamach. Donald was proclaimed chief, probably around 1518.

Donald's son, Donald Gorm, is best remembered for his attempt to restore the ancient Lordship of the Isles. He was proclaimed chief of Clan Donald and Lord of the Isles, and in 1539 he led his men against the great Mackenzie castle at Eilean Donan in Kintail. Macdonald's galleys came under fire from the castle which was commanded by Duncan Macrae. Donald Gorm was shot in the leg by one of Macrae's arrows, which severed an artery, and the chief died from loss of

blood. The feud with the Mackenzies was settled in 1569 at the Council of Perth. Donald
Gorm's son died in 1575, leaving his heir,
Donald Gorm Mor, a minor. When he reached
manhood, he embarked upon a campaign
against the Macleans. The men of Sleat
invaded Mull but, after some initial success,
they were driven back to their galleys. In 1608
Donald, along with his kinsmen Clanranald,
the Maclean of Duart and other leading chiefs,
was invited to meet the king's representative,
Lord Ochiltree, to discuss the royal policy for
the isles. The chiefs disagreed with Ochiltree's
plans, and were consequently imprisoned.
Donald was confined in Blackness Castle, only
being released when he agreed to submit to
the king. He died in December 1616, when he
was succeeded by his nephew, Sir Donald
Macleod, later first Baronet of Sleat. He supported the royalist cause in the civil war, and
when he died in 1643, his son sent four hundred of his clansmen to join Montrose. They
were led by Donald Macdonald of Castleton,
and they returned to the islands only when
the king ordered his forces to disband.

Sleat remained loyal to the Stuart cause
and fought with his clansmen at Killiecrankie
in 1689, when they suffered heavy losses. His
son, Sir Donald, the fourth Baronet, was an
ardent Jacobite, and although he was taken ill
and forced to return home, he left his brothers, James and William, to lead the clan at the
Battle of Sheriffmuir. Despite strong Jacobite
sympathies, the next chief, Sir Alexander, took
no part in the rising of 1745 and the Sleat
estates remained intact. Sir Alexander's second
son, who succeeded as ninth Baronet, was created Lord Macdonald in July 1776.

Sir Godfrey, the eleventh Baronet and
third Lord Macdonald, became a professional
soldier and served in the Peninsular War of
1808–14, achieving the rank of lieutenant general. He married Louisa, natural daughter of
the Duke of Gloucester, brother of George III.
He did not, however, contract a marriage

Macdonald of Sleat

which was legally recognised in England until
1803, by which time his wife had borne him
three children. They subsequently had ten
more. Although Lord Macdonald's eldest son
was legitimate in Scots law, he was not so
under the law of England. Macdonald therefore settled upon him the substantial estates
he had inherited from his mother, who was
the heiress of the old Anglo–Norman family of
Bosville of Thorpe in Yorkshire. He decreed
that his eldest son should change his name to
Bosville, while the eldest son born after the
marriage was recognised in England should
have the chiefship of Clan Donald and the
peerage. A private Act of Parliament was procured in 1847 to regulate the position in
accordance with the chief's wishes. However,
in 1910, Alexander Bosville, grandson of
Macdonald's eldest son, obtained a declarator
in the Court of Session that his grandfather
was legitimate and he was therefore entitled to
resume the name of Macdonald and the
Scottish baronetcy, a decision which over-
turned the settlement which had been reached
in the previous century.

MACDONNELL OF GLENGARRY

G lengarry lies in Lochaber, part of the ancient kingdom or province of Moray once ruled by the Picts. Ranald, a son of the Lord of the Isles, had five sons, including Alan, the progenitor of Clanranald, and Donald. Donald married firstly Laleve, daughter of Maciver, by whom he had a son, John. He took as his second wife a daughter of Fraser of Lovat, and had two further sons, Alexander and Angus. John died without heirs and he was succeeded by his half-brother, Alexander, considered by some historians to be the first true chief of Glengarry, but usually counted as the fourth.

It was not until the late fifteenth century that Glengarry played an independent part in the politics of Clan Donald. Royal policy to pacify the Highlands required that the traditional rights of chiefs should be replaced with feudal relationships, in which the Crown was acknowledged as ultimate superior. James V received the submission of most chiefs, and even lofty Clanranald accepted charters in 1494. Alexander of Glengarry did not receive a Crown charter at this time, which may suggest that he continued to have a rebellious attitude, but in 1531 he finally submitted to royal authority, and was pardoned for all past offences. On 6 March 1539, Alexander received a Crown charter to the lands of Glengarry and Morar, half the lands of Lochalsh, Lochcarron and Lochbroom, together with the Castle of Strome. However, this did not stop Alexander from following Donald Gorm of Sleat in his attempt to reclaim the Lordship of the Isles. The rebellion swiftly collapsed when Donald was killed while attacking Eilean Donan Castle. Glengarry was among the island chiefs tricked into attending on James V at Portree, whereupon they were seized and imprisoned in Edinburgh. Glengarry remained in the castle until the king's death in 1542, and he himself died in 1560. His son, Angus, the new chief, seems to have been politically astute, and he was able to use the influence of his father-in-law, the Laird of Grant, to regain his ancestral estates by charter of James VI in July 1574.

Angus's son, Donald, who succeeded him as eighth of Glengarry, is reputed to have lived for more than a hundred years and ruled his clan for at least seventy. He obtained a charter under the great seal in March 1627, erecting his lands of Glengarry into a free barony. However, he had not always enjoyed such royal favour. Donald had been infuriated by the treatment of his kinsmen a year earlier, when they had been invited to dinner on board the ship of Lord Ochiltree, the king's representative, to discuss royal policy for the isles. They disagreed with the king's plans, and were consequently arrested and imprisoned on the mainland. In February 1609, Donald was warned by the Privy Council to stop harbouring fugitives from the isles, and to appear before them on 25 March in that year to answer for his conduct. He failed to appear, and was denounced as a rebel. When Charles I's religious policies brought him in direct conflict with many of his Scottish subjects, Glengarry was too old for active campaigning. Effective leadership of the clan passed to his grandson, Aeneas, who became the ninth chief when his grandfather died on the very day of Montrose's victory at Inverlochy. Aeneas was with Montrose at that victory, as well as at Dundee and Auldearn. Five hundred of Glengarry's men fought in the Marquess's most impressive pitched battle, when he routed General Baillie at Kilsyth. When Montrose was surprised by a strong force of Covenanter cavalry at Philiphaugh, he barely escaped with his life, and made his way to safety in the Highlands. He was sheltered by Aeneas at Invergarry Castle. Aeneas's devotion to the Stuart cause was so strong that he led his men south into England, only to be utterly defeated by Cromwell at Worcester in September 1651. Glengarry made good his escape, but his estates were forfeit under the Commonwealth. At the Restoration his loyalty was rewarded when he was created a peer, taking the title of

Macdonnell of Glengarry

'Lord Macdonell and Aros'. The honour was short-lived; when he died in 1680 without issue, his peerage became extinct. The Stuart monarchs called upon the Macdonells again when they returned to claim their throne in 1715, and at the Battle of Sheriffmuir, when the captain of Clanranald was killed, Alasdair, eleventh of Glengarry, is said to have rallied the dismayed Highlanders by throwing up his bonnet and crying, 'Revenge today and mourning tomorrow'. On 9 December 1716, James VIII, the 'Old Pretender', issued a patent of nobility under his hand and great seal, raising Alasdair to the peerage as Lord Macdonell. The title was, of course, only recognised by Jacobites. Alasdair Ruadh, the thirteenth chief, was captured by an English frigate when hurrying from France to join the rising of 1745. He was conveyed to the Tower of London and was not released until 1747.

The chiefs of Glengarry have served their country ably in the field in the last two centuries. General Sir James Macdonell, brother of the fourteenth chief, was one of the heroes of the Battle of Waterloo in 1815. The present chief, who attained the rank of air commodore, is one of the few surviving fighter pilots of the Battle of Britain of 1940.

MACDOUGALL

ARMS
Quarterly, 1st & 4th, Azure, a lion rampant Argent,
armed and langued Gules;
2nd & 3rd, Or, a lymphad Sable, sails furled and a
beacon on the topmast Proper

CREST
(on a chapeau Gules furred Ermine)
A dexter arm in armour embowed fessways couped
Proper, holding a cross crosslet fitchée erect Gules

MOTTO
Buaidh no bas (To conquer or die)

SUPPORTERS
(on a compartment embellished with bell heather)
Two lions Azure, armed and langued Gules and
imperially crowned Or

STANDARD
The Arms in the hoist and of two tracts Azure and
Argent, upon which is depicted the Badge in the first and
third compartments and the Crest in the second compart-
ment, along with the Motto 'Buaidh no bas' in letters
Azure upon two transverse bands Or

BADGE
A demi-lion rampant Azure, langued Gules and
imperially crowned Or issuant from a chaplet of bell
heather

PLANT BADGE
Bell heather

This clan takes its name from Dougall, Somerled's son, who, after his father's death in 1164, held most of Argyll and also the islands of Mull, Lismore, Jura, Tiree, Coll and many others. The Celtic Christian name Dougall, or Dugald, is derived from the Gaelic 'dubh-gall', meaning 'black stranger'. His royal descent was acknowledged by the king of Norway, and he styled himself 'King of the South Isles and Lord of Lorne'. His son, Duncan, and his grandson, Ewan, built castles to defend their broad dominions, including Dunstaffnage, Dunollie and Duntrune on the mainland, and Aros, Cairnburgh, Dunchonnel and Coeffin on the islands. Dunollie, a crag rising up over seventy feet, was probably fortified as early as the sixth century and was to become the chief seat. Duncan also built Ardchattan Priory, where the Macdougall chiefs were buried until 1737.

Ewan held his island possessions from the king of Norway and his mainland ones from the king of Scots, and he found it hard to remain loyal to both. A choice was forced upon him in 1263, when King Haakon of Norway arrived off Oban with a huge fleet for his planned invasion of the west coast of Scotland. Ewan declined to join the invasion and because of the old blood ties, Haakon left him in peace. However, Ewan saw that neutrality would ultimately lead to disaster, and attacked part of the Norse fleet near Mull. The Vikings were utterly defeated at the Battle of Largs, and three years later all of the Hebrides were ceded by Norway to Scotland.

Their influence in Argyll brought them into conflict with the Campbells, and in 1294 John Macdougall, the Lame, led the clan against them. At the path of Lorn, between Loch Avich and Scammadale, the Macdougalls were intercepted, and although Sir Colin Campbell was killed, there was considerable slaughter on both sides.

The marriage of the fourth chief, Sir Alexander Macdougall, was disastrous for his clan. His wife was the sister of John Comyn, Lord of Badenoch, whose son, generally called the Red Comyn, was stabbed to death by Robert the Bruce in the Greyfriars Church in Dumfries in May 1306. This started a blood feud with Bruce's family and the Macdougalls, who had supported Wallace and the cause of Scottish independence, now became implacable enemies. Shortly after his hurried coronation at Scone, King Robert was forced to retreat before the victorious English into Argyll, hoping to reach his Campbell allies. The Macdougalls surprised the king at Dalrigh near Tyndrum. The king escaped, but it is said that on his discarded cloak was found a magnificent example of Celtic jewellery which was later known as the 'brooch of Lorne', and it became one of the clan's great treasures. Two years later Bruce led three thousand battle-hardened veterans into Argyll against them. John of Lorne set an ambush for the king's army at the narrow pass of Brander, but after a savage engagement they were broken and forced to flee. The king formally forfeited the Mac-dougall lands, most of which passed to the Campbells in recognition of their loyalty.

Standard

The Macdougalls were never to regain their island possessions, but to a large degree their fortunes were restored when Euan Macdougall married a granddaughter of Robert the Bruce. Most of the mainland estates were re-granted by a royal charter of David II. When the last Macdougall Lord of Lorne died, leaving an only daughter who had married Sir John Stewart, the lordship passed to that family. The chiefship then devolved to a line which had supported Bruce and had been granted Dunollie Castle, which the chief had forfeited in 1314.

Macdougall

During the troubled times of the early seventeenth century the Macdougalls were generally royalist, and in 1645 Alexander Macdougall led five hundred of his clansmen into battle. After the defeat of the Marquess of Montrose, a Covenanting army under David Leslie was sent to Argyll to deal with royalist sympathisers.

On the restoration of the monarchy the Macdougall lands were again restored. Their loyalty to the Stuarts was proved again when the twenty-second chief, Iain Ciar, fought in the rising of 1715 at the Battle of Sheriffmuir. The chief was forced into exile, but later returned to Scotland to live as a fugitive until he was pardoned in 1727. His son, Alexander, although certainly a Jacobite sympathiser, did not join the Forty-five, although his brother and some clansmen fought at Culloden. Alexander built a more modern house behind Dunollie Castle and it was extended in the mid nineteenth century by the twenty-fifth chief, Vice Admiral Sir John Macdougall of Macdougall. He had a distinguished naval career and actively promoted the development of the port of Oban. Three of his sons were to become chiefs in succession,

MACDOWALL

name from Galloway, the district in the south-west of Scotland which took its name from the Galli, or Gaelic settlers of the seventh and eighth centuries. Fabulous legends exist surrounding the foundation of the princedom of Galloway, and even the scholarly Nisbet could not resist narrating that Dovall of Galloway killed Nothatus the Tyrant in 230 BC. The royal house of Galloway apparently also resisted the Romans, and Nisbet asserted that from these early deeds the lords charged their shield with a fierce lion royally crowned.

The Lords of Galloway were certainly powerful, scattering their ancient princedom with well-endowed abbeys and priories. Fergus of Galloway, who flourished in the reign of David I, appears to have divided his princedom between his sons. One of his sons, or perhaps a grandson, was called Dougal. The last of the native Lords of Galloway, Alan, died around 1234. His daughter, Devorgilla, had married Balliol, Lord of Barnard Castle. Their son, John, claimed Galloway in right of his mother. He also claimed the throne of Scotland. Balliol, as Lord of Galloway, granted a charter of the lands of Garthland to Dougal in 1295. A year later, Dougal and Fergus M'douall appear on the Ragman Roll of nobles swearing fealty to Edward I of England. Dougal's grandson, Fergus, third of Garthland, was sheriff depute for Kirkcudbright in the reign of David II. His grandson, Sir Fergus Macdowall, the fifth Laird, was taken prisoner by the English at the Battle of Homildon in 1401. Uchtred, the ninth of Garthland, married Isabel Gordon of the branch of that great family who controlled Lochinver. Uchtred and his son, Thomas, were both killed at the Battle of Flodden in September 1513, along with James IV and the flower of Scottish chivalry.

Dynastic dispute was also to claim the life of John, the eleventh Laird, when he rode to oppose the invading army of Henry VIII at

Pinkie near Musselburgh in 1547. He had taken the precaution of passing his estates to his son, Uchtred, the twelfth Laird of Garthland, before going to war. This Uchtred was to become implicated in the Raid of Ruthven in August 1582, when the Earl of Gowrie and other Protestant nobles kidnapped the youthful James VI, holding him at Ruthven Castle and later at Edinburgh. The young king tried to maintain his composure in the pres-

Standard

ence of this threat to his person, but ultimately burst into tears. One of the conspirators, the Master of Glamis, exclaimed, 'No matter for his tears; better children weep than bearded men'. The king later escaped. It is not known what part Uchtred played in the conspiracy, but it was sufficient for him to require a pardon in 1584 and a fresh charter from the king to the barony of Garthland and Corswall. Uchtred's elder son, Uchtred Macdowall of Mondurk, may also have been implicated in treasonous activities and forfeited. He is styled 'of Mondurk', while his younger brother, Thomas, appears in a deed of 1591 as 'appar-

ent of Garthland', indicating that he was expected to succeed to his father's title. However, Uchtred of Mondurk appears eventually to have succeeded, as it was his eldest son, John, who received confirmation as heir to his father's estates in October 1600, and was styled 'fourteenth Laird of Garthland'.

The sixteenth and seventeenth Lairds, James and William, were both MPs for Wigtownshire for much of the seventeenth century. William and his wife, Grizel Beaton, had fourteen children. His grandson, James Macdowall, became Lord Provost of Glasgow. The twenty-first Laird was an advocate at the Scottish Bar. He was elected to Parliament and sat in the House of Commons at Westminster from 1783 until his death in 1810. He was succeeded by his nephew, William, who sold the original Garthland in Galloway, but transferred the name to his estate at Lochwinnoch in Renfrewshire. He and his brother died unmarried, and the title and estate passed to Lieutenant General Day Macdowall. The chiefly family emigrated to Canada at the end of the nineteenth century. Henry, twenty-eighth chief, was called to the Bar in British Columbia in 1920. The present chief still lives in Canada, but he has reacquired some of the ancient Galloway lands, and supports clan events in this country.

MACGREGOR

The Clan Gregor held lands in Glenstrae, Glenlochy and Glenorchy. Sir Iain Moncreiffe believed that they were descended from the ancient Celtic royal family through the hereditary Abbots of Glendochart, a descent which may be proclaimed in the motto, 'Royal is my race'. There is no evidence to support the tradition that Gregor was the son of Kenneth Macalpin. He may have been Griogair, son of Dungal, who is said to have been a co-ruler of Alba, the kingdom north of Central Scotland, between AD 879 and 889. Most modern historians agree that the first certain chief was Gregor 'of the golden bridles'. Gregor's son, Iain Camm, One-eye, succeeded as the second chief sometime prior to 1390.

Robert the Bruce granted the barony of Loch Awe, which included much of the Macgregor lands, to the chief of the Campbells. In common with many royal gifts of the time, it was left to the recipient to work out how he would take possession of it. The Campbells had already built the stout Castle of Kilchurn, which controlled the gateway to the western Highlands. They harried the Macgregors, who were forced to retire deeper into their lands until they were largely restricted to Glenstrae.

Iain of Glenstrae, the second of his house to be called 'the Black', died in 1519 with no direct heirs. The Campbells supported the succession of Eian, who was married to the daughter of Sir Colin Campbell of Glenorchy. Eian's son, Alistair, fought the English at the Battle of Pinkie in 1547 but died shortly thereafter. In 1660 Colin Campbell of Glenorchy, who had bought the superiority from his kinsman, Argyll, refused to recognise the claim of Gregor Roy Macgregor to the estates. For ten years Gregor waged war against the Campbells. He had little choice but to become an outlaw, raiding cattle and sheltering in the high glens. In 1570 the Campbells captured and killed him. His son, Alistair, claimed the chiefship, but was unable to stem the tide of persecution which was to be the fate of the 'Children of the Mist'.

John Drummond, the king's forester, was murdered after hanging some Macgregors for poaching. The chief took responsibility for the act, and was condemned by the Privy Council. In April 1603 James VI issued an edict proclaiming the name of Macgregor 'altogidder abolisheed', meaning that those who bore the name must renounce it or suffer death. Macgregor, along with eleven of his chieftains, was hanged at Edinburgh's Mercat Cross in January 1604. Clan Gregor was scattered, many taking other names, such as Murray or Grant. They were hunted like animals, flushed out of the heather by bloodhounds. Despite their savage treatment, the Macgregors actually fought for the king during the civil war. When the Earl of Glencairn attempted a rising against the Commonwealth in 1651, he was joined by two hundred of the clan. In recognition of this, Charles II repealed the proscription of the name, but this was promptly reimposed when William of Orange deposed Charles's brother, James VII.

Macgregor

Standard

It was at this time that the legendary Rob Roy Macgregor came to prominence. Born in 1671, a younger son of Macgregor of Glengyle, he was forced to assume his mother's name of Campbell. His adventures have been immortalised and romanticised by Sir Walter Scott's novel, *Rob Roy*, but there is little doubt that he was a thorn in the government's flesh until his death in 1734. When the Stuart flag was raised in 1715, he attached himself to the Jacobite cause, although acted largely independently. After the indecisive Battle of Sheriffmuir, he set out plundering at will. In one raid he put Dumbarton into panic, caus-

ing the castle to open fire with its cannon. He is buried in the churchyard at Balquhidder.

The persecution of Clan Gregor ended in 1774, when the laws against them were repealed. In order to restore their clan pride, it was necessary to re-establish the chiefs. A petition subscribed by eight hundred and twenty-six Macgregors declared General John Murray of Lanrick to be the proper and true chief. He was, in fact, a Macgregor, being a descendent of Duncan Macgregor of Ardchoille who died in 1552. The general had served extensively in India before being created a baronet in July 1795. His son, Sir Evan, was also a general and later Governor of Dominica. He married a daughter of the fourth Duke of Atholl, for whom he built the House of Edinchip, until recently the home of the present chief. Sir Evan played a prominent part in the 1822 visit of George IV to Scotland, where he and his clansmen guarded the honours of Scotland. He proposed the toast to the 'chief of chiefs' at the royal banquet in Edinburgh.

The father of the present chief, Sir Malcolm Macgregor, served in the navy during the First World War, being decorated not only by his own country, but also by France.

ARMS
*Quarterly, 1st & 4th, Or, an eagle displayed Gules,
beaked and membered Sable, charged on the breast
with a plate;
2nd, Argent, a lymphad, sails furled, oars in saltire Sable,
flagged Gules, with a beacon on top of the mast Proper;
3rd, Argent, a sinister hand fessways Gules holding a
cross crosslet fitchée Azure*

CREST
A dexter hand holding a dagger in pale Proper

MOTTO
Per ardua (Through difficulties)

SUPPORTERS
*(on a compartment embellished with white heather)
Two cows Argent, langued Gules, hooved Sable*

STANDARD
*Azure, a St Andrew's Cross Argent in the hoist and of two
tracts Gules and Or, upon which is depicted the Crest
along with the Motto 'Per ardua' extended in the fly in
letters Sable*

PINSEL
*Or, bearing upon a Wreath of the Liveries a dexter hand
holding a dagger in pale both Proper within a strap
Gules, buckled and embellished Argent, inscribed in
letters Or with the Motto 'Per ardua', all within a circlet
Argent inscribed with the title 'MacIntyre of Glenoe' in
letters Sable and on the fly an Escrol Gules bearing in
letters Or this Slogan 'Glenoe' surmounting a sprig of
white heather*

PLANT BADGE
White heather

I n Gaelic, the name Macintyre is rendered 'Mac-an-T'saoir', meaning 'son
of the carpenter'. A traditional
account dates the origins of the name to the
early twelfth century, when Somerled was
establishing his lordship in the Western Isles.
After Olav the Red, Norse King of Man and
the Isles, resisted Somerled's ambitions, he
then resorted to diplomacy, and sought the
hand of the king's daughter, Ragnhild, in marriage. Somerled's nephew, Macarill or Maurice,
assured his uncle that he could devise a
scheme to win the bride. It is said that
Macarill sabotaged Olav's galley by boring
holes in the hull, which he then plugged with
tallow. He contrived to be a passenger on the
king's galley, and went well supplied with
wooden plugs. Heavy seas washed out the tallow and the galley began to founder, at which
point Macarill promised to save the king's life
if he would promise his daughter's hand to
Somerled. The pact was sealed, and the plugs
used to stop the leaks. Macarill was thereafter
known as the 'wright' or 'carpenter', and found
high favour with his uncle.

Macarill's descendents later established
themselves on the mainland where, according
to legend, they were warned by a spirit only to
settle where a white cow in their herd came to
rest. The land they settled was the rich and
fertile Glen Noe by Ben Cruachan on Loch
Etiveside. By the end of the thirteenth century
the Macintyres were foresters to the Lord of
Lorn, an office they held through the passing
of the lordship from the Macdougalls to the
Stewarts and finally the Campbells.

As the family records have been lost, the
Macintyre chiefs cannot be listed with any
accuracy, but the first chief of record was
Duncan, who married a daughter of Campbell
of Barcaldine. Duncan died in 1695 and was
buried in Ardchattan Priory in a tomb worthy
of his rank. Through the Barcaldine connection, the Macintyre chiefs claim descent from

Robert the Bruce. The civil war in Scotland provided a convenient excuse for many clans to settle old scores. The Earl of Argyll was not only leader of the Covenanter faction in the Scottish Parliament, but he was also the implacable foe of many clans whose fortunes had been eclipsed by the rise of the Campbells. The earl's lands were ravaged, but royalist forces commanded by Alasdair Macdonald, 'Colkitto', spared Glen Noe on the grounds that the Macintyres were kinsmen. Many Macintyres subsequently joined Colkitto's army, including the chief's piper. The chief, however, was with Argyll at Inverlochy in February 1645 when the Campbells were surprised by Montrose and routed.

Macintyre

Standard

James, the third chief, was born around 1727. He was sponsored by the Campbell Earl of Breadalbane and studied law, being regarded as a good scholar and a poet. On his father's death he returned to Glen Noe. When Prince Charles Edward Stuart raised his father's standard at Glenfinnan in 1745, James would have joined him but for the influence of his Campbell wife and neighbours. Many clansmen, however, slipped away and fought under Stewart of Appin at Culloden. The great Macintyre bard, Duncan Ban, fought for the house of Hanover at the Battle of Falkirk in 1746. A monument to the poet's memory was erected in 1859 near Loch Awe.

The Macintyres originally held their lands by right of the sword, but they had acquired feudal obligations to the Campbells. The payments were purely symbolic until the early eighteenth century, when Campbell of

Breadalbane persuaded the Macintyre chief to pay a cash rent. The rent was then progressively raised to a point where Donald, the fourth recorded chief, was unable to pay, and he emigrated to America in 1783, leaving his brother, Duncan, to manage the estate. Duncan struggled on until 1806, when he, too, left the glen. The chiefly line continued to honour their Scottish origins in America, preserving the armorial great seal, signet ring and quaffing cup. In 1955 Alasdair Macintyre of Camus-na-h-erie recorded arms in the Lyon Court as cadet of the chiefly house of Macintyre. The shield was quite different from that which clan historians believed to be correct. This unhappy state of affairs was corrected in 1991, when James Wallace Macintyre of Glenoe, ninth of the recorded chiefs, matriculated the correct undifferenced arms. The Macintyres once more take their seat on the Council of Clan Chiefs, and even Duncan Ban's lonely monument is more accessible, with a Forestry Commission stopping place from which it may be viewed.

MACKAY

I n Gaelic, this name is rendered as 'Macaoidh', 'son of Hugh'. Exactly who Hugh was is uncertain. Sir Iain Moncreiffe suggested that the name comes from a branch of the ancient Celtic royal house who disputed the throne in the twelfth and thirteenth centuries. He asserted that the Mackays descend from Aedh, who was the last Abbot of Dunkeld, first Earl of Fife, and the elder brother of Alexander I. Aedh's wife was the granddaughter of Queen Gruoch, wife of Macbeth. Malcolm Macaedh, who was married to a sister of Somerled of the Isles, became Earl of Ross. He died in 1168. Malcolm's son-in-law became Earl of Caithness. He was also lord of the lands of Strathnaver where, by the fourteenth century, the clan appears to have become established in its recognised form.

Iye was chamberlain to Walter, Bishop of Caithness, in 1263. Angus Dubh, sixth in descent from the Chamberlain, married Elizabeth, sister of Donald Lord of the Isles and granddaughter of Robert II, around 1415. This indicates the importance the clan had achieved, as such a marriage would not have been contemplated, except on political grounds. Angus is said to have been able to call out four thousand men from his lands at Strathnaver. From this pinnacle of power, the clan spent the next five centuries fending off their predatory neighbours, the Earls of Sutherland. They were ultimately to lose the lands to the Sutherlands in 1829. (For a detailed study, see *Chief of Mackay* by Dr Ian Grimble, published in 1965.)

In 1556 Iye Mackay, then the chief, was captured by the Sutherlands and sent as a prisoner to Edinburgh Castle. His grandson, Sir Donald Mackay, was created a Baronet of Nova Scotia on 28 March 1627. A year later he was elevated to the peerage as Baron Reay. Lord Reay was a distinguished soldier who fought for Charles I in the civil war. He was to have been created Earl of Strathnaver, but the royal patent was not completed. He went into exile in Denmark, where he died in February 1649. His second son, Angus, became a colonel in the Danish army. He married Catherine of Killernan and is ancestor of the Mackays of Melness. His elder son, John, the second Lord Reay, also fought for Charles I. His second wife was Barbara, daughter of Hugh Mackay of Scouri. Her father was better known as General Mackay, who commanded the forces of William and Mary at Killiecrankie in 1689. John's second son, Aenas, was Brigadier General of Mackay's Scotch Regiment in the service of the States General of Holland. The family settled in the Netherlands, where they prospered. Barthold Mackay was created Baron Ophemert in the Netherlands in June 1822.

Mackay

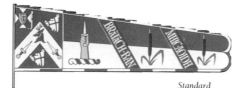

Standard

In Scotland, the chiefly line passed to cousins from time to time, when the chief died without heirs. Eric, the ninth Baron Reay, got heavily into debt. The Earls of Sutherland encouraged him to borrow money, having first had their lawyers ensure that the Mackay lands were pledged as security. The Sutherlands acquired the entire estates when Eric died unmarried in 1875. The succession passed to his cousin, the Baron Ophemert who became tenth Lord Reay. His son, Donald, the eleventh Baron, was Governor of Bombay, Under Secretary of State for India and a Knight of the Thistle. He was additionally created a peer of the United Kingdom, but this title became extinct on his death in 1921. The family maintained their links with the Netherlands, and on the eleventh Baron's death the title passed to his Dutch cousin, whose father had been Prime Minister of that country. Lord Reay died within months of succeeding to the title, which then passed to his fifteen-year-old son. The new chief became a British subject in 1938 and worked in the Foreign Office during the Second World War. He retained his Barony and Castle of Ophemert which escaped damage during the German occupation, although in 1966 an unexploded shell was dredged up from the moat.

There have been many distinguished Mackays in recent times. James Mackay prospered in business, becoming chairman of the P & O shipping line. He was created Earl of Inchcape in 1929. In October 1987, Donald Mackay, now Lord Mackay of Clashfern, was appointed Lord Chancellor of Great Britain. Formerly a professor of mathematics, he entered the law as a second career. He is the first Scot who is not a member of the English Bar, to be appointed head of the English judicial system.

MACKENZIE

The surname itself is rendered in Gaelic as 'Maccoinneach', meaning 'son of the fair bright one'. It has been suggested that the name alludes to the pagan god Cerunnos, who is often depicted as having a stag's head or antlers; this may be one explanation for the gold stag's head on the chief's shield. The Mackenzies were one of the clans who held lands in Ross between Aird on the east coast and Kintail on the west. They are believed to share a common ancestry with Clan Matheson and Clan Anrias, all three descending from the Celtic dynast Gilleoin of the Aird, who lived at the beginning of the twelfth century. By 1267 the family seem to have been settled at Eilean Donan, the great Mackenzie stronghold at the mouth of Loch Duich.

By the fifteenth century the earldom of Ross formed part of the patrimony of the Macdonald Lords of the Isles, and at that time the Mackenzie chief could call out two thousand warriors to do his bidding. Alexander Mackenzie of Kintail attended the Parliament at Inverness summoned by James I, at which the king imprisoned the Lord of the Isles with some of his important chiefs. The Mackenzie chief was too young for this fate, but he quickly learned to whom he should pay allegiance, a lesson which succeeding Stewart monarchs were to hammer home to the other Highland chiefs, and he obtained royal charters to his lands of Kintail in 1463. The Mackenzies weathered the storms which the Stewarts unleashed on the Macdonalds, so that their fortunes waxed as the Macdonalds' waned. Alasdair of Kintail raised his clan against the last Earl of Ross and was rewarded by James III, who granted him extensive lands taken from the defeated earl. The splendid tomb of his son, Kenneth, in the full armour and panoply of a knight, can still be seen in Beauly Priory. In 1508, Kintail was erected into a free barony.

By the beginning of the seventeenth century the Mackenzie territory extended from the Black Isle to the Outer Hebrides. They gained the island of Lewis from its former Macleod rulers and Lochalsh from the Macdonells. Their western stronghold was at Eilean Donan Castle where they installed the Macraes as hereditary constables. The Macraes were fierce in defence of their Mackenzie overlords, becoming known as 'Mackenzie's shirt of mail'. In 1609 the chief was raised to the peerage as Lord Mackenzie of Kintail. Fourteen years later, his son was created Earl of Seaforth. Lord Mackenzie's brother, Sir Roderick Mackenzie of Coigach, was to found the line created baronets in May 1628 and, in 1702, Earls of Cromartie. They made their chief seat at Castle Leod, a name chosen to demonstrate their connection with the Macleods of Lewis.

Mackenzie

Standard

The Seaforth Earls embraced the reformed church and were signatories of the National Covenant in 1638. They fought against Montrose during his campaigns in 1645–46, the chief's standard being taken at the Battle of Auldearn. The execution of Charles I appalled Seaforth, who hurried to join Charles II in exile in Holland. He died before Oliver Cromwell's final victory at Worcester in 1651. His heir joined in the rising against the Commonwealth in 1653, which ended with the defeat of the royalists by General Monck at Loch Garry. Seaforth made his peace with Cromwell in January 1655.

The family did not waiver in their support of the Catholic James VII, and Seaforth fought at the Battle of the Boyne in 1690. He was already a Knight of the Thistle, but the exiled king made him a marquess. The fifth Earl was charged with treason for his participation in the rising of 1715, and his titles were forfeited. Although his grandson was made Earl of Seaforth again, the male line came to an end in 1815. The Earls of Cromartie were also Jacobites, and George, the third Earl, fought at the Battle of Falkirk in 1746. He and his son, Lord Macleod, were surprised and captured at Dunrobin Castle in April 1746. The earl's titles were forfeit. His son, John, was pardoned in 1748 and in 1777 he raised two battalions of Highlanders and served in India with the rank of major general. For his services the forfeited estates, but not the title, were restored to him. His descendent, Anne, was created Countess of Cromartie in her own right in 1861, with a special destination of the earldom in favour of her second son, Francis. The present Earl of Cromartie is her descendent. Throughout the nineteenth century the right to the chiefship was disputed. However, this was put to an end when the father of the present earl matriculated his arms in June 1980. He was officially recognised by the Lord Lyon as 'Cabarfeidh', chief of the Mackenzies.

MACKINNON

The Mackinnons, a branch of the great Siol Alpin, descendents of Kenneth Macalpin, are of royal descent from Fingon, grandson of Gregor. 'Fingon' in Gaelic means 'fair-born'. The clan slogan is 'Cumhnich Bas Alpin' 'Remember the death of Alpin'. Alpin was slain by Bruch, King of the Picts, in 837. Findanus, the fourth chief, brought Dunakin into the clan around 900 by marrying a Norse princess. The castle, properly called Dun Haakon, was a broch (a circular dry-stone tower) commanding the narrow sound between Skye and the mainland. The enterprising Mackinnons ran a heavy chain across the sound, and levied a toll on all passing ships. King Haakon IV assembled his fleet of longships beneath the castle of his namesake before the Battle of Largs in 1263. His defeat there effectively ended Norse domination of the islands. Findanus also held land on Mull.

The Mackinnons on Arran gave shelter to Robert the Bruce during his time as a fugitive, helping him make his escape to Carrick. After the king's victory at Bannockburn they were rewarded with land on Skye. The chiefs were then styled 'of Strathardale', and lived at Dunringall Castle. Dunakin passed to another branch of the family. A branch of the chiefly family became hereditary abbots of Iona. Fingon, son of Gilbride, was Master of the household to the Lord of the Isles before becoming Abbot of Iona, the crucible of the Celtic church. Known as the Green Abbot, he was a powerful churchman, and lent encouragement to a rebellion against the Lord of the Isles for which his brother, Neil, Gilbride's eldest son, was put to death. The last hereditary abbot was John Mackinnon, the ninth chief, who was also Bishop of the Isles. He died around 1500.

The Mackinnons regularly feuded with the Macleans, and incidents flared up from time to time. One encounter in particular provides a good illustration of the Gaelic sense of humour. The Macleans seized some Mackinnon lands on Mull while the chief was visiting in Skye. On learning of the outrage, he gathered his men and discovered that the Macleans were celebrating with a great feast at Ledaig. Ascertaining that the Macleans were all in a drunken stupor, Mackinnon caused his men each to cut and trim a fir tree, and plant all of them around the hall. He himself placed one in front of the door along with a naked sword. The next morning the Macleans, seeing they were surrounded by the plant badge of Clan Mackinnon, realised that they could all have been slaughtered, and promptly withdrew from Mackinnon land.

The Scots kings since the reign of James IV had slowly undermined the power of the island chiefs. In 1606 James VI sent Lord Ochiltree to Mull to make proposals to the chiefs on his plans for government of the isles. When they disagreed with Ochiltree's plans, he seized the chiefs and imprisoned them in castles on the mainland. In 1609, Lachlan Mackinnon of that Ilk and other chiefs were forced to subscribe to the Statutes of Iona, which placed many restrictions upon their power. English was to become the language of the chiefs and firearms were banned. Despite this, the Mackinnons were loyal to the Stuarts, and fought in the army of Montrose at the Battle of Inverlochy in 1645. Their young chief, Lachlan Mor was, at the time in the custody of Argyll. In 1650, Lachlan raised a regiment which fought on the royalist side at the Battle of Worcester in 1651. The chief was created a knight banneret by Charles II on the field of battle.

The clan remained loyal to the Stuarts in the next century, and sent one hundred and fifty men to join the Earl of Mar at the Battle of Sheriffmuir in 1715. For this act the chief was declared forfeit for treason. The Mackinnons were also out during the Forty-five, marching to Edinburgh to join Prince Charles. They fought at Culloden, where the Stuarts dreams of the Crown were crushed.

Mackinnon

The prince was sheltered by the Mackinnons in a cave, and Iain Og, who was over seventy years old, sent for his galley to take the prince to Mallaig, avoiding two Government warships on the way. He was less fortunate on the return voyage, however, and was captured in Morar. He was incarcerated in a prison ship at Tilbury, where he languished until 1750.

When Iain Og died in 1756, his son, Charles, succeeded, but this line died out in 1808. In 1811, William Mackinnon, MP for Dunwich in England, matriculated arms in the Lyon Court, showing his descent from Daniel, second son of Sir Lachlan Mor, who had emigrated to Antigua after a quarrel with his father. The new chief was a prominent parliamentarian, and sat for thirty-five years. He was succeeded by his son, the thirty-fourth chief, who was high sheriff of Kent in 1885. The chief's second son, Sir William Mackinnon, served in the Grenadier Guards, becoming director of recruitment at the War Office during the First World War. He was made a Knight Grand Cross of the Order of the Bath and a Knight of the Royal Victorian Order. The present chief is Sir William's granddaughter, Anne Mackinnon.

MACKINTOSH

T he word 'toisech', meaning 'leader'
can also be translated as 'chief' or
'captain'. According to the
Mackintosh seanachies, the first chief was
Shaw, second son of Duncan Macduff, Earl of
Fife of the royal house of Dalriada. Shaw
Macduff accompanied Malcolm IV on an expedition in 1160 to suppress rebellion in
Morayshire. He was made constable of
Inverness Castle around 1163, and granted
land in the Findhorn valley. The lands of Petty
were to become the heartland of the clan and
the burial place of the chiefs. His son, Shaw,
the second chief, succeeded him in 1179, and
was confirmed in his patrimony by William
the Lion. Ferquhar, the fifth chief, led his clan
against the army of King Haakon of Norway at
the Battle of Largs in 1263. He was killed in a
duel in 1265, leaving his infant son, Angus, as
heir. Angus was brought up at the court of his
uncle, Alexander of Islay, the Lord of the Isles.
A splendid match was arranged for him in
1291, when he married Eva, the only daughter
of Dougal Dal, chief of Clan Chattan in
Lochaber. Eva brought with her the lands of
Glenloy and Loch Arkaig. Angus and Eva lived
on Clan Chattan lands at Torcastle, later with-
drawing from Lochaber taking up residence at
Rothiemurchus. Thereafter the Clan Chattan,
which developed into a confederation of what
were later to become independent clans, was
led by the Mackintosh chiefs, although their
right to do so was unsuccessfully challenged
by the Macphersons over the centuries.
Mackintosh and Clan Chattan history is thus
inextricably entwined.

The sixth chief supported Robert the
Bruce during the War of Independence.
Ferquhar, the ninth chief, was induced to surrender the chiefship, in his own right and for
those of his successors, in favour of Malcolm,
the son by a second marriage of William, the
seventh chief. He was a strong leader who
greatly extended the influence of the clan. His

lands stretched from Petty far into Lochaber. His continuing feud with the Comyns had its origin a century before when they had warred against Robert the Bruce. In 1424, the Comyns forcibly took possession of the Mackintosh lands at Meikle Geddes and Rait. Malcolm Mackintosh retaliated by surprising some leading Comyns at Nairn and putting them to the sword. The Comyns then invaded the Mackintosh homeland of Moy and tried, unsuccessfully, to drown the Mackintoshes in their fastness on the island of Moy.

The feud was to have been ended at a feast of reconciliation in the Comyn's castle at Rait. However, a Comyn lad was in love with a Mackintosh and disclosed to her that the bringing in of a black bull's head to the feast was to be a signal for the hosts to massacre their guests. On the appearance of the bull's head, it was the Comyns who were surprised by the ferocity of their forewarned guests' assault, and as a result it was they who were slaughtered. The Mackintoshes were now well-established at Moy and dominated the south-eastern approaches to Inverness

Mackintosh

Standard

The Mackintoshes fought for Montrose throughout his campaigns in support of Charles I. They remained loyal to the Stuarts in 1715, and Lachlan Mackintosh led eight hundred clansmen to swell the Jacobite ranks under the command of his cousin, Brigadier William Mackintosh of Borlum. They were defeated at the Battle of Preston and many clansmen were transported to the Americas. Angus, twenty-second chief of the Mackintoshes, was a captain in the Black Watch Regiment when Prince Charles Edward Stuart landed in Scotland in 1745. In the absence of her husband, the chief's wife, Lady Anne, daughter of Farquharson of Invercauld, raised men for the prince. Command was

given to MacGillivray of Dunmaglas. They contributed to the prince's victory at Falkirk, following which he arrived at Moy on 16 February 1746 to be received by Lady Mackintosh. The prince's bed is still in the modern Moy Hall. An attempt was made by a force of fifteen hundred Government troops to capture the prince at Moy, but they were deceived by five of Lady Anne's retainers into believing that they had blundered into the midst of the entire Jacobite army, and they fled. The incident was known thereafter as 'the Rout of Moy', and the chief's wife nicknamed 'Colonel Anne'. The Mackintoshes and their Clan Chattan allies suffered heavy losses at Culloden.

On the death of the twenty-eighth chief in 1938, the title passed to his cousin, Vice Admiral Lachlan Mackintosh of Mackintosh. In a complicated decision by the Lyon Court in 1942, the leadership of Clan Chattan passed to Mackintosh of Torcastle. The Admiral died in 1957 with the new and more convenient Moy Hall replacing the vast Victorian baronial mansion, still uncompleted. He was succeeded as Mackintosh chief by his son, Lachlan, who is Lord Lieutenant of Lochaber, Inverness, Badenoch and Strathspey.

MACLACHLAN

This name is Norse, and Lochlainn was the name of the senior branch in Tirconnell of the Ui'neill descendents of the pagan King Niall of the Nine Hostages. Until 1241 the MacLochlainns were virtual rulers of Ulster, until they suffered defeat at the hands of King Brian O'Neill. Their chief, Donall MacLochlainn, was killed in the battle, along with most of his immediate kin. The name appeared in Scotland by the thirteenth century, when Lachlan Mor lived on the shores of Loch Fyne. Lachlan was a great warrior and a descendent of the Irish kings.

In 1292, Archibald Maclachlan was one of the twelve barons whose lands were formed into the sheriffdom of Argyll. Ewen Maclachlan appears on the Ragman Roll as a noble of Scotland, swearing fealty to Edward I of England in 1296. Gillespie, probably the son of the chief, supported Robert the Bruce and attended his first Parliament at St Andrews in 1308. He is also recorded in a charter of 1314, where he granted a stipend to the friars at Glasgow from his lands of Kilbride. By the early fifteenth century the chiefs were described as 'Lords of Strathlachlan'. In 1436, Iain, Lord of Strathlachlan, granted a charter to his cousin, Alan, creating him seneschal of the lands of Glassary in Argyll. Donald Maclachlan confirmed a grant to Paisley Abbey of an annual payment, again from the lands of Kilbride. The Maclachlans recognised the rising power of the Campbells in Argyll, and allied themselves to the earls. Iain Maclachlan witnessed a bond by Stewart of Appin in favour of the first Earl of Argyll in 1485. His son, Archibald, married a daughter of the chief of the Lamonts. From this marriage came Lachlan Maclachlan who, as part of the Earl of Argyll's suite, travelled to France for the marriage of James V. The king's wedding, to the eldest daughter of Francis I of France, was held in Paris.

In 1615, the Maclachlan chief, Lachlan

Og, led his clan in Argyll's foray against the Macdonalds of Islay. He had previously obtained a charter to his lands from James VI in 1591, but in 1633 he procured an Act of Parliament confirming him as Laird of Maclachlin. His lands, which were enumerated in the Act, extended to over thirty-four farms in Strathlachlan and Loch Fyne.

The civil war allowed many clans an opportunity to settle old scores, and the Maclachlans fought with their neighbours, the Lamonts. Lachlan Maclachlan of that Ilk accepted a commission in 1656 from Oliver Cromwell, the Lord Protector, to be justice of the peace for Argyllshire. His son, Archibald, the fifteenth chief, received a charter in 1680, erecting his whole lands into the Barony of Strathlachlan with Castle Lachlan as its seat. He died in 1687 shortly before his clan embarked upon the first of the Jacobite campaigns.

The Maclachlans fought for Viscount Dundee at Killiecrankie in 1689, and the Maclachlan chief himself was present at the raising of the standard of James VIII, the 'Old Pretender', in Scotland in 1715. The Maclachlans followed the Earl of Mar to the Battle of Sheriffmuir. It is said that the chief was harried by the Campbells until his death in 1719, for his part in the rising. In 1745 the Maclachlans rallied to Prince Charles Edward Stuart, making their way through Campbell country in time to join the prince at Prestonpans. The chief was appointed to the prince's staff as commissary-general. When the Jacobite army invaded England, it was Maclachlan who was sent north to Perth to summon reinforcements. His strongest entreaties for haste were of no avail, and fresh troops idled at Perth while the tide of fortune turned against the prince. The retreat from Derby did not dismay the Maclachlan, who led

Maclachlan

three hundred of his clansmen to Culloden. He was riding to order the Highland advance when he was killed by a stray cannon shot. The Maclachlan colours were burned on the Duke of Cumberland's orders by the public hangman at Edinburgh. Castle Lachlan was left in ruins and the chief's family was forced to flee. Lachlan was declared forfeit for treason, but as the estates had been conveyed to his son over a decade before the rising, they escaped untouched. A new mansion house was built in the nineteenth century in sight of the ruins of the ancient castle.

During the Second World War, the chiefship was assumed by Marjory Maclachlan of Maclachlan, the twenty-fourth chief. Her father, Major John Maclachlan, had commanded the Argyllshire Volunteer Regiment during the First World War. He was Vice Lord Lieutenant of Argyll and a member of the Royal Company of Archers (the monarch's bodyguard in Scotland).

MACLAINE OF LOCHBUIE

ARMS
Quarterly, 1st, Argent, a lion rampant Gules;
2nd, Or, a lymphad sails furled, oars in saltire Sable,
flagged Gules;
3rd, Or, a dexter hand fessways couped Gules, holding a
cross crosslet fitchée Azure;
4th, a tower embattled Argent masoned Sable

CREST
a branch of laurel and a branch of cypress in saltire surmounted of a battle axe in pale all Proper

MOTTO
Vincere vel mori (To conquer or die)

SUPPORTERS
Two wolves Proper

The Maclaines of Lochbuie formed an important part of the clan structure of the Hebrides. They are descended from Gillean of the Battleaxe, a fierce warrior who lived in the mid thirteenth century and held lands in Mull and Morvern. Gillean and his three sons fought valiantly at the Battle of Largs, and they were well received by Alexander II. He was succeeded by Gille-Iosa, whose son, Malcolm, fought at the head of his clan at Bannockburn. Iain Dubh, Malcolm's son, was the father of Eachainn Reaganach, Hector the Stern, founder of the Macleans of Lochbuie, and Lachlan Lubanach, Lachlan the wily, who founded the Macleans of Duart. These are the two main independent branches of the family, each with their various cadets, and the spellings of the names of both remained identical until the late sixteenth century.

Hector was granted lands in Mull by the Lords of the Isles around 1350 and he sat on the Council of the Isles, as did subsequent Lochbuie chiefs until the forfeiture of the lordship in 1493. Hector chose a site for his castle on Mull at the head of Loch Buie on the lands formerly held by the Macfadzeans. Moy Castle, a typical Scottish tower house, was built in the late fourteenth century and was the chief's residence until 1752, when Lochbuie House was built. Lochbuie held land on Mull, Scarba, Jura, Morvern, Locheil, and the bailliary of the south part of Tiree and of Morvern. Lands were also granted in Duror and Glencoe but they were never taken into possession. In 1542 the lands held by the sixth Lochbuie chief were united into the barony of Moy.

One of the most famous legends associated with the clan is that of the headless horseman. Prior to 1538 the fifth chief, Iain Og, had a son, Ewan, who lived on a crannog, or artificial island, in Loch Sghubhain just north of Lochbuie. Ewan's wife, who earned the nickname, 'the black swan', pressed Ewan continuously to ask his father for more land. Ewan at last consented, but when he confronted his father a heated argument ensued which resulted in their setting a time and place for battle. They met at Glen Cannir, with Iain Og supported by the Macleans of Duart. In the heat of battle, Ewan left himself open to the swing of a claymore, which completely severed his head from his body. His horse kept galloping with the headless body held in place by the stirrups. The horse eventually stopped and Ewan's body was buried on that spot which is still marked by a cairn. His body was later taken to Iona, where his gravestone can still be seen. It is said that whenever a member of the family is about to die, hoofbeats of Ewan's horse will be heard and his headless ghost may be seen in his green cloak galloping through the night on his black charger.

John Mor, seventh chief, was renowned as an excellent swordsman. When an Italian master-at-arms challenged Scottish nobles to meet him in duel John Mor accepted the challenge, and fought and killed him in the presence, and to the delight, of the king and the court. His son, Hector, eighth of Lochbuie, initiated the spelling of the surname 'Maclaine', which became the accepted spelling by subsequent chiefs. Murdoch Mor, tenth chief, fought alongside the Marquess of Montrose in 1645 and thereby forfeited his lands, which were not restored until 1661. The twelfth chief, Hector, was the victor in the first battle of the Jacobite campaign of James VII when, in 1689, at Knockbreck in Badenoch, he overcame five troops of horse sent by Mackay's army to intercept him. He also participated in the Battle of Killiecrankie later that year in which the Highlanders almost annihilated Mackay's forces.

John, seventeenth chief, was host to Dr Samuel Johnson and James Boswell on the last stop of their famous tour of the Hebrides in 1773. Boswell said of John, 'Lochbuie proved to be a bluff, comely, noisy old gentleman, proud of his hereditary consequence and a very hearty and hospitable landlord'. John had

Maclaine of Lochbuie

a plaque placed above the door of Lochbuie House to commemorate the visit.

One of the more colourful Lochbuie chiefs was Murdoch, twenty-third of Lochbuie, born in 1814. It is reported that, after his late arrival to a formal dinner in Oban, the Duke of Argyll sent a butler to ask him to come and sit at the head of the table. Murdoch retorted, 'Where Lochbuie sits is the head of the table'. Murdoch, along with the Duke of Argyll, founded the Argyllshire Gathering and Ball in 1871. He had a distinguished military career, and while serving as military correspondent of *The Times* during the Franco–Prussian War in 1871, was awarded the Iron Cross by the Kaiser. Murdoch's son and heir, Kenneth Maclaine, the twenty-fourth chief, made a mark for himself by going on the stage as a singer to try to forestall the closure of the Lochbuie estates. Unfortunately, the onset of the First World War made it impossible for him to avoid the inevitable, and the entire estates of some thirty thousand acres were lost. Kenneth served with distinction throughout the war, being awarded the Military Cross twice and the Croix de Guerre with Palm.

MACLAREN

ARMS
Or, two chevronels Gules, accompanied by a lymphad sails furled and oars in action Sable in base

CREST
A lion's head erased Sable crowned with an antique crown of six (four visible) points Or, between two branches of laurel issuing from the Wreath at either side of the head both Proper

MOTTO
Creag an Tuirc (The boar's rock)

On Compartment
Ab origine fidus (Faithful from the first)

SUPPORTERS
(on a compartment semée of laurel leaves)
Two mermaids Proper, their tail-parts Argent, each holding in her exterior hand a laurel branch paleways Vert

STANDARD
In the hoist, Azure, a saltire Argent, impaled with the Arms of MacLaren, of this Livery Gules upon which is depicted the Badge along with the Slughorn 'Creag an Tuirc' extended in the fly in letters Or

BADGE
A mermaid Proper, her tail part upended Argent, holding in her dexter hand a spray of laurel paleways Vert, and in her dexter hand a looking-glass Proper, mounted Gules

It is possible that there are two quite separate origins of this name, one arising in Perthshire around Balquhidder, and the other in Tiree in Argyll. In Argyll, the family are said to descend from Lorn, son of Fergus MacErc, founder of the kingdom of Dalriada in the sixth century. In Gaelic, they are Clann Labhruinn. However, the eponymous ancestor is generally given as Laurence, Abbot of Achtow in Balquhidder, who lived in the thirteenth century. The lands of the Church were often held by hereditary lay noblemen who had the courtesy title of abbot. Balquhidder was part of the ancient princedom of Strathearn and the heraldic device associated with the district is the mermaid. The Maclaren supporters are thus related to the mermaid crest of the Murrays.

In the Ragman Roll of 1296, which lists the Scots nobles who gave allegiance to Edward I of England, are three names identified as belonging to the clan; Maurice of Tiree; Conan of Balquhidder; and Leurin of Ardveche. The Maclarens probably fought at Bannockburn under the standard of Malise, Earl of Strathearn. In 1344, the last Celtic Earl of Strathearn was deprived of his title when the Maclarens came under pressure from their more powerful neighbours. Balquhidder passed into the hands of the Crown, and in 1490, a Stewart was appointed the royal baillie. In 1500 James IV granted the lordship to his mistress, Janet Kennedy, and the Maclaren chief found that his land had become part of another barony. Balquhidder later passed to the Murrays of Atholl. When the Campbell persecution of the Macgregors drove them from their own lands into Balquhidder, the Maclarens lacked the power to stop them. The Macgregors plundered the Maclaren lands, bringing fire and death in their wake. The chiefs appealed to the Campbells who demanded, as the price of their protection, that the Maclarens acknowledge them as feudal superiors. The Crown, however, continued to regard the Maclarens as an independent clan, and they are listed in the Acts of Parliament for the suppression of unruly clans in 1587 and 1594.

Standard

Maclaren

The Maclarens fought for Montrose, in the cause of Charles I, at Inverlochy, Auldearn, Alford and Kilsyth. At the end of the century, when the Stuarts again called for aid, the Maclarens joined James Graham of Claverhouse, Viscount Dundee, who was mustering resistance for James VII following him to fight at Killiecrankie in 1689. The Maclarens were 'out' in the Fifteen, taking part in the Battle of Sheriffmuir. They also flocked to the standard of Prince Charles Edward Stuart, the 'Young Pretender', in 1745. The clan followed the prince from his victories at Prestonpans and Falkirk to the ill-fated Battle of Culloden in 1746. At the battle they were on the right of the line with the Appin regiment under Lord George Murray, brother of the Duke of Atholl. A Gaelic-speaking chieftain, the dashing and romantic Lord George led the Highlanders in one last great charge, which broke the Hanoverian front line, but this was not enough to win the day. Donald Maclaren was captured and carried off to Edinburgh. Balquhidder was ravaged by Hanoverian troops. Donald escaped while being taken to Carlisle for trial by hurling himself down a track which none of the redcoats dared to follow. He remained a fugitive in Balquhidder until the amnesty of 1757.

The Maclarens continued to farm at Achtow until 1892. The father of the present chief was recognised by the Lord Lyon as Maclaren of Achleskine and chief of the Maclarens. He acquired part of the ancient clan territory, including the clan heartland, Creag an Tuirc, the Boar's Rock, which is also the clan's war cry. He died in 1966, when he was buried with his ancestors in the Old Kirk of Balquhidder.

MACLEAN

This name in Gaelic is rendered as 'MacGille Eoin', 'son of the servant of St John'. It has also been suggested that there is an alternative derivation from 'leathan', meaning 'broad' or 'broad-shouldered'. However they spell their name, the Macleans descend from Gilleathan Na Tuaidh, Gillean of the Battle-axe. He may well have been the brother of Fergus Macerc, descended from the royal house of Lorn. Gillean fought at the Battle of Largs when the army of the Norwegian King Haakon was defeated, ending the Norse hegemony over the Hebrides in 1263. His son signed the Ragman Roll as Gillemoir Macilyn in 1296, swearing fealty to Edward I of England. Gillemoir's great-grandson, Iain Dhu Maclean, settled in Mull. Of his sons, Lachlan Lubanach was progenitor of the Macleans of Duart and Eachainn Reaganach (Hector) founded the Maclaines of Lochbuie. The other major cadets, the Macleans of Ardgour and Coll, descend from Lachlan. The Macleans of Duart married into the family of John of Islay, the first Lord of the Isles, and it was a match from which they gained great power and prestige. By the end of the fifteenth century, the Macleans owned most of Mull, Tiree, Islay, Jura and Knapdale, with Morvern in Argyllshire and Lochaber.

The politics of the isles were always turbulent, but the Macleans were particularly at odds with the Mackinnons. Lachlan Lubanach's son, Red Hector of the Battles, was a renowned warrior who fought for the Lord of the Isles at Harlaw in 1411. Red Hector and Sir Alexander Irvine of Drum met in single combat. After the duel, in which neither was dishonoured, they both died of their wounds. James IV was the first Scottish king seriously to attempt to bring the isles under royal control, and the pragmatic Macleans supported him. Lachlan of Duart was killed with the king at Flodden in 1513.

The rising power of the Campbells in the

late sixteenth century brought them into opposition with the Macleans. Inter marriage was a traditional way to avoid unnecessary feuds, and several Campbell marriages were arranged. One went badly wrong when the chief, Lachlan Maclean, married Lady Elizabeth Campbell, daughter of the second Earl of Argyll. The match was not a happy one, and Maclean decided upon drastic action: he marooned her upon a rock, leaving her to drown. She was rescued by passing fishermen who took her to her kin. Maclean was run through in Edinburgh by his wife's brother in 1523.

The Campbells and the Macleans were at least united in their Protestant faith and their dislike of the Macdonalds. Sir Lachlan Mor Maclean harried the Macdonalds of Islay, causing such carnage that, in 1594, he and the Macdonald chief were declared outlaws by the Privy Council. Lachlan redeemed himself when he fought for the king at the Battle of Glenlivet in 1594. He was killed fighting on Islay in August 1598, whereupon his sons took revenge in the form of a massacre which is said to have lasted for three days.

Sir Lachlan Maclean was created a Baronet of Nova Scotia on 3 September 1631. He was passionately devoted to Charles I and called his clan out to join Montrose, who had been appointed the king's captain general. He died in 1649, after which his son, Sir Hector, took up the cause, losing his life at the Battle of Inverkeithing in 1651. This left Hector's four-year-old-brother, Alan, as the heir. Sir Alan died in 1674, leaving another child to inherit the chiefship. The estates were by now heavily in debt. By 1679 the Campbells had gained possession of Duart and most of the Maclean estates. When the Stuarts once again called for aid against their rebellious subjects, the Maclean chief hurried to their standard. Sir John, the fifth Baronet, fought for James VII at Killiecrankie in 1689. The Campbells had little difficulty in obtaining the rest of the Maclean estates as a reward for their loyalty to the new régime.

Maclean

The Macleans were out in the rising of 1715, and Sir Hector Maclean was given a Jacobite peerage in 1716. He was exiled in France where he founded, and was the first Grand Master of the Grand Lodge of Freemasons in Paris. Sir Hector returned to Edinburgh in 1745 to pave the way for the rising of that year, but he was arrested and was imprisoned in the Tower of London until 1747. He died at Rome in 1750. The clan was led throughout the Forty-five by Maclean of Drimmin, who was killed in the Highland charge at Culloden. Duart Castle fell into ruins, but the chiefs, seeing the Jacobite cause was lost, served their country with distinction. All the chiefs from that time have been soldiers. The eighth Baronet achieved the rank of general, while Sir Fitzroy, the tenth Baronet, fought at the Battle of Sebastopol of 1854–55. Duart was reclaimed by the chiefs in 1911 and has been restored as their seat. The father of the present chief was Chief Scout of the Commonwealth and Lord Chamberlain to HM The Queen. He was created a life peer as Lord Maclean of Duart.

MACLENNAN

In Gaelic this name is rendered as 'MacGille Finnan', 'son of the follower of St Finnan'. Who St Finnan's disciple truly was is now lost in the mists of time. The history of the Maclennans is made particularly complex by the fact that until 1976 there had not been a recognised chief for over three hundred years.

The Maclennans settled around Kintail, and they were related to the Logans, who also held lands in Easter Ross. (The Logans were to become most prominent in the Lowlands, where they became Barons of Restalrig, near the Port of Leith.) However, other historians have suggested that the original name of the clan was Logan, and that it was not until the fifteenth century that the name Maclennan was adopted. According to this version of the family's origins, Gillegorm Logan led his men towards Inverness to prosecute a feud against the Frasers. Gillegorm was ambushed at Kessock and he and most of his men were slain. The Frasers captured Logan's pregnant wife, intending either to kill the child, or perhaps to raise him as a fosterling, a common Highland method of obtaining influence over a rival clan. The son was born, but was so deformed that he was allowed to live, and was placed with the monks at Beauly, entering the church in due course. He disregarded the decree of Pope Innocent III enjoining the celibacy of the clergy, preferring to follow the Celtic practice, and he married and had several children. He was the 'Gille Finnan', and his sons honoured his memory by adopting a new name.

Whatever the truth of this story, the heraldry of the chief proclaims the link between the Logans and the Maclennans, as each bear the heart and passion nails which allude to the pilgrimage of Sir Robert and Walter Logan accompanying the heart of Robert the Bruce to the Crusades. The expedition, led by Sir James Douglas, never saw the Holy Land. The Scots knights reached Spain, where they were enlisted to fight the Moors. This seemed compatible with their vows, as the Moors were heathens occupying Christian lands. But Douglas was killed in the Battle of Teba, and the crusade came to an abrupt end. The shield also alludes to the Maclennans' connection to the Mackenzies, whose banner was the 'caberfeidh', so called from the deer's head in the centre. The Maclennans, along with the Macraes, were staunch supporters of the Mackenzies, and may at one time have been custodians of the great castle at Eilean Donan. It was in the service of the Mackenzie chief that the clan came to great prominence. The Marquess of Montrose had rallied many Highland clans to the royalist cause in 1645. He was, however, equally opposed by many, including the Covenanter Earl of Seaforth, then chief of the Mackenzies. The men of Kintail, led by the Maclennan chief, Ruaridh, a red-bearded giant standing well over six feet tall, carried Lord Seaforth's standard. The forces of the Covenant engaged Montrose at Auldearn on 9 May 1645. The marquess was heavily outnumbered but his strategic genius more than compensated. He massed his banners, hoping to deceive the enemy as to the location of his main force. The ruse succeeded, forcing the Covenanters to mass their forces for a full assault. Montrose outflanked Seaforth, turning the tide of battle in his favour. The Maclennans were sent an order to withdraw, but it was never delivered. Ruaridh and his men fought to the last, defending Seaforth's standard. They were finally cut down by the Gordon cavalry.

The decimated clan played little part in any of the Jacobite risings, although eleven Maclennans are recorded as being taken prisoner after Culloden. After the terrible defeat, the clan system began to fall apart, with many Highlanders emigrating to other

Maclennan

parts of the world. There are Maclennan Mountains in New Zealand and a Maclennan County in Texas in the United States.

Ronald Maclennan of Maclennan was recognised by the Lord Lyon, King of Arms, as chief of this name under the process of selection known as the 'ad hoc derbhfine'. He was not a bloodline chief, although he was a member of the only Maclennan family to have matriculated arms since 1672. He carried out a great deal of research into the clan history, and published this in 1978. He traced the clan's origins to the ancient royal Celtic families of Ireland and Scotland through Aengus Macgillafinan, Lord of Locherne around 1230.

The family also developed a great tradition as pipers. Maclennans were town pipers in Inverness in the early sixteenth century, played at the Battle of Waterloo, and regularly won modern competitions. This is commemorated by the heraldic supporters which the chief selected when his arms were matriculated.

MACLEOD

ARMS
Quarterly, 1st & 4th, Azure, a castle triple-towered and embattled Argent, masoned Sable, windows and porch Gules (MacLeod of that Ilk);
2nd & 3rd, Gules, three legs in armour Proper, garnished and spurred Or, flexed and conjoined in triangle at the upper part of the thigh (Royal House of Man)

CREST
A bull's head cabossed Sable, horned Or, between two flags Gules, staved of the First

MOTTO
Hold fast

On Compartment
Murus aheneus esto (Be a wall of brass)

SUPPORTERS
(on a compartment embellished with juniper plants)
Two lions reguardant Gules, armed and langued Azure, each holding aloft in his interior paw a dagger paleways Proper, hilted Or

STANDARD
The Arms in the hoist and of two tracts Azure and Argent, upon which is depicted the Badge in the first and third compartments, and the Crest in the second compartment, along with the Motto 'Hold fast' in letters Argent upon two transverse bands Gules

PINSEL
Azure, the Crest within a strap Argent with buckle and furniture Or, bearing the Motto 'Hold fast' in letters Sable, all within a circlet Or bearing the title 'MacLeod of MacLeod' in letters also Azure and in the fly an Escrol Argent environing a branch of juniper Proper and bearing the Motto 'Hold fast' in letters Gules

BADGE
A bull's head Sable, horned Or, between two flags Gules, staved of the First, within a chaplet of juniper Proper, ensigned of a chapeau Gules furred Ermine

PLANT BADGE
Juniper

It is generally held that Leod was the younger son of Olaf the Black, one of the last Norse kings of Man and the North Isles. Olaf died around 1237, and Leod inherited the Islands of Lewis and Harris, with part of Skye. Marriage to the daughter of the Norse seneschal or steward of Skye brought the family to Dunvegan, which remains the chief's seat to this day. When King Haakon of Norway was defeated at the Battle of Largs in 1263 he was forced to relinquish his residual claims to the Western Isles, leaving Leod in possession of almost half the Hebrides. The clan consisted of two main branches, the Macleods of Lewis, later 'of the Lewes', named after a son of Leod, Thorkil or Torquil (the 'Siol Torquil'), and the Macleods of Skye, named after another son of Leod, Tormod (the 'Siol Tormod'), who established their seat at Dunvegan.

The spirit of independence which this clan inherited from its Norse ancestors did not make them easy subjects of the Crown, although Tormod's son supported Robert the Bruce in the War of Independence. Historians have noted that virtually no royal charters were granted to confirm the Hebridean chiefs in their lands and titles. The Macleods were, of course, more concerned at the growing power of the Macdonalds. The Macleods followed the Lord of the Isles to the Battle of Harlaw in 1411, but when James IV set out to break Macdonald power the Macleods were successful in steering a path through the tortuous politics of the time. However, the Macleods, who did not owe the possession of their lands to any gift of the Stewart monarchs, were forced to accept a royal charter which did not include all that was theirs by right. James V continued the royal policy of suppressing the power of the Hebridean chiefs, and the survival of the Macleods is to a large degree due to the talent of the eighth chief of Dunvegan, Alasdair Crotach, 'Hump-backed'.

Alasdair not only avoided the wrath of James at a time when many other island chiefs were imprisoned or dispossessed, he actually advanced the interests of the clan. He secured a title to Trotternish in 1542 which had long been disputed with the Macdonalds of Sleat. The famous fairy tower at Dunvegan Castle was constructed on Alasdair Crotach's orders, and he also rebuilt the church of Rodel in Harris where he was later entombed. The church and his tomb are considered two of the finest monuments in the Hebrides. He also had a flair for the dramatic, which enabled him to win a wager with James V. The chief is said to have been challenged on a visit to the royal court to admit that nothing in the isles could match the grandeur maintained by the king. Alasdair replied that he had a finer table and candlesticks than any the court could provide. When James V came to visit Dunvegan he found that Macleod had set out a feast on a high flat hill, known as 'Macleod's tables', facing Dunvegan, and the whole scene was lit by clansmen in all their Celtic finery, holding aloft flaming torches. The king conceded defeat.

Alasdair died in 1547 and was succeeded by his eldest son, William, who swiftly followed his father to the grave, leaving his only daughter, Mary, a young girl under the guardianship of the Earl of Argyll. The chiefship was seized by one of Mary's kinsmen, Iain Dubh, who promptly killed any of his rivals who came within his grasp, forcing Mary's only surviving uncle, Norman, to flee. Iain held Dunvegan until 1559 when, as royal justice was about to lay hands upon him, he fled to Ireland where he was later killed. Mary ceded her rights to her uncle Norman, who became the chief. Norman's second son, Ruaraidh Mor, succeeded as the fifteenth chief in 1595. He was knighted by James VI and he continued the work of Alasdair Crotach, establishing Dunvegan as the cultural centre of the isles. He was described in a contemporary report as 'a very lordly ruler'. No chief of the Macleods can avoid at least once calling Rory Mor to memory. A great drinking horn, named

Macleod of Harris

after the fifteenth chief, is kept at Dunvegan and forms an integral part of the rite of passage of every Macleod chief. The horn, which holds a bottle and a half of claret, must be drained at one draft 'without setting down or falling down'. The present chief successfully maintained the honour of his family by performing this feat in less than two minutes.

The Macleods of the Lewes, leaders of the 'Siol Torquil', who had never fully accepted the ascendancy of their cousins at Dunvegan, were forced to do so when the head of that family, Torquil Macleod of the Lewes, was killed in 1597, and the barony passed to Sir Rory Mackenzie of Cogeach, husband of Torquil's daughter, Margaret. The representation of the 'Siol Torquil' passed to the Macleods of Raasay, senior cadets of the Lewes house. In 1988 Torquil Macleod of Raasay rematriculated his arms to be recognised by the Lord Lyon as Macleod of the Lewes, 'Chief and Head of that Baronial House under the MacLeod of MacLeod'. His standard is divided into three tracts, indicating his rank as a major baron-chieftain. The Mackenzies occupied Lewis, and to this day their chief, the Earl of Cromartie, calls his seat Castle Leod, although it stands on the mainland north-east of

Inverness. The Macleods were not immune from mainland politics. The eighteenth chief led his clan into England to fight in the royalist cause at the Battle of Worcester in 1651. Cromwell's forces won an overwhelming victory, and over five hundred Macleods were

Macleod of the Lewes (Lewis)

killed in the battle. Although loyal to the Stuarts, the terrible loss at Worcester prevented the Macleods from taking a leading roll in the rising of 1715. They believed the arrival of Prince Charles Edward in 1745, without a substantial French army, to be ill-conceived, and bluntly refused to join his standard. However, the Macleods of Raasay followed the prince, taking many of the chief's clansmen

with them. Dunvegan's official rebuff to the 'Young Pretender' saved them from the wrath of the Hanoverian government following the disaster at Culloden, and their estates were spared.

The Macleods of Raasay had also acquired, by royal charter in 1571, the lands of Assynt in Sutherland, and from them the MacLeods of Assynt descended. Assynt became synonymous with treachery, when Neil of Assynt sheltered Montrose at his Castle of Ardvreck after the Battle of Carbisdale in 1650. Assynt, to claim the reward on the marquis's head, betrayed him into Argyll's hands and the scaffold. The name of Assynt came to the fore once more, when Norman Macleod, born near the ruins of Ardvreck Castle in 1780, became one of the most renowned Calvinist preachers of his day. He took his congregation from Assynt to Nova Scotia to found a religious community which later followed him like a biblical prophet from Canada to Australia and, finally, New Zealand. Norman's zeal found an echo in the twentieth century when the Reverend Dr George Macleod of Fuinary became, in 1937, leader of the Iona Community dedicated to the restoration of the cradle of the Celtic Church in Scotland. Twenty years later his work was recognised when he was created a life peer as Lord MacLeod of Fuinary.

The most treasured relic of the clan is the Fairy Flag of Dunvegan, called in Gaelic 'am Bratach Sith'. Theories abound as to how this fragile fabric, said to have magical properties, came into the chief's possession. It has been claimed variously to be the robe of an early Christian saint and the war banner of King Harold Hardraade of Norway, who died in 1066, but principally it is said to have been woven by fairies to be used by the chief in time of dire need. Belief in its power is strong, and on at least two occasions the magic of the flag has been called on to turn defeat into victory. Sir Reginald Macleod of Macleod had the Fairy Flag mounted in a specially sealed frame. An expert from the Victoria and Albert Museum in London discussed with Sir

Reginald the various possible origins of the flag, but avoided any reference to the supernatural. The chief listened politely, and at the conclusion of the thesis, simply said, 'You may believe that, but I know that it was given to my ancestor by the fairies'.

The castle at Dunvegan has been renovated and remodelled. Sympathetic Victorian additions have done nothing to detract from the grandeur and elegance of what is still the chief's home, inherited from his grandmother, Dame Flora Macleod. An active clan society and the present chief have continued Dame Flora's work to maintain Dunvegan and promote the fellowship of clansmen throughout the world.

MACMILLAN

The Macmillans are Celts descended from an ancient royal house and from the orders of the Celtic church. In the sixth century, the Irish prince, St Columba, established his church on Iona, thereafter the cradle of Christianity in Gaelic Scotland. The Columban church permitted priests to marry, and it faced increasing pressure from the papacy after the arrival in Scotland of Queen Margaret, under whose influence more European practices were introduced. Malcolm's son, Alexander I, tried to integrate the two traditions when he appointed Cormac, a Columban, as Bishop of Dunkeld. Cormac had numerous sons, one of whom, Gillie Chriosd, or disciple of Christ, was the progenitor of the Macmillans. As a Celtic priest, the bishop's son would have had a distinctive tonsure: the Celts shaved their hair over the front of the head, rather than in the Roman manner of a ring around the crown. The Celtic tonsure was described as that of St John, which is rendered in Gaelic, 'Mhaoil-Iain'. Macmillan is therefore son of one who bore the tonsure of St John. An alternative form, 'Mac Ghillemhaoil', 'son of the tonsured servant', was favoured by the Lochaber branch of the clan.

The clan appears to have moved to the shores of Loch Archaig in Lochaber when David I abolished the mormaership of Moray, and settled the region with Norman knights. They were well established by the end of the thirteenth century when the death of Margaret, the Maid of Norway, at Orkney in 1290, set in motion the events which were to lead to the War of Independence. Robert the Bruce settled his dispute with John, the Red Comyn, by stabbing him to death in the Greyfriars Church at Dumfries. The Comyns and their allies rose in fury, and the new king was forced to flee into hiding in the Highlands. He was sheltered by Maolmuire, the Macmillan chief, at his home at Ben

Lawers. The chief's brother, Gilbert, Baron of Ken, stayed with the king, and the clan fought at Bannockburn. He is the presumed ancestor of the Macmillans of Brockloch, a large Galloway branch of the clan. Despite this, when Robert's son, David II, opposed the Lord of the Isles, the Macmillans, who were generally considered loyal to the Lordship of the Isles, were expelled from the area of Loch Tay around 1360. John of Islay granted them lands at Knapdale. Alexander, fifth of Knap, and twelfth chief of the clan, has left the two most enduring Macmillan memorials, a round tower and a Celtic cross. Castle Sween is one of the oldest fortresses in Scotland, and Alexander married Erca, daughter of Hector Macneil and heiress to the castle. He probably built the round tower on the north-west of the castle, known afterwards as Macmillan's Tower. A fine cross was also erected by him, or in his memory, in the churchyard at Kilmory. One of the finest examples of Celtic art, it shows the chief himself hunting deer.

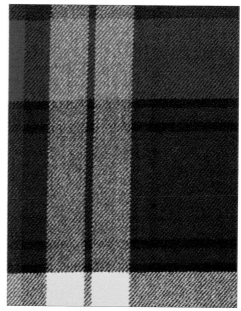

Macmillan

Standard

In time, the direct line became extinct and the chiefship passed, in 1742, to Macmillan of Dunmore, whose lands lay on the side of Loch Tarbert. The Macmillans were not noted Jacobites. John Macmillan of Murlaggan, whose line were later to head the Lochaber Macmillans, refused to join Prince Charles Edward unless the Stuarts renounced the Catholic faith. Murlaggan's eldest son defied his father and the Macmillans formed a company of Locheil's regiment which fought at Culloden; both sons died in the battle. Donald Macmillan of Tulloch, was induced to surrender to the Duke of Cumberland under the impression that he and his men had been promised protection, but they were transported to the Caribbean without trial. Hugh Macmillan guided the prince from Fasnakyle

at the mouth of Glen Afric over the hills to Loch Arkaig after Culloden.

Alexander Macmillan of Dunmore, sometime Depute Keeper of the Signet, an important legal post in Edinburgh, died in July 1770. He designated his cousin's son, Duncan Macmillan, also a lawyer, as his heir. This line, who were styled the Lagalgarve Macmillans, seem not to have had a full appreciation of their standing as chiefs of a great clan, although they served their country well. William Macmillan, Duncan's brother, served as captain of marines under Admiral Nelson on his flagship HMS *Victory*.

It was Captain William's great-grandson, General Sir Gordon Macmillan, father of the present chief, who reawakened the chiefly memory. Even he was not aware that he was the hereditary chief of the Clan Macmillan until he sought to matriculate arms to fly over Edinburgh Castle, of which he had been appointed governor. In fact, arms had been designed, showing him to be a cadet of the chiefly house, when his true pedigree was discovered by the Rev. Somerled Macmillan. Sir Gordon established the seat of the chiefs at Finlaystone House in Renfrewshire.

MACNAB

The name Macnab derives from the
Gaelic 'Mac An Aba', 'child of the
abbot'. According to tradition, the
progenitor of this great clan was Abraruadh,
the Abbot of Glendochart and Strathearn, the
younger son of King Kenneth Macalpine.
Abraruadh, the Red Abbot, was descended
from King Fergus of Dalriada and a nephew of
St Fillan, founder of the monastery in
Glendochart in the seventh century.

One of the earliest records of the family is
to be found in a charter of 1124. Malcolm de
Glendochart was one of the Scottish noblemen
who submitted to Edward I of England and his
name appears on the Ragman Roll of 1296.
Angus Macnab was brother-in-law of John
Comyn, murdered in 1306 by Robert the
Bruce, and he joined with Macdougall of Lorn
in campaign against the king which almost led
to his capture at Dalrigh in Strathfillan in
1306. When Bruce's power was consolidated
by the victory at Bannockburn in 1314, the
Macnab lands were forfeit and their charters
destroyed.

The fortunes of the clan were to some
degree restored in 1336, when Angus's grandson, Gilbert, received a charter from David II.
When the Lord Lyon considered the succession of the Macnab chiefs in 1954, he ruled
that Gilbert should be considered the first
undisputed chief (although he was perhaps the
twentieth). Gilbert was succeeded in his lands
of Bothmachan or Bovain by his son, Sir
Alexander, who died around 1407. By this
time the Macnab lands included Ardchyle,
Invermonichele and Downich. In 1522 the
lands of Ewer and Leiragan were granted to
Mariat Campbell by her husband, Finlay
Macnab, who died at Eilean Ran on 13 April
1525. His second son, John, succeeded to the
estates and married Eleyn Stewart. John's son,
Finlay, married twice and had a daughter and
two sons by his first marriage and, it is
believed, another ten sons by his second. The

eldest of the issue of the second marriage, John Roy or Bain, the red or fair, is the ancestor of the present chief. Finlay was a man of peace intent upon protecting his lands and people from being plundered by the foraging royalist forces of Montrose in the mid 1640s. His son, known as 'Smooth John', did not follow his father's peaceful ways, and led the Macnabs to join Montrose and contributed to the royal victory at Kilsyth. He was appointed to garrison Montrose's own Castle of Kincardine. General Lesley besieged the castle, but the whole garrison broke through the Covenanter lines and fought their way clear. John was, however, captured and taken to Edinburgh where he was sentenced to death. He contrived to escape on the eve of his execution and led three hundred of his clansmen at the Battle of Worcester in 1651.

Robert, the fourteenth chief, was apprenticed to study law under Colin Campbell of Carwhin, and he married the sister of John Campbell, Earl of Breadalbane. This strong Campbell connection constrained him from supporting the Jacobite rising in 1715, although many of his clansmen drew their swords for the 'Old Pretender'. The fifteenth chief, a major in the Hanoverian army, was taken prisoner by Jacobite forces after the Battle of Prestonpans and confined in Doune Castle.

Standard

Francis Macnab succeeded as sixteenth chief, and although within the clan he is renowned as a notable producer and consumer of whisky, he is more generally known as 'The Macnab' of Raeburn's outstanding portrait. He inherited a great burden of debt, and despite considerable personal efforts, he owed over £35,000 when he died in 1816. He had never married, and was succeeded by his nephew, Archibald, who made desperate efforts to

Macnab

extricate the estate from debt. In 1823 a writ of foreclosure was issued, and Archibald was forced to flee to Canada, where he eventually obtained a grant of land in the Ottawa River Valley. Eighty-five settlers came to the estate, which he renamed Macnab. When an official enquiry was threatened into allegations of excessive rents there, he fled to Orkney, then to London, and finally to France, where he died in 1860. Sarah Anne, the eldest of his children, was recognised as the eighteenth chief, but she died unmarried in Italy in 1894.

It was established that the Arthurstone branch of the chiefly family was now entitled to succeed and the de jure chiefship passed to James William Macnab. He served in the East India Company and was succeeded by his eldest son, James Frederick, rector of Bolton Abbey. His only son, James Alexander, succeeded as twenty-first de jure chief. In 1954, he relinquished the chiefship to his uncle, Archibald Corrie Macnab, who had acquired the Killin estate to enable him to become the twenty-second de facto chief. Archibald died in 1970 when the succession reverted to James Charles, the eldest son of James Alexander, who is the present and twenty-third chief.

MACNAGHTEN

The Macnaghtens are one of the clans who claimed descent from the great Pictish rulers of Moray. The name Nechtan, which may mean 'pure' or 'clear', was popular in at least one branch of the Pictish royal line. In the thirteenth century there are records of three brothers, Gilchrist, Athe and Gilbert, the sons of Malcolm Macnachten. Gilchrist received from Alexander III a charter in 1267 granting him the keepership of a castle warding the narrow Pass of Brander, the gateway to the west.

By coming to Loch Awe, the Macnachtens became neighbours of the powerful and acquisitive Campbells. When Robert the Bruce set out to gain the throne, the Campbells were quick to come to his support while the Macnachtens, under the influence of Macdougalls, opposed him. Macnachtens formed part of the Macdougall host that fought against Bruce's army at the Pass of Brander in 1306, and later at Dalrigh near Tyndrum. The Macnachtens appear to have changed their allegiance and a Baron Macnachten, possibly Alexander of that Ilk, is recorded fighting at Bannockburn in 1314. The Macnachtens gained little from their late change of heart, and from that point on the Campbells dominated Loch Awe. Alexander, the chief who may have fought at Bannockburn, took for his second wife Christina Campbell. When she was widowed in 1361, Christina granted to her cousin, Sir Colin Campbell of Lochow, her marriage portion of one third of the Macnachten lands. Alexander's son, Duncan, succeeded to the remaining lands. He made his seat at Dunderave, which was thereafter the territorial designation of the chiefs. In 1478, Duncan's heir, Alexander, acknowledged the Campbell Earls of Argyll as feudal superiors and accepted a charter to his lands from the earl's hands. His grandson, yet another Alexander, was knighted by James IV and followed the king to Flodden in 1513, where he was one of the few survivors. He died two years later. He had married twice and had six sons, the eldest of whom succeeded his grandfather in 1527. The second son, Ian, acted as tutor to his nephew and was the father of Ian, or John, Dhu, who may be the 'Shane Dhu' credited with founding the Irish branch of the family.

In 1548 Gilbert Macnachten succeeded as chief. When he died without issue, the succession devolved upon his younger brother, Alexander. He started the rebuilding of Dunderave Castle on Loch Fyne and it was completed by his son, Iain, in 1596. In 1627 the Macnachten chiefs raised a force of bowmen to go to the siege of La Rochelle to assist the French Huguenot rebels in their fight against Cardinal Richelieu, effective ruler of France. The chief was in high favour at the court of Charles I, and served as a Gentleman of the Privy Chamber. However, the expense of the French expedition and the extravagance demanded by living at court forced Macnachten to mortgage his lands.

Macnaghten

Standard

Alexander died in 1630, followed shortly afterwards by his childless heir, leaving Dunderave in the hands of Alexander's brother, Malcolm of Killearn. Malcolm's son, Alexander, was a fervent royalist, and when he succeeded to the chiefship he called out his clansmen, accompanied by Argyll's son, for the abortive rising against the Cromwellian occupation led by the Earl of Glencairn in 1653. The expedition was sheer folly, and earned Macnachten the enmity of Argyll. He was knighted after the Restoration in 1660, but through Argyll's influence he was later denounced as an outlaw. The lands were almost entirely lost through debt, and Iain, the next chief, who succeeded in 1685, inherited little more than an empty title. He joined the forces of Graham of Claverhouse, the 'Bonnie'

Viscount Dundee, fighting for James VII at Killiecrankie in 1689. He was denounced as a Jacobite rebel, and his remaining lands were forfeited. His younger son, John, was the last chief of this line. He was forced to make a formal disposition of the remainder of the estate in 1710 to Sir James Campbell of Ardkinglas. He died leaving no legitimate heir.

John Macnaughten, known as 'Shane Dhu', appeared in Ireland as secretary to his kinsman, the Earl of Antrim, in 1580. On the extinction of the Dunderave line his great-grandson, Edmond, was pressed to become chief. He declined, but his son, Edmund Alexander, was recognised as chief in 1818. When he died in 1832 he was succeeded by his brother, Francis, who was a judge in Madras and Calcutta. He was created a baronet in 1836. Sir Edward, fourth Baronet, was a distinguished lawyer who became a Lord of Appeal in 1887 with the life peerage of 'Baron Macnaghten of Runkerry'. He was succeeded by his son, Sir Edward, whose sons both succeeded to the title, but were killed in the First World War. Sir Francis, eighth Baronet, succeeded his nephews, and is the father of the present chief.

MACNEACAIL

T he islands of Lewis and Skye remained part of the Scandinavian kingdom of Man and the Isles until 1266, and it seems likely that, in common with the Macleods, the Macneacails were of high Norse descent. The name-father of the Clan Nicail or Nicolson, a name popular in Scandinavia, must have flourished in the mid thirteenth century. The Macleods of Lewis appear to have extended their considerable possessions through marriage with the Macneacail heiress in the fourteenth century. The ancestral Nicail, therefore, probably lived in Lewis, where he and his ancestors would have served the kings of Man and the Isles in a mixed Norse and Gaelic environment. It has also been suggested that the Macneacails formed a large part of two Viking bands which ravaged the east coast of England and established colonies from which sprung the houses of Nicholl and Nicholson in North-umberland and Cumberland. They also spread to the area that is present day Argyllshire and, it is claimed, sent warriors to participate in the tribal wars in Ireland. (Centuries later, some members of the extended clan settled in the north of Ireland during the plantation, and today their descendents are to be found in Counties Donegal and Tyrone with the names Nichols, Macnicols, O'Niocals and Nickells.)

The first chief on record early in the fourteenth century is John, son of Nicail. He appears in the company of leading Hebridean chiefs, Macdonald, Macdougald and Macruairi, descendents of Somerled, who had rested control of the southern Hebrides from Man. John was, perhaps, the leading man in Lewis. In the next generation most of the clan lands passed to the Lewis Macleods, but the main line continued, finding a home in the Trotternish Peninsula in Skye. Later, they followed the Macdonald Lords of the Isles and sat on their council. Tradition and ancient songs maintain that James V was entertained at Scorrybreac during his expedition in 1540 to subdue the island chiefs. After the collapse of the Lordship of the Isles, the clan followed the Macdonalds of Sleat, and fought alongside them during the civil war. Later in the seventeenth century, the chief, Donald, was minister of Kilmuir in Skye, and many of his descendents also followed into the Protestant ministry. It was around this time that the surname became generally anglicised as Nicolson, although it remained MacNeacail in Gaelic.

The Macdonalds of Sleat were Jacobites, and participated in the rising of 1715. After the Stuart defeat they were forfeited, and were more cautious in the Forty-five, when neither they nor the Macleods of Dunvegan came out for Bonnie Prince Charlie, the 'Young Pretender'. However, many Skye men did follow their prince, including the Macleods of Raasay and a band of Nicolsons who joined the Stuarts of Appin and fought at Culloden. It is said that most of them returned with their lives but bearing the scars of that bloody conflict.

In the nineteenth century the clan was badly affected by the Highland clearances. The chief was forced to abandon Scorrybreac and his family settled in Tasmania, where the present chief was born. The loss of the lands, including the traditional burial ground of Snizort, where over a hundred chiefs were buried, was severely felt. Many of the clansmen were evicted from their crofts and sought refuge in emigration, but those that were allowed to remain played their part in the slow revival of the Highlands and islands. Some were prominent in the agitation which resulted in the passing of the Crofters Act of 1886, which signalled the beginning of a new social order in the Highlands. Sheriff Alasdair

Nicolson was a member of the Commission that fathered the Act.

Until a decision of the Lyon Court in 1989, there had been much confusion between the west Highland, or Hebridean clan, and those who became established on the mainland and anglicised their name to 'Nicholson'. A petition was brought forward by Lord Carnock, to be recognised as chief of the whole name and arms of Nicholson. This was granted, but thereafter the Lord Lyon additionally granted a petition to Ian Nicholson of Scorrybreac to be recognised as chief in his own right of the west Highland Clan Macneacail, thereby changing his name and designation to Iain Macneacail of Macneacail and Scorrybreac, taking his designation from the lands of Scorrybreac near Portree in the Isle of Skye. Nicolson is still a common name in Skye, and the sense of family solidarity there remains strong. The greatest Gaelic poet of modern times, Sorley Maclean, is a Nicolson on his mother's side. Oral tradition in the family has preserved some Nicolson songs of considerable antiquity and great beauty. In 1989, the chief unveiled a cairn at Portree, erected by subscription in memory of the Nicolsons of Scorrybreac and their place in seven hundred years of Hebridean history. The portion of ancient Scorrybreac acquired by the clan is presently being developed as a national park, and is being partially re-forested with trees indigenous to Skye.

Another strong link with the homeland was recently forged when Burke Nicholson, a prominent clansman from Atlanta, Georgia acquired the castle and barony of Balvenie. The castle, once home of the Earls of Atholl, also gives its name to a famous whisky.

MACNEIL

The Clan MacNeil claims descent from Niall, a descendent of Aodh O'Neil, King of the North of Ireland at the beginning of the eleventh century. Aodh was twentieth in descent from Niall of the Nine Hostages, the pagan fifth-century founder of the mighty U'Neill dynasty. Niall came to the island of Barra in the Outer Hebrides around 1049, and is reckoned the first chief. 'Barra' means the 'isle of St Barr', but it is uncertain whether this is St Fionnbharr, the founder of Cork, or St Barr, great-grandson of Niall of the Nine Hostages. Neil Macneil, fifth of Barra, was described as a prince at a Council of the Isles in 1252. He was still the chief when King Haakon's army was defeated at Largs in 1263, ending the Norwegian domination of the Hebrides. His son, Neil Og Macneil, is believed to have fought with Robert the Bruce at Bannockburn. He was rewarded with lands in north Kintyre, which were added to his barony of Barra.

The ninth chief, Gilleonan, received a charter of Barra and Boisdale from the Lord of the Isles in 1427. His namesake, the twelfth chief, was one of the island lords tricked into attending on James V at Portree. Promised safe conduct, they were promptly arrested and imprisoned. Barra was held until the king's death in 1542, when he was released by Regent Moray, who sought to use the island chiefs to counterbalance the growing power of the Campbells. His son was one of the chiefs who supported the last Lord of the Isles in his alliance with Henry VIII of England in July 1545. The treaty they signed, which agreed to accept the English king as overlord of the isles, proclaimed the ancient enmity between the isles and the realm of Scotland. In March 1579 the Bishop of the Isles made a complaint of molestation against Macneil of Barra. His grandson, the fifteenth chief, was no less troublesome. He was denounced so many times before the Privy Council that he has been described as a 'hereditary outlaw' and was known as 'the Turbulent' or 'Ruari the Tatar'. He has also been described as the last of the Vikings, raiding from his island Castle of Kisimul. The king eventually issued letters requiring that his loyal vassals 'extirpate and root out' the chief and clan of Macneil. Ruari, who lived by the sword, was probably not surprised when his own nephews launched an attack on Kisimul in 1610. They captured their uncle and placed him in chains. His eldest son, Neil Og, became chief. He had a more conventional attitude towards central authority, and was appointed a Colonel of Horse by King Charles. He fought at the Battle of Worcester in 1651. His grandson, Roderick Dhu, the Black, was well received at court, and in August 1688 he received a Crown charter of all the lands of Barra erected into a free barony.

Macneil

Standard

The Macneils were Jacobites, and Black Roderick led his clansmen to fight for James VII at Killiecrankie in 1689. He remained loyal to the cause and rallied to the 'Old Pretender' at the Rising of 1715. His two sons, Roderick and James, went into exile in France. They returned on their father's death and, for his Jacobite sympathies, Roderick was consigned to a prison ship, the *Royal Sovereign*. He was later taken to London and was not released until July 1747. The estates, however, were not forfeited.

The clan prospered until the time of the twenty-first chief, General Roderick Macneil who was forced to sell Barra in 1838. The gen-

eral had no children, and the chiefship passed to a cousin, whose line had emigrated to America at the beginning of the nineteenth century. It was from the New World that the father of the present chief came to reclaim Kisimul, together with the greater part of the island of Barra, in 1937. He devoted a great part of his life to the restoration of Kisimul, which is once again the home of the chiefs. His work was praised by the late Sir Iain Moncreiffe of that Ilk, one of Scotland's greatest traditionalists, in these words: 'It is often complained that some chiefs have sold their old clan territory and emigrated. Here is an outstanding example of the reverse; a chief who devoted his life and fortune to returning from the New World to rebuild the ruined home of his forefathers.' His son, who is a Professor of Law, divides his time between Barra, Edinburgh and the USA.

ARMS
Parted per fess Or and Azure, a lymphad of the First, sails furled, oars in action and tackling all Proper, flag and pennon flying Gules, in dexter canton a dexter hand fessways couped holding a dagger erect, in sinister canton a cross crosslet fitchée all of the Third

CREST
A cat sejant Proper

MOTTO
Touch not the cat but a glove

SUPPORTERS
Two Highlandmen in short tartan jackets and hose of the tartan of the House of Cluny-Macpherson, helmets on their heads, dirks at their left sides, and targets on their exterior arms, their thighs bare, and their shirts tied between them

STANDARD
The Arms in the hoist and of two tracts Or and Azure, upon which is depicted the Crest three times along with the Slughorn 'Creag Dhu' in letters Or upon two transverse bands Gules, accompanied by two sprigs of heather Proper in the fly

PLANT BADGE
White heather

This is a name derived from the Gaelic, 'Macaphersein', meaning 'son of the parson'. The old Celtic church had married clergy, and the Clan Macpherson is believed to have been founded by Muireach (or Murdo) Cattenach, who was a priest of Kingussie in Badenoch. The Macphersons formed part of the great Clan Chattan Confederation. In the first half of the ninth century, Clan Chattan was led by a chief called Gille Chattan Mor, one of whose sons was forcibly resettled in Lochaber by Kenneth Macalpine around 843. The chief would appear to have been named in honour of St Cattan, and may have been the lay prior of Ardchattan in Lorn.

Macpherson tradition has it that in 1309 Robert the Bruce proposed granting the lands of Badenoch to the chief of the Macphersons (perhaps Ewan Ban MacMhuirich), on condition that he destroyed Bruce's enemies, the Comyns. They carried out the king's wishes with alacrity. Ewan Ban had three sons: Kenneth of Clunie, Iain of Pitmain and Gillies of Invereshie, and the Macphersons are sometimes known as the Clan of the Three Brothers.

In 1370, a raiding party of Camerons lifted cattle from the Clan Chattan lands. They were confronted at the junction of the Rivers Spey and Truim at Invernahavon by the Macphersons, Mackintoshes and Davidsons. An argument arose between the Macphersons and the Davidsons as to who should take the right wing, traditionally the place of seniority or honour. Mackintosh adjudicated in favour of the Davidsons, whereupon the Macphersons refused to take part in the battle. The Camerons were apparently gaining the upper hand when the Mackintosh sent his bard, posing as a Cameron, to taunt the Macphersons for cowardice. The Macphersons soon charged into battle, and the Camerons were routed. The feud between Clan Chattan and the

Camerons continued for many years. In 1396 a battle of champions was fixed to be held on the North Inch of Perth before Robert III and his whole court, and Sir Walter Scott gave a vivid description of this bizarre encounter in *The Fair Maid of Perth*.

Andrew Macpherson, reckoned as the eighth chief, acquired the abbey-castle grange in Strathisla in 1618. His son, Euan, was a great royalist, and fought with Montrose during the civil war. Duncan Macpherson of Cluny, the tenth chief, lost his claim to lead Clan Chattan in 1672 when the Privy Council and the Lord Lyon, King of Arms, ruled in favour of a Mackintosh. As Duncan had no sons, he was succeeded as chief of the Macphersons by Lachlan Macpherson, fourth Laird of Nuid, in 1722.

His son, Euan of Cluny, became a famous Highland leader in the Forty-five. During the retreat from Derby he defeated a numerically superior force at Clifton Moor in Westmorland. After the defeat at Culloden, Cluny was able, through the faithful support of his clansmen, to escape capture by Hanoverian troops for nine years, despite a reward of £1,000 for his capture. He finally escaped to France in 1755.

Macpherson

Standard

William Macpherson the Purser, ancestor of the present chief, was killed at Falkirk in 1746. The Purser's nephew, James Macpherson of Balavil witnessed the redcoats burn Cluny's Castle in 1746. He was the publisher of the supposed translation of the Gaelic poet, Ossian, in 1761. The authenticity of the poetry was doubted by contemporaries, but it was hugely popular: a copy was carried by Napoleon Bonaparte throughout all his campaigns. The Emperor also commissioned a painting based on the Ossianic legends for his state apartments in Rome.

Duncan Macpherson of Cluny, 'Duncan of the Kiln', was born in 1748 while his mother took refuge in a corn kiln. He accepted the ultimate defeat of the Jacobites, and fought for the government during the American Wars of Independence. The Macpherson estates were returned to him in 1784, twenty years after his father's forfeiture. Due to a faulty lease and debts incurred by a son, the Cluny estate was bankrupt by the end of the nineteenth century. Macphersons, however, continued to serve the country in many parts of the world, and thanks to the co-operation of clan members, the principal relics of the chiefs were purchased at an auction in 1943. These form the basis of the clan museum. The present chief is possibly the first to sit as a judge of the High Court of England, but his seat is a handsome castle in Blairgowrie.

MACTHOMAS

homas, a Gaelic-speaking Highlander
known as Tomaidh Mor, from whom
the clan takes its name, was a
descendent of the Clan Chattan Mackintoshes,
his grandfather having been a son of William,
eighth chief of the Clan Chattan. Thomas lived
in the fifteenth century, at a time when the
Clan Chattan Confederation had become large
and unmanageable, and he took his kinsmen
and followers across the Grampians, from
Badenoch to Glenshee, where they settled and
flourished, being known as Mccomie, a pho-
netic form of the Gaelic, as well as Mccolm
and Mccomas. To the government in
Edinburgh, they were known as Macthomas,
and are so described in the roll of the clans in
the Acts of Parliament of 1587 and 1595.

The early chiefs ruled from the Thom, on
the East Bank of the Shee Water opposite the
Spittal of Glenshee, thought to be the site of
the tomb of the legendary Diarmid, of the
Fingalian saga. In about 1600, when the
fourth chief, Robert Mccomie of Thom, was
murdered, the chiefship passed to his brother,
John Mccomie of Finegand, who lived about
three miles down the glen, and Finegand in
turn became the seat of the chief. Finegand is
the corruption of the Gaelic, 'feith nan ceann',
meaning 'burn of the heads', which is said to
be a reference to the fate of some unfortunate
tax collectors who were killed and whose severed heads were tossed into the burn. The
Macthomases consolidated their power in the
glen and became well established at Kerrow
and Benzian, and up into Glen Beag. The seventh chief, John Mccomie, more properly
known as Iain Mor, has passed into the folk-
lore of Perthshire and Angus as McComie
Mor. Tax collectors appear to have been particularly offensive to him, especially those of
the Earl of Atholl. The Earl enlisted a champion swordsman from Italy, whom he hoped
would slay McComie, but the swordsman was
himself slain by his intended victim.

The Macthomases supported Charles I, and Iain Mor joined Montrose at Dundee in 1644. When Aberdeen fell to royalist forces it was Iain Mor who captured Sir William Forbes of Craigievar, the sheriff of Aberdeen and Covenant cavalry commander. After Montrose's defeat at Philiphaugh, the chief withdrew his men from the struggle and devoted his energies to his lands and people, extending his influence into Glen Prosen and Strathardle. He purchased the Barony of Forter in Glenisla from the Earl of Airlie. Forter Castle had been burned eleven years earlier and so Iain Mor built his house at Crandart on the bank of the River Isla, a few miles north of the castle ruins. Despite his earlier royalist sympathies, Iain Mor admired the stability of the government brought by the Common-wealth, with the attendant prosperity it brought to Scotland. This soured his relation-ship with his royalist neighbours, including Lord Airlie.

Macthomas

Standard

At the Restoration in 1660, the local roy-alists took their revenge. Macthomas was fined heavily by Parliament and Lord Airlie took legal action to recover the forest at Canlochan, although it was actually part of the Fortar estates. Airlie's suit prevailed, but the chief refused to recognise the decree and continued to pasture his cattle on the disputed land. Airlie, in turn, exercised his legal right to lease the land to Farquharson of Broughdearg, a cousin of Iain Mor, which led to a bitter fam-ily feud. In an affray on the 28 January 1673 at Drumgley just west of Forfar, at a spot now known as McCombie's Field, Broughdearg was killed, along with two of Iain Mor's sons. The feud continued, and crippling law suits and fines ultimately ruined the Macthomases, and after Iain Mor's death in 1676 his remaining sons were forced to sell their lands.

The Macthomas chief is mentioned in Government proclamations in 1678 and 1681, but the clan was now drifting apart. Some moved south into the Tay valley where their name became Thomson, or to Angus in Fife where they are found as Thomas, Thom or Thoms. The tenth chief, Angus, took the sur-name Thomas, and later Thoms, and settled in northern Fife where he and his family farmed successfully. They moved to Dundee at the end of the eighteenth century, acquiring the estate of Aberlemno near Forfar.

In Aberdeenshire the name became cor-rupted to Mccombie, as well as the anglicised forms Thom and Thomson. William Mccombie of Tillifour, descended from the youngest of Iain Mor's son, was MP for South Aberdeenshire at the end of the nineteenth century, and is today regarded as the father of Aberdeen-Angus cattle breeding. The fifteenth chief, Patrick Hunter Macthomas Thoms of Aberlemno, was Provost of Dundee from 1847 to 1853. He was succeeded by his son, George, an advocate and a great philanthropist. In 1967 George's great-nephew was officially recognised by the Lyon Court as MacThomas of Finegand, eighteenth chief.

MAITLAND

It seems certain that the Maitlands descend from one of the companions of William the Conqueror who later settled in Northumberland. The name is found in many early charters as Matulant, Mautalant or Maltalant. It has been suggested that this was a nickname, meaning 'bad' or 'poor wit'. This seems highly unlikely, however, and Nisbet adds 'Quasi mutilatus in bello', 'As if mutilated in war', as an alternative translation. Sir Richard Matulant acquired the lands of Thirleston, Blyth and Hedderwick, and became one of the most considerable barons in the Borders in the reign of Alexander III. Thirlestane came to him by his marriage around 1250 to Avicia, heiress to Thomas de Thirlestane. Sir William Mautlant de Thirlstane supported Robert the Bruce in his struggle for the crown, witnessing the great victory at Bannockburn a year before his death. His son, Sir Robert Maitland, inherited not only his father's lands, but also received a charter to the lands of Lethington near Haddington from Sir John Gifford around 1345. He was survived by three sons: John, William and Robert of Shivas; the latter is the assumed ancestor of the Aberdeenshire Maitlands whose senior line lived at Balhargardy near Inverurie. William's successors styled themselves 'of Lethington', while his older brother, John, became embroiled in the conspiracies of his kinsman, George Dunbar, Earl of March, with the English. Sir Robert Maitland, William's son, surrendered the Castle of Dunbar to the Earl of Douglas, and thereby escaped being involved in the subsequent ruin of his uncle, John. Sir Robert's heir, William Maitland of Lethington, received a charter of confirmation to the lands of Blyth, Hedderwick and Tollus. His great-grandson was killed at Flodden in 1513. The Flodden knight's heir, Sir Richard Maitland, was a man of extraordinary talent who was appointed a judge of the Court of Session and

Keeper of the Privy Seal. He was also a distinguished poet and historian, and died in 1586 at the age of 90.

Sir Richard Maitland's eldest son, William, has passed into the annals of Scots history as Secretary Lethington, confidante of Mary, Queen of Scots. He fell from favour after he took part in the conspiracy to murder Mary's secretary, David Rizzio, but within the year he was allowed to return to court. He supported Mary's marriage to Bothwell, but later joined the nobles who opposed the queen at Carberry Hill, and fought against her again at the Battle of Langside. He attended the coronation of the infant James VI in July 1567, but kept in secret communication with Mary during her escape from Lochleven Castle. He intrigued with all who were prepared to support his exiled queen, and ultimately, in 1571, Parliament proclaimed Lethington a traitor. He died in Leith on 9 June 1573. The secretary's only son, James, died without issue, and the estates passed to his brother, Sir John, first Baron Maitland. His only son was created first Earl of Lauderdale in 1616. He was President of the Council and a Lord of Session.

The earldom passed to his son, John, in 1645, when the fortunes of the family reached their zenith. He went as a Scots commissioner to the Westminster Assembly of Presbyterian divines in 1643. In 1647 he promoted the king's cause, and the Scots Parliament agreed to send an army into England on behalf of Charles in return for certain undertakings on the Church from him. Lauderdale was sent to Holland to persuade the Prince of Wales to join with the Scots. He fought alongside Charles at the Battle of Worcester, where he was captured, and he spent nine years in the Tower of London. After the Restoration, Lauderdale rose to become the most powerful man in Scotland, ruling virtually as viceroy. In 1672 he was created Duke of Lauderdale, but this title died with him. The duke employed Sir William Bruce to convert his castle at Thirlstane into a renaissance palace. The fam-

Maitland

ily earldom passed to his brother, Charles.

Although Prince Charles Edward Stuart stayed at Thirlstane and his army camped in the parklands after the victory at Prestonpans, the family were not noted Jacobites, and they escaped the forfeiture which ruined so many other families after the Forty-five. General Sir Peregrine Maitland commanded the Foot Guards at Waterloo, and Napoleon later surrendered to Captain Frederick Maitland RN, commanding HMS *Bellerophon*. Sir Thomas Maitland (died 1824), known as 'King Tom', was in turn governor of Ceylon, the Ionian islands and Malta. In the twentieth century, Field Marshal Sir Henry Maitland-Wilson commanded in the Middle East during the Second World War. Politics has always fascinated the Maitlands. In 1968 Patrick Maitland, a distinguished journalist and former MP, became the seventeenth Earl. The family traditions have been maintained by his eldest daughter, Lady Olga Maitland, who now sits in the House of Commons. Among their many honours the Earls of Lauderdale are hereditary bearers of the national flag of Scotland, an office which they regularly perform on State occasions.

MAKGILL

ARMS
Gules, three martlets Argent

CREST
A phoenix in flames Proper

MOTTO
Sine fine (Without end)

SUPPORTERS
*Dexter, a horse at liberty Argent, gorged with a
Viscount's coronet and thereto affixed a chain, maned and
hooved Or;
sinister, a bull Sable, horned, unguled, collared and
chained Or*

Black, in his work, *Surnames of Scotland*, suggests that this name derives from 'Mac an ghoill', meaning 'son of the lowlander' or 'son of the stranger'. The name seems to have become established in Galloway prior to the thirteenth century. Maurice Macgeil witnessed a charter of Maldouen, Earl of Lennox, to the church of St Thomas the Martyr of Arbroath in 1231. Sir James Makgill, who was a prominent Edinburgh merchant and a descendent of the old Galloway family, became Provost of Edinburgh during the reign of James V. He quickly embraced the reformed religion. He had two sons, of whom the elder, Sir James Makgill, purchased the estate of Nether Rankeillour in Fife. He studied law at Edinburgh, where he was soon recognised as an able scholar. In June 1554 he became a member of the College of Justice, and in August of that year a Lord of Session. He took the judicial title, 'Lord Rankeillor'. He was a friend and supporter of the reformer, John Knox. Queen Mary returned from widowhood in France to reclaim her throne of Scotland in 1561, and Rankeillor became one of her Privy Councillors. He was one of the nobles who were jealous of the influence exercised by the queen's Italian secretary, David Rizzio. On 9 March 1566, a group of noblemen led by Patrick, Lord Ruthven, burst into the apartments of the queen (who was six months into her pregnancy), dragged Rizzio from her side, and stabbed him to death. Makgill was heavily implicated in the murder, so when Mary took revenge for the outrage he was deprived of his judicial rank and forced to flee from Edinburgh. He was later pardoned, but ordered to remain north of the Tay. Later, through the influence of Regent Moray, he was restored to his offices in December 1567. He was one of the commissioners who attended the regent on his journey to York to present accusations against the exiled Queen Mary, and was later sent by Moray to London. He was ambassador to the court of Elizabeth of England in 1571 and 1572. During his absence his house in Edinburgh was attacked by supporters of the queen, and his wife was killed. He himself died in 1579. His younger brother, who had acquired the lands of Cranston-Riddell, was also appointed to the Court of Session in 1582. He had held the post of Lord Advocate, which he did not relinquish until 1589. He took the judicial title, 'Lord Cranston-Riddell'. He was succeeded in March 1594 by his son, David, who followed him onto the Bench. He was succeeded by yet another David, the third Laird of Cranston-Riddell, who died without male issue in May 1619. His brother, Sir James Makgill, was created a Baronet of Nova Scotia in 1627 and appointed a Lord of Session in 1629. By letters patent dated 19 April 1651, he was elevated to the peerage with the titles of 'Viscount Oxfuird' and 'Lord Makgill of Cousland'. He died in May 1663. He was succeeded by his son, Robert, the second Viscount who had a son and heir, Thomas, by his second wife, Lady Henrietta, only daughter of the Earl of Linlithgow. Thomas died in 1701, five years before his father, leaving no issue. The viscountcy was claimed by the son of the second Viscount's eldest daughter, Christian, but this was challenged in 1734 by James Makgill of Nether-Rankeillor, sixth in descent from Lord Rankeillor. The House of Lords refused to uphold his claim, but equally denied that of Christian's son, William Maitland, and the title became dormant. Christian's younger sister, Henrietta, later assumed the title of Viscountess of Oxfuird, without establishing her legal right thereto, but in any event she

Makgill

died in 1758 without issue.

The estates of Nether-Rankeillor passed through an heiress to the The Honourable Frederick Maitland, sixth son of the Earl of Lauderdale. The family thereafter assumed the name Maitland Makgill, and when David Maitland Makgill of Rankeillor became heir of line to the Crichton viscountcy of Frendraught, they then styled themselves Maitland Makgill Crichton. It was a member of this family who established his right to the chiefship of the Crichtons and, abandoning his additional surnames as required by Lyon Court decree, was recognised in 1980 as Crichton of that Ilk. In 1986 Crichton's kinsman, George Hubbard Makgill, was recognised as the thirteenth Viscount of Oxfuird and chief of the Makgills.

MALCOLM (MACCALLUM)

The Maccallums derive their name from 'Mac Ghille Chaluim', 'son of the disciple of Columba'. They settled in Lorn, probably towards the end of the thirteenth century. 'Maol', or 'shavenhead', became synonymous in Gaelic for 'monk', and thus 'Maol Chaluim' can also be translated as 'monk' or 'disciple of Columba'. The historian Dr Ian Grimble challenges the thesis that Maccallum and Malcolm are simply interchangeable versions of the same name, asserting in his work, *Scottish Clans and Tartans*, that the name Colm was common throughout all the areas of Celtic settlement. Malcolm appears as a distinct surname in Dunbartonshire and Stirlingshire as early as the fourteenth century, and no less than four Scottish kings were so named.

Ronald Maccallum of Corbarron was appointed constable of Craignish Castle in 1414. Donald McGillespie Vich O'Challum, received a charter of the lands of Poltalloch in the parish of Kilmartin in Argyll from Duncan Campbell of Duntrune in May 1562. The Reverend Archibald Maccallum, translator of parts of the bible into Gaelic, succeeded his cousin to become the fourth Laird of Poltalloch in 1642. His son, Zachary, the fifth of Poltalloch, was a noted swordsman who had been educated at St Andrews University. Zachary also succeeded to the estates of Corbarron, which were left to him by a kinsman. Neil Maccallum, son of Zachary's younger brother, Duncan, served in the French navy, and was reputed to have been the natural father of the Marquis de Montcalm, who was later to defend Quebec against what may well have been his own kin. The Highland regiments scaled the Heights of Abraham, defeated the Montcalm forces and ended French rule in Canada.

John Malcolm of Balbedie, Lochore and Innerneil, chamberlain of Fife in the reign of Charles I, had four sons: Sir John was created a Baronet of Nova Scotia in 1665; Alexander became the judge, Lord Lochore; James fought with Viscount Dundee at Killiecrankie in 1689, and Michael. This distinguished family, today represented by the eleventh Baronet, bears a version of the chiefly arms of Mac-Callum, suitably differenced as determinate cadets, which may provide some evidence of a transitional link between the two names. However, although heraldic authorities often assert that armorial bearings assist in authenticating genealogies, this evidence is by no means conclusive. It is, however, without doubt that it was not until the late eighteenth century that Dugald Maccallum, ninth of Poltalloch, changed his surname to Malcolm. According to the late Sir Iain Moncreiffe, this was for aesthetic reasons.

George Malcolm of Burnfoot near Langholm in Dumfriesshire married Margaret, sister of Admiral Sir Thomas Pasley of Craig, Baronet, in 1761. They were blessed with a large family including three sons, all of whom were to become Knights of the Order of the Bath, two as generals and one as an admiral. General Sir John served extensively in India, and in 1800 he became the first British representative at the court of the Shah of Persia since the reign of Charles II. He wrote several works on India, and in 1815 published a history of Persia still regarded by historians as being of great merit. His brother, Admiral Sir Pultney Malcolm, is perhaps best remembered as naval commander at St Helena when the Emperor Napoleon was imprisoned there after his defeat at Waterloo in 1815. The admiral seems to have had some sympathy for the fallen emperor's plight. When asked by Napoleon if it was his government's intention to keep him on the island till his death, Malcolm replied, 'I do fear so'.

John Winfield Malcolm, who succeeded to the chiefship in 1893, had a distinguished Parliamentary career, representing first Boston in Lincolnshire in England, and then Argyll, from 1886 to 1892. In June 1896 he was

Malcolm (Maccallum)

raised to the peerage as Baron Malcolm of Poltalloch, but the title became extinct when he died without issue. He was succeeded by his brother, Edward, who was an engineer and much involved in local government. He had two sons, Major General Sir Neil Malcolm, who served in India and Africa, and throughout the First World War, and Sir Iain, who succeeded to the chiefship. Sir Iain followed his uncle, Lord Malcolm, into politics, and was a Member of Parliament until 1919, when he was appointed one of the government's directors on the board of the Suez Canal Company. He was made a Knight of the Order of St Michael and St George and a member of the French Legion of Honour, and the Khedive of Egypt invested him with the Grand Cordon of the Order of the Nile. In 1902 he married Jeanne Langtry, daughter of the famous Edwardian actress and friend of Edward VII, Émilie (Lillie) Langtry. It was widely believed that Jeanne was, in fact, the daughter of Prince Louis of Battenberg, a name now famous in its anglicised form of Mountbatten.

The chief's seat is still at Duntrune Castle, where the family have lived for centuries.

ARMS
Azure, a bend between six cross crosslets fitchée Or

CREST
*On a chapeau Gules furred Ermine, two wings, each of
ten pen feathers, erected and addorsed, both blazoned as
in the Arms*

MOTTO
Pans plus (Think more)

SUPPORTERS
*(on a compartment embellished with Scots fir seedlings)
Two griffins Argent, armed and beaked and winged Or*

STANDARD
*Azure, a St Andrew's Cross Argent in the hoist and of two
tracts Or and Azure, upon which is depicted the Badge in
the first compartment, and the Crest in the second and
third compartments, along with the Motto 'Pans plus' in
letters Azure upon two transverse bands Argent*

BADGE
*A demi-nobleman, bearded Proper, in robe Gules furred
Ermine, with a conical hat Gules furred Ermine, embel-
lished with a tall feather Or, quilled Azure, within an
oval chaplet of Scots fir banded of ribbands Azure and
Or, and ensigned with the comital coronet of Mar*

Mar was one of the seven ancient kingdoms or provinces of Scotland whose
rulers were known by the title of
'mormaer'. Its territory lay in that part of
Aberdeenshire largely between the Rivers Don
and Dee. Donald, Mormaer of Mar, fought at
the Battle of Clontarf, where the High King of
Ireland, Brian Boru, drove back the invading
Norsemen in 1014. In the charter erecting the
Abbey of Scone in 1114, the Mormaer of Mar
is named as Rothri, and he is given the latin
title 'Comes' which generally equates to the
modern rank of earl. Rothri was succeeded by
Morgund, second Earl of Mar, who witnessed,
some time before 1152, charters to the Abbey
of Dunfermline. William, the fifth Earl, was
one of the Regents of Scotland and Great
Chamberlain of the Realm in 1264. His son,
Donald, was knighted at Scone by Alexander
III in September 1270. He witnessed the marriage contract of Princess Margaret of Scotland
with King Eric of Norway, and later acknowledged Eric's daughter, Margaret, the Maid of
Norway, as the lawful heir to the throne.
When the child died at Orkney on her way to
claim her kingdom, events were set in motion
which were ultimately to lead to the field of
Bannockburn.

The Earls of Mar supported the Bruce
claim to the throne, and Donald's eldest
daughter, Isabel of Mar, became the first wife
of Robert the Bruce. Her brother, Gratney, the
seventh Earl, married Robert's sister,
Christian, further strengthening the Bruce
alliance. Gratney died around 1305, leaving an
only son, Donald, to succeed to the earldom.
He was captured at Methven in 1306 and
taken as a hostage to England, where he
remained in captivity throughout the struggle
for Scotland's freedom. He was released after
the victory at Bannockburn, when several prisoners, including the wife, sister and daughter
of King Robert, were exchanged for the Earl of
Hereford. In 1332 Mar was chosen to be

regent of the kingdom, a post he held for only ten days. On the eve of his election, Edward Balliol appeared in the Forth with an English fleet. Meeting little opposition, Balliol marched into Perth while Mar hurriedly gathered his troops to confront the invaders on the banks of the River Earn. Balliol's forces were heavily outnumbered, but the Scots army lacked discipline and effective leadership. In the dead of night, on 12 August 1332, the English crossed the river by a secret ford and fell upon the Scots army in their sleep, routing them totally. The Earl of Mar was among the fallen. Thomas, the ninth Earl, died without issue, and the title passed to his sister, Margaret, and through her, to her daughter, Isabel. She took as her second husband Alexander Stewart, the natural son of the feared Wolf of Badenoch. She granted the life-rent of the earldom to her Stewart husband, but reserved succession to her own lawful heirs. She died without issue around 1407, and her kinsman, Robert, a descendent of Elyne, daughter of the seventh

Mar

Standard

Earl, became 'de jure' thirteenth Earl of Mar. His son, Thomas, was denied his lawful title when James II claimed the earldom through the alleged rights of Alexander Stewart, Countess Isabel's husband. The title was then bestowed firstly on the king's son, Prince John, and later, in 1562, on James Stewart, the illegitimate half-brother of Mary, Queen of Scots. In 1565 Queen Mary granted a charter to John, eighteenth Earl, restoring the title. The queen declared that she was 'moved by conscience to restore the lawful heirs to their just inheritance of which they have been kept out by obstinate and partial Rulers and Officers'.

John, the twentieth Earl, was appointed governor of Edinburgh Castle in 1615. He was also a judge of the Supreme Court until 1630. The earls were not supporters of Charles I's religious policies, but when it became clear that support of the Covenant meant armed opposition to the king, both the earl and his eldest son, John, Lord Erskine, took up arms in the royalist cause. The earl entertained Montrose in 1645 in his castle at Alloa. Lord Erskine accompanied the king's captain general and rode at the Battle of Kilsyth in August 1645. The family estates were forfeited until Charles II came to the throne in 1660. Charles, the twenty-second Earl, raised the 21st Regiment of Foot, or Royal Scots Fusiliers, in 1679, and became its first colonel. John, the twenty-third Earl, was created Duke of Mar in 1715 by the exiled James VIII, although for his Jacobite loyalties all his Scottish honours were ultimately forfeited. The earldom was restored to John, twenty-fourth of Mar, by Act of Parliament in 1824. In 1875 the House of Lords ruled that the title of Earl of Mar claimed by Walter Erskine, twelfth Earl of Kellie, was different from the ancient dignity of Mar. There is accordingly an Earl of 'Mar and Kellie', the chief of the Erskines, who should not be confused with the Countess of Mar.

MARJORIBANKS

ARMS
Argent, a mullet Gules, on a chief Sable a cushion Or

CREST
A demi-griffin Proper, issuant from a crest coronet Or

MOTTO
Et custos et pugnax (Both a preserver and a champion)

SUPPORTERS
*Dexter, a man garbed in the robes of a Doctor of Divinity
in the Church of Scotland of the 19th Century Proper;
sinister, a man garbed in the robes of a Writer to the
Signet of the 18th Century Proper*

Princess Marjorie, only daughter of Robert the Bruce, married Walter, High Steward of Scotland, in 1316. She was thus the mother of the first of the royal Stewarts, and received as part of her marriage settlement lands in Renfrewshire which became known as Terre de Marjorie, later Marjoribanks. The name is pronounced 'Marchbanks', and Nisbet asserts that the family who acquired the lands of the princess and took her name were originally kin to the Johnston Lords of Annandale. He finds evidence for this in the family's coat of arms, which incorporates a gold cushion and a star. The Johnstons bear three gold cushions, and in heraldry a star often alludes to a spur-rowel, which is part of Lord Annandale's crest.

The Marjoribanks came to prominence in the early sixteenth century, when the Court of Session, the Supreme Court of Scotland, was reinstituted in its modern form by James V in 1532. Thomas Marjoribanks of that Ilk was one of ten advocates appointed as procurators, or pleaders, before the Lords of Session. Four centuries before the introduction of legal aid the Scottish Courts recognised the need for the poor to be represented by able lawyers, and in March 1535, Thomas was appointed advocate 'for the puir' with a salary of £10 Scots per annum. He willingly accepted the post, but waived his right to the salary. His public-spirited nature was rewarded when he became Lord Provost of Edinburgh in 1540, representing the city in the Parliament of that year, and again in 1546. He had acquired land at Ratho near Edinburgh by a charter of 1539 which enabled him, ten years later, to assume the title, 'Lord Ratho', on his appointment as a judge. He became the Lord Clerk Register and acquired more land at Spotts and in Annandale.

Lord Ratho had two sons: John, who died during his father's lifetime, and James, who was the ancestor of Sir Dudley Marjoribanks,

Baronet, created 'Baron Tweedmouth' in 1881. Sir Dudley was MP for Berwickshire from 1853 until his elevation to the House of Lords. His son and heir, Edward, was also MP for Berwickshire and First Lord of the Admiralty from 1905 to 1908. He was created a Knight of the Thistle and a brigadier in the Royal Company of Archers (the monarch's bodyguard in Scotland). The title became extinct in 1935, when the third Baron died without male issue.

After Lord Ratho died, the chiefship devolved on his grandson, and John's son, Thomas, who sold Ratho in 1614. The family acquired lands at Balbardie around 1624. Christian Marjoribanks, believed to have been Ratho's granddaughter, married George Heriot, goldsmith and financier to James VI, founder of the famous Edinburgh school which still bears his name. Heriot was so wealthy that he reputedly kept his purse filled with gold, and to the citizens of Edinburgh he was known as 'Jinglin' Geordie'. Andrew Marjoribanks of Balbardie and of that Ilk was another distinguished lawyer who was appointed Writer to the King in 1716. He acted as agent for Lord Torphichen and was commissary of Edinburgh, an important post in the administration of estates of the deceased. His grandson, Alexander, brought the family full circle when he acquired the Barony of Bathgate, which had also formed part of Princess Marjorie's dowry. He was convenor of Linlithgowshire for over thirty years, and in 1824 voluntarily surrendered his baronial rights to allow Bathgate to become a burgh, with Alexander as its first Provost. Alexander was ultimately succeeded by his seventh son, the Reverend Thomas Marjoribanks, Minister of Lochmadden and later of Stenton in East Lothian. In 1861 he sold the estates of Balbardie and Bathgate to the trustees of Stewart's Hospital. His eldest son, Alexander, succeeded in 1869, but although he married twice, he died childless and was succeeded by his brother, the Reverend George, who was also minister of Stenton. Two more ministers of religion were to hold the chiefship until it passed to William Marjoribanks of that Ilk, father of the present chief. Will Marjoribanks was an ecologist and worked on major conservation projects for the government of Sudan in Khartoum.

Northfield House, on the outskirts of Prestonpans in East Lothian, became the property of Joseph Marjoribanks, an Edinburgh merchant, around 1608. Recent restoration has revealed some of the finest sixteenth-century tempera wall and ceiling decoration still surviving in Scotland. A traditional L-shaped laird's mansion, it still bears above the door the arms of Marjoribanks and the motto, 'exep the Lord buld inwae bulds man'. A variation on the motto of the city of Edinburgh, 'Nisi Dominus Frustra' (Without the Lord man builds in vain), it seems an apt epithet for this industrious clan.

MATHESON

In common with many clans, the Mathesons suffer from the anglicisation of their name from more than one possible Gaelic derivation. Black attributes the name to the Gaelic, 'Mic Mhathghamhuin', meaning 'son of the bear'. (From this derivation, the chiefs' arms carry two bears as supporters.) Others have suggested that MacMhathain means 'son of the heroes'. However, as bears have long been a totem associated with courage and strength, the underlying meaning remains largely the same. There is also, of course, a Lowland derivation, which is simply 'son of Matthew'.

It is not known whether the Mathesons are of pure Celtic descent, but given the immense influence of the Norse over the Western Isles, it is perfectly possible that some of their blood was intermingled. They seemed to have settled around Lochalsh, Lochcarron and Kintail, where they were granted lands by the great Celtic Earls of Ross. In 1262, a Scots army invaded Skye at the command of Alexander III, who was determined to free the isles from the Norwegian kings. One of the leaders of Alexander's expedition is recorded as Kjarnac or Cormac Macmaghan. After the Battle of Largs the following year, the Western Isles came under the domination of the Macdonalds as Lords of the Isles, and the Mathesons seemed to have sided with them. They fought for Donald, Lord of the Isles, in 1411 at the Battle of Harlaw where Alasdair, the chief, was captured. The Mathesons were said, at that time, to number over two thousand warriors. Macmakan supported the Earl of Ross, whom James I suspected of treason. To discourage such ideas among his nobles, the king seized the earl at Inverness in 1427 and executed him.

As the power of the Lords of the Isles waned, so did the fortunes of the Mathesons. They found themselves uncomfortably set between the powerful and feuding Macdonalds and Mackenzies. However, some found time for less warlike pursuits, and Dougal Mac Ruadhri Matheson was Prior of Beauly between 1498 and 1514, and sat in Parliament. The chiefs, however, were less fortunate, and in 1539 Iain Dubh was killed defending Eilean Donan Castle. He had become constable of the great Mackenzie stronghold after marrying the widow of Sir Dugald Mackenzie. All the genealogies agree that the undisputed chiefship rested in Murdoch Buidhe, or 'yellow haired', who died around 1602. He had two sons, Roderick and Dugall. Dugall, styled 'of Balmacara', became chamberlain of Lochalsh in 1631. He was the ancestor of John Matheson of Attadale whose grandson, John, was forced to sell the Highland estates. He married his kinswoman, Margaret, daughter of a branch of the family which had settled in Sutherland. The Mathesons were baillies to the Earls of Sutherland in the late fifteenth century, and they settled on the north side of Loch Shin. Donald Matheson of Shiness fought

Matheson

Standard

against the Jacobites during the rising of 1715. Alexander, eldest son of Margaret and John, joined, with his uncle James, the merchant adventurers engaged in trade in India and China. In 1827, they founded the trading house of Jardine Matheson. Alexander was able to use his wealth to purchase the Barony of Lochalsh in 1851, having previously acquired Ardintoul and Inverinate, also part of the ancient clan lands. He was MP for Inverness from 1847 to 1868, and was created a baronet in 1882.

Meanwhile, the chiefship had descended through the line of Dugal of Balmacara's elder brother, Roderick. His family acquired Bennetsfield in the Black Isle in 1688. John,

second of Bennetsfield, was, unlike his Sutherland cousins, a Jacobite who fought at the Battle of Culloden. When the prince's army was defeated, John escaped and, according to story, fell into the hands of Hanoverian officers who were unaware of his Jacobite sympathies. He gave them some advice on the location of sound building stone, and returned safely to his home as a result. When John died without issue in 1843, the chiefship passed to his nephew and subsequently to a cousin, Heylan Matheson. His son, Colonel Bertram Matheson of that Ilk, was confirmed in the chiefship by the Lord Lyon in 1963. The Matheson baronets had continued to prosper, and Sir Torquhil, fifth Baronet, was a distinguished soldier who served in the Boer Wars and through the First World War, eventually rising to the rank of general. He was decorated by his own country, France and Russia. The chief, Colonel Bertram, nominated General Sir Torquhil as 'tanastair' (successor). Major Sir Torquil succeeded his father as sixth Baronet in 1963 and Colonel Bertram as chief in 1975, thus uniting the baronetcy and the chiefship. Sir Fergus succeeded his elder brother as seventh Baronet and chief in 1993.

MENZIES

Mesnieres in Normandy was the original home of the Norman family who in England rendered their name as Manners, and were ancestors of the present Dukes of Rutland. Sir Robert de Meyneris appeared at the court of Alexander II, where he gained royal patronage, rising to become chamberlain in 1249. Sir Robert received grants of lands in Glen Lyon and Atholl, reinforced by a grant to his son, Alexander, of Aberfeldy in Strathtay, in 1296. Alexander also acquired the lands of Weem and made a splendid marriage to Egidia, daughter of James, the High Steward of Scotland. His son, Sir Robert, was a companion-in-arms of Robert the Bruce, and was rewarded with lands in Glendochart, Finlarig, Glenorchy, and Durisdeer.

It was the eighth chief, another Sir Robert Menzies, who built the castle at Weem around 1488. Weem was plundered in 1502 by Stewart of Garth during a dispute over the ownership of lands in Fothergill. Janet Menzies had married a Stewart about a century earlier, and Garth claimed the lands as part of her tocher, or dowry. Menzies appealed to the Crown, and James IV found in his favour, ordered Stewart to make restitution, and erected the Menzies lands into the free barony of Menzies in 1510. In 1540 James Menzies of Menzies married Barbara Stewart, daughter of the third Stewart Earl of Atholl and cousin to Lord Darnley, the future King Henry. Despite both their Stewart and royal links, the chiefs opposed Charles I, and Menzies was harried by Montrose. The great marquess sent a messenger to him seeking to enlist support but, whether by accident or design, the envoy was wounded. Montrose retaliated, and in the skirmishing which ensued the Menzies chief was fatally wounded. His son, a major in the Army of the Covenant, was killed when Montrose caught Argyll unprepared at the Battle of Inverlochy. The Menzies families in the north took an independent line from that of their Perthshire chiefs. Sir Gilbert Menzies of Pitfodels was with Montrose throughout his campaigns, and was present at Inverlochy when his chief's son was killed.

In 1665, Sir Alexander Menzies was created a Baronet of Nova Scotia. His brother, Colonel James Menzies of Culdares, ancestor of the present chief, was a veteran of the civil war who, it was claimed, had survived no less than nine serious wounds. Another of Sir Alexander's brothers had died fighting for the royalists at the Battle of Worcester in 1651. The chiefs opposed the religious and political policies of James VII, and when he was forced from his throne in 1688, Menzies declared for Queen Mary and her husband, the Prince of Orange. However, clan loyalties were yet again divided, and although Major Duncan Menzies of Fornock led his Highlanders in the charge at the Battle of Killiecrankie in 1689 which broke the Government troops, they faced in the ranks of General Mackay's army, hundreds of their Perthshire kinsmen.

Standard

When the Stuarts once more called on their loyal subjects to rise in 1715, Menzies of Culdares quickly rallied to the standard of the 'Old Pretender'. Culdares was captured at Dunblane after the rising. After spending many years in exile in Maryland in America, he was released and returned to Glen Lyon, where he devoted his time to forestry and land improvement. When the 'Young Pretender' landed in Scotland in 1745, Culdares was beyond active campaigning, but sent the prince a fine horse. However, the clan was out in force under Menzies of Shian who, with his son, was killed during the campaign. The Menzies lands at Glen Lyon provided shelter for refugees from Culloden, including members of the prince's personal staff.

Menzies

At the end of the eighteenth century, the Menzies name gained momentary prominence when James Menzies, a merchant in Weem, was one of the leaders of a protest by thousands of men and women against the Militia Ballot Act, passed in fear of a French invasion in the wake of the Revolution of 1789. The Act compelled all men between the ages of nineteen and twenty-three to submit to a ballot as recruits for the army. Menzies and his citizen army forced Sir John Menzies and the Duke of Atholl to swear that they would not implement the Act, and even tried to arm themselves with weapons from the Campbell castle at Taymouth. But they were no match for regular troops, scattering at the first sign of serious opposition.

The Menzies baronetcy became extinct on the death of Sir Neil Menzies of Menzies, eighth Baronet, in 1910. His sister, Miss Egidia Menzies, succeeded to the estates, but on her death in 1918, they were sold. Menzies Castle fell into a dilapidated state, and during the Second World War was used as a Polish army medical stores depot. It was saved from ruin in 1957, when it was purchased by the Menzies Clan Society. The present chief lives in Australia.

MOFFAT

The Moffats are an ancient Borders family who were influential and powerful as far back as the time of Sir William Wallace. The ancestor of the Moffats most likely gave their name to the town of Moffat in Dumfriesshire. The origin of the name itself is thought to be Norse. William de Mont Alto, progenitor of the Movats, married the youngest daughter of Andlaw, who came to Scotland from Norway during the tenth century. Over the years the name softened to Montealt, then Movat, through Movest, eventually settling at Moffat in its modern form. In the twelfth century the family was of sufficient importance to be designated in deeds and records as 'de Moffet', showing the family were considered to be principal lairds, or landowners.

In 1268, Nicholas de Moffet was Bishop of Glasgow, and the armorial bearings of the different branches of the family seemed to indicate a connection with the church. Robert the Bruce, as Lord of Annandale, granted four charters of land in the barony of Westerkirk to the Moffats in 1300. One of these was to Adam Moffat of Knock who was granted 'the same Barony in Eskdale'. Both he and his brother fought at the Battle of Bannockburn in 1314, along with many Moffat clansmen. They remained the Lairds of Knock until 1609, when the land was sold to the Johnstones. They were also tenants of Midknock for six hundred years, until 1905. In 1336 the king of England granted a safe conduct to William de Moffete and others described as 'coming as ambassadors from David de Brus' – in fact, David II, son of Robert the Bruce. In 1337, Walter de Moffet, Archdeacon of Lothian, was appointed ambassador to France.

Although there were Moffats in Moffat before 1300, the names of the earliest lairds are not known. They were granted the feu of Granton (not to be confused with the port on the River Forth) and Reddings in 1342 by Sir

John Douglas, Lord of Annandale. These remained the principal holdings of the family until 1628, when the lands passed to the Johnstones as a result of overwhelming debt. Other properties of the Moffats in Upper Annandale were Corehead, Ericstane, Braefoot, Meikleholmside, Newton, and Gardenholm. The Moffats also held the lands of Auldtoun, now known as Alton. One Robert Moffat, born there around 1560, was designated 'Moffat of that Ilk', but there were no Moffats in Auldtoun after 1672, and little is known of what happened to this branch after that time.

In 1759, the last Moffat in Gardenholm died and the family moved to Craigbeck in modern Moffatdale. Two brothers, James and David Moffat, moved from Granton to Crofthead in Moffatdale sometime after 1658. James's son, William, was the progenitor of the Craigbeck branch of the family. The Moffats were tenants of Crofthead and Craigbeck until 1920, when Francis Moffat, who died in 1937, purchased Craigbeck and Garrowgill, thus restoring a landed position to the descendents of Granton after three centuries of landlessness. In 1909 this Francis also bought Bodesbeck, which had been Moffat land in 1589, almost a hundred years prior to the acquisition of Crofthead and Craigbeck. His son, William, added to the estate by the purchase of Hawkshaw in Tweedsmuir in 1911, and Fingland in 1935. When he died in 1948 he was one of the biggest sheep farmers in southern Scotland, owning some ten thousand acres. His son, Francis, remained in Craigbeck until 1977, when it was sold on his retiral from farming. Bodesbeck, Hawkshaw and Fingland are still farmed by Moffats.

Another branch of the Moffat family farmed Garwald in Eskdalemuir. This was first leased to them in 1744, and they remained there until 1950. They were also at Craick in Borthwick Water for more than a century from 1817. The Garwald Moffats have now died out in the male line. Other lands settled by Moffats as the family scattered were Sundaywell and Lochurr. They were there

Moffat

from the latter part of the seventeenth century for over three hundred years. They were very successful farmers and founders of the renowned Lochurr herd of native Galloway cattle.

The Moffats, like many other Borders families, were raiders and reivers, and had many feuds with other clans. Their most notable enemies were the powerful Johnstones. In 1557 the Johnstones murdered Robert Moffat, possibly then the clan chief, and burned a building in which a number of leading Moffats had gathered. They slaughtered all those who tried to escape. From that date the Moffats were considered a leaderless clan, until 1983, when the late Francis Moffat, after many years of research, was recognised as hereditary clan chief, and the Lord Lyon confirmed to him the undifferenced arms of Moffat of that Ilk. His daughter, the present chief, succeeded to the title on his death in April 1992.

Moffats have branched out all over the world, many achieving fame, such as the Reverend Robert Moffat who was patriarch of African missions and founded the Kuruman mission. His daughter married David Livingstone.

MONCREIFFE

This name is derived from the feudal barony of Moncreiffe in Perthshire. The lands themselves take their name from the Gaelic, 'Monadh croibhe', 'Hill of the sacred bough'. The plant badge of the clan is the oak, presumably the sacred tree. Moncreiffe Hill, which dominates the south-east Perth valley, was a stronghold of the Pictish kings, thereby connecting the clan with the lands of Atholl and Dundas, both held by branches of the Picto–Scottish royal house. The late Sir Iain Moncreiffe of that Ilk, Albany Herald and chief of the clan, asserted that the coat of arms of the red royal lion on a silver shield, were the colours of the house of Maldred, Regent of Cumbria and brother of Duncan I. This indicates that they were early cadets of Maldred's line, who was himself of the ancient royal house of Ireland, a descendent of King Niall of the Nine Hostages. The three main lines of the family descend from the eighth Laird of Moncreiffe, who died around 1496, and are distinguished by the spelling of the name. The Moncreiffes of Moncreiffe are the chiefly line, while the principal cadets are the Lords Moncreiff of Tulliebole and Moncrieff of Bandirran, from whom the Scott-Moncreiffs and the Moncreiffs of Kinmonth descend. In the sixteenth century one family joined the famous Scots Guard of Archers of the Kings of France and established no less than three noble French families. The Marquis de Moncrif was one of the unhappy French nobility who met his end on the guillotine during the French Revolution.

In a charter of Alexander II in 1248, Sir Matthew de Muncrephe received lands in Perthshire. Among the many Scottish noblemen who pledged loyalty to Edward I of England in 1296 were Sir John de Moncref and William de Monncrefe. Malcolm Moncreiffe of that Ilk, the sixth Laird, was a member of the council of James II, and received a new charter incorporating his

Highland and Lowland estates into the barony of Moncreiffe. He died around 1465, when he was succeeded by his son, the seventh Laird, chamberlain and shield bearer to James III. He married Beatrix, daughter of James Dundas of that Ilk, and died sometime prior to 1475, murdered by Flemish pirates. His grandson, Sir John Moncreiffe, was killed at the Battle of Flodden in 1513 along with his cousin, John, Baron of Easter Moncreiffe. He was succeeded by his son, William, the tenth Laird, who supported the Douglas Earls of Angus and was fined for refusing to attend the Court in 1532 that condemned the beautiful and talented Lady Glamis to be burned as a witch, when her sole crime was to be a Douglas by birth. William was captured at the rout of Solway Moss in 1542, and was imprisoned for a time in the Tower of London. On his release, he embraced the Protestant religion, being one of the barons who subscribed to the Articles in the General Assembly of the Church of Scotland in 1567.

Moncreiffe

Standard

The twelfth Laird, Sir John Moncreiffe, was sheriff of Perthshire, and in April 1626 he was created a Baronet of Nova Scotia. The title included a nominal grant of 1,600 acres in Canada, to be called New Moncreiffe, but the grant was never taken up. John was, however, unable to support the king's religious policies, and he signed the National Covenant in 1638. His son, John, personally raised a company of the King's Scots Guards by warrant of Charles II in 1674. He was heavily in debt, and in 1667 he secured a Crown charter confirming a family arrangement whereby the barony of Moncreiffe was sold to his kinsman, Thomas, a descendent of the eighth Laird. Thomas succeeded in 1683 to the chiefship of the name, while the baronetcy passed to Sir John's brother. In 1685 a second Moncreiffe baronetcy was created when Thomas, now the fourteenth Laird, was himself created a baronet by James VII, as Moncreiffe of that Ilk. He became Clerk of the Exchequer, treasurer in Scotland and later baillie of the Regality of St Andrews. He commissioned a new seat at Moncreiffe, the first major country house completed by Sir William Bruce in 1679. The house remained the family seat until it was destroyed by fire in November 1957, claiming the life of Sir David Moncreiffe of that Ilk, Baronet, the twenty-third Laird. It was this tragedy which led to the chiefship of Sir Iain Moncreiffe, the great Scottish herald and historian. The twenty-third Laird's sister, Miss Elizabeth Moncreiffe of Moncreiffe, was next in line for the chiefship, but she declared that it was her wish that it be assumed by her cousin, Sir Iain, the Baron of Easter Moncreiffe, while she retained the feudal barony of Moncreiffe. She built a modern country house on the site of the old seat which incorporates the doorway reclaimed from the ashes of the burned house. Sir Iain died in 1985 and the chiefship reverted to Miss Moncreiffe.

MONTGOMERY

A lthough the actual derivation of this name is obscure, the Norman family who bore it held the Castle of Sainte Foy de Montgomery at Lisieux. One tradition asserts that the name refers to a hill and a Roman Commander called Gomericus. Roger de Mundegumbrie, whose mother was the niece of the great-grandmother of William the Conqueror, accompanied his kinsman on the invasion of England and commanded the van at Hastings in 1066. He was rewarded with Chichester, Arundel and the Earldom of Shrewsbury. He soon consolidated his possessions, and then invaded Wales, where he captured the Castle of Baldwin, to which he gave his own name of Montgomery. There was later to be not only a town, but an entire county of this name.

The first Montgomery who appears on record in Scotland is Robert, who obtained the lands of Eaglesham in Renfrewshire. He appears as a witness in a charter to the Monastery of Paisley around 1165. It is generally supposed that Robert, a grandson of Earl Roger, accompanied Walter Fitz-Alan the first High Steward of Scotland, when he came to Scotland to take possession of lands conferred upon him by David I. Eight centuries later the Montgomerys still held lands in Renfrew and Ayrshire. John de Montgomery and his brother are listed on the Ragman Roll, rendering homage to Edward I of England for their estates in 1296. A later Sir John, the seventh Baron of Eaglesham, was one of the heroes of the Battle of Otterburn in 1388, capturing Sir Henry Percy, the renowned Hotspur. According to a vivid Borders ballad, Hotspur and Montgomery met in hand-to-hand combat, and Montgomery carried the day. The Percys paid a great ransom for the release of Hotspur, building for Montgomery the castle of Polnoon. The hero of Otterburn cemented his good fortune by marrying the heiress of Sir Hugh Eglinton, thereby acquiring the Barony of Eglinton and Ardrossan. His son, Sir John Montgomery of Ardrossan, was one of the hostages for James I, and took for his second wife Margaret, the daughter of Maxwell of Caerlaverock. He was succeeded by his eldest son, Alexander, a member of the king's council who was sent on several important missions to England. He was created Lord Montgomery sometime prior to 31 January 1449. Hugh, the third Lord Montgomery, supported Prince James in rebellion against his father, James III, and fought at the Battle of Sauchieburn in 1488. Montgomery was rewarded with the grant for life of the island of Arran and the keepership of Brodick Castle. More honours followed, and in the year after Sauchieburn he was made baillie of Bute and Cunningham. But Cunningham was claimed by the Glencairns, and a feud arose during which Eglinton Castle was burned. In either 1507 or 1508, Lord Montgomery was created Earl of Eglinton. He escaped the carnage of Flodden Field in September 1513, and was part of the Parliament at Perth in October of that year which proclaimed the infant James V king. Hugh, the second Earl, succeeded his grandfather in June 1545, but died a year later, and his son, another Hugh, became the third Earl. A devout Catholic, the Earl rejected the Reformation and staunchly supported Mary, Queen of Scots, throughout her troubled reign. He fought for her at the Battle of Langside, where he was taken prisoner. He was imprisoned and declared guilty of treason, but remained unrepentant until 1571, when he was convinced to accept James VI. He sat in the Parliament in Stirling in September of that year. Twice married, he died in 1585, leaving two sons and two daughters. His daughter, Margaret, married Robert, Earl of Winton, and their son was later to succeed as the sixth Earl of Eglinton.

Margaret's brother, the fourth Earl, fell victim to his family's ancient enmity with the Cunninghams of Glencairn. In 1586 the earl was riding from Eglinton to Stirling when he was attacked by John Cunningham, brother of the Earl of Glencairn, with several of his close

Montgomery

kinsmen and retainers. Eglinton was shot dead, probably by John Cunningham of Colbeith. The Montgomerys on discovering the murder, killed every Cunningham that came in their path. Colbeith was pursued, and when captured was cut to pieces on the spot. The infant who succeeded his murdered father as fifth Earl was brought up by his maternal uncle, Robert Boyd of Badenheath. He was a favourite of James VI. When he died without issue, the Eglinton title passed to Alexander Seton as heir of line. A rigid Protestant, the new Earl of Eglinton could not accept the religious policies of Charles I, and he fought in the Army of the Covenant during the civil war. He was able to accept Charles II, who had agreed to his Scottish subjects' terms concerning religion, and he was made a colonel of the King's Lifeguard of Cavalry. He was captured at Dumbarton and remained imprisoned in Berwick until the Restoration in 1660.

The thirteenth Earl organised the celebrated tournament at Eglinton Castle in 1839 which set out to recapture the spectacle of medieval jousting. The present chief is the eighteenth Earl of Eglinton and ninth Earl of Winton.

MORRISON

ARMS
Per bend sinister Gules and Argent, a demi-lion rampant issuant Or, armed and langued Azure, holding in his paws a battleaxe, the shaft curved, of the Third, axehead of the Fourth in chief, in base, issuing from the sea undy Vert and Or, a tower Sable, windows and port Or, over all a bend sinister embattled Azure, charged with an open crown Or, jewelled Gules, between two fleur de lis Argent

CREST
Issuant from waves of the sea Azure crested Argent, a mount Vert, thereon an embattled wall Azure masoned Argent, and issuing therefrom a cubit arm naked Proper, the hand grasping a dagger hilted Or

MOTTO
Teaghlach Phabbay (Pabbay family)

On Compartment
Dun Eistein

SUPPORTERS
(on a compartment consisting of two timber logs of drift-wood Proper floating in the sea Azure crested Argent) Two dolphins hauriant Vert issuant from the waves

STANDARD
The Arms in the hoist and of two tracts Gules and Argent, upon which is depicted the Crest in the first and third compartments, and the Badge in the second compartment, along with the Motto 'Dun Eistein' in letters Or upon two transverse bands Azure

PINSEL
Gules, bearing the foresaid Crest within a strap and buckle Proper, inscribed with the Motto 'Teaghlach Phabbay' in letters Or, all within a circlet Or bearing the title 'Morrison of Ruchdi' in letters Azure and in the fly a strand of driftweed Proper, surmounted of an Escrol Argent bearing the Motto 'Dun Eistein' in letters Sable

BADGE
A tower embattled Sable, port and windows Or, issuant from the sea wavy Azure crested Argent, upon the battle-ments two hands couped Proper grasping a broadsword in pale Or

PLANT BADGE
Driftweed

This ancient name highlights the problems created by the anglicisation of Gaelic names. It seems quite likely that there are three quite distinct origins – two Hebridean and one mainland. In County Donegal, the O'Muirgheasains, whose name means 'sea valour', were bards, and keepers of the holy relics of St Columcille at Clonmany. It is believed that a branch of this family found its way to Habost on the north-east coast of Lewis. Meanwhile, further to the south, Ghille Mhuire, or 'servant of the Virgin Mary', was, according to tradition, washed ashore, having survived a shipwreck by clinging to a piece of driftwood. This is commemorated in the clan's plant badge. The Virgin's servant has been claimed as a natural son of King Olav, and therefore half-brother of Leod, the progenitor of the Macleods. However Olav's son came ashore, he married the heiress of the Gows, or Clan Igaa, who held Pabbay in the Sound of Harris. The Gows were noted armourers. Their descendents were thereafter known as Mhic 'ille Mhuire. In 1346 Cedhain, son of MacIain of Ardnamurchan, married the heiress of the Morrisons of Lewis, but whether this was a descendent of Ghille Mhuire or O'Muirgheasain is disputed. Perhaps the two families had by this time inter-married as the learned origins of the O'Muirgheasains would have qualified them for the post of hereditary brehon, or judge, which the Morrisons certainly were on Lewis by the late thirteenth century. Cedhain was compelled to take his wife's name which, as he was a descendent of the great Somerled, King of the Isles, suggests that she was of equal rank, and probably a descendent of King Olav. The match brought the Morrisons even closer to the Lords of the Isles, and this, together with the office of brehon, gave them power and influence. In 1493 the Crown finally broke the power of the Macdonald Lords of the Isles, but was in no position to establish royal justice. There followed almost two centuries of feuds and unrest. The Morrisons were not a numerous clan and tried to live at peace with their more aggressive neighbours. The Macaulays of Uig killed Donald Ban, the brother of John Morrison the Brehon, at Habost. When the Morrisons retaliated by raiding Uig, the Macaulays appealed to their allies, the Macleods of Lewes. The Brehon was soundly defeated at the Caws of Tarbert, whereupon a strong force of Macaulays and Macleods invaded the Morrison lands. The chief was captured and imprisoned at Rodil. He managed to escape, but the Macleods used their influence with the king to have him declared an outlaw. As every man's hand was now turned against him, Morrison resorted to desperate measures and kidnapped one of the Macleod heiresses. He agreed to surrender her in exchange for a royal pardon. The girl was apparently released, none the worse for her ordeal. The feud was carried on by the next chief Uisdean, or Hucheon, who invaded north Harris. Once again, the Macleods intervened, and Iain Mor Macleod engaged the Morrisons at Clachan on Taransay. It is said that Hucheon was the only Morrison to survive the battle, swimming over two miles to the mainland despite serious wounds.

Morrison

Standard

The power of the Morrisons on Lewis survived the defeat, only to be finally broken when Hucheon, on his death bed in August 1566, confessed to being the natural father of Torquil, until then accepted as the lawful son of Roderick Macleod of Lewes and his wife, Janet Mackenzie. Macleod disinherited Torquil, set aside Janet as an adulteress and took a third wife. She bore two sons, Torquil Dubh and Tormod. The older Torquil, now half-brother to the Morrison chiefs, allied himself to the Mackenzies of Kintail who, through him, claimed the island of Lewis. In the bloody war which followed the Morrisons sided with the Mackenzies against the Macleods, and both Hucheon's successor, Iain Dubh, and his son, Malcolm Mor, were killed. The Mackenzies were ultimately victorious when, on 14 February 1577, Regent Morton forced the Macleods to recognise Torquil's right to succeed to the Macleod lands. Torquil then drove the Morrisons, his erstwhile allies, from their lands, and Lewis thereafter became a Mackenzie fief. The Morrisons later returned to settle in Ness, but the power of the brehons was forever lost.

On the mainland the Morrisons, whose senior representatives were the Morrisons of Bognie in Aberdeenshire, appear to have no connection whatsoever with their Hebridean namesakes, but are descendents of Maurice, a Norman name derived from the Latin, 'Mauricius', meaning 'dark-skinned', or 'swarthy'. Although individuals of the name distinguished themselves both in Scotland and abroad, it was not until the twentieth century that a clan society was established and the chiefship vested in the Morrisons of Ruchdi.

MUNRO

The country of the Munros lies on the north side of the Cromarty Firth. Known as Ferindonald, from the Gaelic 'Fearainn Domhnuill', or 'Donald's Land', a reference to the traditional founder of the chiefly family, these lands comprised most of the adjoining parishes of Kiltearn and Alness. The clan occupied the fertile coastal strip alongside the firth, and they spread up the river valleys into the uplands around Ben Wyvis. Beyond the bounds of Ferindonald, the Lairds of Foulis had, by the fourteenth century, acquired lands on the west coast in Loch Broom and northwards in the border between Ross and Sutherland.

Donald, ancestor of the Munros of Foulis is said to have received his lands in Ross-shire as a reward for helping Malcolm II against invaders from Scandinavia. Members of the family are also said to have fallen in the Scots armies at Bannockburn in 1314 and at Halidon Hill. The first chief authenticated by record evidence was killed in defence of the Earl of Ross in 1369. When James I came to Inverness to assert his authority in 1428, he seized many leading Highlanders, and while some were executed or imprisoned, others, including a group of Munros, were pardoned for past offences. The clan does not seem to have been unduly combative, but two minor skirmishes are recorded, although not firmly dated. In one against the Mackenzies at Bealach nam Broig at the back of Ben Wyvis, the chief and many of his family were killed. In the other at Clachnaharry near Inverness, a younger son of the then chief lost his hand fighting against the Mackintoshes.

The chiefs also held public office under the Stewart monarchs, and Sir William Munro was killed in 1505 on the king's business in Wester Ross; his son was the royal lieutenant there ten years later. In 1547 the chief was slain at the Battle of Pinkie with many of his men, resisting an English invasion. Early in her short reign, Mary, Queen of Scots, visited Inverness during her northern progress, and when the castle gates were shut against her by the constable, who was a Gordon, the Munros gave her loyal support. She later spent some time hunting in the neighbourhood. During her son's long minority, Munro of Milntown, and then his chief, Robert Mor Munro, had charge of the Crown lands of Ross and the Black Isle. Munro, as a baron of Scotland, had attended the Reformation Parliament of 1560, and his son, Hector, was Dean of Ross in the reformed church before succeeding as chief in 1588.

James VI and his advisers were determined to bring the Borders and the Highlands more fully under Crown control, and here they looked to the clan chiefs as their principal instrument. The Laird of Foulis figures in a roll of Highland landlords attached to an Act of Parliament in 1587, and three years later Hector Munro was one of those required to find security for the good behaviour of his tenants and adherents, even those living on other men's lands.

Munro

Standard

When more peaceful times came, military service abroad had its attractions, and many Munros fought under Gustavus Adolphus of Sweden in the Thirty Years' War in Germany. Two successive chiefs, Robert Dubh and Sir Hector, died on the Continent, the latter shortly after having been created a Baronet of Nova Scotia.

General Robert Munro commanded the army sent by the Scottish Parliament to Ireland in 1642. A long minority in the chiefship from 1635 to 1651 coincided with the period of civil war. Sir Robert Munro was sheriff of Ross under the Commonwealth and Protectorate, and had his lands raided and his tenants abused, while his brother, George,

later commanded the king's forces in Scotland from 1674 to 1677. The Revolution of 1688, which brought William and Mary to the throne of the deposed James VII, was supported by Sir John Munro of Foulis, a devout presbyterian. Dr Alexander Monro of the Fyrish branch refused to abandon his allegiance to the Stuart monarchy, and as a consequence lost his offices as principal of Edinburgh University, minister of the High Kirk of St Giles, and Bishop-elect of Argyll. The clan, however, followed their chief, and throughout the period of Jacobite unrest from 1689 to 1746, supported the Government.

Events during the Forty-five had left Foulis Castle a semi-ruin, and the chief, Harry Munro set about a programme of rebuilding after the rising. However, the castle and grounds were again to fall into neglect, but when Sir Hector Munro inherited the estate in 1884 he once more made it a family home. The castle is mentioned in documents from as early as 1491. Sir Hector's grandson, Captain Patrick Munro of Foulis, completed a programme of restoration begun in 1955, and Foulis now stands much as it did when it took its present form over two centuries ago. The present chief is Captain Patrick's son.

MURRAY

ARMS

Quarterly, 1st, paly of six Or and Sable (Atholl);
2nd, Or, a fess chequy Azure and Argent (Stewart);
3rd, Argent, on a bend Azure three stags' heads cabossed
Or (Stanley);
4th, Gules, three legs in armour Proper, garnished and
spurred Or, flexed and conjoined in triangle at the upper
part of the thigh (Isle of Man);
en surtout, on an inescutcheon Azure, three mullets
Argent within a Royal Tressure Or (Murray) ensigned of
a Marquess' coronet Or (Marquessate of Tullibardine)

CRESTS

Dexter, on a Wreath Argent and Azure a mermaid
holding in her dexter hand a mirror and in her sinister
a comb all Proper (Murray);
centre, on a Wreath Or and Sable a demi-savage Proper
wreathed about the temples and waist with laurel, his
arms extended and holding in the right hand a dagger, in
the left a key all Proper (Atholl); sinister, on a Wreath
Argent and Azure, a peacock's head and neck Proper,
accompanied (one on either side) by two arms from the
elbows Proper, vested in maunches Azure doubled Argent

MOTTOES

Dexter, Tout prest (Quite ready);
centre, Furth fortune and fill the fetters;
sinister, Praite (Ready)

SUPPORTERS

(on a compartment embellished with juniper)
Dexter, a savage Proper, wreathed about the temples and
loins with juniper, his feet in fetters, the chain held in his
right hand Proper; sinister, a lion rampant Gules, armed
and langued Azure, gorged with a plain collar of the Last
charged with three mullets Argent

STANDARD

Azure, a St Andrew's Cross Argent in the hoist and of two
tracts Or and Sable, upon which is depicted the Badge of
Atholl in the first compartment, the centre Crest (above)
in the second compartment, the dexter Crest (above) in
the third compartment, and the sinister Crest (above) in
the fourth compartment, along with the words 'Furth
fortune and fill the fetters' in letters Argent upon three
transverse bands Azure, the words separated by
mullets Argent

GUIDONS

1 (for the Dukedom and Earldom of Atholl) Sable, the
Badge of Atholl, and in the hoist per pale dexter, Azure, a
St Andrew's Cross Argent and sinister, paly of six Or and
Sable and in the fly the words 'Fill the fetters' in letters
Gules
2 (for the Chiefship of the Name of Murray) per fess
Argent and Azure, a mermaid as in the Crest, and in the
hoist per pale dexter, Azure, a St Andrew's Cross Argent
and sinister, Azure, three mullets Argent, within a double
tressure flory counterflory Or, and in the fly the words
'Tout prest'

BADGE

A hand paleways grasping a key Proper, issuant from and
within a chaplet of juniper Proper and ensigned with the
coronet of a Duke (Atholl)

PLANT BADGES

Juniper, for Atholl and butcher's broom, for Murray

The progenitor of this family was Freskin, who flourished in the twelfth century. While it has been claimed that he may have been a Pict, it is more likely that he was a Flemish knight, one of many of that bellicose and ruthless group of warlords who were employed by the Norman kings to pacify their new realm of England after the Conquest. David I, who had been brought up at the English court, sought to employ such men to help him hold the wilder parts of his kingdom, and he granted lands in West Lothian to Freskin. The ancient Pictish kingdom of Moray, in Gaelic, 'Moireabh', was also given to Freskin, to put to an end the remnants of the old royal house. In a series of politically astute moves, he and his sons inter-married with the house of Moray to consolidate their power. There seems little doubt that royal Pictish blood flowed in the veins of Freskin's descendents, and the lines descending from Freskin are linked heraldically by their use of three stars and the colours blue and silver in some fashion on their coats of arms. The Earls of Sutherland descend from what is thought to be Freskin's eldest son. In charters, Freskin's other descen-dents were designated 'de Moravia', and this, in Lowland Scots, became 'Murray'.

Sir Walter Murray, who became Lord of Bothwell in Clydesdale through marriage to an Oliphant heiress, was one of the regents of Scotland in 1255. He started construction on Bothwell Castle, which was to become one of the most powerful and visually striking strong-holds in Scotland. It was the seat of the chiefs until 1360, when it passed into the possession of the Douglases. The third Murray Lord of Bothwell died a prisoner in the Tower of London, whereupon his heir, Sir Andrew Murray, took up the cause of Scottish inde-pendence and rose against Edward I of England in 1297. He was joined by Sir William Wallace who, when Murray was killed at the great victory of Stirling Bridge, assumed command of the Scottish forces. Historians have suggested that, as Murray had shown considerable skill in pitched battle, which

Murray

Wallace sorely lacked, the whole war against the English might have taken a very different course had Sir Andrew survived Stirling Bridge. Sir Andrew's heir, the fourth Lord, fell at the Battle of Halidon Hill in 1333. The lord-ship of Bothwell passed to the Douglases when the fifth Lord and chief died of plague in 1360, and his widow, Joan, took as her second husband the third Earl of Douglas.

There were many branches of the name who disputed the right to the chiefship, and it was not until the sixteenth century that the Murrays of Tullibardine are recorded using the undifferenced Murray arms in the armorial of Lord Lyon Lindsay of 1542. This work pre-dated the establishment of the Lyon register in 1672, and is considered to be of equal author-ity. The Tullibardine claim seems to have rested upon descent from Sir Malcolm, sheriff of Perth, around 1270, who was a younger brother of the first Lord of Bothwell. In order to consolidate their position, the Tullibardines promoted two 'bands of association' in 1586 and 1598, whereby the numerous Murray lairds recognised the chiefship of Sir John Murray, later first Earl of Tullibardine. Among the signatories were the Morays of Abercairny in Perthshire. Sir John Moray had married a daughter of the ancient Celtic royal house of Strathearn around 1320, and as part of her dowry she brought the lands of Abercairny. Sir Iain Moncreiffe has pointed out that when Sir John's son, Sir Alexander, succeeded to Abercairny, he was probably the nearest heir to the house of Bothwell. Although by this family arrangement the Murrays of Tullibardine gained the ascendancy, Abercairny continued to prosper. The neo-gothic seat of the lairds was the largest house in Perthshire until it was demolished to make way for a more conveniently sized but still elegant twentieth-century mansion. Although the bands entered into put beyond doubt the rights of the Murrays of Tullibardine to be chiefs of the clan, Abercairny still ranked high in the family, and in a magnificent portrait of Colonel James, the sixteenth Laird, in his finery, commissioned for George IV's visit to Scotland in 1822, three eagles' feathers (normally worn only by a chief) can be seen in his bonnet.

Standard

Sir John Murray of Tullibardine was created first Earl of Tullibardine in 1606. His son and heir married Dorothea Stewart, heiress to the Earls of Atholl. She brought with her a vast estate of over two hundred thousand acres. The Stewart earldom of Atholl became a Murray earldom in 1629, and a marquessate in 1676. In 1703 the Murrays reached the pinnacle of the peerage when they were created Dukes of Atholl. The first Duke's younger son, Lord George Murray, was the great Jacobite general and the architect of the early successes of the rising of 1745. Most military historians concur in the view that, if Lord George had been allowed sole command of the Jacobite army, the 'Old Pretender' might well have gained his throne. His elder brother, the duke, supported the Hanoverian Government. Lord George had already spent many years in exile

as a result of his Jacobite sympathies, and at first was unwilling to join Prince Charles when he raised his father's royal standard at Glenfinnan. He is believed to have been persuaded by a personal letter from his exiled sovereign, sent to him by the prince. He wrote a poignant letter to his brother on 3 September 1745, explaining his intentions and asking his forgiveness for opposing him in doing what he thought was 'just and right as well as for the interest, good and liberty of my country'. A Gaelic speaker, his strategic skills were matched by his personal courage and popularity with his Highlanders. But his sound advice was ignored by the prince, and the tide of fortune turned against the Jacobites. Lord George Murray led a charge at Culloden which broke the Hanoverian ranks, although this was not enough to prevent the overall defeat. He died in exile in the Netherlands in 1760. Culloden was the last time that the Highlanders of Atholl went to war, but the ceremonial guard of the chiefs – which became known as the Atholl Highlanders – still has the unique honour of being the only private army in the realm. In 1845 Queen Victoria presented colours to the Atholl Highlanders, and they regularly attend upon the present duke on ceremonial occasions.

Another unique honour passed to the family in 1736, when the second Duke inherited through his grandmother the sovereignty of the Isle of Man. As Lords of Man, the Dukes issued their own coinage and held their own Parliament. Although the third Duke transferred the sovereignty to the British Crown in 1765, the Atholl arms still display the trinacria, the symbol of the island.

Another royal connection was established when Sir David Murray was granted the lands of Scone by James VI in 1600. On the lands stood the ancient hill on which the kings of Scots were crowned, a ceremony which last took place in 1651, when Charles II was proclaimed king. Sir David was created Lord Scone and later Viscount of Stormont. His descendents became the Earls of Mansfield who built the magnificent Scone Palace which is their home today. The first Earl of Mansfield was one of the greatest jurists of his time, and rose to become Lord Chief Justice of England. His direct descendent, the seventh Earl of Mansfield, has held high Government office as a minister for Scottish affairs.

Although the heraldry of the Dukes of Atholl includes three separate crests (one each for Murray, Tullibardine and Atholl), the present chief has indicated that the demi-wildman and the motto, 'Furth fortune and fill the fetters', alluding to the capture of the last Lord of the Isles by the Earl of Atholl in 1475 – should be used as the crest badge for all Murray clansmen.

NAPIER

The Napiers have a long and ancient history and are descended, through the Earls of Lennox, from the Celtic royal families of Scotland and Ireland. One suggested derivation of the name is from the officer of the royal household who was in charge of linen, the 'naperer'. However, there is no evidence to suggest that this title was much used in Scotland, and in common with many families, a more stirring and poetic origin of the name is offered. One of the knights of the Earl of Lennox, possibly a younger son, distinguished himself in battle during the reign of William the Lion. After the victory, the king singled out the young knight praising his valour which he said had 'nae peer'. The earliest certain reference to the name appears in a charter of Malcolm, Earl of Lennox, sometime prior to 1290, which granted lands at Kilmahew in Dunbartonshire to John de Naper. The Napiers were to hold lands at Kilmahew for eighteen generations, until the estate was sold in 1820.

The first Laird of Merchiston, Alexander Napier, was a prominent Edinburgh merchant who amassed a fortune and became Lord Provost of the city. In common with most prosperous merchants of the time, he converted part of his wealth into land, obtaining a charter to the lands of Merchiston in 1436. His son, Sir Alexander Napier, later to be Lord Provost of Edinburgh also, rose high in royal favour. He was wounded while rescuing the widow of James I and her second husband, Sir James Stewart, from rebels who had captured them. James II honoured Napier by making him Comptroller of the Royal Household in 1440, and Vice Admiral of Scotland in 1461. His son, John, the son-in-law of the Earl of Lennox who was executed in 1444, did not press his family's claim to the earldom. He was killed at the Battle of Sauchieburn in 1488. His heir, Alexander, and his grandson were both killed at Flodden in 1513, and the Battle of

Pinkie in 1547 claimed another Napier heir.

The most famous of the name is the seventh Laird of Merchiston, John Napier, who developed the system of logarithms. His son, Archibald, who succeeded to Merchiston in 1617, accompanied James VI when he travelled to England to claim his new throne, and was sworn a Member of the Privy Council in 1615. He became a judge and was Lord Justice Clerk of Scotland from 1623 to 1624. He was first created a Baronet of Nova Scotia in 1627, and later in that year raised to the peerage as Baron Napier of Merchiston. He married Margaret, daughter of the fourth Earl of Montrose, and sister of the great Marquess. The brother-in-law of the king's captain general could scarcely avoid the obligations of kinship, and Napiers supported the king throughout the civil war. Lord Napier died in 1645 and his only son, Archibald, second Baron Napier, was forced into exile when Scotland became part of the Commonwealth. He died in the Netherlands in 1660.

Archibald, third Lord Napier, petitioned the Crown for a new patent to the barony, extending the succession to heirs female, including his sisters. The title passed to the only child of his eldest sister, Sir Thomas Nicholson of Carnock, and then to his aunt, Margaret Napier, wife of John Brisbane, Secretary to the Admiralty in the reign of Charles II. Baroness Napier was succeeded by her grandson, Francis Scott, who became the sixth Baron and adopted the name and arms of Napier.

Three grandsons of the sixth Lord Napier served throughout the Napoleonic Wars, each attaining the rank of general and the Order of the Bath. General Sir Charles conquered Sind in India, now part of Pakistan, and his statue can still be seen in Trafalgar Square, London. Francis, the eighth Lord, was an ensign when he was captured during the American War of Independence. He survived the ordeal, and

Napier

later sat in Parliament as a representative Scottish peer, from 1796 to 1823. The ninth Lord was Chief Superintendent for Trade with China in 1833. He determined that Hong Kong should be annexed. His son, another Francis, became the tenth Lord Napier in 1834. A gifted academic, he received degrees from the Universities of Glasgow, Edinburgh and Harvard. He became a diplomat and was highly regarded in Washington prior to the outbreak of the American Civil War. He was a friend of Jefferson Davis, later to be the only president of the Confederate States of America. He was ambassador to the Netherlands, Russia and Prussia. He served as acting Viceroy of India in 1872. A Knight of the Thistle, he was created Baron Ettrick of Ettrick in the peerage of the United Kingdom in July 1872. On his return to Scotland he became chairman of the newly created Crofters Commission.

The present chief, fourteenth Lord Napier and fifth of Ettrick, is Comptroller to the Household, and Private Secretary to HRH The Princess Margaret.

NESBITT

This name derives from the lands and barony of Nesbit near Edrom in Berwickshire. The lands are probably named after a geographical feature, possibly meaning nose-shaped hill or nose-bend. The name is now best known in clan circles through the work of Alexander Nisbet (1657–1725), one of the greatest Scottish authorities on heraldry. His *System of Heraldry* is still a classic work, and was reproduced in facsimile form as recently as 1984. He established his own connection with the chiefly line and must be regarded as authoritative on the pedigree of his own family. In his own words, 'the lands of Nesbit were of ancient denomination for, in the reign of King Edgar, son of Malcolm Canmore, in whose reign surnames came first to be hereditary, they were donated to the monks of Dunfermline to pray for the soul of his father, and for the health of his own.'

Black lists William de Nesbite as witness to a charter by Patrick, Earl of Dunbar, to Coldingham Priory around 1160. Thomas Nisbet was Prior of Coldingham from 1219 to 1240. Philip de Nesbit appears in the Ragman Roll submitting to Edward I of England in 1296. James, John and Adam Nisbet also appear on the roll, and it is likely that Adam is the same person as Adam Nisbet of that Ilk, who received a charter from Robert the Bruce to the land of Knocklies, the feudal obligation being the provision of one knight for the king's army. Adam, or perhaps his son and namesake, continued in royal favour, and distinguished himself in the service of David II, defending the southern borders. Adam was succeeded by Philip Nisbet, who appears in important charters of the Earls of Dunbar, and he, in turn, was succeeded by his son, Adam. Adam's great-great-grandson, Philip Nisbet, married a daughter of Haldane of Gleneagles, and their heir was Alexander Nesbit.

Alexander was a fervent royalist and was

devoted to Charles I. He was appointed sheriff of Berwickshire, but when the king's policies led to military confrontation with his Scottish and English subjects, Nesbit and his sons joined the king's standard at Oxford. His eldest son, Philip, was abroad when the civil war began, but he soon returned, and was knighted and given command of a regiment. He was lieutenant governor of Newark-upon-Trent, which was besieged by the Scottish army under General Leslie. He left Newark and became one of the officers of James Graham, Marquess of Montrose, becoming one of his most trusted officers. Montrose was surprised by a strong force of Covenant cavalry and defeated at the Battle of Philiphaugh, where Nisbet was taken prisoner. He was subsequently executed at Glasgow on 28 October 1646, along with Alexander Ogilvie, the Younger, of Innerquharity at Glasgow. Ogilvie was barely twenty years of age, and his execution was considered an act of savagery, even in those bloody times. Two of Philip's brothers, Alexander and Robert, were also killed in the war. The youngest brother, Adam, survived to become the father of Alexander Nisbet, the heraldic writer.

Nisbet was trained as a lawyer but soon acquired a passion for history and heraldry. He published his first work, an essay on cadency, in 1702. His great work, *System of Heraldry,* was published in Edinburgh in two volumes in 1722, with more editions following in 1742, 1804 and 1816. He died in 1725.

There were numerous other distinguished families of this name, including the Nisbets of Paxton, Dean, Dirleton and Cairnhill. The Nisbets of Dirleton produced a line of distinguished lawyers, including two judges, Lord Dirleton and Lord Eastbank. The present

Nesbitt

descendents of the Nisbets of Cairnhill reside in the splendid Adam mansion of The Drum on the outskirts of Edinburgh.

In February 1994, the Lord Lyon recognised Robert Anthony Ellis Nesbitt as chief of the name and arms of Nesbitt (or Nisbit). The new chief established that he was the only grandson of Robert Chancellor Nesbitt, MP, who recorded arms in 1933, setting out his descent from the Reverend Philip Nisbet, grand-uncle of Alexander, the heraldic writer. He asserted that he was the heir of the noble house of Nisbet of that Ilk 'for aught yet seen'. His petition was accepted, and the undifferenced arms, with the grant of supporters, standard, badge, slughorns and pinsel, assigned to the new chief subject to the proviso that another claimant has ten years to seek to re-open the case, after which time the judgement is unassailable.

NICOLSON

Although the Macneacails or Macnicols of the west Highlands and islands are, according to their heraldry, apparently linked to the Nicolsons of that Ilk, there is little genealogical evidence available to explain this. The chiefs of both clans bear gold shields charged with the heads of birds of prey, with red hawks for Macneacail and red falcons for Nicolson. The Nicolsons are of Norse descent, perhaps derived from the personal name Olsen, 'Nic' in Gaelic signifying 'daughter of'. It could also be a corruption of Nicolassen. The Norse raided all round the coasts of Scotland and north England, and during the centuries of conquest, they established many permanent settlements. The name Nicolson can be found all through Tyneside and Yorkshire. Some sought fresh pillage on the northern coast of France, whence came their Norman descendents, who invaded England again in the eleventh century, and settled in Scotland during the reign of David I. The Macneacails who settled in the Hebrides first populated Lewis, but eventually made their home and chief seat at Scorrybreac in Skye.

Haakon IV, the last Norse king to invade Scotland, sent an advance party under Anders Nicolassen, his foster brother and one of his chief barons. Nicolassen plundered Bute before joining the main fleet off Largs. The Norsemen were defeated, but there is a persistent tradition that Nicolassen eventually settled in Scotland after he was sent as an envoy from Norway to conclude the Treaty of Perth, which finally ceded sovereignty over the isles to the kings of Scots.

James Nicolson was a lawyer in Edinburgh who died around 1580. He married Janet Swinton of the ancient Borders family, and they had two sons. John, the heir, became an advocate, while his brother, James, entered the Church. James was Moderator of the General Assembly of the Church of Scotland in 1595, and minister at Meigle. When James VI re-established episcopal authority in the reformed Church, he appointed James Bishop of Dunkeld in 1606. He was bishop for less than a year, dying in August 1607. His son became an advocate, but his grandson returned to the cloth as minister of Tingwall in Shetland. John, the bishop's elder brother, had acquired the lands of Lasswade by a charter of 1592 from Sinclair of Dryden. His son, John, was created a Baronet of Nova Scotia as Nicolson of that Ilk and Lasswade on 27 July 1629. He was succeeded in that title by his grandson, who was Commissioner of Parliament for Edinburgh in 1672. In 1826 the direct male line failed, and a descendent of the Bishop of Dunkeld from the branch established in Shetland by the bishop's grandson, became the eighth Baronet.

Another baronetcy had been conferred on the family in 1637, when Thomas Nicolson, a son of John Nicolson of Edinburgh, became the first Baronet of Carnock near Stirling. Sir Thomas, third Baronet of Carnock, married Jean, eldest daughter of Archibald, second Lord Napier, in 1668. When the third Lord Napier died in 1683, his nephew, Sir Thomas's son, then fourteen years old, became the fourth Lord. He had been the fourth Baronet since his father's death in 1670. He died only three years later, under-age and childless, and the Napier title passed to other heirs and the baronetcy to his cousin, Nicolson of Tillicoultrie. Sir George, the sixth Baronet, served as a professional soldier in the Netherlands, retiring to live at The Hague in 1746. All three of his sons were officers in Scottish regiments in the service of the States of Holland. The last of this line, Sir David Nicolson, died at Breda in 1808.

The Carnock title then passed to another cousin, Major General Sir William Nicolson, only son of George Nicolson of Tarviston. The general saw service in America, India, Ireland and Mauritius. He died in 1820 to be succeeded by his son, Admiral Sir Frederick Nicolson. The admiral's eldest son, Frederick,

Nicolson

was killed fighting the Zulus in 1879, and it was his second son, Arthur, who succeeded in 1899. Sir Arthur had entered the diplomatic service, holding posts in Peking, Berlin, Constantinople and Tangiers, before becoming ambassador to Spain in 1904. He was ambassador to the imperial court at St Petersburg from 1906 to 1910, when he was appointed Permanent Under Secretary of State for Foreign Affairs, a post he held until 1916. He was showered with honours during his distinguished career, including the Orders of the Bath, St Michael and St George, Royal Victorian, and Indian Empire. Foreign governments also recognised his merit, awarding him some of their highest decorations, including the Grand Cross of the French Legion of Honour. In June 1916 he was created Baron Carnock of Carnock. The fourth Lord Carnock, who had inherited not only the peerage and baronetcy of Carnock, but also the baronetcy of Lasswade and of that Ilk, followed his ancestors into the law, practising as a solicitor in London. In 1985 he matriculated his arms, and was recognised by the Lord Lyon, King of Arms as Nicolson of that Ilk, chief of the Clan Nicolson.

OGILVY

The lands of Ogilvy are in Angus. The name derives from the old British, 'Ocel-fa' or 'high plain'. Angus was a kingdom in Pictish times ruled by a mormaer, one of the ancient Celtic nobles of Scotland who became the first earls. The title of Mormaer of Angus became Earl of Angus. Gillebride, Earl of Angus, gave the lands of Ogilvy to his son, Gilbert, some time before 1177. Patrick de Ogilvy appears on the Ragman Roll of nobles swearing fealty to Edward I of England in 1296.

The Ogilvys became hereditary sheriffs of Angus in the fourteenth and fifteenth centuries. When Sir Patrick Ogilvy commanded the Scottish forces fighting with Joan of Arc against the English, he was styled 'Viscomte d'Angus'. Sir Walter Ogilvy, younger son of Ogilvy of Wester Powrie, was appointed Lord High Treasurer of Scotland in 1425. In 1430, he was an ambassador to England, and four years later attended Princess Margaret on her marriage to the Dauphin, heir to the throne of France. He had numerous sons, including his namesake, Walter, who was to become ancestor of the Earls of Seafield and Deskford. His eldest son, Sir John Ogilvy of Lintrathern received a charter to the castle and lands of Airlie in 1459. Sir John's son, Sir James Ogilvy of Airlie, was appointed ambassador to Denmark in 1491 and advanced to the ranks of the peerage as Lord Ogilvy of Airlie in the same year.

The fourth Lord's eldest son, James, was killed at the Battle of Pinkie in 1547. The seventh Lord Ogilvy was created Earl of Airlie in April 1639.

The family was to suffer much in the service of the Stuart monarchs. The earl and his sons joined Montrose to oppose the enemies of Charles I, and the earl fought with distinction at Montrose's victory at Kilsyth. Sir Thomas, the earl's second son, raised his own regiment to fight with the royalists, but was killed at the scene of another of Montrose's victories, at Inverlochy, in February 1645. The eldest son, Lord Ogilvy, was with Montrose at Philiphaugh when the marquess was surprised by a strong force of Covenanter cavalry under General Lesley. Ogilvy begged Montrose to flee, as he was the only person who could rally the king's supporters. Montrose escaped, but Ogilvy was captured. He awaited execution in the grim castle at St Andrews, where his sister came to say her last farewell. She exchanged clothes with her brother, who passed in her place, unnoticed by the guards. He lived to inherit his father's earldom and see the Restoration.

The Ogilvys rallied to the Stuart cause in the following century, joining the Earl of Mar in 1715. Lord Ogilvy was attainted, but was allowed to return home in 1725. His titles were not restored and he died in 1730, when his younger brother, John, assumed the style, 'Earl of Airlie'. His son, David, raised a regiment comprised mostly of Ogilvys to fight for the 'Young Pretender' in 1745. The regiment fought at Culloden in 1746. After the defeat, Ogilvy escaped to France, entering royal service there and obtaining the rank of general. It was not until 1896 that an Act of Parliament confirmed the restoration of the earldom to another David, the sixth Earl. His son, David, the seventh Earl, was a Scots representative peer from 1850 to 1881. He was created a Knight of the Thistle. The eighth Earl (or tenth, ignoring the attainder) led his regiment, the 12th Lancers, in a charge to save the British artillery at Diamond Hill near Pretoria in June 1900 during the Second Boer War. The Boers were denied the guns, but the earl lost his life in the encounter.

The Ogilvys also held the earldoms of Findlater and Seafield. James Ogilvy, younger son of the third Earl of Findlater, was created Earl of Seafield in 1701. Seafield was a prominent unionist, and supported the Act of Union

Ogilvy

of 1707. In 1711 the Earl of Seafield also inherited his father's title of Findlater. On the death of the fourth Earl of Seafield, the Findlater title became dormant. Seafield was claimed by the earl's cousin, Sir Lewis Grant, in 1811, when he took the name Grant-Ogilvie.

The present chief, as did his father, serves as Lord Chamberlain to HM The Queen. This royal link was reinforced when the Honourable Angus Ogilvy, the chief's brother, married HRH Princess Alexandra. The chief's seat is at Cortachy Castle.

The family name is also renowned in Scotland's religious history. Born in Banff in 1579, John Ogilvie was a Jesuit priest who worked in central Scotland. He was arrested and hanged at Glasgow Cross in 1615 for his defence of the spiritual supremacy of the papacy. He was beatified in 1927 and canonised in 1976. He is the only officially recognised martyr in post-Reformation Scotland.

PRIMROSE

This name is taken from the lands of Primrose in the parish of Dunfermline. It has been suggested that it came originally from the old British, 'prenn rhos' meaning 'tree of the moor'. The Primroses were well settled in Fife, and particularly around the Abbey of Culross, by the fifteenth century. Henry Primrose, who was believed to be born sometime prior to 1490, had four sons and one daughter. Gilbert, his grandson, was one of the Ministers of the reformed church at Bordeaux, and afterwards of the French church in London. He was appointed Chaplain to James VI and Charles I, and became Dean of Windsor in 1628. Another grandson, James Primrose, was Clerk of the Privy Council in Scotland.

When James Primrose died in 1641, he was succeeded in the office of Clerk to the Privy Council by his eldest son by his second marriage, Archibald. A staunch royalist, Archibald Primrose rallied to the banner of the Marquess of Montrose after his victory at the Battle of Kilsyth. He was the king's lieutenant at Philiphaugh, where he was captured when the royal army was surprised by a strong force of cavalry. He was tried and found guilty of treason, and although his life was spared on the orders of Argyll, he was held in prison until Montrose was ordered by Charles I to disband his army and leave the kingdom. Primrose was released and knighted by the king. In 1648 he joined in the Engagement, a scheme to rescue Charles I from the English Parliamentarians, and although the plan was a failure, he survived to join Charles II on his march into England in 1651. The king created him a baronet. He fought at the Battle of Worcester, and after Charles fled into exile, the Primrose estates were sequestrated. They were restored after the Restoration of 1660, and Primrose was appointed a judge of the Supreme Court and Lord Clerk Register of Scotland. He took the title, 'Lord Carrington'.

He was opposed to the policies of John Maitland, Duke of Lauderdale, and resigned his offices, but he was later to be Lord Justice General, from 1676 to 1678. He acquired the barony of Barnbougle and Dalmeny between Edinburgh and South Queensferry, which remains the seat of the family to this day. His eldest daughter married Sir John Foulis of Ravelston, who assumed the name of Primrose. His grandson, Sir Archibald Primrose of Dunipace, was executed at Carlisle in 1746 as a Jacobite. The Lord Justice General was succeeded by his son, Sir William Primrose, and his son, Sir James Primrose of Carrington, was elected Commissioner of Parliament for Edinburgh in 1703. In November of that year he was elevated to the peerage as Viscount Primrose.

The second Viscount died unmarried in 1706, and when his brother, Hugh, the third Viscount, left no issue, the title lapsed. Archibald Primrose, born in 1664, was the only son by the second marriage of Sir Archibald, the Lord Justice General, who left to him the estate of Dalmeny. He served in Hungary in the imperial army in 1680. On his return to Scotland, he opposed the policies of James VII. He was appointed a Gentleman of the Bedchamber after the accession of William and Mary. He was Commissioner of Parliament for Edinburgh from 1695 to 1700, when he was created Viscount of Rosebery, Lord Primrose and Dalmeny. On the accession of Queen Anne he was advanced to the rank of earl. In 1707 he was a Privy Councillor, and was appointed a commissioner for the Treaty of Union. After the union he was one of the sixteen peers elected to represent Scotland in the House of Lords. His daughter, Mary, married a cousin, Sir Archibald Primrose of Dunipace. His son, James, succeeded as second Earl of Rosebery, but also claimed the dormant family title of Viscount Primrose. The third Earl was a representative peer, and in 1771 he was made a Knight of the Thistle. He died in 1814, when he was succeeded by his son, Archibald John, as fourth Earl of Rosebery. A Member of Parliament for Hellston and later

The full achievement of the Earl of Roseberry

Carlisle, Primrose was created a baron of the United Kingdom with the title of 'Lord Rosebery' in 1828. This gave him a permanent seat in the House of Lords. Like his father, he, was made a Knight of the Thistle (in 1840), and three years later he was appointed Lord Lieutenant of Linlithgowshire. His son, using the courtesy title, 'Lord Dalmeny', was MP for Stirling from 1833 to 1847, and was a Lord of the Admiralty from 1835 to 1837. He was succeeded by his son, Archibald Philip, who was Under Secretary for the Home Office from 1881 to 1883. He was thereafter to hold high office, first as Secretary of State for Foreign Affairs, and later as Prime Minister. He was extremely popular with Queen Victoria, who bestowed upon him the rare personal honour of the Royal Victorian Chain, while his political services were recognised when he was created Earl of Midlothian, Viscount Mentmore, and received sundry other subsidiary peerages.

The family seat at Dalmeny is of considerable architectural interest, and houses a splendid collection of paintings and furniture. Although still very much a family home, it is now open to the public.

RAMSAY

ARMS
Argent, an eagle displayed Sable

CREST
A unicorn's head couped Argent armed Or

MOTTO
Ora et labora (Pray and work)

SUPPORTERS
*Dexter, a gryphon with wings displayed Proper
(Ramsay); sinister, a greyhound Proper gorged with a
collar Gules charged with three escallops Argent (Maule)*

A ram in the sea is said to have been an emblem on the seal of an abbey in Huntingdon in the eleventh century. When David, Earl of Huntingdon, travelled north to claim his kingdom of Scotland in 1124, he was accompanied by many young Norman noblemen keen to share in their over-lord's heritage. These may have included Sir Symon de Ramesie who received a grant of land in Midlothian from David and who witnessed several important charters, including one to the monks of Holyrood in 1140.

The de Ramesie family prospered, and by the thirteenth century there were five major branches: Dalhousie; Auchterhouse; Banff; Forfar; and Clatto. William de Ramsay of Dalhousie was a member of the king's council in 1255 during the minority of Alexander III. His son, or perhaps his grandson, also called William, appears on the Ragman Roll, swearing fealty to Edward I of England in 1296 as Ramsay 'de Dalwolsy'. Dalhousie later declared for Bruce, becoming one of the signatories to the open letter to the pope, now known as the Declaration of Arbroath, which declared Scotland's independence in 1320. He had at least two sons, William and Alexander. Alexander was a renowned knight, and for his many services he was made sheriff of Teviotdale in 1342. This aroused the jealousy of the Douglases, who claimed the office as their own. Sir William Douglas of Liddesdale fell upon Alexander with a strong force of men and imprisoned him in Hermitage Castle, where he was starved to death. Alexander's brother, William, also endured captivity when he was captured at the Battle of Neville's Cross in 1346. The English were apparently kinder jailers than Douglas, as William lived to tell the tale.

In 1400, Sir Alexander Ramsay held Dalhousie Castle in Midlothian against a siege by Henry IV of England, and resisted so res-olutely that the English were forced to withdraw. His descendent and namesake, Alexander Ramsay, was killed at Flodden in 1513, when Dalhousie passed to his son, Nicolas, who was to be a staunch supporter of Mary, Queen of Scots. After Mary's final defeat the Ramsays acknowledged her son as James VI. They were later to be handsomely rewarded for saving that monarch's life. In 1600 John Ramsay, one of Nicolas's great-grandsons, killed the Earl of Gowrie and his brother, Alexander Ruthven, who were apparently attempting to kidnap the king in what became known as the Gowrie Conspiracy. John was created Earl of Holderness and Viscount Haddington by a grateful king. George Ramsay, the new earl's eldest brother, also attained high rank when he was created Lord Ramsay in 1618. Ramsay's eldest son, William, opposed the religious policies of Charles I and raised a cavalry regiment for Parliament. He fought at Marston Moor, and was part of General Lesley's force which surprised Montrose at Philiphaugh in 1645. He had been created Earl of Dalhousie in 1633.

The Ramsays were thereafter to continue in military and public service down to the present day. They served in all the great campaigns of the eighteenth and nineteenth centuries on the Continent, in Canada and in India. The ninth Earl was Governor of Canada from 1819 to 1828, and commander-in-chief of India from 1829 to 1832. His son also served as Governor General of India from 1847 to 1856, during a period of great expansion of British interest on the sub-continent. He was created Marquess of Dalhousie in 1849, but this title died with him in 1860, although the older earldom passed to a cousin from whom the present Earl descends.

Many other branches of the family have also produced persons of distinction and rank. Admiral the Honourable Sir Alexander Ramsay, the younger son of the fourteenth Earl, married HRH Princess Victoria of Connaught, granddaughter of Queen Victoria. Their son, Captain Alexander Ramsay of Mar,

Ramsay

and his wife, the Lady Saltoun, chief of the Frasers, are, by HM The Queen's personal wish, members of the royal family. Sir Gilbert Ramsay of Banff, descended from Neis de Ramsay, physician to Alexander II around 1232, was created a Baronet of Nova Scotia in 1666. The Ramsays of Balmain, whose title of 'Lord Bothwell' was forfeited for treason in 1488 and later given to the Hepburns, restored their fortunes by being created baronets, first in 1625 and again in 1806.

Fighting was not the only talent of this family. Andrew Ramsay, better known as the Chevalier de Ramsay, left Scotland for France in 1708. His academic excellence was soon recognised, and he became mentor to the Prince de Turenne. The King of France appointed him a Knight of the Order of St Lazarus, and for a time he was tutor to both the Jacobite princes, Charles Edward and Henry, later Cardinal York. Alan Ramsay, the great eighteenth-century poet, and his son, the distinguished portrait painter, were descended from the Lairds of Cockpen, cadets of the chiefly house. Dalhousie Castle is now a hotel, and the chief seat is Brechin Castle in Angus.

The Rattrays take their name from the barony of Rattray in Perthshire which has been in their possession since the eleventh century. The estate includes the ruins of the Pictish 'rath-tref', or 'fort dwelling', which stands on a serpent-shaped sandy mound which is itself associated, by local tradition, with pagan rites. The heraldic supporters of the family are two knotted serpents.

The first Laird of Rattray of record is Alan, who witnessed several charters of William the Lion and Alexander II. His grandson, Eustace Rattray, was captured at the Battle of Dunbar in 1296 and taken prisoner to England. His son, Sir Adam Rattray, appears on the Ragman Roll swearing fealty to Edward I of England in 1296. Adam was succeeded by his son, Alexander, who was one of the barons who sat in the Parliament at Ayr in 1315 to determine the succession to the throne. Alexander's brother, Eustace, who was to succeed him as the sixth Laird, was accused of complicity in a plot to depose Robert the Bruce and charged with treason. He was later acquitted.

Sir Silvester Rattray of Rattray was ambassador to England in 1463, and inherited large estates around Fortingall in Atholl from his mother. This aroused the jealousy of the powerful Earls of Atholl. After Silvester's death, his son, Sir John, who had been knighted by James IV in 1488, succeeded to the estates. His eldest son died while serving as a professional soldier in the Netherlands, leaving, as well as another two sons, two daughters, the eldest of whom, Grizel, had married John Stewart, Earl of Atholl. The earl promptly claimed half the Barony of Rattray in her right. He also induced his wife's younger sister, Elizabeth, to convey her alleged share of the barony to him. Sir John's second son, Patrick, was driven from Rattray Castle in 1516 by Atholl and forced to take refuge in Nether Kinballoch, where he was engaged in building a new house of Craighall. He was not, however, beyond Atholl's reach, and in 1533 he was murdered.

Silvester Rattray, Sir John's third son, succeeded his murdered brother, and because of Atholl's continuing threats he petitioned the king for dispensation to be legally recognised as heir before the courts in Dundee, rather than in Perth, which would have been the normal practice; the Earl's influence was great in Perth, and Silvester considered a visit to the town too dangerous. He was in turn succeeded by his son, David Rattray of Craighall, who had three sons, the second of whom, the Reverend Silvester Rattray of Persie, became the first minister of Rattray after the Reformation.

The laird's eldest son, George, was murdered in 1592, and his young son, Silvester, succeeded to the title. He was tutored by his uncle, the Reverend John Rattray, and on achieving his majority, he promptly allied himself to the powerful Earls of Errol, seeking greater security for his family. He died in 1612, leaving three sons. David, the eldest, was a staunch royalist who fought for Charles I, and Craighall endured a short siege as a consequence. John, the youngest, suffered more personally when he was captured after the defeat of Charles II at Worcester in 1651 and incarcerated in the Tower of London.

Standard

During these turbulent times the family sought to consolidate their lands. Patrick Rattray obtained a new charter to their lands, a charter of Novodamus, under the great seal in 1648, so uniting the barony of Kinballoch with Rattray and their other associated parishes into one free barony of Craighall-Rattray. The new barony, which passed to Patrick's eldest son in 1682, also laid claim to the Rattray lands seized by the Earls of Atholl.

Rattray

His only son, Thomas, entered the Church and rose to be first Bishop of Brechin, then of Dunkeld, and in 1739 Primus of Scotland. He was an ardent Jacobite, and his second son, John, became physician to Bonnie Prince Charlie, the 'Young Pretender', and followed him throughout the campaigns of the Forty-five. He was captured after the Battle of Culloden, but was reprieved on the intervention of Duncan Forbes, Lord President of the Court of Session. The bishop's eldest son, James, sheltered Jacobite fugitives at Craighall.

The twenty-second and twenty-third Lairds died without heirs, and the estates passed to a cousin, the Honourable James Clerk Rattray, sheriff depute of Edinburgh. Sir James Clerk Rattray, the twenty-sixth Laird, was a distinguished soldier who rose to the rank of general and was created a Knight of the Bath in 1897. He served in the Crimea and in the defence of Lucknow during the Indian Mutiny of 1857–58.

The family's military traditions were continued by the present chief who served in the Scots Guards throughout the Second World War and was mentioned in dispatches. The family seat is still at Craighall-Rattray.

ROBERTSON

The Robertsons descend from Crinan, Lord of Atholl and hereditary lay Abbot of Dunkeld. From Crinan sprang the royal house of Duncan I, King of Scots, whose third son, Melmare, was ancestor of the Earls of Atholl. The Robertsons are more properly called Clan Donnachaidh, from Duncan, fifth in descent from Conan of Glenerochie, a younger son of Henry, Earl of Atholl. Duncan supported Robert the Bruce, and his clan fought at Bannockburn. Duncan later seems to have fallen into the hands of the English, at either Durham or Neville's Cross. He died in 1355, succeeded by Robert, from whom the general surname of the clan is taken. Robert's brother, Patrick, was ancestor of the principal cadet house of Lude. Lude, now a comfortable county house which dominates the skyline of Blair Atholl above Glen Tilt, was erected into a barony in 1448. Alexander Robertson of Lude joined Montrose and fought for Charles I at Tippermuir. Lude was burned by Cromwell's forces in retaliation.

The clan's fame and fortune was assured in 1437, following the murder of James I at Perth. Robert, known as Riach, the Grizzled, captured Sir Robert Graham, the king's assassin who was later put to death with considerable savagery. Although the chief received the tangible reward of having his lands of Struan erected into a free barony, he was also granted a symbolic memorial by additions to his coat of arms. Subsequently, the chief of Clan Donnachaidh bore as his crest a hand holding aloft an imperial royal crown, and on the compartment under his shield a naked man in chains, representing the regicide. Robert Riach died of wounds received in battle in 1460, and the chiefship passed to his eldest son, Alexander. The clan feuded with their neighbours, the Stewarts of Atholl. William, the sixth chief, was killed trying to recover lands seized by them. The eighth chief was murdered, and his brother inherited an estate riddled with debt. A large part of the family lands were sold off, but in 1606, John Robertson, a prosperous Edinburgh merchant who claimed kinship to the chiefly family, obtained a charter under the great seal in his favour. He then reconveyed the lands to Robertson of Struan, that is, transferred the title without exchange of money.

When the chiefship passed to an infant, Alexander, in 1636, the leadership of the clan devolved upon his uncle, Donald. Donald, who was generally known as the Tutor of Struan, was a staunch adherent to the royalist cause, and he fought with the Marquess of Montrose in all of his campaigns. Montrose commissioned him colonel on 10 June 1646. At the Battle of Inverlochy, where Montrose fell upon the surprised Argyll after a long forced march, the Robertsons played a major part in putting the king's enemies to flight.

Robertson

Standard

The next chief, Alexander, was just eighteen years old, and had been at university in St Andrews when his father died, followed almost immediately by his elder brother in 1688. He had been destined for an academic life, and has passed into history as the 'poet chief'. After James VII's final defeat in 1690, the Robertson estates were forfeited, and the gallant and talented young chief joined the exiled court in France. He saw some service in the army of the French king, but was allowed to return to Scotland under a general amnesty granted by Queen Anne. He did not seek any formal pardon from a Crown he still considered to be usurped, and he called out his clan in 1715 when the standard of the 'Old Pretender' was raised. He was twice captured by Government forces, and on each occasion contrived to escape, finally fleeing to exile

again in France. He once more took advantage of a general amnesty and returned to Scotland in 1725. However, he would take no oath of allegiance to the house of Hanover. Despite all he had suffered for the Stuart cause, he hastened to the side of Prince Charles Edward Stuart, although his age precluded him from active campaigning. He died in 1749 without issue.

The chiefship passed to his kinsman, Duncan Robertson of Drumachuine, but he could not take up the family estate as he had been forfeited in his own right for his participation in the rising of 1745. His son, Alexander, the fifteenth chief, had the barony of Struan restored to him by the Crown in 1784. Alexander also died without issue, and was succeeded by a kinsman who received a charter of confirmation to the barony of Struan on 23 June 1824. When George, eighteenth chief, sold the barony of Struan in 1854, he reserved for himself and his heirs the right and privilege of interment in the family burial ground for the members of the family of Struan. The chiefs thereafter lived on their estates in Jamaica, but have now returned to take up farming in Kent.

ROLLO

ARMS
Or, a chevron between three boars' heads erased Azure, armed Proper, langued Gules

CREST
A stag's head couped Proper

MOTTO
La fortune passe partout (Fortune passes over everywhere)

SUPPORTERS
Two stags Proper

STANDARD
Azure, a St Andrew's Cross Argent in the hoist and of two tracts Or and Azure, upon which is depicted the Badge three times, along with the Motto 'La fortune passe partout' in letters Azure upon two transverse bands Argent

BADGE
A hind Argent unguled Or langued Gules

The Rollos, like many families of Norman origin, can trace their roots to the feared Norsemen who raided the coast of Scotland in the seventh and eighth centuries. Sigurd Rollo was Jarl of Shetland and Orkney, and his son, Einar, was a renowned Viking who not only raided Scotland, but parts of his Norwegian homeland for good measure. He was harried by the Norwegian king, Harald I, and eventually turned his attention to the northern coast of France. His descendents became established as Dukes of Normandy, and their spirit of conquest brought them to the shores of England in 1066. Erik Rollo accompanied his uncle, William the Conqueror, on the invasion, and it is believed that his son or grandson, Richard, followed David I when he left the English court to reclaim his Scottish throne. The name first appears on record in a charter of around 1141 granted by Robert de Brus. Black's *Surnames of Scotland* lists numerous variants for the spelling of this name, and one Robert Rolloche obtained from David II lands near Perth in 1369.

The fortunes of the chiefly family were established in February 1380, when John Rollok, secretary to David, Earl Palatine of Strathearn and brother of Robert II, received a charter from the king of the lands of Duncrub. His son, Duncan Rollo of Duncrub, was Auditor of State Accounts until his death in 1419. William Rollo of Duncrub received a charter on 26 August 1511, erecting his lands into a free barony. He probably died at the Battle of Flodden in 1513 along with his elder son, Robert. Andrew Rollo then inherited the estates, and consolidated his position by marrying his cousin, Marion, heir to David Rollo of Manmure. One of his younger sons, Peter, became Bishop of Dunkeld and a judge of the Court of Session. His grandson, Sir Andrew Rollo, was knighted by James VI.

The family were staunch supporters of the

king during the civil war. Their loyalty was rewarded when Charles II created Sir Andrew Lord Rollo of Duncrub at Perth in January 1651. However, by 1654, Oliver Cromwell was firmly in control of Scotland, and Lord Rollo was fined £1,000 for his royal connections. Lord Rollo's fifth son, Sir William Rollo, was a gifted soldier and one of Montrose's lieutenants. He commanded the left wing of the royal army at Aberdeen in 1644, and followed the marquess on his famous forced march over mountainous terrain which surprised the forces of Argyll and led to the victory at Inverlochy. When Montrose thrust south, the royalist forces were themselves trapped by an unexpected force of Covenanter cavalry at Philiphaugh. Rollo was captured and beheaded at Glasgow in October 1645. It is perhaps indicative of the complex politics of Scotland at this time that William's brother, James, second Lord Rollo, was married first to the sister of the Marquess of Montrose and then to the sister of his rival, the Marquess of Argyll.

Rollo

Standard

Andrew, the third Lord, supported the Revolution of 1688 that brought Queen Mary and her husband, Prince William of Orange, to the throne. Despite this, his son, the fourth Lord Rollo, was a staunch Jacobite who attended the great hunt at Aboyne in August 1715, which was in reality a secret council to plan the rising of that year. He fought at the Battle of Sheriffmuir but surrendered, along with the Marquess of Huntly, to General Grant. He was imprisoned for a time, but pardoned in 1717. He had seven children, and died peacefully at Duncrub in March 1758. His eldest son, Andrew, fifth Lord Rollo, became a professional soldier, although he did not embark upon his career until the relatively late age of forty. He fought at Dettingen in 1743, and by 1758 he commanded the 22nd Regiment of Foot. He was sent to the Americas, where he fought under General Murray in the last campaign to secure Canada as a British possession. In 1759 he was sent to capture the French Caribbean island of Dominica which, although heavily fortified, he took with a force of only two thousand five hundred men. In 1760 he was raised to the rank of brigadier general. He fought for two more years in the Caribbean, during which time both Barbados and Martinique fell to the British. However, his health was severely affected by the climate, and he returned to England in 1762, dying at Leicester in 1765.

Military service continued to draw the Rollos into the ranks, and the seventh Lord Rollo fought with distinction at the siege of Pondicherry in India, commanding a force of marines. John, eighth Lord Rollo, was an officer in the 3rd Regiment of Guards, and fought on the Continent between 1793 and 1795. In June 1869 the tenth Lord Rollo was created Baron Dunning in the peerage of the United Kingdom, thereby securing, under the law at that time, a permanent seat in the House of Lords. The present chief, the thirteenth Lord Rollo and fourth Baron Dunning, still lives in Perthshire.

ROSE

This Norman family has no connection with the ancient Celtic family of Ross. Ros near Caen in Normandy was a fief of William the Conqueror's brother, Odo, the bishop famous for his war-like character and for the tapestry named after his see of Bayeux.

The de Ros family appear to have been strongly connected with two other Norman families, the de Boscos and the de Bissets. All three families disappear from records in Wiltshire and Dorset where they first settled after the Conquest, and re-appear in the middle of the thirteenth century around the Moray Firth area. Elizabeth de Bisset, whose family owned the lands of Kilravock, married Andrew de Bosco, and their daughter, Marie, married, around 1290, Hugo de Ros, whose family lands were at Geddes. Hugh's father had been witness to the foundation charter of the Priory of Beauly erected by Sir John Bisset of Lovat. Hugh and Marie established their home at Kilravock, which has remained the designation of the chief and the family's home to this day. The Barons of Kilravock supported the cause of Scottish independence, and captured Invernairn Castle for Bruce in 1306.

Hugh, fourth of Kilravock, married Janet Chisholm, daughter of the constable of Urquhart Castle. She brought with her extensive lands at Strathnairn and also an addition to the family's coat of arms. The Rose shield bore water bougets, which are said to allude to the leather water containers used by knights crossing the desert during the Crusades. The union with Janet Chisholm was marked by adding her family's boar's head to the Rose shield, as appears on the arms of the present chief. Hugh, fifth of Kilravock, lost all the family's writs and charters when Elgin Cathedral, where they had been placed for safe keeping, was burned by the Wolf of Badenoch. His son, John, was forced to reconstruct the family's titles to their landholdings, and obtained charters from James I, the Earl of Ross and the Chisholm.

Around 1460 the seventh Baron built the present Tower of Kilravock, as he lived in unsettled times with unruly neighbours. Stout walls were allied with sound politics, and the Roses entered into alliances with many of their neighbours. When the Earls of Ross were forfeited in 1474, Hugh Rose received a charter under the great seal dated March 1475 of his lands of Kilravock and Geddes. Despite his treaties with powerful nobles, the Mackintoshes seized the tower in 1482, although they soon surrendered it. The Roses had intended to secure the estates of their near neighbours, the Calders of Cawdor Castle, by marrying Muriel Calder, the family's heiress, to Hugh, the grandson and expected heir of Kilravock. Muriel was, however, carried off by the Campbells, and later married to a younger son of Argyll. Cawdor has remained a Campbell stronghold ever since.

Rose

Standard

Hugh eventually inherited Kilravock as tenth Laird. Although known as the Black Baron, he was, in fact, an extremely accomplished man, and managed to live through one of the most turbulent periods of Scottish history in peace and harmony with all his neighbours and the factions which gained ascendancy from time to time. Mary, Queen of Scots, stayed at Kilravock, and afterwards wrote to him as her trusted friend. Some copies of her letters are kept in the museum at the castle. When the queen's son, James VI, visited Kilravock, it is said that he treated the baron like a father, ordering him not to remove his hat in the royal presence.

The Roses had supported the Reformation, and despite their hitherto cordial relations with the royal family, the thirteenth Baron opposed the religious policies of Charles

I and signed the National Covenant. He led his clan against Montrose at the Battle of Auldearn in 1645. However, when the king was handed over to Parliament by the Scots army, Rose led a regiment of dragoons in the Duke of Hamilton's expedition which planned to rescue the king. He raised the regiment at his own expense, and at his death in 1649 he left the estates heavily burdened with debt.

At the outbreak of the Jacobite rising of 1715 the Roses declared for the Government. Arthur Rose was killed leading a detachment of the clan to seize Inverness. On the eve of the Battle of Culloden on 14 April 1746, Kilravock entertained Prince Charles Edward Stuart, while the Duke of Cumberland occupied the Rose's town house at Nairn.

Lieutenant Colonel Hugh Rose, twenty-fourth Baron of Kilravock, had a distinguished military career, commanding the 1st Battalion, the Black Watch. His son was killed at El Alamein in 1942. He himself died in 1946, to be succeeded by his daughter, the present chief.

Kilravock is still the clan seat and the chief's family home, but it is also a Christian guest house, as an expression of the family's Christian traditions and the personal convictions of Madam Rose.

ROSS

I n the ancient Celtic tongue, a ros was a promontory, such as the fertile land between the Cromarty and Dornoch Firths. Those who bore the name rose to be Earls of Ross, and it is believed that the first Earl, Malcolm, who lived in the early twelfth century, allied his family to O'Beolan of the great Irish royal house of Tara, by the marriage of his daughter. The clan was sometimes also referred to as Clan Anrias, or Gille Andras, alluding to Anrias, a distinguished O'Beolan ancestor. It has also been suggested that another variation, 'MicGille Andras', 'son of the follower of St Andrew', derives from one of the ancient earls who was devoted to Scotland's patron saint.

In 1214, Alexander II led his army to the north to put down the rebellion of the son of Donald Bane, a rival claimant to the throne. He was aided by the chief of Clan Ross, Fearchar Mac an t'sagirt, which in English acclaimed him to be 'son of the priest,' alluding to his O'Beolan descent from the hereditary Abbots of Applecross. Fearchar was knighted by his king, and by 1234 he was formally recognised in the title of Earl of Ross. The earl's son, William, received grants of land in Skye and Lewis. William's son, also William, was abducted around 1250 during a revolt against the earl's rule, and was rescued with help from the Munros, who were rewarded with grants of land and became closely connected to their powerful benefactors.

The Rosses were prominent in Scottish affairs and supported an alliance with Llewellyn the Welsh Prince, against the English. They fought at the Battle of Largs against the Norse invasion in 1263, and spoke in Parliament of 1283 in support of settling the succession to the throne on the infant Princess Margaret, the Maid of Norway. Young William survived to succeed his father as chief and Earl of Ross, leading his clan through the turmoil of the struggle to win Scotland's independence. He was one of those who swore fealty to Edward I of England in 1296, and when he was captured at the Battle of Dunbar in the same year, he was sent as a prisoner to London. He was later released, but again fell into the hands of the English in 1306, when he was forced to surrender Bruce's wife and daughter, whom he was protecting and who had taken sanctuary at the shrine of St Duthac at Tain. The king was at first enraged, but when the earl sued for pardon he received it, and the reconciliation was cemented by the marriage of Ross's son to the king's sister, Princess Maud. The clan fought with distinction at Bannockburn, and the earl's seal was affixed to the great Declaration of Arbroath in 1320. Hugh, the brother-in-law of Bruce, fell at the Battle of Halidon Hill in 1333.

The last chief to hold the earldom was another William, who died in 1372. Euphemia, his only daughter, claimed the earldom as Countess of Ross, but it eventually passed through the Macdonalds of the Isles into the hands of the Crown in 1476. The chiefship devolved upon William's younger half-brother, Hugh of Balnagowan.

Ross

Standard

The Rosses were royalists in the civil war, and David, the twelfth chief, led almost a thousand of his clansmen against the forces of Oliver Cromwell at the Battle of Worcester in 1651. The royalists were defeated, and Ross and many of his men were taken prisoner. The chief was imprisoned in the Tower of London in 1653, while many of his clansmen were transported to the colonies in New England. His son, another David, succeeded to the chiefship when he was only nine years of age.

David died, without an heir, in 1711, and the chiefship passed to his kinsman, Malcolm Ross of Pitcalnie. The once-proud estate of Balnagowan had been terribly burdened with debt, and was eventually purchased by General Charles Ross, brother of Lord Ross of Hawkhead, whose family were from the Lowlands and were truly 'de Roos' of Norman descent. As such, they were, genealogically, complete strangers to the Celtic Earls of Ross but nevertheless managed to obtain a matriculation in the Court of the Lord Lyon of the undifferenced arms of Ross. Pitcalnie continued to be regarded as the chief by the clan, and he was acknowledged by the great Simon Fraser, Lord Lovat, who wrote in 1740 hailing him as 'brother chief'. In the risings of 1715 and 1745 the clan as a whole avoided Jacobite intrigues, although Malcolm, the Younger of Pitcalnie, joined the 'Old Pretender'.

The chiefship was restored to the true line in 1903, when Miss Ross of Pitcalnie rematriculated the undifferenced chiefly arms. The chiefship eventually passed in 1968 to her heir, David Ross of Ross and Shandwick, a descendent in the direct male line of Mac an t'sagirt, who was Earl of Ross more than seven-and-a-half centuries ago. The chief's grandfather, Sir Ronald Ross of Shandwick, was a pioneer of modern medicine who discovered the cause of malaria. He was awarded the Nobel Prize for Medicine in 1902.

RUTHVEN

ARMS
Paly of six, Argent and Gules

CREST
A ram's head couped Sable armed Or

MOTTO
Deid schaw

SUPPORTERS
Two goats Sable, armed unguled and ducally gorged Or,
with chains also Or reflexed over the back

STANDARD
Azure, a St Andrew's Cross Argent in the hoist and of two
tracts Argent and Gules, upon which is depicted the
Badge in the first compartment, and in the second and
third compartments the Crest, that in the second compartment being ensigned of an Earl's coronet, along with the
Motto 'Deid schaw' in letters Argent upon two transverse
bands Azure

BADGE
A man in armour Proper, on his head a morion plumed
Argent and Gules, having basses paly Argent and Gules,
and over his left shoulder a scarf Argent and Sable nowed
upon the right hip, his dexter arm elevated and his sinister hand grasping the hilt of his sword Or

SLUGHORN
Tibi soli (For you alone)

The lands of Ruthven in Perthshire take their name from the Gaelic, 'Ruadhainn' meaning 'Dun uplands'. The family are Norse in origin, and first settled in East Lothian, but they were in Perthshire by the end of the twelfth century. Swein is recorded as giving lands, including Tibbermore, to the Monks of Scone, between 1188 and 1199. His grandson, Sir Walter Ruthven, was the first to adopt the name. Sir Walter's second son, Sir William, is listed among many of the Scottish nobility who swore fealty to Edward I of England in 1291 and in 1296. Despite this, in 1292, he led thirty men to help Sir William Wallace at the siege of Perth. He was also with Sir Christopher Seaton when Jedburgh was reclaimed from English hands. After Perth was recaptured in 1313, Robert the Bruce appointed Sir William to be sheriff of the royal burgh, then called St Johnston. The office was held by the family for many generations.

Sir William Ruthven of Balkernoch, a descendant of William the sheriff, spent three years in England between 1424 and 1427 as a hostage for the ransom of James I. He was considered a substantial nobleman, whose annual income was stated to be four hundred merks (about £100 at the time). His great-grandson was created a Lord of Parliament in 1488, as Lord Ruthven, by James III. Lord Ruthven married twice. His sons by his first wife were granted a letter of legitimisation in 1480. His eldest son, William, Master of Ruthven, was killed at Flodden in 1513.

William, second Lord Ruthven, succeeded his grandfather in 1528, and in the following year was elected Provost of Perth. He was appointed a judge of the Supreme Court in 1539. He was also one of the early supporters of Protestantism, and in 1543 he spoke out in Parliament in favour of the Scriptures being made available to all. He married Janet, eldest daughter and co-heiress of Patrick, Lord

Halyburton of Dirleton. By this alliance, Dirleton Castle and extensive lands in East Lothian came to the Ruthvens. Patrick, third Lord, succeeded his father in 1552. In March 1556 Patrick Ruthven and his son, William, were among Lord Darnley's co-conspirators when Queen Mary's secretary and favourite, David Rizzio, was killed in her presence at the Palace of Holyrood House. They both fled to England when abandoned to their fate by Darnley. William succeeded to the family title in June of that year and returned home, having received a royal pardon. He was among those who conducted Queen Mary to Lochleven Castle, where she was forced to abdicate. He voted against the queen's divorce, and was at the coronation of the infant James VI in 1567 at Stirling. He was Treasurer of Scotland during the king's minority, and was created Earl of Gowrie in 1581.

Ruthven

Standard

A year later Gowrie and several other nobles abducted James VI to remove him from the influence of the regents, the Earls of Arran and Lennox. What became known as the Ruthven Raid saw James being detained for ten months by the conspirators. When the king regained his freedom he appeared at first to be forgiving, but Gowrie was later arrested and beheaded for treason in 1584. The estates and titles were restored in 1586 to William's son, James, the second Earl of Gowrie, who died two years later at the age of thirteen years. His brother, John, the third Earl, was educated at Edinburgh and Padua University, where it was later alleged he practised black magic. On his return to Scotland in 1600, he and his brother, Alexander, were killed in their town house at Perth in a mysterious affair which became known as the Gowrie Conspiracy. There was little clear evidence of

what, if anything, the Ruthven brothers planned, but they were declared by Parliament to be traitors, and although they were physically beyond punishment, their very name was decreed out of existence. The family coat of arms was publicly debased, their estates forfeited and the title of Gowrie was forever outlawed. Sir Thomas Ruthven, who descended from a younger son of the second Lord Ruthven, partly restored the family reputation when he was raised to the peerage as Lord Ruthven of Freeland in 1651.

It was only in the twentieth century that the family honour was completely restored. The Honourable Alexander Ruthven, second son of Walter, Baron Ruthven of Freeland, was a distinguished soldier. He fought in the Sudan in 1898, where he won his country's highest decoration for valour, the Victoria Cross. He was appointed Governor General of Australia in 1936. He was offered a peerage in his own right, and according to family tradition, declared that he would only accept this provided he was created Lord Gowrie. His wish was granted, and his triumph was capped when a new earldom of Gowrie was created in 1945. The present earl is a noted art expert.

SANDILANDS

This name comes from the lands of Sandilands in Clydesdale. The family who were later to bear the name, may originally have fled to Scotland from Northumberland in the reign of Malcolm III. Sir James de Sandilands distinguished himself in the wars against the English, and was rewarded with a royal charter to his lands by David II. He married Eleanor, the only daughter of Sir Archibald Douglas, Regent of Scotland, who was the widow of Alexander Bruce, Earl of Carrick. Sandilands received from his brother-in-law, Lord Douglas, the lands of Calder in Lothian. Sir James was killed at the Battle of Halidon Hill in 1333. His son, James Sandilands of Calder, was one of the hostages sent to England for James I, who was only returned to Scotland two years before his death. He was heir presumptive to the Douglas estates and should have inherited them on the death of the second Earl of Douglas, but they went instead to George, Earl of Angus, Douglas's natural son. James was succeeded by his son, John. The Sandilands found themselves in opposition to their Douglas relatives as they were unshakeable in their loyalty to James II. John Sandilands and his uncle, James, were assassinated at Dumbarton by Patrick Thornton on the orders of the Douglas faction. James Sandilands then inherited the estates and married an heiress, Margaret Kinlock of Cruvie. One of their sons, James Sandilands of Cruvie, established the line later to become Lords Abercrombie.

Sir James Sandilands of Calder, a friend of the Protestant reformer, John Knox, was also preceptor of the powerful religious and military Order of the Knights of St John, whose headquarters were at Torphichen in West Lothian. When in 1560 the Scots Parliament declared the abolition of all Papal jurisdiction Sir James found himself the legal representative of an isolated Catholic religious establishment marooned in a sea of fervent reformers. He also appears to have undergone a genuine personal conversion to the new faith. He was promptly excommunicated by Rome and stripped of his office in the Order. His successor was, of course, unable to take up his new post in Scotland and for all practical purposes, Sandilands was still responsible for the Order's affairs on a day-to-day basis. The dilemma was how to secure the future of hundreds of tenants and others who depended on the Order for their livelihoods from the horrors of piecemeal confiscation. The example of Henry VIII and the English monasteries was only too clear and recent a lesson to be ignored. Sandilands took the only legal steps open to him and resigned all the Order's lands to the crown and received a re-grant in his own name for the princely sum of ten thousand crowns and an annual rent of five hundred merks. He also deposited a large sum with Belgian bankers which ultimately made its way into the Order's treasury in Malta. The Preceptors of Torphichen had sat as peers in Parliament as 'Lord St John of Torphichen', an interesting example of a title vested in an office as opposed to a family. Sir James kept his parliamentary rank, being created a hereditary peer as Lord Torphichen. He died without issue, and the new title devolved on James, the grandson of his elder brother, who succeeded as second Lord Torphichen. The first Lord's half-brother, Sir James Sandilands of Slamannan, was a Gentleman of the Bedchamber to James VI and later keeper of Blackness Castle. The second Lord had four sons, two of whom were to succeed to the family title. John, the fourth Lord, although a supporter of Charles I strongly advised against the plan known as the Engagement, which sought to invade England in 1648 to rescue the king, in return for certain conditions, after he had been handed over to Parliament by the Scots army. The plan was ill-conceived, and ended in disaster.

The full achievement of Lord Torphichen

James, seventh Lord Torphichen, took his seat in Parliament in 1704 and was a supporter of the Treaty of Union. He served in the army on the Continent only returning to Scotland at the outbreak of the rising of 1715. He fought at the Battle of Sheriffmuir. In 1722 he was appointed by George I one of the Commissioners of Police. His eldest son was wounded during the campaigns of 1745 against the forces of Bonnie Prince Charlie, the 'Young Pretender', and he later died of consumption. His second son, Walter, who had embarked upon a career in the law, succeeded to the title while sheriff of Midlothian. James, the sheriff's son, was a colonel in the Coldstream Guards and was elected a representative peer to the House of Lords from 1790 to 1800. He was succeeded by his first cousin, James, from whom the present Lord Torphichen, who still lives at Calder, is lineally descended.

SCOTT

The Latin word 'Scotti' originally
denoted the Irish Celts, and later the
Gaels in general. However, Black, in
his *Surnames of Scotland*, notes that in the earliest certain record of the name (in a charter
of around 1120), Uchtred 'Filius Scott' bears a
remarkably Saxon personal name, if the family
were truly of Celtic origin. Henricus le Scotte
witnessed a charter by David, Earl of
Strathearn, around 1195. A Master Isaac
Scotus witnessed charters by the Bishop of St
Andrews at the beginning of the thirteenth
century.

Four generations after Uchtred, Sir
Richard Scott married the daughter and
heiress of Murthockstone, and thereby
acquired her estates. Sir Richard was
appointed ranger of Ettrick Forest, which
brought the additional lands of Rankilburn
into the family demesne. The new laird built
his residence at Buccleuch, and the estates
generally became known by this name. His
son, Sir Michael, second Laird of Buccleuch,
proved a staunch supporter of Robert the
Bruce, and distinguished himself at the Battle
of Halidon Hill in 1333. He was one of the few
that escaped the carnage of that disastrous
day, but he later fell at Durham in 1346. He
left two sons: Robert, the third Laird; and
John, who founded the important cadet house
of Synton, from whom the Lords of Polwarth
were to descend. Robert died around 1389,
probably from wounds received at the Battle of
Otterburn. Robert, fifth of Buccleuch, succeeded to the family estates when his father,
Sir Walter, was killed in battle in 1402. He
consolidated the family's estates, acquiring in
1420 half of the lands of Branxholm. The sixth
Laird exchanged Murthockstone for the
remainder of Branxholm. He was active in the
struggle of the Crown to suppress the powerful Douglas faction, and received tracts of
Douglas land when the king's cause prevailed.
Branxholm became a free barony in 1463, held

on the annual payment to the Crown of a red rose on the feast day of St John the Baptist.

By the end of the fifteenth century, the Scotts were among the most powerful of the Borders clans, and the chief could easily call upon a thousand spears to enforce his will. In common with most Borders families, the Scotts quarrelled with their neighbours, and in particular with the Kerrs of Cessford. The feud flared up when Sir Walter Scott of Buccleuch tried to free the young James V, then being held by the Earl of Angus at Darnick just west of Melrose. On 25 July 1526 he launched his attack, and in the ensuing fray Kerr of Cessford was killed. Sir Walter himself was also wounded. Buccleuch fought at the Battle of Pinkie in 1547, and four years later was appointed warden of Liddesdale and the middle marches. The Kerrs were, however, only biding their time, and they set upon Sir Walter in the High Street of Edinburgh on 4 October 1552 and killed him. The feud was brought to an end when Sir Thomas Kerr of Ferniehirst married Janet Scott, sister of the tenth Laird of Buccleuch. The tenth Laird was a keen supporter of Mary, Queen of Scots, until his death in 1574. His son, another Walter Scott, succeeded to the estates as a youth. He went on to become a daring military leader, being known to his admirers as the Bold Buccleuch, a man much in the mould of his vigorous ancestors. He rescued his vassal, William Armstrong, known as Kinmont Willy, from the previously impregnable fortress of Carlisle in 1596.

James VI's accession to the English throne was followed by a royal policy to pacify the Borders, and so Lord Scott sought military adventure on the Continent fighting for the Prince of Orange in the Netherlands. His son, Walter, also commanded a regiment for the States of Holland against the Spanish, and was advanced to the title of Earl of Buccleuch in 1619. The second Earl, Francis, supported the National Covenant and opposed the religious policies of Charles I. He led his horsemen against Montrose at Philiphaugh, a defeat which marked the turning point in the king's

Scott

war in Scotland. He died in 1651 at the early age of twenty-five, and was succeeded by his four-year-old daughter, Mary, Countess of Buccleuch. She was married at the age of eleven to Walter Scott of Highchester by special sanction of the General Assembly of the Church of Scotland, but died in March 1661, aged only fourteen years. She was succeeded by her sister, Anne, who was considered one of the greatest heiresses in the kingdom and consequently worthy of a splendid marriage. Charles II sought her hand for his illegitimate son, James, Duke of Monmouth, and when the marriage was agreed Monmouth assumed the name of Scott. On the day of the marriage in April 1663, the couple were also created Duke and Duchess of Buccleuch, with numerous subsidiary honours. Monmouth later rose in rebellion against the Crown, and was executed in July 1685. His titles were forfeit, but as Anne Scott had been specifically created Duchess of Buccleuch, her title was unaffected. The duchess was succeeded by her grandson, Francis, second Duke of Buccleuch. The Buccleuch art collection, maintained in the family's three great houses of Drumlanrig, Bowhill and Boughton, is internationally renowned.

SCRYMGEOUR

ARMS
Gules, a lion rampant Or armed and langued Azure holding in his dexter forepaw a crooked sword or scymitar Argent

CREST
A lion's paw erased in bend Or holding a crooked sword or scymitar Argent

MOTTO
Dissipate (Disperse)

SUPPORTERS
(on a compartment embellished with rowan)
Two greyhounds Argent collared Gules, and behind the Shield in saltire two representations of the Royal Banner of Scotland, videlicet:- Or, a lion rampant Gules armed and langued Azure within a double tressure circonfleurdelise Gules, ropes and tassels of the last (as insignia of the Honourable Office of Bearer for the Sovereign of the Royal Banner of Scotland)

STANDARD
Azure, a St Andrew's Cross Argent in the hoist and of the Livery Gules semée of flaming fires Or, upon which is depicted the Crest ensigned of an Earl's coronet, along with the Motto 'Dissipate' extended in the fly in letters Or

PINSEL
Or, upon a torteau within a strap of leather Proper, buckled and embellished Or inscribed of the Motto 'Dissipate' in letters of the Field, the Crest upon a Wreath of the Liveries, all within a circlet Or fimbriated Vert bearing the title 'Scrymgeour, Earl of Dundee' in letters Gules, the same ensigned of an Earl's coronet Proper, and in the fly an Escrol Gules surmounting a sprig of rowan bearing the Motto 'Dissipate' in letters Or

BADGE
A flaming fire Proper (displayed on each side of the Crest)

PLANT BADGE
Rowan

This name is probably derived from the old English, 'skrymsher', meaning a 'swordsman'. The family appears to have been well established in Fife long before their subsequent connection with the city of Dundee. The chiefs were later to be created constables, and then Earls of Dundee, and also hereditary royal standard bearers.

The herald, Sir Iain Moncreiffe of that Ilk, asserted that the Scrymgeours are probably descendents of the great Macduff Earls of Fife, and may have claimed their office as standard bearer from their early Celtic origins. It was customary for Celtic armies to be accompanied by sacred holy relics, usually borne by a hereditary keeper. The Scrymgeours may therefore have carried a sacred relic, possibly the pastoral staff of St Columba, which was later replaced by a consecrated heraldic banner. They were confirmed as banner bearers by Sir William Wallace and Parliament on 29th March 1298, during the struggle for Scottish independence. Scrymgeour is named as Alexander, son of Colyn, son of Carin. He was one of the first to declare for Robert the Bruce, and obtained from him on 5 December 1298 a charter confirming the rights granted by Sir William Wallace. This is the only contemporary document to have survived in which the names of Wallace and Bruce are mentioned together. Sir Alexander was captured by the English and hanged at Newcastle in 1306 on the direct orders of Edward I. He was succeeded by another Alexander, who rode as royal banner bearer at the Battle of Bannockburn in 1314.

Vast lands at Glassary in Argyll came to the family around 1370 with the marriage of Alexander Scrymgeour to Agnes, heiress to Gilbert Glassary of that Ilk. The family continued to prosper, and the seventh constable of Dundee acquired the lands of Dudhope near the city in 1495. They later built a handsome castle on the lands, which was to be their seat until 1668. The Argyll estates were controlled from Fincharn, and it was from there that John Scrymgeour of Glassary marched to carry the royal banner on behalf of the chief, his infant nephew, to the fateful field of Flodden in 1513, where he was mortally wounded. The Gaelic title of the Scrymgeours is 'Mac Mhic Iain', and according to local tradition, Fincharn Castle on the shores of Loch Awe was burned down by an angry bridegroom when an early Mac Mhic Iain attempted to steal his bride.

Sir James Scrymgeour received a new charter to his estates at Holyrood House on 25 November 1587. He was confirmed in all the family's grants of honours, with lands, privileges and titles being destined to his male heirs bearing the name and arms of Scrymgeour. He was one of the commissioners sent to Denmark to negotiate the marriage of James VI to Princess Anne, and in 1604 he was appointed a commissioner to negotiate a political union with England. He died in 1612. He was succeeded by his son, John, who entertained James VI at Dudhope Castle in 1617. He was raised to the peerage by Charles I as Viscount of Dudhope and Baron Scrymgeour of Inverkeithing in November 1641. The second Viscount of Dudhope was sent with the Scottish Covenanter forces sent to assist the English Parliament against Charles I. He fought at the Battle of Marston Moor in July 1644, where he received a fatal wound. He was succeeded by his son, John, who adhered to the royalist cause, and commanded a cavalry regiment under the Duke of Hamilton in 1648 and fought at the Battle of Worcester in 1651. He escaped after the royal defeat and joined the army of General Middleton in the Highlands, eventually being captured in 1654. At the Restoration in 1660 he was rewarded with the earldom of Dundee. He died in 1668

without issue and his castles, estates and royal offices were seized by the Duke of Lauderdale upon a legal pretext. Lauderdale sent soldiers to carry off all of the Scrymgeour charters and papers from Dudhope Castle. He then had it declared that there were no lawful heirs, and the estates reverted to the Crown. He then procured from the king a grant of the titles and estates to his own brother, Lord Chattan. In 1686 the estates passed to John Graham of Claverhouse who two years later was created Viscount of Dundee. The famous 'Bonnie Dundee' was killed at the Battle of Killiecrankie in 1689, and his estates were forfeited, whereupon they passed to the Douglases.

The estates should have devolved on the death of the earl to John Scrymgeour of Kirkton, who was the great-grandson of the fifth Constable of Dundee. His grandson, David Scrymgeour of Birkhill, sheriff of Inverness, married Catherine, daughter of Sir Alexander Wedderburn of Blackness, Baronet, and their son, Alexander, succeeded in 1788 as heir of line of David Wedderburn of Wedderburn to that family's title and estates. The family continued to assert their right to the ancient titles and honours bestowed upon their ancestors, and at the coronation of Edward VII, Henry Scrymgeour Wedderburn carried the standard of Scotland. His grandson succeeded in a case before the House of Lords, and was recognised as the eleventh Earl of Dundee. In 1954 he was also created a peer of the United Kingdom as Baron Glassary to enable him to take up Government office, ultimately becoming Deputy Leader of the House of Lords. His son, the twelfth Earl and present chief, has followed his father into politics in the House of Lords. The family seat is still at Birkhill north of Cupar in Fife.

SEMPILL

A name known in Renfrewshire from the twelfth century, its origin is obscure. The suggestion that it is a corruption of 'St Paul' seems unlikely, as is the tradition that the 1st of the name had a reputation for being humble or simple. Robert de Sempill witnessed a charter to Paisley Abbey around 1246, and later, as chamberlain of Renfrew, a charter of the Earl of Lennox. His two sons, Robert and Thomas, supported Robert the Bruce, and both were rewarded by the king for their services. The elder son received all the lands around Largs in Ayrshire which had been confiscated from the Balliols. Thomas received a grant of half of the lands of Longniddry.

The lands of Eliotstoun, which became the territorial designation of the chiefly line, were acquired prior to 1344. Sir Thomas Sempill of Eliotstoun fell at the Battle of Sauchieburn fighting for James III in June 1488. His only son, John, succeeded to the family estates, and early in the reign of James IV – probably in 1488 – he was ennobled with the title, Lord Sempill. He founded the Collegiate Church of Lochwinnoch in 1505, and rebuilt the castle at the eastern end of the loch which he renamed Castle Semple. Like his father, he followed his king into battle, and died on the field of Flodden in September 1513. His eldest son, William, succeeded to the title, obtaining a charter to the lordship with the assistance of the Regent Albany, in 1515. He favoured the betrothal of the infant Mary, Queen of Scots, to the son of Henry VIII of England. His son, Robert, Master of Sempill, was constable of the king's Castle of Douglas, and was taken prisoner by the English at the Battle of Pinkie in 1547. Sometimes called the Great Lord Semple, he supported the Queen Regent, Mary of Guise, widow of James V. In 1560 his castle was attacked and seized for his opposition to the Reformation. He was a faithful adherent of Queen Mary until the death of

Darnley, and thereafter he joined those who sought to promote Mary's son as King James VI. He fought against the queen and Bothwell at the Battle of Carberry Hill, and was one of the signatories of the warrant to confine the queen in Lochleven Castle. He led the van of Regent Moray's army at the Battle of Langside in 1568, and for this and other services he received a charter to the abbey lands of Paisley, which had been forfeited from Lord Claud Hamilton. Hamilton later regained the lands.

Standard

The murder of the regent was a setback to Sempill's ambitions, and in 1570 he was imprisoned for a year. By his second wife Lord Sempill had a son, John, who was castigated by the reformer John Knox as Sempill 'the dancer'. In 1577 John was accused of treason and conspiring to assassinate the Regent Morton. He was denounced by one of his own alleged accomplices, and was sentenced to be hanged, drawn and quartered. The sentence was commuted to imprisonment by the influence of his family and friends, and he was later released. His elder half-brother, Robert, succeeded as fourth Lord Sempill in 1572. He assisted at the baptism of Prince Henry in 1594, and attended personally on the queen at the banquet held in celebration in the great hall of Stirling Castle. He was appointed Privy Councillor by James VI, and sent as ambassador to Spain. He would not renounce the Catholic faith, and therefore held no other high public office. In 1608 the General Assembly of the Church of Scotland excommunicated him as 'an obstinate papist'.

The fifth Lord took little part in court intrigue or politics, but concentrated on his estates, where he is said to have lived in considerable splendour. He was succeeded by his brother, Robert, who also led a largely private life, but he supported the royalist cause in the civil war, and was fined under the Commonwealth as a consequence. His first two sons died without issue, and he was succeeded by his third son, Francis. The eighth Lord Sempill embraced the Protestant faith, and was the first Sempill to sit in Parliament since the reign of Mary, Queen of Scots. He died without issue in 1684, when he was succeeded by his elder sister, Anne, under a deed of entail which had been confirmed by the Crown in 1685. The baroness obtained a new charter to the title on 16 May 1688, in terms of which the title descended in default of any male issue, to her daughters, and with a special reservation to any of her heirs. Three of her sons were to succeed to the title.

Francis, Anne's eldest son and the tenth Lord, was an implacable opponent of the union with England, and voted in Parliament against every article. He died unmarried in 1716, and was succeeded by his brother, John, who had supported the Hanoverian Government during the rising of 1715. John also died unmarried, and the title passed to his brother, Hew, a professional soldier who had made a reputation fighting on the Continent. At the Battle of Culloden, on 16 April 1746, he held the rank of brigadier general, and fought with his regiment on the left wing of the Government army.

In 1835 the title once more passed to the female line, when Maria Janet Sempill succeeded her brother, the fifteenth Lord. The title passed once more into the safe hands of a lady, when the present chief, the twentieth in line of the peerage, succeeded her father in 1965.

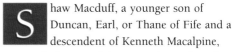

ARMS

Quarterly, 1st, Or a lion rampant Gules, armed and langued Azure;
2nd, Argent, a fir-tree growing out of a mound in base seeded Proper, in the dexter canton a dexter hand couped at the wrist holding a dagger point downwards Gules;
3rd, chequy Argent and Azure, and on a chief of the Second three mullets of the First;
4th, Or, a galley sails furled Azure, flagged Gules, oars in saltire of the Last

CREST

A dexter cubit arm couped and holding a dagger erect all Proper

MOTTO

Fide et fortitudine (By faith and fortitude)

SUPPORTERS

(on a compartment, embellished with red whortleberry and on the dexter a Scots pine-tree Vert, coned Or, and on the sinister an oak-tree Proper, acorned Or, along with the Slogan 'Tordarroch')
Two wild cats rampant Proper, each collared and chained Argent, and pendent from each collar a mullet of the Last

STANDARD

The Arms in the hoist and of two tracts Or and Gules, upon which is depicted the Badge three times along with the Motto 'Fide et fortitudine' in letters Vert upon two transverse bands Argent

BADGE

A dexter cubit arm couped and holding a dagger erect all Proper, within and issuant from a chaplet of fir, oak and red whortleberry also Proper, banded Or and Gules

Shaw Macduff, a younger son of Duncan, Earl, or Thane of Fife and a descendent of Kenneth Macalpine, was made keeper of the strategic royal castle at Inverness by Malcolm IV. His heirs, the 'Mhic an Toiseach', the 'sons of the Thane', consolidated their power around Inverness in support of the royal government. Shaw's grandson, Shaw Macwilliam, acquired important lands at Rothiemurchus in 1236. Beset by the belligerent power of their neighbours, Clan Comyn, his son, Ferquhard, sought alliance with the powerful Macdonalds by marrying Mora, daughter of Angus Mhor, Lord of Islay. In 1291, Ferquhard's son, Angus, sixth chief of Mackintosh, married Eva, daughter of Dougall Dall, the descendent of Ghillechattan Mhor. From this union emerged the large tribal confederation to be known as the Clan Chattan and the first chief of Clan Shaw, John, Angus and Eva's second son.

The feud with the Comyns led the confederation to support Robert the Bruce; they fought at Bannockburn in 1314 and took part in the Scottish invasions of England in 1318 and 1319. The second chief, Shaw Macghillechrist Mhic Iain, a great-grandson of Angus and Eva, was generally known as 'Sgorfhiaclach' meaning 'bucktooth'. He was raised with his cousins at the Mackintosh seat at Moy, and it seems certain that he was present at the Battle of Invernahavon in 1370. Shaw was elected captain of Clan Chattan for the legendary raid of Angus in 1391 under the Wolf of Badenoch. The long-standing feud between Clan Chattan and the Camerons, which had led to the Battle of Inverahavon, continued to threaten the stability of the region, and it was proposed that a trial by combat of champions should be used to settle the dispute. Shaw 'Bucktooth' was appointed to lead Clan Chattan to the appointed battleground at the North Inch of Perth in September 1396. Sixty Highlanders fought before an illustrious audience including Robert III and the Dauphin of France.

Aedh, the grandson of Shaw 'Bucktooth', settled at Tordarroch in 1468. Occupying a strategic site above the fort on the River Nairn, he and his followers became a powerful force in their own right, known as Clan Aedh or Ay. While the Shaws, or Clan Ay, were consolidating their power in Strathnairn, the chief of Mackintosh was murdered in 1524, leaving an infant son, William. To the outrage of the local chiefs, the Earl of Moray seized the boy, allegedly as his guardian. Clan Chattan retaliated against Moray, and Alan Ciar MacIain led Clan Ay in raiding the earl's lands. Heavy fines forced Alan Ciar to sell the feu of Rothiemurchus to the Earl of Huntly.

On 22 May 1543, a Clan Chattan band was signed at Inverness, and Angus Macrobert of Tordarroch was one of the signatories. Again, on 4 April 1609, Tordarroch signed the great Clan Chattan band of union and manrent at Termit, on behalf of Clan Ay and his Rothiemurchus cousins.

Shaw of Tordarroch

Standard

The clan continued to prosper, and by 1691 Duncan Shaw, Laird of Crathienaird, had risen to be chamberlain to the Earl of Mar.

William Mackintosh of Borlum called out Clan Chattan to fight for the Jacobite cause on 15 September 1715 at Farr near Tordarroch. Robert, the Younger of Tordarroch, and his brother, Angus, led the Shaw contingent, which was noted for its discipline, equipment and bravery. After the collapse of the rising at Preston, both Robert and Angus were imprisoned. Robert died soon after his release in 1718. Angus was transported to Virginia until he was pardoned in 1722. He never recovered from his experience or the death of his brother, and although a Jacobite, he refused to call out his clan for Bonnie Prince Charlie in

1745. Many Shaws, however, rallied to the prince's standard, including James Shaw of Crathienaird. Lady Anne, wife of the Mackintosh chief, called out the whole Clan Chattan. Two of her most trusted lieutenants were James and John Shaw of Kinrara. Later, as the Government forces marched north, Angus of Tordarroch's oath to the Hanovarian Government was stretched to breaking point. When the armies met at Culloden, he had to be restrained by his wife from joining his kinsmen.

In 1970, the Lord Lyon recognised Major Iain Shaw of Tordarroch, father of the present chief, in the undifferenced arms of the name, in a line of unbroken continuity to the ancient earls of Fife.

The tartan illustrated is Shaw of Tordarroch. However, it is equally correct to wear the green Shaw (derived from the regimental tartan of the Black Watch) in memory of Fearchar Shaw who was executed at Towerhill in 1743 for refusing to serve overseas when the regiment had been promised that no such service would be demanded of it. Fearchar and two comrades were made an example of to discourage further mutiny and quickly became heroes in their native Highlands.

SINCLAIR

ARMS

Quarterly, 1st, Azure, a lymphad at anchor Or, flagged Gules, sails furled Argent, oars in saltire Or within a Royal Tressure Or (Earldom of Orkney); 2nd & 3rd, Or, a lion rampant Gules, armed and langued Azure (Sparr-Nithsdale); 4th, Azure, a three masted ship Or, flagged Gules, under sail Argent (Earldom of Caithness); overall a cross engrailed and counterchanged Argent and Sable (Sinclair)

CREST

A cock Proper, armed and beaked Or

MOTTO

Commit thy work to God

SUPPORTERS

Two griffins Gules, wings elevated, armed, beaked and winged Or

STANDARD

Azure, a St Andrew's Cross Argent in the hoist and of four tracts Or, Azure, Argent and Gules, upon which is depicted the Crest in the first compartment, the 1st Badge in the second compartment, the 2nd Badge in the third compartment, and the 3rd Badge in the fourth compartment, along with the Motto 'Commit thy work to God' (in letters Gules) upon three transverse bands (Argent)

BADGES

1st, a unicorn sejant Proper, armed, maned and tufted Or; 2nd, a demi-bear Proper, muzzled Or, issuing from the circlet of an Earl's coronet Proper; 3rd, a mermaid Proper, crined Or, holding in her dexter hand a looking glass Proper framed Or, and in her sinister a comb also Or

PLANT BADGE

Whin

St Clare-sur-Elle lies in the Pont d'Eveque region of Normandy. Such romantic origins are hard to call to mind in the traditional pronunciation of the name – *Singklar*. No certain records exist but it is likely that Norman knights from St Clare came to Scotland to seek land and fortune during the reign of David I. Henry de St Clair of Herdmanston near Haddington founded a line in 1163 which was raised to the peerage as Lord St Clair, a title still borne today. The chiefs, the Earls of Caithness, descend from Sir William St Clair, a sheriff of Edinburgh who was granted the barony of Roslin in 1280. His eldest son, Sir Henry, swore fealty to Edward I of England in 1296, and the family generally favoured the Balliol claim to the throne. However, as the struggle for Scottish independence became paramount, the St Clair's gave their loyalty to Bruce, and they fought at Bannockburn in 1314. Sir Henry received a grant of lands around Pentland in 1317 as his reward. Sir Henry's son, Sir William, was a favourite of King Robert, and he accompanied Sir James Douglas on his expedition to the Holy Land with the heart of the king. The Scots knights did not see the Holy Land, but joined the king of Aragon in his fight against the Moors of Spain. St Clair and Douglas were both killed, and the pilgrimage was abandoned. William's tomb is in the chapel at Roslin, which remains one of the finest chapels of the late-medieval period in Scotland. His grandson, Henry St Clair, became Earl of Orkney through his mother, Isabel. Haakon VI, King of Norway, who had previously controlled the islands outright, recognised the title in 1379. Henry conquered the Faroe Islands in 1391 and discovered Greenland. He is now believed to have voyaged as far as the Americas, possibly landing in both Nova Scotia and Massachusetts.

The third Earl was High Chancellor of Scotland between 1454 and 1458. He was granted the earldom of Caithness in 1455 in compensation for the loss of his claim to the lordship of Nithsdale. James III married Princess Margaret of Denmark in 1468 and her father, unable to pay her dowry in cash, pledged Orkney and Shetland in lieu. The islands were never redeemed by the Danes, and became part of Scotland. The earldom, or princedom, of Orkney was conveyed by the St Clairs in 1470, to James III. William settled the earldom of Caithness on the eldest son of his second marriage, and the Roslin lands on his younger son. It was around this time that the spelling 'Sinclair' came into general use. The second Earl of Caithness died at Flodden in 1513 following his royal master, James IV.

The chiefship followed with the earldom of Caithness, and the fourth Earl, George, was as fierce as any of his Viking ancestors. He imprisoned his own son, the Master of Caithness, for making peace with the Morays without his permission.

Standard

George, the sixth Earl of Caithness, was forced to sell off much of the family lands in 1672, being greatly burdened with debt. He died without issue in 1676, and Sir John Campbell of Glenorchy claimed the earldom, being in possession of most of the mortgaged estates. Glenorchy promptly married the widowed countess. The right to the title in the estates was disputed by George Sinclair of Keiss, a descendent of a younger son of the fifth Earl. Keiss took possession of the estates by force, but when he met the Campbells in a pitched battle on the banks of Altimarlech

Sinclair

near Wick, it is said so many Sinclairs were killed that the Campbells were able to cross the water without getting their feet wet. The Sinclairs regained the earldom in 1681 by an order of Parliament.

The St Clairs of Roslin laid claim to be hereditary Grand Master Masons of Scotland. In 1736, when forty-four Scottish Freemasons' Lodges met in Edinburgh to found the Grand Lodge of Scotland, William St Clair appeared as a candidate for Grand Master. He played his trump card by offering to surrender his hereditary rights, and promptly became the first elected Grand Master.

The remains of Rosslyn Castle near Edinburgh and the splendid chapel associated with it are still in family hands. In 1805, the earldom of Rosslyn passed to Sir James St Clair Erskine, Baronet, whose descendants care for these jewels of Scottish architecture today.

SKENE

The traditional origin of this name is found in an eleventh-century legend of the Robertsons. It is said that a younger son of Robertson of Struan saved the life of the king by killing a savage wolf with only his small dagger, or 'sgian'. He was rewarded with a grant of lands in Aberdeenshire which he named after the weapon which had brought him the good fortune, and the family thereafter were named for their ownership of this land. The feat is commemorated in the chief's shield, which displays three wolves' heads impaled on daggers, or as they have now been blazoned, 'durks'.

The first recorded bearer of the name was John de Skeen, who lived during the reign of Malcolm III. After Malcolm's death, he supported Donald Bane, a rival to the succession of King Edgar. His lands were forfeited, and they were only restored when the Skenes joined the army of Alexander I marching against rebels in the north in 1118. His great-grandson, John de Skene, held the lands during the reign of Alexander III, and his son, Patrick, appears on the Ragman Roll in 1296, submitting to Edward I of England. However, the Skenes staunchly supported Robert the Bruce, and after his victory their lands were erected into a barony. Adam de Skene was killed at the Battle of Harlaw in 1411. Four generations later, Alexander Skene de Skene is listed among the dead on the ill-fated field of Flodden in 1513. Yet another Skene laird fell at the Battle of Pinkie in 1547.

The Skenes were not Covenanters, and for their support of Charles I they were forced into exile. The chief took service with the Swedish armies under King Gustavus Adolphus. In 1827 the direct line of the Skenes of Skene died out and the estates passed to a nephew, James, Earl of Fife.

Other prominent branches of the family include the Skenes of Dyce, Halyards, Rubislaw and Curriehill. Sir John Skene of

Curriehill was a prominent sixteenth-century lawyer who was appointed to the Supreme Court Bench in 1594, taking the title, 'Lord Curriehill'. He was knighted by James VI, and his son was created a Baronet of Nova Scotia in 1626. Sir John's 2nd son, John Skene of Hallyards, also rose to high judicial office as the Lord Clerk Register. One of the Skenes of Hallyards later founded Skeneborough on the shores of Lake Camplain in Canada. James Skene of Rubislaw was a close friend of the novelist, Sir Walter Scott, and is said to have provided Scott with some inspiration for both *Quentin Durward* and *Ivanhoe*. William Forbes Skene, the celebrated writer and historian, was appointed historiographer royal for Scotland in 1881.

Standard

Skene

On 17 February 1994, the Lord Lyon recognised Danus George Moncrieffe Skene of Halyards as chief of the name and arms of Skene. The matriculation also recognises the new chief's son, Dugald, as heir apparent. Danus Skene of Skene, who is a teacher with degrees from the Universities of Sussex, Chicago and Aberdeen, matriculated his arms as Skene of Halyards in 1992. It was established that John Skene of Halyards, son of Sir John Skene and his wife, Barbara Forbes of Cragievar, was lineally descended from the second son of James Skene of that Ilk, who died around 1604. John of Halyards, matriculated his arms in the Lyon register in 1672,

differenced from the chiefly arms by the addition of a gold crescent on the shield. In the petition of Danus Skene, it was asserted that there was good reason to believe that, on the death of Alexander Skene of that Ilk with no issue in April 1827, the succession passed to the next most senior line – the Skenes of Halyards. This argument was accepted subject to the proviso that the Lord Lyon's decision was 'for aught yet seen', which means that if a rival claimant, nearer in blood to the old chiefly line, comes forward in the next ten years, then the case can be re-opened. As no other claimant has emerged in the past one hundred and sixty-seven years, it seems reasonable to conclude that the Skenes once more have a bloodline chief under whose standard they can rally.

SPENS

This name is believed to be derived from the old French, 'despense', used to describe the custodian of the larder. This may originally have been an office within the monastic system, but from the thirteenth century onwards the name Spensa, or Dispensa, is used to describe royal officials. Roger 'dispensator' witnessed a deed recording the transfer of lands near Dallas in Inverness-shire in 1232. John Spens is listed as baillie of Irvine in 1260. Henry Spens witnessed a charter by Robert, Earl of Fife, in 1390, and it was in that ancient earldom that the family was to prosper. Henry de Spens of Lathallan swore fealty to Edward I of England, and his name appears on the Ragman Roll of 1296. He died around 1300, when his son, Thomas, succeeded. He is mentioned in two charters of Robert the Bruce.

By the early fifteenth century, the family had risen to considerable prominence, which entitled John Spens of Lathallan to sit in the Parliament called by James I at Perth in 1434. John married Isabel, daughter of Sir John Wemyss, and had three sons. Patrick, the youngest, was a member of the Guard of Scots Archers sent by James II to Charles VII of France in 1450. He settled in France, and his descendents were the prominent family of Spens-Destinot de Lanere. The 'Garde Ecossaise', as they were later known, were to become the personal bodyguard of the French kings until the revolution of 1789. Thomas, the second son, entered the Church and rose to high office. He was appointed Bishop of Galloway and later Lord Privy Seal, a post he held until 1470. He was translated to the bishopric of Aberdeen in 1459, and being considered a clever and shrewd negotiator, he was regularly employed on state business. In 1449 he was sent to conclude a marriage contract between the heir to the Duke of Savoy and Arabella, sister of James II. Two years later he was sent as ambassador to negotiate a truce with England. He died in Edinburgh in 1480, and his tomb is in the splendid chapel of Roslin.

The heir to Lathallan, Alexander Spens, married the sister of the great Scottish admiral, Sir Andrew Wood, and received a charter from James II, creating him constable of Crail harbour. The Spens link with the sea may have been forged two hundred years earlier in the exploits of Sir Patrick Spens, possibly from the cadet house of Wormieston, commemorated in the ballad which bears his name. Sir Patrick was in command of the ship which took Princess Margaret, daughter of Alexander III, to Norway for her marriage to King Eric in 1281. On the return voyage, the Scottish ship went down with all hands.

During the reign of Mary, Queen of Scots, the loyalties of the family were divided. Sir John Spence of Condie was Lord Advocate, but adhered to the reformed Church. When commanded by the queen to prosecute the reformer, John Knox, for alleged treason, he did so with no great zeal, and Knox was acquitted. David Spens of Wormieston, however, was a loyal subject of Mary, and was denounced as a rebel by the Parliament summoned by Regent Lennox in August 1571. David was one of the ringleaders of the attempt to seize Lennox at Stirling in September of that year, and he was given the task of taking the regent personally to hold as hostage. According to one narrative, Spens followed his orders to keep Lennox secure so literally that when some of the conspirators decided to kill the regent, Spens stopped a pistol shot by throwing himself in front of his prisoner. Tragically, when supporters of Lennox came to his rescue, they killed Spens on the spot, despite the regent's attempts to save his unlikely saviour. However, the family were later reconciled to James VI, who sent Sir James Spens of Wormieston as ambassador to Sweden, where a branch of the family settled, rising high in the Swedish nobility as Counts Spens.

Dr Nathaniel Spens of Craigsanquhar in Fife was president of the Royal College of Physicians in 1794. He was a prominent member of the Royal Company of Archers (the monarch's bodyguard in Scotland) and a famous portrait of him hangs in Archers' Hall in Edinburgh. One of his descendents, Sir William Spens, was vice-chancellor of Cambridge University from 1931 to 1933. Another kinsman, John Spens, WS, is the Albany Herald to the Court of the Lord Lyon, King of Arms.

STIRLING

ARMS
Argent, on a bend Sable three buckles of the Field

CREST
Issuing out of an antique coronet Or a hart's head couped Azure

MOTTO
Gang forward

On Compartment
Castrum et nemus strivelense (The castle and wood of Stirling)

SUPPORTERS
Two Caledonian Bulls Proper, gorged and chained Or

The great town and Castle of Stirling lie at the crossroads of Scotland, which many account for the derivation of the name, which means 'place of strife'. The castle has been a silent witness to many of the greatest events in Scottish history, most of which have been associated with strife, murder and battle.

Thoraldus, who appears in a charter of David I granted around 1147, held the lands of Cadder. His descendent, the fifth Laird of Cadder, Sir Alexander de Strivelyn, died in 1304. His heir, Sir John de Strivelyn, was killed at the Battle of Halidon Hill in 1333. His grandson, Sir William, had two sons. The succession passed through the line of his first son, William, for four generations, and then passed to the grandson of the second son, Sir John de Strivelyn, third Laird of Cragernard. Sir John was governor of the royal Castle at Dumbarton and sheriff of Dunbartonshire. He was appointed armour bearer by James I, and Comptroller of the Royal Household. He was knighted in 1430. His son, William acquired the lands of Glorat from the Earl of Lennox. He also held Dumbarton Castle, an appointment later passed to his son, George, who defended it for the Crown from 1534 to 1547. He fought at the Battle of Pinkie in 1547, later dying of wounds that he received there. His great-grandson, Sir Mungo Stirling of Glorat, was a staunch adherent of Charles I, who knighted him in recognition of his bravery. Sir Mungo's son, George Stirling, was created a Baronet of Nova Scotia in 1666. The family were also granted a royal augmentation to their arms of a double tressure, similar to that which appeared on the royal arms of Scotland, in recognition of their loyalty to the Stuart dynasty.

The Stirlings obtained the lands of Keir in Perthshire in the mid fifteenth century. When Prince James, son of James III, rebelled against his father, Sir William Stirling of Keir was one of his supporters, and when the prince succeeded as James IV he was high in that monarch's favour. His descendent, Sir Archibald Stirling of Keir, from whom the Stirlings of Garden also descend, was a prominent lawyer who supported the king during the civil war, and on the Restoration of the monarchy in 1660 was appointed to the Supreme Court with the title of 'Lord Garden'. The Lairds of Keir remained loyal to the Stuarts, and fought in both the risings of 1715 and 1745. James Stirling of Keir was imprisoned and his estates were forfeited for his part in the Fifteen, but they were later restored.

In the nineteenth century, William Stirling of Keir travelled widely throughout Spain and the Middle East, later writing numerous books, including a life of Velasquez. He became MP for Perthshire and succeeded his maternal uncle in the Maxwell baronetcy of Pollock in 1865. Keir is still a family home, and is one of the most splendid sporting estates in Scotland.

The Stirlings of Faskine in Lanarkshire claim descent from a nephew of William the Lion, but were actually a colateral branch of the Stirlings of Cadder. John Stirling, descended from this house, became Lord Provost of Glasgow. He died in 1709. Sir Walter Stirling of Faskine served in the Royal Navy, subsequently being appointed commander-in-chief of the fleet at the Nore by George III. He was offered a baronetcy, which he declined. His eldest son, who was a Member of Parliament, was, however, created a baronet on 15 December 1800. This title is now extinct. His second son became a vice-admiral, and his grandson also attained high naval rank. As Rear Admiral Sir James Stirling of Drumpellier, he fought in the war against America in 1812, and was later made Governor of Western Australia. In 1852 he served as Junior Lord of the Admiralty, and his last command was of the fleet off China.

Another baronetcy was bestowed upon the family when James Stirling, Lord Provost of Edinburgh, received the honour in recognition of his actions to suppress riots in the city in 1792. This title became extinct on the death of his only son while serving in the Coldstream Guards.

The Stirling family's historic connection with Dumbarton Castle was continued into the twentieth century, when Sir George Stirling, ninth Baronet of Glorat, was appointed keeper of the castle in 1927. Today, the family still holds high office: Lieutenant Colonel Stirling of Garden is the Lord Lieutenant of Stirlingshire. The present chief succeeded on the death of his father, Sir Charles Stirling of Cadder, in 1986. Sir Charles was a distinguished diplomat who was made not only a Knight of the Order of St Michael and St George, but also of the Royal Victorian Order, which is exclusively the gift of the Crown for services to the royal house.

The stewards, or seneschals, of Dol in Brittany came to Scotland via England, when David I returned to claim his throne in 1124. They soon rose to high rank, being created hereditary high stewards of Scotland. By judicious marriage to Marjory, daughter of Robert the Bruce, they acquired the throne on the death of the Bruce's only son, David II. Robert Stewart, who reigned as Robert II, bestowed upon his younger son, John, the lands of Bute, Arran and Cumbrae. The king erected the lands into a county, and conferred the office of hereditary sheriff on his son. The grant was confirmed by a charter in the year 1400 by Robert III.

James, sheriff of Bute between 1445 and 1449, was succeeded by his brother, William, who was also keeper of Brodick Castle on Arran. His grandson, Ninian Stewart, was confirmed in the office of sheriff of Bute together with the lands of Ardmaleish, Greenan, the Mill of Kilcattan and Corrigillis. In 1498, James IV created Ninian hereditary captain and keeper of the royal Castle of Rothesay, an honour still held by the family to this day and which is shown in their coat of arms. He married three times, and was succeeded in 1539 by his son, James, who suffered during the struggle between the Earl of Lennox and the Earl of Arran, Regent of Scotland. In 1570, James was succeeded by his son, John, who attended Parliament in Edinburgh as Commissioner for Bute. The family favoured the spelling of their name introduced by Mary, Queen of Scots, and the present chiefs still use it to this day.

Sir James Stuart of Bute was created a Baronet of Nova Scotia by Charles I in 1627. Early in the civil war, he garrisoned the Castle of Rothesay, and at his own expense raised soldiers for the king. He was appointed royal lieutenant for the west of Scotland, and directed to take possession of Dumbarton

Castle. Two frigates sent to assist him fell foul of stormy weather, and one was completely wrecked. Ultimately, Sir James was forced to flee to Ireland when the forces of Cromwell were victorious. His estates were sequestrated, and he was forced to pay a substantial fine to redeem them. His grandson, Sir James Stuart of Bute, was appointed to manage the estates and to be colonel of the local militia on the forfeiture of the Earl of Argyll in 1681. He supported the accession of Queen Mary and William of Orange, and later, in the reign of Queen Anne, he was made a Privy Councillor and one of the commissioners for the negotiation of the Treaty of Union between Scotland and England. In 1703 he was created Earl of Bute, Viscount Kingarth and Lord Mount Stuart, Cumra and Inchmarnock. But by 1706, the earl was convinced a union with England would be a disaster for his country, and he opposed it vehemently. When he realised that Parliament would vote in favour of the alliance, he withdrew from politics entirely. He married the eldest daughter of Sir George Mackenzie of Rosehaugh, the celebrated Lord Advocate and heraldic writer. After the succession of George I, the Earl of Bute was appointed Commissioner for Trade and Police in Scotland, Lord Lieutenant of Bute and a lord of the bedchamber. During the rising of 1715 he commanded the Bute and Argyll militia at Inveraray, and through his vigilance kept that part of the country peaceful. His second son, having inherited his mother's estates of Rosehaugh, took the surname Mackenzie. He became a Member of Parliament and later envoy to Sardinia, Keeper of the Privy Seal and Privy Councillor.

John Stewart, the third Earl, was tutor to Prince George and became his constant companion and confidante. When his royal friend became George III, Bute was created a Privy Councillor and First Lord of the Treasury. He concluded a treaty with France in 1763 which brought the Seven Years' War to an end, but the terms were unpopular, and he was vilified by the press of the day. He retired from public life, having employed Robert Adam to build a

Stuart of Bute

splendid house at Luton Hoo in Bedfordshire. His heir, John Lord Mount Stuart, was born in 1767. He married the heiress of Patrick Crichton, the Earl of Dumfries. He succeeded his father as Earl of Bute in 1792, and in 1796 he was advanced to the rank of marquess. The second Marquess consolidated the family fortunes and expanded the estates on business-like lines. He was a noted industrialist who was largely responsible for modern Cardiff, where he developed the docklands to rival Liverpool. By 1900 millions of tons of coal were being handled there, making Cardiff the greatest coal port in the world. John, the third Marquess, inherited vast wealth at the tender age of six months. He grew to be a scholar, with wide interests, including heraldry, archaeology and mysticism. He rebuilt Castel Coch and Cardiff Castle as tributes to the high art of the Middle Ages.

The present chief, better known as the racing driver, Johnny Dumfries, succeeded his father, the sixth Marquess in 1993. The late Lord Bute was passionately concerned for Scottish heritage, and his efforts were recognised by a knighthood shortly before his death.

SUTHERLAND

ARMS
Gules, three mullets Or, on a bordure Or a Royal Tressure Gules

CREST
A cat-a-mountain sejant rampant Proper

MOTTO
Sans peur (Without fear)

SUPPORTERS
(on a compartment embellished with cotton-sedge plants) Dexter, a savage man wreathed about the head and loins with laurel Proper, holding in his exterior hand a club Gules resting upon his shoulder; sinister, another like savage sustaining in his sinister hand and against his shoulder, upon a staff ensigned of a coronet of an Earl, a bannerette Gules, charged of three mullets Or

PLANT BADGE
Cotton-sedge plant

A territorial name from the county of Sutherland in the north-east of Scotland. Sutherland was the 'Sudrland', or 'Southland', of the Norsemen who had by the tenth century conquered all of the islands of Scotland and much of the mainland as far south as Inverness. The family are probably of Flemish origin, descended from Freskin, whose grandson, Hugh, was granted land in Moray around the year 1130 by David I. Hugh acquired estates in Sutherland and was referred to as Lord of Sutherland. His son, William, became Earl of Sutherland around 1235, at a time when earldoms were accorded only to near kin of the Scottish kings. Hugh's brother, also William, remained in Moray. His family took the surname Murray, and he is the ancestor of the many powerful families who bear this name, including the Dukes of Atholl. The clan evolved around this powerful chief, who was strong enough to hold and protect the cathedral town of Dornoch.

Kenneth, fourth Earl of Sutherland, was killed with the regent of Scotland and three other earls while fighting against the English in 1333 at the Battle of Halidon Hill. William, the fifth Earl, was married first to Princess Margaret, daughter of Robert the Bruce and sister of David II. His son by her was heir to the throne prior to 1361, when he died of plague. William was murdered in 1370 by the Mackays in a feud which was to last for at least the next four centuries. Robert, the sixth Earl, William's son by his second marriage, built Dunrobin. He married the niece of Robert III in 1389. John, the eighth Earl, was declared unfit to manage his own affairs in 1494 at the insistence of his son-in-law, Adam Gordon, a younger son of the Earl of Huntly. He brought a further charge of idiocy against the earl's heir, and rounded things off with a charge of illegitimacy against Alexander Sutherland, the younger son of the eighth Earl, who was ultimately mysteriously murdered. Adam Gordon's wife then succeeded to the Sutherland lands and titles.

John, the sixteenth Earl, resumed the ancient surname of Sutherland, and in 1715, was Lord Lieutenant for the north of Scotland, including the islands. He called out his men for George I, and garrisoned Inverness against the Jacobites. His son, William, the seventeenth Earl, reconciled the Sutherlands to their ancient enemies, the Mackays, and settled the ancient feud at the start of the rising of 1745. The Earl of Cromarty, commanding the Jacobite forces in the north, occupied Dunrobin Castle but was defeated and captured by Sutherland's militia. Dunrobin thus became the first British castle to be captured with bloodshed in time of war.

The death of the seventeenth Earl, leaving an only daughter, Elizabeth, led to a legal battle over the succession to the title. Her right as a woman to succeed was challenged by the nearest male heirs, George Sutherland of Forse and Sir Robert Gordon of Gordonstoun, a descendent of the second marriage of the twelfth Earl. The House of Lords heard the case on 21 March 1771, and decided in Elizabeth's favour, confirming her as Countess of Sutherland in her own right. She married the Marquess of Stafford, of the prominent Leveson-Gower family. He was later created first Duke of Sutherland in 1833.

The first Duke was a keen reformer and progressive planner. He set up new industries on the coast and achieved his ends by ruthlessly clearing his tenants off the land, abandoning the customary obligations of a chief to his clan. He virtually destroyed the old ways of life in Sutherland, uprooting the pastoral inhabitants of the hills and glens and moving some of them to modern housing on the coast to work in industries, such as distilling, which he had financed. Stafford lost a great deal of money in his schemes, and although he was hated at first, he came to be respected by some at his death, although many could never forgive the clearances which his

Sutherland

policies had required.

The second Duke transformed Dunrobin from a traditional Scottish castle into a vast palace in the French chateau style through the work of the architect, Sir Charles Barry. Dunrobin was badly damaged by fire in 1915 and was later restored and partly remodelled by Sir Robert Lorimer. The third Duke contributed nearly a quarter of a million pounds for the building of the Highland railway, and had his own line built from Golspie to Helmsdale.

On the death of the fifth Duke, the chiefship of the clan and the earldom of Sutherland devolved upon his niece, Elizabeth, the present Countess of Sutherland. The dukedom, however, did not die out, and was inherited by the Earl of Ellesmere, a descendent of a younger son of the first Duke. There is accordingly now a separate earldom and dukedom of Sutherland, and the holders of both titles still live in Scotland. The fairy-tale Castle of Dunrobin, the principal seat of the chiefs and the largest house in the Highlands, remains in the family's possession, but is now open to the public.

SWINTON

ARMS
*Sable, a chevron Or between three boars' heads erased
Argent*

CREST
A boar chained to a tree Proper

MOTTO
J'espere (I hope)

On Compartment
Je pense (I think)

SUPPORTERS
*Two boars rampant Sable, armed, crined and unguled Or,
langued Gules*

BADGE
A boar's head erased Sable, armed Or, langued Gules

This family seems to be of Saxon origin, descended from nobles prominent in the kingdom of Northumberland which straddled the present-day border between England and Scotland. The name is said traditionally to have been acquired for their bravery and clearing the country of wild boar, and the family arms allude to this legend. The name is, however, more likely to be territorial. The village of Swinewood in the county of Berwick was granted by Edgar, son of Malcolm III, to Coldingham Priory in 1098. The Swintons' possession of their lands was confirmed by a charter of the Prior of Coldingham in the reign of William the Lion.

Edulph de Swinton received a charter, one of the first recorded in Scotland, confirming his property at Swinton from David I around 1140. Henry de Swinton appears on the Ragman Roll as one of the nobility swearing fealty to Edward I of England in 1296. He was joined in this by his brother, William, priest of the church of Swinton. Sir John Swinton, great-grandson of Henry, was a distinguished soldier and statesman in the reigns of Robert II and Robert III. He was a commander at the Battle of Otterburn in July 1388 when the Scots won the day, although their leader, Douglas, was slain. Swinton's second wife was the Countess of Douglas and Mar, but they had no issue. His third wife was Princess Margaret, who bore Swinton a son, later Sir John Swinton of Swinton, reckoned to be the fifteenth Lord of the name. He was a doughty warrior who fought at the Battle of Beaugh in France in 1420. Although the credit for this is claimed by others, he is said to have been the knight who slew the Duke of Clarence, brother of Henry V of England. The incident appears in Sir Walter Scott's poem, 'The Lay of the Last Minstrel'. He was killed at the Battle of Verneuil in France in 1424.

Sir John Swinton was among the band of

Scottish barons who signed the bond of protection of the infant James VI in 1567 against the Earl of Bothwell on his marriage to the child's mother, Queen Mary. In 1640 Sir Alexander Swinton, twenty-second of that Ilk, became sheriff of Berwickshire. He died in 1652, leaving six sons and five daughters. His second son, Alexander, was appointed to the Supreme Court of Scotland in 1688, taking the title, 'Lord Mersington'. The eldest son, John, was colonel for the regiment of Berwickshire, and at the Battle of Worcester in 1651, he was taken prisoner, and his brother, Robert, died in an attempt to carry off Oliver Cromwell's standard. John was later appointed by the Lord Protector to the Council of State he established to assist in ruling Scotland in 1655. His involvement with Cromwell led to his being tried for treason in 1661, and although he escaped the block, his estates were forfeited and he was imprisoned for six years. He died in 1679 and was succeeded by

his son, Alexander, who later died without issue. Alexander's brother, Sir John, succeeded as the twenty-fifth Laird of Swinton who, after a successful career as a merchant in Holland, returned to Scotland in the wake of the Revolution of 1688 which brought William of Orange to the throne with his wife, Queen Mary.

His father's forfeiture was rescinded, and Swinton sat in both the Scottish Parliament and, later, in the British, at Westminster. John Swinton of that Ilk, the twenty-seventh Laird, became a member of the Supreme Court in 1782, taking the title, 'Lord Swinton'. Captain George Swinton, descended from the Swintons of Kimmerghame, a cadet of the chiefly house, was Lord Lyon, King of Arms, and Secretary to the Order of the Thistle from 1926 to 1929. Major General Sir John Swinton, who still resides at Kimmerghame, is the Lord Lieutenant of Berwickshire. The present chief lives in Canada.

URQUHART

ARMS
Or, three boars' heads erased Gules, armed Proper and langued Azure

CREST
Issuant from a crest coronet Or, a naked woman from the waist upwards Proper, brandishing in her dexter hand a sword Azure, hilted and pommelled Gules, and holding in her sinister hand a palm sapling Vert

MOTTO
Meane weil speak weil and doe weil

SUPPORTERS
(on a compartment embellished with wallflower having four petals of yellow)
Two greyhounds Proper collared Gules, with leashes reflexed over their backs Or

STANDARD
The Arms in the hoist and of two tracts Gules and Or, upon which is depicted the Crest in the first compartment, the Badge in the second and third compartments, and in the fourth compartment a spray of wallflower Proper, flowered Or of four petals, along with the Motto 'Meane weil speak weil and doe weil' in letters Or upon three transverse bands Azure

PINSEL
Or, issuant from a crest coronet Or a naked woman from the waist upwards Proper, brandishing in her dexter hand a sword Azure, hilted and pommelled Gules, and holding in her sinister hand a palm sapling Vert within a strap Gules, buckled and embellished Or inscribed with the Motto 'Meane weil speak weil and doe weil' in letters also Or all within a circlet Argent fimbriated Sable bearing the title 'Urquhart of Urquhart' in letters Gules, and in the fly on an Escrol Gules surmounting a sprig of wallflower Proper flowered with four petals Or the Slogan 'The Urquhart' in letters Or

BADGE
A mermaid Proper, tailpart Gules, crined Or, and holding a harp Or

SLUGHORN
Trust and go forward

The name Urquhart is derived from a place name, Airchart, which is first recorded in an early life of the great Celtic saint, Columba. Today there is a Castle Urquhart on the banks of Loch Ness, and parishes of the same name in Elgin and the Black Isle. The meaning of the word itself has been variously translated from the Gaelic, including 'woodside', or 'by a rowan wood', or 'fort on a knoll'. One legend associated with Castle Urquhart concerns Conachar of the royal house of Ulster, who is said to have come to Scotland to fight for Malcolm III and was rewarded with the castle. Conachar was out hunting with his faithful hound when they were attacked by a massive and savage wild boar. Conachar was on the point of being gored when his dog attacked the beast, and although it died in the effort, it saved his master. This tale of a noble rescue from death in a hunting accident is common throughout Celtic history, but it is offered by some as an explanation of the boars' heads and the hounds which appear on the arms of the Urquhart chiefs.

Willliam de Urchard is said to have defended the Moote of Cromarty against supporters of the English Crown in the time of William Wallace. The Urquharts were hereditary sheriffs of Cromarty from the reign of David II. In the early sixteenth century, Thomas Urquhart of Cromarty is said to have sired twenty-five sons, seven of whom were killed at the Battle of Pinkie in 1547. The eldest son was Alexander, one of whose younger sons, John Urquhart, commonly known as the Tutor of Cromarty, was guardian of his famous grand-nephew, Sir Thomas Urquhart, who was himself born on the day of the day of the Battle of Pinkie.

Thomas Urquhart was knighted by James VI. His son, Sir Thomas Urquhart of Cromartie, was a student at Kings College in Aberdeen at the age of eleven. By the age of thirty he had become a scholar, writer of note and a soldier, and was knighted by Charles I in 1641. After the king's defeat in the civil war he travelled on the Continent and became familiar with the works of the French poet, Rabelais. His translation of Rabelais' work is still considered to be a masterpiece. Literary undertakings did not prevent his rejoining the royalist army, and he fought at the Battle of Worcester in 1651 where he was taken prisoner. He was imprisoned in the Tower of London, and while there published his family tree, which traced the origins of the Urquhart family to Adam and Eve. This may have been true, but it is doubtful whether Urquhart could have submitted appropriate proofs to satisfy the rigours of the present day Court of the Lord Lyon. When released, he returned to the Continent, where he died in 1660, allegedly from laughter while celebrating the Restoration.

Urquhart

Standard

Captain John Urquhart of Craigston, born in 1696, was ultimately a man of great wealth, but the origins of his fortune were shrouded in mystery. He was, however, called 'the pirate' by his family. He had been recruited into the Spanish navy, and probably amassed his fortune from the prize money paid for captured enemy vessels. He narrowly escaped death at the Battle of Sheriffmuir, fighting for the Jacobite cause. The Urquharts of Craigston rose to such social eminence that they were able to secure the services of the great Henry Raeburn to paint family portraits. Adam, son of William Urquhart of Craigston, became sheriff of Wigton. Craigston Castle in still in family hands.

Colonel James Urquhart rose for the 'Old Pretender' in 1715, and was severly wounded at the Battle of Sheriffmuir. In the last years of his life, he was the principal Jacobite agent in Scotland. With his death in 1741 the chiefship passed to his cousin, William Urquhart of Meldrum, a cautious Jacobite who avoided the disaster at Culloden. His cousin, Adam Urquhart of Blyth was more open in his loyalties and was a member of Bonnie Prince Charlie's court-in-exile at Rome. The last of this line, Major Beauchamp Urquhart, was killed in the Sudan at the Battle of Atbara in 1898.

In 1959, a descendent of the Urquharts of Braelangswell, whose family had emigrated to America in the eighteenth century, established his right to be chief of Clan Urquhart. The title of 'Urquhart of Urquhart' is now held by Wilkins Urquhart's son, Kenneth Trist Urquhart, recognised as the twenty-sixth chief of the clan. His seat in Scotland is now established at the ancient Urquhart stronghold of Castle Craig on the southern coast of the Cromarty Firth which was gifted to his father by Major Iain Shaw of Tordarroch as a unique symbol of amity between two great Highland names

WALLACE

T here are two principal theories for the origin of this name, both of which indicate an ancient British origin. The Waleis were originally Britons from Wales who held land in Shropshire and who may have come north with David I. More plausibly, it is believed that they were Britons who settled in the ancient kingdom of Strathclyde, having been driven north in the tenth century. The name is certainly found in records by the twelfth century in Ayrshire and Renfrewshire. Richard Walensis of Riccarton held land near Kilmarnock as a vassal of the High Steward of Scotland sometime before 1160. His grandson, Adam Walays, had two sons, the eldest of whom succeeded to the family estates in Ayrshire. Malcolm, Adam's younger son, received Elderslie and Auchinbothie in Renfrewshire. Malcolm was the father of the great Scottish patriot, Sir William Wallace of Elderslie.

Adam de Waleys appears on the Ragman Roll of nobles paying allegiance to Edward I of England in 1296, but Malcolm of Elderslie was one of very few Scottish nobles who bravely refused to submit to Edward. He and his eldest son, Andrew, were both executed. His wife fled with her younger son, William, to the protection of relatives near Dundee. William gathered a number of young men around him, including a cousin from the Riccarton branch of the family. When he heard that Sir John Fenwick, his father's executioner, was marching towards Dundee with a packed train of plunder from Scottish churches and monasteries, he determined to have his revenge. He met Fenwick at the path leading over Lowden Hill in Lanarkshire, and killed him. His success brought him many new followers, but to gain the support of the nobility he allied himself with Sir Andrew Murray, who was raising a revolt in the northeast. They were joined by the Grahams, the Campbells and the Earl of Lennox. There then began one of the earliest guerilla campaigns in military history. The English, unable to capture Wallace, indiscriminately executed a number of the Scots nobility, including his uncle, who had been lured into their hands to discuss possible peace terms. A full-scale revolt commenced in the south-west of Scotland, but when a strong English army marched to suppress it, resistance melted. Wallace was forced to flee to the north, where he gathered a small force. By 1297 he had gathered enough popular support to lay siege to Dundee. The English sent another great army under the Earl of Surrey and Hugo de Cressingham. Wallace met the English at Stirling Bridge, where his superior tactics carried the day against overwhelming English odds. He was knighted and granted the title 'Guardian of Scotland'. However, the guardian was defeated at a set-piece battle at Falkirk, when the English superiority of numbers finally prevailed and the Scots were defeated. Wallace escaped, but was later betrayed and taken to London, where he was tried for treason. At his trial it was argued that, as he owed no allegiance to the English king, no treason had been committed, but the outcome was predetermined, and Wallace was executed with great brutality.

Wallace

Standard

The Wallaces of Craigie descended from the uncle of the great patriot. They obtained the estate by marriage to the heiress of Sir John Lindsay of Craigie, and in 1669 Hugh Wallace of Craigie was created a Baronet of Nova Scotia. Sir Hugh married Esther Kerr, daughter of the Laird of Little Dean but sadly their only son was brain-damaged. On Sir Hugh's death, his grand-nephew, the grandson of his brother, the Reverend William Wallace of Falford, became the second Baronet. He was a distinguished lawyer who rose to the rank of

Lord Justice Clerk, the second-highest judge in Scotland. The third Baronet left an only daughter, and was succeeded by his brother, who had married a daughter of Sir Hew Wallace of Wolmet. Sir Thomas Wallace was the fifth Baronet, and when his son, a captain in the Guards, predeceased him, the estates passed to his daughter, Frances. In 1760 she married John Dunlop of Dunlop, the friend of the poet Robert Burns. His eldest son, Sir John Dunlop, succeeded his maternal grandmother as sixth Baronet of Craigie, and assumed the name of Wallace.

The representation of the chiefly line then passed to another cadet branch, the Wallaces of Cairnhill, who had lived in Jamaica for several generations. Through marriage to an heiress, they inherited estates in Ayrshire at Busbie and Clancaird. In 1888, Captain Henry Wallace of Busbie and Clancaird established himself as chief of the name. Robert Wallace of that Ilk received both the French and Belgian Croix De Guerre during the First World War. His son, Malcolm, who served in the Second World War, Korea, and Borneo, rose to the rank of colonel. He was succeeded in 1991 by his brother, Ian, the thirty-fifth chief.

WEDDERBURN

Wautier de Wederburn, who rendered homage to Edward I in 1296, is the first of this name who appears on record in Scotland. The lands of Wederburn lay in Berwickshire. References can also be found to John de Wedderburn living in 1364, and William de Wedderburn living between 1426 and 1452. However, the lands of Wedderburn passed at an early date to the family of Home.

Following the decline of the Borders Wedderburns, the family seems to have settled in Forfarshire. By the year 1400, four distinct yet closely related Wedderburn families could be found in Dundee and at Kingennie in Forfar. One of the Dundee families was that of James Wedderburn, whose three sons, James, John and Robert, were among the earliest Scottish Protestant reformers. They united to round the famous Guide and Godlie Ballads, otherwise known as the Wedderburn Psalms. From the eldest of these brothers descended James Wedderburn, Bishop of Dunblane in 1636, who, as the friend of Archbishop Laud and those responsible for introducing a new liturgy to the Church, was driven from Scotland in 1638. He retired to Canterbury, where he is buried in the cathedral. Two Dundee families are now extinct in the direct male line of Walter Wedderburn of Welgait and David Wedderburn, ancestor of the lairds of Craigie.

The fourth and by far the most important family of this name sprang from Robert Wedderburn. His grandson, Alexander, was clerk of Dundee from 1557 to 1582. Alexander's son, Wedderburn of Kingennie, was a favourite of James VI, and accompanied him to England in 1603. On his return to Scotland, the king presented him with a ring from his own hand. His descendents obtained a Crown charter in 1708 erecting the lands of Easter Powrie into a barony to be called Wedderburn. This branch of the family became extinct in the male line on the death of David Wedderburn of Wedderburn in 1761, and the estates passed to the Scrymgeours, who thereafter added the additional surname of Wedderburn to their own name. His brother, James, had a son, Alexander of Blackness, who was one of the commissioners to the Treaty of Ripon in 1641 and one of the deputation who went from Scotland to meet with the ill-fated Charles I at Newcastle in 1646. His son, Sir John Wedderburn, was an advocate at the Scottish Bar and Clerk of the Bills. He was created a baronet by Queen Anne in 1704. His grandson, Sir John, entered the army, and married and died in 1723. He had sold Blackness to his cousin, Sir Alexander, who also succeeded to the baronetcy. Alexander was deposed from the office of Clerk of Dundee for Jacobite sympathies. His eldest son was also a Jacobite, and served as a volunteer in Lord Ogilvy's regiment at the Battle of Culloden, where he was taken prisoner. He was convicted and executed for treason in 1746, when the baronetcy was forfeited. His eldest son, who was also at Culloden, survived and fled to Jamaica.

Sir David Wedderburn of Balindean, who was MP for Perth and Postmaster-General for Scotland, succeeded to the chiefship of the family, and in 1775 was created a baronet. Alexander Wedderburn, the great-grandson of the judge, Sir Peter Wedderburn of Gosford, became a distinguished lawyer in his own right, and Solicitor General for Scotland. He spoke against the Government's policies in the American colonies, and predicted that they would break away from the British Empire. He was created Lord Loughborough in 1780 and Earl of Rosslyn in 1801. He was succeeded in the earldom by his nephew, Sir James St Clair Erskine.

The chiefship of the family is now held within the family of the Scrymgeour-Wedderburns, the Earls of Dundee. By family arrangement, the chiefship of Wedderburn is held by the eldest son of the earl who is himself chief of the Scrymgeours. When the Wedderburn chief succeeds to the earldom, the chiefship passes to his heir.

WEMYSS

T his name is derived from the Gaelic 'uaimh', meaning 'cave', and is believed to be taken from the caves and ciffs of the Firth of Forth in that part of Fife where the family made its home. Wemyss in Fife has been the seat of the chiefs since the twelfth century. They are one of the few Lowland families directly descended from the Celtic nobility through the Macduff Earls of Fife.

In 1290, Sir Michael Wemyss and his brother, Sir David, were sent with Scott of Balwearie to Norway to bring back the infant Queen Margaret, the 'Maid of Norway'. In 1296, Sir Michael swore fealty to Edward I of England, but he changed his allegiance to Robert the Bruce, and Wemyss Castle was sacked by the English. In 1315 Wemyss witnessed the Act of Settlement of the Scottish Crown by Robert the Bruce at Ayr. His son, Sir David, was one of those who appended his seal to the famous Declaration of Arbroath in 1320. Sir David appeared again, as one of the guarantors for the release from English imprisonment of David II, and his son was one of the hostages for his ransom, as his descendent, Duncan, was later to be for the liberation of James I.

Sir David de Wemyss was killed at Flodden in 1513. His grandson, Sir John, fought under the Earl of Arran at the Battle of Pinkie in 1547. He was a great supporter of Mary, Queen of Scots, and it was at the newly enlarged Castle of Wemyss that she first met her future husband, Henry, Lord Darnley. In 1559 Sir John was made lieutenant of Fife, Kinross and Clackmannan, and led his men in the queen's army at Langside in 1568. His great-grandson, John Wemyss, was born in 1586. He was the second-born, but eldest-surviving son of Sir John Wemyss of that Ilk, by his second wife Mary Stewart. John was knighted in 1618 and created a Baronet of Nova Scotia in 1625, with a charter to the barony of New Wemyss in that province of Canada. Created a baron in 1628, he was later advanced to the title of Earl of Wemyss, the patent being presented to him personally by Charles I at Dunfermline. He was High Commissioner to the General Assembly of the Church of Scotland, a Privy Councillor and one of the Committee of the Estates. He died in 1649, and was succeeded by his only son, David, the second Earl. He died in 1679 after a lifetime nurturing the resources of his estate, particularly his salt and coal mines. Besides building on a large harbour at Methil, he greatly improved Wemyss Castle, where he entertained, in both 1650 and 1651, the newly crowned Charles II. Predeceased by his son, the title and estates fell to his daughter, Margaret, Countess of Wemyss, who married her cousin, Sir James Wemyss, later created Lord Burntisland. David, the third Earl succeeded his mother in 1705, when he took his seat in Parliament and was sworn a Privy Councillor and nominated one of the commissioners for the Treaty of Union with England. In 1707 he was constituted Vice Admiral of Scotland.

The fourth Earl, born in 1699, was described as 'a man of merit universal benevolence and hospitality the delight both of small and great'. He married Janet, heiress of Colonel Francis Charteris of Amisfield. In the Jacobite rising of 1745, the fourth Earl's eldest son, David, Lord Elcho, joined Prince Charles in Edinburgh. Appointed colonel of a troop of royal Horse Guards, he accompanied the prince into England, and was with him until his defeat at the Battle of Culloden. Elcho then escaped to France, and took part in the State entry of Prince Charles into Paris the following year. He was convicted of treason in his absence, and his estates were forfeited to the Crown. He continued to reside in France, and died childless in Paris in 1787. Consequent

Wemyss

upon the attainder, the Jacobite earl was succeeded by his second son, Francis, who changed his name to Charteris, the family name of his maternal grandmother. It is from Francis that the present Earl of Wemyss and March, whose seat is the magnificent Adam mansion of Gosford, is descended.

The estates in Fife and the chiefship of the name of Wemyss devolved upon the Earl's third son, the Honourable James Wemyss. He was MP for Sutherland, and married Lady Elizabeth Sutherland in 1757. His great-grandson married Millicent, the granddaughter of William IV, who, on the death of her husband in 1864, successfully took over the running of the estate for thirty years. Her son, Michael, married Lady Victoria Cavendish-Bentinck, the last surviving god-daughter of Queen Victoria. The present chief, David Wemyss of Wemyss who married Lady Jean Bruce, daughter of the Earl of Elgin, still has his principal seat at Wemyss Castle in Fife.

The Armigerous Clans and Families of Scotland

KEY TO SOURCES FOR ARMS

In those instances where alternative arms of a chiefly family exist, the sources for those listed in this section of the book are indicated in the text by superscript numerals and explained below:

[1] *The Public Register of All Arms and Bearings in Scotland.* The numbers given refer to particular volumes of the Lyon Register·

[2] Pont's Manuscript.

[3] Alexander Nisbet *System of Heraldry.*

[4] *Burke's General Armoury.*

[5] *Burke's Peerage.*

[6] Sir James Balfour-Paul *The Scots Peerage.*

[7] Balfour's Manuscript.

[8] Sir Robert Forman's Manuscript (often erroniously called Workman's Manuscript).

[9] Charles Norton Elvin *A Dictionary of Heraldry.*

[10] Sir George Mackenzie *Science of Herauldrie.*

[11] Thomas Crawfurd's Manuscript.

[12] R. R. Stoddart *Scottish Arms.*

[13] James Arnott *The House of Arnot.*

[14] Sir James Balfour-Paul *Ordinary of Scottish Arms.*

[15] Lyndsay of the Mount's Armorial.

ABERCROMBY

ARMS (of Birkenbog LR 1/117)[1]
Argent, a chevron Gules between three boars' heads erased Argent

CREST
A falcon rising belled Proper

MOTTO
Petit alta (He seeks high deeds)

On Compartment
Mercy is my desire

SUPPORTERS
Two greyhounds Argent collared Gules

The lands of Abercromby lie in the parish of the same name in the ancient kingdom of Fife. The earliest record of the name is found in the Ragman Roll in 1296, when William de Abercromby did homage to Edward I of England for his lands in Fife. The senior line of this family died out in the early seventeenth century and the representation of the line passed to the house of Abercromby of Birkenbog in Banffshire. The Abercrombys were to be no strangers to religious discord over the centuries. The lands of Birkenbog were originally church lands, and in 1362 the Earl of Mar confirmed to Alexander Abercromby his grant of lands by the Bishop of Aberdeen. Robert Abercromby, born in 1534, was a Jesuit priest who was violently opposed to the Reformation and to reform of the Scottish church, and is credited with the conversion to Catholicism of Queen Anne, wife of James VI, before her death. He was ultimately driven into exile when a substantial reward was offered for his capture. In 1637 Alexander Abercromby of Birkenbog was created a Baronet of Nova Scotia, but despite this royal favour he was to become a fervent Covenanter, strongly opposed to the attempts of Charles I to impose an episcopal church in Scotland. The Marquess of Montrose, in his famous campaign to restore the power of the king in Scotland, expressed his royal master's displeasure by quartering his troops on Birkenbog. David Abercromby was another Jesuit who studied abroad and returned to his native land to oppose the Protestant faith. He

was instead converted to it and published an important tract against papal power in 1682. Patrick Abercromby, third son of the Laird of Fetterneir, a branch of the House of Birkenbog, became a distinguished doctor, having graduated from the University of St Andrews in 1685. He travelled extensively abroad and on his return established a high reputation in his chosen field, being appointed personal physician to James VII. His brother, Francis, also enjoyed royal favour, being raised to the peerage under the title, 'Lord Glassford', a title limited to his own lifetime. A younger son of the first Baronet of Birkenbog had succeeded to estates at Tullibody in Clackmannanshire. This branch of the family was to prove most distinguished, producing two generals and a judge of the High Court. Sir Ralph Abercromby, born in 1734, was considered to be one of the greatest military reformers and has been credited with the restructuring of the army which was ultimately to defeat the threat of Napoleon. He was a professional soldier, entering the army in 1756 as a colonel in the 3rd Regiment of Dragoon Guards. By 1781 he had risen to the rank of colonel in the King's Irish Infantry. He served throughout the Seven Years' War and acquired considerable experience in that service. In 1795 he was appointed commander-in-chief of the British forces fighting against the French in the West Indies. His campaign met with great success and several new possessions fell to the British Crown, including the Spanish island of Trinidad. His most famous campaign, however, was to be in Egypt, where he commanded the troops who captured the strategic fortress of Aboukir and defeated the French in the decisive Battle of Alexandria. The general himself died of wounds he suffered during the engagement. His contribution to the ultimate defeat of Napoleon was recognised by his country when his widow was created a peeress in her own right, as Baroness Abercromby of Aboukir and Tullibody. Sir Ralph's younger brother, Sir Robert Abercromby, was also a general who was created a Knight of the Order of the Bath and commander-in-chief of the British forces in India. He was later to hold the post of governor of Edinburgh Castle for almost thirty years. Three sons of Sir Ralph also rose to high rank. His eldest son succeeded to the title of 'Lord Abercromby', while his second son became a general. James Abercromby became speaker of the House of Commons and was raised to the peerage as Lord Dunfermline. The various peerage titles are now all extinct but the house of Birkenbog still flourishes.

ABERNETHY

ARMS[3]
Or, a lion rampant Gules surmounted of a ribbon Sable

CREST[8]
A raven Sable, beaked and membered Gules

MOTTO[6]
Salus per Christum (Salvation through Christ)

SUPPORTERS[6]
Two falcons Proper, belled Or

A name of uncertain origin, according to Black, but probably from the lands of the same name in Strathearn. The name of the parish of Abernethy refers to a former Pictish royal residence, and an early Christian settlement in the reign of Nethan or Nectan, around 600. Orme, Abbot of Abernethy, granted part of the tithes of the abbey lands to the new abbey at Arbroath. Sir William de Abernethy was implicated in the murder of Duncan, Earl of Fife in 1288 and was condemned to die in prison. However, the fortunes of the family did not suffer greatly, and William de Abernethy, called Lord Saltoun, affixed his seal to the Declaration of Arbroath in 1320. David II added to the family holdings the lands of Rothiemay. Margaret, heiress of the last Abernethy Lord Saltoun, married Sir Alexander Fraser of Philorth whose son was declared by Parliament in 1669 to be Lord Saltoun. The arms of Abernethy are now to be found quartered with those of Fraser in the achievement of the present chief of that name, Lady Saltoun. Nisbet gives the principal cadet to be Abernethy of Auchnacloich, who used the arms of Abernethy differenced by a bordure. The name of Abernethy also lives on in the styles and titles of the Duke of Hamilton, whose ancestor, the first Marquess of Douglas, was additionally created Lord Abernethy in 1633. John Abernethy, a distinguished physician, is credited with assisting in the discovery of fulminate of mercury which, as an explosive, contributed to the development of modern handguns.

ADAIR

ARMS (of Kinhilt LR 1/241)[1]
Per bend Or and Sable three dexter hands apaumee and erect two and one Gules

CREST
A man's head couped and bloody

MOTTO
Loyal au mort (Loyal unto death)

The origin of this Gaelic name appears to be a variation of Edzaer and the first of the name is generally held to have been a son of Duvenald, a leader at the Battle of the Standard in 1138 and grandson of Donegal of Morton Castle, a descendent of whose had a charter from Robert the Bruce of the lands of Kildonan. Sir Andrew Agnew states, in his work on the hereditary sheriffs of Galloway, that 'in the Lochnaw charter chest various deeds prove the name Edzaer and Adair to have been interchangeable with the Galloway Adairs. In a charter dated 1625 the name is spelt in both forms on the same page'. Many of the Galloway Adairs went to Ulster during the time of the Elizabethan plantation and settled mainly in County Antrim. One Patrick Adair who settled in Antrim around 1641 became famous as the author of a major work on the rise of the Presbyterian Church in Ireland. James Adair, who died around 1783, was an American pioneer and wrote one of the earliest histories of the American Indians. The principal families recorded in the registers at the Lyon Court are those of Kinhilt and Genoch. Sir Robert Shafto Adair descended

from the house of Kinhilt was created a baronet on 2 August 1838 and his son was raised to the peerage as Baron Waveney of South Elmham, Suffolk. The peerage became extinct but the baronetcy devolved upon a younger brother, whose line continues to this day.

ADAM

ARMS (of Blair-Adam LR 11/8)[1]
Argent, a mullet Azure pierced of the Field between three cross crosslets fitchée Gules (quartered with Littlejohn and Brydon)

CREST
A cross crosslet fitchée Gules surmounted by a sword in saltire Proper

MOTTO
Crux mihi grata quies
(The cross gives me welcome rest)

The antiquity of this name is not in any doubt but it came to particular prominence in the family of Robert Adam, the celebrated architect, born in Kirkcaldy in 1728. Prior to this, however, Adam, Sub-Prior of Melrose, is shown as Abbot of Cupar in 1189, and Adam son of Adam is a witness to a charter by William Bruce to Adam of Carlisle of the lands of Kynemund. One Duncan Adam is stated by Anderson to have accompanied James, Lord Douglas, on his pilgrimage to the Holy Land with the heart of Robert the Bruce. William Adam, the father of the architects, Robert and James, and himself a distinguished architect, claimed descent from the knightly line of Duncan Adam. The Adam brothers were responsible for some of the most splendid classical buildings inside and outside

Scotland, the inspiration for which they drew from studying classical architecture in Italy for several years between 1754 and 1757. They have to their credit the homes of some of the most noble families in the land, including Hopetoun House, Culzean Castle and Gosford House, and in England Sion House, one of the seats of the Duke of Northumberland, and Luton Park in Bedfordshire. James Adam is known particularly as designer of Portland Place in London. The Adelphi buildings in the Strand in London are named after the two brothers, who participated jointly in this project. The family continued to give distinguished service through the line of John Adam of Blair Adam, which remains the family seat to this day. The Right Honourable William Adam of Blairadam was an eminent Scottish lawyer and is credited with the introduction of trial by jury in civil cases in Scotland. His son, Admiral Sir Charles Adam, was a Member of Parliament and Governor of Greenwich Hospital. General Sir Frederick Adam was wounded at Waterloo in 1815 and subsequently went to India to become Governor of Madras.

AIKENHEAD

ARMS (LR 1/238)[1]
Argent, three acorns slipped Vert

CREST
A demi-savage holding in his dexter hand three laurel slips fructed Proper

MOTTO
Rupto robore nati (We are born in a weak condition)

The ancient barony of Aikenhead was in Lanarkshire. Gilbert de Lakenhaued rendered homage for his lands in 1296. Black lists William de Aikenhead as a baillie of the burgh of Rutherglen in 1376 and William de Aikenhed as a notary public in Irvine in 1444. The connection with the legal profession appears to have been maintained, as James Aikenhead, claiming to represent Aikenhead of that Ilk, advocate and one of the commissioners of Edinburgh, is recorded as having been granted arms between 1672 and 1673 in the Lyon Court register. Nisbet states that this James was the son of David Aikenhead, Lord Provost of Edinburgh, described as 'eminent for his loyalty and virtue'. However, Black states that this is the same Lord Provost who features in a rhyme alluding to his face: 'if what is said were justly said, that head of Aiken timbers made, his fyrie face had long ago set all his head in blazing glow'. The barony of Aikenhead was apparently sold in the time of the Lord Provost's father but the name is still common in Lanarkshire.

AINSLIE

Although the surname of Ainslie is of great antiquity in Scotland, it was already prominent in England before the Norman Conquest. The Saxon lords of Annesley in Nottinghamshire held large estates, but they fled in the face of the advancing forces of William the Conqueror to Scotland, where they were received generously by Malcolm III. They soon became settled in lands around Dolphinstone. William de Ainslie, a canon of Glasgow Cathedral, witnessed a charter by Walter, Bishop of Glasgow, around 1208. In 1221 Thomas de Ainslie was one of the mediators appointed to settle a dispute between the monks of Kelso and the bishopric of Glasgow. Sir Aymer de Aynesley was a Borders knight sent to treat with the English to settle the marches in 1249. There are two references to the family in the Ragman Roll listing those who submitted to Edward I of England in

1296: John de Anesleye of Roxburghshire and Johan de Anesley of Cruwfurt in Lanarkshire. Robert de Ainslie, Baron of Dolphinstone, accompanied his kinsman Patrick, Earl of Dunbar and March, on a crusade to the Holy Land between 1248 and 1254. It seems likely that the Laird of Dolphinstone who swore fealty to Edward I was the crusader's son, John. The Ainslies were opposed to Robert the Bruce in his campaign to win the Scottish Crown and paid for this by the forfeiture of their estates. However, the family returned to favour when William de Ainslie, who had married Helen Kerr (of the family from which the present Duke of Roxburgh descends), became a favourite of Robert II. The estates of Dolphinstone were restored to him in 1377. The Ainslies secured their fortunes by strategic alliances by marriage with other prominent Borders families. They intermarried with the Pringles, Douglases, Homes and Kerrs. Marjory, daughter of John Ainslie, married Mark Kerr of Cessford, a doughty warrior known as the Terror of the Borders. He was killed at the Battle of Pinkie in 1547. Robert Ainslie, a lawyer who was to become a friend and confidant of the poet Robert Burns, was born on 13 January 1766. He made the poet's acquaintance in Edinburgh in the spring of 1787, and they travelled through the Borders together, Ainslie being received at Burns' family home. He later visited Burns at Ellisland where he was given a manuscript copy of *Tam o' Shanter*, which he later presented to the writer Sir Walter Scott. One of his brothers, Sir Whitelaw Ainslie, was medical superintendent of the Southern Division of India and the author of a detailed work on Indian native medicine. He was a regular contributor to the *Edinburgh Magazine,* and wrote a number of plays. Sir Robert Ainslie was the British ambassador to the Ottoman Empire at Constantinople from 1776 to 1792. He also served as a Member of Parliament and was created a baronet in 1804. He is now best remembered for three volumes of drawings and sketches of Egypt. The Ainslie arms clearly allude to their early crusading exploits

but even in more recent times they have enjoyed high military rank. General Charles de Ainslie commanded the 93rd Highland Regiment, which has now passed into legend as the 'Thin Red Line', at the Battle of Balaclava in 1854. The family were also distinguished lawyers, and David Ainslie of Costerton, who died in 1900, left a fortune amassed from his legal practice to build the Astley Ainslie Hospital in Edinburgh. There is a memorial to the Ainslie family on the wall of the parish church of South Leith.

AITON

ARMS (of that Ilk LR 1/113)[1]
Argent, a cross engrailed between four roses Gules

CREST
A hand pulling a rose Proper

MOTTO
Decerptae dabunt odorum (Roses plucked will give sweet smell)

This name, perhaps more commonly spelt 'Ayton', probably derives from the lands of Ayton in Berwickshire. The name itself is given by Black to mean a town on the banks of the River Aye. The original progenitor of the family is believed to have been an Anglo–Norman knight, Gilbert, who obtained the lands of Aiton in the eleventh century, and assumed the name as his designation. Steffan, son of Swan de Aeitun, granted lands to Coldingham Priory, around 1170. There is believed to have been an ancient castle at Ayton, which would undoubtedly have been the scene of many border disputes, and Matthew of Ayton is listed as a Scots prisoner held at Chester Castle in 1296. The principal family ended in an heiress who married

George Hume, and the greater part of the family lands then passed into that family until James, son of the sixth Earl of Hume, had his estates forfeited for following the Jacobite cause in the rising of 1715. Andrew Ayton is listed by Macgibbon and Ross as a 'Master of the Works' who made purchases for the king, collected the tax of spears in Fife and conveyed money to the Master of Artillery. He superintended works at Stirling Castle until 1511. According to Anderson, this Andrew was a son of the house of Ayton of that Ilk and he received lands at Denmuir in Fife. Sir Robert Ayton was a distinguished poet and some time ambassador to the German Emperor and secretary to Henrietta Maria, wife of the ill-fated Charles I. The traditional family lands are dominated by the great Castle of Ayton which is one of the triumphs of Victorian baronial architecture. The present owner is a former Grand Master Mason of Scotland who is no doubt proud of the connection, through the land, to a former Master of the King's Works at Stirling Castle.

ALLARDICE

Black states that this is not a very common name, 'but all who hold it believe in their descendent from the old family which was settled on the banks of the Bervie water'. The ancient barony of Allardice, sometimes styled

'Alrethes', lies in Kincardineshire near the parish of Arbuthnott. Nisbet states that William the Lion granted a charter to the family of the lands of Allrethis, and since that time the surname of the family has been taken

ARMS (of that Ilk)[3,4]
Argent, a fess wavy Gules between three boars' heads erased Sable

CREST[4]
A demi-savage holding in the dexter hand a scimitar all Proper

MOTTO[4]
In the defence of the distressed

from those lands. Thomas Allardice of that Ilk received lands from David II, and Sir James Allardice was Clerk of the King's Treasury and Archdeacon of Moray around 1478. In 1662 Sir John Allardice of that Ilk, described by Anderson, as 'Chief of that ancient family', married Mary, sister of the Earl of Menteith. This line ended when the last heir of Allardice, Sarah Allan, married Robert Barclay of Urie, MP for Kincardineshire in 1776. Their granddaughter, Margaret Barclay Allardice, claimed, by descent from her Allardice blood, the earldoms of Strathearn, Monteith and Airth, as last of the line descended from Prince David, son of Robert II. She assumed by royal licence of 2 July 1883 the name and arms of Barclay-Allardice. The family continued to prosper, having taken up residence in England, but the present successors to this noble line now use the name of Barclay alone.

ANDERSON

ARMS[3]
Argent, a saltire engrailed Sable between four mullets Gules

As St Andrew is the patron saint of Scotland, it is perhaps not surprising that the name 'son of Andrew' is common over much of the country. The Gaelic derivation of the name 'Gilleaindreas', gives the name 'Macandrew' and other variations. Grimble states that although arms were granted to an Anderson of that Ilk in the sixteenth century, the name is so widespread that no exact place of origin can be established. Black lists Andersons as burgesses of Peebles, and also in the county of Dumfries. John Anderson was commissioner to Parliament for Cupar in 1585. Alexander Anderson was a famous mathematician born near Aberdeen, who later settled in Paris, where he published works on geometry and algebra. His kinsman, David Anderson of Finshaugh, had a similar scientific bent and is renowned for removing, by the application of science and mechanics, a large rock obstructing the entrance to Aberdeen harbour. William Anderson published his famous biographical history of the people of Scotland, *The Scottish Nation,* in three volumes in 1863. He praised the more charitable activities of the family by stating that David Anderson (the rock remover) was also 'rich enough and generous enough to found and endow a hospital in Aberdeen for the maintenance and education of ten poor orphans'. In the twentieth century, the name is remembered for the famous Anderson shelters, bomb shelters designed on the orders of John Anderson, Viscount Waverley, during the Second World War. There is no chiefly line at present but the major cadet branches have been identified as those of Dowhill, West Ardbreck and Candacraig. The Anderson Clan Society was formed in 1973 and is now active throughout the world, and a clan room and archival display are maintained at Wisby House, Kirtlebridge in Dumfriesshire.

ARMSTRONG

ARMS (of Mangerton)[3]
Argent, three pallets Azure

CREST
An arm from the shoulder, armed Proper

The legends and traditions of this powerful Borders family hold that the first of the name was Siward Beorn ('sword warrior'), also known as Siward Digry ('sword strong arm'), who was the last Anglo–Danish Earl of

Northumberland and a nephew of King Canute, the Danish king of England who reigned until 1035. The family is said to have been related by marriage both to Duncan, King of Scots and William the Conqueror, Duke of Normandy and King of England. The name was common over the whole of Northumbria and the Borders, and the Armstrongs became a powerful and warlike border clan in Liddisdale and the debateable border land. Black lists Adam Armstrong as being pardoned at Carlisle in 1235 for causing the death of another man and Gilbert Armstrong, steward of the household of David II, as ambassador to England in 1363. The Armstrongs continued to expand their influence into the valleys of the Esk and Ewes, and in about 1425 John, brother of Armstrong of Mangerton, in Liddisdale, built a strong tower. The Armstrongs were said to be able to raise three thousand horsemen and at one point were in virtual control of the debateable land. In 1528 the English warden of the marches, Lord Dacre, attacked and raised the Armstrong tower but the Armstrong response was to burn Netherby. The Armstrongs' power was seen as a threat by James V to his own authority and, according to tradition, the king tricked John of Gilnockie to a meeting near Hawick, where the king hanged the laird without further ado. The historian Pitscottie attributes to Armstrong the brave retort that 'King Harry would downweigh my best horse with gold to know I were condemned to die this day'. King James was to rue his treatment of the Armstrongs when they failed to support him at the Battle of Solway Moss in 1542. The union of the Crowns in 1603 brought an official end to the Anglo–Scottish border wars and the last of the Armstrong lairds was hanged in Edinburgh in 1610 for leading a reiving raid on Penrith. A ruthless campaign followed as the Crown attempted to pacify the Borders. The families were scattered and many sought new homes in Ulster, particularly in Fermanagh. Armstrong is now among the fifty most common Ulster surnames. There have been many distinguished Armstrongs, including Sir Alexander Armstrong, the Arctic explorer and, in keeping with the Armstrong spirit of adventure, the most far-travelled must be Neil Armstrong, the first man to walk upon the moon. There has been no trace of the Armstrong chiefs since the dispersal of the clan in the seventeenth century, but a powerful and active clan association is in existence and the Clan Armstrong Trust was established in 1978.

ARNOTT

ARMS[13]
Argent, a chevron Sable, between three mullets Gules

The origin of this name appears to be territorial, from the lands of that name in the parish of Portmoak in Kinross-shire. Black states that the family was settled there from the middle of the twelfth century and the lands were in the possession of Michael de Arnoth in 1284. According to Nisbet, the family of Arnott of that Ilk held lands in Fife, and Michael De Arnoth was sent as one of two knights escorting Duncan, Earl of Fife, as ambassador to England in 1340. David Arnott, Archdeacon of Lothian in 1502, later became Bishop of Galloway. Sir Michael Arnott of that Ilk was created a baronet by Charles I on 27 July 1629. His successors favoured military careers and held high rank for the next five generations. This line became extinct when the sixth baronet died without heirs. The other principal families are listed as Arnott of Woodmiln, Balkaithlie, Balcormo and Eastrynd. Hugo Arnott, who succeeded to the Balcormo estates through his mother and assumed the name 'Arnott of Balcormo', was a well-known lawyer, antiquarian and historian who, in 1785, published a work on celebrated criminal trials in Scotland. His appearance as a principal character in Kay's *Edinburgh Portraits*, demonstrates his renown as a character in that city.

AUCHINLECK

ARMS (of that Ilk LR 1/241)[1]
Argent, three bars Sable

CREST
An ear of rye Proper

MOTTO
Pretiosum quod utile (What is useful is valuable)

Nisbet states that the chiefs of this surname had lands in the county of Angus, and took their name from those lands. However, there is also a barony of Auchinleck in Ayrshire, and in 1300 the Laird of Auchinleck is reputed to have followed Sir William Wallace to Glasgow where he fought and slew the Northumbrian Earl Percy. Black states that John of Aghelek, otherwise Achinfleck, is the first recorded of the Angus family of the name and did homage in 1306. The origin of the name may be purely descriptive of the topography of the land it describes: 'auchen' seems to be applied to raised or higher land separating areas of water, while 'lech' may indicate dead, in the sense of barren or sterile. The Angus Auchinlecks held the office of hereditary armour bearers to the Earls of Crawford and lived in the substantial tower known as Affleck near the village of Monikie. The tower passed out of the hands of the family but still stands to this day (it is described in Nigel Tranter's *Fortified House in Scotland*, volume four). The family married into the distinguished family of Boswell, through one of the daughters of Sir John Auchinleck of that Ilk, and adopted the style 'of Auchinleck'. James Boswell, the famous biographer of Samuel Johnson, was a member of this family. General Sir Claude Auchinleck was commander-in-chief in India in 1941 when Winston Churchill, the British Prime Minister, assigned him to lead the Allied offensive in the western desert of Egypt and India. He led the British Eighth Army at the first battle of El Alamein in July 1942. The battle was indecisive, and Auchinleck was replaced by Bernard, later Field Marshal, Montgomery, who went on to lead the Eighth Army in a second attack on El Alamein in October, breaking Rommel's Afrika Korps and securing an important victory for the Allies at a crucial time in the war.

BAILLIE

ARMS (of Lamington LR 10/75)[1]
Quarterly, 1st & 4th grand quarters, Azure, nine stars of six points wavy three, three, two and one, Or (Baillie); 2nd grand quarter, counterquartered, (I) & (IV), Argent, a chevron Gules, between three boars heads erased Azure, langued of the Second, on a chief wavy of the Third a sphinx couchant of the Field (Cochrane); (II) & (III), Argent, on a saltire Sable, nine lozenges of the Field (Blair); 3rd grand quarter, counterquartered, (I) & (IV), Gules, three lions rampant Argent (Ross); (II) & (III), Argent, a man's heart Gules, within a fetterlock Sable, on a chief Azure, three boars' heads erased of the Field (Lockhart)

CRESTS
*(1) A boar's head erased Proper (Baillie)
(2) Issuing from a naval crown Or, a dexter arm embowed vested Azure cuffed Argent, the hand holding a flagstaff Proper thereon hoisted the flag of a rear admiral of the white being Argent a cross Gules, and thereon the words 'St Domingo' in letters of gold
(3) A horse trotting, Argent*

MOTTO
Quid clarius astris (What is brighter than the stars?)

The most likely derivation of this name is from the French 'baillie', meaning 'bailiff' or 'steward'. This was an office of great importance in medieval times. One of the earliest records of the name appears in 1311 when William de Baillie appears as juror in a case concerning land in Lothian. Nisbet records that, according to family tradition, the Baillies of Lamington were truly a branch of the great house of Balliol, Lords of Galloway and sometime kings of Scots. The family was said to have changed its name due to the unpopularity of the Balliol kings after the succession of Robert the Bruce. There is, however, no real evidence to support this tradition, particularly as the name Balliol remained fairly widespread in Scotland after that time. William Baillie of Hoprig was knighted by David II in 1357 and received a royal charter to the barony of Lamington in 1368. The lands remained in the family until the present time. Sir William established the family fortunes and from him are descended the Baillies of Carphin, Park, Jerviston, Dunrogal, Carnbroe, Castlecarry, Provand and Dochfour. Alexander Baillie, a younger son of Lamington, fought at the Battle of Brechin in 1452 and was rewarded by the Earl of Huntly with the lands of Dunain and Dochfour near Inverness. He was also appointed constable of Inverness Castle. The family played a prominent part in affairs around the Highland capital, and formed alliances by marriage to many notable local families. Cuthbert Baillie of Carphin was Lord High Treasurer to James IV in 1512. Sir William Baillie of Provand was called to the Bench in 1566, taking the title of 'Lord Provand'. He was Lord President of the Court of Session from 1565 to his death in 1595. The principal house of Lamington suffered the vagaries of fortune after having risen high in royal favour when Sir William Baillie married Janet Hamilton, daughter of James, Earl of Arran and Duke of Chatelherault. He was made Master of the Wardrobe to Queen Mary in 1542. Faithful to her daughter, Mary, Queen of Scots, they fought at the Battle of Langside in 1568, after which the estates were declared forfeit. His grandson was the famous General Baillie who was soundly defeated by the Marquess of Montrose at the Battles of Alford and Kilsyth in 1645. The general had two sons, both of whom married daughters of the Lord Forrester of Corstorphine, to whose estates they eventually succeeded. The Reverend Robert Baillie, descended from the house of Jerviston, was a renowned Protestant minister and chaplain to the Covenanter armies in 1639. His daughter, Margaret, was to marry a Walkinshaw of Barrowfield, ancestor of the celebrated Clementina Walkinshaw, the mistress of Prince Charles Edward Stuart, the 'Young Pretender'. Robert Baillie of Jerviswood was also a staunch Protestant, whose outspoken views on civil and religious liberty were ultimately to result in his death. A cadet of the Lamington family, he was planning to emigrate to South Carolina in 1683, believing that there was no escape from the oppression of the government of the time. He was also in correspondence with leaders of the faction opposed to the succession of James VII in England, and prior to his intended journey he went to London to consult with the Duke of Monmouth (later involved in a rebellion, and executed) and others. Baillie had no connection with any conspiracy to overthrow the government but he was nevertheless arrested and charged with conspiracy to commit high treason. He was convicted in the High Court at Edinburgh on 24 December 1684 and sentenced to be hanged the same day. His family was forced to flee to Holland and the estates were not restored until the overthrow of James VII in 1688. Lady Grizel Baillie, the poet and songwriter, who died in 1746, was the wife of George, the ill-fated Laird of Jerviswood's son. This branch of the family was ultimately to succeed by marriage to the earldom of Haddington, a title which they still hold. In 1894, James Evan Baillie of Dochfour married the daughter of the first Baron Burton, the great Victorian industrialist. Lord Burton died without male issue and the peerage has now passed to the Baillies of Dochfour, who still have a great estate on the shores of Loch Ness.

BAIRD

ARMS (of Auchmedden LR 1/120)[1]
Gules, a boar passant Or

CREST
A gryphon's head erased Proper

MOTTO
Dominus fecit (The Lord has done this)

The coat of arms of this family proclaim the legend of its origin which, like so many, involves a feat of strength which saves the life of a king. This version states that the first Baird saved William the Lion from a wild boar. The name appears to be territorial, from lands held by the family in Lanarkshire near the village of Biggar. Henry Debard witnessed a deed by Thomas De Hay between 1202 an 1228. Richard Baird received land at Meikle and Little Kyp in Lanarkshire, during the reign of Alexander III. Anderson states that Fergus Debard, John Bard and Robert Bard, who swore submission to Edward I of England at the end of the thirteenth century, are supposed to be of the family of Baird of Kyp. The principal family of the name came to be that holding the lands of Auchmedden in Aberdeenshire, whose influence in that county was strengthened by marriage into the powerful Keith family, Earls Marischal of Scotland. James Baird, a younger son of the house of Auchmedden, became an advocate in Edinburgh and his son, John, was created a baronet and then a High Court judge under the title of 'Lord Newbyth'. His splendid house of Newbyth in East Lothian still stands. The estate of Auchmedden passed into the hands

of the Earls of Aberdeen and, according to local tradition, a pair of eagles which had regularly nested on the nearby crags left the area, fulfilling an ancient prophecy by Thomas the Rhymer, that 'there shall be an eagle in the craig while there is a Baird in Auchmedden'. Lord Haddow, eldest son of the Earl of Aberdeen, married a younger daughter of William Baird of Newbyth, and the eagles returned. They reputedly fled again when the estate passed to another branch of the Gordon family. Sir David Baird, who succeeded his second cousin in the baronetcy of Newbyth, was one of the leading soldiers of his time and saw action in India and throughout the Napoleonic Wars. The name gained prominence again in the twentieth century through John Logie Baird, the pioneer of television. In 1926 he demonstrated the first television transmission, and he remained heavily involved in its development until his death in 1946.

BALFOUR

ARMS (LR 32/16)[1]
Argent, on a chevron Sable, an otter's head erased of the Field

CREST
A dexter arm in armour erect the hand holding a baton in bend Gules tipped Argent

MOTTO
Fordward (Forward)

SUPPORTERS
Two otters rampant Proper

The lands of Balfour, or Bal-orr, lie in the parish of Markinch in Fife. The Orr is a tributary of the River Leven. According to tradition, the lands were given to Siward, a Northumbrian, during the reign of Duncan I. The earliest dependable record of the name is a charter of William the Lion in favour of Michael de Balfour around 1196. Sir Duncan de Balfour supported the cause of Sir William Wallace and was killed at the Battle of Blackironside in 1298, although the engagement was a great victory for the Scots. Sir

John Balfour of Balfour died in 1375 and his estates passed to his only daughter, Margaret, wife of Sir Robert de Bethune. The Bethunes of Balfour were to flourish and figure prominently in Scottish history through such personalities as Cardinal Bethune and Mary Beaton, celebrated as one of the 'four Maries', the ladies-in-waiting of Mary, Queen of Scots. The Balfours continued through the descendents of Adam, the brother of Sir John Balfour, who married into the powerful Macduff Earls of Fife. Adam died of wounds sustained at the Battle of Durham in 1346 and his son was brought up in the household of the earl. He prospered greatly by his family connections and from him descend the Balfours of Denmylne, Forret, Torry and Kinloch. James Balfour of Denmylne was killed at the siege of Roxburgh in 1460 and his son John died, along with the greater part of the Scottish nobility, at the Battle of Flodden in 1513. Sir Michael Balfour was Comptroller of the

Household to Charles I and fought for the king's cause during the civil war. Sir James Balfour, son of Sir Michael Balfour of Denmylne, was created Lord Lyon, King of Arms, in June 1630. He was a distinguished heraldic scholar and antiquary who wrote a number of important treatises on heraldry. He was also a chronicler of the Scottish monarchy, and his *Annals and Short Passages of State* was published in book form almost two centuries later, in 1824. Sir Andrew Balfour, Baronet, also of the house of Denmylne, was a distinguished botanist and founder of the Botanic Garden of Edinburgh (which now flourishes as the Royal Scottish Botanical Garden). He was also a noted physician and the first president of the Royal College of Physicians in Scotland. He died in 1694. Sir James Balfour of Forret was knighted in 1674 and elevated to the Supreme Court in Edinburgh taking the judicial title, 'Lord Forret'. He was subsequently appointed judge of the High Court of Justiciary. Another branch of the family, the Balfours of Burleigh, were raised to the peerage with the title of 'Lord Balfour of Burleigh', in 1606. The fifth Lord Balfour of Burleigh brought the family's fortunes to a very low ebb at the start of the eighteenth century. He formed a strong romantic attachment to a girl considered to be of 'unsuitable' family, and his father sent him abroad, hoping that time and distance would cool his ardour. The infatuated Master of Burleigh swore his undying love to the girl and promised that if she married anyone else

in his absence he would kill him. Time passed and the girl put aside Balfour's threat and married Henry Stenhouse, a local schoolmaster. On his eventual return the Master of Burleigh made immediate enquiry after his love, and on learning the truth, sought out the schoolmaster and shot him in the shoulder. Stenhouse died of his wounds some days later. Balfour was tried before the High Court in August 1709 and despite a most ingenious defence he was sentenced to death. He escaped from prison by changing clothes with his sister, and he went into hiding. He succeeded to the title on the death of his father in 1713. He joined the cause of the 'Old Pretender' in the rebellion of 1715, for which he was declared a traitor. His title and estates were forfeited by an Act of Attainder in November 1715. He died unmarried in 1757. The attainder was reversed in 1869 in favour of Mary, the heir of Lord Balfour's sister, who had bravely taken his place in the condemned cell. Alexander, sixth Lord Balfour of Burleigh, was a Knight of the Thistle and Secretary of State for Scotland from 1895 to 1903. Arthur James Balfour, who was descended from the Balfours of Balbirnie, was Prime Minister from 1902 to 1905, and was created Earl of Balfour in May 1922. In 1843, William Balfour of Trenabie in Orkney proved his descent from the principal family, and received a grant of supporters from the Lord Lyon, King of Arms, as representer and head of the house. The arms were rematriculated in 1936.

BANNATYNE

This name is often alternately rendered as 'Ballantyne', and even in the same family the two forms can be found used interchangeably in the same generation. The origin of the name seems likely to derive from the lands of Bellenden in Selkirk. The lands of Glenmaddy, the 'wolf glen', lie on the south bank of the Euchan Water in Nithsdale, and they came into the possession of the Bannatynes in the fifteenth century. Roland Bannatyne of

Glenmaddy also received lands in the barony of Sanquhar from Lord Crichton in 1548. The land grant was witnessed by John Bannatyne of Cog. The Laird of Cog did not fare as well at the hands of the Crichtons as his kinsman, as in May 1557 John Crichton received lands forfeited from John Bannatyne of Cog who was now a fugitive from the law. In 1499 Patrick Bellenden obtained a charter from the Earl of Morton of the lands of Auchinoul in

Midlothian. His daughter, Catherine, married Oliver Sinclair, a favourite of James V and general of the Scottish army at the rout of Solway Moss in 1542. His son, Thomas, was appointed a judge of the Court of Session in 1535, and in 1539 he was raised to the rank of Lord Justice Clerk, a post subsequently held by both his son and grandson. George Bannatyne, a compiler of Scottish poetry of the fifteenth and sixteenth centuries, was born in Newtyle in Forfarshire on 22 February 1545. His collection of poetry was written during a period of retirement at Bannatyne House in Forfarshire, during the plague which ravaged Edinburgh in 1568. His work was considered so important by the Scottish literary giant, Sir Walter Scott, that he named after him the literary club which he founded in 1823. The Bannatyne Club subsequently published George Bannatyne's work in book form, along with many other previously inaccessible Scottish works. Richard Bannatyne was secretary to the Scottish Protestant reformer, John Knox, and compiler of *Memorials of Transactions in Scotland from 1569 to 1573*. He appeared on several occasions before the General Assembly of the Church of Scotland to speak on behalf of John Knox when he was ill. After Knox's death in 1572, Bannatyne was appointed by the Church to put in order all the papers left by him. He completed the task in 1575 and died in September 1605. Sir Lewis Bellenden of Auchinoul accompanied James VI on his journey to marry the daughter of the king of Norway in 1589. He was thereafter sent to the court of Elizabeth I of England, where he strongly promoted his royal master's ambitions to be recognised as the queen's heir. He was rewarded for his services by numerous grants of land, including the barony of Broughton (now part of the city of Edinburgh). James Bannatyne of Newhall was also made a judge in February 1626, taking the title, 'Lord Newtyle'. The Bannatynes of Kames are recorded as being in possession of their lands and the Castle of Kames as early as the fourteenth century. The castle, which would originally have been a single defensive tower, was later extended by the addition of a fine mansion house by Sir William Bannatyne, later Lord Bannatyne, in the early eighteenth century. Lord Bannatyne was a distinguished lawyer and judge who thrived in the intellectual and literary circles of eighteenth-century Edinburgh. He died at the age of 91 in 1833. His Edinburgh mansion, Whiteford House, is now a retirement home for ex-servicemen. The Ballantynes of Peebles were to become extremely prominent in the Scottish wool trade in the eighteenth century, a connection which they carry on to the present day. In 1829 they were instrumental in the establishment of the trade in Scottish tweed.

BAXTER

A name which, like so many others, is derived from an occupation: in this case, that of baker. The importance of bread as a staple food meant that the baker's was a role of importance and was vital to the existence of any household. The name appears throughout Scotland, and those on the west coast are generally held to be dependents of the Clan Macmillan. In Fife, however, the name achieved independent prominence, and Baxters are found witnessing important documents in the thirteenth century. Black lists Reginald Baxter as a witness to a gift to the church of Wemyss between 1200 and 1240, and Jeffrey le Baxtere of Lissithe in the county of Forfar taking an oath of fealty in 1296. He suggests that, as Forfar maintained a royal residence at that time, these Baxters may have been bakers to the royal household – an early version of 'by appointment'. The name is still prominent in Fife, where until recently, the Baxters of Earlshall resided in their baronial castle which has one of the finest painted heraldic ceilings in Scotland.

BELL

ARMS (of Provesthaugh LR 1/250)[1]
Azure, a fess between three bells Or

CREST
A roe feeding Proper

MOTTO
Signum pacis amor (Love is the token of peace)

The Borders family of Bell may well descend from a Norman follower of David I who reigned until 1153 and was, by the end of the thirteenth century, well established in Dumfriesshire, Berwickshire and Perthshire. The name may derive from the French 'bel', meaning 'fair' or 'handsome'. Since the derivation is descriptive, common ancestry cannot be assumed for all those bearing the surname. The arms attributed to the principal family are in the nature of canting, or punning, heraldry, alluding to the pronunciation of the name rather than its origin. The suggestion that it relates to living beside a bell tower seems far fetched. The Bells participated in the Borders disturbances as one of the riding clans of border reivers. In the thirteenth century Gilbert Le Fitzbel held lands in Dumfries. Sir David Bell was Clerk of the Wardrobe to Robert II. In 1426 William Bell's lands of Kirkconnel were confirmed by James I under a charter recorded in the register of the great seal. The Bells, along with other Borders families, became increasingly turbulent throughout the fifteenth and sixteenth centuries. The Crown's determination to pacify the Borders led in 1517 to the Clan Bell receiving royal letters of warning to keep the peace. The tower of Blacket House was destroyed in a raid by the English in 1547. After the union of the Crowns in 1603 the family suffered much the same fate as the other border reivers: many emigrated to the new plantation lands in Ulster, where the name is among the twenty most numerous in that province. Others settled further afield throughout Australia and New Zealand. The descendents of the Lairds of Blacket House stayed in the realm but moved to the cities where they contributed substantially to learning and in particular medical science. Andrew Bell, founder of the Madras system of education, was born at St Andrews in 1753. The college founded in his native town and named after his system is still a respected seat of education today. Dr Joseph Bell, great-grandson of Benjamin Bell of Blacket House, who was himself a distinguished surgeon, is said to have inspired Sir Arthur Conan Doyle to create his great detective, Sherlock Holmes. General Sir John Bell was a distinguished soldier during the Napoleonic Wars and a friend of the Duke of Wellington. Scottish lawyers encounter the name of Bell in their study of *Principals of the Law of Scotland* by George Joseph Bell, Professor of Scots Law at the University of Edinburgh in 1829. More recently, Alexander Graham Bell was a pioneer in the development of the telephone. Although the Bells were a Borders family, there are others of this name who are of Highland origin, and in that case, Bell is held to be a sept of Macmillan.

BELSHES

ARMS (of that Ilk LR 1/250)[1]
Paly of six Or and Gules, a chief vairy Azure and Or

CREST
A greyhound's head couped Argent collared Azure

MOTTO
Fulget virtus intaminata (Virtue shines unstained)

The barony of Belshes is part of the lordship of Jedburgh in the county of Roxburghshire. Black states that the name may derive from Bellasis, near Coulommières in Seine-et-Marne, France. There were lands of the same name in Northumberland. Richard de Belchis had sufficient status to own a seal, which is shown by Henry Lang in his catalogue, *Ancient Scottish Seals* (published in 1850), as appended to a deed in 1296. Nisbet gives the principal family as Belches of that Ilk and shows a cadet family, Belches of Tofts. Alexander Belches of Tofts was a burgess of Glasgow in 1631. The direct line of the family ended in the eighteenth century.

BETHUNE

ARMS (of Balfour LR 4/21)[1]
Quarterly, 1st & 4th, Azure, a fess between three mascles Or (Bethune); 2nd & 3rd, Argent, on a chevron Sable, an otter's head erased of the First

CREST
An otter's head erased Argent

MOTTO
De bonnaire (Gracious)

A name principally believed to derive from the French town of the same name, lying in the department of Pas de Calais. There is also a quite separate Highland derivation as an anglicised form of the Gaelic, 'Macbheatha'. This means 'son of life', and the family were renowned physicians in the thirteenth and fourteenth centuries. According to tradition, Macbheatha came to Scotland from Ireland in the thirteenth century as part of the retinue of Margaret, wife of Angus, the Lord of the Isles. Macbeths or Beatons were found as physicians throughout the Western Isles. Their influence and skills were lost in the upheaval brought to the Highlands and Islands in the wake of the overthrow of the Stuart monarch in 1688. The first de Bethunes are believed to have come to England in 1066 with William the Conqueror. The Bethunes accompanied Richard the Lion-Heart, King of England, on his crusade to the Holy Land, and one is said to have been held prisoner with the king when he was held to ransom by the Duke of Austria. The first record of the name in Scotland appears around 1165, when Robert de Betunia was a witness to a charter of lands near Tranent in East Lothian. The principal possessions of the family appear to have been in Fife and Angus. Sir Robert de Betune rendered homage to Edward I of England in the Ragman Roll of 1296. The commentary on the Ragman Roll states that the seal of Robert de Betune was 'a fesse and on a chief a file of three pendants'. This is very similar to the arms used in more modern times. The Bethunes, despite having adopted the political expedient of appearing to support the English cause, soon became faithful supporters of Robert the Bruce. Alexander de Bethune was knighted by the king for his bravery in battle. He was killed at the Battle of Dupplin in August 1332. Robert de Bethune married the heiress of Sir John Balfour of that Ilk, and their son succeeded to the extensive Balfour estates, thereafter being designed 'Bethune of Balfour'. Sir David Bethune, second son of Sir John Bethune of Balfour, acquired the lands of Creich in Fife during the reign of James IV. He had been a boyhood friend of the king and remained a court favourite. He was appointed Lord High Treasurer of Scotland. His daughter, Janet, was to become the wife of James Hamilton, Earl of Arran and a nephew of James III. Janet's son rose to be Regent of the kingdom and Duke of Chatelherault in France. From the family of Bethune of Balfour, many names famous in

Scottish history were to descend, including James Bethune, Archbishop of St Andrews and Chancellor of Scotland, and his even more illustrious nephew, Cardinal Bethune or Beaton. David Bethune, the last cardinal and primate of Scotland before the Reformation, was born at Balfour in 1494. He studied at the University of St Andrews and later at Paris, where he became an expert in canon and civil law. He entered the priesthood and when, in 1523, his uncle became Archbishop of St Andrews, he was appointed Abbot of Arbroath. He was a man of great industry, zeal and influence, and in 1538 he received the red hat of a cardinal of the Holy Roman Church. He was determined to stamp out the growing threat of Protestantism, and embarked upon a campaign of persecution. Protestant heretics were condemned to death, including the celebrated George Wishart, the most renowned preacher of his time. The martyrdom of Wishart was to prove a fatal mistake for the cardinal. On 29

May 1546, William Kirkcaldy of Grange, James Melville of Raith and several others seized the cardinal in his castle of St Andrews and killed him. The body of the murdered cleric was hung from the castle battlements. Robert Bethune, a younger son of the Laird of Creich, accompanied the young Mary, Queen of Scots to France on her marriage to the heir to the French throne. On the queen's return to Scotland in 1561 he was appointed a Master of the Royal household and keeper of the Royal Palace at Falkland. His eldest daughter, Mary Bethune, has passed into history as one of the famous 'four Maries', the queen's ladies-in-waiting. The family contracted many spectacular alliances by marriage into other noble houses, including the Earls of Rothes, Glencairn, Lindsay and Wemyss. The Earls of Lindsay still hold lands in Fife, and bear the name and arms of Bethune, placing them in precedence to their equally ancient Lindsay ancestry.

BEVERIDGE

ARMS (LR 2/91)[1]
Vert, two beavers combatant Or the base wavy Argent and Azure

CREST
Out of a mural crown Or a demi beaver Proper

MOTTO
Perseverando (By persevering)

On Compartment
Forward

SUPPORTERS
Two beavers Proper

The name of this family, prominent in Fife, is stated by Black to derive from an old English name, meaning 'Beaver Island'. This is amply displayed in their coat of arms which

shows two beavers standing on the sea. In 1302 Walter Beverage is shown as a juror at an inquest in St Andrews. David Beverage was cup bearer to James V in 1534. The family remained prominent and acquired the estate of Brucefield in Fife. James Beveridge was the collector of offshore dues in the Port of Leith and in 1821 his son, Samuel Beveridge, founded a legal practice which still serves the Port of Leith. In 1985 this law firm petitioned the Lord Lyon, King of Arms, for a grant of arms in its own right, and received a version of the two beavers standing on the sea, forever linking the firm symbolically with the family of its founder.

BINNING

Nisbet lists not only a principal family designed 'of that Ilk' but also Binning of Easter Binning and Binning of Wallyford. He states that the arms of Easter Binning are differenced from the principal family by placing a

silver wagon on the black bend, thus alluding to the family tradition, dating from the reign of David II, that one of the family went with seven of his sons concealed in a wagon full of hay and captured Linlithgow Castle, then held by English forces. The origin of the name itself is said by Black to be territorial, and derive from an old barony of that name in the parish of Uphall West Lothian. The family must have assumed some prominence, as Sir John Benyng was governor of the lands and possessions of the Order of St John of Jerusalem in Scotland around 1388. The order was powerful throughout Europe at that time, and their Preceptory of Torphichen was a major holding. Black also lists Binnings as prominent burgesses in Aberdeen in the fifteenth century. The name was common around Edinburgh in the seventeenth century. It survives as a title of the Earls of Haddington. Sir Thomas Hamilton was created Lord Binning on 19 November 1613. The heir to the earldom of Haddington traditionally uses the courtesy title, 'Lord Binning'.

BISSET

A name said to be of Norman origin and brought to Scotland when William the Lion returned from captivity in England in 1174, accompanied by young noblemen seeking fortune in Scotland; among these were the Biseys. They appear, along with other Norman families, to have been successful in establishing themselves, and they gained land in Morayshire. The power of the family spread, and persons bearing the name were witnesses to several charters in the thirteenth and fourteenth centuries. Thomas de Bissat witnessed a charter of Alexander III to Paisley Abbey. However, the rising fortunes of the family were eclipsed by an act of personal vengeance: in 1242 at a tournament held in Haddington, Walter Byset, Lord of Aboyne, was defeated by the youthful Earl of Atholl. Byset, in a fit of anger, is alleged to have murdered the earl while he slept and set fire to his house to conceal the crime. Walter and his nephew John fled to Ireland and later to England. The feud apparently followed the fugitives, as a pardon was later granted to the son of the Earl of Atholl for slaying some Bysets in Ireland. The principal line is now held to be that of Lessendrum, who are among the oldest families in Aberdeenshire. The name still flourishes there and in Moray. There have been several prominent lawyers of the name, including the exotically named Habakkuk Bisset, Writer to the Signet during the reign of James IV, and Peter Bisset, Professor of Canon Law at the University of Bologna in Italy.

BLACKADDER

This is a territorial name from the lands of Blackadder on the river of that name in Berwickshire. 'Adder' is from the old English word 'awedur', meaning 'running water' or 'stream'. Black lists Blakadir de Eodem (of that ilk) holding lands in the earldom of March in 1426. The family became embroiled in the constant Borders feuds and extended their lands by grants from James II, bestowed as a reward for repelling English raids with great ferocity. The Borders holdings of Blackadder of that Ilk were taken into the family of Home by the marriage of Beatrix and her younger sister, the only heirs of their father Robert, to younger sons of Home of Wedderburn in 1518. According to Anderson, this was achieved in the following manner: 'Andrew Blackadder followed the standard of Douglas at Flodden in 1513 and was slain along with two hundred gentlemen of that name on that disastrous field leaving a widow and two daughters, Beatrix and Margaret, who at the time were mere children. From the unprotected state of Robert's daughters, the Homes of Wedderburn formed a design of seizing the lands of Blackadder. They began by cutting off all within their reach whose affinity was dreaded as an hereditary obstacle. They attacked Robert Blackadder, the Prior of Coldingham, and assassinated him. His brother, the Dean of Dunblane, shared the same fate. Various others were dispatched in like manner. They now assaulted the Castle of Blackadder where the widow and her two young daughters resided. The garrison refused to surrender but the Homes succeeded in obtaining possession of the fortress, seized the widow and her children, compelling them to the marriage by force. The two daughters were contracted to younger sons, John and Robert in 1518 and as they were only in their eighth year, they were confined in the Castle of Blackadder until they became of age.' Whatever the truth of this story, the Home possession of the estates was challenged by a cousin, Sir John Blackadder, who held the lands of Tulliallan. Sir John sought assistance from Parliament but, as was so often the case at that time, the matter was ultimately resolved by steel. Sir John Blackadder was beheaded in March 1531 for the murder of the Abbot of Culross in a dispute over land. He was succeeded in the barony of Tulliallan by his brother Patrick, who again renewed his dispute against the Homes for the family lands. Again, Anderson accused the Homes of treachery in the story of Patrick's murder in an ambush near Edinburgh, where he was to meet the Homes to try to resolve their differences. The Blackadders thereafter relinquished their claim to the Borders lands, and Sir John Home was created Baronet of Blackadder in 1671. They continued to hold the estate and Castle of Tulliallan, and the family prospered. They acquired further lands in Clackmannanshire and Perthshire by successful marriages into the families of Bruce and Oliphant. The Reverend John Blackadder was a prominent presbyterian minister who suffered under the persecution of the Covenanters in the late seventeenth century. Elizabeth Blackadder has been one of Scotland's most distinguished twentieth-century painters. Tulliallan now houses the Scottish police training establishment.

BLACKSTOCK

ARMS (of that Ilk)[3]
Argent, three trunks of trees couped, under and above, two and one Sable

There appears to be no certain origin for this name but Blakstok of that Ilk appears in Workman's manuscript and is stated by Nisbet to bear a coat of three black tree trunks on a silver field. Black states that the name may be territorial but he could trace no place of that name. William Blackstock witnessed a deed in 1517 and the name arises again as a clerk of court in 1524. Blackstocks are listed as owning property in Edinburgh in the sixteenth and seventeenth centuries.

BLAIR

The word 'blair', or 'blàr', means 'open plain', and is found commonly throughout Celtic Scotland; for example, Blair Atholl and Blairgowrie. Nisbet records Blair of that Ilk, an ancient family in Ayrshire, receiving land as early as 1205 near Irvine. William de Blar was a witness to a charter of Alexander III to Dunfermline Abbey. Anderson asserts that the

ARMS[3]
Argent, on a saltire Sable nine mascles of the First

CREST
A stag lodged Proper

MOTTO
Amo probos (I love the virtuous)

family was probably of Norman origin and certainly their martial prowess brought them considerable lands and influence. Sir Bryce Blair of Blair was executed by the English at Ayr in 1296. His nephew and heir, Roger de Blair, was a comrade-in-arms of Robert the Bruce and received royal favour after the victory of Bannockburn in 1314. The family continued to grow in prominence and made alliances by marriage with the powerful families of Kennedy, Montgomery and Cochrane. Pitcairn's *Criminal Trials of Scotland* notes that on 18 May 1545 John Blair and his son Patrick were required to find security for their good behaviour after consorting with the enemies of the queen (Mary of Guise) at Ancrum. Madeleine Blair of Blair married William Scot, second son of John Scot of Malleny, who assumed the surname of Blair, and continued to reside at Blair in Ayrshire. Colonel Frederick Blair of Blair was decorated for bravery during the First World War, and was an aide-de-camp to George V. The Blairs also flourished in Perthshire where the Blairs of Balthyock may descend from a younger son of the Ayrshire knights. Thomas Blair, the second of Balthyock, received a charter of the lands of Ardblair, Baldowie and Balgillo in Forfarshire in 1399. The direct line of Balthyock ended in an heiress in the eighteenth century but the family of Blair-Oliphant still reside in Ardblair Castle near Blairgowrie.

BLANE

ARMS (of Blanefield LR 2/39)[1]
Argent, on a fess Sable a star between two crescents of the First, in base a rose Gules

CREST
The sword of Justice paleways Proper

MOTTO
Pax aut bellum (Peace or war)

SUPPORTERS
Dexter, a lion rampant Gules armed and langued Azure, sinister, a gryphon rampant Proper

A prominent name in Ayrshire. Black states that it may be of Celtic origin, being derived from Macgilleblaan whom he cites as a witness to a grant of land in Dumfries in the twelfth century. The name indicates a follower of St Blaan·or Blane, believed to have been a Celtic saint and possibly a grandson of Aiden, King of Dalriada. As is the case in so many names derived from adherence to a Saint, the origin may relate to land dedicated to the church in his or her name. Patrick M'Blayne was a witness in Wigtownshire in 1484 and Thomas M'Blayne was clerk and notary in the diocese of Glasgow in 1618. The family became firmly established in Ayrshire when Gilbert, the fourth son of Blane of Blanefield, was created a baronet on 26 December 1812 for his services as a physician to William IV. His son and heir, Hugh Blane, served in the Scots Guards at Waterloo three years later. The family continued in military service throughout the nineteenth century in the Crimean War, the Indian Mutiny and then in the First World War where the last baronet, Sir Charles Blane, was killed in the naval Battle of Jutland, on 31 May 1916.

BLYTH

The ancient barony of Blyth lay in the lordship of Lauderdale where the name is still common. The Blyth valley in Northumberland was an early centre of the salt industry and was controlled by the powerful Norman Delaval family. The Scots name may well have its origin in a Northumbrian knight who settled in the Borders. William de Blyth rendered

ARMS[2]
Argent, on a fess Gules between three crescents of the Last as many garbs Or

homage for his lands in Chirnside in 1296. The coat of arms described by Nisbet is believed to be of considerable antiquity, but no recording has ever been made of these

arms in the registers at the Lyon Court. Black records that Blyth was also a common name among the Borders gypsies, one Victorian 'queen of the gypsies' being Esther Faa Blyth. A dynasty of American actors, which included Lionel and Ethel Barrymore, was founded by Herbert Blythe, son of an East India Company surveyor, who died in 1905.

BOSWELL

ARMS (LR 9/79)[1]
Argent, on a fess Sable three cinquefoils of the First

CREST
A falcon Proper, hooded Gules, jessed and belled Or

MOTTO
Vraye foi (Have faith)

Universally accepted as of Norman or French origin, Black offers two derivations of the name – either from a vill, or manor, near Yvetot in Normandy, or from Beuzevill near Bolbec. The 'sieur', or Lord de Bosville, is said to have been one of the Norman commanders at the Battle of Hastings in 1066. Robert de Boseuille witnessed several charters in the reign of William the Lion and it must be presumed that the Boswells were among the knights who accompanied David I back to Scotland after his stay at the English court. Walter de Bosville was taken a prisoner at Dunbar in 1296 and William de Bosville rendered homage in the same year. His son, Richard, also received land from Robert the

Bruce near Ardrossan. A younger son of the Borders family is said to have been the first to settle in Fife, marrying Mariota, daughter and co-heiress of Sir William of Lochore. The family acquired the barony of Balmuto, which they held until the early eighteenth century. Sir Alexander of Balmuto was among the slain at Flodden in 1513. Boswells also fell in the royalist cause at the Battle of Worcester during the civil war in 1651. The family acquired the lands of Auchinleck and were to become lawyers of great eminence. Robert Boswell became a High Court judge, assuming the title of 'Lord Balmuto', and Alexander Boswell was also elevated to the Bench in 1756, assuming the title, 'Lord Auchinleck'. His son, James, was the famous biographer of Dr Samuel Johnson. Sir Alexander Boswell, the biographer's son, was created a baronet in 1821. Another distinguished Boswell was Robert Boswell, Writer to the Signet, who held the post of Interim Lord Lyon, King of Arms, from 1795 to 1796.

BRISBANE

ARMS (of Bishopton LR 1/122)[1]
Sable, a chevron chequy Or and Gules between three cushions of the Second

CREST
A stork's head erased holding in her beak a serpent nowed Proper

MOTTO
Dabit otia Deus (God will give repose)

Nisbet states that Brisbane of Bishopton is the most ancient and principal family of this name. The name may be of Anglo–French

origin, coming from 'bris bane', meaning 'bone breaker'. Black lists William Bris Bone as an archer sent from Berwick to Roxburgh in 1298. Several de Bris Banes witnessed deeds in the fourteenth and fifteenth centuries. The Brisbanes of Bishopton acquired the lands of Killincraig in Largs in the fifteenth century and by a royal charter, dated 1695, their estates were erected into a barony and thereafter they styled themselves 'Brisbane of Brisbane'. Nisbet asserts that the cushions which appear in this family's coat of arms are an allusion to an office of authority. General Sir Thomas Brisbane, Baronet, fought throughout the Peninsular War (1808–14), commanding a brigade in Wellington's army. In 1820 he was appointed Governor of New South Wales in Australia. He founded an observatory during his tenure of office and in 1828 was awarded the gold medal of the Royal Astronomical Society. In 1833 he was elected president of the Royal Society of Edinburgh. The Australian city of Brisbane is a lasting memorial to his work.

BROUN

ARMS (of Colstoun LR 1/21)[1]
Gules, a chevron between three fleur de lis Or

CREST[5]
A lion rampant, holding in the dexter paw a fleur de lis Or

MOTTO[5]
Floreat magestas (Let majesty flourish)

In its more usual form of Brown, this is an extremely common name and in most cases is simply a reference to colouring. Black, however, asserts that those of a Celtic origin may be named after their descent from the native judges, known as 'brehons'. The Lowland name achieved prominence in East Lothian in the early twelfth century, when Sir David Le Brun witnessed the laying of the foundation of the Abbey of Holyrood House in 1128. He gave lands to the new abbey in return for prayers for the health of his son. The Brouns of Colstoun enjoyed considerable royal favour which may have been assisted by their claim to descent from the royal house of France. The arms which they bear contain the three gold lilies of France. The family prospered and married into other noble families around Haddington, including the powerful Hays, who owned the lands of Yester and were ancestors of the marquesses of Tweeddale. Sir Patrick Broun of Colstoun was created a Baronet of Nova Scotia in 1686 and this title is still borne by his direct lineal descendent who now lives in Australia. Robert Brown, born at Montrose in 1773, was a distinguished botanist who was to contribute important original work on the plant life of Australia. In 1828 he published his work on experiments on fine powder suspended in water which revealed the phenomenon to be named 'Brownian motion'. George Brown of Edinburgh moved to Toronto in Ontario, in 1843. He became a newspaper proprietor and founder of the Toronto Globe. He was influential in the acquisition by Canada of the Northwest Territories. He served in Parliament and entered the Senate in 1873. He was fatally shot by a disgruntled former employee in 1880.

BUCHANAN

ARMS (LR 1/122)[1]
Or, a lion rampant Sable, armed and langued Gules, within a double tressure flory counterflory of the Second

CREST
A dexter hand holding up a ducal cap (Proper), tufted on the top with a rose Gules, within two laurel branches in orle (also Proper)

MOTTO
Clarior hinc honos (Hence the brighter honour)

SUPPORTERS
Two falcons Proper, armed Argent, jessed and belled Gules

The earliest family of this name hailed from the shores of Loch Lomond, which were granted by the Earls of Lennox to one Absalon around 1225. 'Buth chanain' is Gaelic for 'house of the canon', and Absalon may have been a clergyman or from one of those families dedicated to the service of the ancient Celtic Church. In 1282 Morris of Buchanan received a charter confirming him in his lands with baronial rights. He also held the small island of Clarinch, the name of which was afterwards to become the battle-cry of the clan. The Buchanans supported the cause of Bruce during the War of Independence and the fortunes of the family were thus assured. Sir Alexander Buchanan travelled with other Scottish nobles to fight for the French against Henry V of England, and fought at the Battle of Beauge in Normandy in March 1421. Buchanan's exploits during this battle are given as one explanation for the heraldry of this family: it is said that Sir Alexander killed the Duke of Clarence and bore off his coronet as a trophy, hence the ducal cap held aloft in the crest. The shield, which is virtually the Royal Arms of Scotland, differenced only by changing the lion and the double tressure of fleurs de lis from red to black. This is said to allude to the marriage of Sir Walter Buchanan to the only daughter of Murdoch, Duke of Albany and Regent of Scotland. The regent was ultimately beheaded by his cousin, James I, in 1425, when his vast estates were confiscated. Albany's son had died childless and the Buchanans were the nearest relatives to this disinherited branch of the royal family. The arms are said to mourn the family's loss of status. Also descended from the chiefly family were the Buchanans of Arnprior who held lands in Perthshire around Kippen. The Lairds of Arnprior lived in some style and were nicknamed the 'kings of Kippen'. Walter Scott relates a tale said to explain this title. James V was fond of travelling in disguise, using a name known only to his close friends and attendants. The king arrived at Arnprior to be met by a grim retainer who advised him that

the laird was at dinner and could not be disturbed. The king retorted by asking him to tell the king of Kippen that 'the Goodman of Ballengeich is come to feast'. When Buchanan heard these words, he knew at once that it could only be the king at his door and begged his royal forgiveness. The laird was killed at the Battle of Pinkie in 1547. The ancient lands of Buchanan were to have been passed at the death of the last chief in 1682 to Buchanan of Arnprior, but instead were sold to meet heavy debts. The mansion house of Buchanan is now in the possession of the Graham Dukes of Montrose. Perhaps the most famous Buchanan was the distinguished poet and Protestant reformer George, who was born at Killearn in Stirlingshire in 1506, the third son of Buchanan of Drumikill. He moved to Paris around 1520 to continue his education and travelled extensively on the Continent, embarking upon a literary career. He returned to Scotland around 1560 and in April 1562 he was appointed tutor in classics to the young Mary, Queen of Scots. He received a measure of royal favour but this did not prevent his launching vicious attacks upon the queen in his writings. He was appointed preceptor and tutor to the young James VI after the abdication of his mother, and he is generally credited with laying the foundations for that monarch's considerable academic prowess as well, unfortunately, as poisoning the child's mind against his mother. James Buchanan was the fifteenth president of the United States of America. There has not been a recognised chief since the late seventeenth century.

BUTTER

ARMS (of Gormack LR 1/123)[1]
Argent, a cross Sable between four mens' hearts Proper

CREST
Two hands issuing from a cloud in dexter, extended to the sinister and drawing an arrow in a bow all Proper

MOTTO
Dirigit Deus (God directs)

A name of great antiquity in Perthshire where the Butters have held land around Fascally near Pitlochry since the twelfth

century. Black suggests that the name may derive from the Gaelic 'bothar', meaning 'cattle road'. In 1554 John Butter of Gormok was declared an outlaw for participating in the murder of George Drummond of Leidcreif during a feud with the Blairs of Balthyock. The Butters' belicose tendencies continued, and on 24 November 1598 Patrick Butter was indicted for besieging the House of Ashintully and imprisoning the laird, Andrew Spalding. The family was to channel its undoubted martial prowess into service in the armed forces, and in the 1850s Lieutenant Colonel Archibald Butter of Faskally served in the Crimea and survived the Indian Mutiny. The present head of the family, Major Sir David Butter of Pitlochry MC, is HM Lord Lieutenant of Perthshire and is related by marriage to the Russian former imperial house of Romanov. HM Queen Elizabeth is godmother to his eldest daughter.

BYRES

A name taken from possession of the ancient barony in the county of Haddington. Byres Castle is now a ruin, but it occupied a highly defensible position over the fertile farmland of this rich county. The barony passed to the family of Lindsay but the Byres family became prominent and wealthy merchants. John Byres of Coates acquired the estate of Coates on the outskirts of Edinburgh and became lord provost of the city. Sir John Byres of Coates added the lands of Warriston near Edinburgh to his inheritance and fought for the king during the civil war, when he was knighted for his services. His fine seventeenth-century mansion of Coates still stands and now forms part of the world-famous St Mary's Cathedral Music School. The family continued to prosper and acquired the barony of Tonley in Aberdeen which became the chief seat of the family. Major Patrick Byres fought at the Battle of Culloden and thereafter fled to France where he entered the service of Cameron of Lochiel in the French Royal Scotch Regiment. The direct line passed through an heiress to the distinguished Aberdeen family of Moir of Overhill, but they assumed the additional surname of Byres and continue to live on the family lands to this day.

CAIRNS

The lands of Cairns are to be found in the parish of Mid Calder near Edinburgh. Black asserts that the first of this name recorded is William de Carnys who witnessed a charter in 1349. William de Carnys and his son, Duncan, held the baronies of Easter and Wester Whitburn, and many individuals of this name are mentioned in deeds in the counties of Midlothian and West Lothian. The name is still common around Edinburgh. The Cairnses were quick to see the advantage of emigration to the new settlements in Ulster and the name arises in Ulster from early in the sixteenth century. Hugh Cairns was raised to the peerage as Lord Cairns in 1867 and was promoted to the rank of earl in 1878. His coat of arms proclaims his descent from the ancient family of Cairns of that Ilk, bearing the same three gold martlets on a red field differenced only by a silver border bearing three green trefoils. He was a distinguished lawyer and was appointed to the office of Lord Chancellor of Great Britain in 1876. Sir William Cairns was Governor of Queensland in Australia from 1875 to 1877. The northern city and port which bears his name was founded in 1870 and is now one of Australia's most important tourist centres.

CALDER

ARMS (LR 1/582)[1]
Or, a hart's head cabossed Sable attired Gules

This name may be of territorial origin, being derived from the Scots word for a small stream. As a place name, it is found throughout Scotland; for example, in East and West Calder near Edinburgh, and Calderwood near Glasgow. Anderson asserts that the name came to prominence in Scotland through a French knight, Hugo de Cadella, who was created Thane of Calder, later to be known as Cawdor, in Nairnshire. Black lists Hugh de Kaledouer as a witness to a charter of land near Montrose around 1178. However the name arose, the Calders were great nobles with considerable lands around Inverness from the fourteenth century onwards. The substantial tower which still stands at the heart of the fine Cawdor Castle was built by the Calders around 1454. They inter-married with other local families, particularly the powerful Rose family, Barons of Kilravock. Their ascendency came to an end when Archibald Campbell, Earl of Argyll, was, along with Hugh Rose of Kilravock, appointed guardian to the infant female heir of the Calder family. Campbell determined to remove the child to Inverary to be educated as part of his family. He was opposed by her uncles, Alexander and Hugh Calder, who pursued the child and her Campbell escort into Strathnairn, but after considerable loss of life, she was safely delivered to Inverary. She was brought up as a Campbell and married Sir John Campbell, son of the Earl of Argyll. Muriel, the last of the Calders, died around 1575 but her descendent, John Campbell of Cawdor, was raised to the peerage as Lord Cawdor in 1796, and his son was created first Earl Cawdor in 1827. The present Earl Cawdor still lives in Cawdor Castle, seat of his Calder ancestors. The name of Calder did not disappear, however, and the Calders of Asswanly received lands near Elgin in 1440. This family obtained a baronetcy of Nova Scotia in 1686. The most notable member of this branch of the family was Admiral Sir Robert Calder who saw substantial service during the Napoleonic Wars. Sir James Calder was an advisor to the Ministry of Supply during the Second World War. Calders are still to be found around Inverness; for example, Douglas Calder, sometime President of the Royal Incorporation of Architects in Scotland, was appointed director of planning for the newly created Highland Region in 1974.

CALDWELL

ARMS (of that Ilk)[3]
Argent, three piles issuing from the chief Sable and in base four bars wavy Gules and Vert

The derivation of this name from the old English 'cealdwielle', meaning 'cold stream', makes it impossible to state a definite territorial origin for the name. Certainly, old lands of that name are found in Renfrewshire, and the oldest record of a family bearing this name coming to prominence is in that district. Black records William de Caldwell holding land in 1342. Nisbet states that the Caldwells of that Ilk wore on their coat of arms four bars wavy to show water related to the name. He states that 'this family continued for many hundreds of years in good reputation, by inter marriage with many honourable families and ended of late in the person of John Caldwell of that Ilk, one of the commissioners for the shire of Renfrew about the year 1693'. A branch of the family had emigrated to County Fermanagh in Ulster, where they purchased a fine castle which they renamed Castle Caldwell. Sir James Caldwell fought for William of Orange in Donegal in 1690. The name was also carried by settlers to the New World. Caldwell, New Jersey was the birth place in 1837 of Grover Cleveland, President of the United States. Erskine Caldwell, who died in 1987, was one of Americas greatest novelists.

CALLENDER

ARMS[3]
Sable, a bend between six billets Or

'Coille-tor', or 'woodhill', is the supposed derivation of the lands of Callender in Stirlingshire from which this family takes its name. The barony is believed to have been bestowed upon the first notable of this name around 1246. Nisbet relates the fascinating but unlikely story that the first of this name was a Roman from a fort near Ardoch, close to the modern town of Callender, and whose office it was to gather fuel for the fort – thus he was named 'Calloner', from the Latin, 'calo', meaning 'log of wood'. Nisbet also states that the Callenders of that Ilk were clerks to the king; this could account for the billets which appear on the coat of arms and may represent sheets or scrolls of paper. Patrick Callender of that Ilk supported the cause of Edward Balliol, and his lands were forfeited by David II. The lands were granted to Sir William Livingstone by a charter dated 10 July 1347, and to secure his undisputed right to these lands he subsequently married Christian, the daughter and heiress of the forfeited Patrick. In 1641 Sir James Livingstone was raised to the peerage with the title Earl of Callender. Callender House is one of the largest stately homes in Scotland and is now in the care of the public authority. Hugh Callendar, a noted physicist, researched extensively in thermodynamics. He was Professor of Physics at the Royal College of Science in 1902. His son, G. S. Callendar, propounded the theory of climatic change brought about by industrial combustion, processes known as the Callendar effect, in 1938. His work is now used by scientists studying the greenhouse-effect theories of global warming.

CARRUTHERS

ARMS (of Howmains LR 1/128)[1]
*Gules, two chevrons engrailed between three
fleurs de lis Or*

CREST
A seraphim volant Proper

MOTTO
Promptus et fidelis (Ready and faithful)

The name arises in Dumfriesshire and appears to allude to an ancient British fort called Caer Rydderch or Rhythyr. Black asserts that this means 'fort of Rydderch', which appears to be a form of personal name. The family rose in the thirteenth century to be stewards of Annandale under the Bruces. Black narrates the career of Nigel de Karruthers, a cleric who was Rector of Ruthwell in 1380, rose to become Canon of Glasgow Cathedral in 1351, and was named as chancellor to Robert, Steward of Scotland, in 1344. The family around the same time acquired the lands of Musfald (now Mouswald). The Carruthers were included in the roll of unruly clans in the West Marches in 1587. In 1563 John Carruthers of Howmains was indicted, along with Edward Irvine of Bonshaw and several others, for an assault on Kirkpatrick of Closeburn and slaying several other sundry persons. The Mouswald line ended in Simon Carruthers who was killed in a border raid in 1548, and the lands passed to the Douglases of Drumlanrig by marriage to the Mouswald Carruthers heiress. The family of Howmains continued to prosper and their lands were erected into a free barony in 1542. The estate of Howmains was lost when financial disaster overwhelmed the family in 1772, but a younger son of the last laird had acquired the estate of Dormont in Dumfriesshire which the family holds to the present day. Lieutenant Colonel Francis Carruthers served in Egypt and in the Boer War, and was assistant direc-

tor at the War Office from 1915 to 1919. He was a brigadier in the Royal Company of Archers (the monarch's bodyguard in Scotland) and Lord Lieutenant of Dumfries.

CHALMERS

ARMS (LR 1/133)[1]
Argent, a demi lion rampant Sable issuing out of a fess Gules and in base a fleur de lis of the last

CREST
The head and neck of a lion Sable langued Gules

MOTTO
Avance (Advance)

A name derived from the office of chamberlain to the king. Herbertus, whose family appears to have held lands in Ayr and Lanarkshire, was 'camerarius regis scotiae', or Great Chamberlain of Scotland, from 1124 to 1153. His family possessed the barony of Gadgirth from that time and Nisbet comments that they assumed the name De Camera, in the same manner as the family of the Great Stewards assumed that of Stewart when they ascended to the throne, alluding to the office of their original dynastic founder. James Chalmer of Gadgirth was a fervent Protestant reformer, admired even by his fellow reformer

John Knox for his zeal. The name is also found in Aberdeenshire, where the Chalmers of Balnacraig and those of Cults and Aldbar are believed to have sprung from entirely separate stock from their Ayrshire namesakes. These families also played a prominent part in public affairs. Major General Sir William Chalmers, a distinguished soldier, is reputed to have had three horses killed under him at the Battle of Waterloo in 1815. Dr Thomas Chalmers, born in 1780, was one of the most influential theological writers of his time. He was appointed Professor of Divinity at Edinburgh in 1828 and he became the first moderator of the Free Church of Scotland after the Disruption of 1843, when the Church of Scotland split in two. He sought to apply Christian ethics to economic issues and worked to relieve need among the urban poor. A splendid statue of him stands in Princes Street in Edinburgh.

CHEYNE

ARMS (of Esslemont LR 1/269)[1]
Azure, a bend between six crosses pattée fitchée Argent (quartered with Marshall of Esslemont)

CREST
A cross pattée fitchée Argent

MOTTO
Patientia vincit (Patience conquers)

A name of great antiquity, believed to be of Norman or French origin, from Quesney near Coutances. The name means 'oak plantation'. According to Black, some early clerks confused the word for 'oak' with that meaning 'dog', and erroneously styled the name 'Canis'. Ricardus de Chenai witnessed a gift to the Hospital of St Peter of York around 1158. The earliest record of the name in Scotland appears

to be William de Chesne who witnessed a charter by William the Lion around 1200. Sir Reginald le Chein was Great Chamberlain of Scotland from 1267 to 1269; he held the lands of Inverugie as well as immense estates in Caithness. Another Sir Reginald signed the Declaration of Arbroath in 1320. Anderson narrates that Sir Reginald le Chein, who died in 1350, was survived by two daughters in the following manner: Cheyne was renowned throughout the lands as a mighty hunter and longed for a male heir to his vast estates. When his wife was safely delivered of a daughter, in a rage, he ordered the child to be killed. A subsequent daughter was condemned in the same way. The years passed and no male heir was born and he began to lament his childless family. At length, on some great festival, he noticed two young ladies far outshining the rest in beauty and accomplishment. He expressed to his wife his admiration of these girls and the cruel fate which had persuaded him to order the death of his daughters who, if they had been allowed to live, would have been about the age of these beauties. His wife confessed her justifiable disobedience and introduced the young ladies to him as his own daughters. Sir Reginald was overjoyed and acknowledged them as his heirs to the lands of Esslemont, which had become the principal seat of the family by marriage with the heiress of Marshall of Esslemont. There were several cadet lines holding lands at Straloch, Dundarg and Pitfitchie. The lands of Esslemont eventually passed into the hands of the Gordons in the early eighteenth century, a branch of which noble family still resides there to this day. Sir William Cheyne, who died in 1932, was a distinguished surgeon and bacteriologist who was a pioneer of antiseptic surgical methods in Britain.

CLELLAND

ARMS (of that Ilk LR 1/128)[1]
Azure, a hare salient Argent with a hunting horn about his neck Vert garnished Gules

CREST
A falcon upon a glove sinister Proper

MOTTO
For sport

The name is said to derive from the lands of Kneland or Cleland in the parish of Dalziel in Lanarkshire. The Clellands of that Ilk were hereditary foresters to the Earls of Douglas, which may account for the device on their coat of arms of a hare with a hunting horn about its neck. Black lists Alexander Kneland of that Ilk as the husband of Margaret, sister of the patriot and independence leader William Wallace. Kneland fought in the War of Independence against the English and is believed to have fought at Bannockburn in 1314, and for his services received extensive lands, including some within the barony of Calder in West Lothian. Alexander Cleland of that Ilk and his cousin William were both killed at Flodden in 1513. Alexander Cleland of that Ilk who was related to the Earl of Bothwell, third husband of Mary, Queen of Scots, was implicated in the murder of Lord Darnley, the queen's second husband, along with other members of his family. His grandson, Alexander, married the sister of Lord Bargeny, and their son, on inheriting Hamilton land from his mother, sold the lands of Cleland to a cousin.

CLEPHANE

ARMS (of Carslogie LR 1/587)[1]
Argent, a lion rampant Gules in the dexter chief point an esquire's helmet Proper (quartered with Douglas of Kirkness)

CREST
A hand holding a helmet Proper

MOTTO
Ut sim paratior (That I may be the more ready)

SUPPORTERS
Two unicorns Argent, horned, hoofed and maned Sable

The Clephanes are said by Black to be an offshoot of an ancient family in England deriving their name from Clapham in Sussex, where they are believed to have settled shortly after the Norman Conquest. The progenitor of the Scottish family is believed to have been Aluns de Clephane, who settled in Lauderdale in the reign of William the Lion. He witnessed a charter around 1200. In a donation to the Monastery of Kelso he is designed 'Alans de Clephane, Vicecom. de Lawder'. The family acquired the lands of Carslogie in Fife, which was to become their principal seat. According to Anderson, Alan Clephane of Carslogie fought with Robert the Bruce in 1314 at the Battle of Bannockburn, where he is said to have lost his right hand; he subsequently had one made in steel to replace it, fitted with springs to enable him to wield his sword. Much of the family holdings in Lauderdale appear to have been lost by the early seventeenth century. Major General William

Clephane sold the remainder of the barony lands prior to his death in 1804, and the House of Carslogie became the residence of an English clergyman. The eldest daughter, the last of the Clephanes of Carslogie, married the Marquis of Northampton, and the famous steel hand was reputed to be in the possession of that family.

COCKBURN

ARMS (of Langton LR 1/129)[1]
Argent, three cocks Gules (quartered with Weapont)

CREST
A cock crowing Proper

MOTTO
Accendit cantu (He rouses us with song)

SUPPORTERS
Two lions Gules, that on the dexter guardant

There is uncertainty about the source from which this distinguished family may take its name. It may be that the name comes from land called Cukooburn in Roxburghshire. As the Scots word for 'cuckoo' is 'gowk', it is unlikely that this was its derivation. Also, the fact that the family heraldry consists of cockerels does not assist this theory, as canting, or punning, heraldry usually illustrates the sound of the bearer's name rather than its origin. Anderson suggests that the name may be a corruption of the old English name 'Colbrand'. Peres de Cockburne rendered homage to Edward I of England, and his name appears in the Ragman Roll of 1296. Sir Alexander de Cockburn married the daughter of Sir William de Vipont, owner of the lands of Langton in Berwickshire, who fell at the Battle of Bannockburn, and the said lands passed into the Cockburn family. Sir Alexander was suc-

ceeded by a son of the same name who, on 10 February 1373, was created hereditary usher, an office thereafter held as an adjunct to the barony of Langton by a charter of James IV in 1504. This honour was to cause one of the family some inconvenience. Balfour's Annals narrate that the office of great usher had been usurped by John, Earl of Wigtown. A committee of Parliament had been appointed to consider the complaint and report. Langton was not prepared to wait for such long-winded deliberations, and when the king entered the Parliament chamber he stepped forward, baton in hand, protesting his rights against those of the Earl of Wigtown. The king, offended at such disruption, immediately had the protesting great usher committed to Edinburgh Castle as a prisoner. He was released later that day on the petition of Parliament. The original chiefly line sold the barony and estate of Langton to a cousin who was created a baronet in his own right in May 1671. His successors still appear on the Roll of Baronets. Other distinguished Cockburns have included Lord Cockburn (1779–1854), a distinguished judge and author, and Sir George Cockburn, who conveyed the Emperor Napoleon to his final exile on the island of St Helena.

CONGILTON

This name first comes to prominence in East Lothian around the parish of Dirleton, which is famous for its impressive castle. Black states that the family may have come from Congilton in Cheshire and to have

given that name to their new possessions in Scotland. Robert de Congaltoun is listed as witnessing a charter granted in 1182. Walter de Congilton witnessed a charter of Dryburgh Abbey around 1224. The arms as recorded in

ARMS (of that Ilk LR 1/271)[1]
Quarterly, 1st & 4th, Argent, a bend Gules, overall a three point label Sable; 2nd & 3rd, Argent, a fess Sable between two cotises Azure

CREST
A bee Proper

MOTTO
Magna in parvo (Much in little)

the Lyon register have the simplicity expected of a very ancient family and at least one cadet branch, Congilton of Dirleton, is also recorded in Nisbet. They appear to have married into other prominent East Lothian families and were still active around Haddington in the late seventeenth century when William Congilton was appointed a justice of the peace for that county.

CRAIG

ARMS (of Riccarton LR 1/130)[1]
Ermine, on a fess Sable three crescents Argent

CREST
A chevalier on horseback in full charge grasping a broken lance in bend Proper

MOTTO
Vive Deo et vives (Live for God and you shall have life)

This surname derived from the Scottish word for a steep or rocky cliff, found as a prefix to place names throughout the realm. It is, therefore, impossible to identify any particular point of origin. Black states that in the fifteenth century there were three families of that name styling themselves 'of that Ilk'. Whatever the origin, the Craigs of Riccarton were to become the most noted family of this name. Sir Thomas Craig of Riccarton was a great institutional writer on feudal law in Scotland. Born around 1538, he studied at the University of St Andrews before proceeding to Paris where he studied both civil and canon law. His great work, *Jus Feudale,* is still referred to by Scottish lawyers today. Anderson records that he was admired by James VI and was present at the royal entry

into London and the coronation of James as king of England. The name of Craig continued to be associated with the law, and William Craig was raised to the Supreme Court Bench with the title, 'Lord Craig'. He retired from the Bench in 1812. The estate of Riccarton passed, through marriage to a daughter of Sir Thomas Craig, to the family of Gibson, who assumed the additional surname of Craig. Sir James Gibson-Craig was an eminent Edinburgh politician who was created a baronet for political services. He was a great supporter of the work of Sir Walter Scott. Sir James Craig, his family and followers, left Scotland for Ireland in 1610, as part of the plantation of Ulster. His descendent, James Craig of County Down, was the son of a self-made whiskey millionaire and was a main organiser of the Ulster Volunteer Force in the struggle against Home Rule in Ireland in the 1920s. He became the first Prime Minister of Northern Ireland in 1921 and was elevated to the peerage, taking the title, 'Viscount Craigavon'. The new town of Craigavon in County Armagh was named after him. He died in 1940.

CRAWFORD

The family of Crawford is believed to be of Norman origin, taking their name from the barony of the same name in Lanarkshire. The early names of the principal families are all Norman, although some scholars have asserted an Anglo–Danish ancestry. According to tradition, Reginald, son of the powerful Earl of Richmond, was one of the Norman knights

established by David I. The Crawfords feature in the legendary incident which led to the foundation of the Abbey of Holyrood when the king's life was saved from a stag in 1127: Sir Gregan Crawford, together with divine intervention, was instrumental in saving his royal master's life. In 1296, Sir Reginald Crawford was appointed sheriff of Ayr. His sister,

ARMS (LR 10/58)[1]
Quarterly, 1st & 4th, Gules, a fess ermine, 2nd & 3rd,
Argent a stag's head erased Gules

CREST
A stag's head erased Gules, between the attires a cross
crosslet fitchée Sable

MOTTO
Tutum te robore reddam (I will give you safety
by strength)

SUPPORTERS
Two bulls Sable, armed and unguled Or

Margaret, married Wallace of Elderslie, and was the mother of Sir William Wallace, the great Scottish patriot. The Crawfords rallied to their cousin in his struggle against English domination. The family of the sheriff of Ayr also produced the main branches of this family, who were styled 'of Auchinames' and 'of Craufurdland'. The chiefly family is generally reckoned to be that of Auchinames in Renfrewshire, who received a grant of their lands from Robert the Bruce in 1320. Sir William Crawfurd of Craufurdland was one of the bravest men of his time and was knighted by James I. He fought with the Scots forces in the service of King Charles VII of France and was wounded at the siege of Creyult in Burgundy in 1423. John of Craufurdland followed James IV to the sorry field of Flodden where, in company with much of the flower of Scottish chivalry, he died. The Lairds of Auchinames, too, fell at Flodden and, a generation later, at Pinkie in 1547. Sir Thomas Craufurd of Jordanhill also fought at the Battle of Pinkie but was luckier than his cousin, being captured and later ransomed. He became a member of Lord Darnley's household when he married Mary, Queen of Scots. In 1569 he denounced Maitland of Lethington and Sir James Balfour as being the true conspirators in the murder of Lord Darnley. He did not, however, sympathise with the plight of the deposed queen, and in 1570 captured

Dumbarton Castle from her forces with just one hundred and fifty men. The splendid Castle of Craufurdland was much extended by the sixteenth Laird in the seventeenth century. John Walkinshaw Craufurd, the twentieth Laird, was a distinguished soldier who, after entering the army at an early age, rose to the rank of lieutenant colonel and was present at the victory of Dettingen in 1743, also distinguishing himself at Fontenoy two years later. Despite his faithful service to the house of Hanover, he was an intimate and faithful friend of the Jacobite Earl of Kilmarnock, and he accompanied his ill-fated friend to the scaffold as a last act of comradeship. He received the earl's severed head and attended to the solemnities of his funeral. This act of charity resulted in his name's being placed at the bottom of the army list. However, he restored his fortunes and in 1761 he was appointed falconer to the king. Despite his devotion to his friends, he did not seem to share a similar affinity for his family. He died in 1793 and in his will left his entire estates to Sir Thomas Coutts, the eminent banker. The deed was, however, contested by Elizabeth Craufurd, who eventually won her case in the House of Lords in 1806, and the ancient estates passed back to the rightful heir. This branch of the family thereafter united the houses of Houison and Craufurd, and they still live at Craufurdland. Sir Alexander Craufurd of Kilbirnie was created a baronet in June 1781. His son, Robert, commanded the Light Division in the Peninsular War (1808–14) and died in 1812, leading his troops on an assault on the fortress of Ciudad Rodrigo. A grateful nation erected a monument to him in St Paul's Cathedral in London. Hugh Crawfurd, twenty-first Laird of Auchinames, emigrated this century to Canada, having sold the ancient family lands.

CROSBIE

The origin of this surname is somewhat obscure but some suggest that it relates to one who dwelt beside a market cross or the crossroads of a major highway. Another suggestion is that it relates to the bearer of the cross, and may be an allusion either to the

ARMS (of Holm LR 1/486)[1]
Gules, a cross Or

CREST
Out of a mount the trunk of a tree sprouting out new branches all Proper

MOTTO
Resurgam (I shall rise again)

Crusades or to an office within the Church. Black lists the surname as being common in Wigtownshire and Dumfriesshire. The families which came to prominence were those living in Dumfries and bearing the territorial styles 'of Oultis' and 'of Holm'. They were followers of the Bruce family. Iuone de Cosseby witnessed a charter by Robert de Brus to Arbroath Abbey between 1178 and 1180. The name appears in numerous charters in Annandale and Moffat throughout the late twelfth and early thirteenth centuries. Andrew Crosbie of the family of Holm was a celebrated lawyer who practised at the Scottish Bar in the eighteenth century. He is credited by Anderson as being the model for Councillor Playdell in Sir Walter Scott's novel, *Guy Mannering*. He is also said to have been the only person to have maintained his own opinion against Dr Johnson on his famous visit to Scotland in 1774. The fortunes of the family collapsed in a bank crash and the famous advocate died in poverty in 1785. In Ireland, what may have been a branch of the same family were created baronets in 1630, and the family remained prominent in Ireland to the twentieth century. The baronetcy became extinct in 1936.

CUMMING

ARMS (LR 1/569)[1]
Quarterly, 1st & 4th, Azure, three garbs Or (Cumming); 2nd & 3rd, Argent, three bends Sable, each charged with as many roses of the Field (Penrose); overall, in an escutcheon Argent, is placed the Arms, Crest, Motto and Supporters of Gordon of Gordonston viz: Quarterly, 1st & 4th, counterquartered, (I), Azure, three boars' heads couped Or, armed and langued Gules (Gordon); (II), Or, three lions' heads erased Gules (Badenoch); (III), Or, three crescents within a Royal Tressure Gules (Seton); (IV), Azure, three fraises Argent (Fraser); 2nd & 3rd grand quarters, Gules, three stars Or (Sutherland), all within a bordure of the Last. On a wreath of the Liveries of these Arms is set for Crest a cat salient Proper, armed Azure, and in an Escrol above the Crest this Motto 'Sans crainte' and for Supporters is placed on the dexter a greyhound Proper gorged with a collar Gules charged with three buckles Or, and on the sinister, a savage Proper, wreathed about the head and middle with laurel Vert, brandishing a club Proper

CREST
A lion rampant Or, in his dexter paw a dagger Proper

MOTTO
Courage

SUPPORTERS
Two horses Argent

The family is Norman in origin, the name derived from Comines near Lisle in northern France, on the frontier with Belgium. They claimed to be directly descended from the Emperor Charlemagne. Robert de Comyn came to England with William the Conqueror in 1066 and was given lands in Northumberland. His grandson, William, came to Scotland in the reign of David I, who bestowed lands upon him in Roxburghshire. He eventually rose to become Chancellor of Scotland. William's nephew, Richard, married a granddaughter of Donald Bane, later Donald III, second son of Duncan I. In the early thirteenth century as a result of good marriages they held three earldoms: Monteith, Menteith, and Atholl and Buchan. When Alexander III was killed near Burntisland, two Comyns, both direct descendents of Duncan I, were appointed to the council of six guardians of Scotland. They were Alexander Comyn, Earl of Buchan, and 'Black John' Comyn, Lord of Badenoch. After the death in 1290 of the child queen Margaret, the 'Maid of Norway', and granddaughter of Alexander III, at least six claimants to the throne (including John Balliol, brother-in-law of the Black Comyn, Robert Bruce, grandfather of the future king, and the two Comyn guardians) invited Edward I of England to decide who should succeed to the Scottish throne. He agreed, providing the chosen successor recognised him as overlord of Scotland, a demand which the

Scots were not in a position to resist at that time. Edward's choice was John Balliol, but resistance broke out again, with the claimants taking sides and switching allegiances in the struggles to win the throne and to break free of England. In 1306, Robert the Bruce, grandson of the original claimant, invited Red Comyn to a meeting in the church of the Greyfriars in Dumfries in the hope of negotiating a compromise. They quarrelled, daggers were drawn and Comyn was stabbed to death in the church, an act for which Bruce was excommunicated. Comyn's son was defeated in a skirmish with Bruce and fled to join the English. He was killed at the Battle of Bannockburn in 1314. The fall of the Badenoch Comyns removed the family from the centre of Scottish politics, but many branches had been established which contin-

ued to thrive. The name generally became spelt 'Cumming', and the Cummings of Altyre were recognised as the chiefly line. Sir Alexander Cumming of Altyre was created a baronet on 21 May 1804. Sir William Gordon-Cumming of Altyre, fourth Baronet, served with the Scots Guards in the Zulu War of 1879 and later in the Guards' Camel Regiment. He is perhaps best remembered for his part in the Royal Baccarat Scandal, in which the Prince of Wales, later Edward VII, became the first member of the royal family to give evidence in a civil court in an action for slander rising out of an accusation of cheating at a game of cards. The family acquired the estate of Gordounstoun which is now well known because of the famous public school established there.

CUNNINGHAM

ARMS (LR 1/53)[1]
Argent, a shakefork Sable

CREST
A unicorn's head couped Argent armed Or

MOTTO
Over fork over

SUPPORTERS
Two cunnings (coneys) Proper

This is a territorial name found in Ayrshire. It is likely that it derives from 'cuinneag', meaning 'milk pail' and the Saxon 'ham', meaning 'village'. The first to take the name was Warnebald or perhaps his son, Robertus, who received a grant of the land of Cunningham, somewhere between 1160 and 1180. A story also states that Malcolm, son of Friskin, obtained the lands of Cunningham from Malcolm III by sheltering him in a barn and covering him with hay. This is said to give rise to the shake-fork in the family arms and the motto, 'Over fork over'. This is a charming legend, but Sir George Mackenzie states that the arms are an allusion to the office of Master of the King's Stables. Another explanation runs that the Cunninghams were great allies of the

Comyns, whose shield bore sheaves of corn. When that great dynasty was overthrown by the Bruces, the Cunninghams adopted the shake-fork used to 'fork over' sheaves of corn, as an ingenious reference to their former allies. It is certain that the Cunninghams were well settled in their lands and the parish of Kilmaurs by the end of the thirteenth century. Hervy de Cunningham, son of the Laird of Kilmaurs, fought for Alexander III against the Norwegian invaders at the Battle of Largs in 1263. He received from his king in the following year a charter of confirmation to all his lands. The family were supporters of the Bruces in their fight for Scottish independence, although in common with a great many of the Scottish nobility, their name appears on the Ragman Roll, swearing fealty to Edward I of England in 1296. Bruce was generous towards his supporters after his great victory, and the lands of Lamburgton were added to Kilmaurs by royal charter in 1319. Sir William Cunningham of Kilmaurs was one of the Scottish noblemen offered to David II's English captors as substitute hostages in 1354. His son, also William, married Margaret, the elder daughter and co-heiress of Sir Robert Denniston of that Ilk, and through her acquired substantial lands, including Finlayston in Renfrewshire and Glen Cairn. Sir William's grandson was created Lord Kilmaurs in 1462 and later Earl of Glencairn. A younger brother was ancestor to the Cunninghams of Caprington who were later to achieve prominence of their own. Other distinguished branches of the family include the Cunninghams of Cunninghamhead, Aiket, Robertland and Corsehill. However, the fortunes of the family remained firmly in the hands of the main line, the Earls of Glencairn. The fifth earl was a Protestant reformer and a patron of the reformer, John Knox. He has been accused of being in the pay of the English, who saw the Reformation as an opportunity to discomfort the Scottish Crown. Whatever the case, Glencairn rose against Mary, Queen of Scots, and was one of the commanders at the Battle of Carbery Hill where she surrendered in 1567. Glencairn is said to have ordered the destruction of the Chapel Royal at Holyrood. The Cunninghams also were among the Scottish undertakers of the Plantation of Ulster, and Sir James Cunningham, who was married to a daughter of the Earl of Glencairn, was granted five thousand acres in County Donegal. The name is now among the seventy-five most common names in Ulster. The ninth earl threw in his lot with Charles II in his bid to gain his father's throne. He raised a force in 1653 to oppose General Monck, who was governor of Scotland. In August he went to Lochearn in Perthshire where he met with some chiefs of the Highland clans, and with a body of fighting men, took possession of Elgin in 1654. He announced his commission on behalf of the king to raise all of Scotland against the Protector, Oliver Cromwell. The rising was a failure, but Glencairn escaped with his life and after the Restoration he was appointed Lord Chancellor of Scotland. The title is now extinct. Sir John Cunningham of Caprington, a distinguished lawyer, was created a Baronet of Nova Scotia by Charles II in 1669. Other prominent Cunninghams include Alexander Cunningham, eighteenth-century historical writer, who was British envoy to Venice from 1715 to 1720. Charles Cunningham was famous for his historical paintings, some of which still hang in the Hermitage Palace in St Petersburg and in Berlin. Sir William Cunningham of Robertland was a friend of the poet Robert Burns. Alan Cunningham, poet and writer, whom many believe was only eclipsed by Burns himself, was born at Blackwood in Dumfriesshire in 1784. His work was supported by Sir Walter Scott who, on Cunningham's death in 1828, provided for his two sons.

DALMAHOY

The family took their name from their lands: the barony of Dalmahoy lay in Midlothian, just south of Edinburgh. The first recorded member of the family was Henry de Dalmahoy, whose name, like many other nobles of the time, appears on the Ragman Roll of 1296, as he swore fealty to Edward I of England. In the reign of Robert II, Richard de Dalmahoy, the third of that Ilk, was named on the Burrow's Rolls as a Free Baron of Lothian. Clearly at this time they were an important local family. On 17 July 1572, Alexander Dalmahoy of that Ilk was a member of the assize for the trial of George Wilkie and his son, Robert, for treason. The Wilkies were accused of plotting with the Earl of Huntly, Kirkcaldy of Grange and others at Edinburgh after they had been outlawed in 1571. In 1579 the same Alexander Dalmahoy, his brother William, his uncle John and five others, were indicted for besieging the House of Warriston, the property of William Somerville, the year before. They were apparently acquitted of all charges. In October 1581, Dalmahoy was one of twenty-four gentlemen and six ministers chosen by the General Assembly of the Church of Scotland to consider the question of what should be done with the temporal powers of the bishops when that office was abolished. (The Commissioners concluded that Parliamentary powers should be vested in the General Assembly and that their civil and criminal judicial duties be vested with the head bailiffs in their own jurisdiction.) In 1614 Sir John Dalmahoy was knighted by James VI. He also obtained the hereditary

office of Under Master of the Royal Household, an office in which he was confirmed by Charles I. This entitled the family to incorporate an augmentation to their coat of arms of a red baton powdered with gold thistles and ensigned on the top with an imperial crown. In 1679, John Dalmahoy of that Ilk was raised to the rank of baronet by Charles II. The second Baronet married Aicia Paterson, daughter of the Archbishop of Glasgow. Sir Alexander, fourth Baronet, was an officer in the service of the French king, and was created a Knight of the Order of St Louis. On his return to Scotland he lived at Carriden near Linlithgow. He was succeeded by his cousin, Sir John Hay Dalmahoy, who was a scholar at Hertford College, Oxford, and in holy orders. He died in 1800 leaving no issue, and the title became extinct.

DALRYMPLE

ARMS[5]
Quarterly, 1st, Or, on a saltire Azure nine lozenges of the Field (Dalrymple); 2nd, Or, a chevron checky Sable and Argent between three water bougets of the Second (Ross); 3rd grand quarter, counterquartered; (I) & (IV), Quarterly, 1st & 4th, Gules, three cinquefoils Ermine; 2nd & 3rd, Argent, a galley, sails furled, Sable; the whole within a bordure compony Argent and Azure, the first charged with hearts Gules, the second with mullets Argent (Hamilton); (II) & (III), Gules, on a fess between three crescents Or as many mullets Azure (De Franquetot); 4th grand quarter, counterquartered; (I) & (IV), Gules, on a chevron between three cinquefoils Argent, as many round buckles Azure (Hamilton); (II) & (III), Gules, three martlets Argent (Makgill)

CREST
A rock Proper

MOTTO
Firm

SUPPORTERS
Two storks, each holding in its beak a fish, all Proper

The family take their name from the land they acquired, which is now part of the parish of Kyle in Ayrshire. The name itself could be derived from several different sources. Many writers believe it stems from 'dal-a-chrumpuill', the Gaelic for 'dale of the crooked pool', although this may be unlikely, as Gaelic never prevailed in the district. The more romantic derivation is 'dal-ry-mole',

denoting the 'valley of the slaughter of kings'. There is a tradition that before the Christian era, two kings, Fergus and Coilus, fought in the valley and were slain. However, the most likely derivation is from the old Saxon 'dahl hrympel', and the land does have a very rumpled or puckered appearance. The first documentary evidence of a person bearing the name is obtained from a charter of Robert II in May 1371, confirming Kennedy of Dunmore (ancestor of the present Marquess of Ailsa) in part of the barony. Three generations of Dalrymples are mentioned in the charter. In 1377 the same John Kennedy obtained another charter for the remaining lands in the barony. In 1540, William de Dalrymple acquired the lands of Stair-Montgomery in Ayrshire on his marriage to Agnes Kennedy, granddaughter of Malcolm de Carrick de Stair, and thus became the first Dalrymple of Stair. The family seem to have been in the forefront of the Protestant Reformation, and fought at Langside against Mary, Queen of Scots in 1568. James Dalrymple of Stair, born in May 1619, was to be one of the most eminent lawyers and statesmen of his day, eventually being raised to the peerage as Viscount Stair. At the age of fourteen he went to Glasgow University and in 1637 received the degree of Master of Arts. The following year he commanded a company of foot in the Earl of Glencairn's regiment. In 1641, while still in uniform, he became the Professor of Philosophy at Glasgow, a post he resigned in 1647. In 1648 he was called to the Scottish Bar, becoming an advocate. He was secretary to the commissioners, and sent to Breda to invite Charles II to return to Scotland and assume his father's throne. While there, he was appointed a parliamentary commissioner for the administration of justice in Scotland, an appointment approved by that most talented of administrators, Oliver Cromwell. At the Restoration, Dalrymple was made one of the Lords of Session by Charles II, and knighted. In 1671 he became Lord President of the Court of Session, the highest judicial post in Scotland. His political skills failed him, however, when he offended the Duke of York, later James VII, and he deemed

it expedient to resign his high office and flee to the Netherlands. He returned with William of Orange and was reappointed Lord President and created Viscount Stair in 1690. He died in 1695 in his seventy-sixth year. Stair's work on Scots Law, *Institutions of the Law of Scotland*, became the cornerstone of modern Scottish civil law, and the work of the great Lord President is still frequently referred to in cases before the Courts of the present day. The second Viscount was also a lawyer who was later to become Lord Advocate and first Earl of Stair. The second Earl was an army officer of considerable skill who was aide-de-camp to, and campaigned with, the Duke of Marlborough in the early years of the eighteenth century. He attained the rank of field marshal, and became ambassador to the court of Louis XIV of France. The present Earl is captain general of the Royal Company of Archers (the monarch's bodyguard in Scotland), and Gold Stick-in-Waiting to HM the Queen.

DALZIEL

Since 1259 over two hundred different forms of this name have been recorded, from Dalzeel to Diyell and including the abbreviation 'DL', which approximates its proper pronunciation. The name is of territorial origin from the old barony of Dalziel in Lanarkshire. The name itself derives from the Gaelic 'dal-gheail', meaning 'white meadow', so named because of the colour of the local clay soil. There are also some from Shetland who bear the name; there, it derives from the island of Yell. The hanged man on the family's coat of arms is said to have come from the time of

Kenneth II, when a member of his court retrieved the body of the king's friend from a gibbet in enemy held territory with the words, 'I Dare', which is now the family motto. Thomas de Dalziel is mentioned as a baron of Scotland in the Ragman Roll of 1296, swearing fealty to Edward I of England. He became one of the patriots who joined Robert the Bruce in the struggle for Scottish independence. Sir William de Dalziel, 'a brave and humorous Knight', who had lost an eye at the Battle of Otterburn in 1388, accompanied Sir David Lindsey of Glenesk to the famous London Bridge Tournament in 1390, in which Lindsey was victor. He is said to have suggested that by the laws of the tourney all should be equal and therefore have had one eye put out! Sir Robert Dalzell was created Earl of Carnwath in 1639. His son, Robert, the second Earl, was an active supporter of the Marquess of Montrose, commander of the forces of Charles I in the civil war in Scotland. Lord Clarendon attributed the royalist feat at Naseby to the Earl of Carnwath's stopping the king's horse and re-directing the charge. The fifth Earl, Sir Robert, fought with the Old Pretender in the Jacobite rising of 1715, which resulted in the forfeiture of his title and estates. Sir Thomas Dalyell of The Binns in West Lothian was from one of the oldest cadets of the name. He was an emi-nent cavalier officer who fought bravely for the king during the civil war. After the execu-tion of Charles I he vowed never again to shave, a vow that he kept. In contemporary descriptions his white and bushy beard 'reached almost to his girdle'. He fought with the royalist forces at the Battle of Worcester in 1651, where he was captured and committed to the Tower of London. He escaped and went to the Continent, where he entered the service of the Tsar of Russia, who made him general of cavalry. He served with the Tsar's feared cossacks, and his later opponents were to refer to him as 'the muscovy beast who had roasted men'. There is, however, no evidence that Tam Dalyell engaged in any more atrocious behav-iour than was normal for the standards of the time. In 1666, after Dalyell's return, Charles II appointed him commander-in-chief of the forces in Scotland. In 1681 he raised a regi-ment, which has since seen much distinguished service, under the popular name, The Scots Grays. His fierce reputation was put to good use when he was charged with the suppression of the Covenanters, and his dra-goons destroyed effective Covenanter resistance in the Battle of Rullion Green near Edinburgh. The House of the Binns was built by the general's father in 1623 and thereafter altered at various times. Its present form dates from around 1820, and it is still the home of the Dalyells, the present baronet being Tam Dalyell, the prominent Labour Member of Parliament.

DAVIDSON

ARMS (LR 18/62)[1]

Quarterly, 1st & 4th, Argent, on a fess Azure, between a dexter hand couped accompanied by two pheons in chief and a pheon in base Gules, a buck lodged Or (Davidson); 2nd & 3rd, Argent, a wolf's head erased Or, armed and langued Gules (Bayne of Tulloch)

CREST
A stag's head erased Proper

MOTTO
Sapienter si sincere (Wisely if sincerely)

This family had bonded with the Clan Chattan in the early part of the fourteenth century when Donald, the third son of Robert Comyn and grandson of the Comyn murdered by Robert the Bruce at Dumfries, married Slane Mackintosh, daughter of the sixth Mackintosh Chief. David is recorded by Macfarlane as being Slane's son and his family and their followers were known as Clan Dhai, as the name of Comyn was prescribed around 1320. Thomas Comyn or Cumming, son of Donald's elder brother, was exempted from the prescription and gave rise to the Cummings of Altyre and their cadets. The Davidsons, or Clan Dhai, are recorded in Macfarlane's account of *Geneologies of the Family of Mackintosh,* as being virtually wiped out as a fighting force at the Battle of Invernahaven in 1370. At Invernahaven the Mackintoshes, along with their Clan Chattan supporters, the Davidsons and the Macphersons, gathered to oppose a strong force of Camerons who had marched into Badenoch intent on slaughter and plunder. A dispute arose between the Davidsons and the Macphersons concerning the right to command and when the Mackintoshes supported the Davidsons' claims the Macphersons, considering themselves insulted, left the field. The Camerons exploited their enemies' confusion, and in the ensuing battle the Davidsons seem virtually to have been destroyed. The Macphersons were goaded into joining the fray, and the Camerons were ultimately put to flight. Later historians attribute another battle of these clans, held on the North Inch of Perth in 1396, to a conflict between the Clan Dhai and the Macphersons, based upon Lowland accounts of 'Clan Claci or Clan Clanquevil' opposing Clan Chattan. However, by the sixteenth century accounts of the battle clearly stated the participants to be Clan Chattan and Clan Cameron, with the bulk of the evidence pointing to the inclusion of the rival Davidsons and Macphersons in the Clan Chattan forces, all fighting their old and continuing enemies, the Camerons. It has been said that after the Battle of North Inch the family of the chief of the Davidsons moved north and gave rise to the Davidsons of Cantray and Tulloch. There is little doubt that well before the end of the fourteenth century the name Davidson is recorded in the east and north-east coastal towns of Perth, Dundee and Aberdeen. The best recorded is the alderman and customar of Aberdeen (collector and distributor of the royal dues and taxes in the town), Sir Robert, named variously as Davisoun and David Filius in civic records of the day. In 1411, he led a contingent from the burgh to fight at the Battle of Harlaw, where he was killed. He was a friend of the Earl of Mar, a son of the Wolf of Badenoch, and some evidence suggests the possibility that Robert could have been a son or grandson of the first Comyn, David. By the sixteenth century the name could be found from Aberdeen in the north to Ayr in the south, and was associated with either the early armorial motif of a running deer transfixed through the body with an arrow, or the more stylised three arrow heads with a lying deer, all pointing to actual supposed common stock and origin. There are no records of Davidsons holding property in the easternmost and oldest-established part of Cromarty before a Donald Davidson and an Alexander Davidson are listed in July 1670 as

'in the council', and probably living in the new town of Cromarty, suggesting, according to local historians, that they were not an established burgess family prior to the mid seventeenth century. There was a family of Davidsons at Samuelston in the Borders, and references to those of that name can be found along with Elliots, Robsons and Turnbulls, as wild and unruly families in the debatable lands. Alexander Davidson was known as Clerk Davidson, and was the town clerk and a writer in Fortrose. He married on 25 November 1689 Elizabeth Bremner, second daughter of a burgess of Fortose. Alexander had two sons: Henry, first Laird of Tulloch, who became a merchant in London and was succeeded by his brother, Duncan, who became a Member of Parliament. He was a great favourite of Queen Victoria, whom he used to visit during her stays at Balmoral. He was her Lord Lieutenant of Ross-shire. Tulloch Castle was extensively restored in 1922 by the renowned architect Sir Robert Lorimer, but the castle and estates have since been sold. However, it still stands as a focal point for Davidson traditions, along with other relics such as the suit of armour of the Provost of Aberdeen killed at Harlaw, which is still preserved by the City Council. Only a few stones mark the site of Invernahaven. The Clan Davidson Association, first formed in 1909, had been inactive for some time until it was revived recently and now vigorously seeks to unite Davidsons throughout the world. A direct descendent of the Davidsons of Tulloch, now living in New Zealand, is seeking to matriculate arms in the Court of the Lord Lyon and claim the chiefship.

DENNISTOUN

The name is territorial in origin from the old barony of Danzielstoun. The manor took its name from a man named Daniel, who may have been of Norman extraction. Buchanan of Ochmar suggests that the family sprang from a younger branch of the Earls of

Lennox but this is doubtful. The name was gradually softened, through use, to Dennistoun. Sir Hugh Danzielstoun, or Denzilstone, of that Ilk, was one of the barons who submitted to Edward I of England, although his name does not occur on the

ARMS (LR 3/60)[1]
Argent, a bend Sable

CREST
*A dexter arm in pale Proper, clothed Gules, (issuing out
of the Wreath) and holding an antique shield Sable
charged with a mullet Or*

MOTTO
Adversa virtute repello (I repel adversity with fortitude)

SUPPORTERS
*Dexter, a lion rampant Gules, armed and langued Azure,
sinister, an antelope Argent, armed Azure, hoofed Or*

Ragman Roll of 1296. His granddaughter, Elizabeth Mure of Rowallan, married Robert II in 1347 and was the mother of Robert III. This gave rise to the proud saying of the Dennistouns that 'Kings come of us, not we of Kings'. This close royal connection brought extensive holdings to the family, together with the governorship of Dumbarton Castle. Robert de Danielstoun was one of the nobles who stood as hostage for the ransom of David II in 1357. In 1370 he was the commissioner for the peace treaty with England. He succeeded his father as sheriff of Lennox and was keeper of Dumbarton Castle. On his death in 1399, his brother, Walter, forcibly took possession of Dumbarton Castle, claiming that it was now the possession of the family, and held it until 1402. His kinsman, Robert III, offered him the vacant bishopric of St Andrews as compensation for his surrender of the castle. The offer was generous but Walter died before he could take up his new office. William de Danielstoun was an officer of the royal household, both to Robert III and his son the Duke of Rothesay. His widow, Lady Marjory, received a royal pension after his death in 1393. By the seventeenth century the designation of the principal family had become that of their estate at Colgrain and they became embroiled in the conflict between Charles I and Parliament. John Dennistoun of Colgrain fought for the royalist cause throughout the civil war and joined in the ill-fated attempt by the Earl of Glencairn to restore the monarchy in 1653. The royalists were completely defeated, and although Colgrain succeeded in saving his estate from forfeiture, he died of wounds he received in the conflict. By the middle of the nineteenth century the family had reached the pinnacle of local aristocratic society. Dennistoun of Dennistoun commanded the cavalry militia of Dunbartonshire and was Deputy Lord Lieutenant. Other branches of the family became prominent Glasgow merchants, and John Dennistoun was MP for the city from 1837 to 1847.

DON

ARMS (of Newton LR 1/136)[1]
Vert, on a fess Argent three mascles Sable

CREST
A pomegranate Proper

MOTTO
*Non deerit alter aureus (Another golden branch
will succeed)*

A name, probably derived from the Anglo–Saxon word 'don' or 'dun', meaning 'open plain' or 'valley'. Black lists this as being a common surname in the Mar district near Aberdeen, and a prominent family of this name possessed lands in Monteith in Perthshire. It was this family that produced Sir Alexander Don of Newton, later named Newton Don, in Berwickshire, who was created a Baronet of Nova Scotia on 7 June 1667. Sir Alexander Don, Baronet, married the sister and co-heir of the last of the Cunningham Earls of Glencairn, and their son was MP for Roxburghshire for many years. The family married into the line of the Wauchopes of Niddrie, who were prominent Edinburgh nobles in the seventeenth and eighteenth centuries. The family combined these two great names and the baronetcy title is still held by the Don-Wauchopes, although the family lands passed into other hands.

DOUGLAS

ARMS (LR 1/143 and 231)[1]

Quarterly, 1st, Azure, a lion rampant Argent crowned with an Imperial Crown Or (Earldom of Galloway); 2nd, Or, a lion rampant Gules, armed and langued Azure, surmounted of a ribbon in bend Sable (Abernethy); 3rd, Argent, three piles Gules (for Wishart of Brechin); 4th, Or, a fess checky Azure and Argent, surmounted of a bend Sable charged with three buckles of the Field (Stewart of Bonkill); overall, on an escutcheon Argent, a man's heart ensigned of an Imperial Crown Proper and on a chief Azure three stars of the Field (Douglas)

CREST

A salamander Vert encircled with flames of fire Proper

MOTTO

Jamais arrière (Never behind)

SUPPORTERS

(on a compartment comprising a hillock, bounded by stakes of wood wreathed round with osiers) Dexter, a naked savage wreathed about the head and middle with laurel and holding a club erect Proper; sinister, a stag Proper, armed and unguled Or

The Douglases were one of Scotland's most powerful families. It is therefore remarkable that their origins remain obscure. The name itself is territorial and it has been suggested that it originates from lands by Douglas Water received by a Flemish knight from the Abbey of Kelso. However, the first certain record of the name relates to a William de Dufglas who, between 1175 and 1199, witnessed a charter by the Bishop of Glasgow to the monks of Kelso.

Sir William de Douglas, believed to be the third head of the Borders family, had two sons who fought against the Norse at the Battle of Largs in 1263. William Douglas 'The Hardy' was governor of Berwick when the town was besieged by the English. Douglas was taken prisoner when the town fell and he was only released when he agreed to accept the claim of Edward I of England to be overlord of Scotland. He later joined Sir William Wallace in the struggle for Scottish independence but he was again captured and died in England in 1302. His son, 'The Good Sir James', patriot and founder of the Black Douglases was killed in battle in Spain, carrying the heart of his life-long friend, King Robert the Bruce to the Holy land. Douglas and his knights had joined the king of Castille's crusade against the

Moors and in 1330, near Teba in Andalucia, they were cut off from the main Christian force and heavily outnumbered when they were attacked by the enemy. Sir James was killed leading the charge against the Moors but the casket containing Bruce's heart was recovered from the battlefield and returned to Scotland where it was interred in Melrose Abbey.

Marriage to a Stewart princess brought wealth and prestige to his great nephew, the second Earl of Douglas, later to die in his moment of victory at Otterburn in 1388. Sir James' illegitimate son, Archibald 'The Grim', became the third Earl and consolidated the family's position. He successfully defended Edinburgh Castle against Henry IV of England in 1400 but died a year later. Archibald, the fourth Earl, married James I's sister and in 1437, on the death of James I, he was one of the council of regents, and later lieutenant general of the kingdom. Both he and his son were killed fighting the English in France.

Despite this and other setbacks, in the early fifteenth century the Douglases had become so powerful that they were seen as a threat to the nation's stability. In 1440 the young sixth Earl and his brother were invited by a rival to dine in Edinburgh Castle with the ten-year-old James II. A black bull's head, the symbol of death, was brought in, and the Douglas boys were dragged away, given a mock trial, and beheaded. The young king was horrified, but twelve years later he invited their cousin, the eighth Earl, under a promise of safe conduct, to Stirling Castle where he was murdered with the king himself striking the first blow. The ninth Earl prudently spent much of his adult life in England. When he returned in 1484 with a small invading army to recover his possessions, he was captured and confined in Lindores Abbey. He died in 1491, the last of his line.

Meanwhile, another of Sir James' great nephews, George, first Earl of Angus, was the first of the Red Douglases. He too married a

Stewart princess and the Red Douglases soon rose to as great a prominence as the family had held hitherto; this was largely due to the success of Archibald, fifth Earl of Angus, known as 'Bell the Cat'. He is said to have gained his nickname from an incident in 1482 when a number of the Scots nobility plotted the downfall of certain unpopular favourites of the king. One of the conspirators told the tale of mice seeking deliverance from a cat: all agreed that a bell should be suspended from the cat's neck to signal its approach, but the question was, which mouse had courage to fasten the bell? Angus is said to have immediately cried 'I shall bell the cat'. The favourites were murdered, and Angus gained his nickname. He subsequently became Lord Chancellor of Scotland. His grandson, the sixth Earl, made himself guardian of James V by marrying Margaret Tudor, the young king's widowed mother. He was still taking the field against the English when over the age of sixty.

James, Earl of Morton, younger brother of the seventh Earl was a bitter enemy of Mary, Queen of Scots. He was one of the murderers of her secretary, David Rizzio, and was deeply implicated in the assassination of her second husband Lord Darnley. A brutally effective regent during the infancy of James VI, he fell from power in 1581 and was duly executed.

William, eleventh Earl of Angus and first Marquess of Douglas, was a Catholic and an ardent supporter of Charles I during the civil wars. He was created marquess in 1633 and lived in princely style at Douglas Castle. He joined Montrose after the Battle of Kilsyth in 1645 and was present when Royalists forces were surprised by Covenanter cavalry at Philiphaugh later that year when he barely escaped with his life. He made peace with Cromwell's government, although he was fined £1,000.

William, brother of the second Marquess became, through marriage, Duke of Hamilton in 1660. The titles of Marquess of Douglas, Earl of Angus and several others were ultimately all to devolve on the Dukes of Hamilton and the eldest son and heir of that house is always styled 'Marquess of Douglas and Clydesdale'. Other branches of the family include the Earls of Morton, and the Marquesses of Queensberry, who gave their name to the famous rules of boxing. The Douglas-Hamiltons are the heirs male of the house of Douglas but are barred, under Lyon Court rules, from matriculating as chiefs because of their hyphenated surname. Angus Douglas-Hamilton, the fifteenth Duke, is an engineer, former RAF test-pilot and author. His seat is at Lennoxlove near Haddington.

DUNLOP

ARMS (of Dunlop LR 4/31)[1]
Argent, a double headed eagle displayed Gules

CREST
A dexter hand holding a dagger erect all Proper

MOTTO
Merito (Deservedly)

This name arises in Scotland around the lands of Dunlop in the district of Cunningham in Ayrshire. The name may be from 'dun lub', meaning 'fort at the bend'. The name may also derive from 'dunlapach', meaning 'muddy hill'. The name is recorded around 1260, when Dominus Willelmus de Dunlop is noted as a witness in a deed concerning the Burgh of Irvine. The name appears also in the 1296 Ragman Roll of those nobles submitting to Edward I of England. Constantyn Dunlop of that Ilk appears to have been summoned to Parliament as a minor baron at the end of the fifteenth century, and the name appears regularly in the charters of other prominent Dumfries and Ayrshire families of that time. The family continued to reside at Dunlop, and James Dunlop of Dunlop commanded a brigade under Wellington during the Peninsular War of 1808–14, obtaining the rank of major general. His eldest son was MP for Ayr and was created a baronet in 1838. This title became extinct in 1858. Another branch of the family were prominent Glasgow shipowners and merchants, and Sir Thomas Dunlop was created a baronet in 1916. He was Lord Provost and Lord Lieutenant of Glasgow from 1914 to 1917, and was decorated by several other countries. The name is, of course, now synonymous with the famous rubber company. In 1771 John Dunlop founded the first newspaper in the USA, *The Pennsylvania Packet*. He was also the printer of the Declaration of Independence.

EDMONSTONE

ARMS (Of Ednam LR 1/144)[1]
Or, three crescents Gules

CREST[8]
A camel's head and neck Proper

SUPPORTERS[8]
Two camels Proper

The Edmonstones are first noted as being prominent in Scotland around Edinburgh where lands of that name are to be found. 'Tun' means 'noble residence' or 'small village'. The 'Edmund' is suggested by Black to have been Aedmund, son of Forn, witness to a charter by Thor, son of Swane, in 1150. Henry de Edmundston witnessed a charter around 1200. Sir John de Edmonstone seems to have been a person of note at the court of David II, being employed on various embassies to England. He received as reward the barony of Boyne in Banffshire. Nisbet states that John Edmundstone received the barony of Ednam, which became the family's principal designation, from Robert II. He married Isabel, widow of James, Earl of Douglas, who was the king's own daughter. This is confirmed in a subsequent royal charter where David de Edmistoun is designed as 'our kinsman'. The family also acquired the lands of Duntreath, and numerous cadet houses have sprung from the main stem. James VI appointed Sir William Edmundstone of Duntreath to be captain of Doune Castle and steward of Monteith. The lands of Edmonstone near Edinburgh came to the family of Wauchope of Niddrie, and one of that name took the title of Lord Edmonstone when appointed to the Supreme Court Bench. Sir Archibald Edmonstone of the Duntreath line was created a baronet in 1774. The fifth Baronet of Duntreath was groom-in-waiting to Edward VII from 1907 to 1910.

FAIRLIE

ARMS (LR 4/25)[1]
Or, a lion rampant and in chief three stars Gules

CREST
A lion's head couped Or

MOTTO
Paratus sum (I am prepared)

This family first appears in Ayrshire as proprietors of the lands of Fairley (the village of Fairley near Largs still exists today). Nisbet, in his commentary on the Ragman Roll of those who submitted to Edward I of England in 1296, states that Robert de Ross was heritor to the lands of Fairly in Cunningham whence the family took its name. The arms of Ross and Fairly both contain a lion rampant but this is such a common feature of Scots heraldry that little can be deduced from it. The name also arose around Edinburgh, and William Fairlie received lands at Inverleith from Robert I. The Fairlies of Braid claimed descent from a natural son of Robert II, and Nisbet cited as evidence of this theory the fact that they bore the red lion rampant on a gold shield of the royal house. There is, however, no other evidence to substantiate this claim. The family of Braid claimed the chiefship of the name when the original Ayrshire line failed. They acquired, by purchase, the lands of Little Dreghorn in Ayrshire which they renamed Fairlie. This line also failed to produce a male heir, and Sir William Cunningham of Robertland, Baronet, who had married the sister of the last Laird of Fairlie, assumed the additional name of Fairlie in 1781.

FALCONER

ARMS (of Halkerton LR 1/100)[1]
Azure, a falcon displayed between three mullets Argent, on his breast a man's heart Gules

CREST
An angel in a praying posture Or, within an orle of laurel Proper

MOTTO
Vive ut vivas (Live that you may have life)

SUPPORTERS
Two falcons Proper

A name derived from the office of falconer, one who breeds or trains falcons or hawks for sport. Many great houses would have maintained their own falconer, and the principal family claimed to be falconers to the king. Nisbet lists the first recording of this name to be Ranulph, son of Walter, falconer to William the Lion around 1200. The falconer received from his king lands in the Mearns which were then named Hawkerton, being another reference to his office. Robert Falconer de Halkertoun is shown on the Ragman Roll swearing allegiance to Edward I of England in 1296. The family prospered and lands were obtained at Newton and Balendro. They achieved particular prominence in the seventeenth century when Sir David Falconer of Newton was appointed Lord President of the Court of Session in Edinburgh in 1682. Sir Alexander Falconer of Halkertoun was also appointed a judge of the Court of Session and took the title of 'Lord Halkertoun'. He was raised to the peerage as Baron Falconer of Halkertoun in 1647. The family also saw military service. The Honourable William Falconer was killed at the Battle of Quebec in 1759. Adrian, eighth Lord Falconer, succeeded his cousin George Keith, as Earl Marischal, and the title of 'Falconer' is now borne as a subsidiary title of the Earls of Kintore.

FENTON

ARMS (of that Ilk)[3]
Gules, a bend engrailed Argent

This family held the lands bearing their own name at Dirleton in East Lothian. They were powerful nobles, and the castle at Dirleton remains one of the finest examples of thirteenth-century fortified architecture. Sir William Fenton, styled 'Lord of Beaufort', was one of the auditors at Berwick of the competing claims for the Scottish throne between Bruce and Balliol. According to Nisbet, this noble, or perhaps his son, married Cecilia Bisset, co-heiress of William Bisset, Lord of Lovat. The principal seat of Lord Lovat, near Beauly, is still known as Beaufort Castle. The lowland Fentons ended in an heiress who married Whitelaw of that Ilk. Sir Thomas Erskine, first Earl of Kellie, received the titles of 'Viscount Fenton' and 'Baron Dirleton' as reward for rescuing James VI from the Gowrie conspirators. The title is still borne by the present Earl of Mar and Kellie, chief of the Clan Erskine.

FLEMING

Fleming, derived from the French, 'le Fleming', indicates the origin of the family as Flanders. The once-powerful medieval principality is now split between the Netherlands, Belgium and France. The Flemish were enterprising merchants who traded with England, Scotland and Wales in the latter part of the twelfth century. Baldwin, a distinguished Flemish leader, settled with his followers in Biggar in Lanarkshire, under grant of David I, and he became sheriff of Lanark under Malcolm IV and William the Lion. This office

ARMS (LR 1/56)[1]
*Quarterly, 1st & 4th, Gules, a chevron within a double
tressure flory counterflory Argent; 2nd & 3rd, Azure,
three fraises Argent*

CREST
A goat's head erased Argent, armed Or

MOTTO
Let the deed shaw

SUPPORTERS
*Two harts Proper attired with ten tynes Or, each gorged
of a collar, Azure charged with three fraises Argent*

appears to have been hereditary for some time. Nine Flemings signed the Ragman Roll, swearing fealty to Edward I of England in 1296, although one of the signatories, Sir Robert Fleming, was among the first to join Robert the Bruce and assist him after the death of the Comyn at Dumfries in 1306. Sir Malcolm Fleming of Cumbernauld was created Earl of Wigton in 1342 by David II for his help in keeping him safe from Edward Balliol and the English. His grandson, Thomas, sold the earldom to Archibald Douglas, Lord of Galloway, in 1371, which was confirmed by Robert II. Sir Malcolm Fleming of Biggar and Cumbernauld was knighted by Robert III and was one of the hostages for release of James I from his English captivity in 1423. He was a friend and counsellor of William, sixth Earl of Douglas, and was a member of the party which went to Edinburgh Castle on the invitation of Governor Livingstone and Chancellor Crichton in November 1440. Douglas, his brother David, and Fleming were summarily arrested, briefly and hurriedly tried and then beheaded. His younger son, Sir Robert, had the forfeited lands returned to him by James II

when it was held that his father had 'died at the faith and peace of His Majesty'. He was created a Lord of Parliament some time before 1460. His grandson, John, the second Lord Fleming, was one of the lords appointed as guardians to James V in his infancy in July 1515. John became Chancellor of Scotland in 1517. He was assassinated on 1 November 1524, while out hawking, by John Tweedie of Drummelzier and others. The third Lord Fleming, Malcolm, was Great Chamberlain of Scotland, and married Janet Stewart, the natural daughter of James IV. He was killed at the Battle of Pinkie in 1547. The fourth Lord Fleming accompanied the young Queen Mary to France in 1548 to marry the heir to the throne. He continued as Great Chamberlain of Scotland for life, and was one of the eight commissioners to the royal wedding in 1558. He was amongst those taken ill at Dieppe on the return journey, supposedly poisoned. Three of the party died immediately and Fleming a fortnight later in Paris. John, sixth Lord Fleming, was recreated Earl of Wigton in 1606. The family were Jacobites and the earl attended James VII after the Revolution of 1688. He opposed the Treaty of Union, voting against every article in the Parliament of 1706. At the rising of 1715 he was arrested by the governor of Edinburgh Castle. The title became dormant with the death in 1747 of Charles Fleming, who had succeeded his brother in the earldom. The most distinguished bearer of this name in recent times has been Sir Alexander Fleming, who discovered penicillin.

FLETCHER

ARMS (LR 3/35)[1]
Sable, a cross flory between four escallops Argent

CREST
*A demi bloodhound Azure, langued Gules, gorged with a
ducal crown Or*

MOTTO
Dieu pour nous (God for us)

SUPPORTERS
Two griffins Proper

The name Fletcher is derived from the French *flechier* – an arrow maker. The word was such a common trade name that it became used in Gaelic as *fleisdear*. In the eighteenth century, some families went full circle and anglicised the name Mac-an-leistear back into Fletcher. One band of Mac-an-leistear settled in Glenorchy in Argyll sometime after the 11th century and became arrowmakers to the MacGregors. Small groups of Mac-an-leisters settled in glens belonging to other clans, for whom they presumably made arrows. The earliest recorded chief was Angus Mac-an-leister, who was born around 1450. Duncan Campbell of Glenorchy coveted the Mac-an-leister lands, and as he was high in the favour of James VI, he had royal authority to maintain a large band of armed retainers which he employed in a campaign of violence and intimidation. He deliberately provoked a dispute with the chief of the Mac-an-leisters, and trumped up a charge of murder against him. Mac-an-leister was compelled to sign a deed ceding his family lands to the Campbells and thereafter they were only tenants in Glenorchy.

Archibald, the ninth chief, led the Mac-an-leisters in the first Jacobite rising in 1715. His younger brother, John, called them out again in the Forty-five, although his brother, the chief, provided some men for the Hanoverian forces under his Campbell landlords, thereby avoiding forfeiture.

Andrew Fletcher of Saltoun, 'the Patriot', was one of the fiercest opponents of political union with England. Born in 1653, he became MP for Haddington in 1678. He was forced to flee to Holland after joining Monmouth's rebellion against James VII. He became the leader of the Anti-Union Country Party in the last Scottish Parliament, predicting that England would ruin Scotland's economy.

FORRESTER

ARMS (LR 43/42)[1]
Argent, three bugle horns Sable, garnished Vert and stringed Gules

CREST
A hound's head erased Proper collared Gules

MOTTO
Blaw hunter blaw thy horn

SUPPORTERS
Dexter, a bloodhound Proper, collared Gules; sinister, a greyhound Proper, collared Gules

It is possible that this family is of Celtic druidic origin, descending from Marnin the Forester, who held lands in Dunipace, Stirlingshire, about 1200. Sir Adam Forrester, first of Corstorphine, is generally regarded as the founder of the clan. He was an ambassador, merchant, Provost of Edinburgh, Keeper of the Great Seal of Scotland and Deputy Chamberlain of Scotland. In 1376 he acquired the estate of Corstorphine in Midlothian (now part of Edinburgh), where Corstorphine Castle (now demolished) and the Collegiate Church of Corstorphine, with the effigies of three of the chiefs, were built by the family. The Dower House of the Lords Forrester now houses a local-history museum.

Adam's son, Sir John Forrester the elder, also became Keeper of the Great Seal of Scotland and was Chamberlain of Scotland and Keeper of the Household to James I. Sir James, the seventh chief, was killed in the disastrous Battle of Pinkie in 1547. The tenth chief, Sir George Forrester, was created a Baronet of Nova Scotia and raised to the peerage as Lord Forrester of Corstorphine, in 1633. On his death the baronetcy title became dormant, and it still awaits a claimant. James and William Baillie, the sons-in-law of the first Lord, assumed the name and arms of Forrester and inherited the title under a re-grant of the peerage. James, an ardent royalist, was fined heavily by Cromwell and the estates became burdened with debts. He was murdered in 1679 by his mistress, Mrs Christian Nimmo, when his brother, who was mad, inherited the title. The fifth Lord, Colonel George of the Grenadier and Life Guards fought under Marlborough at Oudenarde and Malplaquet in Flanders in 1708 and 1709, and was wounded in the Battle of Preston in 1715. Eventually the male line died out and the title descended through heiresses to the Earls of Verulam. The chiefly family had several landed cadets, one of whom, Sir John Forrester of Niddry, died at the Battle of Flodden in 1513. Two French cadet branches, Le Forestier du Buisson-Sainte-Marquerite, and Le Forestier de Foucrainville, in Normandy, descend from Sir Adam, and M. Jean Le Forestier is their head. There was a Stirlingshire branch, the Forresters of Garden, heritable keepers of the Torwood to the Scottish kings (the Torwood was a Royal forest and hunting ground, and may have been a sacred Celtic grove known to the Romans as Medionemeton, or Mid Grove). They owned the barony of Garden, with the Tower of Garden as well as the Torwood, where the ruins of Torwood Castle still stand. Sir Duncan, first of Torwood, was Comptroller of the Royal Household to James IV. Sir David, fourth of Torwood, was killed in the Battle of Pinkie in 1547. The family were virtually hereditary provosts of Stirling burgh; no fewer than eight of them held this office. The Church of the Holy Rude in Stirling has the Forrester Aisle, a former private family chapel. A cadet of Garden was the first of the Fifeshire Chieftains, the Forresters of Strathendry, who built Strathendry Castle, a sixteenth-century tower house in Leslie in Fife, where both Mary, Queen of Scots and Oliver Cromwell stayed. Strathendry Castle is the only inhabitable Forrester stronghold today. The Lords Forrester of Corstorphine have been recognised as chiefs of this Lowland clan since the seventeenth century. The potential chief is Sir John Duncan Grimston, Baronet, seventh Earl of Verulam, sixteenth Lord Forrester of Corstorphine, and patron of the Clan Forrester Society. His seat is Gorhambury in St Albans in Hertfordshire, with its fine Palladian mansion. His heir, Viscount Grimston, is the Master of Forrester. Forresters fought and died at the following battles: Sauchieburn, Pinkie and Langside in Scotland; Halidon Hill, Flodden and Preston in England; Oudenarde and Malplaquet in Flanders; and the many battles of the Le Forestier cadets, including the Battle of Ivry. They were accessories to the murder of David Rizzio, secretary and close friend of Mary, Queen of Scots, and also in Mary's imprisonment in Holyrood House. They held important posts, including those of Keeper of the Great Seal of Scotland; secretary to the king; Chamberlain of Scotland; Master of the Household to James I; Comptroller of the Royal Household to James IV and to his wife, Margaret Tudor; Grand Provisor to Queen Arabella; sheriff of Edinburgh and Lothian; keepers of Edinburgh, Stirling and Skipness Castles, and governor of Belle Island; Bishop of Brechin and Abbot of Balmerino; and heralds to French kings, Normandy King of Arms and Picardy Herald. Among the clan relics and heirlooms is the Corstorphine Pendant, an armorial pendant of gilded bronze, in the Royal Scottish Museum; Sir Duncan Forrester's *Antiphony*, a fifteenth-century vellum book of Eastertide Music, in the Church of the Holy Rude in Stirling; and the Corstorphine Casket of carved oak mounted in silver, a reputed gift from Margaret Tudor, wife of James IV.

FOTHERINGHAM

The name in Scotland comes from the parish of Inverarity in Angus and is probably a corruption of Fotheringhay, a manor in Northamptonshire, because of the resemblance in ancient script between 'ay' and 'm'. The manor was one of those held by David of Huntingdon, later David I of Scotland. By an unlikely tradition, the name of Fotheringay is supposed to belong to a Hungarian who came with the retinue of Edward Atheling whose sister, Margaret, married Malcolm III. Huwe de Fotheringeye rendered homage to Edward I of England, appearing on the Ragman Roll of 1296, in common with many of the Scottish nobility. During the reign of Robert III, John Fotheringhame acquired the lands of West Powrie in what was then part of Forfarshire. It is believed the land was acquired through marriage to a daughter of the Ogilvies of Auchterhouse around 1399. In 1481, Nicholas

ARMS (LR 12/42)[1]
*Quarterly, 1st, Ermine, three bars Gules (Fotheringham);
2nd, Gules, a lion rampant Or, armed and langued Azure
with a scimitar in his dexter paw Proper, hilted and pommelled of the Second all within a bordure of the Field
(Scrymgeour); 3rd, Argent, a lion rampant guardant
Gules, crowned Or, in the middle chief a crescent all
within a bordure of the Second (Ogilvy); 4th grand quarter, counterquartered, (I) & (IV), Or, a fess chequy Azure
and Argent; (II) & (III), Argent, a galley her oars in
action Sable, all within a bordure Azure charged with
eight buckles Or (Stewart)*

CRESTS
(1) A griffin segreant Proper (Fotheringham)
(2) A lion's paw erased holding a scimitar Proper

MOTTOES
(1) Be it fast
(2) Dissipate (Disperse)

SUPPORTERS
*Two Savages, wreathed about the middle with laurel,
each carrying over his exterior shoulder a club all Proper*

Fotheringham of Powrie attempted to deprive the widow of the Earl of Montrose of her lands at Dunbog in Glenesk. Nicholas was among the many Scottish nobles who died at Flodden in 1513. Sir Alexander Fotheringham of Powrie, an ardent supporter of Charles I, was taken prisoner at Alyth and sent to England in 1645. He died in exile in France in 1652. His grandson, David, was a renowned equestrian and was particularly fond of horse breeding. He matriculated the family's coat of arms at the Lyon Court around 1677. Thomas Frederick Fotheringham, a captain in the Scots Fusiliers, served with distinction throughout the Crimean War (1853–56). He married Lady Charlotte Carnegie, sister of the ninth Earl of Southesk. Their son, Walter, succeeded to the handsome estates of Grandtully and Murthly in Perthshire, together with the two splendid castles which still stand on these estates. Murthly was originally a royal hunting lodge and its main tower was probably built at the beginning of the fifteenth century. It was sub-stantially extended in a classical style in the seventeenth and eighteenth centuries. The ballroom, in the east wing of the house, is par-ticularly splendid.

FULLARTON

ARMS (of that Ilk LR 1/150)[1]
Argent, three otters' heads erased Gules

CREST
An otter's head erased Gules

MOTTO
Lux in tenebris (Light in darkness)

This name is often spelt 'Fullerton', and the principal family of this name held the barony of Fullarton in Ayrshire. The name itself may be a derivative of 'fowler', and relate to the keeping of birds, or may come from 'fuller', meaning a 'bleacher of cloth'. The fam-ily are said to be of Anglo–Saxon or Norman origin, and the first recorded instance of the name occurs towards the end of the thirteenth century, when Alunus de Fowlerton founded and endowed a convent of Carmelite or White Friars at Irvine towards the end of the thir-teenth century. Adam de Fowlerton received a charter to the lands of Fowlerton, granted between 1283 and 1309, from James, High Steward of Scotland. Fergus de Foulertoun received the estate of Kilmichael on Arran, confirmed by a royal charter of Robert III on 26 November 1391. Reginald de Fowlertoun of that Ilk was taken prisoner at the Battle of Durham in 1346. He remained a prisoner of the English king for many years. The family remained in royal favour and extended their land holdings considerably over the next cen-tury. James Fullerton of Fullarton married the daughter of a kinsman, Fullerton of Dreghorn, at the beginning of the seventeenth century and the principal family thereafter was styled 'of Fullarton and Dreghorn'. The family fol-lowed a fairly martial career thereafter, John Fullarton rising to the rank of colonel in the army of Louis XIII of France. Sir Archibald Fullarton of Kilmichael served throughout the Peninsular War (1808–14), during which he was severely wounded at the Battle of Salamanca. John Fullarton, second son of the Laird of Carstairs, was elevated to the Supreme Court Bench in 1829, taking the title of 'Lord Fullerton'.

GALBRAITH

This surname is said to derive from the Gaelic for 'strange or foreign Briton'. Black states that it may simply mean 'the Briton's son'. In Gaelic the clan were known as 'Clann a' Bhreatannaich'. The original Galbraith seems therefore to have been one of those who fled from the south to live among the Gaels of Strathclyde. Gillescop Galbrath witnessed a charter by Malduin, Lord of Lennox, around 1208. At the beginning of the reign of Alexander II further charters were witnessed and William, son of Galbrat, received land in Lennox at Buthernockis and Kincaith. The Galbraiths of Bathernock, afterwards Baldernock, became the principal family of this name, from whom were descended the Galbraiths of Culcreuch whose splendid castle still stands to this day. There is some evidence that the Galbraiths were related to the mighty Celtic Earls of Lennox, as in one charter Alwin, Earl of Lennox, referred to Gillespie Galbraith as 'nepote nostro' ('our nephew'). In the twentieth century two members of the family of Galbraith of Barskimming, cadets of Culcreuch, have served as Members of Parliament for constituencies in Glasgow. John Kenneth Galbraith has been one of the most influential economists of the twentieth century.

GALLOWAY

A territorial name from the former Celtic princedom and the modern district in south-west Scotland. The name can be found in Dunbartonshire from about the sixteenth century. There were other families bearing this name who later appeared on the east coast of Scotland. Robert Galloway, author of 'poems, epistles and songs in the Scottish dialect', was born in 1752. He was originally a shoemaker, but became a bookseller and librarian in Glasgow. He died in 1794. General Sir Archibald Galloway was a distinguished soldier who served in the East India Company for thirty-five years. He became chairman of the company in 1849. He was created a Knight of the Order of the Bath and died in 1850. The name is now perhaps best known for the rare breed of native Scottish cattle still found in the district.

GARDEN

This name is frequently spelt 'Gardyne', and Black states that a family 'long of that Ilk' hailed from the barony of Gardyne in the parish of Kirkdon in Angus. They built a strong and splendid tower, which was extended in the late sixteenth and seventeenth centuries. Gardyne Castle is one of the most unusual and attractive examples of Scottish vernacular architecture. The Gardynes seem to have been almost permanently quarrelling with the nearby Guthries, whose even more impressive Castle of Guthrie was only a few miles away. Patrick Gardyne of that Ilk was slain in 1578 by William Guthrie, and in the feud that followed both sides appear to have suffered heavy casualties. There are two accounts of the origin of the feud: according to the Gardyne version, Patrick and his kinsman Robert were slain on Carbundow Moor in 1578, and those deaths were avenged by the killing of Alexander Guthrie in Inverpeffer in 1587 by Thomas Gairden. The Guthrie account holds that Alexander Guthrie was murdered by his cousin, Thomas Gairden of Legatston, and that he was avenged by his nephew, William Guthrie, who slew the said Patrick. Whatever the cause of the feud, the result was ultimately a victory for the more powerful Guthries and David, the tenth Laird,

sold the castle and much of the lands and acquired the estate of Lawton. In 1603 he married Janet Lindsay, daughter of Sir David Lindsay, Lord Edzell. This family failed in the direct male line and is now represented by Bruce-Gardyne of Middleton. The arms of a black boar's head on a silver shield are borne by the family of Gardyne of Troup, descended from Gardyne of Banchory. The first Laird of Troup was a son of the house of Banchory who was sent by Charles I to assist Gustavus Adolphus, King of Sweden, during the Thirty Years' War. He saw distinguished service and remained at the Swedish court until 1654. He returned to Scotland and purchased the lands of Troup in Banffshire, which remain in the family to this day.

GARTSHORE

ARMS (of that Ilk LR 1/310)[1]
Argent, a St Andrew's cross between four holly leaves Vert

CREST
An eagle displayed Proper

MOTTO
Renew my age

The lands of Gartshore are in the parish of Kirkintilloch in Dunbartonshire. The family of Gartshore of that Ilk was of great antiquity and held charters to their lands of Gartshore dating from the reign of Alexander

II. On the death without issue of Patrick Gartshore of that Ilk, the estates devolved upon a younger brother and they remained within the family until they passed to the line of the Murray Baronets of Ochtertyre at the beginning of the nineteenth century. John Murray assumed into his surname the additional name of Gartshore. The most noted member of this family appears to have been Dr Maxwell Gartshore, who wrote extensively in the mid eighteenth century; his works are considered the basis of modern obstetrics.

GAYRE

A Celtic origin has been suggested for this name derived from 'gèarr', meaning 'stocky'. The present chiefly family, however, authoritatively assert that the name hailes from Cornwall, where the de Kayres were lords of many manors. The name as it arises in Orkney and Shetland may have a separate origin, deriving from the Norse, 'geirr', meaning 'spear'. A cadet of the line of Otys Gayre of the

manor of Gayre in Cornwall settled in Ross-shire around 1649. The Maccullochs had until this time held the lands of Nigg, but these passed to the Gayres through marriage to Katherine Macculloch. Alexander Gayre of Nigg and his son, Thomas, extended the family's holdings. In 1679 Thomas became a notary public. Thomas, fourth Laird of Nigg, was notary public at Fort Rose and chancellor of

ARMS (LR 66/25)[1]
Quarterly, 1st & 4th, Argent, a fleur de lis Sable, in the dexter chief point a mullet Vert (Gayre); 2nd & 3rd, Ermine, a fret engrailed Gules (McCulloch of Nigg)

CREST
Issuing from a crest coronet Or, of four (three visible) strawberry leaves, a mount Vert

MOTTO
Super astra spero (I hope beyond the stars)

On Compartment
Sero sed serio (Late but in earnest)

SUPPORTERS
(on a compartment embellished with variegated bay or laurel Proper, berries Purpure) Dexter, a lion rampant Sable, armed and langued Gules holding with the dexter forepaw a lance Or pointed Argent, charged on the dexter shoulder with a Knot of Savoy Or; sinister, an ermine Proper langued Gules holding with the sinister forepaw a staff Or entwined with ivy leaves Proper fructed Purpure, charged on the sinister shoulder with a Knot of Savoy Or

STANDARD
The Arms in the hoist, and of two tracts Argent and Vert semée of sprigs of golden or variegated bay or laurel Proper fructed Purpure, upon which is depicted a lion

rampant guardant Sable supporting a spear Or pointed Argent in the first compartment, the crest and a fret engrailed Gules in the second compartment, and a fleur de lis Sable charged with a mullet Or, on a wreath Or composed of four roses Gules, seeded Gold, barbed Vert, set saltireways in the 3rd compartment, along with the Slughorn 'An Gayre' in letters Or upon two transverse bands Gules

ADDITIONAL BADGES
(1) A cross moline Sable (granted by the Chief Herald of Ireland); (2a) on a mount Vert a castle with three turrets Proper masoned Sable, fenestrated and port and caps Gules, flagged Argent a fleur de lis Sable; (2b) a fleur de lis Sable ensigned of a coronet Or (granted by the Council and Bureau of Heraldry of South Africa)

PINSEL
Vert, a mount Vert issuant from a crest coronet Or within a strap of leather Sable buckled and embellished Or inscribed with the Motto 'Super astra spero' in letters Or all within a circlet Or bearing the title 'Gayre of Gayre and Nigg' in letters Gules and in the fly an Escrol Or surmounting a sprig of variegated bay or noble laurel Proper, berries Purpure, bearing the Slogan 'An Gayre' in letters Gules

PLANT BADGE
Variegated bay or noble laurel Proper berries Purpure

GUIDON
Barry of five Argent and Vert a cross moline Sable

the diocese of Ross. He became a prosperous merchant and councillor for Cromarty which was at the time a prominent sea port. The Gayres became embroiled in the eighteenth-century ecclesiastical disputes which raged throughout Scotland. In 1756 the royal candidate for the church at Nigg was strongly opposed by Thomas Gayre, although the Crown candidate was eventually inducted. The Gayres became Dissenters, and William Gayre supplied land at Balchreggan to build a church. The church was seized at the end of the century by Lord Akerville when the lease came to an end, and he tore it down to build

Shandwick House. The house itself fell down, which the faithful attributed to the wrath of the Lord. The present chief has virtually rebuilt the clan after distinguished service in the Second World War. He served for a time as Minister of Education with the Allied government of occupation in Italy, and was awarded by King Umberto an augmentation to his coat of arms of the royal knots of Savoy. He has established his seat at Minard Castle in Argyll and is a noted heraldic expert, having published numerous works on heraldry and related subjects.

GED

ARMS (of that Ilk LR 1/310)[1]
Azure, three geds hauriant Argent

CREST
A pike's head Proper

MOTTO
Durat ditat placet (It sustains, it enriches, it pleases)

'Ged' is the Scots word for a pike. There are several lands named after this fierce fish, which may also be given in the plural as ged-

des. The arms of both Ged and Geddes show three pike, and this is clearly canting, i.e. merely a pun upon the bearer's name. The English name for such a fish is 'luce', and various Norman families named De Lucy, also have coats of arms with these fish. There may therefore have been a Norman knight come to Scotland who found that his De Lucy shield earned him the Scots name of Ged or Geddes. (The perils of relying upon heraldic evidence, however, can be demonstrated by the fact that one of the editors of this work bears as part of his arms, three lucies, or geds, and his descent from an English knight of Shropshire in 1425 has no relation to either Ged or Geddes, or to de Lucy.) Black relates that one William Geddes was killed in 1558 in a feud with the family of Tweedie, and there is an entry in the records of the Privy Council granting respite (i.e., pardon or reprieve) to James Tweedie of Drumelzier for the cruel slaughter of William Geddes. William Ged, a goldsmith in Edinburgh, is credited with a great improvement in the science of printing, when in 1725

he invented stereotyping. He moved to London in 1729 where he went into partnership to establish his process. William Ged died without seeing his invention properly established, but his fame did prove of benefit to his family. James, his son, a captain in the Duke of Perth's regiment fighting for Prince Charles Edward Stuart in the Forty-five, was captured after the defeat of the prince at Culloden and condemned to death. The Duke of Newcastle was persuaded, on account of his father's work, to intercede, and James Ged was released in 1748.

GIBSONE

ARMS (of Pentland LR 2/52)[1]
Gules, three keys fesseways, wards downwards, in pale Or

CREST
A pelican vulning Proper

MOTTO
Pandite coelestes portae (Open ye heavenly gates)

SUPPORTERS
Two angels Proper

This name is said by Black to derive from the personal name 'son of Gib' (Gilbert). Johun Gibson surrendered the Castle of Rothesay in 1335. The family rose to prominence in Fife, and the Gibsons of Durie were to found a dynasty of lawyers when Sir Alexander Gibson was elevated to the Bench with the title of 'Lord Durie' in 1621. He married a daughter of Sir Thomas Craig of Riccarton, the celebrated expert on feudal law. The arms which they bear are said to refer to one of the fifteenth-century lairds of Durie who received a grant of armorial bearings from the pope, alluding to the keys of St Peter. They purchased the barony of Pentland near Edinburgh in 1633, and the imposing family mausoleum still stands in Old Pentland Graveyard. They became baronets of Nova Scotia. This did not occur entirely without mishap, and Sir Walter Scott relates in his *Minstrelsy of the Scottish Border,* the harrowing tale of the alleged kidnapping of Alexander

Gibson, the seventeenth-century Lord President of the Court of Session. The story goes that Willie Armstrong was due to stand trial for having stolen a cow. The authorities had let it be known that they were determined to make an example of Willie, who was the last member of a notorious family of border reivers. Willie's wife, fearing the death penalty for her husband, sought the assistance of the Earl of Traquair hoping that he could sue for clemency. Traquair apparently agreed to this, provided that Willie, on escaping the scaffold, should in turn agree to abduct Gibson of Durie before he was able to give an anticipated opinion against His Lordship in a land dispute pending before the Court. Scott captured Traquair's evil scheme in his verse, 'If auld Durie to heaven were flown, or if auld Durie to hell were gane, or if he could be but ten days stown my bonny braid lands would still be ma ain'. Will was released and, as good as his word, he fell upon Lord Durie in a darkened close off the Canongate in Edinburgh and held him confined near Moffat. The Lord President was assumed to have died in some manner, and after an interval of mourning, a new Lord President was appointed. The Traquair case was called again and judgment given for the earl, who presumably ordered Lord Durie's release. He came back to Edinburgh three months later, a broken man and died at Durie in June 1644. The family continued to reside at Durie and though many are buried within their barony of Pentland, they never built a family seat there. Sir John Gibson, sixth Baronet, assumed the additional surname of Carmichael on inheriting estates through his mother, a sister of the Earl of Hyndford. Sir Thomas Gibson Carmichael, eleventh Baronet,

was Governor of Madras from 1911 to 1912 and of Bengal from 1912 to 1917, and was raised to the peerage as Baron Carmichael in 1912. The representation of the family had devolved upon the daughter of the fourth baronet, whose son had taken the name of Gibson in 1810.

GLADSTAINS

ARMS (of that Ilk LR 1/311)[1]
Argent, a savage's head couped distilling drops of blood and thereupon a bonnet composed of bay and holly leaves all Proper within an orle of eight martlets Sable

CREST
A gryphon issuant holding a sword in her dexter talon Proper

MOTTO
Fide et virtute (With faith and valour)

This name is variously spelt, but appears to derive from the old English 'glede stan', which means 'rock of the hawk'. The ancient lands associated with this name appear to have been in Teviotdale, and there is still land by this name near the village of Biggar in Lanarkshire. Herbert de Gledstanes is shown on the Ragman Roll of nobles giving their submission to Edward I of England in 1296. William de Gledstanes witnessed a charter around 1354. Black suggests that this may be the same person as Sir William of Gledstanes who was present at the Battle of Poitiers in 1356. The name being of territorial origin, however, means that such connections must always be considered dubious. John Gladstanes who claimed descent from Gledstanes of that Ilk was appointed to the

Supreme Court Bench in January 1542. George Gledstanes was made Bishop of Caithness in 1600 and in 1606 was translated to the archbishopric of St Andrews. He died in May 1615. The most prominent family claiming descent from Gledstanes of that Ilk, were the Lairds of Toftcombs near Biggar. They became prosperous merchants in the port of Leith, and John Gledstones (born on 11 December 1764) was to move to Liverpool and become the first Baronet of Fasque. He amassed a considerable fortune and marked his Scottish origin by endowing a splendid new church at Leith and making considerable gifts to Trinity College Glenalmond, the Scottish public school. One of his younger sons was William Ewart Gladstone, the great nineteenth-century Prime Minister, who is also remembered for the distinctly shaped bag named after him. The family name was standardised as Gladstone by royal licence on 10 February 1835. The Prime Minister's son was raised to the peerage as Viscount Gladstone, but this title became extinct in 1930. The main line, however, still continues to this day bearing the undifferenced arms.

GLAS

This name is more commonly spelt 'Glass', and is probably derived from 'glas', the Gaelic adjective meaning 'grey'. It may be a shortened form of MacGillieglais, meaning 'son of the grey lad'. The name is recorded in the Lyon registers as 'Glas of that Ilk'. Glass of Ascog on the isle of Bute is listed as a notable family from as early as the fifteenth century.

Black records a grant of land to Alexander Glas in 1506. Nisbet also lists the family of Glass of Sauchie, whom he declares to be related to the chiefly family, due to the similarity of their heraldry. The Reverend Alexander Glas, possibly of the Sauchie branch, became renowned for the religious sect known as the 'Glassites', which he

ARMS (of that Ilk LR 2/82)[1]
Argent, a fleur de lis between three mullets within a bordure Gules

CREST
A mermaid holding in her dexter hand a comb and in her sinister a looking glass all Proper

MOTTO
Luctor non mergor (I struggle but am not overwhelmed)

On Compartment
Pro patria non unquam non paratus
(Nothing I would not do for my country)

SUPPORTERS
Two horses Argent bridled and saddled Proper the housings Gules fringed Or

founded. His teachings opposed the established Church, holding that every meeting of Christians constituted a church within itself. He was expelled from the Church of Scotland but he was not otherwise penalised, and he wrote a number of controversial pamphlets which were widely read after their publication in 1762. Anderson, however, narrates the fate of a much less fortunate member of this family, John Glas, master mariner. He was apparently educated into the medical profession and afterwards became captain of a merchant vessel plying trade to Brazil. He became involved in a scheme to form a new settlement on the coast of Africa, but this was not successful and for a time he was imprisoned by Spanish authorities. He was released on the intervention of the British government. In 1765 he set sail with his wife and daughter for the return to England, having on board all that he possessed, including a considerable amount of gold. The crew mutinied near the coast of Ireland and murdered Captain Glas and threw his wife and daughter overboard. The mutineers attempted to conceal their crime by alleging there had been a shipwreck, but they were ultimately forced to confess and were executed in October 1765.

GLEN

ARMS (of that Ilk)[2]
Argent, three martlets Sable

CREST
An arm embowed, vested Sable, in the hand Proper a heart Gules

The lands of Glen, from which the family of Glen of that Ilk took its name, are in the parish of Traquair in Peeblesshire. A magnificent castle still stands on these lands, although it was built for the family of Tennant, now Lords Glenconner. Colban de Glen received a charter from Robert the Bruce in 1328 confirming him in his lands in the sheriffdom of Peebles. Thomas de Glen was granted a safe conduct to travel to England in 1422. John Glenn travelled considerably further when he was launched from Cape Canaveral in Florida, USA, in the space capsule *Friendship VII*, to orbit the earth on 20 February 1962. He was thereafter elected a senator for the state of Ohio and made an unsuccessful attempt to become the Democratic Party candidate for the presidency of the United States in 1984.

GLENDINNING

ARMS (of that Ilk)[10]
Quarterly, Argent and Sable, a cross parted per cross indented counterchanged of the Second and First

The family of Glendinning of that Ilk takes its name from the ancient territory of that name, which comprised a considerable part of Teviotdale and Dumfries. Black states that a charter was granted to Adam de Glendonwyn of part of the lands and baronies of Clifton and Merbottle in Roxburghshire in the reign of Alexander III. Sir Adam de Glendonwyn was a supporter of Robert the Bruce and a companion of Sir James Douglas on his pilgrimage to take the heart of Bruce to the Holy

Land. The connection with the house of Douglas remained strong, and Sir Simon Glendinning was killed in the battle between the Douglases and the Percys at Otterburn in 1388. The power of the family grew, and another Sir Simon Glendinning was a favourite of James II who extended his Borders land-holdings. The family also became hereditary baillies of Eskdale. In 1458 they obtained the barony of Parton in the Stewartry of Kirk-cudbrightshire, and this was to become the territorial designation of the main family. The fortunes of the family were reversed when

John Glendinning, eleventh Baron of Parton, joined Montrose in his campaign against the opponents of Charles I in the civil war. He was denounced as a traitor and all his goods were forfeited. He fled to the Continent and remained there until the Restoration. Anderson states that the male line of this family ended in 1720 when Agnes Glendinning married James Murray of Conheat. Black, however, points out that the death of William Glendinning of that Ilk is recorded in the commissary papers for Kirkcudbright in 1798.

GRAY

The surname is originally French, being first borne by Fulbert, Great Chamberlain of Robert, Duke of Normandy, who granted him the castle and lands of Croy or Gray in Picardy which he thereafter assumed as the family surname. His daughter, Arlotta, is said to have been the mother of William the Conqueror. In England several families from this source were raised to high rank, and spelt their name 'Grey'. From the Dukes of Suffolk came the amiable and accomplished Lady Jane Grey, who was an innocent victim of the ambitions of her father. She was proclaimed Queen of England and reigned for nine days in 1553, but she perished on the block in February 1554. In Scotland, John de Gray was a witness to donations in favour of the Monastery of Coldstream during the reign of Alexander III. He was descended from Lord Grey of Chillingham in Northumberland, and became steward to the Earls of March. Like

many others, the Grays swore fealty to Edward I of England in the Ragman Roll of 1296, but they were soon following Robert the Bruce on the long fight for Scottish independence. Sir Andrew Gray was one of the first to scale the rock of Edinburgh Castle when it was taken from the English in 1312. He was rewarded with several grants of land, including Longforgen in Perthshire, for his services to the Crown. One of his descendents, another Sir Andrew, was one of the Scottish nobles who met James I at Durham from his return from captivity in England. He was created Lord Gray in 1444. Patrick, Master of Gray, son of the second Lord Gray, was a Gentleman of the Bedchamber to James II, and when the king stabbed the Earl of Douglas, Gray struck the next blow with a battleaxe. His son, the third Lord Gray, became Lord Justice General of Scotland in 1506. Patrick Gray of Butter-gask, the fifth Lord, was taken prisoner at the Battle of Solway Moss in 1542, and was ransomed for £500 sterling. He was one of the first promoters of the Reformation in Scotland, and in 1567 joined in the defence of the infant James VI. Patrick, Master of Gray, the seventh Lord, was a great favourite of James VI but became embroiled in the intrigues of the time, including the death of the king's mother, Mary, Queen of Scots. He was eventually tried for treason but on the intercession of the Earl of Huntly and Lord Hamilton his life was spared and he was exiled. Andrew, eighth Lord Gray, was lieutenant of the 'Gens D'Armes' in France under Lord Gordon. He was ordered to be banished from the kingdom by Order of the Estates for being with the Marquess of Montrose in 1645, but the sentence was never carried out. In 1649 he was excommunicated by the General Assembly of the Church of Scotland for his Catholicism. In 1639 Lord Gray resigned his honours to Charles I and obtained a new patent in favour, after himself, of his daughter Ann who had married William Gray, younger of Pittendrum. William, like the rest of the family, was a staunch royalist, and he commanded a regiment, which he had raised mostly at his own expense, at the Battle of Worcester in 1651. He was killed in a duel by the Earl of Southesk in 1660. For a time the title passed to the Earls of Moray, but on the death in 1895 of the fourteenth Earl of Moray and eighteenth Lord Gray, the title passed to his niece, Eveleen, Baroness Gray in her own right. The present Lord Gray is barred from the chiefship of his family by a famous decision of the Court of the Lord Lyon in 1950 – the case of Gray Petitioner, which established that in Scots heraldic law the bearing of a compound, or double-barrelled name, was an absolute bar to assuming the chiefship of a Scottish clan or family.

GUNN

ARMS (of Banniskirk LR 56/63)[1]
Argent, on a sea in base undy Azure, a three-masted ship Gules, flagged of Scotland (Azure, a saltire Argent) sails furled Proper, on a chief Gules, a buckle between two mullets pierced Or

CREST
A dexter cubit arm attired in the proper tartan of Clan Gunn, the hand Proper grasping a basket-hilted sword blade Gules, hilted Argent

MOTTO
Aut pax aut bellum (Either peace or war)

BADGE
Within a chaplet of juniper an arm naked, the hand Proper grasping a basket hilted sword, blade Gules, hilted Argent

GUIDON
The Arms in the hoist, of this livery Argent upon which is depicted the badge along with the motto 'Aut pax aut bellum' extended in the fly in letters Gules

PINSEL
Argent, bearing upon a Wreath of the Liveries Argent and Gules, the said Crest within a strap of leather Proper, buckled and embellished Or, inscribed with the motto, 'Aut pax aut bellum' in letters of the Field, all within a circlet, Or, fimbriated Vert, bearing the title 'Gunn of Banniskirk' in letters Gules, and in the fly an Escrol Gules, surmounting a sprig of juniper Proper, bearing the Slogan, 'Clyth' in letters of the Field

Gunni came to Caithness at the end of the twelfth century when his wife, Ragnhild, inherited estates there from her brother, Harald, Jarl of Orkney. His wife was descended from St Ragnvald, founder of the great cathedral of St Magnus at Kirkwall. Gunni, whose name itself meant 'war', was descended from Viking adventurers. His grandfather, Sweyn, had been killed in 1171 on a raid in Dublin. The first chief of Clan Gunn to appear definitively in records was George Gunn, who was crouner, or coroner, of Caithness in the fifteenth century. The proper Celtic patronymic of the Gunn chiefs was 'MacSheumais Chataich', but George Gunn was more widely known as 'Am Braisdeach Mor', the 'great brooch-wearer', so called for the insignia worn by him as coroner. He is said to have held court in his castle at Clyth in such splendour as to rival any Highland chief. The Gunns' traditional enemies were the Keiths who, from their castle at Ackergill, challenged the Gunn chiefs both for the political hegemony of the region and for the land itself. As with most feuds which were truly fought for wealth and power, a convenient personal insult was provided to justify the constant bloodshed as an affair of honour. It was claimed that Dugald Keith coveted Helen, daughter of Gunn of Braemor. The girl stoutly resisted Keith's advances but he, on learning that the object of his desire was to be married to another man, promptly surrounded her father's house, slew many of the inhabitants and carried the hapless girl to Ackergill. She threw herself from the Castle Tower rather than submit to her kidnapper. The Gunns repeatedly raided Keith territory but they suffered defeat in 1438 at the Battle of Tannach Moor and again in 1464 at Dirlot in Strathmore. Having suffered considerable loss of life, both families agreed to meet to settle their differences in what was probably intended to be a battle of champions. Each side were to bring twelve horse, but when the Keiths arrived they had two warriors on each horse and, as they outnumbered the Gunns, a slaughter ensued. The chief and four of his sons were killed and the great coroner's brooch stolen. The chief's remaining son, James, from whom the Gaelic patronymic probably derives, avenged his family in due course by killing Keith of Ackergill and his son at Drummoy. The Gunns were now fighting for their very existence. The Earls of Caithness and Sutherland entered into a pact to destroy Clan Gunn, probably sealed at Girnigoe Castle around 1586. There were a number of indecisive encounters and heavy casualties were inflicted on both sides. The Gunns strengthened their connection with the Mackays when Gunn of Killearnan married Mary, sister of Lord Reay, the Mackay chief, and the next Gunn chief thereafter married Lord Reay's daughter. The son of this marriage, the sixth chief, was generally known as Donald Crottach, 'the hunchback'. It was in his time that the house at Killearnan was destroyed, apparently due to an accident with gunpowder. The lands of Killearnan themselves were lost through debt. About the same time the fortunes of one of the branches of the clan reached their pinnacle, although not on its native soil. The Gunns of Braemore were the descendents of Robert, a younger son of 'Am Braisdeach Mor', and were generally known as the Robson Gunns. Although he was a Catholic, Sir William Gunn, brother of the Robson chieftain, took service in the army of the Protestant king of Sweden and rose to command a battalion. He later fought for Charles I, who conferred a knighthood on him in 1639. He returned to the Continent, entering the service of the Holy Roman Empire, and married a German baroness. He became an imperial general and was created a baron of the Holy Roman Empire in 1649. Debt also overcame the Gunns of Braemore, who were forced to sell their estates at the end of the eighteenth century. The Gunns of Killearnan obtained a new estate at Badenloch, where they sought to revive the splendour of their ancestors with pipers and all the other panoply of Highland chiefship. The Gunns did not rally to the standard of the exiled Stuarts, and in the Jacobite rising of 1745 they fought on the government side. The eighth chief served as a regular Highland officer and was killed in action in India. The chiefship passed to a cousin in whose line it remained until the nineteenth century, when the tenth Macsheumais Chataich died without an heir. The clan is presently led by a commander, Iain Gunn of Banniskirk, a descendent of a seventeenth-century Caithness laird, who has been appointed under a commission from the Lord Lyon, King of Arms. Petitions have been presented recently to the Lord Lyon seeking to establish representation to the bloodline chiefs, and it is to be hoped that a successful claimant will be found.

HALIBURTON

The name of Haliburton is territorial, derived from lands in Berwickshire. The lands were first called Burton or Burghton, but a chapel was built there and the place was then referred to as Holy or Haly Burton. Nisbet, however, prefers the view that the church took its name from a holy man named Burton. Walterus de Halyburton confirmed a donation of his church of Halyburton to the Abbey of Kelso in 1176. Walter's great-grandson, Sir Henry Halyburton, swore allegiance to Edward I of England in 1296, and his name

ARMS (of Pitcur LR 1/160)[1]
Or, on a bend Azure between three boars' heads erased Sable as many lozenges of the First

CREST[1]
A negro's head couped at the shoulders and armed with a helmet Proper

MOTTO[3]
Watch well

SUPPORTERS[1]
Two cats Proper

appears on the Ragman Roll. Sir Henry's grandson, Sir Walter, was taken prisoner by the English at the Battle of Durham in 1346 and was finally ransomed along with David II in 1357. Another Walter Halyburton was one of the hostages for James I in 1424. In 1439 he became High Treasurer of Scotland, and a Lord of Parliament a year later. His wife, Lady Isabel Stewart, was the eldest daughter of the Regent Albany and widow of the Earl of Ross. John, second Lord Halyburton, married Janet, daughter of Sir William Seaton of Seaton, and they had two sons, each of whom bore the family title. When the sixth Lord Halyburton died in 1506 he left three daughters. The

eldest, Janet, married William, Lord Ruthven. The title thereafter descended through Lady Ruthven. Her grandson, William, was created Earl of Gowrie in 1581. All the Gowrie titles were forfeited after the execution of the third Earl and his brother for alleged treason. James Halyburton of Pitcur, a descendent of the principal family, was Provost of Dundee for thirty-three years, from 1550 until 1583. He was a great supporter of the Reformation, and he fought alongside the Regent Moray and the enemies of Queen Mary at the Battle of Langside in 1568. In 1570 he assisted Regent Lennox in dispersing troops under the command of the Earl of Huntly, fighting for Queen Mary. He died in 1588 at the age of seventy. Sir George Halyburton, a later member of this family, became Lord President of the Court of Session in 1642, having been knighted by Charles I at Holyrood nine years earlier. He was a member of a commission for revising and arranging the laws of Scotland, and his report was accepted and passed by Parliament in 1649.

HALKERSTON

ARMS (of Rathillet LR 1/167)[1]
Or, three falcons' heads erased Gules

CREST
A falcon's head erased Proper

MOTTO
In ardua nitor (I endeavour in difficulties)

SUPPORTERS
Two falcons Proper, hooded and belled Or

Another name derived from the sport of falconry, so beloved of medieval monarchs. The lands of Hawkerton in the Mearns were held as a feu of the king's falconer. The arms of three red falcons' heads on a gold shield are both canting, or punning, and a reference to the office of the bearer. Johan de

Haukerstone of the shire of Edinburgh, is shown on the Ragman Roll as rendering homage to Edward I of England in 1296. Black states that his seal is shown bearing an eagle, but at this time an eagle would have been a representation for any form of bird of prey. The name was common around Edinburgh in the fifteenth and sixteenth centuries and there are still lands known as Halkerston near the village of Inveresk in Midlothian. One of the streets of Edinburgh was known as Halkerston's Wynd named after either John or David Halkerston. The latter was killed in 1544, when the city was assaulted by English troops. The principal line became the Lairds of Rathillet in Fife.

HALKET

This family is believed to have taken its name from the lands of Halkhead in Renfrewshire. Black suggests that the place

name may have originally meant Hawk-wood. Sir Henry Hackett was witness to a charter in 1230. The house of Pitfirran has long been

ARMS (of Pitfirrane LR 1/166)[1]
Sable, three piles Argent, on a chief of the Second a lion passant guardant Gules

CREST
A falcon's head erased Proper

MOTTO
Fides sufficit (Faith is sufficient)

SUPPORTERS
Two falcons Proper

accepted as the principal stem, and they have held their lands in Fife since the fourteenth century. They were already established when they obtained the lands of Luphannan and Ballingall from David II sometime prior to 1370. Philip Hagat, Lord of Ballingall, is recorded in 1390 in writs of Pitfirrane. Sir Robert Halket of Pitfirrane was knighted by James VI, while his eldest son, Sir James, sup-

ported the cause of the Covenanters in the reign of Charles I. He was elected MP for Fife in 1649 and subsequently raised his own cavalry regiment. Sir Charles Halket of Pitfirrane was created a baronet in 1662. His line ended in an heiress, Janet, who married Sir Peter Wedderburn of Gosford, created a baronet in 1697. He inherited the estate of Pitfirrane but was obliged to assume the name and arms of Halket. General Sir Colin Halket commanded a brigade of the German legion throughout the Peninsular War (1808–14) and was severely wounded at Waterloo. Sir Peter Arthur Halket of Pitfirrane, eighth Baronet, saw distinguished service with the 42nd Highlanders during the Crimean War and carried the Queen's Colour at the bloody Battle of Alma in 1854. The baronetcy became extinct in 1904.

HEPBURN

ARMS[6]
Quarterly 1st, Gules, on a chevron Argent a rose between two lions combatant of the First (Hepburn); 2nd, Azure, a ship Or, sails furled Argent, within a double tressure flory counterflory of the Second (Orkney); 3rd, Ermine, three chevronels Gules (Soulis); 4th, Or, a bend Azure (Vaux)

CREST
A horse's head couped Argent, bridled Gules

MOTTO
Keep tryst

SUPPORTERS
Two lions rampant guardant Gules

The Hepburn name is territorial, coming from the village of Hebburn in the parish of Chillingham in Northumberland. During the late thirteenth or early fourteenth century, an Adam de Hibburne appears to have been captured by the Scots on one of their many cross-border raids. On his way through East Lothian to Edinburgh, the story goes that he saved the Earl of Dunbar from attack by an unbroken wild stallion. The earl, in gratitude, gifted Adam the lands of North and South Hailes in East Lothian. Adam's son, Patrick, married Eleanor de Brus, Countess of Carrick, who was the niece of Robert the Bruce. She was Adam's second wife and he, her fifth husband. Patrick and his son, another Patrick,

were with James, Earl of Douglas, when he raided Northumbria in 1388. The Scots captured the banner of Henry Percy (the renowned Hotspur), who vowed that the banner would never leave England. At the ensuing Battle of Otterburn the Hepburns managed to save the Douglas standard, a feat which won them the gratitude and protection of that powerful family. Henry Percy, Earl of Northumberland, invaded Scotland in 1400 intent on burning Hailes by way of revenge, but he was driven off by Douglas. Sir Patrick Hepburn became the first Lord Hailes in 1482. His grandson, also Patrick, was created Earl of Bothwell by James IV, who was his cousin. He was also created High Admiral of Scotland, Keeper of the King's Household, Sheriff Principal of Scotland, Keeper of Edinburgh Castle and Lord of Orkney. He was trusted enough to stand proxy for the king at his marriage to Margaret Tudor, daughter of Henry VII of England. It was from this union that James VI was later to succeed to the English throne. Patrick and his son, Adam, were among the many Scottish nobles who died alongside James IV at Flodden in 1513. Adam's son, Patrick, the third Earl, grew up with the leading Borders families and joined their rebellion during the reign of James V, as a result of which he was forced into exile in England. On the death of the king he returned home to attempt to woo Mary of Guise, the king's widow and mother of Mary, Queen of Scots. Henry VIII of England bribed Bothwell and a number of other Scottish nobles to ensure the marriage of the infant Mary to his son Edward, Prince of Wales. A treaty was enacted but later annulled, due to Henry's excessive demands. Mary was instead married to the heir to the throne of France, but after her husband's death returned to Scotland in 1561. She married her weak-willed cousin, Henry Stewart, Lord Darnley. When Darnley, now King Henry, was found strangled in the ruins of his house at Kirk o' Field, there was little public doubt that his death had been contrived by James, fourth Earl of Bothwell, who had already tried to abduct the queen. Bothwell was charged with the murder but was acquitted after filling Edinburgh with his men. He married the queen, a union later said to have been forced upon her, and he was created Duke of Orkney and loaded with other high ranks and titles. Public outrage and the jealousy of other powerful factions ensured that the marriage was not to last, and after various adventures, Mary escaped to England where she was held captive for twenty years, ultimately being executed by her cousin, Elizabeth. Bothwell escaped to Denmark where he was seized and held in the castle at Dragsholm, where he died in pitiful circumstances, chained to a pillar after eleven years of captivity. All his honours were forfeited to the Crown. His mummified body was on display until quite recently. A cousin of the earl, Sir John Hepburn, became a marshal of France and later the first colonel of the Royal Scots Regiment. Sir George Buchan Hepburn became representer of the family and was created a baronet in May 1815. His direct descendent, Sir Ninian, is the present baronet.

HERON

ARMS (LR 6/30)[1]
Argent, two lions rampant affrontée supporting between their paws a rose Gules, slipped and leaved Vert

CREST
A Demi lion Argent holding in his dexter paw a cross crosslet fitchée Gules

MOTTO
Par valeur (By bravery)

below the shield
Ad ardua tendit (He attempts difficult things)

The family of Heron arose in the south-west of Scotland in Kirkcudbrightshire and the Stewartry, claiming descent from the Herons of Chipchase in Northumberland around the eleventh century. The English name appears to have originally been a nickname for a thin man with long legs. Walterus de Hayroun was clerk to William the Lion from about 1178 to 1180. The Herons were among many of the Borders riding clans who were crushed and scattered after the area was pacified by James VI in the decade after 1603.

Some time after the Revolution of 1688, the Herons had their lands at Kerroughtree in Kirkcudbrightshire consolidated into the barony of Heron. A Robert Heron, the son of a weaver born in New Galloway in 1764, became a student at Edinburgh University in 1780. He wrote many books, including a memoir of Robert Burns which has been often quoted. He was also a spendthrift who was often in debtors' prison in London until his death in 1807. Patrick Heron of Heron, Member of Parliament for Kirkcudbright, married Lady Elizabeth Cochrane, daughter of the eighth Earl of Dundonald. Their daughter, Mary, who was to become her father's heiress, married Lieutenant General Sir John Maxwell of Springkell, Baronet. On the death of his father-in-law, Sir John assumed the additional surname, and quartered the arms, of Heron. Sir Nigel Heron-Maxwell, tenth Baronet, is the present representer of the line.

HERRIES

ARMS (LR 18/10)[1]

Quarterly, 1st grand quarter, Argent, a double headed eagle displayed Sable, beaked and membered Gules, surmounted of an escutcheon of the First charged with a saltire of the Second and surcharged in the centre with an urcheon Or (Maxwell, Earl of Nithsdale); 2nd grand quarter, counterquartered, (I) & (IV), Argent, a saltire Sable,in chief a label of three points Gules (Maxwell), (II) &(III), Argent, three urcheons Sable (Herries); 3rd grand quarter, quarterly Gules and Vair, a bend Or (Constable of Everingham); 4th grand quarter, Azure on a bend cotised Argent, three billets Sable (Haggerston)

CREST
A stag's head with ten tynes Argent

MOTTO
Dominus dedit (The Lord has given)

SUPPORTERS
Two savages wreathed about the loins and holding clubs in their exterior hands Proper

This family is said to descend from the Counts of Vendome in France, who bore three hedgehogs (in French 'herissons') on their shield of arms. Chambers suggests that the Scottish Herries could also be a branch of the Anglo–Norman family of Heriz, from Wyverton in Nottinghamshire, who first came to Scotland during the reign of David II. William de Heriz witnessed several charters before 1152. Nigel de Heris had lands in Ettrick during the reign of Alexander II.

William de Herris swore fealty to Edward I of England and appears on the Ragman Roll of 1296 for his lands in Dumfriesshire. Sir Herbert Herries of Terregles was arrested with Murdoch, Duke of Albany, in 1425, and after his later release sat as one of the duke's jurors. He accompanied Princess Margaret of Scotland when she went to France in 1436 to marry the heir to the French throne. His brother, John Herries, fell foul of a dispute with the powerful Douglases, and he was seized and hanged by the Earl of Douglas. Sir Herbert Herries of Terregles, great-great-grandson of the first Sir Herbert, was created a Lord of Parliament with the title of 'Lord Herries' in 1489. His son, Andrew, the second Lord Herries, was slain along with many others of the nobility at the ill-fated Battle of Flodden in 1513. When William, the third Lord, died in 1543, the title passed to his daughter, Agnes, who married Sir John Maxwell, a younger son of Robert, Lord Maxwell. The original title, created in 1489, was destined to heirs general, and therefore permitted succession through the female line. The Maxwells, who in 1667 succeeded to the title of 'Earl of Nithsdale', thereafter quartered the arms of Herries with their own.

HOG

ARMS (LR 1/532)[1]
Argent, three boars' heads erased Azure, armed Or

CREST
An oak tree Proper

MOTTO
Dat gloria vires (A good name gives strength)

SUPPORTERS
Two boars Proper

This is a name of great antiquity in Scotland. Alexander Hog 'de Hogstown' appears on the Ragman Roll swearing fealty to Edward I of England in 1296. Alexander's grandson, Roger, was a burgess of Edinburgh in 1330. He acquired charters to lands around the city during the reign of David II. The family also received land at Sydserf in East Lothian from the Countess of Fife in 1373, thereafter being styled 'of Harcarse'. Sir Roger Hog of Harcarse was appointed a Supreme Court judge in 1677 while his grandnephew, and eventual heir, Roger Hog of Newliston matriculated his arms in volume 1 of the Lyon Court register in 1783. He was recognised as 'representor and Chief of that sirname'. Lt Colonel Steuart Hog of Newliston was an advocate at the Scottish Bar. A member of the Royal Company of Archers, he was appointed Vice-Lord Lieutenant of West Lothian in 1935. His son, Roger, served in both World Wars during which he won the Military Cross. Newliston House still stands on the outskirts of the village of Kirkliston near Edinburgh.

HOPKIRK

ARMS
(of Dalbeath LR 2/133)[1]
*Gules, a saltire engrailed Argent between four
fleurs de lis Or*

CREST
*A dexter hand in armour erect and couped at the elbow
the hand Proper pointing to a crescent in dexter chief
Argent*

MOTTO
Spero procedere (I hope to prosper)

SUPPORTERS
*Two gryphons Proper, winged, beaked, membered
and armed Or*

This name appears to derive from the lands of Hopkirk near Hawick in Roxburghshire. The name may indicate lands dedicated to the Church by either a man named Hob (a diminutive of Robert), or perhaps a member of the ancient family of Hopringle, who held lands near Stow in Roxburghshire in the eleventh century. The name arises in various early charters of land in Roxburghshire, and James Hobkirk is recorded as resident at Carrington in 1574. The principal family were Lairds of Dalbeath. James Hobkirk, a fervent Covenanter, was drowned off Orkney in 1679.

HORSBURGH

ARMS (of that Ilk)[3]
Azure, a horse's head couped Argent

CREST
A horse's head couped Argent

MOTTO
*Aegre de tramite recto (Having safely passed through
a rough path)*

The lands and barony of Horsburgh lie near Innerleithen in Peeblesshire. The ruins of the tower of the same name still stand, and according to Black, 'the first of the race is believed to have been an Anglo–Saxon designated, "horse", or "orse", whose settling on lands on the north bank of the Tweed there reared the castle which communicated the present surname to his descendents'. Simon de Horsbrock witnessed a charter to the monks of Melrose Abbey in the reign of Alexander II. William de Horsboroch is recorded as a notary public in the diocese of Glasgow in 1287. Alexander Horsbrock of that Ilk is recorded in 1479. The arms recorded by Nisbet of a silver horse's head on a blue shield are clearly canting, or punning, on the family name. James Horsburgh, a fellow of the Royal Society, was a distinguished hydrographer at the beginning of the nineteenth century. In 1810 he was appointed hydrographer to the East India Company. He published numerous works on maritime subjects, which were to become standard authorities in that field. The name is still found in the Borders and around Edinburgh. The last of the name to hold the barony was Lady Horsburgh of Horsburgh, through whom it recently passed to the family of Chinnery.

HOUSTON

ARMS (LR 8/45)[1]
*Or, a chevron chequy Azure and Argent, between three
martlets Sable, beaked Gules*

CREST
A sand-glass Proper

MOTTO
In time

SUPPORTERS
Two hinds Proper

The name is territorial in origin, derived from an old barony of the name in Lanarkshire. Hugh de Padinan, who is believed to have lived in the twelfth century, was granted the lands of Kilpeter. By about the middle of the fourteenth century, these lands had become known as Huston. Sir Finlay de Hustone appears on the Ragman Roll swearing fealty to Edward I of England in 1296. The castle of the de Hustones was built on the site of an ancient Cistercian abbey. The family also acquired a substantial barony near Whitburn in West Lothian, where Huston House, which was rebuilt in the eighteenth century, still stands today. Sir Patrick Hustone of that Ilk, who was probably the eleventh chief, married Agnes Campbell of Ardkinglas. Sir Peter Huston fought with the Earl of Lennox on the right wing at Flodden in 1513, where he was killed. His son, Sir Patrick Huston of Huston, was a companion of James V and Keeper of the Quarter Seal. He intrigued with Lord Lennox against the king, and was slain at the Battle of Linlithgow Bridge. The next Sir Patrick, his grandson, was knighted by Mary, Queen of Scots, and accompanied her when she visited Lord Darnley in Glasgow. The nineteenth chief was created a Baronet of Nova Scotia by Charles II in 1668. His son, Sir John, was falconer to Queen Mary and her husband, William of Orange. The fifth Baronet was a prosperous merchant who had substantial interests in America. His son, who was educated in Glasgow, made his home in Georgia, and he and his brother greatly increased the family's colonial estates. They are reputed to have owned over eight thousand slaves when the thirteen American colonies broke from Britain and declared their independence. The Hustons renounced their Scottish titles in favour of their American wealth. From this family descended General Sam Huston, born in 1793, who fought for the independence of Texas from Mexico. He was first president of Texas and later a United States Senator. Sir Robert Houston, descended from a Renfrew branch of the family, was a prominent Victorian shipowner who was created a baronet of the United Kingdom. He is credited with developing the theory of convoys first used during the Boer War.

HUTTON

ARMS (LR 1/330)[1]
Or, a lion rampant Azure between three arrows points downwards two and one Proper headed and feathered Argent, on a chief Gules as many bezants

CREST
A serpent catching at a finger of a man's hand which issues from a cloud all Proper

MOTTO
Si Deus quis contra (If God is for us, who is against us)

The origin of this name in Scotland is obscure. A family called De Hoton is recorded as an ancient and noble family in the county palatine of Lancaster, who were granted arms by the English heralds in the sixteenth century. A Simon de Hotun is listed by Black as juror on an inquest held in Lanark in 1263. Arms were recorded on behalf of Dr John Hutton, whom Nisbet states to have claimed to be a representor of Hutton of that Ilk, and who was chief physician to William and Mary in 1692. James Hutton was an eminent geologist and philosopher, who published in 1795 a major work expounding his theory of geology, which attributed the structure of the solid parts of the earth to the action of fire. He was a fellow of the Royal Society of Edinburgh and his prominence in that city led to his inclusion in Kay's *Edinburgh Portraits*. He is considered one of the founders of modern geology.

INGLIS

There are very early records of this name in the south of Scotland, and Black states that it is derived from the old English for 'Englishman'. Richard Anglicus witnessed a charter of David I to Melrose Abbey sometime prior to 1153. Walter de Inglis, John de Inglis and Philip de Inglis were in possession of considerable lands when Edward I of England

ARMS (of Mainer and Mainerhead LR 1/341)[1]
Azure, a lion rampant, in chief three stars Argent

CREST
A demi lion Argent

MOTTO
Nobilis est ira leonis (The lion's anger is noble)

invaded Scotland in 1296. Sir William Inglis was a knight of great renown in the reigns of Robert II and Robert III: in 1395, he met in single combat Sir Thomas Struthers, the English champion, and killed him on the spot. The Inglises were rewarded with the barony of Manner by royal charter in 1396, and the family subsequently traced their descent from Sir William. Nisbet states that the family were closely connected to the Earls of Douglas and added the three stars of Douglas to their own coat of arms to indicate their dependence upon that great house. The barony of Manner was sold in 1709 and the representation of the family devolved upon Charles Inglis of Craigend who was a lawyer in Edinburgh and who died in 1743. The family of Inglis of

Cramond flourished in Edinburgh, where they acquired great wealth and the lands of Cramond, purchased from the Bishop of Dunkeld in 1624. A fine tower, all that remains of the bishop's palace, still stands in the grounds of Cramond House, the splendid mansion house built by John Inglis of Cramond in 1680 shortly before his death. Sir James Inglis of Cramond was created a baronet in March 1687. His son was Postmaster General of Scotland until 1725. The baronetcy became extinct in 1817 for want of a male heir and the estate passed to Lady Torphichen, daughter of Sir John Inglis. The fine house was not abandoned and at the height of the Victorian era it was a fashionable society address. In 1860 the Duchess of Kent, mother of Queen Victoria, stayed there for several weeks. The queen herself, en route for Balmoral, made an unexpected visit in September 1860 when, along with the Prince Consort, she attended a service in Cramond Kirk. The house is still in use today and belongs to Cramond Kirk.

INNES

ARMS(LR 58/3)[1]
Quarterly, 1st & 4th grand quarters, counterquartered (I) & (IV), Vert, on a chevron between three unicorns heads erased Argent, as many mullets Sable; (II) & (III), Gules, three mascles Or; 2nd & 3rd grand quarters, Argent, three stars (of five points) Azure

CREST
A boar's head erased Proper

MOTTO
Be traist

SUPPORTERS
Two savages wreathed around the head and middle with laurel and holding in the exterior hand a club resting on the shoulder, all Proper

The barony of Innes lies in Morayshire. Berowald, a Flemish nobleman, was granted this barony in 1160 by Malcolm IV. In 1226, Alexander II granted a charter of confirmation to Berowald's grandson, Walter, who assumed the surname of Innes. The eighth Laird, 'Good Sir Robert', who died around 1381, had three sons: Sir Alexander, who later

succeeded as ninth Laird, and who married the heiress of Aberchirder; John, later Bishop of Moray, who restored Elgin Cathedral after it had been destroyed by the Wolf of Badenoch; and George, head of the Scottish Order of Trinitarian Friars. Sir Alexander's son, Sir Walter, was chief for forty-two years until his death in 1454. His son, Sir Robert Innes, the eleventh Laird, fought under the Earl of Huntly at the Battle of Brechin in 1452 and sought to expiate the sins of his life by founding the Greyfriars of Elgin. His eldest son, James, was armour bearer to James III, and entertained James IV at the Castle of Innes in 1490. He and his son, Alexander, were noted patrons of the arts and architecture. Alexander the Proud, the sixteenth chief, was executed by the Regent Morton for the murder of Walter Innes and was succeeded by his brother, John, who resigned his chiefship to his cousin, Alexander Innes of Crommey. He was murdered at Aberdeen in 1580 by his kinsman, Robert Innes of Innermarkie, during a family quarrel. His grandson, Sir Robert, the twentieth chief, was a Privy Councillor who represented Moray in Parliament, and he was created a Baronet of Nova Scotia in 1625. Although a prominent Covenanter, he welcomed the uncrowned Charles II at Garnoch in 1650, and raised a regiment to fight for the royalist cause. He sold the Aberchirder estates but built Innes House. The third Baronet married Lady Margaret Ker through whom Sir James Innes, the sixth Baronet and twenty-fifth chief, succeeded to the dukedom of Roxburgh in 1805. His son was granted an additional title of 'Earl Innes' in 1836. The present Duke of Roxburgh would be the chief of Clan Innes but is barred from the title as he bears a compound, or double-barrelled surname. Walter of Innermarkie, the second son of Sir Robert Innes the eleventh chief, was succeeded by his son, Robert, who was created hereditary constable of Redcastle and married a niece of James II. Sir Robert, fifth of Innermarkie, was created Baronet of Balveny. He built a fine Castle on Speyside, but his son, Walter, lost everything in his support of Charles I. The family continued to support the cause of the Stuarts in exile as did their kinsmen, the Inneses of Coxton. When the present *Register of Arms and Bearings in Scotland* was instituted in 1672, the Lyon Depute was Robert Innes of Blairton. Sir Thomas Innes of Learney, a descendent of the Lairds of Innermarkie, was Lord Lyon, King of Arms from 1945 to 1969 and was one of Scotland's greatest heraldic experts. His son, Sir Malcolm Innes of Edingight, is the present Lord Lyon.

KELLY

The name Kelly, as it arises in Ireland, seems to be a variant of 'O ceallaigh', 'son of Ceallach'. This seems to have been a personal name, possibly meaning 'strife', and has become the second most popular name throughout the whole of Ireland and the sixth most common name in Ulster. There is, therefore, the possibility that the name arises in Scotland from the same derivation, but Black gives other possible explanations. The name may be a variant of Kelloe, an old barony in the lands of Home, in Berwickshire. Kelloe is also a place name in Durham and Kellah is found in Northumberland. William de Kellawe was bailiff to Alexander III in 1278. Richard de Kellow was a witness to a charter in Roxburghshire in 1338. The name is found in its more familiar form in Fife and Angus, where there are two lands bearing this name, including the magnificent Kellie Castle, restored this century by the architect Sir Robert Lorimer. John de Kelly is listed as Abbot of Arbroath in 1373. The Mackellies found in Galloway and Wigtownshire are most likely to be of Celtic descent. The only certain reference to Kelly of that Ilk is found in Nisbet, who describes the arms of a black saltire between four blue fleur de lis all on a gold field. The earldom of Kellie has always been a dignity, or title of honour, of the Erskine family.

KINLOCH

This name seems to be territorial from lands at the head of Rossie Loch in Fife ('ceann-loch' meaning 'head of the loch'). This is a most ancient family, listed as receiving charters to their land as early as the reign of Alexander III. Nisbet states that they bear one of the earliest surnames of the kingdom. John de Kyndelouch had confirmation of the privi-

ARMS (of Aberbothrie – afterwards Sir David
Kinloch of Kinloch Bt LR 1/172)[1]
Azure, a boar's head erased between three mascles Or

CREST
*A young eagle perched and looking up to the sun in
splendour all Proper*

MOTTO
Non degener (Not degenerate)

lege of a millpool in Fife around 1250.
William de Kyndelloch of Fifeshire, appears
on the Ragman Roll of those submitting to
Edward I of England in 1296. George Kinloch,
styled 'of Kinloch and Cruivie', lived through
the reigns of James IV and V and had several
sons, notably Alexander and David, progenitors of the cadet families of Kinloch of Kilrie
and Kinloch of Gourdie. David Kinloch, who
lived towards the end of the sixteenth century,
and may have been a member of one of the
cadet branches, was a noted physician and
traveller. He acquired the lands of Aberbothrie
from James VI in 1616. Another David
Kinloch was created a Baronet of Nova Scotia
in 1685. His son, Sir James Kinloch, second
Baronet, married the heiress of Nevoy of that
Ilk, and for a time this family prospered. Their
son, James, who was styled 'of that Ilk', fought
for the Jacobite cause in 1745 and on the

defeat of Prince Charles Edward Stuart, the
'Young Pretender', at Culloden, his titles and
estates were forfeited. He was captured and
condemned to death but contrived to make his
escape to France. The family lands were subsequently repurchased, but the family left to
reside in England and the estates were sold to
a cousin, George Oliphant Kinloch. The family
fortunes were much restored when Sir George
Kinloch, proprietor of the barony of Kinloch,
and a distinguished member of the Scottish
Bar, received a baronetcy under the style of
'Kinloch of Kinloch'. Another branch of the
family, the Kinlochs of Gilmerton in East
Lothian, also prospered. Sir Francis Kinloch of
Gilmerton was raised to the rank of Baronet of
Nova Scotia in 1686. His son married a daughter of the great civil war general, David Leslie,
Lord Newark. This family intermarried with
other prominent East Lothian houses and
thrived as a result. There is a family connection with the Grenadier Guards, and the tenth
Baronet served in the regiment throughout the
Crimean War. His son was mentioned in dispatches in the First World War, and rose to
the rank of brigadier general in 1917. The
name is also known worldwide through the
famous Highland outfitters, Kinloch Anderson.

KINNAIRD

ARMS (LR 1/103)[1]
*Quarterly, 1st & 4th, Or, a fess wavy between three mul-
lets Gules (Kirkcaldy); 2nd & 3rd, Gules, a saltire
between four crescents Or (Kinnaird)*

CREST
*A crescent arising from a cloud having a star issuing
from between its horns, all within two branches of palm
disposed in orle Proper*

MOTTO
Errantia lumina fallunt (Wandering lights deceive)

On Compartment
Certa cruce salus (Sure salvation by the cross)

SUPPORTERS
*Two naked men wreathed about the loins with oak leaves,
each holding in his exterior hand a garland of laurel,
their interior ankles surrounded by a fetter and the chain
held in the interior hand*

Kinnaird is a territorial name from the district of Gowrie in Perthshire. William the

Lion conferred the barony of Kinnaird on
Radulphus called Rufus, by a royal charter of
1170. Richard de Kinnaird, the great-grandson
of Rufus, was one of the Scottish barons who
swore fealty to Edward I of England and
appears on the Ragman Roll of 1296. Sir
George Kinnaird of Inchture was loyal to the
Crown throughout the civil war and was
knighted by Charles II in 1661. In 1682 he
was raised to the peerage as Lord Kinnaird of
Inchture. Patrick, the third Lord, opposed the
union of the Parliaments; he died in March
1715. The fifth Lord, Charles, died childless
though not before a court case was brought to
prove that the supposed birth of twins to Lady
Kinnaird had never taken place. Lord and
Lady Kinnaird refused to answer any ques-

tions, and the affair was terminated by Lord Kinnaird's declaring the twins dead. He was succeeded by a great-grandson of Sir George. Another George, the seventh Lord Kinnaird, was one of the sixteen Scots representative peers in the House of Lords. His brother, Douglas, an eminent banker, was a friend of the poets Sheridan and Byron, and he also helped to manage the Drury Lane Theatre in London. The eighth Lord Kinnaird, born in 1780, was first a Member of Parliament and later a representative peer of Scotland. He

built Rossie Priory, the family mansion in the Carse of Gowrie. In 1831 the ninth Lord, George Kinnaird, was created Baron Rossie of Rossie in the peerage of the United Kingdom. He was Master of Buckhounds to the Queen and Lord Lieutenant of Perthshire. In 1860 he was created Baron Kinnaird of Rossie. His brother, who was MP for Perth, succeeded him in the family honours. The family still live on the lands they have held for over six centuries.

KINNEAR

ARMS (of that Ilk LR 1/173)[1]
Sable, on a bend Or three martlets (or Kinnerrie birdes [sic]) Vert

CREST
Two anchors in saltire Proper

MOTTO
I live in hope

The lands named Kinnear are near Wormit in the kingdom of Fife. Black lists Symon, son of Michael, giving land from his holdings at Cathelai to the church of St Andrews. This grant was apparently confirmed by Malcolm IV prior to 1164. Descendents of Simon adopted the name from the lands. Sir John de

Kyner appears in the Ragman Roll as submitting to Edward I of England in 1296. Numerous early charters have references to this name, and Henry Kinneir of Kinneir was appointed commendator of Balmarino Abbey in 1574, while John Kinneir of that Ilk was subsequently appointed its baillie. George Kinnear was a banker in Edinburgh at the end of the eighteenth century and his son and heir, James, was a lawyer of some distinction. James Kinnear's descendents continued a legal tradition into the twentieth century, and they bear the family arms differenced with a gold bordure.

KINNINMONT

ARMS (of that Ilk)[2]
Azure, a chevron Argent between three fleurs de lis Or

CREST[4]
An oak tree Vert

MOTTO[4]
Stabo (I shall stand)

This name is of territorial origin from the lands of Kinninmonth in Fife. Odo, seneschal to the Bishop of St Andrews, received a charter of confirmation to his lands of Kynninmonth between 1189 and 1199 from William the Lion. A publication in 1841 on the charters of the archbishopric of St

Andrews states that the charter granted by John, son of Adam, son of Odo, is not recorded, 'but his original deed of consent, executed at the same time, and before the same witnesses with the charter of his father, is still extant; and on his seal we find the family name for the first time: "S'Iohannis de Kinimmund" '. William de Kynemuthe appears on the Ragman Roll of Scots nobles submitting to Edward I of England in 1296. Alexander de Kynimund was preferred to the bishopric of Aberdeen in 1356. In 1438 James Kynimond of that Ilk, asserted his right to the hereditary offices of baillie, steward and marischal of St

Andrews by right through his earlier ancestors. A direct line of the Kininmonts of that Ilk came to an end with the marriage of a sole heiress to Murray of Melgund. Sir William Kininmouth was a distinguished twentieth-century Scottish architect.

KIRKCALDY

ARMS (of Grange LR 1/173)[1]
Gules, a chevron Argent between three stars in chief and a crescent in base Or

CREST
A man's head with the face looking upwards Proper

MOTTO
Fortissima veritas (Truth is the strongest)

The families of this name hail from the lands in Fife where later developed the major town of the same name. The land is said to have been a site of worship for the ancient Celtic church, known as 'Culdees'; hence 'Kil Culdee', which was ultimately corrupted to the more familiar name. Many in early times styled themselves as being 'de Kyr Caudi', and one of the earliest on record is Willilmus de Kyrcaudi, who was in holy orders in Stirling in 1299. Andreas de Kirkaldy was granted a pension by David II in 1363. The principal families appear to have acquired lands at Inchture in Perth and Grange in Fife. The house of Inchture ended very early in the direct line by the marriage in 1396 of Marjory, daughter and heir of John of Inchture, to Reginald, son of Richard Kinnaird of that Ilk. They thereafter styled themselves 'of Inchture', and Lord Kinnaird still resides on the lands of Inchture to this day. However, the family of Grange prospered, Sir James Kirkcaldy of Grange becoming treasurer to James V. His son, William, was renowned as one of the bravest and most accomplished soldiers of his time. After the disastrous Battle of Solway Moss in 1542, James visited the house of Kirkcaldy of Grange, where he was well received by the treasurer's wife, Kirkcaldy himself being absent. The king is said to have predicted that he would die within the next fifteen days. Kirkcaldy of Grange and William were with the king when he died at Falkland Palace on 13 December 1542. Having been advised of the birth of his daughter and only heir, the future Mary, Queen of Scots, the king is said to have expired with the famous words, 'it cam wi' a lass and it will gae wi' a lass'. His words were to be as prophetic as the prediction of his own death. The treasurer's son, William, was a staunch defender of Queen Mary, and held Edinburgh Castle against the forces of her enemies, led by the Regent Morton, until the siege forced him to surrender on 29 May 1573. He was promised fair treatment, but he and his brother were hanged at the Market Cross in Edinburgh. However, the lands were restored to a nephew and in 1664 the family received a baronetcy. The title became extinct in 1739.

KIRKPATRICK

ARMS (of Closeburn LR 1/173)[1]
Argent, a saltire Azure, on a chief of the Second three cushions Or

CREST
A hand holding a dagger in pale distilling drops of blood

MOTTO
I make sure

The name of Kirkpatrick is common in Dumfriesshire, where it derives from a chapel dedicated to St Patrick in the parish of Closeburn. According to tradition, the family of Kirkpatrick of Closeburn have held lands in this dale since the ninth century. They appear in the twelfth century, when Ivone de Kirkpatrick witnessed a charter of the Bruce family. Alexander II granted a charter of confirmation to Ivone of his lands. Roger Kirkpatrick was one of the attendants of

Robert the Bruce at Dumfries when he met and slew the Red Comyn. Kirkpatrick is said to have met the Bruce rushing out of the church exclaiming that he believed he had killed Comyn. Kirkpatrick drew his dagger with the words, 'I'll mak siccar'; the family motto and coat of arms allude to this story. In 1314 he was sent on an embassy with Sir Neil Campbell to England and in recompense the family received the lands of Redburgh. In 1355 Sir Roger Kirkpatrick distinguished himself by taking Caerlaverock and Dalswinton Castles from the English, thus preserving Nithsdale. He was murdered by his kinsman, Sir James Lindsay, in a private quarrel in 1357. The title passed through a nephew to Sir Thomas Kirkpatrick, who had a charter of resignation to the baronies of Closeburn and Redburgh from Robert, Duke of Albany, in 1409. His grandson, another Sir Thomas, was taken prisoner at the Battle of Solway Moss in 1542. The estate again passed through a cousin and in 1685 Sir Thomas Kirkpatrick of Closeburn, for his fidelity to the cause of Charles I, was created a Baronet of Nova Scotia. The mansion house built by the first Baronet was later destroyed by fire. Sir James, the fourth Baronet, sold the estate of Closeburn. William Kirkpatrick, a descendent of the Kirkpatricks of Conheath, was a merchant in Malaga in Spain, who married the eldest daughter of a Belgian baron. His great-granddaughter, Eugenie, became Empress of the French when she married Napoleon III.

LAING

This is clearly a descriptive name, being a reference to 'long' or 'tall'. There can be no certainty as to the first prominent family of this name, but Black lists Thomas Laing as promising, in 1357, that Dumfries would pay part of the ransom for the return of David II from England. John Layng, the Rector of Newlands, rose to be Bishop of Glasgow and treasurer to James III between 1473 and 1474. The name is found frequently in the protocol books of the diocese of Glasgow in the sixteenth century. Malcolm Laing, a lawyer and historian from Orkney, was admitted to the Scottish Bar in 1785. He published a history of Scotland in 1800, and the poems of the Celtic bard, Ossian, with notes and illustrations in 1805. Major Alexander Laing was a renowned eighteenth-century African explorer, most famous for penetrating to the fabled town of Timbuctoo in 1826. He arrived in West Africa in December 1825 and set off into the desert in January 1826. He apparently arrived in Timbuctoo on 18 August, having survived the privations of the desert and attacks by Tuareg tribesmen. He remained for about a month in Timbuctoo but on his return journey he was murdered by his guides. The Most Reverend Cosmo Gordon Lang, descended from a Scottish family, was Archbishop of Canterbury from 1928 to 1942, and officiated at the coronation of George VI. He was raised to the peerage as Baron Lang of Lambeth in 1942.

LAMMIE

Black states that this is a diminutive of Lamb. There may, therefore, be some connection between this name and the Norman family de Agneux, from whom the great family of Agnew of Lochnaw in Wigtownshire descend. Alexander Lambie received a charter from David II of lands in the barony of Crail in Fife, and Liolph and Nigel Lamby appear in Montrose between 1372 and 1379. Andrew Lamby was accused of complicity in the murder of Mary, Queen of Scots' favourite, David Rizzio, in the Palace of Holyroodhouse in

ARMS (of Dunkenie LR 1/348)[1]
Azure, three crosiers paleways in fess Or and a saltire couped in base Argent

CREST
A hand Proper holding a crosier Or

MOTTO
Per varios casus (By various fortunes)

1566. The L'Amys held the lands of Dunkenny as early as 1542; they still held these lands into the twentieth century. The family arms, bearing three bishops' croziers and a saltire in base, may be a reference to the family's connection with the archbishopric of St Andrews and in particular to Archbishop Lamberton, the supposed author of the Declaration of Arbroath and then Chancellor of Scotland. The archbishop has been poetically described by Anderson as 'the most distinguished person of that name, by whose advice and assistance the immortal Bruce was encouraged in his efforts to deliver Scotland from the English yoke'.

LANGLANDS

ARMS (of that Ilk LR 1/178)[1]
Argent, on a chevron Gules three mullets of the First

CREST
An anchor in pale placed in the sea Proper

MOTTO
Spero (I hope)

The family of Langlands of that Ilk are said by Black to derive their name territorially from a property in Peebleshire. Nisbet states the family were of good standing in Teviotdale. They acquired part of the lands of the barony of Wilton in Roxburghshire. Marion, widow of John de Langland, received a charter of land in 1364. Jamie Langland was tenant of lands of Kelso Abbey in 1567. The main line seems to have failed in 1790.

LEARMONTH

ARMS (of Balcomie LR 1/178)[1]
Or, on a chevron Sable three mascles of the First

CREST
A rose slipped Proper

MOTTO
Spero (I hope)

This is a name arising from lands in Berwickshire. The earliest family of note were the Learmonths of Ercildoune in the Merse, to which family Anderson attributes the early Scottish poet, Thomas the Rhymer. Sir Walter Scott, who named Thomas the earliest Scottish poet, believed that he was born between 1226 and 1229 near the village now named Earlstoun in Berwickshire. The prophesies of Thomas the Rhymer were published in 1691. The family married into the Dairsies of Fife and thereby established the principal line of the family in that county. Sir James Learmonth of Dairsie was Master to the Household of James V, and provost of St Andrews in 1446. The family also acquired the lands of Balcomie in Fife, and in 1604 Sir James Learmonth of Balcomie was one of the commissioners appointed to consider a possible political union with England. Alexander Learmonth was a prosperous merchant in Edinburgh and Leith. The family acquired the estate of Parkhall in the early nineteenth century. They latterly assumed the compound surname of Livingston-Learmonth, but still used the ancient Learmonth arms. There is still a substantial residential district of Edinburgh named after this family.

LITTLE

This name is said by Black to be descriptive, meaning 'small'. It is found in Latin documents as 'Parvus'. The problem of all such descriptive names is that it is impossible to assert any certain origin of the name in Scotland. Hugo Parvus was clerk to the king in the reign of William the Lion, some time prior to 1214. Hugo Parvus is also listed as a burgess of Dundee, circa 1202, although it is not known if they are the same person. Nichol Litil served the Earl of Douglas on the West Marches in 1368. The Littles soon established themselves in the Borders, holding lands at Meikledale, Kirkton and Sorbie in Ewesdale. They became part of those turbulent Borders families known as the riding clans, who were, at their height, some of the finest light cavalry ever seen. Edward of Meikledale was a supporter of Sir William Wallace, the patriot, who upheld the independent rights of Scotland against the oppression of Edward I of England. A charter of James I confirmed to Simon Little the lands of Meikledale. Royal government, however, became fearful of the riding clans' strength. James V executed the leader of the Armstrongs, having deceived him and another thirty or so persons into attending a meeting for an apparently peaceful purpose. James VI, after the union of the Crowns, was determined to settle the border wars which had lasted several centuries, and he did so with characteristic Stuart ruthlessness. The Littles, in common with other Borders families, were scattered and many emigrated to Ulster, and then to more distant lands in North America, Australia and New Zealand. The family has been without a recognised chief since the late seventeenth century but there is now an active Clan Little Society and it is estimated that there are some forty-five thousand families throughout the English-speaking world owing allegiance to this name.

LIVINGSTONE

A name which is probably territorial in origin, from lands of the same name in West Lothian. According to one legend, the lands were named after a Saxon called Leving. There is record of one Livingus living during the reigns of Alexander I and David I. Sir William Livingstone, believed to be his great grandson, had three sons. Two of his younger sons appear on the Ragman Roll swearing fealty to Edward I of England in 1296. His eldest son followed David II on his invasion of England in 1346 and was taken prisoner at the Battle of Durham. He was one of the commissioners to England who negotiated the release of the king and was thereafter granted the barony of Callendar. Sir Alexander Livingstone of Callendar was one of the guardians of the infant James II. Following a dispute with William Crichton, another of the guardians, the young king was spirited out of Edinburgh Castle to Callendar. In 1440 the Livingstones were instrumental in persuading the young Earl of Douglas and his brother to attend a banquet of reconciliation in Edinburgh Castle. The Douglases were promptly seized and executed. In revenge, the Douglases imprisoned Livingstone and killed one of his sons. Another son, Sir James Livingstone, was created captain of Stirling Castle and later Great Chamberlain of Scotland. He was raised to the peerage as Lord Livingstone in 1458. He died without issue and the title devolved upon his nephew, John. In 1543 Alexander, the fifth Lord Livingstone, was one of the noblemen chosen to educate the young Mary, Queen of Scots. He accompanied the young queen to France, where he died. William, his son who succeeded him as sixth Lord, was a fierce adherent of Mary's cause and fought for her at the Battle of Langside. In 1600 Livingstone was raised to the rank of Earl of Linlithgow. The second Earl was created Hereditary Constable of the Royal Palace of Linlithgow. His son, George, remained loyal to the Crown during the civil war and the estates suffered, first at the hands of the Army of the Covenant and later the forces of Oliver Cromwell and the Parliamentarians. After the Restoration,

Livingstone was appointed a colonel in the Royal Horse Guards and a Privy Councillor. The family supported the Jacobite cause, and for their part in the 1715 rising the titles were forfeited. The Livingstones of Bachuil had received in early times a grant of lands on the island of Lismore as hereditary keepers of the crozier of St Molluag. The Celtic barony attached to the hereditary keepership was recognised by Parliament. The Barons of Bachuil are still the keepers of this sacred relic and live on their ancient lands on Lismore. The name of Livingstone is also borne as an anglicised version of 'Macleay', meaning 'son of the physician'. Doctor David Livingstone, the famous African explorer and missionary, was descended from the Macleays of Appin.

LOGIE

ARMS (of that Ilk)[7]
Sable, three bars wavy Or

This name is often confused with Logan, but appears to be a quite separate territorial family, and the heraldry of the two names is quite different. Wauter de Logie of Fife appears on the Ragman Roll submitted to Edward I of England in 1296. Sir John of

Logy is mentioned in Sir David Dalrymple's *Annals of Scotland* (published in 1819) as one of the nobles who conspired with Edward II of England and the Earl of Warenne in their invasion of Scotland in 1320. The arms given by Nisbet for Logie of that Ilk are ancient in form but they were never subsequently recorded in the Lyon Court registers.

LUNDIN

ARMS (LR 1/180)[1]
Or, a lion rampant Gules, armed and langued Azure, within a double tressure flory counterflory of the Second, (The Royal Arms of Scotland) all within a bordure compony Argent and Azure

CREST
A lion Gules, issuant from an antique crown Or, holding in its dexter paw a sword erect and in its sinister a thistle slipped both Proper

MOTTO
Dei dono sum quod sum (By the grace of God I am what I am)

SUPPORTERS
Two lions guardant Gules, each having a collar Or charged with three thistles Vert

Originally thought to be derived from lands in Forfarshire and Fife, the name

of Lundin appears to arise from one Robert de London, who came to Scotland before the reign of Alexander II. Philip de Lundin was granted a barony near Largo in Fife, and his brother Malcolm, received lands in Forfarshire. Malcolm's son, Thomas, was appointed doorward (a gatekeeper, or janitor) by William the Lion and was later called by the surname Durward. The doorward's was an important post, and in this case would imply close personal confidence and trust by the king. The Doorwards' son, Alan, was appointed justiciar, and assumed the title 'Earl of Athol', to which he did not appear to have any right. However, he married the natural daughter of Alexander II, and this close royal connection may have promoted the marriage of Robert, natural son of William the Lion, to the heiress of the house of Lundin. Robert assumed the Lundin surname, and thereafter the Lairds of Lundin proudly proclaimed their twice-royal blood, their coat of arms leaving this in no doubt. In 1648 Sir John Lundin of Lundin was succeeded by his daughter, Margaret, whose husband, Robert Maitland, assumed her name and the family coat of arms along with the estates. He joined with the Duke of Hamilton in the engagement for the rescue of Charles I in 1648, and fought at the Battle of Worcester in 1651. He was captured and remained a prisoner for some years until he paid a heavy fine. The line again passed through a female and in 1679 John Drummond received a royal warrant to add his wife's coat of arms, which were virtually those of the Kings of Scots, to his own. He held high office, first as Deputy Governor of Edinburgh Castle, and later as Secretary of State. He was created Earl of Melfort in 1685. He married twice and left his Drummond titles to his second family, as the Lundins were staunch Protestants and the Drummonds were among the most ardent of Jacobites. His son, James Lundin, succeeded to his mother's estates, which his descendents ultimately sold.

LYLE

ARMS[3]
Gules, fretty Or

CREST
A cock Or, crested and barbed Gules

MOTTO
An I may

SUPPORTERS
Two cats Proper

This name appears to be Norman in origin, being derived from D'Lisle, which is often rendered in Latin 'de insula', both meaning 'of the island'. The first of this name in Scotland appears to come from the great Northumberland family of that name and is given as Ralph de Insula, a follower of Walter the Steward, who witnessed a gift of land to the monks of Paisley Abbey around 1170. William de Lile witnessed a charter of certain lands belonging to Paisley Abbey between 1222 and 1233. Alan de Insula witnessed many charters of Alexander, son of Walter the High Steward, prior to 1252. Both John de Lille of Berwickshire and Richard del Isle of Edinburgh rendered homage to Edward I of England and appear on the Ragman Roll of 1296. They acquired the barony of Duchal in Renfrewshire, and they extended their lands during the reign of David II, receiving a charter to the barony of Buchquhan (now Buchanan) in Stirlingshire. Sir Robert Lyle was raised to the peerage as Lord Lyle by James II, and the second Lord Lyle was sent as ambassador to England in 1472. He formed part of that band of noblemen who intrigued against James III and is said to have been present when the king was murdered at Sauchieburn in June 1488. However, he appeared to have been appalled by the actual murder of the king, and joined the Earl of Lennox and other nobles to take up arms to avenge the king's death. The fortunes of war did not favour them, and Lord Lyle was forfeited in 1489. But the estates were restored shortly thereafter, and Lyle enjoyed high judicial office for the rest of his life. This title is now extinct. Another family of Lyles received the lands of Murthill in Forfarshire around 1375. This family produced a number of distinguished soldiers, including Hercules Lyle, who fought in the Forty-Five and was killed at the Battle of Falkirk in 1746. They subsequently acquired the lands of Gardyne by Forfar in Angus, which they still held in the twentieth century.

MACARTHUR

ARMS (LR 70/110)[1]
Azure, a maltese cross Argent, between three antique crowns Or

CREST
A greyhound couchant within two branches of bay all Proper

MOTTO
Fide et opera (By fidelity and labour)

The Macarthurs are Celts, and the family of Arthur is one of the oldest clans in Argyll, so ancient that even in remote Celtic times there was a Gaelic couplet which is freely translated, 'the hills and streams and Macalpine but whence came forth Macarthur?' The Macarthurs supported Robert the Bruce in the struggle for the independence of Scotland, and their leader, Mac-Ic-Artair, was rewarded with lands in mid Argyll, which had belonged to those who had opposed the king. Over the years many descendents of Arthur dispersed, some settling in Skye where one family of Macarthurs set up a famous piping school and were for several generations hereditary pipers to the Macdonalds of Sleat. The most celebrated of this family was Charles, who received his piping instruction from Patrick Og Maccrimmon. Another branch of the family became armourers to the Macdonalds of Islay. Two families of Macarthurs came to the fore in the late 1400s around Loch Awe. There has been a good deal of confusion between the Macarthurs of Loch Awe and the Macarthur Campbells of Strachur on Loch Fyne. The names of some Macarthurs holding prominent positions appear in the fifteenth century in mid Argyll, and by the latter half of the sixteenth century they had gained so much land and power that their neighbours became jealous and Duncan Macarthur and his son were drowned in Loch Awe during a skirmish in 1567. The Earl of Argyll ordered compensation to be made and appointed a nephew, John, son of Finlay, to be leader of the Loch Awe Macarthurs. The direct male line appears to have become extinct in the years around 1780. The Macarthurs of Milton, at Dunoon, had by the middle of the 1680s produced a baillie in Kintyre and a chamberlain to the Marquess of Montrose in Cowal. The Macarthurs also sought their fortune abroad, and Colonel John Macarthur became military deputy governor of St Kitts in the Caribbean. A large number of the clan, many of whom fought on both sides in the Jacobite risings, left Scotland, particularly after the disaster of Culloden in 1746, eventually to settle in the West Indies, America and Canada. John Macarthur went to New South Wales with the 102nd Regiment and became commandant at Parramatta until 1804. He is credited with the foundation of the great Australian wool industry by first crossing Bengal and Irish sheep and later introducing the Merino from South Africa. His sons planted the first Australian vineyard. A Macarthur migrant from Strathclyde landed in America in 1840. His son, Arthur, fought in the civil war and was promoted to lieutenant general in the US army, while his son, Douglas, became even more well known as the commander of the Pacific Theatre in the Second World War. Clan Arthur is at present without a chief, but in 1991 the Lord Lyon appointed James Macarthur of Milton as commander.

MACAULAY

Anderson attributes this clan to one of the branches of the Siol Alpen, from whom also descend the Macgregors. It has equally been asserted that they stem from Almhalidh, a younger son of the Earl of Lennox. Nisbet, in his commentary on the Ragman Roll of 1296, states that Maurice de Arncaple, who submitted to Edward I of England, was the ancestor of the Lairds of Ardincaple, which was to become the principal Macaulay seat. In

ARMS (of Ardincaple)
Gules, two arrows in saltire Argent surmounted by a fess chequy of the Second and First between three buckles Or

CREST
A boot couped at the ankle and thereon a spur Proper

MOTTO
Dulce periculum (Danger is sweet)

1587 Sir Aulay Macaulay of Ardincaple was noted as a principal vassal of the Earls of Lennox. Whether the connection between the Macgregors and the Macaulays was one of descent or not, they became closely connected, and a bond of manrent was entered into on 27 May 1591 between Macgregor of Glen Strae and the Laird of Ardincaple; in it, Macaulay acknowledged the superiority of Macgregor and agreed to pay him tribute in cattle. The historian Skene, while sceptical about the claim that the Macaulays were a sept of Macgregor, stated that 'their connection with the Macgregors led them to take some part in the feuds that that unfortunate race were at all times engaged in, but the protection of the Earls of Lennox seems to have relieved the Macaulays from the consequences which fell so heavily upon the Macgregors'. The Macaulays were certainly keen to renounce any connection with the Macgregors when they were declared outlaw, and Ardincaple was required to find surety for the good

behaviour of his clan in 1610. The fortunes of the family declined, however, and the twelfth and last chief of the Macaulays sold off the estates to the Campbells around 1767. The Macaulays of Lewis asserted that they were of Norse descent, their name meaning simply, 'son of Olaf'. One of the chiefs of the Lewis Macaulays in the sixteenth century was known as Donald Camm, meaning Donald One-Eye. He was so renowned for his great strength and quarrelsome nature that Anderson tells us that there was a Gaelic saying, 'whoever is blind of an eye is pugnacious'. The son of Donald Camm followed the Marquess of Montrose in his campaign for Charles I during the civil war, and died at the Battle of Auldern in 1645. Thomas Babington Macaulay, the nineteenth-century politician and historian, was descended from the line of Donald Camm. He is best remembered for his works, *History of England*, which is still read by historians today, and *Lays of Ancient Rome*. He appears to have made little reference during his life to his distinguished Highland background. He received many honours and was raised to the peerage as Lord Macaulay in September 1857. He died unmarried in 1859 and is buried in Westminster Abbey. Lord Macaulay of Bragar is a distinguished modern Scottish jurist who now sits as a life peer.

MACBRAYNE

ARMS (LR 1/234)[1]
Gules, two lions passant guardant in pale parted per pale Or and Argent

CREST
A dexter arm issuing out of a ducal coronet and grasping a sword all Proper

MOTTO
Fortis ceu leo fidus (Brave as a faithful lion)

This largely Highland name is said to derive from the Gaelic for 'son of the judge'. The brieve, or brehon, was a Celtic judge who was trained in the oral customary law of the Celtic polity, and this office was held in high esteem. The system is said to

have broken down by its becoming hereditary, thus placing great power in the hands of men whose qualifications would necessarily be of an unequal nature and whose judgments could not be seen to be free of bias. Eugenius Macbrahin is listed as a student at the University of St Andrews in 1525. Duncan and Archibald Mcbrain were denounced as rebels in Argyllshire in 1685. Archibald Mcbrain, who died in 1760, brought to the family the estates of Macnaghtan of that Ilk and his son, Donald, quartered the Macbrayn lions with the arms of Macnaghtan around 1773. The family continued to prosper and acquired the lands of

Glenbranter in Argyll. Major John Macbrayne was mentioned in dispatches in the First World War, when he served in the cavalry and was wounded. However, the name is now best known throughout the Western Isles for the MacBrayne shipping lines, without which many of the islands would still be completely isolated. There is a saying in the west which states: 'God made all the earth and is lord of all that it contains/Except the Island shipping lanes that belong to the MacBraynes'.

MACDUFF

ARMS (LR 1/76)[1]
Quarterly, 1st & 4th, Or, a lion rampant Gules, armed and langued Azure (Viscount Macduff and Earl of Fife); 2nd & 3rd, Vert, a fess dancetty Ermine between a hart's head cabossed in chief and two escallops in base Or (Duff of Braco)

CREST
A demi-lion Gules holding in the dexter paw a broadsword erected in pale Proper, hilted and pommelled Or

MOTTO
Deus juvat (God assists)

On Compartment
Virtute et opera (By virtue and deeds)

SUPPORTERS
Two savages wreathed about the head and middle with laurel holding branches of trees in their hands, all Proper

Clan Duff claims to be of the original Royal Scoto–Pictish line, of which Queen Gruoch, wife of Macbeth, was the senior representative. After the death of the king, her second husband, her son Lulach was murdered in 1058. Malcolm III seized the Crown and his son, Aedh, married Queen Gruoch's only living granddaughter. He was created Earl of Fife and hereditary abbot of Abernethy. Fife, symbolically representing the ancient royal line of his wife, became the undisputed second man of the kingdom. He bore on his shield the red lion rampant and was accorded three distinct privileges: to lead the vanguard of the Scottish army; to enthrone the king of Scots at his coronation; and the right of sanctuary for all his kinsmen, even for the crime of murder, if they reached the cross near Abernethy, after which a small fine would be levied instead of more severe penalties. Gille-michael MacDuf was one of the witnesses to the great charter of David I to the Abbey of Dunfermline. At the coronation of Robert the Bruce in 1306 Duncan Macduff, Earl of Fife,

was a minor held by Edward I of England as his ward, and so his sister, Isabel, Countess of Buchan, placed the golden circlet upon the king's head. For this heinous crime, she was imprisoned in a cage suspended from the walls of Berwick Castle when she later fell into the hands of King Edward's army. Duncan married Mary Monthermer, niece to Edward I, and he threw in his lot with his uncle against the Bruce. He was captured and held in Kildrummy Castle in Aberdeenshire where he died in 1336. The earldom passed into the hands of Robert Stewart, later Duke of Albany and Regent of Scotland. The family had lost their great rank but they continued to prosper, and in 1404 David Duff received a charter from Robert III to the lands of Muldavit in Banffshire. John Duff sold Muldavit in 1626, but his half-brother, Adam, was a man of ability who acquired considerable wealth and laid the foundation for the ultimate prosperity of the family. His son, Alexander, improved the family's estates in Banffshire, which he further extended by marriage to Helen, the daughter of Archibald Grant of Ballentomb. A Fife title returned to the family when William Duff, MP for the county of Banff, was created Earl Fife and Viscount Macduff in 1759. He commissioned the building of the splendid Duff House in 1740 which cost over £70,000 to complete, a staggering sum for the time. Sadly, he quarrelled with the architect, and when some structural defects became apparent he abandoned the house and never lived in it again. The house has recently been fully restored and is now open to the public. James, the fourth Earl Fife, fought with distinction during the Peninsular War of 1808–14, being granted the rank of major general. He was wounded at the Battle of Talavera and was made a Knight of the Order of St Ferdinand of Spain. His country honoured his services when he was appointed to the Order of the Thistle. The ancient lineage of the Macduffs received another infusion of the blood royal when Alexander, the sixth Earl Fife, married HRH Princess Louise, the Princess Royal, eldest daughter of the Prince of Wales, the future King Edward VII. He was advanced to the highest rank of the peerage as Duke of Fife in July 1889. By a special reservation in the patent creating the dukedom, the title was to pass, in default of a male heir, to the duke's eldest daughter, Princess Alexandra, and if

she produced no male heirs, to her sister Princess Maude. In 1923, Princess Maude married Lord Carnegie, who was later to succeed to his father's title as Earl of Southesk and chief of the Carnegies. The Countess of Southesk in due course did inherit the dukedom, which passed on her death to her son, James Carnegie, third Duke of Fife. This created the remarkable situation that the heir to the earldom of Southesk and the chiefship of Clan Carnegie also bore the ancient title of Macduff and outranked his own father by two steps in the peerage. The duke has since succeeded to his father's earldom and chiefship.

MACEWEN

There are numerous spellings of this name, which is rendered in Gaelic as 'Maceoghainn'. The sons of Ewen hold that they descend from Ewen of Otter on the shores of Loch Fyne in Argyll. Malcolm MacEwen witnessed a charter by the Earl of Atholl to the church of St Andrews around 1174. The chiefs of the clan seem to have stayed around Loch Fyne and shared a common heritage with the Maclachlans and the Macneils until around 1432, when by a charter of James I, the barony of Otter was confirmed

to Sween Macewen with a destination to the heirs of Duncan Campbell of Loch Awe. Sween is the last Macewen chief on record, and thereafter they appear only as dependents of the Campbells or as broken (clanless) men. In 1598 two hundred Macewens were described as broken Highland men heavily armed and living by robbery. They are listed in an Act of Parliament in 1602, along with other broken clans as subjects of the Earl of Argyll who was made answerable for their good behaviour. Some of this name seem to have become poets or bards, and found patrons among the Campbells and the Macdougalls. Neil Macewen composed a poem on the death of Campbell of Glenorchy in 1630. The Macewens seem to have supported the Jacobite cause, but only as individuals, as they were lacking a chief to call them out as a clan. Sir Alexander Macewen was lately Provost of Inverness.

MACFARLANE

The Macfarlanes are descended from Alwyn, Celtic Earl of Lennox, whose younger son, Gilchrist, received lands at Arrochar on the shores of Loch Long at the end of the twelfth century. Gilchrist's grand-

son, Malduin, sheltered Robert the Bruce when his fortunes were at a low ebb and he was forced to flee through Loch Lomondside to reach the safety of the west Highlands. The Macfarlanes also fought at Bannockburn in

ARMS
Argent, a saltire engrailed between four roses Gules

CREST
A demi-savage brandishing in his dexter hand a broad sword Proper and pointing with his sinister to an Imperial Crown Or standing by him on the Wreath

MOTTO
This I'll defend

SUPPORTERS
(on a wavy compartment) Two Highlanders armed with bows and arrows, all Proper

SLOGAN
Loch Sloy

1314. Malduin's son, Parlan, provided the chief's patronymic, and Iain Macpharlain received a charter of confirmation to Arrochar in 1420. Duncan, the last Celtic Earl of Lennox, was executed by James I, and although the Macfarlanes had a valid claim to the earldom, the title was given by the Crown to John Stewart, Lord Darnley. The Macfarlanes sought to oppose the Stewarts but they proved too powerful and Andrew Macfarlane, the tenth chief, married a younger daughter of Lord Darnley, cementing a new alliance. Thereafter the Macfarlanes followed the new Earls of Lennox in most of the major conflicts of the fifteenth and sixteenth centuries. The eleventh chief and many of his clansmen fell at Flodden in 1513. When the Earl of Lennox threw in his lot with Henry VII of England, the clan followed him, capturing Bute and Arran, but they met with stout resistance at the royal castle of Dumbarton. The Macfarlanes later opposed the invading

English at the Battle of Pinkie in 1547 where Duncan, the thirteenth chief, and his brother were both killed. After the murder of Lord Darnley, Mary, Queen of Scots' second husband, the Macfarlanes opposed the queen and were noted for their gallantry at the Battle of Langside in 1568. Andrew, the fourteenth chief, is said to have captured no less than three of the queen's standards, earning the personal praise of the Regent Moray. The clan's crest and motto alludes to the defence of the Crown of the infant James VI which was secured at Langside. Their loyalty to the Stuarts brought Macfarlane swords to the aid of the Marquess of Montrose when Walter Macfarlane, the sixteenth chief, declared for Charles I. They fought at Montrose's great victory at Inverlochy in 1645. When Oliver Cromwell succeeded in conquering Scotland, adding it to the Commonwealth, the Macfarlane seat at Inveruglas was burned to the ground. Despite their attachment to the Stuarts they could not support James VII, and the chief declared for Queen Mary and her husband, William of Orange, in 1688. The clan does not seem to have played any major part in the Jacobite risings of 1715 and 1745 which may have been because the twentieth chief, Walter Macfarlane, a noted antiquary and scholar, lived in Edinburgh for most of his life. The clan lands at Arrochar were sold off after Walter's death in 1767, and the direct male line of the chiefs failed in 1886. There is presently no chief of the clan.

MACFIE

ARMS (LR 64/54)[1]
Per fess indented Azure and Or, in chief a sword Argent, point downwards, hilted and pommelled of the Second, between two pheons also points downwards of the Last, in base a lymphad Sable, under sail of the Third and flagged of the First, within a bordure chequy Or and Azure

CREST
A demi lion rampant Sable charged with a pheon point downwards Or

MOTTO
Pro rege (For the king)

In modern Gaelic this name is written as 'Maca'phi'. It is usually rendered in English, Macfie or Macphee or Macafie. The name appears to be derived from 'MacDhuibhshith', meaning 'son of the dark fairy'. The origin of this name has been lost in the mists of time. In many countries the remnants of the original bearers of the name have been conferred with mystic powers. Tradition asserts that the Macfies are descended from a seal-woman who had been prevented from returning to the sea. In 1164 Duibhshith was known to have been 'ferleighinn', or 'reader', at Iona when Malcolm IV was king. The Macphees of Colonsay were the hereditary keepers of the records of Man and the Isles. There is little or no trace of these records, which may have been kept at Tynwald, still the seat of the Manx Parliament. One charter which does exist is evidence of the fact that the Lords of the Isles did conduct their business in the ancient Celtic tongue as well as in clerical Latin. There is a tradition that one of the chiefs of Colonsay fought and overcame Sir Gile de Argentine at the Battle of Bannockburn in 1314. He would probably have come to the battle with the Lord of the Isles. The Macphees continued to be loyal to the Macdonalds even after the Hebrides were ceded to Scotland in 1494 by the king of Denmark on the marriage of his daughter, Princess Margaret, to James III. This established the legal claim of the Scots Crown to control of the island kingdoms, a policy which was to be ruthlessly enforced by James IV. In 1615 Malcolm Macphee of Colonsay joined Sir James Macdonald, chief of the Macdonalds, in the southern islands in his rebellion against the Earl of Argyll. Macphee and eighteen other leading conspirators were betrayed to the

Campbells and were forced to sign the Statutes of Iona, abandoning the ancient Lordship of the Isles. (Colonsay was later murdered in 1623 while ignominiously hiding under piles of seaweed.) The Macphees were dispossessed, and some followed the Macdonalds, but most others went to the mainland where they found shelter in Lochaber. Many Macphees are believed to have followed Cameron of Lochiel at the ill-fated Battle of Culloden in 1746. In the middle of the nineteenth century Ewan Macphee became famous as the last Scottish outlaw, when he settled with his family on Eilean Mhic Phee in Loch Quoich. He recognised no law and was an inveterate sheep stealer. Macfie of Dreghorn matriculated arms in the Lyon register in 1864. He was a member of a powerful merchant family with considerable interests in the sugar-refining industry. The company was eventually to be taken over by the present sugar giants, Tate & Lyle. Sadly, many of the clan were so destitute that they could make no permanent home, and today the name is most closely associated with the wandering tin-smiths known as 'tinkers'. There is now an active Macfie Society world-wide and the Lord Lyon has recognised this by granting a commission for the appointment of a clan commander.

MACGILLIVRAY

The Macgillivrays were an important clan in the western isles even before King Somerled, Lord of the Isles, drove the Norsemen out of the area in the middle of the twelfth century. When Alexander II subdued Argyll in 1222, the Clann Mhic Gillebrath were dispersed. Some of the clan remained in Mull and Morvern. Tradition asserts that Gillivray, the progenitor of the clan, placed himself under the protection of the chiefs of the Clan Macintosh. The clan thereafter belonged to the Clan Chattan Confederation. The Macgillivrays were first accurately recorded in Dunmaglas in 1549. At the great gathering of the Clan Chattan in 1609, when

all bound themselves in loyalty to the young Mackintosh chief and in mutual support, the 'haill kin and race of Macgillivray' was represented by Malcolm of Dalcrombie and Duncan Macfarquhar of Dunmaglas. This is a classic example of the use of patronymics and the territorial designations common in the Highlands before the use of what would now be popularly considered surnames became widespread in the eighteenth century. The Macgillivrays were supporters of an episcopacy in the church, and this caused them to be persecuted by their Calvinist and presbyterian neighbours. In common with most of the confederated Clan Chattan families, the Macgillivrays were

ARMS (LR 51/64)[1]
*Quarterly, 1st, Or, a cat-a-mountain sejant guardant
Proper, his dexter fore-paw on the ground, his sinister
fore-paw in a guardant posture and his tail reflexed under
his sinister paw; 2nd, Argent, a dexter hand couped at the
wrist apaumy Gules; 3rd, Azure, a salmon naiant Argent;
4th, Or, a galley sailing sinister-wise Azure, its oars in
saltire and flagged Gules*

CREST
*A cat-a-mountain as afore blazoned for the first quarter
of the field*

MOTTO
Touch not this cat

SUPPORTERS
Two young plants of boxwood

BADGE
*A demi cat-a-mountain passant guardant issuant from a
chaplet quarterly Vert and Or, grasping in his sinister
paw a boxwood sapling*

GUIDON
*The Arms in the hoist, of this livery Gules upon which is
depicted the badge along with the Slughorn 'Dunmaghlas'
extended in the fly in letters Or*

staunch Jacobites, and they fought in both the Fifteen and in the Forty-five. In 1745 the chief

of the Mackintoshes was an officer in a Hanoverian regiment. His wife, a formidable lady with distinct Jacobite sympathies, summoned Alexander Macgillivray and placed him in command of the regiment raised by Clan Chattan. Macgillivray was at the head of his men at Culloden where he fell along with many of his followers, and the graveyard at Dunlichity commemorates the many Macgillivray fallen. After Culloden, many emigrated across the Atlantic where their spirit of independence and fortitude made many successful, particularly as traders. William Macgillivray became head of the Canadian Northwest Company and member of the Legislative Council of Lower Canada. The estates in Dunmaglas were sold off in 1890 and the last Chief is believed to have died in Canada. The Macgillivrays have become organised and active again in this century, and there are clan societies throughout the world.

MACINNES

ARMS (LR 44/79)[1]
*Quarterly, 1st, Azure, a castle of two towers Or, port and
windows Gules; 2nd & 3rd, Or, upon a sea in base undy
Azure and Argent, a lymphad Vert flagged and five visible oars in action Gules; 4th, gyronny of eight Sable and
Or; overall, dividing the quarters, a cross Vert charged
with a millrind between four pheons Argent, accompanied
by two cross crosslets in the flanks and as many cross
crosslets fitchée, in chief and in base, of the said cross all
of the Last*

CREST
*A sinister arm from the shoulder bendways, attired in a
close sleeve of the proper tartan of Clan Aonghais, cuff
flashes yellow with three buttons Or, grasping a bow
Vert, stringed Gules*

MOTTO
Ghift dhe Agus an righ (By the grace of God and king)

This Celtic name is derived from the Gaelic 'Macaonghuis', meaning 'son of Angus'. Grimble notes the earliest reference to the sons of Angus is given in the seventh-century chronicle, *Senchus Fer n'Alban* (*History of the Men of Scotland*). The Scots of Dalriada appear to have been divided into three kindreds: those of Gabran, Lorne and Angus. The kindred of Angus are said to have possessed Islay,

later to be the seat of the Lordship of the Isles. There is, however, little concrete evidence to connect all of this to the MacInneses as a distinct family. They arose around Morvern, and were in possession of Kinlochaline Castle when it was attacked in 1645 by the Macdonalds who had risen for Montrose against the Covenanters, led by Campbell of Argyll. They may simply have held the castle as keepers or captains, however, as they had become by this time quite dependent upon the Campbells. Another section of this family were noted as hereditary archers to the Mackinnon chiefs on Skye, and this is alluded to in the most common crest of this family, which is an arm holding a bow. The main body of the clan followed the Campbells in supporting the Hanoverian cause against the Stuart exiles, but one branch, which had become connected with the Stewarts of Ardsheal, fought for the Jacobite cause. In common with many fragmented families, the Macinneses scattered worldwide during the great periods of emigration and the name is commonly found throughout the English-speaking world, particularly in Canada and New Zealand.

MACKIE

This family were powerful and prominent in Galloway in the sixteenth and early seventeenth centuries. The name is in its derivation similar to Mackay, and the Mackies may be descendents of sons of Aoidh (a descendent of the royal Celto–Pictish house of Moray) who made their way to Galloway and Wigtownshire via Kintyre. The arms of the principal family Mackie of Larg give rise to one of the many legends of family origins based upon feats of martial skill. The story is told that Mackie of Larg was in the company of Robert II and was making much of his prowess as an archer. The king, wearying of

this, pointed to two ravens on a distant tree and invited Mackie to demonstrate his skill. Mackie, no doubt much to the king's chagrin, skewered the ravens with a single arrow. He was thereafter granted the right to bear on his shield the two ravens pierced by an arrow through their neck, together with a lion, alluding to the royal witness to this feat. Sir Patrick Mackie of Larg was one of the original fifty Scottish undertakers of the plantation of Ulster at the beginning of the seventeenth century. He was clearly not an enthusiastic participant, as John, Earl of Annandale, eventually took over some one thousand acres near Donegal that was in the original portion of Sir Patrick. The family also acquired the lands of Bargaly in Kirkcudbrightshire and Auchencairn by Castle Douglas. The family prospered, and Lieutenant Colonel John Mackie of Bargaly served with distinction in the Boer War. There are still Mackies in Kirkcudbright today.

MACLELLAN

The name is Gaelic in origin, deriving from 'MacGille Fhaolain' 'son of the servant of St Filan'. St Filan was a missionary of the old Celtic church, and there is a village in Perthshire named after him. The name Filan itself is derived from the Celtic 'faelchu', meaning 'wolf'. The Maclellans were numerous in Galloway and gave their name to

Balmaclellan in Stewartry. Duncan MacLellan appears in a charter of Alexander II in 1217. Maclellan of Bombie was among the close followers of Sir William Wallace when he left Kirkcudbright for France after the defeat at Falkirk in 1293. In the early fifteenth century it is said there were no fewer than fourteen knights of the name Maclellan in Galloway. Sir Patrick Maclellan of Bombie forfeited his estates for marauding through the lands of the Douglases, the Lords of Galloway. James II restored the lands when Sir Patrick's son, Sir William, captured the leader of a band of gypsies who were terrorising the district. Sir William carried the head of the brigand to the king on the point of his sword. This is one explanation advanced for the origins of the crest of this family, although moors' heads are often considered to be an allusion to the Crusades. In 1452, William, eighth Earl of Douglas, captured Sir Patrick Maclellan, the tutor of Bombie and Sheriff of Galloway, and held him in Threave Castle for refusing to join a conspiracy against the king. Sir Patrick's uncle, who held high royal office, obtained letters ordering the release of Douglas's prisoner. When Douglas was presented with the royal warrant he promptly had Sir Patrick murdered while he entertained his uncle at dinner. Maclellan's death was another example of Douglas's contempt for royal authority which the king was later to repay by executing the earl at Stirling. Although there is little doubt that the celebrated Scots cannon, 'Mons Meg', was made at Mons in Belgium, there is a local tradition that it was the Maclellans who brought the great gun to batter down Threave as part of their revenge on the Douglases. Sir

William Maclellan of Bombie was knighted by James IV but followed his king on the ill-fated invasion of England which ended at Flodden field in 1513. His son, Thomas, was killed at the door of St Giles' Cathedral in Edinburgh by Gordon of Lochinvar in 1526. His great-grandson, Sir Robert, was a courtier both to James IV and Charles I, and in 1633 was raised to the peerage as Lord Kirkcudbright. The third Lord was such a zealous royalist that during the civil war he incurred enormous debts in the king's cause, and completely ruined the estates. The title passed from cousin to brother to cousin, with very few direct male heirs, although at the beginning of the eighteenth century there were two claimants to the title. The dispute was finally settled by the House of Lords in 1761 but the title again became dormant in 1832 when the ninth Lord died in Bruges.

MACQUARRIE

ARMS (LR 43/93)[1]
Quarterly, embattled, 1st & 4th, Vert, three towers in chief Argent masoned Sable; 2nd, Gules, three cross crosslets fitchée Argent; 3rd, per fess Azure and Vert, a lymphad sails furled in chief and a fish naiant in base both Argent

CREST
Issuant from a tower head embattled and crenellated Argent, a dexter arm in armour embowed, the hand grasping a dagger projected fessways all Proper

MOTTO
Turris fortis meus mihi Deus (To me God is my strong tower)

This clan, for long associated with the island of Ulva, derives its name from the Gaelic 'guaire', meaning 'noble'. They are said to have a common descent with the Mackinnons, Guaire being the brother of Fingon, ancestor of the Mackinnons. The historian Skene states, 'the history of the Macquarries resembles that of the Mackinnons in many respects; like them they had migrated far from the headquarters of their race; they became dependent on the Lords of the Isles and followed them as if they had become a branch of the clan'. The first chief that can be referred to with any certainty appears to be

Iain or John Macquarrie of Ulva, who is believed to have died around 1473 and who appeared as a witness in an earlier charter. The suppression of the Lordship of the Isles gave the Macquarries a greater measure of independence but they seem to have generally followed the fortunes of their more powerful neighbours, the Macleans of Duart. John Macquarrie of Ulva supported the attempt of Donald, the last Lord of the Isles, against the Crown in 1545 and he was also one of the chiefs denounced in the same year for traitorous dealings with the English. Macquarrie of Ulva was one of the chiefs summoned to the island of Iona by James VI in 1609, ostensibly to attend a service of reconciliation in that holy place. The king, however, had the chiefs seized and he forced them to sign the Statutes of Iona, ending forever the pretensions of the Lordships of the Isles. The Macquarries followed the Macleans in support of the royalist cause in the civil war, and Ulva himself was slain with most of his followers at the Battle of Inverkeithing against the Parliamentarian troops of Oliver Cromwell in July 1651.

Despite this setback, the family held its lands until the end of the eighteenth century when, in common with many other island lairds, crippling debt forced Lachlan Macquarrie to sell them. However, the family name was not to pass from history, and a cousin of the chiefly house, another Lachlan, rose to the rank of major general in the British army, and was appointed Governor of New South Wales. He held this post from 1809 to 1821, and is best remembered for his strong moral sense which helped to establish a balance of power between the large landowners and the freed convicts and other emigrants seeking a new life in Australia. The Macquarrie River is named after him and he is often termed 'the father of Australia'. He returned to Ulva and bought back much of the family lands. The main chiefly line had failed around 1818 and General Macquarrie's only son, Lachlan, by his marriage to a daughter of Campbell of Airds, died without issue.

MACQUEEN

ARMS[4]
Argent, three wolves' heads couped Sable

CREST
An heraldic tyger rampant Ermine holding an arrow,
point downwards Argent pheoned Gules

MOTTO
Constant and faithful

SUPPORTERS
Two heraldic tygers Ermine

This Celtic name is also given as 'Macsween', or 'son of Sweyn'. They are accordingly of the same descent as the great Clan Donald, claiming kinship with the Irish High Kings. The Macqueens are said to have provided a guard for a daughter of the house of Clan Ranald who married a Mackintosh chief, and they elected to settle around Findhorn and became part of that confederation of clans known as the Clans of the Cat, or Clan Chattan. They were known as Clan Revan, after the leader of the original escort. The principal family became the Lairds of Corriborough and they remained highly regarded among the supporters of the Macdonalds. In 1778 Lord Macdonald of Sleat wrote, 'it does me great honour to have the sons of Chieftains in the Regiment and as the MacQueens have been invariably attached to our family, to whom we believe we owe our existence, I am proud of the nomination'. The Macqueens or Macsweens were numerous throughout the islands. The Reverend Donald Macqueen, minister of Snizort, was a man of such intellect that he even impressed the great Dr Samuel Johnson, who met him on his visit to the Hebrides. The fortunes of the family failed, and the chiefs are believed to have emigrated to New Zealand and the family scattered throughout Scotland and the English-speaking world. The name was not always highly regarded, however: Robert Macqueen, a famous eighteenth-century Scottish judge, was elevated to the Bench with the title, 'Lord Braxfield'. He was feared for his savage sentences and his predeliction for the death penalty. One famous incident is related where he found an old friend, and constant adversary in the game of chess, before him on a capital charge. He is said to have delivered the death sentence and then looked his old friend in the eye and declared, 'and that's checkmate to me'. Professor John Macqueen is a distinguished twentieth-century academic and for many years held the chair of Scottish Studies at the University of Edinburgh.

MACRAE

This Celtic name stems from the Gaelic, 'son of Grace'. The Macraes were most numerous around Kintail in Wester Ross, where they appear to have become supporters of the Mackenzies. Duncan Macrae was constable of Eilean Donan Castle and acquired for

ARMS (of Inverinate LR 27/16 and 54/76)[1]
*Argent, a fess Azure between three mullets in chief and a
lion rampant in base Gules*

CREST
A cubit arm grasping a sword all Proper

MOTTO
Fortitudine (With fortitude)

himself the lands of Inverinate. The Macraes were so fierce in adherence to their Mackenzie overlord that they became known as 'Mackenzie's shirt of mail'. In 1539 the Macdonalds, under Donald Grumach, fourth of Sleat, besieged Eilean Donan Castle as part of their attempt to revive the shattered Lordship of the Isles. Macrae is credited with slaying the Macdonald chief with an arrow, bringing the siege to an end. The fortunes of the Mackenzies prospered and they obtained for themselves the title, 'Earl of Seaforth'. The Macraes basked in reflected glory and were invested with the hereditary constableship of Eilean Donan Castle and also created chamberlains of Kintail. There were numerous cadet houses, including the Macraes of Conchra, Clunes and Feoirlinn. The family was not only renowned for its military prowess. Duncan Macrae, born around 1640 was educated at Edinburgh University and composed Gaelic poetry. Lieutenant Colonel John Macrae, born in 1861, served in the Black Watch, and was both deputy keeper of the Palace of Holyroodhouse and a member of the Royal Company of Archers (bodyguard of the monarch in Scotland). Colonel Sir Colin Macrae of Feoirlinn, who was knighted in 1935, served with distinction throughout the Boer War and was not only a member of the Royal Company of Archers, but also a lieutenant in the bodyguard of the English monarch, the Yeomen of the Guard.

MASTERTON

ARMS (of Parkmill and Gogar LR 1/514)[1]
Argent, a chevron Gules and a chief Azure

CREST
*A stag current bearing on his attyres an oaken slip
fructuated Proper*

MOTTO
Per ardua (Through difficulties)

The lands from which this name derives are of great antiquity in Fife. The name may relate to lands held by a magister, or master, of the great Abbey of Dunfermline. William de Mastertone of the county of Fife appears on the Ragman Roll of 1296, rendering homage to Edward I of England for his possessions. His seal is said to have borne a lion rampant with a rose, devices which form no part of the arms recorded in the Lyon register. However, such heraldic discrepancies were common at this time, and the arms recorded of a red chevron and a blue chief on a silver field have the simplicity which would be expected of medieval arms. Duncan de Mastertone witnessed a charter of Duncan, Earl of Fife, to the abbots of Dunfermline in 1316, and Sir Thomas Mastertone was a canon of the Abbey of Cambuskenneth in 1476. Margaret, daughter of Alexander Mastertone, was nurse to Henry, eldest son of James VI, and received a royal pension. Alan Masterton, a friend and admirer of the poet Robert Burns, composed many of the tunes to accompany the bard's lyrics. He was a teacher at the Royal High School of Edinburgh around 1795, and Burns is said to have written some verses in honour of the composer's daughter.

MAULE

A surname of Norman origin, from Maule in France. It is believed that a younger son of the Sieur de Maule accompanied William the Conqueror on his invasion of England in 1066 and was granted manors in Yorkshire. One of his sons may have accompanied David,

Earl of Huntingdon, when he travelled north to claim his kingdom as David I. The name is found thereafter around Midlothian. William de Maule fought at the Battle of the Standard in 1138, but died without issue, and it is thought that Roger de Maule, probably his brother, was the progenitor of the Maules of Panmure who were to become the principal family. Sir Thomas Maule, Roger's grandson, was governor of Brechin Castle and held it against Edward I of England. He was killed during the siege and his brother, the sheriff of Forfar, was compelled to swear fealty to Edward in 1292. In common with most of the Scottish nobility who submitted to the English king the Maules were quick to support Robert the Bruce and the cause of Scottish independence. Sir Henry Maule was knighted personally by Robert. Bruce's son, David II, appointed Maule governor of the castle of Kildrummy. Sir Thomas Maule of Panmure, grandson of the constable of Kildrummy, fought with the Earl of Mar at the Battle of Harlaw against the Lord of the Isles in 1411, when he was killed. His great-great-grandson,

another Sir Thomas, fell on Flodden field in 1513. The Maules were supporters of the Earls of Lennox in their attempt to rescue James V from the power of the Douglases in 1526. Maule openly opposed the negotiations for the proposed marriage of the infant Mary, Queen of Scots, to the son of Henry VIII of England. During Henry's invasion of Scotland (later known as the 'rough wooing'), Maule was captured and sent to the Tower of London and was only released two years later on the intervention of the French ambassador. Patrick Maule of Panmure was in the retinue of James VI when the king travelled to London to take possession of his new throne. Charles I created him Earl of Panmure and Lord Maule of Brechin in 1646. The earl attended on the king during his imprisonment. His son, Henry, commanded a regiment in the force which was raised to attempt the rescue of the king in 1648. The earl's eldest son and heir, George, fought for the royalists at Dunbar in 1650 and at Inverkeithing, where he was wounded. The Maules came to terms with Cromwell's army of occupation, led by General Monck. James, the fourth Earl, proclaimed the 'Old Pretender' King James VIII at Brechin in 1715. He fought at the Battle of Sheriffmuir, where he was taken prisoner. He was rescued by his brother and they fled to France. His titles and estates were forfeited, but he refused to take part in the general amnesty offered by the house of Hanover, and remained in France until his death. His great-granddaughter married the son of the Earl of Dalhousie, and through her the title passed to the Ramsays.

MAXTON

The lands and barony of Maxton lie in Roxburghshire, and Black suggests the name may be a version of the 'dun' or 'tun' of Maccus. A dun was the fortified dwelling of a Celtic nobleman. Maccus, son of Undwin, is believed to have obtained land in the area from David I some time prior to 1153. The family are believed to have lost the original barony, which passed at the end of the twelfth

century into the hands of Robert de Berkley. Adam de Maxton was elected Abbot of Melrose in 1261, and Alexander de Maxton, styled 'constable of Roxburgh', may be the same individual as appears on the Ragman Roll, submitting to Edward I of England in 1296. Robert de Maxton received the lands of Cultoquhey near Crieff in Perthshire, around 1410. His arms bore three crosses which may

ARMS (of Cultoquhey LR 6/52)[1]
Or, a chevron Gules between three cross crosslets fitchée Azure

CREST
A bee Proper

MOTTO
Providus esto (Be careful)

have been a heraldic reference to the earlier Abbot of Melrose. Robert Maxton died with James IV at the Battle of Flodden in 1513. The

family continued to prosper in Perthshire and they allied themselves by marriage to other local notables, such as the Oliphants and the Grahams of Balgowan and of Murrayshall. James Maxton of Cultoquhey succeeded to the estates of his uncle, Robert Graham of Balgowan, in 1859, and the family has since then borne the compound surname Maxtone-Graham and quartered the arms of both families.

MAXWELL

ARMS[3]
Argent, a saltire Sable, (as displayed on the Arms of the Earl of Nithsdale) viz:- Argent, an eagle displayed Sable, beaked and membered Gules, (Nithsdale), surmounted of an escutcheon of the First, charged with a saltire of the Second (Maxwell), the escutcheon surcharged in the centre with an urcheon, Or (Herries)

CREST
A stag Proper, attired Argent, couchant before a holly bush Proper

MOTTO
Reviresco (I grow strong again)

SUPPORTERS
Two stags Proper, attired Argent

Maccus Well, a pool in the River Tweed by Kelso, is claimed as the origin for this name. Maccus was believed to be a Norse chief who lived in the reign of David I. Sir John Maxwell, Chamberlain of Scotland, died without issue and was succeeded by his brother, Aymer, from whose sons sprang many branches of this family throughout the south-west of Scotland. Sir Herbert Maxwell swore fealty to Edward I of England in the Ragman Roll of 1296. His son, Eustace, held Caerlaverock Castle as a vassal of the English, but later followed Robert the Bruce to Bannockburn in 1314. His descendent, another Sir Herbert, was created Lord Maxwell around 1440, taking his seat as Lord of Parliament. From his second son descended the Maxwells of Monrieth, who were later to be created baronets in 1681. The fifth Lord intrigued with Henry VII of England, although by 1542 James V had appointed him warden of the marches. Maxwell was captured at the Battle of Solway Moss in the same year. John, the

seventh Lord, remained a devout Catholic throughout the Reformation, and his name was linked with a number of plots to restore Mary, Queen of Scots to her throne. After Mary's execution in England in 1587 and the defeat of the Spanish Armada the following year, Lord Maxwell continued to correspond with Philip of Spain, seeking support for a Catholic revolution. Maxwell was killed in 1593 during a feud between his family and the Johnstons, near Lockerbie. The feud contin-ued, however, and the next Lord Maxwell shot Sir James Johnston, who was attempting to reconcile the two warring factions. His brother, Robert, succeeded to the Maxwell title and additionally was created Earl of Nithsdale. His descendent, the fifth Earl of Nithsdale, was a staunch Jacobite who was captured at the Battle of Preston during the ill-fated rising of 1715. He was taken to London, tried and sen-tenced to death for treason. On the eve of his execution, with the assistance of his wife, he escaped from the Tower of London, disguised as a serving woman. The couple fled to Rome where the earl died in 1744. A number of the cadet branches rose to prominence in their own right, including the Maxwells of Cardoness, Monreith, Sprinkel and Pollok, each achieving the rank of baronet. Pollok House, the seat of the Maxwell Baronets of Pollok, was gifted to the city of Glasgow in 1967; in its grounds is the world-famous Burrell Collection of art. James Clerk Maxwell, born in Edinburgh in 1831, was a physicist who made a fundamental contribution to this branch of science through his formulation of electromagnetic theory. Gavin Maxwell, the Scottish author and naturalist who died in 1969, was the youngest son of Sir Herbert Maxwell who descended from the Maxwells of Monreith.

McCORQUODALE

ARMS (of that Ilk LR 1/359)[1]
Argent, a stag Gules attired Or issuing from a fess wreathed of the Second and Third

CREST
A stag at gaze Proper attired Gules

MOTTO
Vivat rex (Long live the king)

This name is derived from the old Norse 'thorketill' which, rendered in English, means 'son of Torquil'. The Norse name is clearly descriptive, relating to the god of thunder and storms. According to Anderson, the founder of the clan was one Thorkil who was part of the Scots army of Kenneth, called Macalpin, who fought against the Picts around 834. The story goes that Alpin, King of the Scots, had been killed in battle prior to Kenneth's arrival from Ireland. The late king's head was fixed upon a spike in the midst of the Pictish camp, and Kenneth offered a grant of land to anyone in his army who would recover the head. Thorkil is said to have accomplished this feat and the king, good as his word, rewarded him with a charter of land. There is no record of this grant, but in 1434, Ewan, son of Ewan Makcorquydill, received a grant of lands, and in the charter he is described as 'Lord of Maintelan'. Black states that this was properly Phanteland and the Mccorquodales of Phantelands were to become the most prominent branch of the Mccorquodale family. Despite the stirring deeds of their possibly mythical ancestor, the Mccorquodales were not all held in high regard and in 1612 they were rebuked by the Privy Council as 'notorious thieves and the supporters of Clan Gregour'. There were still Mccorquodales dwelling on Loch Aweside towards the end of the eighteenth century, claiming direct descent from Torquil (Thorkil), from whom the chiefly line descended. Sir Malcolm Maccorquodale, who died in 1971, was raised to the peerage as Lord Maccorquodale of Newton, but this title is now extinct.

McCULLOCH

ARMS (of Myreton LR 1/185)[1]
Ermine, fretty Gules

CREST
A hand throwing a dart Proper

MOTTO
Vi et animo (By strength and courage)

This name, which in Scotland is found principally in Galloway and Wigtownshire, is of Celtic origin, but a number of alternative derivations has been proposed. The Irish Gaelic 'MacCu'uladh', meaning 'son of the Hound of Ulster', is anglicised as 'Maccullagh'. In Scots Gaelic it is often rendered 'Maccullaich', and translated as 'son of the boar'. They are, of course, very similar, and both are references to descriptive personal names suggesting fierce vigour. There is also a more northerly branch of the family around Oban, descendents of the Macdougalls, who may derive their name from 'MacLulaich', which may mean 'son of the little calf'. This, again, is a descriptive personal name and its significance is obscure. The progenitor of the Argyllshire Mccullochs was said to be Lulach, son of Gilla Comgan, the Celtic Mormaer, or Earl, of Moray. The Galloway Mccullochs first come to prominence when Thomas Maculagh,

'Counte de Wyggtone', appears on the Ragman Roll of 1296, rendering homage to Edward I of England. He may also be the same Thomas Makhulagh who was appointed sheriff of Wigtown in 1305. Mccullochs witnessed various charters throughout the fourteenth century and Sir Patrick M'Owlache is noted as being restored to his lands in 1363, having previously been forfeited, apparently for allegiance to the English. The family also lost the office of sheriff of Wigtown, which passed to the family of Agnew of Lochnaw who still hold this honorary title to this day. In 1488 Quinton Agnew, sheriff of Wigtown, was ordered to restore to Archibald McCulloch twenty-eight oxen, eighty-eight sheep, four horses and other goods. It is recorded in 1507 that the Mcculloch chief, in revenge for a raid on the town of Kirkcudbright, ravaged the Isle of Man, then in possession of the Earl of Derby. The Mccullochs appear to have acquired the lands of Myretoun, which were constituted into a barony around 1566. They were raised to the rank of baronet in 1634, but this title came to an unfortunate end when Sir Godfrey Mcculloch was executed at Edinburgh in 1697 for the murder of William Gordon. The trial was of such celebrity that it is recorded in Pitcairn's *Criminal Trials of Scotland*. The representation of the family passed to cousins, the Mccullochs of Ardwall, and there were other cadets. Major General Sir Andrew Mcculloch of Ardwall served in both the Boer War (1899–1902) and the First World War (1914–18), winning the Distinguished Service Order no less than three times. He was aide-de-camp to George V from 1931 to 1933.

McIVER

ARMS[11]
Quarterly Or and Gules, overall a bend Sable

CREST
A boar's head couped Or

MOTTO
Nunquam obliviscar (I will never forget)

This family of very ancient heritage takes its name from the Gaelic 'Maciomhar', meaning 'son of Ivar'. This is a Norse personal name and it is therefore extremely difficult to determine with any certainty the progenitor after whom this family is named. Black states that Imhair was a Norse chief who joined with Olaf the White, King of Dublin, in his siege and sack of Dumbarton around 870. Doenaldus, son of Makbeth Macyvar, is recorded as one of the perambulators of the boundary between the lands of Arbroath Abbey and the barony of Kynblathmund in 1219. In 1292 the lands of Malcolm McIuyr and others in Lorne were erected into the sheriffdom of Lorne by Act of Parliament. McIan states that Iver was a son of Duncan, Lord of Lochow, and therefore the Macivers were part of the progeny from which was to spring the mighty Clan Campbell. Indeed, it has been suggested that Iver was the elder son and that the Macivers were truly the senior line. In practical terms, this seems to have been of little significance, as the Campbell Lords of Lochow distinguished themselves in battle and succeeded in acquiring the Lordship of Lorne, thereafter becoming earls, and ultimately dukes, of Argyll. Their ascendency over their cousins, the Macivers, does not seem to have gone undisputed, and it is recorded that in 1564 the fifth Earl, in return for Maciver acknowledgment of his chiefship, resigned all claims he might have to receive calps (tribute in cattle or other livestock) from them. The Macivers held the estates of Asknish, and the deeds to their estates bound them to use that name. They remained trusted allies of the Campbells, and in 1572 Duncan Maciver, chief of Asknish, was captain or keeper of Inveraray Castle. His cousin, Charles, the Laird of Ballochyle, is said to have used the names Campbell and Maciver quite indiscriminately, but in May 1589 he is recorded as holding the powerful post of chamberlain of Argyll. Thereafter the fortunes of the Macivers were largely those of the great house of Argyll and they followed Campbell interests throughout the seventeenth and eighteenth centuries. Mcian suggests that it was after the restoration of the Campbell fortunes, after the defeat of James VII and II in 1690, that the Earls of Argyll imposed upon their Maciver supporters the condition that they adopt the surname of Campbell in return for the restoration of their forfeited estates. This is a trite explanation, as there had been so much intermarriage with other Campbell cadets, including the Houses of Dunstaffnage, Ardkinglass and others, that the use of the name and the quartering of arms would have taken place in any event. The principal houses bore into this century the compound surnames of Maciver-Campbell of Asknish and Maciver-Campbell of Ballochyle. There is now an active Maciver Society which has established its headquarters at Strathendry Castle in Fife, and which seeks to promote awareness of the distinctive character of the name.

McKERRELL

ARMS (of Hillhouse LR 56/60)[1]
Azure, on a fess Or three lozenges Gules within a bordure engrailed Argent

CREST
A roman soldier on his march with standard and utensils all Proper

MOTTO
Dulcis pro patria labor (Labour for our country is sweet)

This name may have several derivations, but there seems little doubt that they are of very ancient Celtic origin. Black suggests that it is 'Macfhearghil, son of Fearghal'. According to O'Hart's *Irish Pedigrees,* they descend from Lochlan MacCairhill Roidamna, the future king of Ulster, who fled to Scotland after defeat in battle in 1095. The name is found very early in Carrick, and Recherus MecMaccharil witnessed a confirmation by the Earl of Carrick of a charter granted in the reign of William the Lion. The name also arises as Carleton, a place name found around Kirkcudbrightshire, Wigtownshire and Ayrshire. This is recorded as 'Cairlitoun' in the Whithorn Priory rentals. John Mckerrell of Hillhouse, the first laird, was the grandson of Martin Mckerrell (born *c.* 1490). Martin was directly descended from Sir John Mckirel, the 'chevalier Ecossais' who distinguished himself at the Battle of Otterburn in 1388 by wounding and taking prisoner Rouel de Percy, second in command of the English host. John, fourth of Hillhouse, married Elizabeth, daughter of Robert Wallace, Bishop of the Isles, in 1660, and built a fine new mansion house, replacing the older seat. John, eighth of Hillhouse, born in 1762, is credited with bringing the silk industry to Paisley, and his eldest son, William, was the colonel of the Paisley Volunteers, the first volunteer regiment formed to resist the threatened French Revolutionary invasion of 1792. Colonel Mckerrell's son sought his fortune in India and was master of the mint at Madras. Robert, thirteenth of Hillhouse, sold the estates in 1895. He was a prison commissioner for Scotland and a member of the Royal Company of Archers (the monarch's bodyguard in Scotland). His sister, Henrietta, married Henry, Count Bentink. Charles, fifteenth of Hillhouse, Baron of Dromin, returned in 1990 to the family lands, and established his seat at Lochmaben in Dumfriesshire.

MELDRUM

The ancient barony of Meldrum is in Aberdeenshire. The family are styled as 'Dominus (Lord) de Meldrum' in very early charters. Alexander de Melgedrum, was witness to a resignation of lands by John, Earl of Strathearn, around 1278. Philip and William de Melgedrum were witnesses to the foundation charter by the Comyn Earl of Buchan, of the Hospital of Turriff. William de Melkedrom, sheriff of Aberdeen, appears on the Ragman Roll submitting to Edward I of England in 1296. William Myldrum, a Scots prisoner of war, was executed by the English in 1402. The direct line of Meldrum of that Ilk ended in an heiress, Elizabeth, who married William, son of Sir Alexander Seton, who was killed at the Battle of Brechin in 1452. Another branch of the family, the Meldrums of Crombie, married into the powerful Preston family, and accordingly quarter the Meldrum arms with those of Preston. The name is still widespread in Aberdeenshire.

MELVILLE

The barony of Maleville lay in the Pays de Ceux in Normandy. Guillaume de Malleville was one of the companions of William, Duke of Normandy, at the Battle of Hastings in 1066. de Mallevilles settled in Scotland during the reign of David I, who granted them lands in Midlothian. Galfrid de Maleville was 'vicecomes' of Edinburgh Castle for Malcolm IV. He served as Justiciary of Scotland under William the Lion, the first record of such an appointment. The only daughter of his eldest son, Gregory, married Sir John Ross of Halkhead, carrying with her the earliest Barony of Melville. Agnes's descendent was created Lord Ross by James IV, and the Barony of Melville remained in that family until 1705. It was Galfrid's youngest son, Walter, who was to be the ancestor of the Melvilles of Raith. Sir John de Melville, one of the great barons of Scotland, appears on the Ragman Roll, swearing fealty to Edward I of England in 1296. His lineal descendent, Sir John Melville of Raith, was a favourite of James V, by whom he was appointed Master General of the Ordnance and captain of the Castle of Dunbar. In 1536, and again in 1542, he obtained charters to lands at Murdocairnie in Fife. He was one of the first supporters of the Reformation in Scotland and despite his royal patronage, he earned the emnity of the powerful Cardinal Beaton. He was a friend of some of the conspirators, and was falsely implicated in the cardinal's murder by means of a forged letter sufficient to convict him of treason, and he was executed in 1550. His eldest son, John Melville of Raith, was restored to the family estates by Mary of Guise, the Queen Regent, around 1553. He subscribed to the Articles of July 1567 passed in the General Assembly of the Church of Scotland for the support of the reformed religion. His second son, Sir Robert Melville of Murdocairnie, lived for a time in France before being sent as ambassador to England in 1562. In 1567 he was appointed keeper of the Palace of Linlithgow. He was sent again to England in 1587, by which time Mary, Queen of Scots was under sentence of death. Melville spoke against this outrage with such force that he offended Queen Elizabeth of England who, despite his diplomatic status, threatened to imprison him. In 1589 he was appointed Vice-Chancellor of Scotland. He became a judge, taking the title, 'Lord Murdocairnie', retiring in

1601. In April 1616 he was created Baron Melville of Monymaill. He was succeeded by his son, who was also a judge. In 1627 Charles I created him Lord Monymaill. He died in 1635, when he was succeeded by his cousin, John, third Lord Melville. John's son, George, was created first Earl of Melville in April 1690. A staunch Protestant, he had earlier supported the rebellion by James, Duke of Monmouth, the illegitimate son of Charles II. In June 1685 he was with the Duke when he landed at Lyme from Holland. Monmouth was defeated by the forces of his uncle, James VII, and was executed. Lord Melville was forced to flee to the Continent, his estates being declared forfeit by Parliament. In 1688 he returned with Queen Mary and her husband, William of Orange. His forfeiture was immediately rescinded, he was appointed Secretary of State for Scotland and later became President of the Council. He married the granddaughter of the great Covenanter general, Sandy Lesley, 1st Earl of Leven. His eldest son, Alexander, died without issue, before his father, leaving his younger brother, David, to inherit the earldom. In 1713, he also succeeded through his mother to the earldom of Leven. The fine Castle of Balgonie in Fife, recently substantially restored, was Leven's seat. Thereafter the title of 'Lord Balgonie' has been borne by the heir as a courtesy title. David Melville eventually became commander-in-chief of the army in Scotland, and was a commissioner for the Union of the Parliaments. He sat in the new Parliament at Westminster as a representative peer of Scotland, from 1707 to 1710. The fourth Earl served as a High Court judge from 1741 to 1753. He was succeeded by his son, David, fifth Earl of Melville and sixth of Leven. His second son, William, was killed in the American War of Independence in 1777. Two of his other sons achieved the rank of general. He was succeeded in the family titles by his eldest son, Alexander, in 1802. The seventh Earl was a vice-admiral in the Royal Navy. Viscount Balgonie served in the army, and was decorated with the French Legion of Honour. The father of the present chief, the twelfth Earl of Melville and thirteenth of Leven, served in the 2nd Dragoons (Scots Grays) and was wounded in the First World War. He became a colonel in the Lovat Scouts, Lord Lieutenant of Nairn, and a Knight of the Thistle. The family seat is now at Glenferness in Nairn. Melville Castle, which stands in the ancient barony of Melville, was entirely rebuilt by the Dundas family, who, although they took the title, 'Viscount Melville', have no direct connection with the chiefly family.

MERCER

ARMS (of Aldie LR 1/186)[1]
Or, on a fess between three crosses pattée in chief Gules and a mullet in base Azure as many bezants

CREST
A cross Or

MOTTO
Crux Christie nostra corona (The cross of Christ is our crown)

The French 'mercier', or 'merchant', is generally reckoned to be the most likely origin of this name. The name Le Mercer is fairly common in medieval records throughout England, Scotland and Ireland. The name is, of course, still used to describe the trade of a silk dealer. William Le Mercer witnessed two charters in favour of Kelso Abbey, around 1200. Aleumnus, or Alcunus, Mercer had a grant of lands at Tillicoultry in Stirlingshire from Walter Fitzalan. These lands were resigned to the king in 1261. The principal family were the Mercers of Aldie, who held land around the ancient Abbey of Scone and had the lands of Aldie confirmed to them by a charter of 1362. John Mercer was a counsellor to the king between 1364 and 1367, and was ambassador to England and France. Sir Andrew Mercer received further lands from Robert II in 1378 and 1381. Sir Lawrence Mercer sat as a minor baron in the Parliament of 1481. There were numerous cadet houses, including the Mercers of Inchbrakie, of Newton and Forgandenny, and of Kimrain. The principal family were latterly styled 'of Huntingtower'. William Mercer of Huntingtower, sometime major in the Sixteenth Lancers, entered politics in Australia and promoted the erection of Victoria as a state separate from New South Wales. There are two rhymes relating to this family and their extensive holdings around Perth. One has it 'sae sycker 'tis as onie thing on earth, the Mercers aye are aulder than auld Perth'. The other relates to the endowment of St John's Church in Perth, with the two inshes, or islands, beside the river in return

for the perpetual right of burial in the church-yard. This was a generous gift but led to the inevitable witticism, 'Folk say the Mercers tried the Town to cheat when for just two inches they did win six feet'. Brigadier General Hugh Mercer, who fought under George Washington in the American War of Independence, was said to have been a surgeon at the Battle of Culloden. He fought at the Battles of Trenton and Princeton in America in the winter of 1776–77, and died of wounds sustained during that campaign. The Mercers are still prominent in Perthshire.

MIDDLETON

ARMS (LR 1/168)[1]
Parted per fess Or and Gules, a lion rampant within a double tressure flory counterflory all counterchanged, armed and langued Azure

CREST
Issuing out of a tower Sable, a lion rampant Gules, armed and langued Azure

MOTTO
Fortis in arduis (Brave in difficulty)

SUPPORTERS
Two eagles volant Sable armed and beaked Or

There are various lands named Middleton in Scotland, but it is believed that the family took its name from lands so called near Laurencekirk in Kincardineshire. The lands were confirmed by a charter of William the Lion. Humfrey de Middleton of Kincardyn rendered homage to Edward I of England in the Ragman Roll of 1296, and in the same year Robert de Middleton was taken prisoner at Dunbar Castle. The family came to prominence in the seventeenth century. John, son of Middleton of Coldham, was a professional soldier who joined Hepburn's Regiment in the service of the king of France. He returned to Scotland in 1642 to enter the service of the opponents of Charles I, first as a cavalry commander and later as a general. He was with Leslie's cavalry which surprised Montrose at Philiphaugh in 1645 and pursued him northwards. When the marquess received direct

orders from Charles to disband his forces in 1646, it was General Middleton who negotiated the terms which allowed the king's captain general to take ship for the Continent. However, Middleton was deeply unhappy at the decision to surrender the king to the Parliamentarian army, and subsequently he joined the forces under the Duke of Hamilton which attempted a rescue of the king in 1648. He was taken prisoner after the Battle of Preston but later escaped, rejoining the royalist forces, only to be wounded and captured again at the Battle of Worcester in 1651. He was to be tried for treason, but again escaped, this time to France. In 1654 he again returned to Scotland to join forces with the Earl of Glencairn, but was defeated by General Monck and once more went into exile on the Continent. At the Restoration a grateful Charles II created him Earl of Middleton and Lord Clermont and Fettercairn. He was appointed Lord High Commissioner by the Scots Parliament, and in 1667 was made Governor of Tangier in Morocco, where he died. His only son, Charles, second and last Earl of Middleton, was ambassador to the imperial court at Vienna, and Secretary of State for Scotland. He did not approve of the actions of James VII, but he refused to recognise the Revolution of 1688 and the subsequent accession of Queen Mary and

William of Orange. He was imprisoned in England but, following his father's example, he contrived to escape and fled to France. His sons were captured attempting an invasion of Scotland with the assistance of French troops and were sent to the Tower of London. They were later released, but the title was forfeited and never restored. Sir Thomas Middleton of Rosefarm in Cromarty was a distinguished twentieth-century agriculturalist and deputy director general of the Department of Food Production during the First World War. He was made a Fellow of the Royal Society in 1936.

MONCUR

ARMS (of that Ilk)[8]
Argent, a rose Gules and on a chief of the Last three escutcheons of the First

This name appears in very early charters, and it is suggested that it may derive from the French word 'coeur', meaning 'heart'. Michael de Muncur, a soldier, witnessed a charter by Isabella Bruce, between 1237 and 1248. Andrew de Monctour appears on the Ragman Roll rendering homage for his lands to Edward I of England in 1296. Marriota de Moncur is listed by Black as being Lady de Rossy in 1302. Andrew Moncur of that Ilk gave a bond of manrent to the Earl of Errol in 1541. The Moncurs of that Ilk flourished around Perthshire, and their Castle of Moncur was in the parish of Inchture in the Carse of Gowrie. The Moncurs of Dundee had a high reputation as armourers in the sixteenth century. There are many references to armour made by them and they appear to have been armour makers to the royal court.

MONTEITH

ARMS (of Kerse LR 1/367)[1]
Quarterly, 1st & 4th, Or, a bend chequy Sable and Argent; 2nd & 3rd, Azure, three buckles Or

This name is quite commonly spelt 'Monteath', and was most prominent in Perthshire. The lands of Monteith were held by the family perhaps as early as the twelfth century. Malcolm de Maneteath appears as a witness to a charter of 1237. Kilinus de Mineteth was vicar of Kaledrach in the diocese of Dunblane in 1322. The name is found elsewhere in Scotland: William Mynteith and Patrick Mynteith were both burgesses of Glasgow at the beginning of the seventeenth century. The principal families were those of Kerse and of Duchally. Sir Ruthven Monteath of Duchally was chairman of the Bombay Chamber of Commerce in 1910 and a member of the viceroy's council in India.

MONYPENNY

ARMS (of Pitmilly LR 70/36)[1]
Gules, three cross crosslets fitchée issuing out of as many crescents Argent

CREST
A figure representing Neptune, namely a naked man, bearded Proper, crowned with an antique crown Vert, bestriding a dolphin naiant Or, finned Gules, in waves of the sea Argent and Azure, holding in his sinister hand, bridling the dolphin Gules, and in his dexter hand a trident Azure

MOTTO
Imperat aequor (He rules the sea)

Despite the attractive simplicity of the explanation, this name has nothing whatsoever to do with coinage. Nisbet states that the ancient arms bore a dolphin and from this he conjectured that the Monypennys may originally have been knights from the Dauphinate region of Auvergne in France. The name Magnepenine appears in Normandy towards the end of the twelfth century, and Manipeni and Manipenyn are later found in English documents. The family acquired lands of Putmullin, later called Pitmilly, from the prior of St Andrews at the beginning of the thirteenth century. John Monipenny appears on the Ragman Roll, rendering homage for his lands to Edward I of England in 1296. He may also be the same John Monipenny who was one of the ambassadors to Edward III of England in 1336. The possible connection of the Monypennys with France was re-established in the fifteenth century, when William Monypenny acquired land in France and appears to have resided there for the latter part of his life. In 1447 he was granted a safe conduct to negotiate the marriage of Princess Eleanor of Scotland to the son of the king of France. He had clearly risen to prominence in his adopted country, where he was honoured with the title of 'Baron and Lord of

Conquersault'. He was sent, along with John Kennedy, Provost of St Andrews, on a long mission to Rome via Denmark and Castile. He presumably performed his tasks satisfactorily as he was created Lord Monypenny by James II sometime prior to 1464. The title became extinct when his son, Alexander, died without male issue. Isabel Monypenny, a daughter of the Baron of Pitmilly, was the mother of Cardinal Beaton, the last cardinal and primate of Scotland before the Reformation. David Monypenny of Pitmilly was a distinguished lawyer at the turn of the nineteenth century. He became Solicitor General in 1811 and was thereafter elevated to the Bench with the title of 'Lord Pitmilly'. The Monypennys of Pitmilly, who no longer bear the dolphin on their shield, are still prominent in Fife.

MOUAT

ARMS (LR 2/66)[1]
Argent, a lion rampant Sable crowned with an antique crown Or

CREST
The battlement of a castle Or, issuant therefrom a demi warrior armed and accoutred Proper, holding in his dexter hand a sword Proper hilted and pommelled Or and in his sinister a flag staff thereon hoisted a banner Vert fringed and charged with an antique crown Or

MOTTO
Monte alto (On a high mountain)

On Compartment
Commit thy work to God

SUPPORTERS
Two naked savages wreathed about the head and middle with oak leaves all Proper each holding in his exterior hand a trident Or

This Norman name of 'monthault', rendered in Latin as 'monte alto', is usually translated as 'of the high mountain'. The Monte Altos are known to have settled in Wales and they first appeared in Scotland during the reign of David I. The family swiftly rose to positions of influence and power, acquiring lands in Angus. Robert and Michaele de Muheut witnessed a charter by the Comyn Earl of Buchan, around 1210.

William de Monte Alto witnessed the marking of the boundaries of the lands of the Abbey of Arbroath around 1219. Michael de Monte Alto was sheriff of Inverness in 1234 and witnessed numerous charters of other noble families in the vicinity. Bernard de Monte Alto, a soldier, was among the knights and nobles who accompanied Princess Margaret to Norway for her marriage to that country's King. On their return he, along with many others, was drowned in a shipwreck. William de Muheut features in the Ragman Roll, rendering homage to Edward I of England in 1296, but William de Monte Alto was later one of the signatories to the Declaration of Independence at Arbroath in 1320. He was killed at the siege of Norham Castle in 1327. The name became widespread and is found throughout Scotland from Ayrshire to Orkney. The Lairds of Balquhally in Aberdeenshire were to become the principal family. Axel Mowat, an admiral in the Norwegian fleet in the mid seventeenth century, was reputed to be one of the richest men in Norway, and claimed descent from the Mowats of Balquhally.

MOUBRAY

ARMS (LR 1/565)[1]
*Gules, a lion rampant Argent, crowned with a
ducal coronet Or*

The ancient barony of Mombray in Calvados, France, is the probable origin of this name. Robert de Moubray witnessed a gift to the Abbey of Kelso in the reign of Malcolm IV in the mid twelfth century. Philip de Moubray was a counsellor to the king around 1208 and may have been the son of Robert. Roger de Mubray was sheriff of Edinburgh, Linlithgow and Haddington around 1225. The family appears to have adhered to the cause of Balliol, and much of their lands were forfeited after the victories of Robert the Bruce. However, their fortunes recovered, and they acquired the lands of Barnbugele in Fife. They also acquired the lands of Inverkeithing and the barony of Dalmeny, strategically placed on either side of the principal crossing of the River Forth near Edinburgh. Sir John Mowbray of Barnbugele gave part of his lands to his nephew, William Mowbray of Loch Cairny, by charter in 1511. Nisbet suggests that the Mowbrays enjoyed the favour of several monarchs and that their arms – of a lion rampant wearing a crown – are a mark of this favour. The last Mowbray Laird of Barnbougle was Sir Robert, who died around 1675 without issue. The baronies of Barnbougle, Dalmeny and Inverkeithing, together with the castle of Barnbougle, passed into the hands of the Primroses and still form part of the Earl of Rosebery's estate today.

MOW

ARMS (of Eastmains LR 1/368)[1]
*Azure, a boar's head erased Argent armed Gules between
three mullets of the Second*

CREST
A phoenix rising out of the flames Proper

MOTTO
Post funera faenus (An interest after death)

This name was originally derived from the lands of Molle, latterly Mow, in Roxburghshire. Liuluf de Molle appears to have held land in Roxburghshire at the beginning of the twelfth century and his son, Uctred, held the town of Molle and the patronage of the church there prior to 1152. He later granted the church, with its land and pastures, to Kelso Abbey. Radulf de Molle witnessed the settlement of a dispute regarding money due to the church of Roberton in 1279. The name appears in the spelling 'Mow', when Robert Mow resigned his lands to the king in 1490 for a regrant to John, his brother. Pitcairn, in his *Criminal Trials of Scotland,* records the Mows of that Ilk featuring in several sixteenth-century trials. In 1575 the Laird of Mow was slain at the Battle of Redesweire. The name appears again in the north of Scotland when John Mow is listed as master of singing and a burgess of the town of Elgin. In 1789 John Mow of Mains and his brother, William Mow, Writer to the Signet, applied to the Court to alter the spelling of their surname from Mow, to Molle, the ancient form of their name.

MUIR

This name appears to have two derivations, one Highland and one Lowland. The Gaelic, 'mor,' is translated as 'large' or 'big', and the surname may in some instances simply refer to such physical attributes. Alternatively, Muir is also derived from the Middle English for a 'low grassy hill or heath'. In 1291 Thomas Delamore was executor of the will of Devorgilla, the mother of John Balliol, King of Scots. The chief family of the name

ARMS (LR 1/189)[1]
*Quarterly, 1st & 4th, Argent, on a fess Azure three stars
of the First (Muir); 2nd & 3rd, Azure, three garbs Or
(Cumming)*

CREST
A savage head couped Proper

MOTTO
*Durum patientia frango (I overcome difficulty by
patience)*

SUPPORTERS
Two blackamoors Proper

were the Mures of Rowallan in Ayrshire. At the beginning of the reign of Alexander III, Sir Walter Comyn seized the house and lands of Rowallan from the Mures. However, the lands were restored after Gilchrist Mure distinguished himself at the Battle of Largs in 1263, when he was also knighted for his bravery. Better relations were established with the Comyns by the marriage of Gilchrist to one of the Comyn daughters, through whom he inherited additional estates. His eldest son, Archibald, was killed at the siege of Berwick when the town was sacked by the English and Balliol's army routed. The name appears several times on the Ragman Roll of Scottish nobles submitting to Edward I of England in 1296. Sir William Mure, son and successor to Archibald, was knighted by David II, and sent one of his sons as hostage to England for the ransom of the king. His granddaughter, Elizabeth Mure, married the future Robert II in 1346. The validity of the marriage was later challenged, and a papal dispensation was sought to ensure the legitimacy of their

children, including the future Robert III. The Mures followed James IV to the fateful field of Flodden in 1513, and many of them died along with their king. Mungo Mure supported his relative, the Regent Arran, during the minority of Mary, Queen of Scots, and fought for him at Glasgow in 1543. He carried out significant improvements to the fine Castle at Rowallan, but was killed at the Battle of Pinkie in 1547. The family embraced the new reformed religion and became opponents of Mary, Queen of Scots, but by the end of the seventeenth century they were persecuted as Covenanters. William Mure of Rowallan allowed conventicles to be held in his house, for which he was imprisoned, first at Stirling Castle and then in Edinburgh. The direct line ended soon thereafter, when the estates passed to the Earls of Loudoun. Another prominent branch of the family, the Mures of Abercorn, prospered under the early Stewarts. A member of this branch, Sir Robert Mure, was one of the jury who tried Lord Ruthven for the murder of Queen Mary's secretary, David Rizzio. Sir Robert was a favourite of James VI. Alexander Muir Mackenzie, born in 1764, was a descendent of the line of Muir of Cassencarie and was created a baronet in 1805. John Muir, born at Dunbar in 1838, emigrated to America in 1849. He was a naturalist and first advocate of forest conservation in the United States, being responsible for the establishment of the internationally renowned Yosemite National Park.

NAIRN

The important northern burgh of Nairn lies in the rich lands of Morayshire. One of the earliest records of the name is Adam de Narryn, chaplain of the altar of the Blessed Virgin at Inverness. Alexander Nairn of Sandford was Comptroller of the Royal Household to James II, and commissioner for peace negotiations with England in 1547. Robert Nairne, who held Scotland's highest judicial office as Lord President of the Court of Session, was the father of Robert Nairne of

Strathford, an ardent royalist and supporter of Charles I. He was captured after the Battle of Worcester in 1651 and imprisoned in the Tower of London, where he remained until the Restoration. He was knighted and later in 1681 created a peer, taking the title, 'Lord Nairne'. He had no male heirs and the title was entailed to his son-in-law, Lord William Murray. The second Lord Nairne was a naval officer who supported the Jacobite rising of 1715. He was captured at Preston and sent to

ARMS (LR 10/56 and 29/17)[1]
Quarterly, 1st grand quarter, parted per pale Sable and Argent, on a chaplet four quatrefoils counterchanged (Nairn); 2nd grand quarter, counterquartered, (I) & (IV), Or, on a fess Gules, between three crosses pattée of the Second in chief, and a mullet Azure in base, three bezants (Mercer) (II) & (III), Argent, a chevron Sable, between three boars heads erased Gules (Elphinstone), 3rd grand quarter, counterquartered, (I) & (IV), paly of six, Or and Sable; (II), Or, a fess chequy Azure and Argent; (III), Azure, three mullets Argent, within a double tressure flory counterflory Or, (Atholl); 4th grand quarter, Argent, three martlets Sable, on a comble Azure, a cross Or, a franc-quartier (distinction of a military Count of the French Empire) of the Third, charged with a sword palewise of the Field, hilted and pommelled of the Fourth (Flahault)

CREST
A celestial globe on a stand Proper

MOTTO
Plus ultra (More beyond this)

SUPPORTERS
Dexter, a pegasus Ermine, bridled, crined, winged and unguled, Or, charged on the shoulder with a fleur de lis Azure; sinister, a ratch hound Proper

the Tower of London. He freely admitted his treason and was condemned to death. He was later reprieved, but his title was forfeited. The family remained adherents to the Stuart cause, and the second Lord's son, Robert, followed Bonnie Prince Charlie, the 'Young Pretender', and was killed at Culloden. His brother, John, who commanded two hundred Nairnes at the same battle, escaped with his life to France. The peerage was restored to his grandson, William Nairne, born in 1757, and who became inspector general of the army for Perthshire. He married Carolina Oliphant, the celebrated Jacobite poet credited with authorship of the famous songs, *Charlie is my Darling* and *Will ye no' come back again?* On the death of William's eldest son, the title was claimed by Margaret, Baroness Keith, the granddaughter of Robert Nairne who fell at Culloden. She had married the French ambassador to the Court of St James, the Comte de Flahault, who had been a famous general in the army of Napoleon. In 1704 Sir William Nairne of Dunsinnan (a designation made legendary by its mention in Shakespeare's *Macbeth*, as Dunsinane) was created a baronet. Sir William Nairne, the fifth Baronet was a distinguished lawyer who was appointed to the Bench in 1786 with the title, 'Lord Dunsinnan'. Michael Nairne of Kirkcaldy founded the great Scottish linoleum industry and was to become a great benefactor to his native town. His eldest son, Michael, was created a baronet in 1904. Floor coverings are still marketed throughout the world under the name, 'Nairnfloor'. Charles Nairne, who was born in Perth in 1808, emigrated to America where he became Professor of Philosophy at Columbia University in New York. Ainslie Nairn of Ballincrieff, a descendent of the chiefly house, is one of Scotland's leading lawyers, with particular interest in peerage and heraldic matters.

NEVOY

ARMS (LR 1/194)[1]
Sable, a chevalier on horseback armed at all points cap-a-pie brandishing a scimitar aloft Argent within a bordure Gules

CREST
A pegasus Proper

MOTTO
Marte et arte (By strength and by art)

This name takes its origin from the lands of Nevay in Angus. Adam de Neveth witnessed the marking of the boundary of the lands of the Abbey of Arbroath in 1219. Alexander de Nave, taken prisoner in the wars with England, was given safe conduct to return to Scotland in 1422. John Nevay of that Ilk served as juror on an inquest in Angus in 1558. Black lists James Nevay as taking passage to Sweden in 1579 to become Governor of Westmanland and Dalarne, where he was subsequently murdered. The Reverend John Nevoy was a fervent Covenanter and preacher during the Wars of the Covenant against Charles I. Sir David Nevoy of Nevoy was elevated to the Supreme Court Bench and it is his arms which are now recorded for the family of Nevoy in the Lyon register.

NEWLANDS

ARMS (of Lauriston LR 67/92)[1]
*Per saltire Gules and Or, in chief a cross pattée fitchée at
the bottom Argent, and in each flank a cross pattée fitchée
at the bottom of the First*

CREST
A game cock hooded as a falcon Proper spurred Or

MOTTO
Honour the spur

This is a territorial name from the 'new
lands' erected into a barony in the sheriffdom of Kincardine. There is also a parish in
Peeblesshire of the same name. Black lists
Jasper Newlands of that Ilk, around 1469.
Duncan Newlandis was baillie of Linlithgow in
1493. Janetta Newlands was heir to lands in
the barony of Monkland in 1675. The family
has returned to Kincardine this century and
William Newlands of Lauriston, the distinguished travel writer, has restored Lauriston
Castle, near Montrose. There is now a family
association seeking to link Newlands throughout the world with their Scots ancestry.

NEWTON

ARMS (of that Ilk LR 1/194)[1]
*Vert, a lion rampant Or, on a chief of the Second three
roses Gules*

CREST
A demi-lion Or, brandishing a scimitar Proper

MOTTO
Pro patria (For my country)

This is a name derived from lands in
Midlothian. James and Huwe de Neutone
appear on the Ragman Roll doing homage to
Edward I of England for their lands around
Edinburgh in 1296. Alexander de Newtoun of
Newtoun appears on an inquiry into the
boundaries of lands of Gladmor in 1430. The
name arises in other parts of the country and
may well relate to other places of a similar
name. The name rose to prominence when
Adam Newton was appointed tutor to Prince
Henry, eldest son of James VI, around 1600.
He was installed as Dean of Durham Cathedral
in 1606. He was secretary to the prince until
his death in 1612, whereupon he was
appointed treasurer to the new heir to the
throne, the future Charles I. He was created a
Baronet of Nova Scotia in 1625. He was a formidable Latin scholar and translated several
works at the request of the king. In 1628 he
was appointed as secretary for Wales, which
post he held until his death in January 1629.
He had married a daughter of Sir Thomas
Pukering, Keeper of the Great Seal in the reign
of Queen Elizabeth of England, and the family
ultimately assumed this name in England.

NORVEL

ARMS (of that Ilk)[8]
Sable, on a bend Argent three martlets of the First

A shortened form of 'Normanville', which
supports their claim to be of Norman
descent. Robert Norvyle witnessed a charter of
Sir David de Wemyss in 1373. Johannes
Norwald, Lord of Cardonald, near Paisley,
witnessed a notarial deed in 1413. William
Norwell represented Stirling in Parliament
from 1568 to 1586. Nisbet lists Norvel of that
Ilk claiming descent from Sir Walran de
Normanville, and the arms that this family
bear have the simplicity which heralds associate with early nobility. The name is still
common in central Scotland.

OCHTERLONY

ARMS (of that Ilk and Kelly)[3]
Azure, a lion rampant within a bordure Argent charged with ten buckles Gules

There are numerous variant spellings of this name, including 'Auchterlony'. They all appear to derive from the lands of Auchterlonie near Forfar. John of Othirlony is mentioned in a deed of 1226. Wauter de Oghterloveny of Fife appears in the Ragman Roll, rendering homage to Edward I of England for his lands in 1296. Nisbet asserts that he was the ancestor of Auchterlony of that Ilk. They acquired the lands of Kelly, and William Auchterlony de Kellie was sheriff of Forfar in 1514. There were also Auchterlonys at Kintrocket and Pitforthy in Ayrshire. Descended from the Lairds of Kintrocket was one Major General Ochterlony, who fought in the service of the Russian Tsar during the Crimean War and fell at the Battle of Inkerman in 1854. His family had left Scotland and settled in Russia in 1794. Major General Sir David Auchterlony entered the military service of the East India Company and distinguished himself in campaigns in Nepal. He was created a Knight Grand Cross of the Order of the Bath and became a baronet in 1816. The family still hold land in Forfarshire to this day.

OLIPHANT

ARMS (LR 1/95 [1] and [6])
Gules, three crescents Argent

CREST
An unicorn's head couped Argent armed and maned Or

MOTTO
A tout pouvoir (Provide for all)

SUPPORTERS
Two elephants Proper

The Oliphants were a Norman family who first held lands in England around Northampton. It is said that David de Olifard rescued David, Earl of Huntingdon, later David I of Scotland, at the siege of Winchester Castle in 1141. He travelled north when the earl went to claim his kingdom, and was granted lands in Roxburghshire and made justiciar of Lothian. One of his sons was sent as hostage for William the Lion. The name appears on the 1296 Ragman Roll of Scottish nobles submitting to Edward I of England. In common with most of those forced to swear fealty to the English king, the Oliphants quickly took up the cause of Scottish independence, and defended Stirling Castle. Oliphant was captured at the fall of the great royal fortress and was sent to the Tower of London.

He was subsequently released, and appears as one of the nobles appending their seals to the famous Declaration of Arbroath, asserting to the pope the historic independence of Scotland. The family received the lands of Gask in Perthshire which were erected into a barony. Sir John Oliphant was knighted by Robert II and his son, Sir Laurence of Aberdalgy, was created a Lord of Parliament by James II in 1458. He was ambassador to France in 1491 and later keeper of Edinburgh Castle. His grandson was killed following James IV at the Battle of Flodden in 1513, and his great-grandson was captured at the Battle of Solway Moss in 1542. The fourth Lord Oliphant was a staunch supporter of Mary, Queen of Scots, and was a member of the inquiry which acquitted Lord Bothwell of the murder of Darnley, the queen's second husband. He attended the queen's wedding and fought for her at the Battle of Langside in 1568. His eldest son, Laurence, was implicated in the conspiracy, known as the Raid of Ruthven, to kidnap the young James VI, and was exiled in 1582. The ship in which he sailed was lost at sea. His brother, who succeeded to the title, dissipated the entire estates, but some of the family lands were saved when one of his cousins purchased from him the Gask estate. He died without male issue, but the title was bestowed by Charles I upon the nearest male cousin, Patrick Oliphant. His son, Charles, strongly opposed the Treaty of Union in 1707. The Oliphants were devoted to the Jacobite cause, and the ninth Lord fought at the Battle of Killiecrankie in 1689, and was afterwards imprisoned. He joined with his cousin, Oliphant of Gask, in the rising of 1715. The tenth and last Lord Oliphant played an active role in the campaign of Bonnie Prince Charlie in the Forty-five, escaping first to Sweden and then to France after the defeat at Culloden. He was allowed to return to Scotland in 1763, but never relented in his opposition to the Hanoverians. The peerage became extinct when the tenth Lord died, acknowledging the Laird of Gask as his heir. Lady Nairne, the Jacobite poet, was Carolina Oliphant, daughter of the Laird of Gask, and was named in honour of Prince Charles Edward Stuart. She is credited with writing the lyrics of *Charlie is my Darling* and the equally famous *Will ye no' come back again?* The principal seat of the family is now at Ardblair Castle near Blairgowrie in Perthshire, the home of a direct descendent of the first Lord Oliphant.

ORROCK

ARMS (of that Ilk LR 1/198)[1]
Sable, on a chevron Or between three mullets Argent as many chess-rooks of the Field

CREST
A falcon perched Proper

MOTTO
Solus Christus mea rupes (Christ alone is my rock)

A name derived from lands in the parish of Burntisland in Fife. Symon de Oroc witnessed a deed of lands in favour of Dunfermline Abbey in 1248. This Symon, or perhaps a son by the same name, gave the Abbot of Dunfermline the lands of Muyoch and Cnokduuy, parts of the lands of Oroc. Robert and Symon de Orroc appear in the Ragman Roll, submitting to Edward I of England in 1296. Anderson suggests that the name may refer to the rocky nature of that part of the coast of Fife where the family held its lands. The arms, which include three chess pieces known as rooks, are clearly canting, or punning, on the name. The lands of Oroc in Fife passed to the Bethunes, but the name arises again in Aberdeenshire; Black states this is due to the Fife family's naming new lands in Aberdeen in memory of those lost in Fife.

PAISLEY

ARMS (of Craig LR 1/397)[1]
Azure, on a chevron between three roses Argent as many thistles Vert

CREST
A dexter arm from the shoulder in armour grasping a dagger all Proper

MOTTO
Be sure

This name originates from the lands and barony of Paisley and the great abbey which bore its name. Early records of the name appear in charters witnessed by William Passelew during the reign of William the Lion between 1179–90. William de Passelet witnessed a charter by Alan, son of Walter the Steward, to the abbey around 1150. Dominus John de Passelet, Canon of Glasgow Cathedral, witnessed a gift of part of the lands of Little Govan in 1320. William Passeley, described as a 'merchant of Scotland', obtained an order in 1389 to have goods of his which were being held, released. The name appears in various spellings, and in Dumfriesshire the family of Pasleys of Craig near Langholm came to prominence when Admiral Thomas Pasley distinguished himself in 1794, taking part in the defeat of the French, on what was known as 'the Glorious First of June'. General Sir Charles Pasley was a distinguished military engineer who was with Sir John Moore at the defeat of the French at Corunna in 1809. He established the Royal School of Military Engineering at Chatham, and was created a Knight Commander of the Bath. He is best remembered for his work on pontoon bridges, contained in his thesis, *Military Instruction.* The degree of Doctor of Civil Laws was con-

ferred on him at Oxford in 1844. His son was Agent General of the state of Victoria in Australia between 1880 and 1882, and was responsible for the building of the Houses of Parliament and other public buildings in the state. The Pasley Baronets of Craig are still represented today. A tartan was designed in 1952 and a family society established in 1988, headed by Paisley of Westerlea. The society aims to link Paisleys throughout the world with their homeland in the west of Scotland.

PATERSON

ARMS (of Dunmore LR 1/202)[1]
Argent, in three nests Vert as many pelicans in their piety Or

CREST
A dexter hand issuing out of a cloud holding a branch of laurel, all Proper

MOTTO
Huc tendimus omnes (We all strive for this)

In Gaelic this name is given as 'MacPhadraig', possibly a shortened form of 'MacGille Phadraig', 'son of the devotee of St Patrick'. This indicates that the eponymous ancestor may have been either a churchman (the Celtic church permitted priests to marry) or a layman with an office in the ecclesiastical hierarchy. The Patersons settled on the shores of Loch Fyne around the end of the thirteenth century, and the name soon became widespread in the Lowlands, where it is now among the twenty most common surnames. William Patrison 'gentleman' witnessed a charter in Aberdeen in 1446. James Paterson was sheriff-depute of Inverness in 1563, later becoming Provost of the city. Around this time, William Paterson was born near Dumfries. He was later to found the Bank of

England, although he is perhaps better remembered as the architect of the ill-fated Darien Scheme. This scheme was planned to establish a Scottish colony at the isthmus of Darien in Central America. Many Scots invested heavily in the project and signed on as colonists. The scheme was wrecked by the intrigues of powerful merchant interests in England who convinced the London government to oppose it. Settlers died like flies in the fever-ridden colony, and many of the investors were ruined when it finally collapsed in 1699. The most celebrated episode in the history of this family occurred during the Jacobite rising of 1745. Sir Hugh Paterson of Bannockburn, whose baronetcy title dated from 1686, entertained Prince Charles Edward Stuart in January 1746 at his splendid mansion near the site of the famous battle. It was during his stay that the prince met Sir Hugh's niece, Clementina Walkinshaw, who became his mistress, and later bore him a daughter, Charlotte, Duchess of Albany. Bannockburn House still stands today, looking much as the 'Bonnie Prince' would have remembered it.

PENNYCOOK

The barony and town of Penicuik is in Midlothian. The name may derive from the British, 'pen-y-cok', meaning 'cuckoo's hill'. William de Pennycook was appointed to determine the extent of the lands of

Lethenhop during the reign of Alexander II. Sir David de Penicoke is mentioned in charters of the mid thirteenth century. Two Pennycooks appear on the Ragman Roll, doing homage for their lands to Edward I of England

ARMS (of that Ilk)[2]
*Argent, a bend Azure between three hunting horns Sable
stringed Gules*

CREST
A man winding a horn

MOTTO
Free for a blast

in 1296. Alexander de Penycuyk 'magistr artium' (Master of Arts) was curate of the church of Kilconquhar in Fife around 1463. The name appears frequently among the records of the burgesses and baillies of Edinburgh in the fifteenth and sixteenth centuries. The barony passed into the hands of

the family of Clerk at the beginning of the seventeenth century, and Sir John Clark of Penicuik still resides at Penicuik House to this day. Alexander Pennecuik was an eminent doctor and poet born at Newhall near Edinburgh in 1652. He was the author of *A Description of Tweeddale,* renowned for its wealth of antiquarian and botanical information. Another Alexander Pennycook was a poet and author in Edinburgh in the early eighteenth century. He is the author of *An Account of the Blue Blanket or Craftsman's Banner,* describing the flag used by the craftsmen's guilds in Edinburgh on their rallies in defence of trade rights.

PENTLAND

ARMS (of that Ilk LR 2/77)[1]
*Argent, a fess Azure between three lions' heads erased in
chief and as many crescents in base Gules*

CREST
*A lion's head erased Gules gorged with a collar Argent
charged with three crescents of the First*

MOTTO
Virtute et opera (By virtue and deeds)

The Pentland Hills surround Edinburgh, but the parish of Pentland, which lay between Straiton and Roslin, no longer exists. Adam of Pentland was a monk of the Abbey of Holyrood around 1298. Ralph de Penteland was sent to Montrose with orders to detain a vessel in 1304. The name is found in various documents pertaining to persons living around Edinburgh in the fourteenth and fifteenth cen-

turies. The lands, however, were so close to those of the mighty Norman barons the Sinclair Earls of Caithness and Orkney, that they soon fell under their influence. The Sinclairs sold the barony of Pentland in 1633 to the Gibsones who were to hold the lands into the twentieth century. The Pentlands of that Ilk passed through an heiress to the Campbells, and the arms as recorded in the Lyon register now are quartered. All that remains of Pentland is the churchyard which contains an old family vault of the Gibsones and also the graves of many of the Covenanters who were slain at the Battle of Rullion Green in 1666. They are commemorated on the Martyrs' Monument in Greyfriars Churchyard in Edinburgh.

PETER

ARMS (of Lee LR 77/6)[1]
*Gules, on a bend Or, between four keys in saltire two and
two, between two men's hearts Gules, a hurt charged with
a saltire Argent*

CREST
*Issuant from an antique crown Or, a gothic castle triple
towered Argent, masoned Sable, windows and port Gules,
charged with a man's heart of the Last*

MOTTO
Numquam despera (Never despair)

This name, meaning 'rock' in Greek, was particularly common in Angus and Kincardine. John Peter, a vassal of the Earl of Mar, was charged with aiding outlawed Macgregors in 1636. David Peter was commissary depute, a Court official responsible for the registering of wills, in Peebles in 1645. Alexander Peter was a notary public in Melrose in 1648. A tartan has now been registered for the name, and Edward Leslie Peter, Baron of Lee, resides at Lee Castle near Lanark, which was extensively remodelled in the nineteenth century with magnificent interiors by Pugin (most famous for his work on the Houses of Parliament at Westminster).

PITBLADO

ARMS (of that Ilk)[2]
Vert, a boar's head erased Argent

The lands of Pitblado lie in the parish of Cupar in Fife. Peter Pitblado of that Ilk was a juror on an inquest into lands of Hough and Pitconnochie in Fife in 1505. Alexander Pitblado of that Ilk is also mentioned in a charter of 1563. The arms of a silver boar's head on a green field are clearly ancient, but although they are noted by Nisbet, they have never been recorded in the Lyon register.

PITCAIRN

ARMS (LR 1/395)[1]
Argent, three lozenges Gules

CREST
A moon in her complement Proper

MOTTO
Plena refulget (The full moon shines)

The lands of Pitcairn lie in the parish of Leslie in Fife, and the family are reputed to be one of the oldest of that ancient kingdom. William de Petkaran was a juror at Dunfermline prior to 1249. Sir Hugh de Abernethy granted to his kinsman, John de Pitcairn, the lands of Innernethie. Piers de Pectarne of Fife appears on the Ragman Roll, swearing fealty to Edward I of England in 1296. Andrew Pitcairn and seven of his sons were killed at Flodden in 1513. Nisbet states that Robert Pitcairn, Commendator of Dunfermline Abbey and Secretary during the regency of Moray, Lennox, Mar and Morton, was 'a great timeserver, a great enemy to Queen Mary and a very humble servant of the Regents'. He accompanied the Regent Moray to England in 1568 to justify his proceedings against the queen, and was one of the commissioners at York. The Pitcairns were to prosper as Fife lairds but suffered heavily for their support of the Jacobite cause in the Fifteen and Forty-five rebellions. Pitcairn Island (famous as the last refuge of the *Bounty* mutineers) was discovered in 1767 by Captain Robert Pitcairn. John Pitcairn, a major in the Royal Marines, was in command of the unit which fired the first shots in the American War of Independence. *Criminal Trials of Scotland,* edited by Robert Pitcairn and published in 1833, provides a wealth of information gleaned from trials between 1487 to 1624, and is still regularly consulted by historians and geneaologists.

POLLOCK

ARMS (LR 1/395)[1]
Vert, a saltire Or between three bugles in fess and base Argent garnished Gules

CREST
A boar passant shot through with a dart Proper

MOTTO
Audacter et strenue (Boldly and readily)

The name may derive from the Gaelic, 'pol-lag', meaning 'little pool'. Peter, son of Fulbert, had a grant of Upper Pollock in Renfrewshire in the twelfth century, and took his surname from these lands. He gave the church of Pollock to the recently founded Monastery of Paisley in 1163. He also appears to have held lands in Aberdeenshire, and he bestowed the barony of Rothes on his daughter as part of her dowry. Robert de Pollock also endowed the abbey at Paisley. The name appears twice on the Ragman Roll of nobles rendering homage to Edward I of England in 1296. John Pollock of Pollock, probably the twelfth Laird, supported the cause of Mary, Queen of Scots, and fought at the Battle of Langside. On the defeat of the queen's party, his lands were forfeited. His son, John, was killed at Lockerbie in 1593, supporting his kinsman, Lord Maxwell, in a feud against the Johnstons. The Pollock name was restored when Sir Robert Pollock of Pollock was created a Baronet of Nova Scotia by Queen Anne in 1703 for services to the Crown. He represented Edinburgh in Parliament, and after the

union of 1707 he sat in the British Parliament at Westminster. James Knox Polk, the eleventh president of the United States of America, was the great-great-grandson of Robert Pollock of Ayrshire. His administration was marked by large territorial gains, including Texas and California. Many Pollocks also emigrated to Ulster, where the name is widely found in Antrim and Tyrone. The Poilocks of Newry claim to descend from John Pollock, a younger son of Robert Pollock of Pollock, who came to Ireland from Renfrew in the mid seventeenth century.

POLWARTH

ARMS (LR 1/104)[1]
Gules, three piles engrailed Argent

The lands of Polwarth lie in Berwickshire. There are records of this name in early charters: Adam de Paulwrth witnessed a deed of Patrick, first Earl of Dunbar, sometime prior to 1139; and Ada de Polwarth was witness to a charter of Walter Oliford around 1210. William of Polwarth had letters of protection to travel abroad in 1371. Black asserts that, according to French authorities, Hennes

Polvoir, a Scot living at Tours who painted the standard of Joan of Arc, was a Polwarth. Sir Patrick Polwarth of that Ilk resigned his lands into the hands of his feudal overlord, George, Earl of March, who in turn in 1377 granted them to John Sinclair of Herdmanstown. The lands passed again into the powerful border family of Home and Sir Patrick Hume, second Baronet of Polwarth, was raised to the peerage with the title, 'Lord Polwarth', on 26 December 1690. The title of 'Baron Polwarth' is now borne by the family of Hepburne-Scott.

PORTERFIELD

ARMS (of that Ilk LR 1/395)[1]
Or, a bendlet between a stag's head erased in chief and a hunting horn in base Sable garnished Gules

CREST
A branch of palm Proper

MOTTO
Sub pondere sursum (In difficulty I look upward)

This name and its diminutive, Porter, derive from the office of doorkeeper or janitor of a castle or religious house. The name is also found rendered in Scots as 'Durward'. The office was considerably more important than the modern term would suggest: lands and privileges were attached and,

in the case of royal buildings, the post was often hereditary. The office of durward to the king was for a considerable time hereditary in the family of Lundin. The Lord High Constable of Scotland had, as part of his traditional retinue, his durward guard of partisans who were all gentlemen of good family. The name is widely known through Sir Walter Scott's famous novel, *Quentin Durward*. The family of Porterfield of that Ilk took their name from inheriting the lands or porterfields pertaining to the office of the porter at the great Abbey of Paisley. They grew to have considerable influence in Renfrewshire. John Porterfield of that Ilk obtained from James III a charter of confirmation of his lands of Porterfield in 1460. The Reverend John Scott Porter, minister of the Presbyterian Church in Belfast, was a distinguished theologian, whose family appeared to have been of Scots descent.

His eldest son, who married the only sister of Alexander Horsburgh of that Ilk, was Solicitor General for Ireland between 1881 and 1883, and was created a baronet in 1902.

PRESTON

ARMS (of that Ilk LR 1/202)[1]
Argent, three unicorns' heads erased Sable

CREST
An angel Proper

MOTTO
Praesto ut praestem (I undertake what I may perform)

This name derives from lands which would probably have been part of the endowment of a church or monastery, the priests' town. The name is found both in the north of England and Lowland Scotland. One of the earliest records of this name appears in a charter in 1222: Lyulph held land in Linlithgow, which he donated to the Abbey of Newbattle. Nisbet, in his commentary on the Ragman Roll of Scottish nobles submitting to Edward I of England, identifies Nicol de Prestone, as Preston of that Ilk. Sir John de Preston followed David II in his foray into England in 1346 and was taken prisoner at the Battle of Durham. He was only released after several years' confinement in the Tower of London and payment of substantial ransom. His grandson, Sir Simon de Preston, purchased in 1374 the Castle of Craigmillar, lying three miles southeast of Edinburgh. This impressive castle, although now in ruins, still dominates the surrounding countryside and was one of Mary, Queen of Scots' favourite residences. Sir William Preston of Craigmillar was a member of the Parliament which met in Edinburgh in 1478. Sir Simon Preston of Craigmillar and of that Ilk was Lord Provost of Edinburgh in 1567 and was responsible for obtaining from James VI a charter conveying to the city, the Trinity Church and Hospital for the benefit of the poor. The Prestons of Craigmillar sold their fine castle to Sir John Gilmore around 1661. However, the family had already acquired lands in Perthshire, having been confirmed in the barony of Valleyfield by various Crown charters. George Preston, sixth of Valleyfield, was created a Baronet of Nova Scotia in 1637. His younger son, George, was in command of the garrison of Edinburgh Castle when Prince Charles Edward Stuart entered the city in 1745. Sir Charles Preston, the fifth Baronet, fought during the American War of Independence, and commanded Fort John, which he only surrendered after a long siege. He died without issue in 1800. He was succeeded by his brother, Sir Robert Preston, who purchased the ruined Abbey and Palace of Culross near Dunfermline, which he set out to restore. This magnificent building is now in the care of the National Trust for Scotland and is an outstanding example of Scottish vernacular architecture. John Preston of Fenton Barns was Lord President of the Court of Session from 1609 to 1616. His son was created a Baronet of Nova Scotia in 1628. They named their mansion house in Fife, Preston Hall.

PRINGLE

The arms of this ancient family bear three scallop shells, the scallop being the traditional badge of those on pilgrimage to the Holy Land. Nisbet conjectures from this that the name is a corruption of 'pelerin', or 'pil-grim'. The name first appears in the form 'Hopyringil' in a charter during the reign of Alexander III, around 1270. The family was long to be known as Hop Pringle, and it has been suggested that this is from the Welsh,

ARMS (Torsonse)[3]
Argent, on a bend Sable, three escallops Or

CREST
An escallop Or

MOTTO
Amicitia reddit honores (Friendship gives honour)

'Ap', which, like the Gaelic 'Mac', means 'son of'. The Hop Pringles of Teviotdale may accordingly descend from the son of a pilgrim to the Holy Land, perhaps a crusading knight. The Hop Pringles of that Ilk held substantial lands around Galashiels. The Pringles of Whitsome were supporters of Bruce, and for this suffered the forfeiture of their lands at the hands of John Balliol. They were restored after the Battle of Bannockburn by charter of Robert the Bruce in 1315. The Lairds of Whitsome were allies of the great house of Douglas, and Robert Pringle was squire to James, Earl of Douglas, at the Battle of Otterburn in 1388. Robert survived the battle and received a charter to the lands of Smailholm in Roxburghshire, from Archibald the Grim, Earl of Douglas, in 1408. They built the Tower of Smailholm, perched stubbornly on the rocky hills at Sandyknowe, six miles west of Kelso. The tower still stands today, a lonely but impressive tribute to this family. The tower was well known to Sir Walter Scott, the novelist, whose grandfather owned the farm at Sandyknowe. The son of the Laird of Smailholm, David Pringle, was, together with his four sons, killed at Flodden in 1513. Sir James Pringle of Smailholm was sheriff principal of Ettrick Forrest in 1622. He is said to have sold off a considerable portion of his estates to pay debts incurred by living extravagantly at the court of James VI. Robert Pringle died without issue in 1653, when the representation of the family devolved upon the Pringles of Whytbank. Alexander Pringle of Whytbank was MP for Selkirkshire and a member of Sir Robert Peel's government from 1841 to 1845. Alexander Pringle, thirteenth Laird of Whytbank, served in India throughout the Second World War. The Pringles of Stitchill were raised to the rank of baronet in 1682. Another prominent family descended from the Pringles of Smailholm are the Lairds of Torwoodlee. This family suffered much during the persecution of the Covenanters when their house near Selkirk frequently offered sanctuary to those forced into hiding for their adherence to the Covenant. Other cadets include the Pringles of Haining, Newhall and Lochton. Thomas Pringle, the border poet and writer, was born in Teviotdale in 1789. He became secretary to the Society for the Abolition of Slavery in 1827, and died only a few months after the announcement of the abolition of slavery in 1834. The famous Scottish knitwear, which bears this family's name, has carried its fame throughout the world.

PURVES

ARMS (of Purves LR 1/204)[1]
Azure, on a fess between three mascles Argent as many cinquefoils of the Field

CREST
The sun issuing out of a cloud Proper

MOTTO
Clarior ex tenebris (Brighter from darkness)

SUPPORTERS
Two lynxes Proper

A parvis is an enclosed area in front of a cathedral or church, and the term is often applied to the portico, or porch. Medieval lawyers and academics often gathered in such areas to meet clients and students. The first of this name may, therefore, have some such association. The name may also derive from the Latin 'venire', meaning 'to come'. The lands of Purveshaugh were named after a family who settled in Berwickshire in the eleventh century. William Purveys of Mosspennoch made a grant of lands to Melrose Abbey between 1214 and 1249. William Porveys appears on the Ragman Roll, rendering homage for his lands in Peeblesshire to

Edward I of England in 1296. Alan Purvays de Ercildon witnessed the confirmation of a charter by Patrick, Earl of March, in 1318. Nisbet lists Sir William Purves of that Ilk as head of an eminent family in Berwickshire. Chambers' *Popular Rhymes* prints a parody of the famous couplet praising the Haigs of Bemerside, but showing rather less respect for the Purveses: 'befa' what e'er befa', there'll aye be a gowk in Purves-ha'. Sir William Purves published a work on the revenue of the Scottish Crown in 1681. This book was reprinted in 1897 and is a useful source for both the historian and the genealogist.

RAIT

ARMS (of Hallgreen LR 1/206)[1]
Or, a cross engrailed Sable

CREST
An anchor Proper

MOTTO
Spero meliora (I hope for better things)

This name is said by both Nisbet and Anderson to be of Germanic origin and it is supposed that it was rendered in that language as 'Rhet'. Lands were apparently granted to one of this name near Nairn, and from there the family spread south to Perthshire and Fife. Sir Gervase de Rathe was constable of Invernairn around 1292 and he is presumed to be the same de Rate who appears on the Ragman Roll four years later, rendering homage for his lands to Edward I of England.

Nisbet describes him as Sir Gervais Rait of that Ilk. Sir Alexander Rait is said to have killed the Thane of Calder and fled to live under the protection of the powerful Keith family, the Earls Marischal. The fugitive's son, Mark, married the heiress of the estates of Hallgreen, and this was to be the territorial style thereafter of the principal families. David Rait of Hallgreen and Drumnagar, received a charter of confirmation to his estates from James III. John Rait was Bishop of Aberdeen and died in 1355. Descended from the Raits of Hallgreen were the Raits of Pitforthie and of Anniston. James Rait of Anniston commanded a regiment of lancers in the British Legion in Spain, 1835–37, and was decorated for bravery. In 1838 he married Lady Clementina, a daughter of the Earl of Airlie.

RALSTON

ARMS (of that Ilk LR 1/402)[1]
Argent, on a bend Azure three acorns in the seed Or

CREST
A falcon looking to the sinister Proper

MOTTO
Fide et marte (With fidelity and bravery)

There are two likely explanations of this name, both of which are derived from personal names relating to wolf-like qualities. The northern origin is probably a diminutive of 'hroth'wolfr', meaning 'wolf of fame'. The southern derivation stems from the personal name Ralph, which is itself a diminutive of Randolph, from the old English 'raedwlf', or 'cunning wolf'. Nicolas de Ralston witnessed a charter to the monks of Paisley in 1272. Hew de Ralston appears in the Ragman Roll of 1296, rendering homage to Edward I of England. Jacobus de Raulyston 'dominus eusdern' (of that Ilk) witnessed the election of an abbot of Paisley in 1346. John de Ralston, Bishop of Dunkeld, was appointed Lord High Treasurer of Scotland in 1449. He was ambassador to England in that year and again in 1452. John Ralston of that Ilk sat as arbiter in a dispute between Paisley Abbey and the burgh of Renfrew. Hew de Ralston of Ralston was killed at the Battle of Pinkie in 1547. The estate of Ralston passed in the early eighteenth century to the Earls of Dundonald. The Ralstons of Warwickhill were cadets of the Lairds of Ralston, and continued to flourish around Paisley.

RENTON

ARMS (of that Ilk)[2]
Azure, a chevron Or between three towers Argent

This name appears to be a shortened form of the old English personal name Raegenweald. Renton is thus the 'tun', or small village, of Raegen. The Rentons first appear holding lands around Coldingham in Berwickshire in the reign of William the Lion. They were hereditary foresters of Coldingham, and Ricardus de Renington, 'forestarius', appears in charters of that time. They rose to particular prominence in Berwickshire in the fourteenth and fifteenth centuries. Robert de Rentun witnessed a charter by the Abbot of Kelso around 1225. Symon of Rennyngton rendered homage for his lands to Edward I of England in 1296. The early line is said to have ended in an heiress who married Ellem of Ellemsford, but a branch of the family had acquired the lands of Billy and thereafter the estates of Lamberton. Agnes, daughter of Renton of Billy, married Alexander ('Sandy') Leslie, the great seventeenth century soldier and first Earl of Leven. Sir Thomas Renton was a descendent of the Lairds of Billy, and rose to be personal physician to George I. The king was so pleased by the skill and attention of Dr Renton that he not only created him a knight but ordered a patent to be prepared, with the intention of elevating him to the peerage as Baron Renton. Sir Thomas considered that he had already received too great an honour and modestly declined to accept the title. He frequently accompanied the king on his visits to Hanover. Renton in Dunbartonshire was named after Cecilia Renton, who married into the Smolletts of Bonhill who developed the town in 1782.

RIDDELL

ARMS (LR 1/535)[1]
*Argent, a chevron Gules between three ears of rye,
slipped and bladed Proper*

CREST
A demi greyhound Proper

MOTTO
I hope to share

SUPPORTERS
Two greyhounds Argent collared Gules

One theory for the origin of this name suggests that a family from Gascony may have come to Scotland via Ryedale in Yorkshire. It is much more likely, however, that the name is of Norman origin. Gervase Ridale was a witness to a charter of David I in 1116, and his son, Walter, received a charter of the lands of Lilliesleaf in Roxburghshire. One of his nephews was hostage for William the Lion who had been taken prisoner by the English at the Battle of Alnwick in 1174. Riddells also acquired Swinburn in Northumberland. The lands were subsequently erected into a barony of Riddell. Sir William Riddell of Riddell swore fealty to Edward I of England for his lands in the Ragman Roll of 1296. Sir John Riddell was created a Baronet of Nova Scotia on 14 May 1628, and his lands were erected into the barony and regality of New Riddell. Sir John's third son, William, was knighted by Charles I and later served in the wars in the Netherlands. The Reverend Archibald Riddell, the third son of the second Baronet, was a minister of the reformed church in Edinburgh who was persecuted and imprisoned because he would not renounce his Covenanter beliefs; unlike many others, however, he escaped with his life. Sir John Buchanan Riddell, MP for Selkirk, married in 1805 the eldest daughter of the Earl of Romney. His successors in the title still live in the Borders, although in that part now claimed by England. John Riddel, a prominent seventeenth-century Edinburgh merchant, claimed descent from Galfridus de Ridel. He amassed great wealth from the trade across the Baltic, particularly with Poland, and he became a free burgess of Scotland's capital. His son acquired extensive lands near Linlithgow. He is said to have intrigued with the forces of Oliver Cromwell, becoming a close friend of General Monck. He is credited with having persuaded the general to restore the ancient parish church of South Leith, which Cromwell had ordered to be used as a stable for his troopers. One of Edinburgh's finest churches, it still bears some of the scars of the Parliamentarian troops' occupation. Two generations later, this family acquired the extensive Argyll estate of Ardnamurchan and Sunart. Sir James Riddell, first Baronet of Ardnamurchan, received his title in September 1778. He was superintendent general to the Society of British Fishery and a Fellow of the Society of Arts and Sciences. Sir Rodney Riddell, the fourth and last Baronet, was a distinguished professional soldier who campaigned in New Zealand and during the Afghan War of 1878 to 1880. He died in 1907 and the title became extinct. In 1920, Sir George Riddell of Duns, a prominent newspaper proprietor who had represented the British press at the Versailles peace conference of 1919 was raised to the peerage as Baron Riddell.

ROBERTON

This name is plainly derived from the personal name Robert. The name can be either of Norman or French origin, or from the old English 'hroo-berht', meaning 'bright fame'. Black asserts, following Nisbet, that the manor or lands of Roberton were in the hands of the family who were to assume the name as early as 1200. Robertus de Roberton witnessed a charter by Hugo of Biggar, in favour of the church of Lesmahagow in 1228. The other witnesses to this charter were Reginald of Crawford and Archibald Douglas. This indicates the importance of the deed and the high standing of all those who were party to it. Robert Roberton of that Ilk witnessed a charter around 1250. Stephen de Roberton of Roberton seems to have adhered to the cause of Edward Balliol in the struggle for the crown of Scotland. In 1296 he appears on the Ragman Roll, acknowledging Edward I as his direct and lawful superior. His barony of Roberton was forfeited when Robert the Bruce triumphed and was confirmed as king. The family, however, was not extinguished, as Stephen's son, Symon, obtained by marriage to a daughter of Sir David Hamilton of Cadzow, the lands and estate of Earnock. Lands were later confirmed to the family by a charter under the great seal of Robert II in 1380. The family prospered by a series of splendid marriages into notable families around Lanark. John Roberton of Earnock married firstly, a daughter of Cleland of that Ilk, and then Margaret, daughter of Lord Cathcart. Daughters of the Laird of Earnock married into the great dynasties of Hamilton and Dundas. James Roberton of Earnock served under the Duke of Hamilton in the service of King Gustavus Adolphus of Sweden in 1631. John Roberton was secretary to George I.

ROSSIE

This name is territorial in origin. The Rossies of that Ilk held lands in Fife probably from as early as the late eleventh century. They may have been related to the great Norman family of De Ros, or they may equally have claimed descent from the Celtic Earls of Ross. Robertus de Rossyn was a witness to the perambulation of the boundary between the

ARMS (of that Ilk)[3]
Per bend Gules and Argent, a lion salient counterchanged

lands of the Abbey of Arbroath and the barony of Kynblathmund in 1219. Thomas de Rossi received a charter to the lands of Rossi from Hugo de Malherbe around 1245. Walter de Rossy, burgess of Montrose, appears on the Ragman Roll, rendering homage to Edward I of England in 1296. Nisbet relates that Sir Alexander Rossie of that Ilk had his lands forfeited during the reign of Malcolm III and his estates given to the Earl of Fife. Bernard Rossie received a charter of the barony of Rossie and the lands of Inene in Forfar from Robert III around 1400. David Rossy of Rossy sat as a juror on an inquest on the lands of Ochterlony in 1457.

RUSSEL

ARMS (of that Ilk)[8]
Argent, a chevron Gules between three tadpoles Sable

This name appears to be derived from 'rous', meaning 'red'. This was commonly found among the Normans or French in the personal name Rufus. Walter Russel witnessed a charter in favour of the Abbey of Paisley between 1164 and 1177. John, son of Robert Russel of Duncanlaw, is mentioned in a charter of around 1180. Robert Russel witnessed a deed relating to the lands of Threipland in 1259, and Robert Russel appears on the Ragman Roll, doing homage to Edward I of England in 1296. Anderson relates that the name of Russel came to Aberdeenshire in one Rozel, an English baron who fought at the siege of Berwick and in the Battle of Halidon Hill in 1333. He subsequently settled in Scotland, obtaining the estate of Aden; his family was to be styled 'Russel of that Ilk'. In 1680 Patrick Russel, married to a sister of Archbishop Sharp, purchased the lands of Moncoffer in Banffshire. The Russels of Ashiesteel in Selkirkshire were a prominent local family, particularly distinguished in military service. Colonel William Russel of Ashiesteel was adjutant general of the army of Madras, and served under General Lord Clive throughout all his campaigns between 1756 and 1767. His son, Major General Sir James Russel, also served in India and commanded a brigade of cavalry at the Battle of Mahedpoor in 1830. Alexander Russel was an eminent doctor and naturalist in the mid eighteenth century, and published a *Natural History of Aleppo* in 1756. In England the descendants of Rufus rose to become the powerful Dukes of Bedford. Lord John Russell, third son of the sixth Duke, was sent by his father to Edinburgh University, where he greatly admired the independent and democratic philosophy of the Scots. He entered politics and was the architect of the first Reform Act of 1832, extending the right to vote. He was created Earl Russell in 1861. His grandson was Bertrand Russell, the third Earl and one of the greatest philosophers of the twentieth century.

RUTHERFORD

ARMS (of that Ilk and of Edgerstoun LR 1/207)[1]
Argent, an orle Gules, in chief three martlets Sable beaked of the Second

CREST
A marlet Sable beaked Gules

MOTTO
Nec sorte nec fato (Neither by chance nor fate)

The lands of Rutherford are near Maxton in Roxburghshire, and there are two explanations given of the name's origin. The first states that a man named Ruther guided an ancient king of Scots over a little-known ford in the River Tweed, giving him a victory against the Northumbrians. He was rewarded with a grant of land thereafter, named after the crossing which had brought him such good fortune. The other tradition tells of an English army which foolishly abandoned a strong position on heights above the Tweed to attack a Scottish force on the opposite bank. The English attempted to force a crossing of the river and were soundly defeated. The victorious Scots are said to have named the place Rue the Ford, to commemorate the disaster which befell the English at that spot. Whether or not this was the explanation, the English certainly came to rue the name, as the Rutherfords were fierce in their defence of their lands and eager to raid the rich pickings of Northumberland. Robert de Rutherford witnessed a charter by David I around 1140. Sir Nichol de Rutherford is mentioned in several charters between 1161 and 1272. Sir Richard Rutherford was a favourite of Robert III and witnessed a charter in 1390 in favour of William, steward of the lands of Minto. He was ambassador to England in 1398 and he and his sons were wardens of the marches. One of Sir Richard's younger sons obtained the lands of Chatto and Hunthill. The main line failed, and the lands of Rutherford passed into the hands of the Traquairs. The name, however, continued to be feared in the Borders, and Thomas Rutherford, the Black Laird of Edgerston, was famed for his daring attacks upon the English. His most notable exploit was at the Battle of the Red Swire at Carterfell in July 1575. This came about when the English and Scots wardens of the marches had met to hear mutual grievances and to give redress for complaints. The Scots demanded the surrender of a notorious English brigand named Farnstein. The English warden, Sir John Forster, claimed that Farnstein had fled and could not be found. Sir John Carmichael,

the Scots warden, doubted this and said so to Sir John in plain terms. The English warden retorted with insults regarding Carmichael's family, whereupon the English bowman discharged a flight of arrows among the Scots. The Scots, being taken by surprise, were at first driven back and Sir John Carmichael taken prisoner. However, the Rutherfords and the men of Jedburgh soon appeared and put the English to flight, freeing Carmichael and instead taking prisoner the English warden and a number of his lieutenants. The Lairds of Edgerston further distinguished themselves fighting for Charles I during the civil war. Rutherford raised a troop of horse at his own expense and fought in England until the king surrendered in 1646. However, he took up the royal cause once more, only to be severely wounded and have his whole troop wiped out at the Battle of Dunbar in 1650. Lieutenant General Andrew Rutherford of the Rutherfords of Chatto and Hunthill was raised to the peerage as Lord Rutherford in 1661. He was appointed Governor of Tangier in Morocco in 1663 and was killed in a battle against native forces in 1664. He had been advanced to the earldom of Teviot, but as he died without issue, this title became extinct, the title of 'Lord Rutherford' passing to a cousin. This title is also now extinct. Andrew Rutherford was MP for Leith from 1839 to 1851. He held the office of Lord Advocate and was ultimately elevated to the Bench with the judicial title of 'Lord Rutherford'. Ernest Rutherford discovered the alpha particle and developed the nuclear theory of atomic structure, laying the groundwork for the development of nuclear physics in the twentieth century. He was knighted in 1914 and appointed to the Order of Merit in 1925, and died in 1937.

SCHAW

The Lowland name of Schaw has a quite separate origin from the great northern clan within the Clan Chattan confederation. Schaw was said to be a second son of Duncan,

Earl of Fife, who held the privileged office of cup bearer to the king. Nisbet suggests that they may have acted in this capacity for Alexander II or Alexander III, but there is no

ARMS (of Sauchie)[3]
Azure, three covered cups Or

CREST
A demi savage Proper

MOTTO
I mean well

SUPPORTERS
Two savages wreathed about the head and middle with laurel Proper

certainty of this. The arms of this family allude to their royal office and in this they are similar to the English house of Butler. William Schaw witnessed a charter to the Monastery of Paisley in 1291. The family acquired the lands of Hayley, Wardlaw and Drumchaber in Ayr from James, Great Steward of Scotland, sometime prior to 1309. John Schaw, Lord of Hayley, entered into an agreement with Alan Cathcart which was confirmed by charter under the great seal around 1407. John Schaw of Hayley was part of the Embassy which successfully negotiated the terms of the marriage of James III to Margaret, daughter of the king of Denmark. Andrew Schaw, a younger son of Hayley, received the lands of Sornbeg and Polkemmet in 1477. In 1615 John Schaw received a charter from James VI erecting all his lands into the barony of Sornbeg. The principal family were held to be the Schaws of

Sauchie, near Stirling. John Schaw of Sauchie was Comptroller of the Royal Household to James III. The most unusual story connected with this name is that of Christian Schaw, the eleven-year-old daughter of John Schaw of Bargarran in Renfrewshire, who featured in one of the last witchcraft trials ever held in Scotland. The girl was said to have been tormented by witches at the end of 1696 and the beginning of 1697. In due course, three men and four women were charged with the crime of witchcraft, were condemned to death and were executed at Paisley. Christian clearly survived her supernatural experience and was to become responsible for the establishment of the world-wide trade in thread, based around the town of Paisley. She married in due course and became Lady Blantyre. She was noted for her dexterity in spinning yarn and conceived the idea of manufacturing it into thread. She was encouraged by her younger sisters and neighbours in this enterprise, and a parcel of her thread was sold in Bath, where it was widely acclaimed. She established a modest manufacturing base among the young women of the neighbourhood and the thread was named after her house at Bargarran. Bargarran thread became famous and the industry is still important today.

SETON

It is thought that the village of Sai near Exmes in Normandy had given its name to Seton in Scotland by 1150, when Alexander de Seton witnessed a charter of David I. Sir Christopher Seton, who died in 1306, secured the family's fortunes when he married a sister of Robert the Bruce. He was a witness at Bruce's coronation at Scone in March 1306, and is said to have saved the king's life when he was unhorsed at the Battle of Methven in June of that year. Seton was captured at the same battle and taken to London where he was executed with great brutality. In 1320 Sir Alexander Seton, who was probably his brother, signed the famous missive to the pope, later to be called the Declaration of

Arbroath, asserting the independence of Scotland. He was governor of Berwick from 1327 to 1333 when the town surrendered to the English. The surrender was made all the more bitter by the fact that the English had hanged Seton's son whom they held as hostage. Further tragedy followed when his remaining sons were killed – one fighting Edward Balliol and the other drowning in a sea battle with an English fleet. His daughter, Margaret, succeeded to the estates, and it was her descendents who were created Lords Seton. William, Lord Seton, attended the coronation of Robert II. One of his sons married Elizabeth of Gordon and so was ancestor to the Marquesses of Huntly. George, the third

Lord, was a favourite of James IV and died with his king at Flodden in 1513. The Setons supported Mary, Queen of Scots, and in 1557 the fifth Lord attended the queen's wedding to the Dauphin of Viennois. Seton later became her Privy Councillor, Master of the Household and close personal friend. On the terrible night of the murder of the queen's secretary, David Rizzio, he helped the queen escape, first to his castle at Seton in East Lothian, and thence to Dunbar. After the assassination of the queen's husband, Darnley, it was again to Seton that the queen turned and it was in his castle that the marriage contract with Lord Bothwell was sealed. When his queen was imprisoned in Lochleven Castle in 1568 Seton, with two hundred lances, aided in her escape. He retired to Flanders after the queen's defeat at the Battle of Langside, and tried to enlist foreign aid. He returned to Scotland two years later. In 1581 he was one of the judges at the trial of the Earl of Morton, accused of complicity in the murder of Darnley. His portrait, which now hangs in the Scottish National Portrait Gallery, is one of the most spectacular paintings of his or any other period. His second son, Robert, who succeeded to his father's title, was created Earl of Winton by James VI in 1600. The earl's brother, Alexander Seton, was appointed Lord President of the Court of Session, Scotland's highest judicial office, and then Chancellor of Scotland. He was himself created Earl of Dunfermline in 1606. Staunch Jacobites, the fourth Earl of Dunfermline forfeited his title for his support of Viscount Dundee in 1689, as did the fifth Earl of Winton after the 1715 rising. Other branches of the family include the Setons of Abercorn, who were created Baronets of Nova Scotia in 1663. Sir Alexander Seton of Pitmedden, who took the title, 'Lord Pitmedden' on his appointment to the Supreme Court Bench in 1677, was also created a Baronet of Nova Scotia in 1684. Port Seton, Seton Collegiate Church and Seton House itself all still lie on the coast south of Edinburgh, fitting memorials to this great family.

SKIRVING

A name found generally in East Lothian. Black lists it as one of the commonest surnames in Haddington in the eighteenth century. Black John Skirving was said to have been the Earl Marischal's standard bearer at the disastrous Battle of Flodden in 1513. Alexander Skirving was a burgess of the city of Edinburgh, whose son, Patrick, made up title to his estate in 1667. Lord Braxfield, the notorious eighteenth-century 'hanging judge', sentenced William Skirving, secretary of the radical group, Friends of the People, to fourteen years' transportation in 1793.

SOMERVILLE

This name is derived from Somerville, a town near Caen in Normandy. Sir Gaulter de Somerville accompanied the Duke of Normandy, William the Conqueror, to England in 1066. One of his descendents, Philip of Whichnow, in Staffordshire, instituted the gift of a side of bacon called the 'Dunmow flitch', which is still given today to husbands and wives who have lived together a year and a day without strife or disagreement. William de Somerville, Gaulter's second son, came to Scotland with David I and received lands near Carnwath in Clydesdale. William died around 1142 and was buried at Melrose Abbey. William de Somerville, who, according to tradition, killed the last serpent in Scotland, obtained the lands of Linton around 1174 from Malcolm IV. He later became chief falconer to the king and sheriff of Roxburgh. Sir William de Somerville, fifth of that name, fought for Alexander II, driving back the Norse invasion at Largs in 1263. His son, Sir Thomas appears on the Ragman Roll of nobles forced to swear fealty to Edward I of England in 1296, but the following year he joined Sir William Wallace in the fight for Scottish freedom. Sir Walter Somerville commanded a brigade of cavalry under Wallace at the Battle of Biggar, and was later a steady supporter of Robert the Bruce. His great-grandson, Sir Thomas, was created Lord Somerville around 1430. He was justiciar of Scotland south of the Forth. John, the third Lord, was wounded fighting against the English at the Battle of Sark in 1448 and was present at the siege of Roxburgh in 1460, when James II was killed by an exploding canon. John, fourth Lord Somerville, died without issue and was succeeded by his brother, Hugh, who was taken prisoner after the rout at Solway Moss in 1542. He was ransomed for 1,000 merks and the promise of his support for the proposed marriage of Mary, Queen of Scots to Edward, Prince of Wales, son of Henry VIII of England. He was later arrested for treason but was pardoned. He supported Mary of Guise, the Queen Mother, as Regent of Scotland. Like many nobles who had been secretly intriguing with England, he was an early adherent to the reformed doctrines. However, his son – later the sixth Lord Somerville – opposed the Reformation and voted against the Confession of Faith proposed in the Parliament of 1560. He supported also Mary, Queen of Scots, and fought at the Battle of Langside where he was severely wounded. Hugh Somerville, the seventh Lord, was also a supporter of the queen, but in the shifting politics of the time he later supported her son, James VI, becoming a Privy Councillor. James was entertained by the Somervilles in such splendour that they burdened themselves with debt and had to sell their estates at Carnwath. When the Scots nobility was ranked in 1606 after the union of the Crowns, the name of Somerville did not appear. James Somerville, titular tenth Lord Somerville, served on the Continent, where he gained a considerable reputation as a soldier commanding his own regiment. His grandson, James Somerville of Drum, died from wounds received in a duel with Thomas Learmonth in 1682. In 1723 the Somerville peerage was acknowledged by the House of Lords and John, now thirteenth Lord Somerville, stood for election as a representative peer of

Scotland. He built the elegant House of Drum which still stands on the outskirts of Edinburgh. Mary Somerville who died in 1872 was a noted mathematician and scientific writer as well as a great pioneer of womens' education, and Somerville College in Oxford, founded in 1879, is named after her.

SPALDING

This name takes its origin from the town of Spalding in Lincolnshire. The name is recorded in Scotland as early as 1294, when John de Spaldyn, 'Magister' (Master) witnessed a grant of lands in Aberdeen. Another Spalding is mentioned as a canon of Elgin Cathedral around 1300. He is probably John de Spauyding, who petitioned Edward I of England in 1304 for timber to build his church at Duffus. The Spaldings came to prominence in 1318 at the siege of Berwick by Robert the Bruce. The story goes that Peter de Spalding, a burgess of Berwick, hated the English governor, and aided the besiegers in taking the town. He was rewarded by Bruce in May 1319 with the lands of Ballourthye and Pitmachie in Angus. He was also granted the keepership of the royal forest of Kylgerry. In 1587 the Spaldings appear in an act of Parliament as a clan for whom their chief, chieftain or captain, would be held responsible. The principal family were the Spaldings of Ashintully. John Spalding was a lawyer and commissary clerk of Aberdeen in the reign of Charles I. He is the author of a famous historical work, *Memorials of the troubles in Scotland and England from 1624 to 1645*. His work was originally available only in manuscript form and was first printed in 1792, then reprinted in 1829. An antiquarian society known as The Spalding Club was founded and named in his honour.

SPOTTISWOOD

The barony of Spottiswood lies in the parish of Gordon in Berwickshire. The first person of note recorded is Robert de Spotteswode, who appears in 1296 on the Ragman Roll, submitting to Edward I of England for his land in Berwick. His seal is noted as bearing a wild boar, a device which was to later appear on the arms of Spottiswood of that Ilk. William Spottiswood of Spottiswood fell at the Battle of Flodden in 1513. He had married Elizabeth, daughter of Henry Pringle of Torsonce, and from this union came, in successive generations, two notable Scottish clergymen. The Reverend John Spottiswood of that Ilk was born in 1510. He studied divinity at the University of Glasgow and was converted to the Protestant faith. He went to England and was admitted to holy orders by Archbishop Cranmer. Returning to Scotland, he fell under the patronage of Sir James Sandilands, Lord Torphichen, a fervent Protestant. He was part of the Scottish entourage of Mary, Queen of Scots when she was married to the Dauphin, heir to the kingdom of France. He was also active during the Reformation of the Scottish Church, being one of the six ministers appointed to prepare the first Book of Discipline, as well as being instrumental in framing the Confession of Faith. He was opposed to Queen Mary's Catholicism, and when she escaped from Lochleven Castle in May 1568, he denounced her as 'that wicked woman, whose iniquity, knowen and lawfully convict, deserveth more than ten deaths'. He was appointed superintendent of the churches of Lothian, Berwick and Teviotdale, and died in 1585. His eldest son, also John, was born when his father was minister at Mid Calder near Edinburgh in 1565. Despite his father's vehement attack upon the queen, he rose high in royal favour in the reigns of her son and grandson, and was appointed Archbishop of Glasgow by James VI in 1603. He was a staunch supporter of the king's plans to establish an episcopal, rather than a presbyterian, church in Scotland. In 1629 Charles I translated him to the see of St Andrews, and in 1633 he officiated at Charles' coronation in the Abbey of Holyrood. He was appointed Lord Chancellor of Scotland with precedence before the whole nobility of the realm, an advancement which greatly increased the resentment of the nobility against the king's religious reforms. Archbishop Spottiswood was present at the famous incident in the Cathedral of St Giles in Edinburgh on 23 July 1637, when Jenny Geddes is said to have picked up her stool during the sermon and, throwing it at the celebrant's head, exclaimed, 'Thou false thief, dost thou say Mass at my lug?' The archbishop witnessed the ensuing riot from his throne. The archbishop's grandson, John Spottiswood, was a supporter of the Marquess of Montrose, fighting for Charles I against the forces of the Covenant, and was executed in 1650. Sir Robert Spottiswood, Secretary of State for Scotland, had already been executed in 1646, meeting his end at the hands of 'the maiden', a Scottish version of the beheading machine later to be called the guillotine. Alexander Spottiswood is credited with encouragement of the development of the tobacco plantations of Virginia and the development of that industry in Glasgow. Alicia Spottiswood, wife of Lord John son of the fourth Duke of Buccleuch, resumed the surname of Spottiswood in compliance with her father's will. She was succeeded by her great nephew, John Roderick Spottiswood of Spottiswood, who died in 1946.

STEWART

ARMS (LR 38/11)[1]
Or, a fess chequy Azure and Argent surmounted of a bend engrailed Gules, within a double tressure flory counterflory of the Last

CREST
A pelican Argent, winged Or, in her nest feeding her young Proper

MOTTO
Virescit vulnere virtus (Courage grows strong at a wound)

SUPPORTERS
(On a compartment embellished with seedling oak trees fructed Proper) Dexter, a savage man wreathed about the head and middle with laurel and holding in his right hand a club resting on his shoulder all Proper; sinister, a lion Gules

The Stewarts, who were to become monarchs of the Scots, descended from a family who were seneschals of Dol in Brittany. They acquired estates in England after the Norman Conquest and Walter Flaad, the Steward, moved to Scotland when David I claimed his throne. He was created Steward of Scotland and granted extensive estates in Renfrewshire and East Lothian. He was one of the commanders of the army which defeated Somerled of the Isles in 1164. James, the fifth High Steward, swore fealty to Edward I of England, but later joined Sir William Wallace and on his death, Robert the Bruce, in the struggle for Scottish independence. Walter, the High Steward, married Marjory, Robert's daughter, and when Bruce's son, David II, died childless, he was succeeded by Bruce's grandson, Robert Stewart, who reigned as Robert II. The first Stewart king had many sons. His eldest, John, succeeded to the throne as Robert III; his third son, Robert, Duke of Albany, was Regent during the reigns of his father, his brother and his nephew, James I; his fourth son Alexander, Earl of Buchan, famed as the 'Wolf of Badenoch', was responsible for the destruction of the elegant cathedral at Elgin. When James I became of age, he curbed the power of his cousins of Albany by beheading Robert's son, Murdoch, along with the latter's sons and father-in-law. The royal line of male Stewarts continued uninterrupted until the reign of Mary, Queen of Scots, and as a family they held the throne of Scotland and later that of England in the direct line until the death of Queen Anne in 1714. The present royal family still has Stewart blood, both through Sophia of Hanover, granddaughter of James VI, and the mother of the present queen, formerly Lady Elizabeth Bowes-Lyon. Apart from the royal house, three main branches of the Stewarts settled in the Highlands during the fourteenth and fifteenth centuries: the Stewarts of Appin; of Atholl; and of Balquhidder. The Appin Stewarts descend from Sir John Stewart of Bonkyl, son of Alexander the fourth High Steward. Sir John's younger son, Sir James Stewart, was killed at the Battle of Halidon Hill in 1333. His grandson married the heiress of the Lord of Lorne, and their son became the first Stewart Lord of Lorne. In 1463, the dispossessed Macdougalls murdered the next Lorne heir whose son, Dugald, became the first Stewart to hold Appin. Duncan, second of Appin, was appointed Chamberlain of the Isles by James IV and built Castle Stalker, which was sometimes used as a royal hunting lodge. Duncan Mor, eighth of Appin, took the field under Montrose in 1645 at the Battles of Inverlochy, Auldearn and Kilsyth. He was outlawed and his lands were forfeited, although they were later restored after the accession of Charles II to the throne. The Stewarts of Appin came out in 1715 for the 'Old Pretender', and fought at the Battle of Sheriffmuir. The chief was attainted for treason and fled into exile. Charles Stewart of Ardsheal led the men of Appin during the

rising of 1745, and many fell at the grim field of Culloden, having first gained glory by breaking the Redcoat ranks. Colin Campbell of Glenure, 'the Red Fox', was placed as government factor on the forfeited Stewart estates. His murder in 1752 has been immortalised by Stevenson in the novel, *Kidnapped*. After the chief suspect, Alan Breck Stewart, made his escape, James Stewart, the half-brother of the chief, was tried by a jury comprised entirely of Campbells at Inverary presided over by Argyll himself, and, perhaps not surprisingly, was convicted and hanged. The Stewarts of Atholl descend from a son of the Wolf of Badenoch. James Stewart built a strong castle at Garth and settled there towards the end of the fourteenth century. In 1437 Queen Joanna, widow of James I, married the Black Knight of Lorne who was descended from the fourth High Steward. Her son by this marriage, Sir John Stewart of Balveny, was granted the earldom of Atholl by his half-brother, James II. He supported his brother by commanding the royal forces who suppressed the rebellion of the Lord of the Isles. John, fifth Earl, died with no male issue. His daughter had married William Murray, second Earl of Tullibardine, who was created Earl of Atholl in his own right in 1627. Many Stewart families continued to live around the Atholl lands, many of them claiming direct descent from the numerous illegitimate progeny of the Wolf of Badenoch. They largely transferred their allegiance to the new Murray Earls of Atholl, calling themselves Athollmen. This is commemorated by the right still exercised by the present Duke of Atholl to maintain the Atholl Highlanders as the only private army in the kingdom. The new allegiance was sometimes sorely tried. In 1689 Murray called out the Athollmen for William of Orange, but his baillie defiantly held Blair Castle for James II. In 1715 Atholl again supported the government but his heir, the Marquess of Tullibardine, was a Jacobite. Stewarts flocked to the banner of Bonnie Prince Charlie in 1745. General David Stewart of Garth, an Athollman, was an officer in the 42nd Regiment (the Black Watch) whose book, *Sketches of the Highlanders and Highland Regiments,* did much to popularise his homeland in Victorian England. Stewarts came to Balquidder when William Stewart of Baldorran, grandson of the only son of the Duke of Albany who escaped the persecution of James I, was appointed baillie of the Crown lands of Balquhidder around 1490. The Crown lands were eventually divided and granted to various noble families, and William's grandson, Alexander, settled in Ardvorlich at the end of the sixteenth century. It is generally accepted that the Earls of Galloway now head the principal house of this great name.

STRACHAN

ARMS (of Thornton LR 1/427)[1]
Or, a stag at gaze Azure attired Sable

CREST
A demi stag springing Or holding a thistle in his mouth Proper

MOTTO
Non timeo sed caveo (I do not fear but am careful)

SUPPORTERS
Two greyhounds Argent each charged on the shoulder with a thistle Proper

This name is derived from the lands of Strachan, or Strathachen, in Kincardineshire. 'Strath' is derived from the Gaelic, 'srath', meaning 'broad mountain valley'. In 1200 Walderus de Stratheihen made a grant of lands to the church of St Andrews. John, son of Rudolph de Strachane, gifted lands to the Abbey of Dunfermline which was confirmed by a charter of Alexander III in 1278. The barony of Strachan and the lands of Feteresso passed to the family of Keith from the Strachans by marriage, in the reign of David II, but Sir James Strachan of Monboddo obtained the lands of Thornton in Kincardine.

He had two sons – the elder, Duncan, took the lands of Monboddo, while the younger had the lands of Thornton. Sir Alexander Strachan of Thornton was created a Baronet of Nova Scotia by Charles I in May 1625. The baronetcy passed into the senior line of Monboddo by a charter under the great seal in 1663. Admiral Sir Richard Strachan, sixth Baronet, commanded a squadron during the Napoleonic Wars. On 2 November 1805 his squadron engaged four French battleships that had escaped from Lord Nelson's triumph at the Battle of Trafalgar. Sir Richard captured all four French vessels with little loss of British life. He was created a Knight of the Bath and in 1810 he was granted the Freedom of the City of London. The title became dormant in 1854. William Strachan was born in Edinburgh in 1715. He became a printer and moved to London, where for a time he worked in the same office as Benjamin Franklin, the American statesman, scientist and philosopher. He was a friend of Dr Samuel Johnson and became a Member of Parliament.

STRAITON

ARMS (LR 1/532)[1]
Argent, three bars counter embattled Azure

CREST
A falcon rising Proper

MOTTO
Surgere tento (I strive to rise)

SUPPORTERS
Dexter, a lion rampant Or; sinister, a bloodhound Sable

The barony of Straiton lies in the county of Midlothian on the outskirts of Edinburgh.

There are also baronies of a similar name in Ayrshire and in Fife. Nisbet states that an old family of this name, designed 'of that Ilk', received their lands of Straiton from David I. Alexander Straiton of that Ilk and Andrew Straiton of Craig served in the inquest on the succession of Sir Alexander Fraser of Philorth to the estates of his grandfather. Thomas de Straton of the shire of Edinburgh appeared in the Ragman Roll in 1296. Alisaundre and James de Strachan also rendered homage.

Alexander de Straton was a signatory to the Declaration of Arbroath in 1320. Black suggests that he may be the same Alexander de Straton who is described as 'of our blood' in a charter to him by David II. John de Stratton 'dominus ejusdem' (of that Ilk) witnessed a charter of lands in 1351. Alexander Straiton of Lauriston was killed at the Battle of Harlaw in 1411. The Straitons also held lands in Aberdeenshire and near Inverness. Cristina de Stratone granted a charter in 1451 in favour of the Friars Preachers in Aberdeen.

STRANGE

ARMS (LR 1/559)[1]
Argent, a chevron between three lozenges Sable

CREST
A cluster of grapes Proper

MOTTO
Dulce quod utile (That which is useful is sweet)

This name is often found more commonly as Strang, and is probably derived from the Norman or French word 'étrange', meaning 'foreign'. When rendered as 'Strang', its etymology was believed in the past to derive from the Scots dialect word for 'strong'. Home le Estraunge was in the service of the Scottish king around 1255. Thomas de Strang held land around Aberdeen in 1340. John Strang married, sometime around 1362, Cecilia, sister of Richard Anstruther of that Ilk, and received as part of the marriage settlement some of the lands of Balcaskie. William Strang of Balcaskie is mentioned in deeds around 1466. John Strang of Balcaskie acquired the lands of Ewingston and received a charter of confirmation in 1482. John Strang of Balcaskie was slain at the Battle of Pinkie in 1547. John Strang of Balcaskie sold the estate in 1615 and became a colonel in Cochrane's Scots Regiment. Sir Robert Strange was descended from a younger son of the house of Balcaskie whose family had settled in Orkney at the time of the Reformation. He was intended for a career in the law, but instead took ship on a man-of-war heading for the Mediterranean. On his return he took up the art of engraving. When the army of Prince Charles Edward Stuart entered Edinburgh in September 1745, Sir Robert was appointed to the Prince's Life Guard, where he served until after the defeat at Culloden in 1746. He managed to escape after several months as a fugitive in the Highlands and returned to obscurity in Edinburgh. In 1751 he moved to London, where he engraved several important historical prints and began to receive critical acclaim. In 1760 he left to tour Italy and produced some outstanding engravings. He died in 1792, and is generally considered the father of the art of engraving historical prints.

SYDSERF

ARMS (LR 1/422)[1]
Argent, three fleurs de lis Azure

CREST
An eagle's head couped Gules

MOTTO
Virtute promoreo (By virtue I prevail)

The lands and barony of Sydserf lay in East Lothian but the main estate was later to be called Ruchlaw. The lands were probably named after St Serf. Nisbet suggests that the arms bear the royal fleurs de lis of France, and that the family are of noble French origin. Marior de Sydserfe appears on the Ragman Roll of 1296, swearing homage to Edward I of England for his lands near Edinburgh. William de Sideserf also appears on the roll. The name appears in the register of the Privy Council of Scotland in 1577, as 'Sydserf of that Ilk'. William Sydserf of Ruchlaw received a Crown charter to his lands in 1619. His son, Sir Alexander Sydserf, was a prominent Edinburgh baillie who signed the National Covenant, in defence of presbyterianism, in

1639. He was also a royalist in the civil war and was taken prisoner in 1651, but he was knighted after the Restoration in 1660. Martha Sydserf, the heiress to Ruchlaw, married

Francis Buchan, a scion of the chiefly house of Auchmacoy, in 1791. The family, which is still represented today, were thereafter styled 'Buchan-Sydserf'.

SYMMERS

ARMS (of Baljordie)[2]
Argent, an oak tree in bend sinister surmounted of a bend Gules, charged with three cross crosslets Or

This name is found in a variety of spellings, including Symmers, Simmers, Somers and Summers. The name appears to derive from the old French 'somier', or 'sumpter', meaning 'packhorse'. The name can also be applied to the person who provisions such animals. William Sumer witnessed a charter around

1180. David II granted William Somyr a pension for life in 1326. In 1478, George Somyr was selected to sit upon the inquest to ascertain the lands of Walter Ogilvy of Airlie. A family by this name appears to have acquired the lands of Baljordie in Angus, as early as 1450. In 1682 the Symmers of Baljordie are described in Spottiswood's *Miscellany of Scots History* as 'ane ancient familie and chief of that name'. They were prominent in local affairs until about the middle of the eighteenth century, when the male line failed.

TAILYOUR

ARMS (of Borrowfield LR 54/118)[1]
Argent, a saltire engrailed Sable between two hearts Gules one in chief and one in base and as many cinquefoils in the flanks Vert

CREST
A hand holding a passion cross Gules

MOTTO
In cruce salus (Salvation from the cross)

This name derives from the French 'tailler', meaning 'to cut', and is rendered in Latin documents as 'cissor'. Black states that this is a very common name in early Scots records. Alexander le Taillur is listed as valet to Alexander III in 1276. Bryce le Taillur was one of the Scottish prisoners at the capture of Dunbar Castle in 1296. The Ragman Roll of the same year lists six persons of this name from counties as far apart as Roxburgh and Angus, rendering homage to Edward I of

England. Walter Cissor received a grant of land from David II around 1137. Donald Cissor and Bricius Cissor were witnesses to a deed in Inverness in 1462. The name can also be found in the form Macintaylor. Several Macintaileours were fined in 1613 for sheltering members of the outlawed Clan Gregor. Gillepatrick Tailzeour was sergeant of Dornoch around 1552. James Taylor, who was born in Lanarkshire in 1753, is credited with the first practical application of steam power to vessels for inland navigation. The first paddle-wheel steam boat was launched on 14 October 1788 at Dalswinton and the experiment proved a success, the vessel achieving a speed of five miles per hour. The great paddle steamers which later carried passengers and freight on the North American rivers were derived from Taylor's original work.

TAIT

Black states that this name derives from the old Norse 'titr', meaning 'glad' or 'cheerful'. It was apparently a popular nickname among the Saxons. Thomas called Tayt is

recorded in a document of 1329. Between 1362 and 1370, payments of a pension were made to John Tayt who appears to have been a clerk with the Hospital of Montrose. Andrew

ARMS (of Pirn)[3]
Argent, a saltire engrailed and a chief Gules

Tayt was one of the perambulators of the boundaries of the barony of Yeochrie in 1492. The principal family of this name owned the lands of Pirn in Tweeddale. The family ended in an heiress who married Horsburgh of that Ilk, who thereafter quartered the Tait arms with his own. Archibald Campbell Tait, who died in 1882, rose to be Archbishop of Canterbury.

TENNANT

ARMS (of that Ilk)[7]
Argent, a boar's head couped in chief and two crescents in the flanks Sable

This name derives from the Latin 'tenere', 'to hold'. William Tenent of Crestone is recorded as early as 1296. Thomas Teneunt was one of the witnesses in the inquiry concerning the affairs of the Knights Templar in 1309. John Tenent of Lynhous was a witness to a charter of Lord St John, preceptor of the Order of St John at Torphichen, in 1558. Nisbet describes the seal of Mungo Tennent, burgess of Edinburgh, appended to a deed of 1542 as bearing a boar's head in chief and two crescents in the flanks and in base the letter 'M'. This is remarkably similar to the arms of Tennant of that Ilk described in Balfour's manuscript. Francis Tennent was Lord Provost of Edinburgh and a supporter of Mary, Queen of Scots. He was taken prisoner by the queen's enemies in 1571. James Tennent of Cairns married a daughter of Somerville of Drum. He had been a page to James VI. John Tennent of Glenconner was the factor of the Glencairn estates and a close friend of the poet Robert Burns. His descendent, Sir Charles Tennent, was created a baronet in 1885. His son was raised to the peerage as Lord Glenconner in 1911. He was Lord Lieutenant of Peebles and Lord High Commissioner to the General Assembly of the Church of Scotland from 1911 to 1914. The present Lord Glenconner still resides on the family lands at Glen, near Innerleithen, but also owns the island of Mustique, now an exclusive holiday resort. Sir Ian Tennent, a cousin of Lord Glenconner, was created a Knight of the Thistle in 1990.

TROTTER

ARMS (LR 1/220)[1]
Quarterly, 1st & 4th, Argent, a fess Gules between three mullets in chief Sable and a crescent in base Azure; 2nd & 3rd, Argent, a chevron Gules between three boars heads couped Sable

CREST
A Knight in armour Proper, holding his courser Argent caparisoned Gules

MOTTO
In promptu (In readiness)

SUPPORTERS
Dexter, a lion rampant Gules, armed and langued Azure; sinister, a horse Argent maned and hoofed Or

The name of Trotter is said to derive from the French, 'trotier', a 'runner' or 'messenger'. One legend says that this name was given to a brother of Lord Gifford for delivering a message to James III with great speed. The Borders clan bearing this name was headed by the Trotters of Prentannan in Berwickshire, who followed the Homes on their many forays across the border. One of the Trotter chiefs was killed at Flodden in 1513. A direct descendent fought under the banner of James Graham of Claverhouse, Viscount Dundee, for James VII at the Battle of Killiecrankie. The Jacobite's grandson, the Reverend Robert Trotter, was a distinguished academic who produced a work on the life of Christ and the Apostles which is still considered standard reading in many theology colleges. Dr John Trotter was a surgeon at Tynron in Dumfries who followed his family's Jacobite sympathies, treating and concealing wounded Scots soldiers retreating from England. Other distinguished families of this name include the Trotters of Charterhall, of Catchelraw and of Mortonhall. The name is also now common in Northumberland and Durham. The Trotters of Mortonhall, which lies on the outskirts of Edinburgh, claim to have held their lands as far back as the reign of Robert II. William Trotter of Catchelraw was one of the knights charged with keeping the peace on the Borders under royal warrants of 1437 and 1450. One of his grandsons was treasurer of the city of Edinburgh. They were staunch adherents of Charles I, and in 1645 were fined for assisting the Marquess of Montrose. Robert Trotter of Bush was Postmaster General for Scotland. He died in 1807. Thomas Trotter of Mortonhall was killed serving with his squadron of Dragoons at the Battle of Waterloo in 1815. Other members of the family distinguished themselves in the service of the British Raj in India. The magnificent Mortonhall House now lies in a suburb of Edinburgh.

TROUP

ARMS (of Dunbennan LR 31/31)[1]
Vert, three bucks trippant Or

CREST
A hind's head erased Proper

MOTTO
Veritas vincit (Truth conquers)

The lands of Troup are in Banffshire, although Black records that there is a charter of 1370 which refers to the lands of John of Trowpe in Ayrshire. Hamund de Troup of Lanarkshire appears on the Ragman Roll, rendering homage to Edward I of England in 1296. The seal attached to his homage bears a hawk with a crescent and a star which is quite different from the arms of Troup which are recorded in the Lyon register. The Troup arms, however, may simply be canting, using the word 'trippant' to make a pun on the name. The family seems to have been most prominent in Banffshire and around Aberdeen. Hamelin de Troupe was a prebendary of Aberdeen Cathedral in 1332 and subsequently obtained the living of Inchebrioc in 1345. William de Troup granted a charter of land in the Mearns in 1357. Normand Trupt was made a burgess of Aberdeen in 1611. Nisbet states that the family of Troup of that Ilk ended when an heiress married a younger son of the powerful Keith family. The lands of Troup were sold to Major Alexander Garden, a Scottish soldier in the service of the Swedish Crown in the seventeenth century, around 1654. They remained Lairds of Troup into the twentieth century. The Troups of Dunbennan, who came to bear the undifferenced arms of the family, traced their descent from John Troup of Huntly who lived in the middle of the eighteenth century. His direct descendent, Francis Troup of Dunbennan, was a distinguished architect and engineer who exhibited in the Royal Academy between the two world wars.

TURNBULL

ARMS (of Bedrule)[3]
Argent, three bulls' heads erased Sable (armed vert)

This name, like so many others, has a legend to explain its origins. The sixteenth-century historian, Boece, records that a Borders man by the name of Rule, saved Robert the Bruce by 'turning an angry bull which was set to gore the king'. The king promptly named him Turnbull and rewarded him with lands which were named 'bedrule' after their fortunate new owner. Sadly, like so many such stories, the more likely derivation is from the old English 'trumbald', meaning 'strong'or 'bold'. Black notes that in Teviotdale the name is commonly pronounced 'Trumell', which tends to support the English derivation. The fact that the arms of this family bear three bulls heads is of little assistance, as they are clearly canting, or punning on the name. The Turnbulls were to become one of the most turbulent of the Borders families. Prior to the Battle of Halidon Hill in 1333, Turnbull, accompanied by a huge mastiff, approached the English host and challenged anyone to single combat. He was to regret his audacity. Sir Robert Benhale accepted Turnbull's challenge and, although apparently lacking Turnbull's impressive stature, his skill was such that he dispatched the mastiff with a single blow and then dealt similarly with its master. He apparently severed Turnbull's left arm, promptly followed by his head. The Turnbulls held land throughout the Borders. William Turnbull received a charter from Robert the Bruce in 1315 to land near Philiphaugh, and John

Turnbull received the lands of Hundleshope from David II. John Turnbull, nicknamed 'outwith sword', for his fierce temper, is listed as a Scots prisoner of war in England around 1400. William Turnbull held a papal appointment in 1433 and this same name appears as one of the canons of Glasgow Cathedral in 1452. Stephen Tournebulle represented Scottish interests at the University of Orleans at the beginning of the sixteenth century. William Turnbull, Bishop of Glasgow, procured from the pope a charter to establish a university in the city in 1450. The bishop's vision was realised when the University of Glasgow was founded in 1451. William Turnbull, a noted nineteenth-century American ornithologist, was born in Midlothian in 1820. Herbert Turnbull, who died in 1961, was a distinguished mathematician responsible for major contributions to the study of algebra.

TWEEDIE

ARMS (of Drumelzier)[15]
Argent, a saltire engrailed Gules and a chief Azure

CREST[12]
A bull's head

MOTTO[12]
Thol and think

This famous Peeblesshire family claimed to descend from a water spirit living in the River Tweed. The name is certainly derived from the lands of Tweedie and the family was never lacking in spirit, whether granted to them by a water sprite or not. Chambers' *History of Peeblesshire* states that they had the reputation of being a savage race and another commentator in the eighteenth century described them as 'a powerful and domineering family'. Finlay de Twydyn appears in the Ragman Roll of 1296, submitting to Edward I of England for his lands in Lanarkshire. Roger, the son of Finlay of Twydyn, received a charter to the house and lands of Drumelzier around 1320. They were to hold these lands for more than three hundred years. In 1592,

James Tweedie of Drumelzier was accused of the murder of Geddes of Glenhegdon in Edinburgh. The complaint brought against Tweedie narrates that it was unknown 'how mony slauchters have been committit by James Tweedie of Drymelzier and his friends. The Tweedies of Oliver Castle descend from a younger son of Drumelzier and they obtained their lands from the preceptor of Torphichen in the late fourteenth century. Thomas Tweedie of Oliver Castle was implicated in the murder of Lord Fleming in 1524, and a bloody feud erupted between the families. In 1531 Thomas was exiled from Scotland for three years. Thomas Tweedie received a charter in 1611 from Robert Williamson, Superior of all the Temple lands in Scotland and heritable baillie of the Regality of Torphichen, for which he required to pay one penny annually as feuduty. Captain Michael Tweedie served in the Royal Artillery during the Peninsular War (1808–14). Major General Michael Tweedie also served in the Royal Artillery in the 1850s, throughout the Crimean War and during the

Indian Mutiny. Admiral Sir Hugh Tweedie, born in 1877, had a distinguished naval career: he was aide-de-camp to George V in 1925 and retired as an admiral in 1936, but was recalled at the outbreak of the Second World War. He was created a Knight of the Bath, in addition to holding the French Legion of Honour and the Japanese Order of the Rising Sun.

UDNY

ARMS (LR 1/552)[1]
Gules, a stag's head cabossed Or, between two grey-hounds salient affrontée Argent, collared of the Field, in chief and base three fleurs de lis of the Second

CREST
A fleur de lis Gules

MOTTO
All my hope is in God

SUPPORTERS
Two naked savages, their heads and middles wreathed with oak leaves, with gigantic batons in their exterior hands resting on their shoulders, all Proper

The lands and parish of Udnie lies in Aberdeenshire. The earliest certain record of this family appears in 1406, when Ranald de Uldeny received a charter of his lands from David II. It seems, however, that they had held these lands for a considerable period prior to the charter. Udny Castle, which still stands occupied to this day, is the most obvious evidence of the prominence of this family. The castle, lying about four miles south of Tarves, is a massive fortalice dominating the surrounding countryside. It is believed that building commenced in the first quarter of the fifteenth century and was completed and embellished over the next three generations. The costs of building nearly ruined the family, with extensions being added in the late sixteenth century and gables in the early seventeenth century. During the reign of Mary, Queen of Scots, the Laird of Udney raised his followers in support of the queen's cause; they were equally prominent in their adherence to Charles I against the forces of the Covenant. In 1634 John Udny of Udny acquired property in the Belhelvie area and went to live at Knockhall Castle. In 1693 Knockhall was attacked and captured by Covenant troops under the Earl of Errol and the Earl Marischal. The following year the castle was attacked again and was surrendered by Lady Udny but, as on the previous occasion, her husband, the Laird, escaped. Alexander, the twelfth of Udny, has become famous through his employment of James Fleming, renowned as the last professional fool, or jester, to be retained as part of a nobleman's court. Despite his title, it was the Laird of Udny's fool who saved the family from certain death in a fire which destroyed Knockhall Castle in 1734.

VANS

This is a Norman name, derived from 'vaux' or 'vaus', meaning 'valleys' or 'dales'. The family are said to have come to Scotland in the eleventh century as part of the entourage of Queen, later Saint, Margaret, wife of Malcolm III. They acquired the barony of Dirleton in East Lothian and built the magnificent castle which still dominates the village to this day. McGibbon and Ross, in their great work on the castles of Scotland, comment that the design of Dirleton Castle reflects a strong Norman and French influence. The castle was attacked during Edward I's invasion of Scotland in 1297 and fell only after a long and bitter siege. A nephew of William de Vaus of Dirleton married the heiress to the lands of Barnbarroch in Wigtownshire around 1384. The estate of Dirleton passed into other hands and the principal family of this name was thereafter styled 'of Barnbarroch'. In 1747, John Vans of Barnbarroch married Margaret, only child and heir of Robert Agnew of

ARMS (of Barnbarroch LR 47/109)[1]
Argent, on a bend Gules a mullet in dexter chief of the First

CREST
*On a chapeau Azure furred Ermine a lion rampant
Proper holding in his paws a balance Gules*

MOTTO
Be faithful

SUPPORTERS
*Two savages bearded Proper wreathed about the loins
and temples with laurel Vert and holding in their exterior
hands Proper clubs Gules, resting on their exterior shoulders*

Shauchen, and in return for her substantial inheritance he assumed the additional

surname of Agnew. John Vans Agnew served in the second Boer War and commanded the Scottish Horse Yeomanry during the First World War. The house of Barnbarroch was redesigned and extended in the nineteenth century, and is particularly associated with the architect and landscape gardener, John Loudon, who described and illustrated his improvements in his treatise, *Forming, Improving and Managing Country Houses*. The house was gutted by fire in 1941 and still stands ruined and unoccupied today.

WALKINSHAW

ARMS (of that Ilk LR 1/223)[1]
Argent, upon a mount in base a grove Proper

CREST
A martlet

MOTTO
In season

The lands of Walkinshaw are in Renfrewshire. The family descends from one Douglas, a judge in the earldom of Lennox who, in 1235, made over his lands of Knock, including the Abbey of Paisley, in return for the lands of Walkinshaw. The family were hereditary foresters to the High Stewards of Scotland in the barony of Renfrew and their coat of arms is an allusion to this office. The lands remained with the principal family until they were carried by an heiress to the Walkinshaws of Little Fulwood and thereafter to the Walkinshaws of Garturk who subsequently styled themselves 'of that Ilk'. Other cadets were the Walkinshaws of Burrowfield and of Scotston. The name has passed into Scottish legend through its associ-

ation with Prince Charles Edward Stuart. Clementina Walkinshaw was the younger daughter of a diplomat who had met the exiled James VIII, the 'Old Pretender', in Rome. The 'Bonnie' Prince Charles met the attractive and sophisticated Clementina at Bannockburn House near Stirling, the home of Sir Hugh Paterson, in January 1746. Miss Walkinshaw captivated the prince almost immediately and she became his mistress. She followed him into exile, and although they never married, she presented him with a daughter, Charlotte, on 27 October 1753. The couple later parted and were never reconciled, but Charlotte did finally gain her father's favour. In 1784 he declared her legitimate, created her Duchess of Albany, and conferred upon her the Order of the Thistle. The blood of the Walkinshaws now ran in the veins of a royal duchess, but sadly her mother, Clementina, lost everything in her flight from Paris during the French Revolution and died in poverty in Switzerland.

WARDLAW

ARMS (LR 1/222)[1]
Azure, three mascles Or

CREST
A celestial star Or

MOTTO
Familias firmat pietas (Religion strengthens families)

This name, which is found in several parts of Scotland, derives from 'ward' in the sense of a watch or guard, and 'law', a hill. The wardlaw was evidently an early lookout post. Wardlaw near Beauly was part of the lands of the Norman lord, John Bisset, perhaps as early as 1210. The Wardlaws held lands in Galloway and Fife but, for adherence to the claim of Balliol against Bruce for the crown of Scotland, they were forfeit. They later made peace with the triumphant Robert the Bruce, receiving lands in Roxburghshire and establishing their principal seat at Torry in Fife. Sir Henry Wardlaw of Torry married a niece of Walter, the High Steward of Scotland. His son, named after his mother's illustrious uncle, became Bishop of Glasgow in 1367 and was created a cardinal by Pope Urban VI in 1381. He is buried in Glasgow Cathedral. His nephew, Henry Wardlaw, was also to become a bishop, and in 1410 he founded the University of St Andrews, obtaining a papal charter for it in 1413. The Wardlaws of Torry continued to prosper, and several prominent cadet families acquired substantial estates in their own right. Sir Henry Wardlaw, chamberlain to Queen Anne, wife of James VI, acquired the lands of Pitreavie at the beginning of the seventeenth century. He was created a Baronet of Nova Scotia in 1631. He built a splendid castle in the renaissance style which is still inhabited to this day. However,

the Lairds of Pitreavie were not always known for their hospitality at the castle. When Highlanders, fleeing from Oliver Cromwell's troops after the Battle of Inverkeithing in 1651, sought refuge at Pitreavie, they were driven off, and the laird himself is said to have thrown stones at them from his roof. Sir Henry, third Baronet, married a younger daughter of Halket of Pitfirrane, who was the authoress of a fine ballad relating the Battle of Largs in 1263. The ballad was for long thought to be a genuine product of antiquity and it was published at the private expense of Sir Gilbert Elliot in 1719. The true authorship was not disclosed for a further thirty years. The estates have passed from the family but the baronetcy survives. The Wardlaws of Gogarmount were to produce a number of distinguished lawyers in the nineteenth century. David Wardlaw of Gogarmount, Writer to the Signet, was a noted peerage lawyer who died in 1908. The first Wardlaw Laird of Gogarmount founded the Scottish Widows' Fund, now one of the most prominent insurance investment companies in Europe.

WATSON

ARMS (of Saughton LR 2/178)[1]
Argent, an oak tree (growing out of a mount in base) Proper, surmounted of a fess Azure

CREST
Two hands holding the trunk of an oak tree sprouting the hands issuing out of clouds

MOTTO
Insperata floruit (It has flourished beyond expectation)

SUPPORTERS
Two gryphons Proper gorged of a ducal coronet Or

The sons of Watt, a diminutive of Walter, held land in Edinburgh in the fourteenth century. Thomas Watson of Stenhous sat on

an inquest held at Dunipace near Falkirk in 1426. Sir Donald Watsone is recorded in the records of diocese of Moray in 1493. Thomas Watson of Cupar in Fife was the ancestor of Sir John Watson who was created a baronet in 1895. The third Baronet was killed in the First World War, serving with the 16th Lancers in 1918. He was succeeded by his brother. George Watson was sheriff of Wigtownshire from 1891 to 1925. His son, James, also a lawyer, was town clerk of Nairobi from 1911–1926. George Watson's College in Edinburgh is one of the capital's leading schools.

WAUCHOPE

The lands of Wauchopedale lay in the parish of Langholm in the Borders. Ada de Waleuhop witnessed two charters to the

Abbey of Melrose during the reign of William the Lion. Alan de Walchope witnessed a charter by Thomas de Lundin between 1203 and

ARMS (of Niddrie LR 1/222)[1]
Azure, two mullets in chief and a garb in base Or

CREST
A garb Proper

MOTTO
Industria ditat (Industry enriches)

1214. Robert de Waluchop received part of the lands of Culter near Aberdeen, from Alexander II in 1247. He was one of the twelve Scottish knights appointed by Parliament to meet with an equal number of English knights to settle the border disputes. Robert de Walchop of Kulter swore fealty to Edward I of England in the Ragman Roll of 1296. The Wauchopes were related by marriage to the powerful Comyn Earls of Buchan, which may account for the gold wheatsheaf which appears on their shield (the Comyn arms are three gold wheatsheaves on a blue Field). The principal family were to become the Wauchopes of Niddrie who obtained their lands at Niddrie near Edinburgh, from the Keiths. The Keiths were hereditary Great Marischals of Scotland and the lands were thus named Niddrie Marischal. Gilbert Wauchope of Niddrie received a charter of confirmation from Robert III. The fortunes of the family were severely tried when Robert Wauchope of Niddrie and his son Archibald were forfeited in 1587 for treason and adherence to the Earl of Bothwell. The Wauchopes were, however, restored to royal favour when John Wauchope of Niddrie was knighted by Charles I in 1633. The king was also present at the christening of Sir John's second son, and placed about the infant's neck a gold and enamel chain. This heirloom was in the possession of the family until 1931, when they presented it to the city of Edinburgh, and it can still be seen in the City Museum at Huntly House in the capital's historic Royal Mile. The favoured child was to become a judge in 1672, taking the title, 'Lord Edmonstone'. The family is now represented under the compound surname of Don-Wauchop, John Wauchop succeeding to his kinsman Sir William Don, seventh Baronet of Newton, in 1862.

WEIR

ARMS (of Blackwood LR 4/94)[1]
Argent, on a fess Azure three mullets of the First

CREST
Upon a chapeau Gules furred Ermine a boar statant Azure armed Or

MOTTO
Vero nihil verius (Nothing truer than truth)

The Norman word 'vere', from which this name derives, comes from the same Norse root as the old English 'weir' meaning 'dam'. Ralph de Ver was captured along with William the Lion at Alnwick in Northumberland in 1174. He witnessed a charter of his king of lands in the bishopric of Moray sometime between 1174 and 1184. He also donated land to the Abbey of Kelso, and his brother Robert was a witness. The Weirs of Blackwood in Lanarkshire, who were to become the principal family, claim descent from Ralph de Ver, although they do not appear holding their lands until around 1400. Richard Wer appears in the Ragman Roll, rendering homage to Edward I of England in 1296. In the same year, the sheriff of Edinburgh was ordered to restore to Thomas Le Wer certain forfeited lands. George Were received remission for his part in the burning of the town of Dumbarton in 1489. Major Thomas Weir was captain of the Edinburgh Town Guard in the late seventeenth century and a notable character in the city. In 1649 he formed the escort for the doomed Marquess of Montrose when crowds flocked to the Royal Mile to see him pass in a tumbril driven by the common hangman. Twenty years later, Major Weir had retired but was still well known in Edinburgh for his fervent Protestant beliefs and great gift for prayer, and he regularly held prayer meetings which were well attended. At one such meeting in 1670, Major Weir suddenly announced that he often committed adultery, and had also indulged in incest with his sister. At first his followers refused to believe him, but not only did the major repeat his confession, his sister Jean added a version of her own. She recalled that the devil often took her brother in a fiery coach drawn by six black horses from the West Bow to Musselburgh and back. It was also alleged that the major's walking stick frequently opened doors without any assistance

from its owner. The major was in due course sentenced to death and was burnt at the stake on 11 April 1670. His sister was hanged at the Grassmarket. For long after his death, the people of Edinburgh would claim that the major could sometimes be seen riding about the West Bow on a headless horse, only to vanish in a burst of flames.

WHITEFOORD

ARMS (of Blairquhan LR 1/223)[1]
Argent, a bend cotised Sable between two garbs Gules

CREST
A garb Or standing upright and thereon a dove Proper

MOTTO
Tout est d'en haut (All is from above)

The lands of Whitefoord lay on the River Cart near Paisley. There is no explanation as to why the ford over this river should have been white, but the old English 'whita' was a common personal name. The first to bear the name is said to have been one Walter, who distinguished himself at the Battle of Largs in 1263 and obtained the lands from Alexander, High Steward of Scotland, as a reward. Walter Whitefoord witnessed a charter by Alexander III in the same year. The sheriff of Lanark was ordered in 1296 to restore the lands of John de Wheteford. John de Quhetfur, is described in a notarial instrument of 1413 as 'dominus ejusdem', which translates as 'of that Ilk'. The family arms display two red wheatsheafs, to commemorate a victory by one of the Whitefoords over the English at the time of Robert the Bruce. He is said to have led a surprise attack on the English by creating a causeway over a river, using a great quantity of wheatsheaves. Whatever the truth of this

story, the family grew in power and reputation and acquired considerable estates. They married into the powerful families of Semple, Somerville and Houston. The principal stem of the family ended in 1689. The name was continued by the Whitefoords of Blairquhan, descended from a younger son of Whitefoord of that Ilk. They obtained substantial lands in Ayr and were hereditary coroners of Carrick. James Whitefoord married a daughter of Sir Bryce Blair of that Ilk, and their son, Adam, was created a baronet in 1701. Colonel Charles Whitefoord of Blairquhan was a professional soldier who fought for the Hanoverian cause during the 1745 rebellion. His only son, Caleb, born in 1734, was unable to prove his legitimacy and the baronetcy became dormant. Caleb was an acquaintance of Dr Samuel Johnson and Oliver Goldsmith, and a friend of the great actor David Garrick. He was appointed one of the commissioners to negotiate the peace settlement with America after the War of Independence and became a close friend of the American statesman, Benjamin Franklin. Major General Philip Whitefoord, heir of line to the Baronets of Blairquhan, was a distinguished soldier who commanded the Allied land forces in Norway from 1944 to 1945.

WHITELAW

The lands and barony of Whitelaw lie in the Borders parish of Bowden. There are also lands of this name at Morebattle. John de Wytelowe of the county of Edinburgh appears

on the Ragman Roll, rendering homage to Edward I of England in 1296. John Wytelowe of that Ilk was a juror on an inquiry into the extent of lands at Gladsmuir in 1430.

ARMS (of that Ilk) [4]
Sable, a chevron Or between three boars' heads couped Argent

CREST
A bee erect Proper

MOTTO
Solertia ditat (Skill in riches)

Archibald Whitelaw was Archdeacon of St Andrews and rose to become Secretary of State to James III. Nisbet states that Archibald was a son of Whitelaw of that Ilk. The Whitelaws of that Ilk ended with an heiress, Jean, who married Walter Burnside. The Whitelaws of Gartshore now bear arms only slightly differenced from that of the principal stem. From this family descended William Whitelaw (now Viscount Whitelaw), the distinguished twentieth-century British politician.

WISHART

ARMS (of Pitarrow LR 1/444)[1]
Argent, three piles meeting in point Gules

CREST
A demi eagle with wings expanded Proper

MOTTO
Mercy is my desire

SUPPORTERS
Two horses Argent, saddled and bridled Gules

'Guischard' in old French means 'prudent' or 'wise'. The name being descriptive of a personal quality, the identity of the first person to bear it must be largely a matter of conjecture. Nisbet states that Robert, a natural son of David, Earl of Huntington, was a valiant crusader and was known by such an epithet. William Wishard witnessed a grant in favour of the Abbey of Cambuskenneth around 1200. John Wishard was a witness to the marking of the boundaries between the lands of Conon and Tulloch. William Wischard was a monk at St Andrews in 1250. Lands were granted to Adam Wishart of Logie by the Earl of Angus around 1272. The family also acquired the lands of Pitarro. James Wishart of Pitarro was a judge in the reign of James V. His son, George, born around 1513, was to become one of the first Protestant martyrs in Scotland. He was educated at the University of Aberdeen and on completing his studies, he travelled in France and Germany. He quickly absorbed the new Protestant theology and when he returned to Scotland he soon found himself at odds with the authorities. He was summoned before the Bishop of Brechin to answer a charge of heresy but he elected to withdraw to England instead. He returned to Scotland in 1543 and began to preach publicly at Montrose and Dundee. He then removed to the west of Scotland, preaching around the town of Ayr. Cardinal Beaton ordered the Archbishop of Glasgow to prevent Wishart from preaching. He was saved by the intervention of the Earl of Glencairn and other sympathetic noblemen of the area. The cardinal, however, was not to be thwarted, and he tried to have Wishart assassinated. In December 1545 he was encouraged by friends to travel to Edinburgh to preach. He preached in Leith once and was then advised to leave and withdraw to East Lothian. John Knox, the Protestant reformer, was Wishart's devoted pupil and bodyguard at this time. Wishart realised that he was likely to be captured by his enemies and he ordered Knox to leave him with the words, 'ane is sufficient for a sacrifice'. Wishart was seized and after more than a month in the dungeon of the archbishop's castle at St Andrews he was condemned to death and burnt as a heretic on 1 March 1546. The Wisharts of Logie were to produce another George who was also a distinguished clergyman. A fierce opponent of the Covenanters, George Wishart found himself frequently in the Tolbooth prison in Edinburgh. He was there in 1644 when the army of the Marquess of Montrose, the king's captain general, arrived in the city. Wishart was quickly freed and became Montrose's chaplain, accompanying him to the Continent where he joined the household of Elizabeth of Bohemia, the 'winter Queen', of King Charles I. He was installed as Bishop of Edinburgh in June 1662. His magnificent tomb lies within the ruins of Holyrood Abbey.

WOOD

ARMS (LR 1/222)[1]
Azure, an oak tree Or, growing out of a mount in base Proper, between two cross crosslets fitchée of the Second

CREST
A demi savage wreathed about the head and middle with laurel and holding erect in the dexter hand a club all Proper

MOTTO
Defend

SUPPORTERS
Two savages wreathed about the head and middle as in the crest, each holding a baton resting on his right shoulder

The name of Wood was previously given as 'de Bosco', a Norman name which has become common throughout England. The name also arises as an anglicisation of several Gaelic names which incorporate the word 'coill', also meaning 'wood'. In the mid fifteenth century Andrew Wood, a merchant trader of Leith, was employed by James III to protect the Scottish trade with Holland. In 1481 he defended Dumbarton against a fleet of Edward IV of England. James III granted him lands at Largo and bestowed a knighthood upon him. When that unhappy monarch was forced to flee from his rebellious nobles, he took refuge aboard one of Sir Andrew's ships and crossed to Fife to gather an army. During the Battle of Sauchieburn, Andrew Wood's ships sailed up and down the Forth, taking on board the wounded and afterwards searched for the missing king. After the death of James III Sir Andrew refused to acknowledge the young James IV, whom he considered to be merely a pawn in the hands of his guardians. Sir Andrew was the greatest Scottish seafarer of his time, and his open contempt of the new regime went unpunished. He was entirely restored to royal favour when in 1488, and again in 1490, he defeated English fleets sent to destroy the Scottish merchant trade. James IV used Scotland's emerging naval power in his campaign to suppress the Lords of the Isles. After the fateful Battle of Flodden it was Sir Andrew Wood who was sent to France to invite the Duke of Albany to assume the regency of Scotland. Sir Andrew's grandson was one of the barons of the Parliament of 1560 who subscribed to the Articles for upholding the new reformed religion. After the downfall of Mary, Queen of Scots, he quickly joined those upholding the claims of the infant James VI.

YOUNG

ARMS (of Auldbar LR 1/226)[1]
Argent, three piles Sable, on a chief of the Last as many annulets Or

CREST
A lion rampant issuant Gules holding a sword Proper

MOTTO
Robore prudentia praestat (Prudence excels strength)

This name is clearly personally descriptive but may have been applied to distinguish a father from a son, when both bore the same Christian name. In this instance the name in Scotland would be synonymous with Younger, used to describe the heir to a feudal title. Malmor and Ade, called Young, appear at Dumbarton in 1271. John Young of Dingwall witnessed a charter by the Earl of Ross to Reginald, son of the Lord of the Isles in 1342. Alexander Young was chaplain to the House of the Holy Trinity at Aberdeen in 1439. Peter Young was born at Dundee on 15 August 1544, the son of a merchant. He and his brother were given a very thorough education and in 1569 Peter Young, on the recommendation of the Regent Moray, became assistant preceptor to the three-year-old James VI. He was later to become Almoner to the King, an office that he held until his death. He was employed in a number of embassies and came to enjoy considerable royal favour. He was knighted at Whitehall on 19 February 1605. Sir Peter had a large family, many of whom also rose to enjoy royal patronage. One of his sons, another Peter, was part of the Embassy to King Gustavus Adolphus of Sweden in 1628. Sir Peter Young was to outlive his pupil, James VI, by three years, dying at Easter Seton in January 1628. He was succeeded by his eldest son, Sir James, who had extensive grants of land in Ireland. The name has become common in the counties of Antrim, Tyrone, Down and Londonderry. The descendents of Sir Peter married into numerous prominent families. Margaret Young married Sir John Forbes of Craigievar in 1659. Robert Young married Anna, daughter of Sir William Grahame of Claverhouse. The family sold their original estate at Easter Seton and purchased the lands of Auldbar in 1670. In 1743 the estates were sold to William Chalmers of Hazlehead who was related to the Youngs by marriage. Brigadier Peter Young DSO was a distinguished soldier and military historian. He was awarded the Military Cross on three occasions and was for a time commander of the Ninth Arab Legion, an elite unit of the kingdom of Jordan. He was reader in military history at the Royal Military Academy at Sandhurst and formed the Sealed Knot Society in 1968. The fortunes of this family are so inextricably linked with the Stewart monarchs that it is perhaps fitting that this military history society, dedicated to the study of the English civil war and the Scottish Wars of the Covenant, should have been founded by a descendent of the Youngs of Auldbar.

APPENDICES

Chronology of important dates in Scottish history 400–1886

c. 400

St Ninian brought Christianity to Scotland, establishing a church at Whithorn in Galloway amongst the indigenous people, the southern Picts.

c. 500

An Irish people, the Scoti, established settlements in Kintyre and mid-Argyll. These settlements formed the basis of the Kingdom of Dalriada.

c. 563

St Columba, an Irish missionary, arrived on Iona and established a monastery there two years later. Columba strengthened Dalriada, inaugurating Aidan as king, c. 574. Aidan sought to establish the independence of Dalriada.

794

The Norse invasions of Scotland began.

843

Kenneth Macalpin united the kingdoms of the Picts and Scots and fixed his capital at Scone.

1130

The ancient Pictish province of Moray was forfeited to the Crown. Moray had strong separatist tendencies and a rebellion led by a local noble, Angus, was crushed by David I.

1138

The Battle of the Standard. David I, seeking to exploit the civil wars in England that followed the death of Henry I and the subsequent anarchic reign of King Stephen, invaded England to claim the crown on behalf of Henry's daughter, Matilda. However, his undisciplined army was heavily defeated by the English at Northallerton.

1153

Somerled, the leader of the indigenous people of the Western Isles, challenged Norse supremacy in this region. After victories during 1156-58, the Norse recognised his position as Lord of the Isles.

1263

The Battle of Largs, at which Alexander III defeated Haakon IV of Norway. This effectively ended the Norse threat to Scotland.

1266

The Western Isles and the Isle of Man were ceded by Haakon's successor, Magnus IV, to the Scottish Crown in return for an annual gratuity.

1290–92

The First Interregnum, following the death of Margaret, 'the Maid of Norway'. Scotland's throne was disputed by a dozen contestants, and the prospect of civil war loomed. To avoid this, Edward I of England was invited to choose between the claimants. Edward agreed but only on the condition that all the Scottish nobles acknowledge his claim to be Superior and Lord Paramount of Scotland. All but two agreed to do so.

1292

John Balliol was selected to rule by Edward I of England. Following humiliating treatment at the hands of the English king, Balliol rebelled against Edward's overlordship in 1296.

1296

Edward I invaded Scotland to crush Balliol's rebellion, so precipitating a period of over thirty years of warfare during which time Scotland sought to free itself from English rule. After the fall of Berwick and defeat at the Battle of Dunbar, Balliol resigned his kingdom and left for exile in England. To underline his overlordship of Scotland, Edward removed the Stone of Destiny (on which Scottish kings were crowned) from Scone to Westminster and forced two thousand Scottish nobles, churchmen, burgesses and freeholders to swear allegiance to him, recording this submission on what became known as the Ragman Roll.

1297

Insurgents led by a minor noble, William Wallace, rebelled against Edward and defeated his armies at the Battle of Stirling Bridge. Wallace was an inspirational leader, but his relatively low social status prevented many of the major nobles coming to his aid against the English.

1298

Wallace was defeated by Edward at the Battle of Falkirk. After this battle, Wallace faded into obscurity. He was captured by the English in 1305 and executed in London.

1306

After years of personal enmity between their respective families, John, the Red Comyn, Balliol's nephew, was murdered by Robert the Bruce in Greyfriars Church at

Dumfries. Bruce was crowned king of Scotland later that year but was proclaimed an outlaw by Edward I and was excommunicated for Comyn's murder. Bruce began a guerilla campaign which lasted for several years and succeeded in pushing the English almost completely out of Scotland.

1314

The Battle of Bannockburn. Bruce won a crushing victory over superior English forces, effectively securing Scottish independence.

1320

The Declaration of Arbroath. A letter sent by the nobles of Scotland to Pope John XXII, asserting the independence of Scotland and their support of Bruce as their king.

1326

The first Scottish Parliament met.

1328

The Treaty of Northampton signed between Bruce and Edward II by which England finally recognised Scotland's independence.

1333

Battle of Halidon Hill. Edward Balliol, eldest son of John Balliol, was encouraged by the English to invade Scotland in 1332 and had been victorious in battle at Dupplin Moor. Subsequently driven out, he returned with exiled Scots nobles who had been disinherited because of their opposition to Bruce, and inflicted a heavy defeat on the Scots at Halidon Hill. As David II, Robert the Bruce's son, was still a child, he was sent to France for safety, and the independence of Scotland was placed once more in jeopardy.

1346

The Battle of Neville's Cross. Five years after his return from France, David II invaded England but was defeated at Neville's Cross and was captured, remaining in captivity in the Tower of London for eleven years.

1371

Accession of Robert II, son of Walter, the High Steward of Scotland and Marjorie Bruce, daughter of Robert. Robert II was the first king of the Stewart dynasty.

1427

During the Parliament held at Inverness, James I ordered the imprisonment of fifty Highland chiefs in an effort to secure more centralised control. The chiefs believed that they held lands of their own right, not of the king, and many of them had caused trouble for the Crown – for example, with support for Edward Balliol.

1488

The Battle of Sauchieburn. James III was defeated by an army of disgruntled nobles, led by his son, the future James IV. The king was killed at the battle.

1493

The Lordship of the Isles was broken up by James IV.

1513

The Battle of Flodden. James IV invaded England but was killed, with many of the Scots nobility, in a disastrously executed battle.

1542

Battle of Solway Moss. James V's army was defeated by the English in this rout, at which many Scots nobles surrendered. James died a short time after the battle, leaving his infant daughter, Mary, as queen.

1547

The Battle of Pinkie. Scottish forces were defeated by the English. Henry VIII wished Queen Mary to be married to his son, the future Edward VI, and tried to bring about the match by force. Mary, however, was betrothed to the Dauphin of France, where she was sent the following year and whom she married in 1558.

1560

The Confession of Faith was passed by Parliament. Reformed ideas had been present in Scotland from at least the 1520s, and had been gaining ground since then. By the 1550s many Scots lords were supporters, and they resented the influence in Scotland of the Catholic French under the Queen Mother, Mary of Guise. In 1560 many barons met in Parliament to abolish papal supremacy and the Mass.

1561

Queen Mary's husband had died in 1560, and she was asked by the Scots to return to Scotland the following year. Following her return, Mary continued to use the French spelling of her surname, Stuart, and it became common practice for the royal house of Stewart to be so styled thereafter. She was allowed to continue to practise her Catholic religion and, for the first few years of her reign, negotiated well her way through the complicated religious and political landscape in Scotland.

1565–57

Mary's marriage to her cousin, Henry Stewart, Lord Darnley, precipitated the troubles which led to her deposition. Her son, the future James VI, was born the following year. She became estranged from her husband after his part in the murder of her secretary, David Rizzio, but was later reconciled with him. Darnley was murdered in 1567 and the queen married the Earl of Bothwell, chief suspect in the murder, three months later. She was forced to abdicate in favour of her son in July 1657, and was imprisoned in Lochleven Castle. Her half-brother, the Earl of Moray, became Regent.

1568

The Battle of Langside. Queen Mary escaped from Lochleven, but her forces were defeated at Langside and she fled to England. She was imprisoned for nineteen years and executed by her cousin, Queen Elizabeth of England, in 1587.

1582

The Ruthven Raid. James VI was kidnapped by a group of extreme Protestant nobles and imprisoned in Ruthven Castle. The raid led to the downfall of his kinsman, Esmé Stewart, the Duke of Lennox. The Church of Scotland approved the raid. This had the result that, after his escape the following year, James asserted his authority over the Church, and several ministers were forced to flee to England.

1596–1610

James's campaign to assert his influence over the Church ended successfully with the introduction of an episcopal system of government in 1610, despite vocal opposition.

1597

As part of his ongoing campaign to bring the clans further under central control, James required that all chiefs and lairds should produce titles to their lands, and should provide guarantees of good conduct for themselves and their followers. He entrusted the keeping of order in the Highlands to the strongest families, allowing them to keep their smaller neighbours in check.

1603

After the death of Elizabeth of England, James VI travelled south to take possession of his new kingdom. Both countries were now united under one monarch, although both remained independent, with their own systems of government.

1609

Statutes of Iona. A Crown measure intended to pacify further the Highlands.

1638

The signing of the National Covenant. Charles I had introduced changes in religious practice to the Church of England, and in the late 1630s was attempting to change the liturgy in the Scottish Church. The most obvious manifestation of this was the introduction of the new prayer book the previous year. Scottish Protestants signed the National Covenant to consolidate opposition to the changes.

1643

The signing of the Solemn League and Covenant. Scottish supporters of the National Covenant agreed to give armed help to the English Parliament in their struggles against the king in return for an overthrow of the system of episcopacy in the Church of Scotland, and a return to a presbyterian system of church government.

1644–45

Campaign of Marquis of Montrose in support of Charles I. Montrose had originally been a supporter of the Solemn League and Covenant, but was persuaded by the king to become his captain general in Scotland. He conducted a superb campaign against the Army of the Covenant, winning battles at Tippermuir, Aberdeen, Inverlochy, Auldearn, Alford and Kilsyth. His forces were finally surprised and defeated at Philiphaugh in the Borders by a force of Covenant cavalry.

1648

Charles I had surrendered himself to the Scots, who handed him over to the English Parliament in 1647 in return for £400,000, about one third of the money owed to the Scots army. The king continued to negotiate with the Covenanters, however, and agreed to a limited restoration of presbyterianism in return for armed support. The Scots consequently re-entered the war, this time on the side of the king.

1650–51

Charles II was crowned at Scone following the execution of his father the previous year. He was forced to accept the Solemn League and Covenant. At the Battle of Dunbar in 1651, a numerically superior Scottish force was routed by Parliament's New Model Army, led by Oliver Cromwell. Cromwell's subsequent campaign against the Covenanter army was concluded at Worcester in 1651, when the Scots were crushed. Scotland became part of the Commonwealth, and later the Protectorate. Charles fled to the Continent.

1660

Charles II returned from exile and the monarchy was restored.

1666

The Pentland Rising. Extremist elements among the Covenanters, in protest against the restoration of episcopal government in 1661, marched on Edinburgh from Dumfries. However, at Rullion Green in the Pentland Hills, they were crushed by Government forces under Sir Thomas Dalyell.

1678

In order to suppress the extreme Covenanters in the south-west of Scotland, the Government ordered a 5,000-strong Highland army to march to Renfrew and Ayrshire with orders to disarm the dissidents and live off the land. The plundering of the south-west by this 'Highland Host' left the inhabitants with a lasting hatred of the Highlanders.

1679

Continuing attempts by the Government to suppress Covenanting worship meetings (conventicles) by force led to violence at Drumclog in Lanarkshire when a party of royalist cavalry under John Graham of Claverhouse were routed by the worshippers. This action gathered momentum and with an army of 5,000, the Covenanters marched on Glasgow. However, their rebellion ended with the defeat of the insurgents at Bothwell Bridge.

1689

James VII, a Catholic, succeeded his brother, Charles, in 1685 and immediately undertook to remove the penalties against his co-religionists that had been in force since the early 1660s. In 1688, William of Orange, James' brother-in-law, accepted an invitation from disaffected English Anglican nobles and clergy to depose James and assume the throne. James escaped to France and this 'Glorious Revolution' established William and his wife, Mary, as joint rulers. In Scotland a Convention of the Estates in 1689 formally declared James to have forfeited his throne by vacating it and invited William to become King of Scots.
John Graham of Claverhouse, now Viscount Dundee, raised a Highland army in support of the exiled James and at the Battle of Killiecrankie defeated a larger Williamite force. Unfortunately for the Jacobite cause, he was killed during the battle. His army subsequently failed to take the cathedral town of Dunkeld from its Covenanter defenders and the rebellion effectively ceased.

1692

Massacre at Glencoe. As an example to other rebellious clans, William authorised punitive action against the Maciain MacDonalds of Glencoe, who had been slow in taking the oath of allegiance to the king. The Campbells of Glenlyon duly murdered thirty-eight MacDonalds while acting as their guests, in direct violation of the code of Highland hospitality.

1707

The Union with England. Scotland experienced severe economic and financial hardship in the early eighteenth century and was pressurised into abandoning its political independence by England in return for assistance. Amid great popular unrest, the Scottish Parliament voted for union with its English counterpart although elected to retain its own church, courts and legal system. The separate kingdoms of Scotland and England ceased to exist and were incorporated into a United Kingdom of Great Britain.

1715

The second Jacobite rising. Hoping to capitalise on disaffection among the clans with the Union and the new Hanoverian king, George I, the supporters of the exiled son of James VII, James, 'The Old Pretender', attempted to restore the Stuart dynasty by rebellion. A Jacobite army led by the inept Earl of Mar met Government forces led by the Duke of Argyll at Sheriffmuir and although the battle was inconclusive, it was a tactical defeat for the Jacobites who subsequently retreated and dispersed.

1719

A third Jacobite rising occurred when a party of 300 Spaniards landed to raise the clans who generally refused to be drawn into the scheme. At Glen Shiel, they were defeated by Government troops.

1724

Major General George Wade was appointed commander-in-chief in Scotland with the task of demilitarising the Highlands. He increased the number of garrisons in the region and linked them with an extensive chain of military roads running along the Great Glen.

1745–46

The last Jacobite rising. At Glenfinnan, 'The Young Pretender', Prince Charles Edward Stuart, raised his standard and the Highland clans, in some cases reluctantly, rose in support. The Highland army enjoyed an easy victory at Prestonpans before moving into England. It failed to capitalise on its successes and at Derby abandoned its plans to seize London. In spite of a further victory at Falkirk in 1746, the campaign reached a bloody conclusion at Culloden Moor where the Jacobite army was crushed. Charles escaped to France but his supporters were subject to cruel and bloody repression. The wearing of tartan was proscribed and the clan system was effectively destroyed in the years after Culloden as the Highland chiefs were deprived of their hereditary powers.

1782

The Act proscribing Highland dress was repealed.

1790 onwards

The Highland Clearances. During the first half of the nineteenth century, the Highland estates were reorganised to allow sheep farming at the expense of arable farming. Consequently, tenants were evicted from their holdings and removed to other, less viable parts of the estate. Great hardships often resulted and gradually, emigration to the Lowlands or to the colonies became the inescapable fate of the Highlander. However, the emotive associations of the Clearances have tended to obscure the fact that Highland depopulation in the second half of the nineteenth century was no greater than in comparable areas in the Lowlands and that those who left the land and emigrated often fared better than those who remained.

1886

The Crofters' Holding Act. By the 1880s, crofter discontent at the pattern of land holding in the Highlands became violent and also found direct political expression. To forestall this agitation, the government passed the Crofters' Holding Act which conferred on the crofters security of tenure, rights to inherit, bequeath or assign crofts, fixed rents and the right to compensation for land improvement if they were removed. The act also established the Crofters' Commission to safeguard their rights and manage disputes.

Scottish monarchs and their reigns to the Union of the Parliaments, 1707

Kenneth I (Macalpin)	843–860	William I (The Lion)	1165–1214
Donald I	860–863	Alexander II	1214–1249
Constantine I	863–877	Alexander III	1249–1286
Aodh	877–878	Margaret (Maid of Norway)	1286–1290
Eocha	878–889	[First Interregnum	1290–1292]
Donald II	889–900	John Balliol	1292–1296
Constantine II	900–943	[Second Interregnum	1296–1306]
Malcolm I	943–954	Robert I (the Bruce)	1306–1329
Indulph	954–962	David II	1329–1371
Dubh	962–967	Robert II (Stewart)	1371–1390
Culiean	967–971	Robert III	1390–1406
Kenneth II	971–995	James I	1406–1437
Constantine III	995–997	James II	1437–1460
Kenneth III	997–1005	James III	1460–1488
Malcolm II	1005–1034	James IV	1488–1513
Duncan I	1034–1040	James V	1513–1542
Macbeth	1040–1057	Mary, Queen of Scots	1542–1567
Lulech	1057–slain	James VI	1567–1625
Malcolm III (Canmore)	1057–1093	Charles I	1625–1649
Donald Bane	1093 (deposed)	[The Commonwealth & Protectorate 1651–1660]	
Duncan II	1094 (slain)	Charles II	1660–1685
Donald Bane (restored)	1094–1097	(crowned at Scone 1651, exiled and restored 1660)	
Edgar	1097–1107	James VII	1685–1688
Alexander I	1107–1124	Mary II (jointly with William II)	1689–1694
David I	1124–1153	William II	1689–1702
Malcolm IV (The Maiden)	1153–1165	Anne	1702–1714

Glossary of heraldic terms

abatement   an additional charge used as a mark of dishonour.

accolée   a form of marshalling in which two shields are placed side by side.

accoutred   equipped for the battlefield

achievement   a full coat of arms with crest, helmet, mantling, shield, motto and, where applicable, coronet of rank, supporters and insignia of orders.

additament   an addition to a coat of arms indicative of personal rank, hereditary office or mark of royal favour.

addorsed   back to back.

Aesculapius, rod of   a snake entwined about a rod or staff. This charge is named after the Greek god of healing and usually refers to the medical profession.

affronty (affrontée)   facing the observer.

allerion   an eagle displayed without a beak or legs.

annulet   (i) a ring; (ii) the cadency mark used to distinguish the arms of a fifth son.

antique crown   a crown composed of five or more sharp points mounted on a circlet. This charge is also known as an eastern crown.

appaumy (appaumée)   describes an open hand with the palm facing the observer.

arched   curved in the form of an arch.

argent   silver or white.

armed   (i) describes the horns, tusks, teeth or talons of a beast, monster or bird of prey when of a different tincture from the body; (ii) wearing armour.

armed at all points (armed cap-a-pie[d]) completely encased in armour.

armiger   any person who bears arms by lawful authority.

at gaze   describes a deer standing with its head facing the observer.

at liberty   describes a horse without bridle or saddle.

attires   the antlers of a stag.

attired   having antlers. This term can also refer to the garments of a man or woman.

augmentation   an additional charge to arms, crest, badge or supporters, usually as a mark of honour.

azure   blue.

balance   an apparatus for weighing objects; a beam with two opposite scales.

banded   tied with a band or ribbon.

banner   a square or rectangular flag showing only that part of a coat of arms which appears on the shield. A banner may either be flown from a flagstaff or carried in procession. The banner should not be confused with either the standard or the gonfanan.

bar   a diminutive of the fess occupying approximately one fifth of the total depth of the shield.

barbed   bearded. This term also applies to the leaves of a heraldic rose, the points of an arrow, fishhook or spear, or to the ears of wheat.

barded   describes a horse when bridled, saddled and armoured.

barnacle   an instrument used by farriers to curb horses.

baron   the fifth and lowest rank of the British peerage. This term often refers, mistakenly, to the Scottish rank of Lord of Parliament.

baronet   a hereditary honour outwith the peerage. Derived from the medieval title of knight banneret, it entitles the holder to the prefix 'sir' and to the badge appropriate to this rank which may be used as a heraldic additament.

barrulet   a diminutive of the bar.

barry   describes a field or charge which is divided horizontally into an even number of stripes of alternate tinctures.

base   the lower portion of a shield.

baton (batune, baston)   a couped bendlet. This term can also be used to describe a staff of office or a form of club carried by some supporters.

beaked   describes the beaks of birds or monsters when of a different tincture from the body.

beaver   the face-guard of a helmet.

belled   having a bell or bells attached.

bend   one of the ordinaries; a broad band extending from dexter chief to sinister base.

bend sinister   a bend which runs from sinister chief to dexter base.

bendlet   a diminutive of the bend.

bendwise   descriptive of charges when shown at the same angle as a bend.

bendy   describes a field or charge which is divided diagonally into an even number of stripes of alternate tinctures.

bezant   a gold roundel; originally a Byzantine coin.

billet   an oblong rectangular charge said by some to represent a brick and by others a letter. This charge is classified by some authorities as one of the sub-ordinaries.

blackamoor   a negro.

blazon (blason)   (i) the written description of armorial bearings; (ii) to describe a coat of arms using correct heraldic terminology.

bordure one of the sub-ordinaries; a border round the edge of a shield, generally used as a difference or mark of cadency.

bouget a stylised representation of two leather waterbags supported by a yoke or crossbar.

brisure (brizure) a mark of cadency or difference.

cable a chain or rope attached to an anchor.

cabossed (caboshed) describes an animal's head when depicted affronty and cut off behind the ears leaving no part of the neck showing.

cadency the system whereby a coat of arms is differenced to distinguish the cadets of a family from its head and from one another.

cadet a junior member or branch of a family.

caduceus a winged wand or staff with two snakes entwined around it.

caltrap (galtrap, caltrop) a four-pointed iron device designed so that when strewn on the ground one point was always upwards; it was used in medieval times to maim horses in a cavalry charge.

canting describes a coat of arms which alludes in a punning way to the name or profession of the bearer.

canton one of the sub-ordinaries; a square division of the shield, smaller than a quarter, in one of the upper corners of the shield, usually in dexter chief, often charged and used as an augmentation. In Scottish heraldry, a canton voided is used as a mark of cadency for an adopted child.

cantoned between.

cap of maintenance a chapeau.

cap-a-pie(d) from head to toe; describes a man in full armour.

caparisoned describes a barded horse often covered by an armorial or ornamental cloth.

capuched wearing some specified form of headgear.

cartouche an oval shield.

cat-a-mountain a wild cat.

chapeau a velvet cap lined with fur, indicative of feudo-baronial rank.

chaplet a garland or wreath of flowers or leaves.

charge any device or figure placed upon a shield.

charged describes anything which has a charge placed upon it.

chequy (checky) describes a field or charge which is divided into three or more rows of small squares of alternate tinctures.

chess rook (zule) a stylised chess piece having a bifurcated top.

chevalier a man on horseback, usually a knight in full armour.

chevron one of the ordinaries; an inverted v, issuing from the base of the shield, said to represent the rafters of the gable of a house.

chevronel a diminutive of the chevron, usually borne in twos or threes.

chief one of the ordinaries; a broad horizontal band occupying at most, the top third of the shield.

chough usually blazoned 'Cornish chough'; a bird similar to a corbie or raven with large red beak and legs.

cinquefoil a stylised floral form with five petals.

circonfleurdelise flory counter flory.

claymore strictly, a Scottish two-handed broadsword. The Scottish basket-hilted broadsword is often blazoned 'a claymore'.

close describes a bird with wings closed.

close couped cut off close to the head; no part of the neck showing.

coat armour armorial bearings. This term also applies to a form of loose surcoat, worn over armour, emblazoned with heraldic devices.

cockatrice a heraldic monster with the head, beak, comb, wattles and legs of a cock, a barbed tongue and the wings, tail and body of a wyvern.

colours the principal heraldic colours are gules (red), azure (blue), sable (black), and vert (green). Other colours, less commonly used, are purpure (purple), bleu celeste (sky blue) and murrey (mulberry). This term also refers to certain military and naval flags.

combatant describes two rampant beasts when facing each other.

comble a narrow chief.

compartment a grassy mound or other solid base, often elaborately blazoned, on which the supporters stand.

complement, in her describes a moon when full.

compony (gobony) describes a bordure, pale, bend or other ordinary which is composed of a single row of squares of two alternate tinctures. In Scottish heraldry, the bordure compony is used as a mark of illegitimate descent.

conjoined joined together.

contourné (contourny) facing the sinister.

coney (cony, cunning) a rabbit.

coronet a lesser crown consisting of a cap of maintenance within a circlet of gold. Varying patterns of coronet have been assigned to the five ranks of the peerage. The circlet of a Lord of Parliament or baron's coronet has six (four visible) silver balls, all placed closely together; an earl's coronet has eight (five visible) balls on long spikes, alternating with eight (four visible) strawberry leaves; a marquess's four (two visible) balls on short spikes, alternating with four (three visible) strawberry leaves; a duke's coronet has eight (five visible) strawberry leaves. This form of coronet is also known as a 'coronet of rank' and should not be confused with the 'crest coronet'. Coronets of rank are sometimes represented as the circlet only, omitting the cap and the ermine edging.

cotise (cost) a narrow bendlet, usually borne in pairs and placed on either side of and parallel to a bend.

cotised describes an ordinary when depicted between two of its diminutives.

couchant lying down with head raised.

couché describes a shield when it is placed at an angle.

counterchanged describes a shield which has been divided into a colour and a metal where the charge thereon is tinctured in reverse.

counter compony describes an ordinary which is composed of a double row of squares of two alternate tinctures.

counter flory decorated with fleurs de lis lying alternately head to tail.

couped cut off. This describes any charge that is cut off cleanly with a straight line. When used of an ordinary it means that its ends do not reach the edge of the shield.

couped at all his joints this term, which seems to be peculiar to the Maitland family, describes a lion rampant when depicted with each of its four paws, its head and its tail severed and separated by a small gap from the body.

courant (current) running.

coward describes an animal or monster with its tail between its legs.

crenellated see embattled.

crescent (i) a half moon depicted with horns pointing upwards; (ii) the cadency mark used to distinguish the arms of a second son.

crest a three-dimensional device set upon a wreath, chapeau or coronet and mounted upon a helmet. Crests are now displayed above the shield as an integral part of the full achievement.

crest coronet a coronet of four strawberry leaves, three visible, depicted as part of a crest in place of, or in addition to, the wreath. This form of coronet is sometimes known as a 'ducal coronet'. In Scotland, a clan chief is entitled to petition the Lord Lyon for the grant of a crest coronet to replace the wreath in his coat of arms. Other forms of crest coronet include the antique crown, the mural crown and the naval crown.

crined describes the hair of a human being or a beast's mane when of a different tincture from the body.

crosier (crozier) the staff borne by bishops and abbots and shaped like a shepherd's crook.

cross one of the ordinaries and perhaps the most widely used of all heraldic devices,

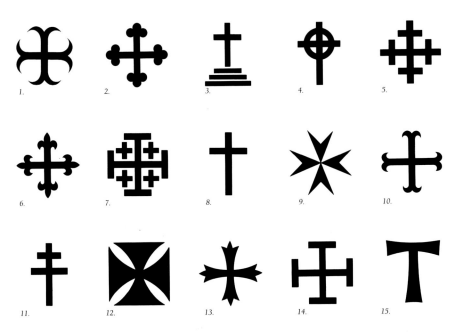

THE CROSS
1. Anchory.
2. Bottony.
3. Calvary.
4. Celtic.
5. Cross Crosslet.
6. Flory.
7. Jerusalem.
8. Latin/Passion.
9. Maltese.
10. Moline.
11. Patriarchal.
12. Pattée/Formy.
13. Patonce.
14. Potent.
15. Tau.

having more variants than any other.

crown an ornamental head-dress of gold and gems denoting sovereign rank. In Scottish heraldry it is depicted as a stylised version of the crown of Scotland.

cubit describes a hand and arm cut off at the elbow.

cuirass armour for the upper body consisting of a breastplate and backplate.

current see courant.

cutlass a form of curved sword similar to a scimitar (a corruption of curtle-axe).

dancetty (dancettée) describes a zig-zag line of partition or edge to an ordinary; similar to 'indented' but with fewer and wider indentations (see **partition**).

debruised describes any charge over which an ordinary or sub-ordinary is placed.

decrescent a crescent with the horns turned towards the sinister.

defamed without a tail.

demi half. This term invariably relates to human or animal charges when depicted from the waist upwards.

dexter the right hand side of the shield as held by the bearer, but the left hand side from the viewpoint of the observer.

diapering a method of decorating uncharged areas of a shield by covering them with scrollwork or geometric patterns, usually painted in shades of the same colour.

difference an addition or alteration to a coat of arms usually marking a distinction between arms of closely related persons.

dimidiation a rare and antiquated form of impalement made by cutting two coats of arms in half vertically and uniting the dexter half of one with the sinister half of the other.

diminutive a narrow version of an ordinary.

displayed with wings outstretched.

dorlach a quiver of arrows or darts.

dormant in a sleeping posture.

double queued having two tails

doubled describes the inner lining of mantling, mantles and chapeaux.

dovetailed describes a line of partition or the edge of an ordinary in the shape of a series of dovetail joints (see **partition**).

dragon a four-legged heraldic monster, invariably depicted with scales, bat-like wings and a barbed tail.

ducal coronet a gold coronet of four strawberry leaves (three visible) set on a rim the jewels of which are shown but not coloured.

ducally gorged having a collar in the form of a ducal coronet.

duke the highest rank of the British peerage

earl the third rank of the British peerage.

earne a white-tailed eagle.

elevated pointing upwards; describes wings

when raised above the head.

embattled describes a line of partition or the upper edge of an ordinary which is indented to resemble the battlements of a tower or castle (see **partition**).

embowed bent or curved.

enfiled pierced through or transfixed.

engrailed describes a line of partition or the edge of an ordinary which is composed of semi circular indents with the points turned outwards (see **partition**).

enhanced placed above its usual position.

ensigned describes a charge which has another charge placed immediately above it.

en surtout over all. This term usually applies to an inescutcheon.

environed encircled by.

eradicated torn up by the roots.

erased torn off, leaving a jagged edge.

erect upright.

ermine white fur with black tails.

ermines black fur with white tails.

erminois gold fur with black tails.

escallop a scallop shell; the emblem of St James, formerly worn as a badge by pilgrims, of whom he is patron.

escarbuncle a rimless wheel of eight spokes radiating from a central boss and terminating in fleurs de lis.

escrol a ribbon on which the motto is placed.

escutcheon a small shield borne as a charge. When a single escutcheon is so used it is normally termed an inescutcheon.

estoile a star of six wavy rays.

expanded displayed.

fenestrated describes windows when of a different tincture from the rest of the building.

fess one of the ordinaries; a broad horizontal band extending across the centre of the shield.

fess point the centre of the shield.

fessways describes any charge placed or borne in fess, i.e. in a horizontal line across the shield.

fetterlock a shackle for a horse.

feudal baron originally the lowest rank of the Scottish peerage, holding lands with baronial jurisdiction. Their obligation to attend parliament was restricted by an act of 1428 and their present statutory rights are defined in the Heritable Jurisdictions Act of 1747. Heraldic additaments appropriate to this rank are the chapeau, robe of estate and standard.

field the background or surface of the shield on which charges are placed.

fillet a very narrow diminutive of an ordinary.

fimbriated edged.

fitchy (fitchée) describes a cross the lower limb of which is pointed. If a cross is blazoned 'fitchy at the foot', it is depicted normally but has a point added to the lower limb.

flank   the sinister and dexter sides of a shield between the chief and the base.

flaunches   a pair of concave indentations, one on each side of the shield. The flaunch is classified by most authorities as one of the sub-ordinaries.

fleur de lis   (i) a stylised lily; (ii) the cadency mark used to distinguish the arms of a sixth son.

flory   decorated with fleurs de lis.

fluke   the large, blunt 'barbs' of an anchor.

fly   the part of a flag furthest from the pole. In long flags such as standards, the devices are described in order reading from the hoist to the fly.

fountain   a heraldic fountain is represented by a roundel barry wavy of six argent and azure.

fraise   a stylised strawberry flower usually depicted as a cinquefoil.

fret   a mascle interlaced by a bendlet and a bendlet sinister. This charge is classified by some authorities as one of the sub-ordinaries.

fretty   a field covered with a trellis pattern of interlacing bendlets and bendlets sinister.

fructed (fructuated)   bearing fruit.

fur   a form of heraldic tincture represented by stylised animal skins. The principal heraldic furs are ermine, ermines, erminois, pean, vair and potent.

furison   the steel used for striking fire from a flint.

furnished   describes a horse which is completely caparisoned.

furred   describes the fur lining of a chapeau or mantle.

fusil   an elongated lozenge. This charge is classified by some authorities as one of the sub-ordinaries.

gamb   the foreleg or paw of an animal, often a lion or bear.

garb   a sheaf of wheat.

garnished   ornamented, decorated.

gauntlet   an iron glove or armour for the hand.

ged   a pike or lucy.

gemels   twins or pairs. Three bars gemels, for example, describes three pairs of barrulets.

gillyflower   a red, five-pointed flower resembling a carnation or pink. A note in volume 1 of the *Public Register of All Arms and Bearings in Scotland* states that this charge should always be depicted as a cinquefoil.

gobonated   see **compony**.

gonfanan (gonfannon, gonfalon)   a rectangular, upright flag suspended from a horizontal bar and emblazoned with a coat of arms. This form of banner is usually associated with the Church.

gorged   collared.

goutte   a drop (of water or blood, for example).

grand quarter   a quarter that is itself quartered to show two or more coats of arms.

gryphon (griffin)   a winged monster with the foreparts of an eagle, including a pair of sharply pointed ears, and the hindparts of a lion. A male gryphon has no wings and has spikes or rays emerging from the body.

guardant   describes a beast or monster with its head turned to face the observer.

guidon   a long flag similar in shape to the standard. The guidon is eight feet long and is assigned by the Lord Lyon to non-baronial lairds who have a following. It tapers to a round, unsplit end at the fly and has a background of the livery colours of its owner's arms. The owner's crest or badge is shown in the hoist and his motto or slogan is lettered horizontally in the fly.

gyron   the lower half of a canton or quarter when divided diagonally from the dexter chief to the fess point. This charge is classified by some authorities as one of the sub-ordinaries.

gyronny   describes a field which is divided by three to six lines all passing through the fess point. (see **partition**).

habited   clothed or vested.

hart   a stag.

hatchment   a lozenge-shaped panel painted with the arms of a deceased person. This panel was placed over the main door of the house where the dead person lay and was often moved to the church after the funeral. The word hatchment is a corruption of achievement.

hauriant   describes a fish in a vertical position with its head upwards.

helmet   defensive armour for the head. In heraldry the helmet bears the crest and its form differs according to rank. The sovereign and princes of the blood have a barred helmet of gold which is always placed affronty. A peer's is silver and faces the dexter. It has a gold grille of five bars and is garnished with gold. The helmet of knights and baronets is of steel. It is placed affronty and has the visor raised. Where this helmet is incongruous, a steel tilting helm garnished with gold may be used. In Scotland, the rank of feudal baron has been assigned the great tilting helm garnished with gold. Esquires and gentlemen bear a steel barrel helm, that of an esquire garnished with gold. The helmet can also be used as a charge.

hilted   describes the handle and guard of a sword or dagger when of a different tincture from the blade.

hoist   the part of a flag nearest to the pole.

honour point   the point of a shield between middle chief point and fess point.

hurchin a hedgehog (see **urchin**).

hurt a blue roundel.

impaled united by impalement.

impalement the arrangement of two coats of arms side by side in the same shield. A husband's arms may be impaled on the dexter with those of his wife on the sinister, and holders of certain offices may impale their personal arms with those of their office, the latter being placed on the dexter.

imperial crown literally, a crown attributed to an empire but commonly used to describe an arched or closed crown as opposed to an open crown or coronet.

in bend
in chevron
in chief
in cross
in fess
in pale
in pile
in saltire

these terms are all used to describe the disposition of two or more charges when arranged along the line of a bend, chevron, chief, etc.; they should not be confused with bendwise, chevronwise, etc.

increscent a crescent with the horns turned towards the dexter.

indented describes a line of partition or the edge of an ordinary which is composed of small indentations and resembles the blade of a saw (see **partition**).

inescutcheon one of the sub-ordinaries; a small shield borne as a charge on a larger shield.

invected similar to engrailed but having the points turned inwards (see **partition**).

issuant issuing or emerging from.

jessed describes a falcon which has leather straps or thongs attached to its legs.

knot entwined cords used as charges or badges. They are generally named after the families who adopted them.

label a horizontal bar with a number of dependent points. A mark of cadency. When used as a permanent difference, it is invariably charged and classified by most authorities as one of the sub-ordinaries.

lamb, holy or paschal (agnus dei) a passant lamb with a halo behind its head, carrying over its right shoulder a staff, topped with a cross to which is attached a gonfanan or pennon.

langued tongued.

leopard in medieval heraldry a lion passant guardant was blazoned as a leopard. This term now refers to the natural beast.

livery colours the principal metal and tincture of the shield. In Scottish heraldry, the wreath is usually described as 'of the liveries'.

lochaber axe a Scottish pole-axe with a strongly curved blade projecting beyond the top of the shaft. Behind the axehead, a large hook was fitted to the top of the shaft and was used to drag horsemen from their mounts.

lodged describes a stag or other deer when couchant.

Lord of Parliament the lowest rank of the Scottish peerage, introduced in the reign of James I. The obligations to attend parliament, being too great a burden on all barons, the practice arose of designating the more considerable peers by this style.

lozenge a diamond-shaped figure used both as a charge and instead of a shield to display the arms of some women and peeresses in their own right. When used as a charge, the lozenge is classified by some authorities as one of the sub-ordinaries.

lozengy describes a field or charge which is divided bendy and bendy sinister thus creating an overall pattern of lozenges.

lucy (luce) a pike (fish).

lure a decoy used by falconers, composed of two wings conjoined, with their tips downwards, fastened to a line and ring. Two wings conjoined, with their tips downwards, are said to be 'in lure'.

lymphad a one-masted galley propelled by oars. It is extensively used in West Highland heraldry.

maned describes a beast with a mane of a different tincture from the body.

mantling a cloth cape, suspended from the top of the helmet and hanging down the wearer's back. It was originally intended to absorb the heat of the sun and in early examples is usually depicted as a plain or scalloped cloth. In later centuries it became much developed by artists to give a decorative surround to the shield, helm and crest.

martlet (i) a bird, similar to the swift or swallow, which is always depicted without legs and feet but with tufts of feathers at the thighs; (ii) the cadency mark used to distinguish the arms of a fourth son.

marquess (marquis) the second rank of the peerage.

mascle a voided lozenge. This charge is classified by some authorities as one of the sub-ordinaries.

mask the face of a fox, always shown cabossed.

masoned describes lines of pointing when of a different tincture from the building on which they appear.

maunch a stylised representation of a medieval sleeve.

membered describes the legs and beak of a bird or the genitalia of a lion or other beast when of a different tincture from the body.

mertrix a pine martin; also termed a martin or martin-cat.

metals the heraldic tinctures or (gold) and argent (silver).

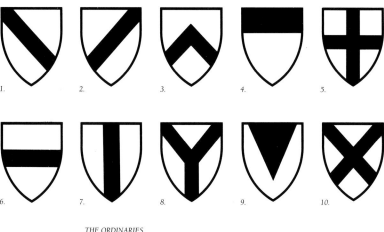

THE ORDINARIES
1. Bend.
2. Bend Sinister.
3. Chevron.
4. Chief.
5. Cross.
6. Fess.
7. Pale.
8. Pall.
9. Pile.
10. Saltire.

millrind (fer-de-moline) a stylised representation of the iron centre-piece of a millstone.

miniver a plain white fur.

mitre the head-dress worn by bishops and abbots.

moor a black man.

mortar a thick, short cannon mounted on a low carriage.

motto a word or short phrase placed in a scroll either below the shield or, as is usual in Scotland, above the crest. It often reflects the sentiments of the armiger or may be of a punning nature relating to his name or arms. The motto of a clansman will often respond to that of his chief.

mound an orb; an emblem of sovereignty consisting of a ball surmounted by a cross.

mullet (i) a five-pointed star; from the french 'molette'- spur rowel; (ii) the cadency mark used to distinguish the arms of a third son.

mural crown a crest coronet in the form of an embattled wall. The mural crown is widely used in civic heraldry and in the past has been granted to distinguished soldiers.

murrey the colour mulberry. An uncommon heraldic tincture.

muzzled describes any animal whose mouth is banded to prevent its biting.

naiant swimming; describes a fish when shown in a horizontal position.

naval crown a crest coronet consisting of alternate representations of the stern and sail of a ship mounted on a circlet. The naval crown is most commonly encountered in the badges of royal navy ships and in the arms of distinguished sailors.

nebuly describes a line of partition or the edge of an ordinary which is deeply waved to represent clouds (see **partition**).

nowed tied in a knot.

or gold.

ordinary a major heraldic charge. Opinions differ as to the number of these charges but most authorities include the bend, bend sinister, chevron, chief, cross, fess, pale, pall, pile and saltire. Specific dimensions are often given for each of the ordinaries. However, as an ordinary may be placed between other charges or be itself charged, these dimensions will inevitably vary.

orle one of the sub-ordinaries; a narrow border running parallel to the edge of the shield but not adjacent to it.

overall (surtout) describes a charge, ordinary or escutcheon which is superimposed on other charges.

pale one of the ordinaries, a broad vertical band placed in the middle of the shield.

pallet a diminutive of the pale.

paly describes a field or charge which is divided into an even number of vertical stripes of equal width in alternating tinctures.

papingoe a parrot.

parted divided.

partition, line of a line which divides the surface of a shield or charge into a variety of geometrical shapes. The direction of a line of partition is indicated by relation to its corresponding ordinary. For example, if a shield is divided horizontally across the middle it is said to be parted 'per fess'. Similarly, the shield can be parted per bend, per bend sinister, per chevron, per pale and per saltire. The term 'quarterly' is used to describe a field which is

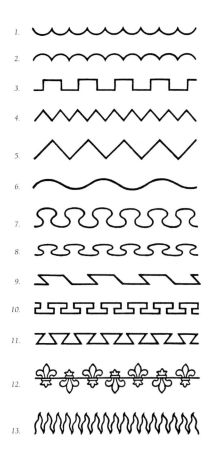

1.
2.
3.
4.
5.
6.
7.
8.
9.
10.
11.
12.
13.

LINES OF PARTITION
1. Engrailed.
2. Invected.
3. Embattled.
4. Indented.
5. Dancetty.
6. Wavy.
7. Nebuly (deep).
8. Nebuly (shallow).
9. Raguly.
10. Potenté.
11. Dovetailed.
12. Flory counterflory.
13. Rayonné.

divided per pale and per fess. A shield which is divided into three parts is said to be 'tierced' and when divided into a number of gyrons or triangular pieces radiating from a centre point, it is blazoned 'gyronny'. Lines of partition may be straight or ornamented. The most common variations are here illustrated and further described elsewhere in the glossary.

passant walking.

passion nail a form of nail generally represented as wedge-shaped and without a head.

pastoral staff see **crosier.**

pean black fur with gold tails.

peerage a hereditary dignity, derived from the crown, devolving on a line of heirs implied or expressed in the instrument or other act of creation. Among the privileges is the right to a seat and vote in parliament.

pegasus a winged horse.

pellet a black roundel.

pendent hanging from.

pennon strictly, a small guidon, four feet long, which, nowadays, is very rarely assigned. This term, however, is more commonly used to refer to a long triangular flag borne at the end of a lance or spear, or flown from the mast of a ship.

peplummed describes a tightly fitting jacket with a short, slightly flared panel or panels extending from the waist.

pheon an arrowhead with the barbs engrailed on the inner edge.

phoenix a fabulous bird similar to an eagle. It is sometimes depicted with a crest of feathers on its head and is always shown emerging from flames.

piety, in her describes a pelican when wounding its breast with its beak and nourishing its young with blood.

pile one of the ordinaries; a triangular charge issuing from the chief and tapering towards the base.

pinsel a small triangular flag granted by the Lord Lyon only to chiefs or very special chieftain-barons for practical use to denote a person to whom the chief has delegated authority to act in his absence on a particular occasion. The flag is 4 feet 6 inches long by 2 feet high, with a background of the main livery colour of the chief's arms. On it is depicted his crest within a strap and buckle bearing the motto and outside the strap and buckle a circlet inscribed with his title. On top of the circlet is set his coronet of rank or baronial chapeau if any. In the fly is shown the plant badge and a scroll with his slogan or motto.

plate a silver or white roundel.

pole-axe a form of pole-arm having a five or six foot shaft with a comparatively small axe-head mounted at the end. At the rear was often a fluted hammer head.

pomme a green roundel.

pommel the rounded knob at the end of a dagger or sword hilt.

popinjay a parrot.

port the door or gate of a castle.

portcullis the protective grille over the gateway of a town or castle. It is usually depicted as a lattice of four horizontal bars and five vertical bars terminating in points at the bottom and with chains attached to the top corners.

potent (i) resembling the head of a crutch; (ii) one of the heraldic furs which is composed of crutch or t-shaped divisions.

proper depicted in natural colours.

purpure purple.

quarter (i) to divide the shield into four or more compartments; (ii) a sub-ordinary occupying one quarter of the shield.

quarterly a term used to signify that the shield is quartered (see **partition**).

quatrefoil a stylised floral form with four petals.

raguly   describes a line of partition or the edge of an ordinary which is ragged or notched resembling the trunk or limb of a tree which has been lopped of its branches (see **partition**).

rampant   describes a beast or monster standing on one hind leg.

ratch hound   a beagle.

reflexed   describes a chain when attached to an animal's collar and then thrown over its back.

reguardant   describes a beast, bird or monster when looking back over its shoulder.

respectant (respecting)   describes two animals when shown face to face.

riband (ribbon)   a narrow bendlet. This term also refers to the ribbon of an order or decoration which may be pendent below the shield.

rising   describes a bird about to take flight.

robe of estate   a ceremonial robe worn by the nobility, usually of rich material with an appropriate arrangement of fur and other trimmings according to rank.

roundel   a disc-shaped charge. The roundel is classified by some authorities as one of the sub-ordinaries.

rowel (revel)   the spiked, revolving disk at the end of a spur; usually depicted as a pierced mullet.

royal tressure   a double tressure flory counter flory as in the royal arms of Scotland.

rustre   a lozenge pierced with a round hole. This charge is classified by some authorities as one of the sub-ordinaries.

sable   black.

salamander   a fabulous reptile, depicted as a lizard-like creature surrounded by flames.

salient   springing.

saltire   one of the ordinaries; depicted in the form of a diagonal cross. Also known as a St Andrew's cross.

sanglier   a wild boar.

savage   a long-haired, bearded man often depicted as being wreathed about the head and loins with foliage.

scimitar   a form of curved sword.

scrip   a bag or purse formerly carried by pilgrims.

seeded   describes the seeds of a rose or any other flower when of a different tincture from the petals.

segreant   describes a gryphon when in the rampant position.

sejant   sitting.

semée (semy)   describes a field which is evenly powdered with an indeterminate number of small charges.

sgian   see **skene**.

shakefork   a sub-ordinary in the form of a pall the arms of which do not reach the edge of the shield.

sinister   the left hand side of the shield as held by the bearer, but the right hand side from the viewpoint of the observer.

skene (sgian)   a Highland knife often depicted in heraldry as a short sword or dagger.

sleuth-hound   a large dog similar to the talbot. A sleuth-hound is of the badges of the Earl of Perth.

slipped   describes flowers and leaves when depicted with the stalk attached.

slughorn   a slogan or war-cry.

splendour, in his   describes the sun when depicted as a disc, sometimes with a human face, environed by rays which may be alternately straight and wavy.

standard   a long, narrow, tapering flag, granted by the Lord Lyon only to those who have a following, such as clan chiefs. As a 'headquarters' flag, its principal use is to mark the gathering point or headquarters of the clan, family or following and does not necessarily denote the presence of the standard's owner as his personal banner does.

The standards of peers and barons have their ends split and rounded; for others the end is unsplit and rounded. At the hoist, the standard usually shows the owner's arms, though some are still granted with the former practice of having the national saltire in the hoist. The remainder of the flag is horizontally divided into two tracts of the livery colours for chiefs of clans or families, three tracts for very major branch-chieftains and four for others. Upon this background are usually displayed the owner's crest and heraldic badges, separated by transverse bands bearing the owner's motto or slogan. The whole flag is fringed with alternating pieces of the livery colours.

The length of the standard varies according to the rank of its owner, as follows:

the Sovereign:	8 yards
Dukes:	7 yards
Marquesses:	6½ yards
Earls:	6 yards
Viscounts:	5½ yards
Lords:	5 yards
Baronets:	4½ yards
Knights and barons:	4 yards

On rare occasions, a uniform length of standard for a decorative display may be laid down by the Lord Lyon.

statant   standing.

stringed   describes the strings or ribbons of musical instruments, bows and bugle horns.

sub-ordinary   one of a group of major charges which are subordinate to the ordinaries. Opinions vary as to which charges should be classed as sub-ordinaries. However, most authorities include the bordure, canton, flaunch, inescutcheon, lable, orle, quarter, shakefork and tressure. The billet, fret, fusil, gyron, loz-

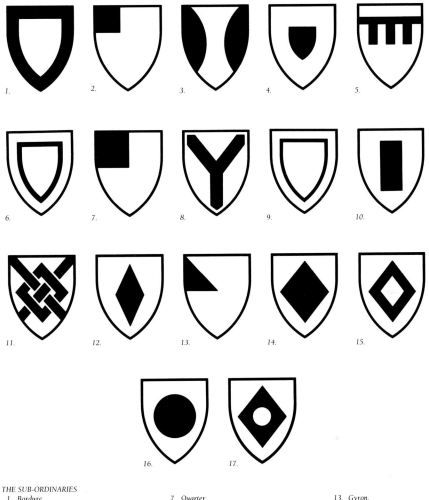

THE SUB-ORDINARIES

1. Bordure.	7. Quarter.	13. Gyron.
2. Canton.	8. Shakefork.	14. Lozenge.
3. Flaunch.	9. Tressure.	15. Mascle.
4. Inescutcheon.	10. Billet.	16. Roundle.
5. Label.	11. Fret.	17. Rustre.
6. Orle.	12. Fusil.	

enge, mascle, roundle and rustre are also classified as sub-ordinaries by some authorities.

supporters additaments, usually human or animal figures placed on either side of a shield as though supporting it.

surmounted describes a charge with another placed upon it.

surtout overall.

sustaining supporting or holding.

talbot a hound or hunting dog.

targe (target) a small circular shield.

tenné (tawny) the colour orange. An uncommon heraldic tincture.

thunderbolt a heraldic charge conventionally depicted as a winged and twisted bar, inflamed at each end and having four forked and barbed darts in saltire issuing from its centre.

tierced divided into three (see **partition**).

tinctures the metals, colours and furs used in heraldry.

tines (tynes) the branches of a stag's antlers.

torse see **wreath**.

torteau a red roundel.

tracts two or more horizontal strips of metal and colour which constitute the field of a heraldic standard. The number of tracts is dictated by the rank of the armiger: two for chiefs of clans or families, three for very major branch chieftains and four for others.

transfixed pierced through.

trefoil a stylised, three-lobed leaf, generally shown slipped.

tressure one of the sub-ordinaries; a diminutive of the orle. Tressures are usually borne double and are often decorated with fleurs de lis or other figures.

trippant   describes a stag or deer when depicted as passant.

triumphal crown   a wreath or garland of laurel.

two and one   describes the disposition of three charges when borne on a shield with two in chief and one in base.

tyger   the heraldic tyger is an imaginary beast resembling a lion with a large wolf-like head and a down-curving tusk on the end of its nose. A natural tiger is blazoned a 'Bengal tiger'.

undy   see **wavy**.

unguled   describes the hooves of an animal when of a different tincture from the body.

unicorn   an imaginary animal resembling a horse with cloven hooves, the beard of a goat, the tail of a lion and a long twisted horn growing out of its forehead.

urchin (urcheon)   a hedgehog.

vair   a heraldic fur represented by rows of small blue and white shield or bell shapes alternately reversed.

vairy   describes vair when depicted in colours other than blue and white.

vambraced   describes an arm clad in armour.

vane   a small flag, often made of metal, found on the caps and turrets of castles and towers.

vannet   an excallop when represented with-out its two projecting 'ears'.

vert   green.

vested   habited or clothed.

viscount   the fourth rank of the British peerage.

voided   describes an ordinary or sub-ordinary consisting only of a fillet border and showing the field or another tincture in the voided area.

voider   similar to the flaunch but not so deeply curved.

volant   flying.

vulning   wounding. Invariably used to describe a pelican pecking at its own breast to produce blood.

wavy   describes a line of partition or the edge of an ordinary which undulates like waves (see **partition**).

winding   sounding a horn or bugle by blowing.

wreath   a twisted length of cloth originally intended to cover the join between crest and helmet. It is conventionally depicted as being composed of six alternate twists of the owner's livery colours. The wreath is often replaced by some form of crest coronet or chapeau. A garland of flowers, leaves or other stylised foliage is also described as a wreath.

wreathed   encircled with a wreath.

wreathy   twisted, in the form of a wreath.

wyvern   a heraldic monster similar to the dragon but having only two legs.

Appendix 4

Alphabetical list of Scottish names associated with clans and families

The subject of septs is a contentious one and one which is difficult to resolve with any degree of historical accuracy. The list below is neither comprehensive nor definitive but is intended solely as a guide to the possible connections a name may have to a recognised clan or family featured in detail elsewhere in this book.

Name	Associated Clan
Abbot	Macnab
Abbotson	Macnab
Addison	Gordon
Adie	Gordon
Airlie	Ogilvy
Airth	Graham
Aitcheson	Gordon
Aitken	Gordon
Alexander	Macalister, Macdonald
Alistair	Macalister
Allan	Macdonald, Macfarlane
Allanson	Macdonald, Macfarlane
Allison	Macalister
Arrol	Hay
Arthur	Macarthur
Askey	Macleod
Austin	Keith
Ayson	Mackintosh
Bain	Macbain, Mackay
Balloch	Macdonald
Barrie	Farquharson, Gordon
Barron	Rose
Bartholomew	Macfarlane, Leslie
Bean	Macbain
Beath	Macdonald, Maclean
Beattie	Macbain
Begg	Macdonald
Berry	Forbes
Beton	Macleod
Binnie	Macbain
Black	Lamont, Macgregor, Maclean
Blake	Lamont
Bonar	Graham
Bontein	Graham
Bontine	Graham
Bowers	Macgregor
Bowie	Macdonald
Bowmaker	Macgregor
Bowman	Farquharson
Boyes	Forbes
Brebner	Farquharson
Brewer	Drummond, Macgregor
Brieve	Morrison
Brown	Lamont, Macmillan
Bryce	Macfarlane
Bryde	Brodie
Buntain	Graham
Bunten	Graham
Buntine	Graham
Burdon	Lamont
Burk	Macdonald
Burnes	Campbell
Burns	Campbell
Caddell	Campbell

Name	Associated Clan
Caird	Sinclair, Macgregor
Cariston	Skene
Carlyle	Bruce
Carr	Kerr
Carrick	Kennedy
Carson	Macpherson
Cassels	Kennedy
Cattanach	Macpherson
Caw	Macfarlane
Cessford	Kerr
Charles	Mackenzie
Christie	Farquharson
Clanachan	Maclean
Clark	Cameron, Macpherson
Clarke	Cameron, Macpherson
Clarkson	Cameron, Macpherson
Clement	Lamont
Clerk	Cameron, Macpherson
Cluny	Macpherson
Clyne	Sinclair
Cobb	Lindsay
Collier	Robertson
Colman	Buchanan
Colson	Macdonald
Colyear	Robertson
Combie	Macthomas
Comine	Cumming (Comyn)
Comrie	Macgregor
Conacher	Macdougall
Connall	Macdonald
Connell	Macdonald
Conochie	Campbell
Constable	Hay
Cook	Stewart
Corbet	Ross
Cormack	Buchanan
Coull	Macdonald
Coulson	Macdonald
Cousland	Buchanan
Coutts	Farquharson
Cowan	Colquhoun, Macdougall
Cowie	Fraser
Crerar	Mackintosh
Crombie	Macdonald
Crookshanks	Stewart
Cruickshanks	Stewart
Crum	Macdonald
Cullen	Gordon
Cumin	Cumming
Cushnie	Lumsden
Dallas	Mackintosh
Daniels	Macdonald
Davie	Davidson
Davis	Davidson
Davison	Davidson

Name	Associated Clan	Name	Associated Clan
Dawson	Davidson	Fyfe	Macduff
Day	Davidson	Gallie	Gunn
Dean	Davidson	Galt	Macdonald
Denoon	Campbell	Garrow	Stewart
Denune	Campbell	Garvie	Maclean
Deuchar	Lindsay	Gaunson	Gunn
Dickson	Keith	Geddes	Gordon
Dingwall	Munro, Ross	Georgeson	Gunn
Dinnes	Innes	Gibb	Buchanan
Dis	Skene	Gifford	Hay
Dixon	Keith	Gilbert	Buchanan
Dobbie	Robertson	Gilbertson	Buchanan
Dobson	Robertson	Gilbride	Macdonald
Dochart	Macgregor	Gilchrist	Maclachlan, Ogilvy
Docharty	Macgregor	Gilfillan	Macnab
Doig	Drummond	Gill	Macdonald
Doles	Mackintosh	Gillanders	Ross
Donachie	Robertson	Gillespie	Macpherson
Donaldson	Macdonald	Gillies	Macpherson
Donillson	Macdonald	Gillon	Maclean
Donleavy	Buchanan	Gilroy	Grant, Macgillivray
Donlevy	Buchanan	Glennie	Mackintosh
Donnellson	Macdonnell	Gorrie	Macdonald
Dove	Buchanan	Goudie	Macpherson
Dow	Buchanan, Davidson	Gow	Macpherson
Dowe	Buchanan	Gowan	Macdonald
Downie	Lindsay	Gowrie	Macdonald
Drysdale	Douglas	Greenlaw	Home
Duff	Macduff	Gregorson	Macgregor
Duffie	Macfie	Gregory	Macgregor
Duffus	Sutherland	Greig	Macgregor
Duffy	Macfie	Greusach	Farquharson
Duilach	Stewart	Grewar	Macgregor, Drummond
Duncanson	Robertson	Grier	Macgregor
Dunnachie	Robertson	Griesck	Macfarlane
Duthie	Ross	Grigor	Macgregor
Dyce	Skene	Gruamach	Macfarlane
Eadie	Gordon	Gruer	Macgregor, Drummond
Eaton	Home	Haddon	Graham
Edie	Gordon	Haggart	Ross
Elder	Mackintosh	Hallyard	Skene
Ennis	Innes	Hardie	Farquharson, Mackintosh
Enrick	Gunn	Hardy	Farquharson, Mackintosh
Esson	Mackintosh	Harold	Macleod
Ewing	Maclachlan	Harper	Buchanan
Fair	Ross	Harperson	Buchanan
Fairbairn	Armstrong	Harvey	Keith
Federith	Sutherland	Hastings	Campbell
Fee	Macfie	Hawes	Campbell
Fergus	Ferguson	Haws	Campbell
Ferries	Ferguson	Hawson	Campbell
Ferson	Macpherson	Hawthorn	Macdonald
Fife	Macduff	Hendrie	Macnaughton
Findlater	Ogilvie	Hendry	Macnaughton
Findlay	Farquharson	Hewitson	Macdonald
Findlayson	Farquharson	Hewitt	Macdonald
Finlay	Farquharson	Higginson	Mackintosh
Finlayson	Farquharson	Hobson	Robertson
Fisher	Campbell	Hossack	Mackintosh
Foulis	Munro	Howe	Graham
France	Stewart	Howie	Graham
Francis	Stewart	Howison	Macdonald
Frew	Fraser	Hudson	Macdonald
Frissell	Fraser	Hughson	Macdonald
Frizell	Fraser	Huntly	Gordon

Name	Associated Clan	Name	Associated Clan
Hutchenson	Macdonald	Macaindra	Macfarlane
Hutcheson	Macdonald	Macaldonich	Buchanan
Hutchinson	Macdonald	Macalduie	Lamont
Hutchison	Macdonald	Macallan	Macdonald, Macfarlane
Inches	Robertson	Macalonie	Cameron
Ingram	Colquhoun	Macandeoir	Buchanan, Macnab
Innie	Innes	Macandrew	Mackintosh
Isles	Macdonald	Macangus	Macinnes
Jameson	Gunn, Stewart	Macara	Macgregor, Macrae
Jamieson	Gunn, Stewart	Macaree	Macgregor
Jeffrey	Macdonald	Macaskill	Macleod
Kay	Davidson	Macaslan	Buchanan
Kean	Gunn, Macdonald	Macauselan	Buchanan
Keene	Gunn, Macdonald	Macauslan	Buchanan
Kellie	Macdonald	Macausland	Buchanan
Kendrick	Macnaughton	Macauslane	Buchanan
Kenneth	Mackenzie	Macay	Shaw
Kennethson	Mackenzie	Macbaxter	Macmillan
Kerracher	Farquharson	Macbean	Macbain
Kilgour	Macduff	Macbeath	Macbain, Macdonald, Maclean
King	Colquhoun		
Kinnell	Macdonald	Macbeolain	Mackenzie
Kinnieson	Macfarlane	Macbeth	Macbain, Macdonald, Maclean
Knox	Macfarlane		
Lachie	Maclachlan	Macbheath	Macbain, Macdonald, Maclean
Laidlaw	Scott		
Lair	Maclaren	Macbride	Macdonald
Lamb	Lamont	Macbrieve	Morrison
Lambie	Lamont	Macburie	Macdonald
Lammond	Lamont	Maccaa	Macfarlane
Lamondson	Lamont	Maccabe	Macleod
Landers	Lamont	Maccaig	Farquharson, Macleod
Lang	Leslie	Maccaishe	Macdonald
Lansdale	Home	Maccall	Macdonald
Lauchlan	Maclachlan	Maccalman	Buchanan
Lawrence	Maclaren	Maccalmont	Buchanan
Lawrie	Maclaren	Maccamie	Stewart
Lawson	Maclaren	Maccammon	Buchanan
Lean	Maclean	Maccammond	Buchanan
Leckie	Macgregor	Maccanish	Macinnes
Lecky	Macgregor	Maccansh	Macinnes
Lees	Macpherson	Maccartney	Farquharson, Mackintosh
Leitch	Macdonald	Maccartair	Campbell
Lemond	Lamont	Maccarter	Campbell
Lennie	Buchanan	Maccash	Macdonald
Lenny	Buchanan	Maccaskill	Macleod
Lewis	Macleod	Maccasland	Buchanan
Limond	Lamont	Maccaul	Macdonald
Limont	Lamont	Maccause	Macfarlane
Linklater	Sinclair	Maccaw	Macfarlane
Lobban	Maclennan	Maccay	Mackay
Lockerbie	Douglas	Macceallaich	Macdonald
Lombard	Stewart	Macchlerich	Cameron
Lonie	Cameron	Macchlery	Cameron
Lorne	Stewart, Campbell	Macchoiter	Macgregor
Loudoun	Campbell	Macchruiter	Buchanan
Low	Maclaren	Maccloy	Stewart
Lowson	Maclaren	Macclure	Macleod
Lucas	Lamont	Maccluskie	Macdonald
Luke	Lamont	Macclymont	Lamont
Lyall	Sinclair	Maccodrum	Macdonald
MacA'challies	Macdonald	Maccoll	Macdonald
Macachounich	Colquhoun	Maccolman	Buchanan
Macadam	Macgregor	Maccomas	Macthomas, Gunn
Macadie	Ferguson	Maccombe	Macthomas

Name	Associated Clan
Maccombich	Stewart (of Appin)
Maccombie	Macthomas
Maccomie	Macthomas
Macconacher	Macdougall
Macconachie	Macgregor, Robertson
Macconchy	Mackintosh
Maccondy	Macfarlane
Macconnach	Mackenzie
Macconnechy	Campbell, Robertson
Macconnell	Macdonald
Macconochie	Campbell, Robertson
Maccooish	Macdonald
Maccook	Macdonald
Maccorkill	Gunn
Maccorkindale	Macleod
Maccorkle	Gunn
Maccormack	Buchanan
Maccormick	Maclean of Lochbuie
Maccorrie	Macquarrie
Maccorry	Macquarrie
Maccosram	Macdonald
Maccoull	Macdougall
Maccowan	Colquhoun, Macdougall
Maccrae	Macrae
Maccrain	Macdonald
Maccraken	Maclean
Maccraw	Macrae
Maccreath	Macrae
Maccrie	Mackay
Maccrimmor	Macleod
Maccrindle	Macdonald
Maccririe	Macdonald
Maccrouther	Macgregor, Drummond
Maccruithein	Macdonald
Maccuag	Macdonald
Maccuaig	Farquharson, Macleod
Maccubbin	Buchanan
Maccuish	Macdonald
Maccune	Macewan
Maccunn	Macpherson
Maccurrach	Macpherson
Maccutchen	Macdonald
Maccutcheon	Macdonald
Macdade	Davidson
Macdaid	Davidson
Macdaniell	Macdonald
Macdavid	Davidson
Macdermid	Campbell
Macdiarmid	Campbell
Macdonachie	Robertson
Macdonleavy	Buchanan
Macdrain	Macdonald
Macduffie	Macfie
Macdulothe	Macdougall
Maceachan	Macdonald of Clanranald
Maceachern	Macdonald
Maceachin	Macdonald of Clanranald
Maceachran	Macdonald
Macearachar	Farquharson
Macelfrish	Macdonald
Macelheran	Macdonald
Maceoin	Macfarlane
Maceol	Macnaughton
Macerracher	Macfarlane
Macfadzean	Maclaine of Lochbuie

Name	Associated Clan
Macfall	Macpherson
Macfarquhar	Farquharson
Macfater	Maclaren
Macfeat	Maclaren
Macfergus	Ferguson
Macgaw	Macfarlane
Macgeachie	Macdonald of Clanranald
Macgeachin	Macdonald of Clanranald
Macgeoch	Macfarlane
Macghee	Mackay
Macghie	Mackay
Macgilbert	Buchanan
Macgilchrist	Maclachlan, Ogilvie
Macgill	Macdonald
Macgilledon	Lamont
Macgillegowie	Lamont
Macgillivantic	Macdonald
Macgillivour	Macgillivray
Macgillonie	Cameron
Macgilp	Macdonald
Macgilroy	Grant, Macgillivray
Macgilvernock	Graham
Macgilvra	Macgillivray, Maclaine of Lochbuie
Macgilvray	Macgillivray
Macglashan	Mackintosh, Stewart
Macglasrich	Maciver, Campbell
Macgorrie	Macdonald
Macgorry	Macdonald
Macgoun	Macdonald, Macpherson
Macgowan	Macdonald, Macpherson
Macgown	Macdonald, Macpherson
Macgrath	Macrae
Macgreusich	Buchanan, Macfarlane
Macgrewar	Macgregor, Drummond
Macgrime	Graham
Macgrory	Maclaren
Macgrowther	Macgregor, Drummond
Macgruder	Macgregor, Drummond
Macgruer	Fraser
Macgruther	Macgregor, Drummond
Macguaran	Macquarrie
Macguffie	McFie
Macgugan	Macneil
Macguire	Macquarrie
Machaffie	Macfie
Machardie	Farquharson, Mackintosh
Machardy	Farquharson, Mackintosh
Macharold	Macleod
Machendrie	Macnaughton
Machendry	Macnaughton, Macdonald
Machowell	Macdougall
Machugh	Macdonald
Machutchen	Macdonald
Machutcheon	Macdonald
Macian	Gunn, Macdonald
Macildowie	Cameron
Macilduy	Macgregor, Maclean
Macilreach	Macdonald
Macilleriach	Macdonald
Macilriach	Macdonald
Macilrevie	Macdonald
Macilvain	Macbean
Macilvora	Maclaine of Lochbuie

Name	Associated Clan	Name	Associated Clan
Macilvrae	Macgillivray	Maclairish	Macdonald
Macilvride	Macdonald	Maclamond	Lamont
Macilwhom	Lamont	Maclardie	Macdonald
Macilwraith	Macdonald	Maclardy	Macdonald
Macilzegowie	Lamont	Maclarty	Macdonald
Macimmey	Fraser	Maclaverty	Macdonald
Macinally	Buchanan	Maclaws	Campbell
Macindeor	Menzies	Maclea	Stewart of Appin
Macindoe	Buchanan	Macleay	Stewart of Appin
Macinroy	Robertson	Maclehose	Campbell
Macinstalker	Macfarlane	Macleish	Macpherson
Maciock	Macfarlane	Macleister	Macgregor
Macissac	Campbell, Macdonald	Maclergain	Maclean
Maciver	Maciver, Campbell	Maclerie	Cameron, Mackintosh,
Macivor	Maciver, Campbell		Macpherson
Macjames	Macfarlane	Macleverty	Macdonald
Mackail	Cameron	Maclewis	Macleod
Mackames	Gunn	Maclintock	Macdougall
Mackaskill	Macleod	Maclise	Macpherson
Mackeachan	Macdonald	Macliver	Macgregor
Mackeamish	Gunn	Maclucas	Lamont, Macdougall
Mackean	Gunn, Macdonald	Maclugash	Macdougall
Mackechnie	Macdonald of Clanranald	Maclulich	Macdougall, Munro, Ross
Mackee	Mackay	Maclure	Macleod
Mackeggie	Mackintosh	Maclymont	Lamont
Mackeith	Macpherson	Macmanus	Colquhoun, Gunn
Mackellachie	Macdonald	Macmartin	Cameron
Mackellaig	Macdonald	Macmaster	Buchanan, Macinnes
Mackellaigh	Macdonald	Macmath	Matheson
Mackellar	Campbell	Macmaurice	Buchanan
Mackelloch	Macdonald	Macmenzies	Menzies
Mackelvie	Campbell	Macmichael	Stewart of Appin, Stewart
Mackendrick	Macnaughton	Macminn	Menzies
Mackenrick	Macnaughton	Macmonies	Menzies
Mackeochan	Macdonald of Clanranald	Macmorran	Mackinnon
Mackerchar	Farquharson	Macmunn	Stewart
Mackerlich	Mackenzie	Macmurchie	Buchanan, Mackenzie
Mackerracher	Farquharson	Macmurchy	Buchanan, Mackenzie
Mackerras	Ferguson	Macmurdo	Macpherson
Mackersey	Ferguson	Macmurdoch	Macpherson
Mackessock	Campbell, Macdonald of	Macmurray	Murray
	Clanranald	Macmurrich	Macdonald of Clanranald,
Mackichan	Macdonald of Clanranald,		Macpherson
	Macdougall	Macmutrie	Stewart
Mackieson	Mackintosh	Macnair	Macfarlane, Macnaughton
Mackiggan	Macdonald	Macnamell	Macdougall
Mackilligan	Mackintosh	Macnayer	Macnaughton
Mackillop	Macdonald	Macnee	Macgregor
Mackim	Fraser	Macneilage	Macneil
Mackimmie	Fraser	Macneiledge	Macneil
Mackindlay	Farquharson	Macneilly	Macneil
Mackinlay	Buchanan, Farquharson,	Macneish	Macgregor
	Macfarlane, Stewart of Appin	Macneur	Macfarlane
Mackinley	Buchanan	Macney	Macgregor
Mackinnell	Macdonald	Macnider	Macfarlane
Mackinney	Mackinnon	Macnie	Macgregor
Mackinning	Mackinnon	Macnish	Macgregor
Mackinven	Mackinnon	Macniter	Macfarlane
Mackirdy	Stewart	Macniven	Cumming, Mackintosh,
Mackissock	Campbell, Macdonald of		Macnaughton
	Clanranald	Macnuir	Macnaughton
Macknight	Macnaughton	Macnuyer	Buchanan, Macnaughton
Maclae	Stewart of Appin	Macomie	Macthomas
Maclagan	Robertson	Macomish	Macthomas
Maclaghlan	Maclachlan	Maconie	Cameron

Name	Associated Clan
Macoran	Campbell
MacO'Shannaig	Macdonald
Macoull	Macdougall
Macourlic	Cameron
Macowen	Campbell
Macowl	Macdougall
Macpatrick	Lamont, Maclaren
Macpetrie	Macgregor
Macphadden	Maclaine of Lochbuie
Macphater	Maclaren
Macphedran	Campbell
Macphedron	Macaulay
Macpheidiran	Macaulay
Macphillip	Macdonald
Macphorich	Lamont
Macphun	Matheson, Campbell
Macquaire	Macquarrie
Macquartie	Macquarrie
Macquey	Mackay
Macquhirr	Macquarrie
Macquire	Macquarrie
Macquistan	Macdonald
Macquisten	Macdonald
Macquoid	Mackay
Macra	Macrae
Macrach	Macrae
Macraild	Macleod
Macraith	Macrae, Macdonald
Macrankin	Maclean
Macrath	Macrae
Macritchie	Mackintosh
Macrob	Gunn, Macfarlane
Macrobb	Macfarlane
Macrobbie	Robertson, Drummond
Macrobert	Robertson, Drummond
Macrobie	Robertson, Drummond
Macrorie	Macdonald
Macrory	Macdonald
Macruer	Macdonald
Macrurie	Macdonald
Macrury	Macdonald
Macshannachan	Macdonald
Macshimes	Fraser of Lovat
Macsimon	Fraser of Lovat
Macsorley	Cameron, Macdonald
Macsporran	Macdonald
Macswan	Macdonald
Macsween	Macdonald
Macswen	Macdonald
Macsymon	Fraser
Mactaggart	Ross
Mactary	Innes
Mactause	Campbell
Mactavish	Campbell
Mactear	Ross, Macintyre
Mactier	Ross
Mactire	Ross
Maculric	Cameron
Macure	Campbell
Macvail	Cameron, Mackay
Macvanish	Mackenzie
Macvarish	Macdonald of Clanranald
Macveagh	Maclean
Macvean	Macbean
Macvey	Maclean

Name	Associated Clan
Macvicar	Macnaughton
Macvinish	Mackenzie
Macvurich	Macdonald of Clanranald, Macpherson
Macvurie	Macdonald of Clanranald
Macwalrick	Cameron
Macwalter	Macfarlane
Macwattie	Buchanan
Macwhannell	Macdonald
Macwhirr	Macquarrie
Macwhirter	Buchanan
Macwilliam	Gunn, Macfarlane
Malcolmson	Malcolm (Maccallum)
Malloch	Macgregor
Mann	Gunn
Manson	Gunn
Mark	Macdonald
Marnoch	Innes
Marshall	Keith
Martin	Cameron, Macdonald
Mason	Sinclair
Massey	Matheson
Masterson	Buchanan
Mathie	Matheson
Mavor	Gordon
May	Macdonald
Means	Menzies
Meikleham	Lamont
Mein	Menzies
Meine	Menzies
Mennie	Menzies
Meyners	Menzies
Michie	Forbes
Miller	Macfarlane
Milne	Gordon, Ogilvy
Milroy	Macgillivray
Minn	Menzies
Minnus	Menzies
Mitchell	Innes
Monach	Macfarlane
Monzie	Menzies
Moodie	Stewart
Moray	Murray
Morgan	Mackay
Morren	Mackinnon
Morris	Buchanan
Morton	Douglas
Munn	Stewart, Lamont
Murchie	Buchanan, Menzies
Murchison	Buchanan, Menzies
Murdoch	Macdonald, Macpherson
Murdoson	Macdonald, Macpherson
Murphy	Macdonald
Neal	Macneil
Neil	Macneil
Neill	Macneil
Neilson	Macneil
Nelson	Gunn, Macneil
Neish	Macgregor
Nish	Macgregor
Niven	Cumming, Mackintosh
Nixon	Armstrong
Noble	Mackintosh
Norie	Macdonald
Norman	Sutherland

Name	Associated Clan
O'Drain	Macdonald
Oliver	Fraser
O'May	Sutherland
O'Shaig	Macdonald
O'Shannachan	Macdonald
O'Shannaig	Macdonald
Park	Macdonald
Parlane	Macfarlane
Paton	Macdonald, Maclean
Patrick	Lamont
Paul	Cameron, Mackintosh
Pearson	Macpherson
Peterkin	Macgregor
Petrie	Macgregor
Philipson	Macdonald
Pinkerton	Campbell
Piper	Murray
Pitullich	Macdonald
Pollard	Mackay
Polson	Mackay
Porter	Macnaughton
Pratt	Grant
Purcell	Macdonald
Raith	Macrae
Randolf	Bruce
Reidfurd	Innes
Reoch	Farquharson, Macdonald
Revie	Macdonald
Riach	Farquharson, Macdonald
Richardson	Ogilvie, Buchanan
Risk	Buchanan
Ritchie	Mackintosh
Robb	Macfarlane
Roberts	Robertson
Robinson	Gunn, Robertson
Robison	Gunn, Robertson
Robson	Gunn, Robertson
Rome	Johnstone
Ronald	Macdonald, Gunn
Ronaldson	Macdonald, Gunn
Rorison	Macdonald
Roy	Robertson
Rusk	Buchanan
Ruskin	Buchanan
Russell	Russell, Cumming
Sanderson	Macdonald
Sandison	Gunn
Saunders	Macalister
Scobie	Mackay
Shannon	Macdonald
Sharp	Stewart
Sherry	Mackinnon
Sim	Fraser of Lovat
Sime	Fraser of Lovat
Simon	Fraser of Lovat
Simpson	Fraser of Lovat
Simson	Fraser of Lovat
Skinner	Macgregor

Name	Associated Clan
Small	Murray
Smart	Mackenzie
Smith	Macpherson, Mackintosh
Sorely	Cameron, Macdonald
Spence	Macduff
Spittal	Buchanan
Spittel	Buchanan
Sporran	Macdonald
Stalker	Macfarlane
Stark	Robertson
Stenhouse	Bruce
Stewart	Stewart
Storie	Ogilvie
Stringer	Macgregor
Summers	Lindsay
Suttie	Grant
Swan	Gunn
Swanson	Gunn
Syme	Fraser
Symon	Fraser
Taggart	Ross
Tarrill	Mackintosh
Tawesson	Campbell
Tawse	Farquharson
Thain	Innes, Macintosh
Todd	Gordon
Tolmie	Macleod
Tonnochy	Robertson
Torry	Campbell
Tosh	Mackintosh
Toward	Lamont
Towart	Lamont
Train	Ross
Turner	Lamont
Tyre	Macintyre
Ure	Campbell
Vass	Munro, Ross
Wallis	Wallace
Walters	Forbes
Wass	Munro, Ross
Watt	Buchanan
Weaver	Macfarlane
Webster	Macfarlane
Whannell	Macdonald
Wharrie	Macquarrie
Wheelan	Macdonald
White	Macgregor, Lamont
Whyte	Macgregor, Lamont
Wilkie	Macdonald
Wilkinson	Macdonald
Will	Gunn
Williamson	Gunn, Mackay
Wilson	Gunn, Innes
Wright	Macintyre
Wylie	Gunn, Macfarlane
Yuill	Buchanan
Yuille	Buchanan
Yule	Buchanan

Genealogy in Scotland by Kathleen B. Cory FSAScot

In Scotland, the main record repositories for the purposes of genealogy are the General Register Office for Scotland, New Register House, Princes Street, Edinburgh, and the Scottish Record Office, HM General Register House, Princes Street, Edinburgh. The General Register Office (GRO) holds statutory (or civil) registers of births, marriages and deaths from 1855 to the present day; Old Parish Registers (OPRs) of births, marriages and deaths which occurred prior to 1855; and census returns for the years 1841–91 inclusive. These records are available for consultation on payment of a search fee.

STATUTORY RECORDS

In 1854 Parliament introduced statutory registration of births, marriages and deaths in Scotland. This Act (17 & 18 Vict. c.80), was to take effect from 1 January 1855, and since that date it has been compulsory, by law, to register all births, marriages and deaths which take place in Scotland.

Statutory birth certificate: This records the name of the parish and the address where the child was born; full names of the child; the date and time of birth; the home address if it is not the same as the place of birth; the names and occupation of the father; the names and maiden surname (M/S) of the mother, and if the parents were alive when the birth was registered; the date and place of parents' marriage (except for births in the years 1856–60 inclusive); and the name and relationship of the informant.

Statutory marriage certificate: This records the name of the parish, the place of marriage (which is not always a church) and the denominational rites (Established Church of Scotland, Roman Catholic, etc.) where the marriage took place; the date; the name of the minister or priest, and the names of witnesses. Also recorded are the full names of the groom; his age; marital status (widower or single);

occupation; and usual address. The names and occupation of the groom's father, and if he was deceased at the time of the marriage; the names and M/S of the groom's mother, and if she was deceased at the time of the marriage. The same information is recorded for the bride.

Statutory death certificate: This records the name of the parish in which the death occurred; the place and date of death; the home address if this is different from the place of death; the full names of the deceased, the age of the deceased; the deceased's marital status together with, where applicable, the name of the spouse (except for the years 1856–60 inclusive); the names and occupation of the deceased's father, and if he was deceased at the time; the names and M/S of the deceased's mother, and if she was deceased at the time; the cause of death and the name of the medical attendant; and the name and relationship of the informant. In some of the 1855–60 death certificates, the place of burial and the name of the undertaker are recorded.

In Scots Law, a married woman retains her maiden surname, and should her death be registered in Scotland, this will be indexed under both surnames. If a woman married more than once, the death should be indexed under all her various surnames, if these are known to the informant.

OLD PARISH REGISTERS

Old Parish Registers consist mainly of Church of Scotland births, marriages and deaths, but they contain less information than do their statutory counterparts. These handwritten registers are available for consultation on microfilm. Microfiche and computer indexes exist for births and marriages but not for deaths. The earliest date of a record still extant is 1553, for the parish of Errol in Perthshire. Non-Church of Scotland records are held in the Scottish Record Office, although occasional entries may be found in the OPRs.

OPR birth and baptismal entries: These record the names of the child; the names, and sometimes the occupation of the father; the maiden surname of the mother; names of witnesses; and the name of the officiating Minister. Seldom are addresses given except in country areas where the name of the farm may be recorded. The date recorded is usually either of the birth or of the baptism, although some registers do record both dates. Where both dates are known, the Mormons choose the baptismal date for their International Genealogical Index (IGI). It is important to note this fact, and not to assume that the date found in the index is always the date of birth. The information from the IGI has been used to produce the new computer index.

OPR marriage entries: These record the names of the bride and groom; sometimes the name of the bride's father but very seldom the name of the groom's father; and only in extremely rare cases, the name of their mothers. The date recorded is that of the proclamation of banns, and not often the date of the actual marriage. When a couple gave intimation of marriage (Proclamation of Banns) they often had to consign a sum of money as a surety for good behaviour before the marriage and a guarantee to marry within forty days of contracting. This sum of money was called a 'Pawn', 'Pand' or 'Pledge', and most of it was retrievable on marriage, provided that the bridal couple had behaved to the satisfaction of the elders of the kirk and the minister; a smaller amount was paid to the poor of the parish. Cautioners (pronounced 'cationers' as in 'nation') were held responsible for the satisfactory behaviour of the bride and groom prior to their marriage.

OPR death or burial entries: Not all parishes kept these records, and in most cases where they are to be found they contain little information of use to the genealogist. Most entries merely show the name of the deceased, with no kinship or age; deaths of children sometimes show the name of the father. Only a very few registers show the name, age, address and cause of death. It was customary for some churches to hire out mortcloths (or palls), and the money collected for these may constitute the only death or burial entry. Other sources to be found in the monumental inscriptions (tombstones). This information is being collated from burial grounds all over Scotland, and these records are held in the GRO and in the library of the Scottish Genealogy Society, 15 Victoria Terrace, Edinburgh.

CENSUS RETURNS
Personal census returns
The main link between statutory records and old parish registers is the census return. It is necessary to know in which parish the subject was born in order to know through which OPR to search for the appropriate entry.

Census returns of the population are taken every ten years. In Scotland such censuses have been taken since 1801, but with a few exceptions, only statistical reports are preserved for 1801–31. Returns for individual households are available (on microfilm) to the public for the years 1841–91 inclusive; they were recorded by district or parish, each one having its own registration number. These were sub-divided into enumeration books, each book having its own number. Headings to show the contents of each column are found at the top of each page of the census return.

The 1841 census return, taken on 7 June, included all the people living in the parish on the previous night. It was the first full census return to be taken, but contains less information than those taken in later years. The 1841 census does not record kinship, and it was the policy, after the age of fifteen, to round down the age to the nearest five years, so 20 will be recorded for age 20–24, 25 will be recorded for age 25–29, 30 will be recorded for age 30-34, and so on.

Unlike the census returns for 1851, 1861, 1871, 1881 and 1891, the returns for 1841 did not record the place of birth of the subject; instead was written 'Y' or 'N' which stands for 'Yes' or 'No' and shows if the subject was, or was not, born in the county where the census was taken. If the subject was born in England or Ireland then 'E' or 'I', or if abroad, then 'F' for Foreign, will denote this.

A double line (//) divided families or households at the same address. A single line (/) dividing the names denoted either another member of the family living with the head of the house but who was not one of the immediate family; or people living in the house who were not related to the head of the house, such as servants and visitors.

The 1851 census return, taken on 31 March, was the first census return to show kinship and the parish or place of birth, if that birth had occurred in Scotland. For births out of Scotland, usually only the name of the country was recorded, and very seldom the name of the parish. (This applies to census returns 1851–91 inclusive.)

The 1861 census return, taken on 8 April, did away with the column relating to a subject's being 'Blind Deaf or Dumb', but now showed the number of children in the household, aged between five and fifteen, who were attending school, and the number of rooms in the house with one or more windows.

The 1871 census return, taken on 3 April, returned to the practice of stating whether the subject was deaf, etc. and added 'Imbecile' or 'Idiot' or 'Lunatic'. There was a column for the number of children at school, this time between the ages of six and eighteen, and it allowed for children being educated at home.

The 1881 census return, taken on 3 April, no longer had a column for the number of scholars, although 'scholar' was recorded in the occupation column.

The 1891 census return, taken on 5 April, was the most detailed. It included the information 'Employer or Employed, but working on own account', and whether the subject was Gaelic- or Gaelic-and-English-speaking (G or G & E).

Census returns in Scotland have continued to be taken decennially since 1891 except for the year 1941, during the Second World War. The latest date available to the public is 1891.

Naval and shipping census returns

Additional to the personal census returns are those pertaining to Scottish shipping in English ports, ships in European ports and shipping at sea. These returns exist only for the years 1861–91.

The 1861 Census Merchant Navy, taken on 7 April, listed persons on board merchant vessels which were in Scottish ports on that night. These ports are named. It records the name and type of ship (fishing vessel, ketch, etc.) and the port to which the ship belonged; the name and surname of each person on board; and each person's age, marital status and place of birth.

The 1871 Census Merchant Navy, taken on 2 April, contains similar information to the above. It records a more detailed list of ports, and Scottish merchant ships in English ports are also shown.

The 1881 Census Merchant Navy, taken on 3 April, listed Scottish Shipping in English and European Ports, and Shipping at Sea. Although these were Scottish ships, the crews were officers and men from all over the world, including Lascar seamen. All names, occupations, places of birth, etc. were recorded.

The 1881 Census Royal Navy, taken on 3 April, listed drill ships and cutters in Scottish ports, and recorded the usual information concerning crews and vessels.

The 1891 Census Merchant Navy was taken in April, but no date was recorded. It listed ships in dock or offshore from ports from Shetland to Wigtown. The usual information was recorded for the crews and vessels.

The 1891 Census Royal Navy was taken in April, but no date was recorded. It listed drill ships, a cruiser and gunboats in Scottish ports, and recorded the usual information for the crews and vessels.

OTHER RECORDS

Records other than the statutory and old parish registers, and census returns, are held in the Scottish Record Office, which is on a split site, with a branch repository, the West Register House, in Charlotte Square, Edinburgh. The building of HM General Register House was started in 1774. It was designed by Robert Adam as a repository for the principal legal registers and the older historical records which were previously kept in the Laigh Parliament House. The main holdings include state papers and administrative records prior to the Treaty of Union in 1707, registers of the Court of Session, High Court of Justiciary, Sheriff, Commissary and other courts; registers of Sasines and Deeds; local records, including local authority records; valuation rolls; church records; gifts and deposits (private archives); and church records of denominations other than Church of Scotland.

The West Register House is a conversion (1968–71) of the former St George's Church designed by Robert Reid and founded in 1811. It is used for modern records and series requiring specialised storage. The main holdings include records of government departments and nationalised industries in Scotland, court processes, maps and plans. Lists, and other guides to records, are available for consultation in the Historical Search Room of the SRO.

Of the records held in the SRO the main ones used by the average searcher for the purposes of genealogy are those following.

Kirk Session Minutes: These include lists of male heads of families who were communicants, and lists of parishioners receiving money, and so are useful pre-census sources of information. They may also include details about illegitimate births, and report the name of the alleged father. The Kirk Session is composed of elders of the congregation with the minister as moderator. They are responsible for the general organisation of the affairs of the congregation, and concern themselves with the religious, moral and social discipline of church members, perhaps less stringently today than was done in the past.

Testaments: In Scotland there are two kinds of Testaments. A Testament Testamentar applies when a person dies testate, i.e. leaves a will and names the executor or executors; and a Testament Dative applies when a person dies intestate, i.e. does not leave a will and the executor (usually a near relative) is appointed by the court. In either case (Testament Testamentar or Testament Dative) an inventory is usually made of the deceased's effects, which used to be described as 'guidis, geir, debtis and soumes of monie'.

Register of Deeds: This contains, among other items, marriage settlements as well as trust depositions and settlements in which mention may be made of children and people nominated as their guardians.

Register of Sasines: After an heir proves to have the right to inherit land etc. or when it is transferred to a grantee rather than to an heir, the act of taking possession is known as sasine or seisin. The Register of Sasines deals with such transactions.

Services of Heirs or Retours: When lands were inherited by an heir and not given to a grantee, a brieve was issued from Chancery. This instructed the sheriff of the county concerned to empanel a jury whose responsibility it was to discover what lands the deceased possessed at the time of his death, and to obtain proof from the heir as to his right to inherit. The jury returned or 'retoured' and the heir could then take possession of his inheritance. Records of the juries' findings are in the Services of Heirs or Retours.

Poll Tax Records: Poll Tax was first imposed by Parliament in 1693, for paying debts due to the army. It was to be levied at the rate of 6 shillings per person and upwards according to a scale based on rank and means, and payment was to be made at or before Martinmas (11 November) 1694. Children and poor persons living on charity were exempt, and their names are listed separately. In 1695 a second poll tax was granted for providing ships of war and maintaining seamen. Two poll taxes were granted in 1698 for clearing the arrears of pay due to land and sea officers and men.

Poll books and lists were made up by the Commissioners of Assessment for the shires, and the magistrates of burghs. The information they contain varies greatly from parish to parish within a county, but the best of them give a record of everybody liable to be taxed over the age of sixteen, and in some cases, of children under the age of sixteen.

Assessed Taxes: By the Act 20 Geo. II, cap 3 (1747) under which assessed taxes were first levied in Scotland, duplicates of all assessments (otherwise called surveys) were ordered to be transmitted to the Office of the King's Remembrancer. These duplicate schedules furnished the necessary checks and charges upon the Receivers-General of the respective duties, as well as upon the collectors in the several counties and burghs. It was also upon them that all prosecutions on account of the duties were founded. On receiving the schedules the King's Remembrancer was required to examine them to see that the assessments or charges were made in strict confirmity with the Acts of Parliament imposing the duties.

Following the Consolidating Acts (38 Geo. III, cap. 40 and 41), the duties on windows, inhabited houses, male servants, carts, carriages and dogs were incorporated on comprehensive assessed taxed schedules. Income tax, and later, property tax, remained on separate schedules. No property tax schedules have been preserved, and there are comprehensive assessed tax schedules for 1798–99 only. There are, however, property tax schedules for Midlothian, 1799–1812.

Valuation Rolls: These are available for every year since 1855 to the present day, and cover every piece of property in Scotland. They show the name and the value of the property, the name of the owner and the name of the tenant and occupier. It is helpful to know the name of the county or burgh, as some of the earlier rolls are not indexed.

Gifts and Deposits (GDs): These are the deposited collections of private papers. They are mostly family muniments, but they also include papers from business firms and lawyers' offices. The collection may contain land titles, legal writs, marriage contracts, wills, correspondence, and estate papers which may be used to trace tenants. For collections not held in the SRO, refer to the survey of muniments in private hands drawn up by the National Register of Archives (Scotland), or NRA(S). A

copy of these surveys may be seen in the SRO and in the manuscript department of the National Library of Scotland, George IV Bridge, Edinburgh, which also holds many family papers.

Muster rolls: When it was an independent nation, Scotland had only a very small standing army, and landowners were compelled to provide forces according to their financial means. The best source of information containing names is to be found in the muster rolls for 1641–1707.

Burgh and Royal Burgh Records: These include council minutes, craft records, burgess rolls, apprentice rolls and their own land registers from the seventeenth century. Indexes to some of the records have been printed by the Scottish Record Society.

Burgess and Guild Records: A burgess was originally an inhabitant of a burgh who held a piece of land there from the Crown, or other superior. In later years, a burgess was a merchant or a craftsman who was influential in burgh affairs. The Burgess and Guild records list the name of the burgess and of the guild brother in a particular burgh. They also show the record of his admission as a burgess, member of his craft, or as an apprentice.

Register of the Privy Council: The Council was the chief administrative body of Scotland before 1707, and dealt with every topic. The Register, 1554–1691, is printed and indexed, and is on the open shelves in the Historical Search Room of the SRO, in Edinburgh.

County Records: A list of these is held in the SRO, but many of these are now held only by local authorities. The poor relief records are mainly those of parochial boards and parish councils, which are classed as county records. These records contain a great deal of personal information about families applying for relief.

Forfeited Estate Papers: These concern the estates forfeited by Jacobites involved in the risings of 1715 and 1745.

Court of Session Records: The Court of Session is the highest civil court in Scotland. These records contain details of civil cases which have come before the Court.

Justiciary Court Records: These contain

details of criminal court cases. Among them may be found the reports on the trials of and other details concerning those who were found guilty and transported.

Consistorial Processes and Decreets: These are papers relating to the various civil jurisdictions exercised by the Ecclesiastical Courts prior to the Reformation, and include causes or actions relative to marriage, legitimacy and divorce, as well as executry. The Commissary Court of Edinburgh, instituted 1563–64, acted as a general court for the whole country for such matters. Local commissary courts retained a more limited jurisdiction. In 1830 almost the whole of the old commissary jurisdiction was transferred to the Court of Session. (See chapter 5 in Gordon Donaldson's *Scottish Church History,* published in 1985 by Scottish Academic Press, for more information on church courts.)

Fasti Ecclesiae Scoticanae: With additional addenda and corrigenda, this records the succession of ministers in the parishes in the Church of Scotland from the middle of the sixteenth century up until 1975, giving details of each minister's family, parentage and education.

Writers to the Signet (WS): Writers to the Signet are solicitors. The Register of the Society of Writers to the Signet (1983) has superseded previous lists and provides details of all members from the fifteenth century to the 1980s.

Commission by the Lord Lyon King of Arms in favour of the ceann-cath

UNTO ALL AND SUNDRY whom these presents do or may concern. We Sir Malcolm Rognvald Innes of Edingight, Knight Commander of the Royal Victorian Order, Writer to Her Majesty's Signet, Lord Lyon King of Arms send Greeting:

Whereas it has been represented to us that the hereditary chiefship of the Clan McX is dormant: that the dormancy of the chiefship of the said Clan has created difficulties in maintaining the wellbeing of the said Clan and of its branches and houses at home and overseas; that in order to preserve the spirit of kinship and clanship and the traditions of the said clan, a *ceann-cath* or Commander of the said clan should be appointed to rally the members of the said clan, to convene meetings thereof and to preside thereat during the dormancy of the chiefship; that the principal landed and armigerous men and women that now are of the Clan McX (*videlicet* . . .) have after due consideration selected and recommended to us Fingal McX as the person of the name and race of McX most fit and deserving for appointment as *ceann-cath* or Commander of the said clan.

Now therefore we after due consideration and investigation being well satisfied as to the good qualities, abilities and loyalty of the said Fingal McX and of his fitness for the said office have approved, received and appointed as we do by these presents approve, receive and appoint the said Fingal McX to be the *ceann-cath* or Commander of the Clan McX both at home and overseas with power and commission to him to do and perform all acts and functions proper to the Commander of the said clan in the personal absence of the hereditary chief thereof in the same manner and to the same effect as if he had been specially appointed and instructed by such hereditary chief; and we ordain that the said Clan McX and all persons belonging thereto shall honour and obey the said Fingal McX as *ceann-cath* or Commander foresaid so long as this commission shall subsist and shall not have been recalled by us; That these presents shall be recorded in the Books of the Lyon Court (probative writs section) in testimony whereof we have subscribed these presents and the Seal of our Office is affixed hereto at Edinburgh.

Index of names

The following list contains all clan and family names featured in this book. Those names marked in **bold** are members of the Standing Council of Scottish Chiefs and can be found in the first section of this book; those marked in ***bold italic*** are of armigerous families and can be found in the second section while the remainder can be found in Appendix 4.

The Arms of the Kings of Scots